CW00751526

The Oxfordshire Record Society

The Life and Times of a Charlbury Quaker: The Journals of William Jones, 1784-1818

Edited by
Hannah Jones

Volume 69

2014

First published in Great Britain 2014
By Oxfordshire Records Society
c/o The Secretary,
Dr Shaun Morley, Tithe Corner, 67 Hill Crescent,
Finstock, Chipping Norton, OX7 3BT

Registered Charity No. 209808

British Library Cataloguing in Publication Data.

A catalogue record for this book is available from the British Library.

ISBN 978-0-902509-78-8

Printed and bound in Great Britain by Berforts Information Press Ltd
www.informationpress.com

Thanks to The Sandford Trust for their generous grant.

The picture on the front cover is from a painting
of the 1840 Yearly Meeting
by Samuel Lucas [LSF picture ref PIC/F035].

The composition must be at least partially fictional, as Jones died in 1838, but he is pictured on the front row: the stooped, white-haired, old man seated fourth from the left, along with other prominent Friends of the time.

Contents

Foreword

In many respects, William Jones is a rather unlovable diarist. He is also a frustrating one. His ceaseless moralizing reads badly nowadays – and it is hard for the reader not to note the increasingly frequency with which acquaintances found an excuse to avoid his words of wisdom as the journals progress. Jones' unwillingness to name many of his associates, his apparent lack of reflection on events around him, and his haziness about places and dates have also deterred many local and family historians from exploiting his work. His diaries have, as a result, remained unread.

Yet, as Hannah Jones shows in this exacting edition of his journals from 1784 to 1818, her namesake deserves more than our condescension. Just like E. P. Thompson's 'obsolete' hand-loom weaver, 'utopian' artisan, and 'deluded' follower of Joanna Southcott, the life of William Jones provides a real insight into late-eighteenth- and early-nineteenth-century history. His diary is more than just the record of one man's religious development – although it is certainly that. It also offers us glimpses of the wider Quaker world of which he was part: a national and a trans-Atlantic world as well as a strictly local one; a world, it is clear, which challenged many of the conventions – not least about gender – upheld by many of Jones' contemporaries.

Perhaps what is most striking about the journal is the faith that it depicts. Like his contemporary, William Blake, William Jones lived in a landscape in which God's hand could be seen everywhere. He glimpsed the divine and was moved by the spirit in Charlbury and Chipping Norton, Burton and Barton, Henley and Hook Norton. In this book, Oxfordshire is God's own county.

Oxford, January 2014

William Whyte
Editor of the Oxfordshire Record Society

Editor's Preface

This journal comprises a full transcript of the first three journals of William Jones, a Charlbury Quaker. I first came across the journals when I was cataloguing the records of the Oxford and Swindon Area Quaker Meeting at Oxfordshire History Centre and I felt that this fascinating resource ought to be opened up to a wider audience.

It would not have been possible to complete this project without the assistance of Josef Keith, archivist, and his colleagues at the Library of the Religious Society of Friends (LSF) in London. They have never failed to respond to any my queries with anything less than unfailing helpfulness and courtesy. I am also indebted to the LSF Library Committee for agreeing to relocate the journals to Oxford to allow me to carry out the transcription. I am hugely grateful for their patience, as the initial six months that I had estimated for the transcription gradually developed into two years!

Thanks must go to my colleague Alison Smith for her painstaking proof reading, and to William Whyte, the general editor of Oxfordshire Record Society for his guidance and suggestions for improvements. Any remaining errors are, of course, my own. Finally I must extend my thanks to Carl Boardman, Mark Priddey, and the rest of my colleagues at Oxfordshire History Centre for their interest, support, and endless supply of biscuits.

Hannah Jones

Introduction

William Jones was born to Quaker parents in Charlbury on 23 October 1760, the only son, and at least third child of William and Hannah Jones. He had at least two elder sisters, Hannah (born 1758) and Elizabeth, more commonly referred to as Betty (born 1759).[1] In the course of his journals he also makes reference to a third sister, Margaret, but it has not been possible to establish her date of birth. William Jones senior was a weaver, a trade to which his son was later apprenticed, and the family were committed Quakers. In the introduction to his first journal, Jones refers to his father borrowing books by other notable Quakers and reading them to his family.[2]

In his introduction, Jones writes that he began to compile his journals 'Now being arived to about the 22 year of my Age'.[3] The first dated entry from the journal is January 1784. He describes the journal as 'Benefical to my Minde... as it caused me to Recolect how I had passed the Day and wether I had done anything that was rong'.[4] Jones went on to compile ten journals, beginning in 1784 and continuing, uninterrupted, until a few days before his death in 1838. The journals, referenced MS.Box 1/2/A-J, remained in the ownership of his family until 1902, when they were deposited with the Library of the Society of Friends, London [LSF] by Jones' great-nephew Frederick Sessions. In addition to journals A-J, there is also a copy of Journal A, referenced M, and a series of five notebooks, two referenced K and L, and three without references. Notebooks K-L cover the years 1790-94, a period which is also recorded in Journal A. The notebooks are less formulaic than the journals, and include details of weather, travel, and business transactions.

Journals A-J remained with the Library until the early 1980s, when they were temporarily withdrawn by another of Jones' descendents, Arthur Bissell. Bissell was Warden at the Society of Friends meeting house on St Giles, Oxford, and, after his retirement, moved to Charlbury where he was instrumental in re-establishing the Friends' meeting there, the meeting which Jones himself had attended. Bissell completed a partial transcription of the journals, but mostly for genealogical purposes and other items of local interest. Following his death, Bissell's transcription and other working papers became part of the papers of the Witney Monthly Meeting[5] deposited at Oxfordshire History Centre.[6] Other than Bissell's partial transcription, no further work has been carried out on the journals until now. This volume comprises the first complete transcription of Journals A,[7] B,[8],and C,[9] together covering the period from 1784 to 1818.

---

1 The National Archives, RG6/Piece 1378/ Fol 46.
2 Library of the Society of Friends, London [abbreviated LSF]: MS. Box 1/2/A, p.6v.
3 LSF: MS.Box 1/2/A, p.12v.
4 LSF: MS.Box 1/2/A, p.12v.
5 Subsequently renamed Oxford and Swindon Area Quaker Meeting.
6 Oxfordshire History Centre, NQ3/1/MS1/1.
7 LSF: MS.Box 1/2/A.
8 LSF: MS.Box 1/2/B.
9 LSF: MS.Box 1/2/C.

Style of Transcription

Each journal has been transcribed in full, line by line, page by page. The pagination is my own. All spellings, abbreviations, use of capitals, and punctuation are as Jones wrote them. The only exception is a small number of passages throughout the journals where Jones has interpolated additional comments above the existing text. To transcribe these passages as they appear in the original journals would render them somewhat incomprehensible and they have therefore been inserted in italics to indicate a break from the line by line transcription. Any insertions made by myself are indicated by the use of square brackets while insertions made by Jones are in parentheses. Information has also been inserted, where possible, about the dates of foundation of the Quaker meetings that Jones visits. This information is derived from David M. Butler's book, *The Quaker Meeting Houses of Great Britain* (1999).

Quaker Dating Conventions

Quakers objected to using those day and month names derived from the names of heathen gods and goddesses and therefore named their days and months sequentially instead. Thus Sunday would be First Day (sometimes abbreviated to FD by Jones), Monday Second Day and so on. Similarly January was First Month, February Second Month, and so on.[10] Jones used this style throughout the journals. The dates have been expanded where necessary.

Themes in the journals

Throughout the journals, a number of specific themes develop and some of these warrant closer examination.

One subject which features frequently and prominently in the journals is the participation of women in Quaker meetings at all levels. In additional to regular attendance at weekly meetings, women are seen to attend Yearly Meeting in London (for example Sarah Jones and Margaret Sessions in 1817),[11] and, perhaps more surprisingly, even to 'appoint' additional meetings in areas where there is no current Quaker population – for example, Broadway[12] and Enstone.[13] One woman Friend, Elizabeth Mintchin/ Mintchon, travels further still. In Journal B Jones writes 'she Signified she had Public Meetings much to her comfort and Perticularly at one Island, ware at a Woman stood up not of our Society, and Expressed in the French Language her Satisfaction of the Meeting'.[14] For women to play such an active role may seem surprising but, at the time Jones was writing, women were on a similar footing to male Friends. Admittedly there were separate Men's and Women's meetings, with the Women's meetings tending to focus on more 'domestic' themes

10 http://www.quaker.org.uk/sites/defaults/files/qcal.doc. Accessed 27 October 2012.
11 LSF: MS.Box 1/2/C, p.175v.
12 LSF: MS.Box 1/2/A, p.72-73v.
13 LSF: MS.Box 1/2/C, p.24v.
14 LSF: MS.Box 1/2/B, p.46.

such as sick-visiting and poor relief, but they were also able significantly to influence the Quaker movement as a whole.

The equal footing of women was a notable feature of the Society of Friends from its foundation. Quakers believed that anyone – man or woman, adult or child, literate or illiterate – might be capable of preaching the word of the Lord. Early Friends strenuously disagreed with the concept that someone needed a qualification or university degree to preach, much less that they should be paid to do so, condemning such figures as 'hireling' preachers. For the Quakers, anyone could spontaneously prophesy at a meeting, regardless of gender, age, or education.[15] As Larson writes 'Since Quakers believed that inspired words came from the same source, the indwelling Spirit of God, it was irrelevant who actually preached at the meeting'.[16]

Nonetheless, some Friends, both male and female, were considered particularly gifted in public speaking. These 'public' or 'ministering' Friends often travelled extensively to spread the word of the Gospel. In cases where these ministering Friends travelled away from home in the service of God, the Society paid their expenses and cared for their families in their absence. Jones pays a visit to the children of Sarah Lambley in 1811 'she being from Home & had been a pretty wile on a religious visit'.[17]

The 'concerns' felt by these Friends to promote the Gospel might merely have been a wish to hold a meeting in an area where there was no established Quaker meeting or could manifest as a desire to travel on a far wider scale. Throughout Jones' journals there are references to 'public' or 'ministering' Friends visiting Charlbury and surrounding meetings. Larson notes that meetings featuring travelling Friends could be a notable local event.[18] Jones records in one instance in 1804 when a meeting at Charlbury called by Joseph Cloud, a visiting Friend, was so busy that the floor of the meeting house collapsed.[19]

However, a more surprising aspect of the Friends who visited Charlbury is the number of American visitors. Between 1784 and 1818, Jones lists at least twenty-three American visitors to Charlbury. Initially to have over twenty Americans visiting a relatively small Oxfordshire village in a 34 year period would seem astonishing, but the close connections between British and American Quaker communities helps to explain this. As already stated, ministering Friends would travel substantial distances when they felt concerned to do so, and travelling across the Atlantic was no exception.

The first Quaker missionaries travelled to North America in 1655, only a few years after the Society of Friends had been established in Britain, and many more travelled in the 1660s as persecution for their beliefs increased. George Fox also

15 Tolles, 1960, p.25.
16 Larson, 1999, p.18.
17 LSF: MS.Box 1/2/C, p.69.
18 Larson, 1999, p.176.
19 LSF: MS.Box 1/2/C, p.11v.

instigated the process of an exchange of epistles between the yearly Meetings in Britain and America, so there was a constant exchange of information and advice travelling in either direction. The exchange of letters between British Quakers and those settling in America helped to cement the bond between the two communities and this was further strengthened by ministering Friends travelling between the two countries, both British Friends travelling to America and vice versa. Tolles compares the process to that of circulation in an organism 'Thus there was a constant circulation of "public Friends", as they were called... giving Friends at the remotest extremities of the Atlantic world a sense of belonging to a single body.'[20]

Whilst it can be seen from the journals that other local Friends, such as Sarah Lambley and Elizabeth Mintchin, felt it necessary to go on extended journeys as part of their ministry, Jones' writing style again makes it difficult to establish what he considered his role in the ministry to be. He never expresses a 'concern' to travel widely or for an extended period of time, although he repeatedly uses the phrases 'felt a conceарn' and 'felt drawings in my minde' when visiting local meetings. From closer reading it would appear that Jones did consider himself to have a role in the ministry. He notes in Journal A that he did 'firmly believe without doubt that the Almighty God has Intrusted me with a Small Gift in the Ministery'.[21] He also refers to an occasion when Friends 'gave me some good Instruction in a very kinde manner respecting my appearing in the Ministery'.[22] In Journal B he writes, 'I think there was no Friend in the Ministery, except Jn° Hankins Wife and myself',[23] and makes a similar comment in Journal C.

Although Jones did not leave home for any sustained periods, he did travel widely around local Quaker meetings in Oxfordshire, Berkshire, and Warwickshire. In the course of journals A-C Jones visits meetings at Burford, Faringdon, Banbury, Reading, Henley, and Radway, in addition to numerous other locations. Furthermore, ministering Friends 'appoint' one off meetings at Enstone, Deddington, Islip, and Great Barrington, all of them attended by Jones. Jones walked to the huge majority of these places. He even remarks in 1806 when he rides from Charlbury to Oxford and then on to Shillingford as a guide for some visiting Friends 'returned home much tired not being used to travel so long a Journey on horseback'.[24]

On three occasions, Jones travelled further still, in order to attend the Quaker Yearly Meeting in London. He first attended in 1810, but comments that he decided to travel there by coach so as not to get lost in the city.[25] He attended again in May 1813 and recorded the following stages of his journey:

> 15th, rode from Charlbury to Oxford, walked to Warborough, then on to Henley, via Shillingford, arrived in Henley around 9pm.

20 Tolles, 1960, p.25.
21 LSF: MS.Box 1/2/A, p.50.
22 LSF: MS.Box 1/2/A, p.138.
23 LSF: MS.Box 1/2/B, p.37.
24 LSF: MS.Box 1/2/C, p.25.
25 LSF: MS.Box 1/2/C, p.55v.

16th, attended Henley meeting, travelled in carriage to Maidenhead

17th, walked to Staines

18th, walked to Brentford

19th, walked into central London

19th-31st, attended Yearly Meeting

31st, walked back to Staines

1st June, walked to Maidenhead, and then on to Henley

2nd, walked to Shillingford

3rd, walked from Shillingford to Charlbury

He travelled to London again in 1816 and journeyed further still, to visit Friends in Gravesend, Strood, and Rochester after the conclusion of the Yearly Meeting. He returned to London by boat and then walked back to Charlbury over the course of three days.

Another subject which appears in the journals is that of the harassment to which he and his family were subjected to on a number of occasions. In May 1798 Jones records that his goods were seized by 'the Constable and Tytheing men'[26] after refusing to join the militia the previous year.[27] He also records an instance in 1816 when local young men came to his house 'with the Engin',[28] broke and sprayed water through the windows, damaging his goods.

Local meetings, particularly those appointed by the special desire of a ministering Friend, were also subject to disruption. Hannah Smith appointed a meeting at Deddington in August 1802 but when Friends visited the town they were unable to secure a venue for the meeting so held it in a grove of trees just outside. A local lawyer disrupted the meeting by sending a man up the trees to prune them whilst the meeting was in progress.[29] Friends were similarly prevented from meeting in Islip: 'friends went thither & Indeavourd to get a place but could not it appear'd the Dean was very much against it & the People ware so much under him as not to spare their Places lest they should offend him'.[30]

However other comments by Jones would appear to suggest that he was generally well received by his neighbours. On several occasions he records that he was invited to attend funerals of neighbours at the local church. In November 1796 he writes 'met with no molestation except having my hat taken from me when I went into the worship hous, it was gave to me again when the people came out'.[31]

26 LSF: MS.Box 1/2/B, p.28.
27 see LSF: MS.Box 1/2/A, p.197v-198.
28 LSF: MS.Box 1/2/C, p.161.
29 LSF: MS.Box 1/2/B, p.96v-97.
30 LSF: MS.Box 1/2/C, p.59v.
31 LSF: MS.Box 1/2/A, p.191.

Reading through the journals, the theme of financial hardship is also apparent. Whilst Jones and his wife do not appear to struggle themselves, he frequently remarks on the price of food and the harshness of the weather, and its impact on the poor. On two occasions in the winter of 1799-1800 he reports on the price of bread and meat,[32] noting similar problems more than a decade later in 1812.[33] He also comments on an extremely late harvest in 1816.[34] Food prices in 1799-1800 prompt him to visit the Overseers of the Poor in Charlbury 'and two more towns' and urge them to assist 'the distressed situations of the poor'.[35] Jones also reports two instances of local Friends grouping together and distributing wood and coal at their own expense. In December 1796 he reports that Friend Spendlove donated £5 worth of wood to the poor, and it being distributed to around 100 people.[36] Similarly, wood and coal is distributed to the poor in January 1814 after a collection is made locally.[37]

The wider tradition of Quaker 'journalling'

Whilst the keeping of a journal for over 50 years, as Jones did, may seem a formidable task to most, the tradition of 'journalling' would have been well known to Jones and his contemporaries. This tradition grew out of Quakerism's identity as a religion focusing on inner spiritual experience. Early Quaker writers, many of them travelling Friends in the Ministry, used journals as a method of recording their spiritual lives. Burr states 'The autobiographical intention of early Friends became a dogma ... of their belief, and to leave behind a journal ... was almost a requirement of faith'.[38]

Many early journals, written between the mid-seventeenth and eighteenth centuries, were written with the intention of publication for didactic purposes. Jones himself states that his father would borrow books 'such as the History of Tho's Ellwood the Journal of Jn'o Gratton and the like', so he would have been well acquainted with the tradition of journal-keeping.[39]

Wright indicates that four of the most influential Quaker journals were published in a short period between 1689 and 1694, those of William Caton, John Burnyeat, Stephen Crisp, and George Fox.[40] These four volumes, similar in style and content, set a tone which would remain unbroken for decades. This can be seen in Jones' work, where phrases such as 'a City that is set upon a hill'[41] are copied directly from Fox's own work. Wright also identifies a number of themes which are typical of a Quaker journal: 'his hesitancy to deliver his first Quaker message in a meeting of

32 LSF: MS.Box 1/2/B, p. 61v and 64.
33 LSF: MS.Box 1/2/C, p.82.
34 LSF: MS.Box 1/2/C, p.167v.
35 LSF: MS.Box 1/2/B, 64v.
36 LSF: MS.Box 1/2/A, p.193v
37 LSF: MS.Box 1/2/C, p.108
38 Burr, 1909, p.235.
39 LSF: MS.Box 1/2/A, p.6v.
40 Wright, 1966, p.193.
41 LSF: MS.Box 1/2/B, p.29.

worship, including his call to the ministry, his missionary journeys, and the general progress of the Quaker movement'.[42]

The role of the journal as a piece of spiritual autobiography also helps to explain some of the apparent peculiarities in Jones' writing style. His purpose in keeping the journal was, as Vann has put it, as a 'spiritual account book'.[43] Jones only records those pieces of information which he feels relevant to his life, and progress, as a Quaker. Therefore the passages recording the charitable distribution of wood and coal to the needy poor are not for self-aggrandisement but to demonstrate provision of relief for the poor.[44] Similarly his comments on the theft of money from the Atkins family, local bankers, and the subsequent run on the bank are not recorded for the purposes of local gossip, nor to gloat on another's misfortune, but to reflect on other people's imprudent behaviour.[45] National events are also commented on, but again from Jones' perspective as a Quaker. For example, he notes the introduction of Income Tax in 1799 by writing 'I being much exercised concearning it, thinking Friends could not pay it and bear a faithfull and Christian Testimonie against War and Oppressing our fellow Mortals'.[46]

However, this writing style – particularly the efforts to mirror journals written by earlier Quakers – means that some details which might be expected in a diary or journal are missing. Details about his home, neighbours, and Charlbury in general are sparse in the extreme. Jones does not indicate where he lives, except for one reference in February 1804 where he notes him and his wife moving to 'Wm Albrights House near their dwelling House'.[47] Nor are any of his neighbours ever named, although he records attending a number of their funerals at various dates.

Similarly, information on Charlbury is limited. Jones supplies very little information about the town and its population directly, but we are able to glean small pieces of information from some of his comments. In Journal A, he records that a man drowned on his way home from Charlbury Fair in October 1790,[48] and in Journal C he records that people visit the town 'to act plays, shows, and such vain amusements'.[49] In Journal C he gives details of the founding of the British School in the town.[50] He also records the instance in January 1804 when Charlbury meeting house was so full of visitors at a public meeting that the floor gave way.[51] In August 1812 Jones records being out in the fields and hearing the church bells rung 'I understood it was to signify a rejoicing on accont of menny of the French People being slain by the English'.[52] Again, many of these comments are made

42 Wright, 1966, p.166.
43 Vann, 1969, p.20.
44 LSF: MS.Box 1/2/A, p.193v and LSF: MS.Box 1/2/C, p.107v.
45 LSF: MS.Box 1/2/C, p.131v.
46 LSF: MS.Box 1/2/B, p.48v.
47 LSF: MS.Box 1/2/C, p.12v.
48 LSF: MS.Box 1/2/A, p.46.
49 LSF: MS.Box 1/2/C, p.82.
50 LSF: MS.Box 1/2/C, p.128v.
51 LSF: MS.Box 1/2/C, p.11v.
52 LSF: MS.Box 1/2/C, p.82.

in the context of Jones' Quaker beliefs, but they do provide us with some idea of contemporary Charlbury.

Jones' writing style can also be seen to develop through the journals, with variations in dating conventions and abbreviations, and even the amount of information recorded, as he endeavours to establish his 'voice' as a Quaker journaller. This is particularly noticeable in Journal A, where gaps of several months can appear between entries. For example, Jones records an entry for 18 October 1784, noting that he attended Monthly Meeting where 'public' or ministering Friends William Barrett and Ann Stait were present.[53] The next entry in the journal is made on 8 November, when he again attends Monthly Meeting.

However, when a comparison is made between these entries in Journal A, and the same period recorded in Notebook K, the differences are surprising. Jones records the same, almost verbatim, entry for 18 October 1784 but the notebook then includes details of what he did every day from there until the entry on 8 November. What is interesting about these entries is that they are a day-to-day record of his life, but are not significant in recording his life as a Quaker. For example, he records that on 19 October he bought '2 sacks Pease of holloway', on 25 October that it was very cold; on 31 October he records a visit from 'Cousin B & Damaris ... from Enstone', and notes that it rained on both 1 and 2 November.[54]

A similar instance occurs in 1787, where Jones makes entries in Journal A for 1 and 3 January. The entry for the latter records a visit to his uncle and cousins in Sibford, Epwell, Brails and Shipstone made between 3 and 7 January.[55] However, the same period in Notebook K records a separate entry for each day between 1 and 7 January, noting who and where he visited, and which Quaker meetings he attended.[56]

Jones therefore appears to have recorded his daily activities in the notebooks, using them as an aide-memoir, but consciously editing the entries before including them in the journals; perhaps even in an attempt to imitate the content of other notable journals. The five notebooks, K-L and the three unlettered volumes, cover the period 1784-1794, which coincide with the earliest period of Jones' journal keeping. There are no notebooks after 1794, either because they have not survived, or because Jones felt comfortable enough with his writing style to stop writing them. Nonetheless, the information recorded in these notebooks provides many of the details lacking from the journals. The names of local tradesmen and neighbours, field names, and financial transactions are of particular interest, and the notebooks themselves provide an invaluable resource to local historians.

53 LSF: MS.Box 1/2/A, p.14v.
54 LSF: MS.Box 1/2/K.
55 LSF: MS.Box 1/2/A, p.21.
56 LSF: MS.Box 1/2/K.

Bibliography

Abbott, Margery Post; Chijioke, Mary Ellen, et al. *Historical Dictionary of the Friends (Quakers)*. Lanham, Maryland: The Scarecrow Press, 2003.

Brailsford, Mabel Richmond. *Quaker Women*. London: Duckworth & Co., 1915.

Brinton, Howard H. *Quaker Journals: Varieties of Religious Experience Among Friends*. Wallingford, Pennsylvania: Pendle Hill Publications, 1972.

Burr, Anna Robeson. *The Autobiography: A Critical and Comparative Study*. Boston/ New York: Horton Mifflin Company, 1909.

Butler, David M. *The Quaker Meeting Houses of Britain, Volumes I and II*.

London: Friends Historical Society, 1999.

Hamm, Thomas D. *The Quakers in America*. New York: Columbia University Press, 2003.

Larson, Rebecca. *Daughters of Light: Quaker Women Preaching and Prophesying in the Colonies and Abroad, 1700-1750*. New York: Alfred A. Knopf, 1999.

Tolles, Frederick B. *The Atlantic Community of the Early Friends*. London: Friends Historical Society, 1952.

Tolles, Frederick B. *Quakers and the Atlantic Culture.* New York: The Macmillan Company, 1960.

Trevett, Christine. *Quaker Women Prophets in England and Wales 1650-1700*. New York: The Edwin Mellen Press, 2000.

Vann, Richard T. *The Social Development of English Quakerism 1655-1755*. Cambridge, Mass.: Harvard University Press, 1969.

Wright, Louella M. *The Literary Life of the Early Friends 1650-1725*. New York: AMS Press, Inc., 196

Map of William Jones' Travels

The Journeys of William Jones
Warwickshire
Northamptonshire
Glos.
Ettington
Armscote
Ticer
(Tysoe)
Worcs.
Shipstone
(Shipston
on Stour)
Worcs.
Campden
(Broad
Campden)
Brailes
Banbury
Warks.
Worcs.
Sibford
Worcs.
Glos.
Long
Compton
Adderbury
Seasonscutt
(Sezincote)
Worcs.
Buckinghamshire
Worcs.
Chipping
Norton
Barton
(Middle Barton)
Stow
(Stow on the Wold)
Charlbury
5 miles
20 miles
Milton
(Milton under
Wychwood)
Gloucestershire
Oxfordshire
Burford
Witney
Oxford
Alvescot
Faringdon
Uffington
Berkshire
Wiltshire
Reading
Newbury
Hampshire
0
10 km
0
5 miles

Dramatis Personae

William Jones

born 23rd October 1760 at Charlbury
son of William and Hannah Jones of Charlbury
occupation: weaver
married Sarah Gilkes, 6th June 1797

'Father'

William Jones (senior), weaver of Charlbury
married to Hannah Jones (senior)
father of Hannah, Elizabeth (Betty), Margaret and William Jones
died 27th March 1796

'Father'

Philip Gilkes of Sibford, father of Sarah Jones (nee Gilkes) and father-in-law of William Jones
died 3rd September 1797

'Mother'

Hannah Jones (senior), married to William Jones (senior)
mother of Hannah, Elizabeth (Betty), Margaret and William Jones
died 22nd June 1799

'Mother'

Sarah Gilkes (senior), mother of Sarah Jones (nee Gilkes), mother-in-law of William Jones

'My Wife'

Sarah Jones (nee Gilkes), daughter of Philip and Sarah Gilkes of Sibford
married William Jones, 6th June 1797

'Sistor Hannah'

Hannah Jones, eldest daughter of William and Hannah Jones
sister to Elizabeth (Betty), Margaret and William Jones
born 2nd June 1758 at Charlbury
died 27th March 1790 at Charlbury

'Sistor Hannah'

Hannah Gilkes, sister of Sarah Giles, sister-in-law of William Jones
married William Corks, 9th May 1807

'Sistor Betty'

Elizabeth (Betty) Jones, second daughter of William and Hannah Jones
sister to Hannah, Margaret and William Jones
born 15th September 1759
married Henry Ma(u)nder, 25th December 1789

'Sistor Margaret'

Margaret Jones, daughter of William and Hannah Jones
sister to Hannah, Elizabeth (Betty), and William Jones
date of birth uncertain
married Robert Sessions, 24th February 1791

'Brother Henry'

Henry Ma(u)nder, husband of Elizabeth (Betty) Ma(u)nder (nee Jones), brother-in-law of William Jones
married Elizabeth (Betty) Jones, 25th December 1789
died c.23rd May 1809

'Brother Robert'

Robert Sessions, husband of Margaret Sessions (nee Jones),
brother-in-law of William Jones
married Margaret Jones, 24th February 1791

'Sistor Mary'

Mary Gibbs (nee Gilkes), sister of Sarah Jones (nee Gilkes), sister-in-law of William Jones
married John Gibbs c.1812
died 24th October 1816

'Brother John Gibbs'

John Gibbs, husband of Mary Gibbs (nee Gilkes)
brother-in-law to William and Sarah Jones (nee Gilkes)
married Mary Gilkes c.1812

Journal A

Page 1

It hath been much upon my Minde to
write some account of my Life and
of the Tryals and Exercises I have met with
from my youth up and of the Dealings and visitation
of the Almighty to mee to let me se how vainitis
and nothing-ness of these Earthly things and
for me to set my Heart upon the things of this World
which in a little wile must Perrish and be no more and
that I must part with these Earthly things and
take up the Cross unto them if I would Injoy
Things more lasting I must minde the guidence
of the pure witness of Truth placed in my Breast
by the Almighty a Measure and manifestation
wareof all have Received sufficient to Inable them
to overcome the Earthly Things and Please the
Almity and make them fit for an Habitation
that will nevver End and full of Joy as sayeth
the Scripture "the Grace of God which bringeth
"salvation hath appeard unto all Men teaching us
"that Denying all ungodlyness and worldly lusts we should live soberly

verso

"Righteously and godly in this Present World looking for
"that Blessed hope and Glorious appearance of the great
"God our Saviour and Jesus Christ who gave Himself
"for us that he might Redeem unto Himself a peculiar
People Zealous of good words and Works."
and this witness of Truth is placed in us when very
young even when very little Children when wee tell
stories or disobey our Father or Mother or do any
thing without their leave which we know they would
not be pleased we should do there is a surest con=
=viction in our own Breast that tells us we have done
what we ought not to have done and we Play
with naughty Children or Speak bad words we are
sensible we should not do so I remmember once
when very young my Sistor told me that there was a
bad Place that burned for Ever and Ever and that
they that ware naughty Children and told stories
would go there but they that ware good would go to
a good place it had such an affect upon my Minde
that I thought I would in=deavour to live better and be more
carefull for I knew I was guilty of telling stories,
I Remmember also when very young I might be about
sevven or Eight years old hearing the Testament

Page 2

and Reading a Chapter to my self, in the Revelation
the ninth Chapter ware it is said "and
when the Angel which had the key of the
Bottomless Pit had Opened it there ascended
out smoke and the smoke thereof Ascendeth
up for Ever and Ever and Locoust came
out of the smoke upon the Earth they ware
not to hurt the green things that ware
upon the Earth but to hurt and Plague all Men
who had not the mark of God in their fore-head,
it affected my Minde very much the thoughts
of the Burning for Ever and Ever which makes
me think it is Exceeding good in Parents to learn
their Children to read when yound which my
Father did me He used to have me Read two
or three Chapters in a day by him when at
Work which was of great use to me to keep me
out of Harms way and to Instruct my Minde
in good thus by having good Parents I was more
Preserved from the Evels snares and Temptations
of the World than menny Children tho I was

verso

strongly a dicted to Play and get out without my
Parents
leave and so neglect my duty to them which I
knew I
ought not to have done having often found
conviction with=
=in my self and condemnation for so doing my
Parents
if they knew it would not let me play at Marvels
in
gaming as other Children used to do which I
believe
since was a very good thing as it was a means of
Preserving my minde from much and scandlous
Company,
when I was about 13 years old I had an intimate
acquaintance that used to come and beg me off
to Play
some afternoons he having no work to do at
which
I was uneasy sometimes and used to tell him it
was a [illegible] time for me to leave off Play but
he would
say twas no harm there was menny Old than
me that Played but still I was not easy, this
young man has since turnd out Bad, and
sometimes he
would come and call me to go a sliding a distance
from home with some more boys but tho I seemed
to delight in it yet I was not quite easy in my
minde

Page 3

and when I came home I used to think I had
done rong that it was not Pleasing to the
Almighty thus going from home teacheth Chil=
=dren to be wild and of a roving Minde,
though my Parents were not very willing I
should go and I believe it very Wrong for Parents
to let them go much from Home amoungst
loose and vain Boys, but bring them up to
work wile young finding some little work for
them to do which would keep them out of harms
way and would teach them how to get a living
tho a little Play sometimes may be no harm
so as they are kept within Bounds and not
sufferd to be out to long for as Solomon
sayeth "Train up a Child in the way he
should go and when He is Old he will not
depart from it." I know I thought their would
be no harm in Play provided I told no stories
and said no bad word but in the way of Play
when the are striving for Marstry and if there

verso

is one that dont minde what He says he will say I
did do so and so whereas I have been sure it has
not
been so and been loth to lose the game hath said
it
was not so the other would say it was so ware=
=by menny stories have been told and sometimes
quarrelling so that I have been Ready to resolve
I would Play no more tho I had a strong In=
=clination for it yet I perceivd I must leave
it of tho it seemd hard work if I would be
found doing my duty and Please the Almighty
as I ought to do, and I often wish'd I had some
work to do to keep my hands out of Mistief
which
tho unpleasent would nevvertheless Preserve my
minde
from doing that which I knew was rong which
makes me think it is a very good thing for
Parents
to finde some Imploy for them, when I was about
14 years old I went to service to a very worthy
Friends
Wm and Hannah Squires who lived not far from
us
He was a verry Considerate Friend who had a
Testimony to bear for the Everlasting Truth
and she was a free familar considerate woman
altho in high circumstances to the Poor as well
as to

Page 4

the Rich, I think as Ever lived being very good
to the Poor working very close her self to make
garments
for them, now wile I lived with them I was weakly
and often poorly so that I could hardly Eate and
when dinner time came instead of being glad I
wish'd
the time over or that I could live with out victuals

the sight of which was ready to turn my stomack
altho my poor inside wanted Food to strengthen it
and when I looked upon others and saw how they
Eate and Drank with great delight but I did
not consider that they had their Tryals and
Exercises of Minde to bear during the course
of the day tho of another nature and I thought
that no Mans affliction or condition was so
bad as mine but I have often times since
seen that those things which we think great
Hardships and bitter things is the Mercie of
the Almighty to us to preserve us from setting
our Mindes on Earthly Things and giving way
to Evel and therefore we ought not to be disconted
nor Repine their at but to bear them with Patience

verso

meekness and Humility of Minde and indeavour to
serve the Almighty according to the Best of our under=
=standing then we should see that in his time we should
come to Injoy Pleasenter Things as sayeth the scrip=
=ture "Menny are the Afflictions of the Righteous but
the Lord Delivereth them out of them all."
and sometimes I was afflicted with the Headake
and sickness, I thought it was sufferd to come upon
me for doing things which I knew to be rong
and I would desire of the Almighty that he would
be Pleas'd to ease my Head and then I would do
so no more and sometimes it would go of and
then I was verry Joyfull and glad and so by
degrees I got over one Bad thing and another,
and now the time drew on that my year
was nigh fulfill'd which I had indeavourd to
bear with Patience and I longed to have the time
up that I might come Home and then I thought
I should grow stronger and Eate more victuals

Page 5

and satisfy myself better because much Company
affected me and here I should be more alone and
freer from Company I thought I would learn
the Trade of weaving which before I had not done
altho I did not much like it but I had felt
what it was to suffer and be exposed to meny
Trying Things as being out in the cold in
the Winter which was bad for me to bear and I
thought I would do any thing to be more by
my self and that now I should bear menny
things with Patience and do them which before
I should have repined at and been unwilling to
have done and now came on another Tryal
to my weak minde I my sistors and first Cou=
=sin who lived at Wm Squires had often talked
of Having the small Pox and she and wee being
out a walking one First day [Sunday] brought it up
a fresh thinking it a verry good time to be Inocula=
=ted she spoke to her Cousins about it and they and
Father and Mother agreed we

verso

should be done on a suddain [illegible] would the Docters
People comming to our House very common wereby we
ware often in danger my sistors seemd willing as for
me things appeard suddain and Trying for I thought
if I run my self into it I should have my self to blame
and I might be very bad and might not live it being
a dangrous distemper wareof menny have Died I thought
if I Died and was not Prepared I should be miserable
for Ever and if my sistors had it and should get well
over it when I came to be in danger I should be often sor=
=rowfull so I thought I would indeavour to live as

well and as good and as self denying as I could
and
give up and have it Earnestly Breathing to the
Almighty
that in his Mercy and good ness to me He would
be
Pleased to spare my Life then I would indeavour
to
live better than what I had done and be more
carefull
how I spent my time these ware my Breathings of
soul to Him, and I believe it wrought some good
more
for I often took menny solitary walk being
desirous to
Please the Almighty and that when in Company
I would
be verry carfull of my Words and Actions that I
might

Page 6

not offend Him and Praised be His Name altho
I had
it more than any of my Sistors yet I had it but
light
getting well over it when I was got out of danger
O!
the Joy and gladness that was in my Minde
and I thought now I must Indeavour to Live as
carefully
and as Righteously as I could according to the
best
of my Understanding in Thankfullness to Him
who
had been Pleased to Preserve my Life
And now I indeavoured to settel to my Trade
with Content tho it did not agree very well
with my Health and to go out but little and
to keep but little Company except it was
to Meetings sometimes my Father would
come and say to me at a Monthly meeting
which was about five or six miles of if
thou wilt come and go take a walk with
me the shalt be welcome and sometimes I
would say I had rather not and then I could
not be easy for there was something in me
that Inclined to go and yet it was a Cross to give
up and then I would give up and go with him

verso

and when I returned I found great satisfaction of
Minde, my Father used to borrow Books such as
the
History of Tho's Ellwood the Journal of Jn'o
Gratton
and the like and in long winter Evenings cause us
to be still and Read to us when he has read of
the dealings of the Lord with them when young
and
How they ware made sensible of His Truth and
made
willing to forsake vanity and Evel and give up all
to obey and follow his leadings and it hath often
af=
=fected my Minde with sorrow I was so bad and
unsteady
in menny Things altho, Older than them and it
would
Put me in Minde of my better end and that I
must
mend my Life if I would Injoy Happiness above
when I had done here.
and thus by degrees the Almighty made me sen=
=sible of His Truth and Power, on Fifth day
[Thursday]s
I had used Pretty constant to leave my work
and go to Meetings in which in Sitting still
thinking of my unfittness to dye the thoughts of

Page 7

Eternity hath affected my Minde Exceedingly the
thought to
if I should die unprepared I must suffer
Everlast=
ing Punishment hereafter shourelly I had better
un=
dergo the greatest Cross Sufferings and
Hardships
in this World which at the longist will not be very
long in Comparison to Eternity and that
Miserable
for Ever without end what Punishment that will
nevver have End, but if we live well here and
walk agree=
=able The Pure Truth in our Own Breast
according

to the best of our Understanding then we shall be
Intitled to happiness hereafter that will nevver End,
O! it is worth striving after and Denying ones
self of those Earthly Pleasures Carnal Delights and
cravings to Injoy Everlasting Happiness and Peace
and that without End,
and now being arived to about the 18 or 19 year of
my Age I was visited with Affliction of Body
for being weakly and growing Pretty fast I stook
Pretty Close to my Loomb which is not very
Healthy work it brought a Pain in my side
which brought me very low I being of that

verso

disposition did not like to Complain unless very bad
therefore I bared it so long that I was so Reduced
and brought so thin that I could hardly work
at times I was so Bound in my Body that I did
not ease my self for two or three days altho I
used to take things opening my Father in the
Harvest time used to take some Corn to Reap weat
a field it being thought the Fresh Air and out
of doors work would help my Health but O!
I was weak altho my disposition was to Work being
always willing to Work if I could that at times I
was so low that I had hardly any Heart to keep
on I being at times very hot but seldom Sweating
which if I did it done me good altho I had a good
appetite to my Food sometimes it seemd to do me
hardly any good
Tho it seemd to do me a little good I took menny
Things which I was Recomended for menny People
out of Love and goodwill to me would Recomend
menny Things I also tried Docters stuff but for want
of Patience to take it in a Regular manner it done

Page 8

me but little or no good and sometimes hurt for I
wanted the Phisitian of Value to Instruct me
How to make Proper use of things and wait with
Patience to se if they would do me any good
and not to be anxious after the Health of my
Body for it was my Poor soul that wanted to
be strengthened and Comforted which if People did
but minde the would not be so very anxious after
this Life but wether they had their Health or no
but wait In faith and Patience up on Him who
could give food to the Sould and Health to the
Body And as I was thus anxious after Life there appe=
ard two strong Desires in me the one desirous
to get well and Injoy Pleasures and the
Friendships of this World the other was after
the Salvation of my Poor Soul which I knew wan=
=ted to be Redeemd from Bondage and to be made fit for an Habita=
=tion in Heaven above
And I wanted to feel forgiveness of the Almighty
for my Sins and Inicquieties for I knew I must

verso

Dye, and if I died in an unprepared State I could nevver
go to Heaven but I Plainly saw that if I would have for=
=giveness for my Poor faults I must live a new Life and
that which I was so Anxious after I must give up
into the Hands of the Almighty viz the Health of the
Body and the Joys of this Life and that I must deny
my self and take up the Cross freely and live a new
Life and say in Truth "Lord thy will be done and
not mine own will." In deed this is a great matter
to give up all into the Hands of the Almighty and say
in Truth come Health come Sickness or wether I Injoy
those Earthly Things or not thy will be done.

Indeed I often thought wile I was seeking for
Health
and Earnestly striving after it by seeking means
to
obtain it and I was spending the Time and got no
better but rather worse without making use of
it for
the Salvation of my poor Soul which I knew lay
at
stake, and should I Dye O! what a wretched
situation
miserable for Ever therefore I thought I will not
strive
so much for Health but indeavour to take up the
Cross

Page 9

And do my duty to the Almight in what way
soever He
shall require it of me for He Plainly Manifestest
my Duty
by the [illegible] of his Truth in my Heart and not
only to
me but to All People that will give up thereunto
and do
it and obey it leadings so I thought I would set to
work and Labour Faithfully if Happily I might
have
time enough to work out my Souls Salvation
with fear
and trembling
there is one Perticular Circumstance or two
which
I ommited in its Proper Place which I cannot be
quite easy without mentioning them I being very
young my Father went out to see his Father who
was very Ill it so proved He Dyed of his sickness
and He staying longer than he Intended I was
very thoughtfull about Him wanting to have
Him come Home I being alone and Intending to
go to meet Him I prayed and Desired of the
Almighty
In mine Heart that I might be favoured to meet
Him and it so Prov'd I did which tho it might be
no more than chance yet I believe it was a

verso

means of bringing my Minde into a more
Humble
and awefull sence of the Devine Being and that
He regards his little ones who Fear wait upon
and
Trust in Him alone,
Another thing which is upon my Minde to
mention
is it being war time there was to be a Militia
drawn in our County a thing which had not
been done befor I been turnd Eighteen was ad=
=vised by some Friends who wishd me well to be
Bound
an Apprentice to my Father to Escape being
drawn
my Parents also ware willing if I thought fitt but
when
I had considerd the thing the thought of
Bondage was
Burthensome to me I also thought if i was Bound
it would
be only to evade the Law and shun the Cross
therefore I thought
I was most Easy not to be Bound but I greatly
desired
in my Heart to the Almighty that I might not be
drawn and I was very thoughtfull about it for
some
time before the time came that the ware to be
drawn
and when the day was that the ware drawn I was
very desirous

Page 10

to know who ware drawn and when I understood
who the ware and that I had Escaped I was very
glad and Humbled in a degree of thankfullness
to the
Almighty for His Mercy and Preservation, not
being
much concerned for the time to come as
thinking perhaps I
might not Live or there might be a change in my
situta=
tion in Life
but to return I being about to give up all to the
Will

of the Almighty as finding nothing else would do
there came a friend to see me as in deed menny came
to se me out of Love to me and in sitting with us
in Silence He was drawn forth to Speak a few words
and Mentioned that Scripture in Isaiah when
He was sent to Hezekiah with this message
"Thus sayeth the Lord set thine House in order
for thou shalt Dye and not Live."
This Awakened me throughly for now believing that
all Hopes of Life was gone and that now I had nothing
to do with these Earthly things but to Prepare for
Death for I Knew not how soon I must Leave this World

verso

---

and be centerd in Eternity either to be miserable for
ever or to be receivd into Everlasting Joy tho he was drawn
to speak thus yet he signifyd he did not know that
it would be so with me or that He had this Perticular
Message to me but as it arose in his Minde but O! I could not get it out of my
Minde Indeed the rest of our Family were Pretty
much affected there with for I think my Father and Mother and
all my Sistors ware Present now I thought I would endeavour
to lead anew Life and give up all to the Will of the Almighty
in Hope He would be Pleased to spare my Life,
And that now I must leave of all my Own notions &
Conceits to attain Health Even in Eating and Drinking
but be guided by the Pure Light of Truth as it guided
and Pointed out my duty not Indulging my Self but
useing what stirring Exercise the strength of my Body would
admit and Eating and Drinking that which I found freedome
in but O! the menny weakness's and Indulgences that I
had gratified my self in it was hard to give up yet by
following this Pure witness of Truth in my Breast and
obeying it I was Inabled by degrees to overcome them.

Page 11

Wm Squires and his Wife of whome I have made men=
=tion of before ware very kinde unto me often lending
me their Horse to ride out when I could not tell
how to walk on foot menny times inviting me me up to
their House to Eate and Dring something which some=
=times I axcepted And He being a Public Friend would
give me good Advice and was a sopport to me in the
Truth now having given up all into the Hands of the
Almighty and Trusting in Him alone I began to Amend
and gain strength,
I remmember after I was got a little better a
a Friend asked me to go a Journey as far
as Enstone and lent me their Horse I axcepted
thereof as thinking the Ride might do me
good In Riding along I was led to contemplate
on Heaven and the Joy there was there it being
free from noise and Disturbances to breake the Peace
of the Minde and I seemd got almost thither But when
I thought my Life would be spared a little longer and looking
on the Earth it appeard to me a Cold Difucult and Exer=
cising Place

verso

Wherein there ware menny Worldly besetments
Frowns and Temptations to wrestle with and over=

=come but there seemed to be someting of the Love
of god in my Heart towards my Parents Friends
and Neighbours and I was willing to Remain Labour=
=ing among those trials and Dificulties if it Pleased
the Almighty in his Fear for the Honour of His
Pure Truth, thus by degrees I got a little better
but I found menny weakness's and Indulgences
of self that I often gave way to which when my
Parents and Sistors saw they would gently tell
me of them and Desire me to leave them of say=
=ing they speak out of Love and goodwill to one
if I Indulged my self in them and in such ways they
might bring on bad Habits and their Admonitions
sunk deep into my Minde and ware a great strength
to me to Inable me to give up all more fully into the
Hands of the Almighty and not to be so carefull after
that food which perrisheth but to seek after that Food

Page 12

which nourisheth up the Soul unto Eternal Life,
so by degrees I got to do a little work and found benifit
thereby sometimes out of doors for I found great
benefit by being out in the Air thinking my self
a little able to work I took to Weaving a little shag
as being willing to do any thing for Peace as my
strength of Body would Admit,
Now being arived to about the 22 year of my
Age I Kept a short Account of my Life and
how I passed my time wrighting a Line or two
Every day as what Perticular things passed or
making a minute of what arose in my Minde
and it was very Benifical to my Minde I believe
as it caused me to Recolect how I had Passed the
Day and wether I had done anything that was rong
and if I had that I might be aware and not do
so on the Morrow, those following are a few of
of the Minutes I made

1784

1st mo [January]"Cannot set to great a Gard on the

'Tongue tho it may seem ever so Clear yet to be
'to Positive is rong the yea or Nea is sufficient

verso

[page left blank]

Page 13

[page left blank]

verso

'Without any more words and that should be
'used with Caution.'
=23 I am very sorry for these three things is
Perticular among menny others'In giving to
'much Liberty to the Tongue in letting in a Spirit
'of Discontent and Indulging my self in things I
'knew to be rong when I did consider and gave no
'way to the Enemies plausable arguements which
'he would throw in my way for its being no Harm'.
[*month obscured*] =11 its good to be content in what situation
'soever we are Placed and persevear in the way
'that brings true and Lasting Peace',
-16 as I continue patient I believe what ever
'Imployment the Almighty shall allot me I
'believe its my duty nevver to be discontentedth
'or uneasy about it but to look to Him for help and strength both in=
'=wardly and outwardly to preserve me from doing
'Evel and teach me to do good'
28th It was recommended in our Meeting to day
than none should Place their dependance on

Page 14

Man or Look for Instrumental help from Him
or them but wait upon and look to the Lord alon,
for help and Instruction' then if any thing was
spoken in Love it would be a deal more Eddifying
'to the Minde',

4mo [April] 26th In the day of Prosperity there is great need to walk
Humbly and Circumspectly befor the Almighty
least the love of the world and the Friendships
should steal upon one at unawares and draw the
minde from the Injoyment of the Pure Truth by
which menny have been brought Into much sorrow
and Trouble for want of watchfullness,
7mo [July] 11th I thankfully acknowledge the Almightys Mercy and
Goodness In that He has for sometime Past preserved
me through menny seeming Difficulties and hardships
beyond my Expectation yet I am so sensible of my own
Weakness that I Humbly crave Divine assistance and
Mercy to strengthen and preserve me for the time to
come

verso

1784

11mo [November] 15 this Morning Set out with Fath'r sistor B and H to the
the Funeral of Aunt Margaret Gibbs of Epwell who Died
of a Cancer in her Breast she was a good woman and
given up to the Will of the Almighty I believe and tho the
Loss of Her be great yet Her gain will be much greater I
believe
9 mo [September]
F[irst] Day 29, it is good to wait upon the Almighty and obey
the Pure light of Truth which openeth the under=
=standing and shews him that to serve his God is the
only way to Injoy true Comfort and to Injoy his
outward gifts,

11 [October] 18 fine Monthly Meeting to day P.B[1]. Friends Wm Barratt
and Ann Stait went with Cousins to witney on Horse=back
'strive to walk in the Faith and Patience of Jesus
tho it may seem hardwork at times yet it brings Peace
that Exceeds all Wordly Things and when one looks
round and sees wath distresss and Hardships some
Poor Creatures undergo to get a living and consider
how much better of we are than they shourdly it must
raise in us great thankfullness and a sympathy

Page 15

for the Relief of Such poor Creatures,
11mo [November] 8th was at Witney Monthly Meeting which was small the
Meeting for discipline held long considering how
little Buisness was done on account of the Negligence
of some Friends in their duty wareby the Affairs
ware hindred and some delayed from time to time
till they ware grewn so out of Place that they ware
wholy neglected, to the sorrow of some Sincear Hearted
Friends
12mo [December] 31st our Friend Wm Squires having been very
Poorly for some time past he departed this Life
this day, the Loose of Him will be greatly felt
by menny I believe, he was a man that was
verry Charitable to the Poor, and tho he was
a Man in a Capaciety to have gotten much
of this Worlds wealth and greatness yet he
declined them, to seek after something more last=
=ing"a Treasure in the Heavens that nevver
"fadeth away;,

verso

---

1 Probably an abbreviation of 'public Friends' – Friends who ministered or preached to the wider public rather than just within established Quaker meetings.

1785

3mo [March] =13 In all our undertakings it is best to have
an Eye to the Witness of Truth within and
act agreeable thereunto for that will preserve
the minde through all Difficulties, and gives
True Satisfaction to the Minde,
22 Nicholas Wald from America vissited our Meet=
=ing and after=wards Fathr and Wm Albright went
with him to Bistor [Bicester],
4
1st Day [Sunday] 27 Barton Meeting[2] to day, It seems a rather
slackness in Friends for I have observed that to
Day nor this time last year none attended Barton
Meeting from Charlbury[3] whereas it had been constontly
attended by sevral from Charlbury and I believe to
good Satisfaction their being menny Neighbours that
generaly came in and the Truth there delivered seemd
to have a good Effect upon some of them
4mo [April] 8th Wm Mathews An Elderly Frd an American
Paid us a visit and wee had a Comfortable Meeting
together of Friends and Others to pretty good Satisfaction I believe

Page 16

4mo [April] 10 Uncle Gibbs from Epwell came home with
sistor Betty from Epwell and return'd back the same
day, was favourd with the Company of another
Friend from America viz George Dellwin
who had a desire also that the Neighbours should
be let know of the Meeting which was accordingly
done and we had a large Meeting in which four
Testimonies ware borne wareby the People
ware directed not to place their dependance on
Man but that they should turn their mindes
inward to their True Teacher Jesus Christ the
Light within "who Teacheth as nevver Man"
"Taught"
6mo [June] 1st In the day of Prosperity it is good to look
back and remmember how it was with us in
the day of Adversiety when the minde was
exercised and brough so low that it hath been
made willing to do any thing to finde Mercy
and axceptance of God, and have Pettioned

verso

the Almighty that if He would be pleased in mercy to bless
them with Health and Strength they would no more
seek to gratify their own Carnall desires but be willing
to bear the Cross in what the Almighty should be
pleased to make known unto them to be their duty
to do by the Opperation of His divine Light upon
their understandings Yet how menny when the
Almighty hath Blessed them with Health and
strength and plenty have given way to the
Inticing Prospects of Worldly greatness for want
of keeping in an Humble watchfullness and over
a greatfull sence of the Obligations the Are under
for his great Mercys and Blessing by waiting
for Strength from Him to Answer His pure
Requirengs, for want of this when they have
come to a true sence of their sad Condition they
have been brought into greater sorrow and dis=
=tress of Minde than before,

Page 17

1785

8 [July] 23rd Samuel Spavall vissited our Meeting
to day
=29 sometimes meeting with grievences and
Troubles the Minde is brought almost to a dis=
=ponding Condition in which Situation it is

2 Earliest recorded reference of meeting 1668.
3 Earliest recorded reference of meeting 1668.

good to Exercise Patience least the Enemy
should take advantage of our Weakness and
so cause us to do or utter things in our own
Wills
Let the Fear of the Almighty be before thine
Eyes, even when thou Refreshest thy self
thy Table, that His blessing may attend it,
9 [August] 14th O! How the Poor are oppress
with hard
Labour and low wages thereby being deprived
of the sufficiences of and nescessories of Life
when
they stand in most need of them, thereby the
Lives
of some are become very sorrowfull, wile the
Rich menny of them are full and at ease,
taking their Pleasure, not sufferring their Eyes,

verso

---

to behold their hardships lest their Compassion
should
be stir'd up thereby and put them in minde of
their
Duty to God, to Improve their Talent which they
have
received also, which will make them willing to
adminis=
=ter Relief and Comfort to the Needy and
Distress'd
8mo [August] 18th being out a Reaping with
Father and Sistor,
came home to meeting, there being two women
Friends to be there who ware upon a Religious
visit to Friends viz Ann Jessop, from America,
and Mary Roe, from London,
11mo [November] 20th sometimes the Outward
Tryals of our
Patience may be an Emblem of that Inward
or Spiritial Labour Performed in Spirit to
god, wherein the Flesh must bear the Cross
with Patience so that the work on Truths behalf
may be freed from Imperfections,

1786

9mo [September] 1st very Cold snow on the
ground my Minde
has been much Exercised to day and I hope it will
prove for my good,

Page 18

1786

1mo [January] =8th through the Exercise of my
minde I
have been made sensible that tis but vain
to fix ones minde upon any Earthly things
because of the Fricquent Disapointments that
attend them,
2mo [February] 7th It is good to be very carefull
how we have to
do with any Evel minded Persons and when
we cannot verry well avoid it we should be very
care=
=full of our Words and Actions to speak and do
nothing but what the Truth will Justify because
if the have any opportunity they take hold of
the least
trifling matter to slander the Truth and them that
strive to walk therein,
3mo [March] 12th = came away from Friend
squires's having Liv'd
with her about half a year she and I not agreeing
verry well in some Perticulars I thought it was
best to part
=15 some when they have been at a meeting and
heard
Truth declared have been throughly sensible
thereof

verso

1786

but in Striving to walk agreeable thereunto they
have
been brought to see their own Weakness and
Unworthy=
=ness to that degree, that they have Despised the
Truth
and turned against it, for want of being low and
hum=

=ble enough that the Power of the Almighty might
work in them, and Inable them to overcome their own
weakness's, and in time make them more Worthy,
4mo [April] 9th very Poorly with a Chillyness, and sickness
O! thought I we must Indeavour to do our Duty as the
Light of Truth makes it manifest, and then what ever
Afflictions befalls us, we shall be the better able to bear
it in True Resignation,
5mo [May] 21st took a walk it being a fine Morn'g the Birds
did sing and the Flowers ware in Blume O! how
Delightfull, there was nothing to grieve and afflict
the minde which for want of watchfullness, and through
the disobidience of some is menny times sadly Oppressed
with sorrow

Page 19

7mo [July] 27th went to Witney with Mary Fardon to the
Burial of her Brothers Daughter a verry hearty
Girl, till sised with a Violent Fever, that quickly
Croped the promising rose before it was quite in
full Bloome,
8mo [August] 9th very Hot and trying to poor Creatures that have
not nescesaries sufficient to support Nature was
it not that the Almighty is carefull over them they
must Perrish, now if some of the Lofty ones ware
sometimes to be Exposed to heats and hardships it
would be a means of Humbling them and letting them
see how much their Days work is behinde hand
and also that it must be done up if ever they come
to Injoy a Place of Happiness Above,
8mo [August] 20th Received the sorrowfull Account of Aunt Ann Hem=
=mings death she was a woman that Indulged herself
giving way to Carlessness and Indolence the Ilness fell
to her Lot at times yet by not being dilegent to
Improve the Oppertunities which the Almighty
afforded Her in being watchfull to follow the Pure

verso

Light of Truth Her Disorder Increased upon her
and Brought her into an Un [illegible] Situation for sometime
before she Dy'd "O that all would be Diligent to Im=
"=prove their Talent wile they have time."
9mo [September] 5th two women Friends had a Meeting appointed here
which was agreeable to Friends viz Mary Pole
and Patience Bright
my Minde being Exercised I made the following
Minute
"The desire of my Heart is to the Almighty that
He would be Pleased to give me strength in the
Difficult and Proving seasons to go through them
without being to low, so as to give way to a
Dijected state of minde least the Enemy should
take the Advantage thereof to the grief of
the Sincear Hearted,
9mo [September] 17th went with Thos French to Seaconcutt [Sezincote]
was at Stowe Meeting which was small and

Page 20

the Life of Truth seem'd scarsely to be felt to strive
amoungst them and some instead of being glad
to go to Meetings to Receive Strength and Com=
=fort to their Souls they seem to be Holdless
about it. O! that the Affairs of the World may
nevver hinder any from going to meetings,
10 [October]=28 our Preparative Meeting to Day held
according to appointment by the Monthly meeting
sevral of the Commity being Present which ware
appointed by the Quarterly Meeting to attend the
Monthly and Preparative Meetings and ware
things ware grown out of Order by slackness
in some Friends to see that they ware put to

Rights
11mo [November] 2nd two women Public Friends one came
from America Paid us a visit at our
Meeting to Day,
11mo 5th took a Comfortable walk, to Chusegood

verso

Company is of great Advantage to the young
People to strengthen their Mindes in the Everlas=
=ting Truth, and bad Company is very hurt=
=full and Dangrous to draw the Minde of from
that which is good,
11mo [November] 30th I have been grieved to see People careless
about their souls welfare, which is of the greatest
moment, far beyond any Earthly Things,
12mo [December] 29th it hath appeared to me to be very Hurt=
=full for young Men and Women to assem
=ble mush together to spend the Evening in
myrth and Vanity because they draw the
mindes of one another of their Guard and from
the Pure Truth and the Rein is let loose to
the Tongue to applause one another and if
there is any one Amoungst them that is more
sollid than the other, and will not do so

Page 21

they Rail at Him Calling him stiff Ignorant
or Foolish, but consider not that they are
the Ignorant and Foolish, and if they
could see their selves they would see that
they ware deceived and that their Mindes
ware drawn from the Pure Innoscient
Truth into sensual delights which must
Perish,

1787

1[January]=1st I am very desireable in my Minde that
I may be more watchfull for the future
to walk agreeable to the gracious Manifes=
=tation of the Pure Truth in mine own Breast

1st [January] 3rd it being a leiserly time that I had not much
work to do took a walk to see my Relations and
Pay them a Visit, went to sibford to see Cousin
Thos French and Wife slept there that night set
out pretty soon in the Morning to Epwell ware I
found Uncles, and Aunts, Pretty well, staid with them
one Night In the Morning set out with Uncle Gibbs,

verso

to sibford week day Meeting[4] after Meeting went to
Brails to see Cousin Jno Hemmings, staid with him
that Night, next morning went with Him to shipstone
with whom I had some Friendly discourse staid one Night with Cousing
Jno Wells who Maried Mary French she being kin
to us and has got a fine Boy, was at their First
day [Sunday] Meeting[5] which seemd to be attended with devine
goodness, after dinner took my Kinde leave of them
and set out for Home Reachd home about six oclock
ware I found my Friends Tolerable well,
4[April]=31 O! How menny are Complaining of Tryals
and HardShips in this thing and the other
Thing when Alas they have no reason to Complain
for If they did but Feel what some Poor Crea=
=tures undergo to get a Living through heats
and Colds and hard Labour they would Perceive
that they ware in a Happy situation,
F[irst] Day [Sunday] 18th of 2nd Mo [February] fine Pleasent Day, to those

Page 22

whose mindes are not disturbed with Cares
and Anxieties that to friquently besets the
Minde wile here espescialy those who do
not walk agreeable to the Pure witness of Truth

4 Earliest recorded reference of meeting 1668.
5 Earliest recorded reference of meeting 1668.

in their own Breast, as it Points out their
Duty to them
3 [March]=18th O! how discontented and Unsettled
are the mindes of menny People, Crying
out if I had but this thing and the other
I should be happy which wen they have ob=
tained it they are still disconted and
in a worse state than before, by seeking
to satisfy their vain desires their Mindes
not being centered in the pure Wisdom which
if the ware to come to it would let them see
what they wanted to give them Content and
True satisfaction, viz Heavenly food to
nourish their Poor sould and then their cra=
=vings desires would be silenced,

verso

4mo [April] 21st An American Friend came here to day
and had a Meeting with Friends his Name
was Zacaria Dicks a Notable Friend and
on the Morrow had a Meeting with sevral Friends
at Chipping Norton[6], to good satisfaction I believe,
sevral states being spoken to, and Friends ware
directed to seek for that Peace which would Indure
beyond the grave, Mentioning the Words of Jesus
"my Peace I leave with you my Peace I give
unto you not as the World giveth give I unto
you." that Peace which is of the World being
subject to Ebbings and flowings, but the Peace
that comes from Jesus would Indure for Ever
Took a Solitary walk alone one Evening
and saw a young woman of our Society In Company
with a young man of a Difrent Religion which
Brought me Seriously to Reflect with sorrow
on the Danger there was In giving way to vain

Page 23

Company and the great need there was to be
on our watch and not give way to the least
selfish desire that might tend to lead the minde
from the pure Truth
the Sixth Month [June] the tenth took a walk to
Milton meeting[7] saw Thomas Mintchens
wife there who used to live at Worster [Worcester], he
having Maried Her from thence a Largish
Meeting but Truth seemed to be oppress therein
the Sixth Month [June] the Eighteenth this ANoon [afternoon]
we are favourd with the Company of two
Woman Friends viz Fr'd Beavington
and the Widdow Boon and a Comfortable
meeting was held the Lukewarm and
Indifrent been spoken plain unto and the
willfull and Stubborn ware warned of their
Dangrous State also the Elderly Friends
ware put in Minde to be Examples and
Incouragers to the younger in the Truth.

verso

1787

6mo [June] the 22nd took a Journey with Sistor to Sibford and
from thence to Banbury Quarterly meeting[8] which
was held on the third day [Tuesday] following
7 [July]=27th Rich'd Gilkes came here to Day from
Devises and had a meeting with Friends
in the Evening He being on a Religious
visit to Friends hereaboutes
8 [August]=5 Observations on the Hardships of the poor
I have observed how hard the Labour causing
their Bones to Ake and their Body to be full
of Pain which is very trying to the Minde
sometimes destitute of Food to strengthen nature
or sometimes lose of Appetite not able to take
something to Inliven their wearies Spirits yet
under the nescesiety of Drudging on or Else
some of their Family must starve or their
Backs go naked O! that these things might
sink deep in the mindes of the Rich and full

6 Earliest recorded reference of meeting 1668.

7 Earliest recorded reference of meeting 1668.

8 Earliest recorded reference of meeting 1654.

that their Harts might be tender so as to Admini=
=ster something to Relieve and Comfort them which

Page 24

I believe would be acceptable to the Almighty
and they found in the Discharge of their Duty
as good Stewards who have Received largly
of the Lords outward gifts and in gratitude
they are willing to be found making good
use of them to the Honnour of his Name

1788

the Third month [March] ye 30th was at meeting to
day which was Small and I have often
took notice that menny seem careless of
attending week=day meetings as tho it was
a matter of great Indifrence thus wasting
their Precious time which they will know the
want of by and by which was given them
to work out their Souls Salvation and that
with fear and trembling for their poor Souls
stand in need of Heavenly food day by day
as much as their poor Bodys do of Earthly
Food which makes me think for all their
great and high Pretentions they are very

verso

Negligent of their Souls Everlasting well=
=fare,
the ninth month [September] the tenth went to C[hipping] Norton M Meet=
ing on foot Truth seemed to be very low in the
meeting yet the Buisness was gone through in Love
and Unity
the ninth month [September] the seventh at meeting to day
was favoured a little with the Refreshing dew
from the Almighty who is pleased to manifest
his will to his Children and also to Refresh
them with His Love and goodness as they
are concearned to retire in ward in their Spirits and
wait upon Him in aweful Silence,
10mo[October] 28 I have observed that when some
are Reached by the Power of Truth to
[text obscured] a Sence of their Poor Condition
and are thereby made willing to give up
and walked Humbly and Circumspectly in the

Page 25

Truth these are often Despised Reproached
and Slandered by others at doing the least
thing Rong on having a bad misfortune
O! that these may not be discouraged
but when they finde their mindes oppress
and have none upon the Earth to trust
in let these turn their mindes Inward and
wait upon the Almighty in a awefull stillness and they will
finde their mindes Strengthened from above
11mo [November] the twenty first there was one of our
Society or at least in profession with
us who Joined hands with a young woman who difred in the
way of worshiping the Almighty to what
we do at which my minde has often been
affected to think that one who desires to walk
in the Straight and narrow path that leads
to Everlasting Happiness should look out into
the world and Desire to have a Companion that

verso

that has no desire to walk in the same path
but on the other will strive to draw him there=
from O! how can such a help meat conduce
to mutual Happiness when instead of asisting him
to persevear in the Right path and to help him
out in Dificulties and Distress's She increases
difficulties and Rejoices when she can draw him
into the Broad path which if they perrish in
will lead to Everlasting misery,
13nth [December] the Seventeenth went to Oxford
Quarterly meeting[9] after the Meeting for
worship the Friends proceeded upon the

9 Earliest recorded reference of meeting 1668.

Buisness which was conducted in Love
I thought if Friends ware more lowly
and walked more in the way of Selfdenial
the would be good Examples to others who
know but very little of that self denying
Life which must be led by all that would
Injoy Everlasting Rest [text obscured] hereafter

Page 26

which must be Obtained by Obeying and following
our Saviours Doctrine who said come unto
me all he that are weary and Heavy
Laden and I will give you Rest Learn
of me for I am meek and Lowly in
Heart and he shall finde Rest to your souls
and also I have found it is very nes=
=cessary to wait upon the Lord and seek
Him often to know his will and also
to beg of Him that He will be pleased
to give us help and Strength to sup=
=port our mindes from being drawn
aside by the Temptations of the Enemy
who often besets us divers ways sometimes
stirring up others to Reproach and Sland=
=er us who are concerned for the good and
prosperity of the Truth O shuredly there
is great need for us often to Retire in Our
mindes to the pure Spirit of Truth which

verso

will let us see the workings of the Carnal
selfish Spirit in us from that which
seeks the good of all and has something of
Life and power in it that is strengthening
and Comforting to the Humble
the Eleventh month [November] the twenty fifth
took a walk to Barton meeting on
foot it is a meeting that is held once
a Quarter for the good of the Neighbours
that do not make a proffession with
us not menny Friends there but a few
Neighbours came in and it seemd to
be a Satisfactory meeting warein Devine
goodness was felt,

1789

the first month [January] the Second this day two

women Public Friends paid us a Visit
viz Rebecca Young and Ann Sumerland,

Page 27

the Second month [February] the fourth I have been
often Exercised in my minde and been
made Sensible of the Exercises Tryals Dis=
=couragments and oppressions some poor
Creatures undergo wile menny that live
at Ease and in fullness have such plenty
that they cannot tell what to with it now
if they would but Look out and Distribute
to these Labouring ones Liberaly it would
give them great satisfaction and I believe
it would be so axceptable to the Almighty
that He would bless the Rest to them and
and Cause them to Injoy his Love and good=
=ness which is better than any Earthly things
the second month [February] the Eleventh Old Wm Barrett
came to day to be at Our Monthly meeting
which was held on the morrow to good satis=
=faction I believe

verso

the second month [February] the fourteenth was favourd
with the Company of Frd Tho's Cash at Meeting
to day and we ware Comforted and Refreshd
together in the Love of Truth I believe,
second month the fourteenth [February] I had to Rem=
=ark that menny there are that are lifted up
in Earthly notions and Earthly wisdom
and Self Righteousness as believing that
would lead them to Hapiness hereafter but
are not following our Saviours Precepts
who sayeth unless a man deny himself
take up his daily Cross and follow me
He cannot be my Disciple, and are
not Enough become acquainted with the
new Birth which cannot do nothing again

=st the Truth but for the Truth and
there mindes is taken of Earthly Things
and set on Heavenly Things which will

Page 28

Indure when all these Earthly things
shall come to an end and be no more
the Second month [February] the twenty ninth
I have made this Remarks that some
marsters and mistress that pretend
to be good Friends frown at their
Servants and think that the meat
and Drink that they Eat is to
good for them as tho they ware not
fellow mortals
the third month [March] the Ninth I have
Remarked when wee are with Friends
in Conversation or others it is very
Nescesary in all our Words to Have
recourse to the Witness of Truth in
our own Breast that we do not speak
words sincerly to get praise or Com=
=mendation or to be thought Religious
but simply to Incourage one another and

verso

Strengthen one another in the Truth or
otherwise it may prove to our great grief
for some that Love Libertys in unlawfull
Things Rejoice to draw others aside to be
Like themselves so seeing that wee are
of our gard they take that oppertunity to
Insinuate to us that if wee be so strict
and Labour in Love to manifest to others
their errors and danger of being drawn
out of the way that leads to peace and
Happiness we shall only meet with Rep=
=roach and be Laughf'd at but Let them
Laughf that will Laughf they that would
Injoy True Peace of minde Here and
Injoy Happiness hereafter must minde the pure
Light of Truth in their own mindes and
obey it in all Things according to the best
of their understanding

Page 29

the third month [March] the thirteenth was at
meeting
and in Sitting in Silence my minde was
very poor and low being sensible of the want
of Heavenly food to strengthen my feeble
minde,
the 3rd Month [March] the sixteenth during
our Pilgrimage here sometimes wee
meet with Discouragments by the sensure
of Some.
and Under a Sence of our Own weakness
and Unwatchfullness to the pure Lead=
=ings of Truth that we are Ready to
Conclude that in keeping to this pure wit=
=ness we are Less comendable and not so
couragous to do good and persevear therein as
some others
who do not pretend to be so strict and
so are Ready to give way and run in
our own wills saying we will be more
couragous but here in Stead of gaining ground

verso

or Strength in the Truth we loose it and are
soon sensible of our own unable ness to do good
and the nescesiety of this Pure witness to guise
and direct us and that it was through the
want of Patience and watchfullness to its
Leadings that we have made no greater pro=
=gress in the Truth and by letting in discour
=agements and Reasoning and not through the
Insuficiency of this Blessed Guide,
the third Month [March] the Nineteenth Sistor
and
I went to Barton Meeting on Friend Squires
Horse the Meeting seemed as tho it would
be small at first yet after a wile the
Neighbours came in young people and
we had a Quiet Comfortable Meeting
in which Incouragment was given to
the weak and feeble Hearted and the Dis=
=orderly Lukewarm and Indifrent

Page 30

walkers ware warned of the Dangrous
situation the ware in if they willfully

Persisted theirin and they ware also
warned to Repent and for sake whatever
they knew to be rong and Live in the fear
of God and obey his Heavenly Manifes=
=tation in their own Breast which if
they faithfully liv'd up thereunto it would
be more to them than all this world could
afford,
the fourth month [April] the third was at meeting
to day which was small O how menny
Plead Excuses Even in the Highist stati=
=on of Life who are for most in tranacting
the Buisness at Monthly and Quarterly
meeting and have but little to do that need
Hinder them from giving no wonder that them
that are poor Have families to provide
for are negligent and slack in attending them

verso

---

when they have such Bad Examples from those
that have nothing to hinder them,
the fourth month [April] the tenth had a largish meeting
to day with the Friends viz Rebecca Jones from
America and Cristianna Husler from York
together with sevral other
Friends who ware so kinde to favour
us with their Company from the Neighbouring
towns, at which Friends ware advised not to be
careless and Cold in their worship to the Almighty
and some ware warned of the Danger they ware
in by Pleading Excuses of Ever being ad=
=mitted to the wedding feast
the fourth month [April] the twenty fourth this
Morning Cousins and I set out for witney
Quarterly meeting Began at 10 oclock fullish
meeting the American Friend had a fine
time in the Morning at which the Friends
ware advised not to attend the Meeting in

Page 31

---

form only but In power which would sanctify the form
the fourth month [April] the fifteenth went to witney
there was a meeting for worship Held before
the meeting for Buisness began in which
Friends ware advised to attend week day
meetings and not to plead Excuses Especi=
-aly those of the Highist rank as preten=
=ding Buisness or some Body to come or
I attended last week and the like having
thereby brought sorrow and darkness over
their mindes instead of Peace but when
they have left their Buisness with a good=
=will to go to meetings they have found such
satisfaction that tho they have had a deal
of work to do yet it has went on with a
deal more Ease and pleasenter that at
other times the fourth month [April] the second took
a little Journey with Sistor Hannah to seasoncutt [Sezincote]

verso

Charingworth &et was at Armscutt Meeting[10] and
I believe it was to good satisfaction it is a meeting
which is held once a quarter for the good of the
Neighbours as well as Friends
the fifth month [May] the twenty fifth was at meeting
which was very dull and heavy there being menny
Sleepy ones there who do not strive against so much
which is a great Hurt to their mindes and
Instead of feeling Refreshment and Comfort in
giving to meetings they come away Cloudy and
under Condemnation and it would look exceeding
well of young People if they would pull of their
Hatts or Stand up it would show that they ware
Consciensely concearned to behave with decency
in worshipping their great Creator,
the Sixth month [June] the Sixth this day Received the
sorrowfull account of Aunt Corks death she liv'd
at Charringworth a Health woman and middle
Aged she had been at Market about 2 miles of
Returned Chearfully but in getting of her Horse

Page 32

---

found her self unwell she said but little but

---

10 First recognised by Monthly Meeting 1668.

Dyed before Morning leaving a largish family
to lament and Mourn for the Lose of so tender
a parent being young and now left fatherless
and Motherless Exposed to struggle through the
Temptation and Troubles of this unceartain
world
a Striking instance to all to lead such a Holy and
Righteous Life that they may not be a fraid of
Death if it should come upon them as a thing in
the Night but be able to give a good account
how they have spent their Time wile here
the Sixth month [June] the twenty Eight there are
menny Tryals and Exercises we poor Creat=
=ures are Exposed to sometimes almost Ready
to overcome and make us give way from
striving to go forward in the Path that
leads to Everlasting Happiness in which
seasons there is nothing better than to Re=
=tire into Stillness and wait upon the Almighty
for strength and incouragment from Him to
inable us to persevear through all showing faith

verso

in His power viz the secret witness of
Truth placed by Him in our own Breast
Sixth Month [June] 29th Sistor Hannah and I
set out for Sibford was at Meeting
a Worthy Friend Joseph Harris had a
Public Testimonie to Bare and He had
to Declare that there seemed to be dry=
=ness in some and a want of water in
their Sisterns Reciting the words of
Calebs Daughter viz to Her Father
Father thou hast given me a South
Land give me also a Land of Water
so He gave her the upper and Nether
Springs,
afterwards went to Banbury Quarterly meeting
at which menny or Sevral Testimonies
ware Born and Friends ware advised
to be plain in their dress Perticularly in

Page 33

the form of the Hat for if the did not con=
=form to the world in that Respect altho
little in appearance yet it being in
the Cross there was a Testimonie Born
thereby or to that Respect,

7mo [July] 8th I make this Remark how unbe=
=coming it is to be proud and value our
selves upon decking our selves and Dis=
=figureing our selves with gaudy appa=
=rell which are but dust and soon
must be laid Level there with as say=
=eth the Scripture Let not your
addorning be that of Platting the Hair
waring of Gold Putting on gay apparrel
but let your addorning be that of the hid=
=den man of the Heart a meek and Qui=
=et Spirit which is of great price with the
Lord
the Seventh month [July] the Tenth did not go

verso

to meeting for which I was Sorry having
generally attended week day meeting which
I have found very Benificial to the minde
and I believe tis to all sober mindes Cleans=
=ing and doing away menny thing that
have Crept in through unwatchfullness
and giving Comfort and Strength when
weary and allmost cast down giving
fresh Life and Vigour to go through their
Buisness with Clearness and Ease
7 Month [July] the 27 was at meeting was
favoured
with a little degree of Comfort but was
Concearned to see menny give way to Sleepy=
=ness day after day o what Thoughts must
they have of the Devine Almighty power
and when we assemble to Worship Him
it should be In a very Humble and Carefull
manner and great Reverence of minde

Page 34

for as we Read in Scripture God is a
Spirit and they that worship Him aright
must worship Him in Spirit and in
Truth for [illegible] the Father seeketh to worship
Him
the seventh month [July] the Thirteenth
was at meeting most
of the young Friends being there
was favoured with a little degree
of Hope that the Almightys watch=
=full Eye was Still over us for good

if we would but be Obidient to His
gracious drawings and minde the
gentle Reproofs of His Power,
Seventh month [July] the 24 Monthly meeting
to day at Witney caried my Sistor
Hannah Behinde me on Horse Back
to Cousins she stay'd there some
days smallish meeting one Testimonie

verso

was Born in which it was Recommended
to Love God who is good to them that Love Him
According to the Scripture He that Hon=
=noureth me I will Honnour but they
that disonnour Me will dishonour them and
Likewise
that they should give up every Thing
that the Almighty Has a Controversy
with and they would Injoy His Blessing
and that they that seek me Early
shall finde me finde a Stay to their
Fasted Troubled mindes after which
meeting for Buisness began which was
gone through in Love and Concord tho truth
Truth seemd low,
the Seventh [July] month I went after meeting
to see Aunt and Cousins took notice how
Cousin set her Cap in a light Airy
manner giving way to Pride and it is found

Page 35

to be of great Hurt to young peoples mindes
to give way of Pride for tho they give way
a little at first yet be giving way by little
and little it groweth on them still they
are so delighted in it and their mindes
are drawn out to love wanton Company
more is the Pity was favoured a little a
Comming Home with a Degree of Peace
which made my Heart Cheearfull,
the Seventh month [July] the thirteenth
was at Meeting most of the young [text
obliterated]
friends being there was favourd [text obliterated]
a little degree of Hope that the
Almightys watchfull Eye was Still
Over us for good if we would but be
Obidient to His gracious drawings and
minde the gentle Reproofs of His Power.
the seventh month [July] the twenty Third
went to C[hipping] Norton on some Buisness

verso

Saw there Cousin John Hemmings
who is very poorly O may he be faith=
=full to Answer the Almightys Requirngs
who seems to be at work upon him so
that he may be made Quite willing to
give up what so ever the Almighty shall
Require of him for His great Names
sake and for His Favour and goodness which
which is Better than all Earthly things
seventh month [July] the twenty fourth took
a walk with Ann Oldaker Part
of the way to Witney after Meeting
the Seventh month [July] the Twenty Eight some
times when we fast Long how poor and
weak our Body's get so in the midst of
all these Earthly things seemingly sufficient
to make us quite happy yet these very things
often hinders the minde from feeling after
and striving for something more Lasting

Page 36

viz Heavenly Food, for want of which
the minde becomes so poor and Discon=
=solate that it cannot Injoy any of
these Earthly Things,
the Eight month [August] the Tenth was favourd
at Meeting to day tho small with a
little of the Refreshing Stream which
comes from that Fountain which is pure
and comes from Him who is the Author of
every blessing and goodness and all the
Righteous partake of when He In His
Mercy is Pleased to hand it fourth to
them in His Love,
the Ninth month [September] the fourth was
favourd at
meeting to day with the Company of a
Public Friend and after a time of Silence
He was drawn forth to Exort the People
to be Inward and weighty in their Spirits
when Assembled together to Worship the
Almighty and to be thankfull for the menny
Favours and Blessings wee injoy to what

verso

menny having done, and that we should be concearn'd
first of all to seek the Kingdom of Heaven and the Righte
=ousness theirof it being the most nescesary Things to conduce
to our Happiness here and our Everlasting Happiness
Hereafter
the Ninth month [September] the fourteenth I have taken notice
How some Friends that pretend to be steady friends
and might be serviceable ones to in the Society
Enjoying menny a blessing and Favour Having
but little to do are sitting down at Ease like
those that are in Ease in Zion Who have a
Talent afforded them by devine Providence ych they
appear to bury their Talent in the Earth not
minding to Improve it as they ought to do but are
a craving after the World and the Things their of
which hath often hurt their Mindes as Sayeth the
Scripture"the Love of Money is the Root of all
Evel which wile some coveted after they have
Erred from the Faith and Pierced themselves through
with menny sorrows."

Page 37

the Ninth Month [September] the twenty Eight fullish
meeting to day most of the Servants being there
and sevral straingers and we ware Comforted
and Refreshed together, and Indeed I Have often
found it very Benefical to my Minde to attend week
day meetings tho. I Know menny are apt to
make Excuses one is pleading buisness keeps him
at Home another he is unwell but O! Remember
what became of them that made Excuses when
they ware Invited to the feast one
Pleaded he had bought a piece of Land and
must needs go see it another he had bought five
yoke of Oxen and I go to Prove them
and another He had maried a wife and so
could not come but what was the Answer to
these when the Servants came and told their
Lord which Excuse they made why truly none
of those that ware bidden shall taste of my
Supper so may wee be carefull that none of us
Plead Excuses and so may be hindred thereby from
attaining that Rest which is immortal.

verso

the tenth month [October] the fourth went to Witney
and from thence with Robert Sessions to Oxford
Meeting Sevral Friends their from Divers
Parts P.B. [public] Friends Elizabeth Mintchin
J. Harris R. Sconce Wm Barrett E. May meeting
Began at Eleven after a time of Silence, sevral
Testimonies Ware born to Stir up Friends and
others to be more Carefull to fear and Serve the
Almighty from Whome Every Blessing Comes and
that when we comes to Worship the Almighty we
should come very Humbley as it is said in Scrip=
=ture How shall I come and appear before the Lord
shall I come with Rams or of Lambs or of ten thou=
sands of Rams no Thou hast no need of these but
the offerring of a Broken Heart and a Contrite Spi=
=rit A Broken Heart and a Contrite Spirit O! Lord
thou wilt in no wise reject and that they should
not Dress themselves up as fine and gay when they come
and appear before Him and indeed at no other time for
His Eye Runs too and fro, beholding the Evel and the
good for He knows who are Sincearly and Truly in
Heart disposed to serve Him Truthfully and who are

Page 38

not for as when good Samuel went to anoint David
to be King over Israel Jesse caused sevven of his
sons to pass befor Samuel and when there came a

tall comly and goodly Person to outward appearance
before Him Samuel said in his Heart shourdly this
is He but I think the Lord answered him this is not
he neither the Lord sees not as man sees the Lord
looks not at the outward appearance but He looks at
the Heart then said Samuel to Jesse hast thou not
another Son or to that Purpose besides there but His An=
=swer was after his manner there is the youngest but he is with the
sheep in the Wilderness and his Answer was Send
and fetch Him whome so Jesse sent for Him and the
Lord said this is He then Samuel took the Oil and pourd
it on His Head and Anointed Him to be King over
Israel and thus having faithfully performed His
Arrand which the Lord sent him to do he took his leave
and returned Whome, so that seeing the Lord looks
at the Heart wee should always Indeavour to Keep
our Conciences free from offence towards God and to=
=wards men,
the tenth month [October] the Eighteenth wrote a Letter to Cousin
William French who lives at Reading, at our Meeting
to day was Favoured with Stillness and great Quietness

verso

Quietness which was a great Comfort to my Minde,
the Tenth month [October] the twenty ninth took a walk to see a
Poor Woman who was In a Decline found She very weak
and Poorly and I believe she took it kindly now the
end of my wrighting this is that those Exceeding Poor
Dijected Despised Poor Creatures who are often looked
upon by the Rich unworthy to be taken notice of on account
of the meanness of their Condition now if the Rich would but
look out for those very Poor Creatures who are Ready to
Perrish for want of a bit of meat and a draft of Drink
(yea and often times I believe disorders and weakness's
are brought on them and their Lives shortned theirby
Menny times) and if they Rich would but go and see
them sometimes and sympathise with them and give them
something often O! How would it cause the Almighty to
Bless them for wee Read he that giveth to the Poor lendeth
to the Lord and He will Repay him but Truly the Lord
lendeth to us to give to the Poor,
the Eleventh month [November] the fifth was at meeting
and In Sitting in Silence Instead of feeling
a degree of Joy my minde was burthened
there appeared a Cloud of darkness over us
which occasioned my minde to be Sorrowful

Page 39

the Eleventh month [November] the twenty second it
being Milton meeting went thither on Horse
back call'd to see John Matthews before
meeting small meeting Especialy the
woman Friends on account of the badness
of the weather after a time of Silence John Mathews stood
up and Exorted the People to Retire into great
stillness of minde to wait upon the Almighty
to know His Commandments and to feel
His pure Word of Truth to arise In their
Hearts to make know their duty to the Almighty
and what they should do and when they
knew it they should leave all Earthly
Things to do His Will and then they would

Finde greater Peace than Worldly Things
could give,
the Eleventh Month [November] the twenty ninth to day was
comforted a little at meeting but our Meeting held
not long on account of the restless of some members I believe which
is a great hurt to the Power of Truth arising and
flowing freely,
the Eleventh month [November] the sixth fullish meeting today of

verso

Friends and in Sitting in Silence together I believe
we ware Favour'd with instruction and Comfort
from the Almighty who is pleased to own and acknow=
=ledge such who are truly concearned to wait
silently upon Him,
the twelfth month [December] the Fourteenth went to Burford
monthly Meeting[11] with Sistor Margrett Sistor Hannah
intended to go but it Proving so wett it was not fit
for she to go she being very weakly a pretty fullish
meeting considering the weather after a time of Silence
a Friend stood up and Spake Signifying there
ware some sensible of their own weakness poorness
and Nothingness without the help and assistance of
the Almighty and that this was an axceptable
state to feel that of themselves they could do no good thing
In which quiet still frame of minde the soul becomes teach=
=able by the pure Spirit of jesus in them which is called
which is called the witness of Truth the light of Jesus
the grace of God which Teacheth every own in their In=
=ward Man what is good and what is Evel what the
ought to do and what they ought to leave undone to please
the Almighty who is pleased thereby to make known the
way that is cast up for the Righteous and Reedmed to

Page 40

---

walk In, and that there was She Thought such
a Solidness and quietness in the Meeting that
was axceptable to the Almighty in which
state they ware fitted to pertake of the bread
which cometh down from Heaven which none
but them which none but them that Worship
the Almighty in Spirit and In Truth can
rightly pertake of,
the twelfth month [December] the Twenty fifth this day my
Sistor Betty was Joined in the Marriage to
Henry Maunder a Convincd Young man
one that had been Convinced of the Blessed
Truth for sometime being of a very sober
and innoscient behaviour,
the twelfth Month [December] the twenty eight it being Barton meet=
=ing with their with Richard Fardon, it being Held once
a Quarter for the good of the Neighbours sevral came in
in and ware very quiet and attentive to what was deliver'd
by a Worthy Friend who Signifyed to the People that He
would not have the think the time to be lost that was
pass'd in Silence and Stillness for they that truly waited upon
the Almighty in Silence and Stillness ware as much instructed

verso

---

as when menny Words ware Spoken for in this Stillness
and Retiredness of minde there was a true Teacher to be

---

11 Earliest recorded reference of meeting 1668.

found within them even the Spirit of truth which would
Teach them what was good and what was Evel what they
ought to do and what they ought to leave undone as the
carfully minded its gentle Instructions Reciting that Scripture
"that the Lord speaks to his people not as formerly by His pro=
=phets but He speaketh to them by His Son Crist Jesus
In the Hearts of the Children of Men and Women"

1790

the first month [January] the Seventeenth at meeting to day in Sitting
with Friends was a little comforted and refreshed I Trust
by the Springings up of the Pure Truth amoungst us,
The Second Month [February] the first was at meeting which was
small the Life of Truth I thought was hardly felt to arise
a mongst us wether it was owing to the Lukewarmness
of the Members or wether the Almighty saw meet to with=
-draw His Countenance from us for some good End I
cannot tell,
The Second month [February] the 28th having felt a Weight
upon my minde for sometime to go Visit a
young man not of our Profession as to Religion
viz Jn'o Turtle He being a Sober steady young man
and it often arose in my Minde that he would

Page 41

become a Quaker if he was Faithfull to the
lie up to the pure Witness
the third month [March] the 5th went to Burford Monthly Meeting
with Father which was pretty full onely one Public=
Testimonie was Born which was to this Effect that every
one should minde their own proper buisness which if they
did it would qualify and fit them to Worship the
Almighty who is the Authur of all Being Axceptabley
the third month [March] the 13 went to the Quarterly Meeting which
was held at Witney and began at ten oclock before friends
proceeded upon the Buisness a Friend had a few Words
to deliver to this Effect that friends should get down low
and Dig deep signifying there was a River the Streams
wareof make glad the Whole Heritage of God who are fav=
=ourd to Drink theirof, and that friends should get low
enough that they might be favoured to drink theirof to
the refreshing their Mindes after which Friends proceeded
upon buisness which was conducted in much Love and
Unity the Chief minute which took up Friends attention
most was respecting the uniteing Berkshire and Oxford=
=shire Quarterly meetings together into one some thinking
it would be of no Service as it would lessen the number
of Meetings and cause them to be at a greater dis from
one another and other being of the minde that ware the

verso

Meetings ware small it might be a means of helping them
and strengthening some mindes in the Truth,
the third month [March] the Twenty fifth Sistor Hannah

who has been very Poorly for these sevral weeks past
and still growing weaker and weaker Her disorder
proving to be the Dropsy, and she having a desire
to se Sistor Betty I went to Burford for Sistor who
came Just time enough to have a little of Sistor Hannahs
Company and for She to ease Her mine to her before
she Died,
the third month [March] the twenty seventh Sistor Hannah still
growing weaker and weaker about one oclock in the
After=noon She Departed this Life having settled Her
Peace with the Lord I believe and infull Asshurance
of being admited into the Kingdom of Everlasting rest
=and Joy amoungst the faithfull that are gone before
she seemed to go of very easy without either Sigh Grown
or Struggle, all of our Family being present and
a friend or two, She was much Resigned to the Will of
Devine Providence for some weeks before she Died
often signifying she was willing to Die if it ware the
will of Providence saying to Her sistor Betty who came

Page 42

from Burford to see she that she was willing to go
and Asked forgiveness of her Parents if she had of=
=fended them at any time in any thing which she was exceeding
carefull not to do being very obidient and dutifull
them to obey them, and I have this to say of she that
she was a very Kinde and Loving Sistor for when
she see me go rong or do anything which I ought
not to do she would give one gentle admonition not
to do so she was very kinde to Her neighbours and
Friends Especialy those who lived up to the pure
Witness of Truth in them and walked agreeable
thereunto according to the best of their understanding
she went of in Her Fathers arms who held her up in
her Bed the Last words she said was I have done
I have done, and tho the Lose of such a good sistor
is cause of Mourning to us who are left behinde
yet to she I trust "Tis Her Everlasting Gain,"
the third month [March] the Thirti'th this day being appointed
for the interment of my Dear Sistor the Corps was
caried to meeting attended by menny Relations and

verso

Neighbours I should have been very glad to have atten=
=ded the Corps to the grave but being very ill could
not yet I was Favour'd with strength to sit with
Friends in the Afternoon for sometime and In sitting
with them I found my minde a little Refreshed and a
Friend had a few words to deliver Recommending
to Friends to minde their True teacher the Witness of
Truth in their own breast which as the took heed to
its manifestation and guidance and follow its leading
it would tend to their everlasting Happiness when
time to them would be no more, or to that Effect,
the fourth month [April] the first very poorly being beset by the
Enemy of all mankind who seeks their misery and Dis=
=truction if the are not carefull to minde the pure light of
Truth in them and obey it which if they then it will let them see the snares

and besetments of the Enemy from that which is right and
and to their Everlasting Happiness, I was so beset
by the Enemy of my soul, that he represented to me
that I should be Miserable for Ever do what I would
I could nevver expect forgiveness for I had sinned against
the Holy Ghost therefore I might take my liberty in Wickedness

Page 43

And not strive to walk uprightly amoungst men there=
=fore I might Indulge my self in gratifying my own
vain Inclination to the full and Speak against the Truth
and them that walk theirin and then I should Live the longer
and Injoy Pleasure for a time but if not I should
Dye and be Miserable for Ever, but O! the Love that was
in me for my Friends and Neighbours at that Time
I thought I had rather dye and be Miserable my self
that live to be the cause of my Friends and Neighbours
to be miserable, and thus I wrestled and strugled in my
minde for some time earnestl breathing and praying to the
Almighty that He would be pleased to spare my Life and
forgive my sins that ware past and if He would I would
with His help and assistance walk before Him more care=
=fully and nevver offend Him any more, and O! the Love
and Goodness of God Almighty to my poor soul that He
gave me some Hopes that He had not quite forsaken me but
if I would walk before Him more humbly and carefully and
circumspectly for the future he would forgive what was past,
and blessed be His worthy Name for Ever who, in His
mercy caused His Sun to Shine in my Heart as a
Morning without Clouds to the Scattering and dis=
=pelling the Clouds of darknes which had so long oppressd

verso

my poor minde during the time I was tried and proved
which was suffered to try me for my good and wether
I would Love the Lord Almighty and His pure Truth
before and above any thing this World could
afford and to overcome the Enemy and I do Earnestly
Breath and Pray to Him that He will be pleased in
His Infinite Love and goodness still to Continue the visit=
ation of His Love and Mercy to me as to Inable me
to see all the Temptations and besetments of the Enemy
and to Inable me to overcome them in Ever degree
that I may Live all the remainder of my days to the Honnor
and Praise of Him who Created me and hath been
so very Mercyfull and good to me more than ever I
do deserve, "Praises be to His Worthy Name for Ever"
the Fifth month [May] the nineteenth being a little recoverd of
my Illness went to Witney for their weekday meeting and
in Sitting in Silence with Friends my Minde was Comforted
the fifth month [May] the thirtieth took a walk to Charingworth
to see Cousin Corks who ware very well on First day [Sunday]
was at Campden Meeting so to Charingworth and from

thence Home, the sixth month [June] the fourteenth it being

Page 44

our Monthly meeting one young married woman appeared
in a public manner, which I believe nevver appeared
in Public before after which the meeting Proceeded
upon Buisness which was gone throug in Love and Unity
the sixth month [June] the Twenty sevventh took a walk to Barton
Meeting and from thence to Banbury Quarterly meeting
a large meeting sevral Public friends ware their
substainchable ones and the people ware directed to
minde the Grace of God which brings salvation and hath
appeared unto all men which as the take heed thereunto
and obey it it would bring them out of a State of diso=
=bidience which all are subject to in their fallon nature
and bring them into a state of axceptance and obidience
to the Will of God and make them become Heirs of
the Kingdom of Heaven when time to them here should
be no more the meeting for buisness was held on
third day and the uniting the two Counties viz Berkshire
and Oxfordshire into one Quarterly meeting was agreed
on after meeting went with some Friends to Adderbury
staid their weekday[12] which was on the morrow after meet=
=ing walked home having a good Journey,
the Seventh month [July] the thirteenth took a walk to Charingworth

verso

to see Cousins there who ware very well and from thence
to Cousins at the Hill Farm and back to Campden meeting
after meeting walk to Cousin Jo's Ashby Seasoncutt [Sezincote]
ware I found them very well except young Cousin
Joseph who was very weak and poorly being in
a decline I believe went from thence to Stow
Meeting Cousin Jo's taking a little walk along
with me after meeting walk'd home having had
a Pleasent Journey for which I was very thank=
=full to Providence,
8mo [August] 11th Having a little Buisness to do at Witney went there
and stoped their weekday meeting at which I found
great Satisfaction to my minde having often found
much Peace of minde in constantly attending weekday
meetings and tho menny Plead that they should go to
meetings on those days ware it not for their Buisness
which then would be neglected but I do believe if they did but
give up and go with a willing minde the would finde
such satisfaction and Clearness to their mindes that would
so fit them for Buisness as to Inable them to do it much
quicker and better than if they had stayed at Home,

Page 45

the ninth month [September] the thirteenth went to C[hipping] norton monthly meeting
a Largish meeting there being a public Friend there on a
religious visit and sevral more Public Friends and we had
a comfortable meeting sevral Testimonies being born and
the Pure Truth was exalted over all I believe after which

12 Earliest recorded reference of meeting 1668.

the meeting proceeded upon Buisness which was Conducted
in Love and Unity,
the tenth month [October] the second our Quarterly meeting being to
be holden at Reading[13] set out on foot Reached that Night Witney
got up pretty early on the morrow and set out with Robert
Sessions for Oxford meeting sevral Friends and Neighbours
ware at it and the meeting was to good satisfaction I believe
after meeting set out with some more Friends for Newbery [Newbury]
Reached Market Elsley that Night and Newbery [Newbury] a little
befor Meeting[14] which began at Eleven and a good meeting I
believe it was sevral Testimonies ware born and the people
ware directed to minde the pure Leadings and witness of Truth
in themselves in every degree which if they did it would lead
them out of all Evel and into all Truth, after meeting set
out for Reading reach'd Cousin Tuties about seven Oclock the meeting
for worship began on the morrow at ten oclock a pretty Large meet=
=ing and sevral living Testimonies ware born to the truth which seemed
to have a good effect upon the peoples mindes after which the Friends
proceeded upon buisness the Answers to the Queries ware Read and sev=

verso

ral remarks made thereon ware the friends saw a deficiency
in order to Stir up the peoples mindes to live near to the pure
Truth that they might answer them in a more Satisfactory man=

13 Earliest recorded reference of meeting 1656.
14 Earliest recorded reference of meeting 1668.

=ner the Buisness was Conducted in much Love, after meeting took
my kinde leave of Cousin Tuties and set out with Friends
for Home reached Shillingford that Night slept at Cousin Ashby's rose
pretty Early in the morning and got to Oxford about Twelve ware
I parted with Friend Barrett Wm Minchin and Joseph Lamb bear=
=ing me company as far as Campsfield ware I took my leave of
them and Reached home about five in the Evening was I found
my friends pretty=well I had a pretty Satisfactory Journey the
Lord Almighty favouring me with Health to hold out better than
I could Expect praises be to His great and Worthy Name
for Ever,
the tenth month [October] the eighteenth the two Counties of Oxfordshire
and Berkshire being United together our Monthly Meeting
was appointed to be holden at Faringdon in Berkshire[15]
went their on Horseback with Father and some more
Friends Reached there alittle before meeting, meeting
began at Eleven after a time of Silence a woman friend stood
up and Spoke signifying that it was our duty to love one
another it being a Sure token that we are Jesus's des=

Page 46

=ciples and also Friends ware exorted to be constant
In their attendance of Weekday meetings,
A Few words arising in my Minde to speak
In the meeting yet under a Sence of my own Weak=
=ness delayed it and put it of Until

15 Earliest recorded reference of meeting 1668.

Just the breaking up of the meeting but being afraid
if I neglected what I believed to be my duty to speak
I stood up and spake what was upon my Minde to
speak and felt True peace of Mind I trust afterwards
got up pretty early in the morning and after taking my
leave of Friend Snellings set out with Friends Squires
for Home Reach'd Home about three Oclock having had
a very pleasent Journey for which I was Truly thankfull
the tenth month [October] the twenty fifth this day the Corroner
came to view the Body of a man who was found drown'd
in Charlbury river he was an Inhabitant of Churchil[l]
and came to Charlbury fair and being a lose man
he got Drunk and has he was returning Home rather
late twas thought He mist his road and so fell into the
River and was drowned a Striking Instance to all to
beware of Drinking to Excess least they should loose their lives
In the midst of their wickedness and so be lanched put of Time into

verso

Eternal misery,
the Eleventh month [November] the fifth having a desire to go and
see my Relations at Epwell got leave of my Parents and
set out on Sixth day [Friday] Morning a foot tooke Chipping=norton
Meeting in my way which was comfortable to me Reached
Epwell in the Evening found my Relations there very
well stayd at Epwell one day on first day [Sunday] Morning went
to sibford meeting after meeting went to see some Cousins
there who appeared glad to se me returned back that after=
=noon to my Relations at Epwell In the morning took my
kinde leave of my Relations there and set out for Braills found
Cousins there very well spent the Evening with Cousins
and two more Friends very Comfortabley in the morning
went from thence to Shipstone called at Upper Brails to se
Friend Gillets found Cousins at Shipstone very well and
they appeard glad to see me called to se Friend Hodgkings
who ware all very well stay'd their week day Meeting which
was on the morrow after Meeting took my kinde leave of
Cousins and set out Home reached Home about Eight oclock
found all my Friends there very well Except Mother who
appeard glad to se me Return safe Praises be to the Almighty
who is worthy for Ever whose Power I Trust preserved me in
this little Journey from doing any thing to the dishonnour of the
Truth I believe which is more my desire than to Injoy any
Earthly Thing.

Page 47

The Eleventh Month [November] the tenth was at our week
=day Meeting ware again a few words came be=
=fore my Minde to speak but not keeping close
to my Guide I speak what was not required of
me which brought great Trouble to my Minde
but Retiring into Stillness and breathing to the
Almighty for forgiveness I found Ease
the Eleventh month [November] the thirteenth took a walk to seasoncutt [Sezincote]
to se Cousin Joseph Ashby Juiner reached there about seven in
the Evening found him very Weak and poorly but he seems in

a Comfortable fram of minde and pretty much resigned to the
will of Providence next morning after Breackfast took my kinde
leave of Cousin Joseph not much expecting to se him any more
in this world and so it proved went from thence to Stow meeting
which was small and thence Home, on the Seventeenth heard
of Cousin Joseph Ashbys Death, on the nineteenth it being the
day appointed for the Buriall of Cousin Joseph Ashby went
to seasoncutt [Sezincote] ware I found a pretty menny Friends Assembled
on the occasion the meeting began at Stow about twelve which

verso

Was pretty large of Friends and Neighbours and sevral Public
Friends who exhorted the people to be carefull how the Spent their
time and to minde and Improve it as they knew not how soon
they might be called upon to give anaccount how the had spent
their time and they should not be like the Unprofitable
who laid up the Talent which he had Received of His Lord In a
Napkin and Hid it in the Earth and when they ware called
upon to give an account how the had Improved it the brought it
to their Lord saying here is thy Talent which thou gavest me
for I knew that thou wast an Auster Man taking up that thou
laidst not down and Reaping that thou didst not sow and the if
Lord Answered him O thou unprofitable servant and Slothfull thou
knewest that I was an Austear man taking up that I laid not
down and Reaping that I did not sow oughtest not thou to have put
my money into the Bank that at my Return I might have put
mine own with Usury, went back to seasoncutt [Sezincote] and spent the
Evening with Cousins and some more Friends sympathising with
them for the loose of their dear Son and Brother, who died in a state
of pure Innosciency I trust and is now admited into the Kingdom
of Joy and Peace and that for Evermore,
the twentieth took my kinde leave of Cousins and set out home
ware I found my friends very well being Truly thankfull
to the Almighty who preserved me I trust and brought me safe
home again to my Fathers House in Peace praises be to His
Great and Worthy Name for Ever,

Page 48

the 12th moth [December] the fifth hearing that Sistor Betty at Burford
was very poorly Sistor Magarett and I went to se she was
at meeting which was rather small yet I think I may truly
say we ware Comforted and Refreshed together with the
renew'd Visitation of Devine Love on the twentieth went to
Oxford Meeting on foot and I think it was as Comfortable
a meeting as ever I was at Sevral Testimonies being born
on truths behalf and there was one friend a Stranger and
she also had a testimonie to bear to the Honnour of Truth
Afterwards friends proceeded upon buisness which was gone
through in much Love, after meeting came back to witney
and home the next morning on the twenty sixth took a
walk to Barton meeting there are no friends living there but

its held once a Quarter it was Established for the good of the
Neighbours living there abouts I believe not menny friends
came but sevral Neighbours and a Comfortable meeting we
had Sevral living Testimonies being Born on Truths behalf

1791

the Second of the first month [January] it being first day took a walk

to Witney was at Both their morning and afternoons meeting
in which my minde was Comforted and refreshed in the Truth
I staying rather late and it growing dark I lost my way a
Comming over the Earth and getting among the Trees my minde
was much Exercised for I Expected or was ready to conclude I
must stay out all Night but being given up to the will of Devine
Providence being very weighty in my minde i at length saw a light

verso

and making up to it it Brought me within my knowledge
which caused me to Rejoice but I believe it will be a warning
to me and may to others to be carefull not to stay out late
if they can very well avoid it
1791 the First month [January] the ninth was at Our Meeting
which was fullish ware after waiting sometime
in Silence upon the Almighty I again found an
Engagement upon my Minde to stand up and Speak
a few Words, which I did and speak in great awe-
=fullness and fear under a Sence of my own great we=
akness and Inability without the Almighty's Assistance
whose Powers I trust Inabled me to discharge my duty
to Him praised be His worthy Name for Ever
the tenth went to Chipping Norton to our Monthly
Meeting a Pretty large meeting considering the weath=
=er sevral Pub.[lic] Friends ware there and Sevral Tes=
timonies ware born in Order to Stir up the mindes
of the People to Retire inward and wait upon the Al=
=mighty to feel the Arisings of his power to manifest
their duty unto them and to lead and guide them into all
Truth, as sayeth the Scripture they that wait upon
the Lord shall renew their strength they shall mount
up with wings as Eagels they shall run and not be

Page 49

weary they shall walk and not faint after which
the meeting of Friends proceeded upon buisness
which was Conducted in Love and Unity sevral
Sober friends ware appointed to visit Friends Fam=
=ilies belonging to our Monthly Meeting
F[irst] [Sunday] Day the Sixteenth of the same month took a walk
to Witney Meeting ware I unexpectedly met with
the Friends Appointed to visit Friends families and
we had two pretty large good Meetings both Morning
and afternoon warein the Devine Power appear'd
Evedently to arise to the strengthening and Comfort=
=ing menny Mindes present menny Living testimo=
=nies Ware born to stir up the mindes of the People
to wait upon God and worship Him in Spirit and in Truth
and on the Eighteenth following we ware favoured

with the Company of the Friends at Charlbury
who
Favoured us with their Company a Considerable
time
in the Evening and I think I may again say we
ware renewedly Favourd with a fresh visitation
of
Devine Love and on the morrow I took with them
to
Aunts of Enstone ware also the the Friends had
a few

verso

by way of Incouragement to Incourage all to
persevear
In the way of Truth,
on the thirtieth following Sistor M and I went to
Burford to see Brother and Sistor there ware
after
a time of Solid Silence sevral Friends ware
drawn forth In testimonie to Exhort the people
to
be resigned to the Will of the Almighty that they
might be searched and tried by His Refineing
Hand
that thereby the Might be made sensible of their
du=
ty to Him or to that Effect
The Second month [February] the third was at
Meeting and
In Sitting with Friends my Minde found
Refresh=
=ment the Sixth, our Preparative meeting was
Held to day not much buisness to do but it was
Conducted in Love and Unity
the thirteenth following it being Milton
prepara=
=tive Meeting felt some drawings in my minde
to be
there but it proving wett prevented my going
on which account my Minde was affected with
sor=
=row being a lover to attend Religious Meetings,
but

Page 50

sorry when through fear I have sufferd any
thing to hinder me or have been prevented
through weakness or Indisposition of Body from
attending them,
the fourteenth was at Our own Monthly Meeting
to day, onely one Public Testimonie born wareby
the People ware directed to minde the pure lead=
=ings of the Light of truth (which is called in
Scripture by divers names as grace light and
Spirit of God and light of Christ, a Measure
and Manifestation wareof all have received su=
ficient to Inable them to work out their own
sould Sal=
=vation that when they have done here they may
Be admited into the Heavenly Kingdom of rest
and Joy ware sorrows shall be no more,)
the seventeenth at Meeting to day was exceeding
low and poor in
my Minde under a Sence of my own weakness and
Unworthiness bein sensible that without the
Almightys
help and Assistance I could do no good Thing
the twenty sevventh Having a minde to go to
Mil=

verso

=ton Meeting and see Jn'o Matthews who was
very
poorly went on foot. was at meeting which
was Small after Sitting with Friends a time
in awefull Silence I believed it to be my duty
to bear a Short Testimonie for the Truth which
I gave up unto in awefull fear least I should not
obey My Father which is in Heaven or at
least I should not Discharge my duty to Him
faithfully
in Speaking what I believed to be my duty to
speak being made willing to give up all and obey
the Almighty according to the best of my
Underst=
=anding, and do firmly believe without doubt
that the Almighty God has Intrusted me with
a Small Gift in the Ministery,
the Second month [February] the Sixth was at
Meeting today
and In Sitting in awefull Silence and Retiredness
of minde waiting upon the Almighty to know
His Will
my Minde felt Inward strength and Comfort
the twelfth finding a little drawings in my Minde
to

go to Stow meeting and see my Cousins at Seasoncutt [Sezincote] got
leave of my parents and went on foot found Cousins at

Page 51

Seasoncutt [Sezincote] Pretty well and I was glad to sit with
them and have a little of their Company
the thirteenth walked from Seasoncutt [Sezincote] to Stow meeting before Meet=
=ing called to see Grandmother and Aunt at Meeting
again also a few words came before my Minde to
speak which I gave up unto and Speak in Much
Humility and found peace in my Own Minde
and I trust and do Earnestly beg of the Almighty
that when ever it shall please Him to Require
and make it know to me to be my duty to speak
in a Meeting appointed to Worship Him that
He will not only make it known to me to be my duty
to speak but that He will give me Strength to
speak plainly and Inteligeably to the People
that what I speaks may be to the Honnour of
His great Name Onely
after meeting took my leave of my Relations and
set out Home ware I found my Friends pretty well
the twentieth took a Ride to Burford to fetch sis=
=tor Betty and little Hannah came behinde
Brother Henry was at their meeting ware also
I was drawn forth to speak a few words on truths

verso

Behalf and found Peace in so doing found
friends there very well after Meeting set out
for Home ware we all arrived safe and found
our Friends Indifrently well,
the twenty fourth it being the day appointed for the
Marriage of Margarett to Robert Sessions sevral Fri=
ends and Relations came on that Account the Meeting
began at 10 oclock in the Morning and it was a good
Meeting to some I believe Friend Barrit being dra=
=wn forth in Public Testimonie to the People to the Ed=
=dification Instruction and Incouragment of Menny pres=
=ent I believe and I also I believed it to be my duty to
Bear a Short Testimonie on truths behalf and do be=
=lieve it had a good Effect and that by so doing I dis=
=charged my duty to the Lord Almighty, after which
the Relations proceeded to Sign the Certificate and it was
done in a good and orderly manner, had a pretty men=
=ny friends to Dinner after which Cousins took their leaves
of Us in love and went for Home
the thirty first smallish Meeting more is the Pitty that
weekday Meetings are so poorly attended,

Page 52

the fourth Month [April] the first was at Meeting after the
Meeting of Worship the Friends proceeded upon the
Preparative Meeting Buisness that it might be ready to go to
the Monthly Meeting which was to be held at Burford
on the Morrow Father and Brother Robert went to it,
the Tenth was at Meeting to day and after Sitting in
Awefull silence I believe my great Lord and Master
Jesus Christ did Require it of me to Stand up and
speak a few Words to discharge my duty to Him but
not keeping low enoughf in my own Minde and near enoughf to
his pure Power which if I had I trust it would have
Inabled me to have discharged my duty fully to Him

but not being on my watch as I might be every
hour
and every Minute I sat down without speaking
enoughf
I believe and not finding ease to my to my Minde
after sometime
I Stood up and speak twice more but not
Minding the leadin=
=gs of the pure truth in all Things I then
Exceeded the
Bounds of Truth and Moderation and so brought
great
sorrow and trouble on my poor minde and I do
ear=
nestly Pray in Secrett to the Almighty that when
Ev=
=er it shall please the Lord to manifest it to me
plainly

verso

---

to be my duty to speak in a meeting He will be
pleased
to Inable me to speak to the Honnour of his
great Name
only, and in much Humility of minde I do
breathe to
Him that He will take away my Life rather than
that
I should live to offend Him in any thing being
thoroughly
sensible of my own poor weakness and
unworthyness without
His assistance of doing any good Thing yet not
my
will Lord but thy pure will be done,
Our Worthy Friend Jno. Hall had a fine
testimonie to
bear in the Meeting on truths behalf and to the
Eddifi=
cation of Friends I believe,
The Eleventh and twelfth being our Quarterly
Meeting
at Witney Father Brother and Sistor Maragarett
went
there on foot found them pretty well at Meeting
one
Testimonie was born which Comforted and
Reffreshed my
poor Minde

on the twenty fourth Having got leave of my
Parents to
go to Sibford meeting. but did not set out till
about 7
oclock went on foot and before I got quite there
I let in
the Reasoning part, that I should not get there
by the time
meeting began and so returned without going to
the Meet=

Page 53

---

ing but O! the sorrow and Trouble of minde I
feel is
so great that I cannot help Expressing it, and I
write
this for no other end but that I and other who
may se
these lines may be carefull that when they feel
anything
upon their mindes to do, they give up and do it
with
a Diligent and a willing Minde, and nevver give
way to the Temptations of the Enemy of the
Truth as I
have done for want of Watchfullness
5mo [May] the Second after I left my work went
to see a Young
Man who has been very poorly for sometime
rather I
believe in a decline he seems of a Contented
disposition
of Minde and appeared to take my Visit kindly
on the sevventh being rather sorrowfull and low
in my
Minde under a sence of my Own weakness my
dear
sistor gave me good advice and I intend to be
minde=
=full of it for the Future
on the Eight was at meeting which was not very
large
and in Sitting theirin my Minde was Exceedingly
desirous
to be drawn into awefull Silence and to wait
upon the
Almighty patiently to know His pure Requireings
and
to do them faithfully when known

on the Eighteenth being poorly and Having a desire to
go to Witney and be at their Meeting and see Cousins
went on foot Reached their Just at Meeting time one testimonie

verso

---

was born by Friend Hannah Smith after Meeting
I went up to se Old Friend Barrett with Whome
I had some discourse concearning the Tryals Exercises
and Probations that attend Mankinde and that at=
=tended my Minde in this Life, and also concearning
the Work of the Ministrey, and He being a good
and experienced Man theirin gave one good advice
that when anything was upon my minde that ap=
=peared to to be my duty to Speak in a Meeting
to give up and Speak it,
1791 the sixth Month [June] the second was at meeting to day and
it was small and my Minde was Exercised poor and
very low theirin under a sence of my own unworthyness with
fervent desires and breathings to the Almighty that He
would be pleased to forgive my past offences that I
had Offended Against Him, and it arose in my Minde
that there was forgiveness if asked for a in humble and
submissive manner in the Name of Jesus
the 4th Having a desire to go to Milton Meeting asked
leave of my Parents and set out on foot reached there
a little before meeting began at Meeting was John Matthews
and several more Public Friends who after sometime of
silence had a few words to speak by way of Testimonie

Page 54

---

wareby the People ware Exorted to minde the pure Light
of Truth within them and obey it in all its leadings and
gidance it would leade and guide them all into the Truth
or to that effect after Meeting went with Brother Henry to
Burford and staid with them all Night
the 12th Having a minde to go to stow meeting as believeing
the Almighty required it of me to go, asked leave of my
Parents and set out on foot Reached there in good time, at
meeting a few words arose in my Minde to Speak and I
was made quite sensible it was my duty to speak and I
Promise with the Almightys assistance that when ever it shall
Please Him in his Love to manifest it clearly to me to be my duty
to speak a few words in a Meeting, to give up and speak
them in His fear being sensible that His Love is better than the Injoyment
of any Earthly Thing, and that His displeasure is more pa=
=infull to be born that the Loss of any Earthly thing or
even Death it self, for to obey is better than Sacrifice and
to hearken that the fatt of Rams, for Rebellion is as the sin
of Witchcraft and Stubbornness is as Iniquiety and Idol=
=atery, after Meeting took a walk to see Cousins at Seasoncutt [Sezincote]
and on the Morrow walked Home, to our own Monthly
meeting which was held at Charlbury at which the Buisness
was Conducted in Love and Unity, on the Morrow a Woman
Friend whose Name was Hannah Wiggams came to pay us

verso

a Visit at Meeting after a time of Silence she had
a pretty deal to speak to the peo=
=ple by way of Testimonie in a solid manner
ware
in she did Exhort Friends to be diligent to labour
Faith=
=fully according to the Talent that had Received
for if
their Talent was not taken from them, if they did
not labour
Faithfully according to the manifestation of the
light of Truth
in them as it Manifested to them to be their duty
their Talent
would not be Improved and then when they ware
called to
give an account by the great Lord who had
Intrusted them with
a Talent the would have no good Account to give
"and so
would be in danger of having it said unto them
as it was
to Him who had received but one Pound and
took and
lapped it up in a Napkin and hid it in the Earth
instead
of Improving it, and I think it was said Unto him
by the
great Lord of all, O thou Wicked and slothfull
Servant
if thou Knewest that I was a hard Marster taking
up
that I laid not down and reaping that I did not
sow
oughtest not thou to have put my money into the
bank
that at my coming I might have received mine
own
with Usuary, now therefore take his pound from
him and
give it to him that hath ten pounds and they said
Lord he
hath ten pounds and He said unto them verily I
say unto you to every one that hath shall be given
but
to him that hath not shall be taken away even
that which

Page 55

He hath, I also believed it to be my duty to speak
two or three
sentences in meeting, on the morrow she went to
Witney
to pay a visit to Friends their I took a walk also
having a desire to be at their Meeting ware also
she had
a pretty deal to say Especialy to Exhort the
Elderly friends
in Particular to prepare for their great and last
Cha=
=inge for they knew not how soon they might be
called
upon to give an account how they had spent their
pre=
=cious time, and that she thought their work lay
behinde
hand and she thought their was great need for
them to be diligent now wile the had the time
and prise
it, after Meeting walked Home with satisfaction
in
my own Minde for which I was truly Thankfull to
the Almighty
the 21st Friend Samuel Smith paid us
a Visit He came from America to visit
Friends in this Nation and on his Account
a Meeting was held to pretty good Satisfaction
on the 24th it Being Barton Meeting took a
walk there it was a pretty large meeting
of Friends and Neighbours and a very Com=
=fortable meeting it was I believe Warein the
Devine power was Exalted over all Sevrall

Verso

Testimonies being born in order to stir up
and arouse the Mindes of the people to prepare
for their latter End,
the 7th month [July] the 4th, it being our
Monthly Meeting
at Witney took a walk their smallish meeting
after
a time of Silence the Friends proceeded upon the
buisness
in much Love and Unity
on the 14th was at our weekday meeting which
was small

and I have often observed that weekday meetings are very
poorly attended more is the pity and I believe it is for
want of Friends giving up their hearts more freely
to serve the Almighty and leave their outward buisness
for the truths sake which if they did I believe the bles=
=sing of the Almighty would attend them and amply
make amends for that little time they spent in going to
Meetings
on the 20th this morning Uncle Gibbs came from Epwell
and brought the sorrowful account of Uncle Wm Hemmings
Death of the same place He was a healthy comely Man
rather middle aged and was taken Ill on Seventh day
and died on Seconday following a Strikeing Instance
to all people to take warning and learn to Live as they
would wish to die, he left a Wife and only Childe to
mourn for a good and Tender Husband but as I believe He

Page 56

had led a Sober and Honest Life so I believe He is gone
to a place of Rest and Happiness that will nevver have End,
on the 21st set out after Meeting for Epwell found Aunt
Hemmings at Epwell pretty well considering her great Loss
on the 22nd it being the day appointed for the Interment of
my Dear Uncle (He was Interd at Sibford) a great menny
Friends and Neighbours assembled on the Occasion, it
was a good meeting to sevral I believe sevral living testimo=
=nies being born by sevral Worthy friends to stir up the
mindes of the people to a diligent watchfull waiting upon
God to feel the arising of his pure witness of Truth in them
which if they would but take good heed thereunto it would
teach them what they should do and what they should
leave undone, In the Afternoon Friend Tho's Harris
had a few words to speak by way of Testimonie to the
Widdow and Friends not to be discouraged at the Tryals
and Exercises that attend us here for the Lord nevver suf=
=fereth us to be tried above what He will Inable us to bear
and more words to that purpose,
on the 23rd took my Kinde leave of my Relations at Epwell
and went to broad Sibford and little Sibford to see some
Friends there and from thence to Brails to see Cousins their
who ware very well walked from their to upper Brails
to see Friend Gillets found them pretty=well Except friend
gilet She who was very poorly

verso

on the twenty fourth it being first day took a walk to Stowerton
to se Friend Gillets and from thence back to Brails Meeting[16]
which was Small their being but very few Friends livving
there but found a little Comfort and refreshment to my poor
minde in Sitting with them, after Meeting set out for Home
call'd to see friend Crossley at Witchford [Whichford] their Daughter

16 Earliest recorded reference of meeting 1668.

having liv'd with we for sometime, Reached Home
about
7 oclock in the Evening safe and well Truly
Thankful
to the Almighty who by His goodness Inabled me
to dis=
=charge my duty to Him according to the
Measure and
manifestation of His pure light of Truth placed
in my
Heart and favoured me with Health Praises
Praises
be to His Great and Worthy Name for Ever,
the 8th mo the 8th in the Evening yesterday came
to
Witney and this morning set out for Faringdon
Monthly Meeting with Brother and Friend
Hawkins
reached their in good time a fullish Meeting
considering
the distance it is from the other places ware the
monthly mee=
=tings are Usualy held, sevral Public Friends
there and one Testimonie born on Truths behalf
by a Woman Friend, warein she had to reminde
the People of the saying of Christ recorded in
Scripture
Behold I stand at the door and knock if any men
hear

Page 57

my Voice and Open unto me I will come into Him
and sup with Him and He with Me, reached
Witney
in the Evening slept at Friend Barretts and next
morning set out with Brother
for Home ware we arived very well having had a
very pleasent Journey for which I was truly
Thank=
=full in my Minde to my Creator,
First day the 15th of the 8mo Father and
Brother
went to Milton to the Burial of John Matthews
a Public Friend who lived there, I believe He
was a Honest disposed Friend and one was loved
the Truth and lived therein and was very loving to
young Friends and desirous that they should be
Instructed and Nourished up in the Truth, He
lived to a good Old Age
on 27th Having a little drawings in my Minde to
go to Campden Meeting asked leave of my
Parents
to go to which they consented walked to
seasoncutt [Sezincote]
to see Cousins their stop'd with them a little and
went from thence to se Cousins at the Upper
House and from thence to the Hill Farm to se
Cousin John Cork and Family spent some little
time with them in an Honest kind and free Con=
=versation with them on the morrow Morning
went

verso

---

to Campden Meeting Cousins going a long with
me
or followed me Small Meeting there being but a
verry
few Friends living there abouts at meeting I was
desirous in minde was desirous to be drawn into
Awefull Silence
to know the Will of the Almighty and what He
would
have me do and then to do it,
went to Campden to Charingworth after Meeting
Friend Beavington was so kind as to go a little
way
with me found Cousins there pretty well spent
the afternoon with them in a free and Loving
manner, after Breakfasting with Cousins
on the morrow morning took my kinde leave of
them
and walked Home, ware I found my Friends
very well I having had a very pleasent Journey
being favoured with Health and I found things
more easy than I did expect to find them
Thanksgiving praises glory and Honnour be
given to my great Creator who is worthy to be
served obeyed and Honnoured for Evermore
on the 4th of the 9th [September] was at meeting
which was fullish
and after Sitting a time in Solid Silence the
Meet=
=ing broke up and afterwards the Friends
proceeded
upon the preparative meeting buisness, the
Quarterly

Page 58

Meeting Queries ware Answered pretty near to
what the Questions required and the buisness
was Conducted in Love and Unity,
on the 7th Having a little buisness to do for
Father
at Burford took a walk thither to see Brother and
Sistor found them pretty well,
on the 11th having a desire to go to Eden[17]
Meeting in
Buckinghamshire went thither and got to
Meeting
in good time which was fullish to what I did
Expect at Meeting was Comforted in my Minde
being sensible of the Love and goodness of the
Al=
=mighty to arise amoungst us in our Silent sit=
=ting together and waiting upon the Lord,
after Meeting went to Byfield to se Cousin Wells
who ware pretty well, slept there and on
the Morrow after spending part of the Day
with them in a Loving manner took my kinde
leave of them and set out Home ware I arived
in the Evening truly Thankfull in my Minde
to the Almighty who I trust preserved me by
His Mercy and goodness and brought me
safe Home again
Praises be to His great and worthy Name
for Ever,

verso

on the 17th Having a little desir to go again to
Eden Meeting took a walk thither, smallish
Meeting but I think I may again say we ware
renewedly favoured with the springings up of
the Love of God amoungst us in our Silent sit=
=ting together a waiting upon Him I was out
two Nights it being about 26 miles,
On the twenty fifth it being our Quarterly Meet=
=ing at Oxford took a walk thither with Bro=
=ther Robert fullish meeting two Testimonies
ware
born to the Honnour of Truth I believe, sevral
Neighbours comming in and seemed very atten=
=tive to what was Delivered, after Meeting set
out for Home ware I found my Friends very
well Having had a good Journey for which I
was Thankfull to Providence,
Second or Third of the Tenth Month [October] it
being our
Monthly Meeting to day Sistor Betty came from
Burford and the Meeting was pretty large and
a very Comfortable Meeting I think one public
Testimonie
was born in the Honour of the truth after which
the Friends proceeded upon the buisness which

Page 59

held pretty long two Friends ware received
into Membership with us viz a Young Woman
and a young Man and I believe both more
sincear and upright walkers in the truth
than menny that are edducated in our profession
on the fifteenth having a desire to go to Epwell
and
se my Relations asked leave of my parents and set
out on foot reached there about five in the
Evening
found them pretty well on the 16th walked to
Sibford went
to se sevral Friends before meeting at Meeting a
Testimonie was born to stirup the Mindes of the
peo=
=ple to Improve their gifts and Talents which
they
had received from the Almighty for if they did
not they
would when they had done here they would be set
amoungst
the goats wen they had done here or to that
purpose
after Meeting refreshed myself at Aunt Gilkes
and set
out for Home ware I arived very well having had a
pleasent Journey and truly Thankful in my Minde
to the Al=
=mighty whose Power I Trust preserved me in
this little
Journey from doing any thing against Him or His
pure Truth
on the 27th received the sorrowful account
Brother Roberts

17 There is no evidence for an Eden Quaker Meeting in Buckinghamshire. There is however evidence of a Quaker meeting at Eydon in Northamptonshire. Jones' comment on p.58v that the distance to the meeting is approximately 26 miles from Charlbury would bear this out.

Fathers death He was Returning Home late at Night and

verso

Missing his way slipt into the water and was drowned
a Striking Instance for all to prepare to live as they would
wish to Dye for we know not how soon any of us may be
called upon to give an account how we have spent our time
the Eleventh Month [November] the 4th Having a desire to be at
Milton week day Meeting took a walk thither small
Meeting yet in sitting with Friends I found much
comfort and peace of minde and believe Friends
that were present did the same who do give up them=
=selves freely to attend week=day meetings
on the fifth having a desire to attend Armscutt [Armscote] meeting
which is holden once a quarter asked leave of Parents
which they consented to went on foot walked to Brails
to se Cousins there and friend Gilletts who ware very
well and appeared glad to see me, on the sixth went
to Armscutt [Armscote] with Cousin Wm Hemmings and John
Gillett saw there sevral of my Relations it was a pretty
large Meeting menny Friends and Neighbours also
being present and menny living Testimonies ware
born to Incourage the people to walk in fear of the
Lord and to Incourage them to persevear in the strait

Page 60

and Narrow path that leads to Eternal Life
walked to Brails after meeting on the sevventh after
Breackfasting with Cousins took my leave of them
and walked Home ware I found my Friends pretty
=well having had a pleasant Journey for which I was
thankfull to Providence
on the thirteenth it being first day of the week
we ware favoured with the Company of two
Public Friends at our Meeting one of them
had a Testimonie to bear on behalf of the Truth
on the fourteenth it being our Monthly Meeting
at Witney went their on foot, a pretty lar=
=ge Meeting on the Account of a Committe of
Friends being appointed to attend the same
to Examine whether the Legacies and Gifts
left to Poor Friends &et ware properly dis=
=tributed sevral Friends attended the Oc=
=cation and sevral good testimonies ware born
by sevral worthy Friends,

verso

---

on the seventeenth was at our meeting to day and
in Sitting with Friends my minde was filled
with a degree of peace altho the number was
but small,
on the twenty sixth having felt a little drawings
in my minde to go to Stow and be at their Meeting
Asked leave of my Parents to go to which they consented
to walked to seasoncutt [Sezincote] in the Afternoon ware I found
Cousins mostly pretty well on the Morrow morning
walked from thence to stow Meeting, and in Sitting
in awefull silence a waiting upon the Lord I think
I may say in Truth, tho our number was Small
we ware favoured with His Love and goodness to
the Comforting and Incourageing our poor mindes who
trusted in Him after Meeting called to see Grandmother
and Aunt Jones who ware pretty well then walked
Home reached home about six in the evening ware
I found my Friends pretty well for which and all

other mercies I am truly thankfull to Devine Providence
on the eleventh took a walk to Burford to see Brother
and sistor their and be at their Meeting and at the

Page 61

Monthly Meeting on the morrow found Brother and
sistor pretty=well a pretty large Comfortable meeting
one Testimonie born by a young Man I believe not
Eighteen years of age, the substance of what he had
to deliver to friends was this, this people draw near to
me with their lipps but their souls are far from me
the make a great profession of the Lord but it is a doubt
they are far from Him in Possession and it was a Complaint
of the Prophet formerly against the People they draw near
to me with their lips but their Souls are far from me
after which the Meeting was Concluded with a Solem
Prayer, on the morrow our Monthly Meeting was held
at Burford warein Sevral Testimonies ware born in
order to stir up the People, to Indeavour to retire in their mindes
that the might come to sit every one under their own Vine
and Under their own Fig Tree ware none could make them
afraid
on the eighteenth of the twelfth month [December] it being first
day after Meeting took a walk to Enstone to se Aunt
and Cousin there and in Sitting with them it ap=
=peard to be my duty to speak a few words amoungst
them to incourage them to be diligent to attend religious

verso

Meetings and wait upon the Lord to fell after
His love and Goodness to be near to strengthen their
Mindes in the Truth, and in so doing I found
Peace to attend my Minde,
on the twenty eight of the twelfth mo: [December] having a little
buisness to do at Witney and it being the day on which
their meeting is held chose to go on that day that
I might be at their meeting having generaly
felt great satisfaction in atending weekday mee=
=tings both at Home and abroad two friends appeard in Testimonies
ware by friends ware exhorted to be diligent in attend=
ing weekday meetings, and altho the may meet with
menny difficulties and probations in this Life in serving
the Lord yet if they put their trust in Him His
power would preserve them through all or words
to that Import,

1792

it being the first day of the week and the first day

of the first mo: [January] having walked to Witney last night
this morning set out with old friend Barritt
and some other friends for Oxford quarterly Meeting, a pretty menny
Friends and Neighbours at meeting and we ware

Page 62

Devinely favoured I believe with the fresh Visita=
=tion of the Almighty in that He was pleased to
favour us with His living power and presence
to the Comforting of menny Hearts present I be=
=lieve sevral Testimonies being born in order to
stirup the people a diligent watchfullness and
waiting upon God to know His Will and then to
do it, after which the meeting was Concluded in
awefull Prayer,

on the 2nd friends transacted the buisness but be=
=fore they entered there upon sometime was spent
in waiting upon the Lord, and sevral Testimonies
ware born, to stirup the people to minde the pure
light of Christ within them and Obey it
after meeting walked to Witney with Friend Barrett
and slept there, and in the morning took my leave
of them and walked Home,

1792

1st mo [January] the 5th was at our meeting to day and in Sitting
with a very few friends, in the openings of the pure
truth upon my Minde I trust Devine Providence made
it known to me plainly that it was my duty to speak

verso

a few words amoungst them, which I gave up unto
and speak them, with care, and found great peace
of minde in so doing,
the 8th it being first day [Sunday] Friend Barrett came to se'us
and was at our Meeting warein he was drawn forth
in Testimonie to exhort friends to be carefull how
they spent their precious time as they knew not how soon
the great Lord of all would call them to give anaccount
how they had spent it,
the ninth it being our Monthly meeting at C.[hipping] Norton a
pretty large meeting sevral friends appearing in Public
after which the friends proceeded upon the buisness
which was Concluded in much Love and Unity
on the 27th feeling a little drawings in my minde to go to
Chipping Norton and be at their week day meeting walked
to it, and after Sitting with Friends sometime in
Silence it appeared to be my duty to speak a few words
amoungst them and I gave up and speak them in the
fear of the Almighty what appeared to be my duty to
speak in much humility and found Inward peace
in so doing,
the fifth was at our Meeting which was pretty large and
after a time of Silence, in the springings up of the pure

Page 63

Love of truth I found it to be my duty to speak a few
words amoungst them which I gave upunto and speak
them and found Inward peace in so doing
our preparative meeting also which was conducted in much Love
the 12th it being our Monthly meeting we ware favoured
with the Company of Timothy Beavington of whose company
we ware glad, together with the Company of sevral other
public Friends Friend Beavington had a pretty deal to
speak by way of Testimonie, afterwards the Friends
proceeded upon the buisness which was Conducted in
Love and Unity,
the 22nd having a little buisness to do at Witney I so ordered
it to go and be at their weekday Meeting and after
a time of Solid Silence I speak a few words amoungst
friends tho in much fear least I should offend the
Almight, afterwards found true peace in so doing
on the twenty sixth took a walk to Stow Meeting
at meeting after a time of Solid silence a few
words arose in my minde which appeared to be my

duty to speak in the meeting and I speak them
in an awefull frame of mind and found inward
Peace in so doing, went to se grandmother and
Aunt
Ann Jones she is very poorly seems to be in a
Decline

verso

---

afterwards took a walk to seasoncutt [Sezincote]
and in the morning
set out for Home in my way called again to see
Grand
=mother and Aunt sat with them sometime and I
trust a sitting together we ware favoured with the
springings up of the Devine Love amoungst us
to the
comforting of our poor mindes,
on the third month [March] the tenth having
drawings in my
minde to visit the friends at Faringdon meeting
walked
to Witney and asked Friend Hankins if he found
freedom to go with me which after some
consideration
he did, In the morning he and I walked over
together
at meeting I trust we ware favoured with the
over=
=shadowings of Divine Love but friends seems
very
cold in their love for the pure truth there and
much
out of order with coming up in their duty in
their
preparative meeting not doing so much as to ap=
=point one Friend to attend the monthly
meeting
after meeting Friend Hankins and I walked to
Witney very comfortabley, slept at Friend
Barritts
on the morrow our Monthly meeting was held at
Witney a considerable number of Friends there
and it appeared to be a good Meeting warein
Providence was pleased to favour us with His
goodness, after a time of Silence two Friends had

Page 64

---

a few words to speak by way of Testimonie
after which the Friends proceeded upon the
buisness which was gone through in Love and
Unity, after Meeting walked home
on the twenty fifth was at our meeting which was
pre=
tty full considering the small number of friends
be=
=longing thereunto
on the twenty fourth was favoured with the
company
of our Friend Thomas Cash out of Cheshire who
had a meeting here to good satisfaction I believe,
on the twenty fifth friend Cash intending to be at
C,[hipping]
Norton and have a meeting there, I took a walk
there in company with sevral Friends, and a
Comfortable Meeting I trust it was, sevral neig=
=hbours being present as well as friends and we
ware favoured with the springing up of Devine
Love to the comforting and refreshing our poor
mindes
on the fourth month the first it being Barton
Meeting took a walk thither a pretty large
meeting
of Friends and Neighbours (it is a meeting that
is held
there for the benifit of the sober Neighbours)
sevral
public Friends being there and sevral Testimonies
ware born I believe to the Honnour of the great
Crea=
=tor of all Things, after which the meeting was
Concluded

verso

---

in Prayer to Him that he would be pleased to
Indow His Children with Wisdom to labour in
His truth in that way which He should be pleased
to make known to them to be their duty to
labour in
or words to that import I also had a few words
to speak in the meeting and in so doing I found
peace to my minde
2[February]=2nd of the fourth mo, took a walk
to Burford monthly
Meeting found Brother and sistor there very well
a pretty
fullish meeting at meeting after waiting upon the
Lord

a wile in Silence I had a few words to speak amoungst
friends, the buisness was gone through in Love and Unity
3[March]=3 took a walk to milton to the burial of Sarah Brunsdon
Daughter of Jn'o Mathews She was taken away suddenly
as it ware in the bloom of youth leaving a Husband
and two little Children to lament for the great loss
of so loving a Wife,
1st 8th [August] to day at meeting was favoured with the company
of sevral Friends who being on their Journey for Witney
Quarterly meeting, and a good meeting it was sevral
Testimonies being born to the honnour of truth and a prayer
was put up to the great Creator of all things that He
would be pleased to draw more and more nearer and
nearer to Him and His Truth or words to that Import,

Page 65

2=9th [September] took a walk with sevral Friends to the Quarterly
meeting at Witney a pretty large good meetings
both fore and after=noon sevral living Testimonies
ware born to Recomend all to wait upon their great
Creator and mind the direction of His inward guidance
and witness of truth in their mindes a measure wareof
all have received sufficient to inable them to work out
their own souls Salvation,
F[irst] [Sunday] Day 15. was at meeting today and after sitting a wile
in Silence a few words arose in my minde to speak
amoungst friends and after I speak them I found peace
to my minde praises be to my great Creator who
has hitherto inabled me to discharge what I
believed to be my duty to Him faithfully
on the 22 took a walk to stow to se Aunt and Nanney Jones
who is very poorly she seems rather in a decline was
at their meeting which was small yet found my Minde
comforted and refreshed therein
on the 29, at our meeting to day was favoured to day with
the good company of Friend Barritt
5mo [May] 2, took a walk to Brails monthly meeting a pretty
large meeting warein the Devine Power appeard to
arise amoungst us sevral testimonies being born in order

verso

to stirup the mindes of the people to wait upon God to
feel after His power to arise in them to guide them in
the path that leads to true peace, after meeting walked
with Uncle Gibbs to Epwell and on the morrow to a little meet=
=ing at Radway after meeting walked Home
on the 6, took a walk to Chipping Norton meeting
on the 13 we ware favoured with the company of sevral neighbouring
friends at meeting and I trust we ware renewedly favoured
with the springings up of Devine Love amoungst us to the
Uniteing us one near to another,
on the 24th went to C[hipping] Norton Monthly Meeting a
pretty comfortable meeting sevral Testimonies being
born by sevral Worthy friends to the honnour of
the great Creator of all things I believe afterwards
friends proceeded upon buisness which was gone through
in Love and Unity,

on the twentieth took a walk to Burford to see Brother
and Sistor found them Indifrent well was at their
meeting which felt Comfortable to me a Young man
of about Eighteen years old being drawn forth in

Page 66

1792

Awefull and Solem Prayer, after meeting took a walk
up to Friend Huntleys ware we had a little meeting
with the scollers in the School
on the 27th was at meeting to day which was not very
large yet a sitting with friends my minde was a little comforted
and refreshed
6mo [June] the 3rd feeling a little drawings in my minde to be at Witney meeting
took a walk thither was at both their morning and afternoon
meetings which to me felt pretty Comfortable Devine Love
appear to arise amoungst us to the uniteing us one near to the
other
on the 10th was at meeting and a Sitting with Friends my
Minde was a little Comforted and it appear to be my duty
to speak a few words amoungst them, in so doing I found
peace
on the 11th was our Monthly meeting and it was holden here, it
was a pretty full meeting, and altho held in Silence I believe
it was a Satisfactory meeting the buisness being conducted
in Love and Unity,
on the 14th was at our weekday meeting which was pretty full con=
=siddering the smallness of our Number, and it is Comfort to
sincear honnest Hearted friends to se friends carefull and Dili=
=gent constantly to attend weekday Meetings
on the 15th this day was favoured with the Company of friend John
Weal out of Wilt=shire on whose account a meeting was held to good
satisfaction I trust it being pretty large, sevral Testimonies being

verso

born to strengthen and Incourage the sincear in Heart
7mo [July] 24th this morning set out with Brother Robert for the
Quarterly Meeting to be holden at Banbury walked to
Southnewington meeting[18] which was small their being
but very few friends living there yet in sitting with them
my minde was comforted being sensible that the goodness
of Providence was near to us, in the Evening took a
walk to Milton to se Friend Thomas Harris of Milton
who was very well, on the morrow walked to ban=
=bury called to se Uncle Aunt and Cousins
the Quarterly Meeting was large sevral Substancial
Friends being there and sevral Testimonies ware
born on Truths behalf by which the people ware
Exhorted not to put their trust nor dependance in man
but in the Lord alone that is able to lead and preserve
them in the path that leads to true peace and Happi=
=ness, the afternoon meeting I believe was held to good
satisfaction
on the 26th the meeting for buisness was held before
they entered much upon buisness sevral good Testimonies

18 Earliest recorded reference of meeting 1668.

ware born in order to stirup the mindes of the people
to be diligent to attend their religious meetings for the
Worship of Almighty God and to be carefull how they

Page 67

behaved when assembled to Worship Him, as they might
be called upon to give anaccount how they had spent
their time and they knew not how soon and more to that
purpose, the Buisness held pretty long there bein a
pretty deal to do but it was concluded in Love and Unity
after meeting walked with Brother to Southnewington
on the Seventh in the Morning took my leave of
Cousins and walked to Friends Harriss of Milton and
from thence with Him to Adderbury Meeting a pretty
fullish meeting of Friends, and I believe I may say
in truth we ware greatly favoured in our sitting together
with the springings up of Devine Love amoungst is to
the Uniteing us near one to the other, after meeting walked
with Friend Harris to dinner afterwards walked Home
he being so kind as to go part of the way with me to show
me the road reached home very well being truly
Thankfull to providence who may be pleased to preserve me
in this little Journey in healt and to favour me with peace
in my own bossom at my return,
F[irst] [Sun]Day 1st of the seventh month [July] this morning took a walk to Shutford
meeting[19] which was small their being but very few Friends
living their abouts yet in Sitting with them few my minde was
Comforted under a Sence that devine Love was felt amoungst us
after Meeting walked to Friend Jarrots to Hornton, on the
morrow set out pretty early and walked to Sibford ware I called
to se Friend Rich'd Holtom and Friend Jo's Lamb and walked with

verso

Friends from thence to Hooknorton Monthly Meeting[20] a comfortable
Meeting after a time of Silence a friend had to reminde the
People to be good Examples in their conduct amoungst men as
they might be preachers of Righteousness by setting good exam=
=ples in their Conduct and behaviour amoungst men as much
or more than by Woords afterwards proceeded upon the
buisness which was Conducted pretty much in Love and Unity
dined at friend Halls afterwards walked Home,
on the 12, was at our Meeting which was small yet in sitting
with friends my Minde was refreshed and Comforted
on the 14, Having asked leave of my Parents to go to Hornton to se
Martha Jarrot in Hopes to obtain her for a Wife if Pro=
=vidence saw meet to bless me with suxcess set out about
one and walked thither in the afternoon, took an oppertunity
and oppened my minde to old Friend Jarrot but she was
unwilling to give Her consent, slept there,
on 15th took my leave of Friend Jarrot and set out with
her son for Shutford Meeting which was small yet my

19 Earliest recorded reference of meeting 1668.

20 Earliest recorded reference of meeting 1668.

minde was refreshed and Comforted their at being sensible
that Devine Love was felt amoungst us after meeting walked
to Epwell found Aunt Uncle and Cousins there very
well walked from thence to sibford weekday Meeting
which felt a little comforting to my minde after Meet=
=ing went to se a Friend and then walked Home ware

Page 68

I found my Friends very well for which I remain thankfull
on the 25th having a little buisness to do at Witney
I so ordered it for to go on that day on which their
meeting is held, was at meeting at meeting it ap=
=peared to be my duty to stand up and speak
a few words amoungst them to Incourage them
to wait upon the Lord for His assistance and I
hope it will also prove instructing to my own minde
on the 29th took a walk to Stow meeting about 10 miles
distant from Charlbury, Small meeting yet a sitting
with Friends my minde was a little comforted
called to se Grandmother and found Her Indifrent
well considering the great Loss she has lately met
with as that of a dear and only Daughter
after meeting took my leave of Grandmother and
Friends and walked home,
on the 8mo [August] the 4th finding a little drawings in my minde
to be at Armscutt [Armscote] meeting, a meeting that is held
once in a quarter of a year, asked leave of my
Friends and walked to Shipstone in the afternoon
called at long=Compton to see Friend Harris's,
found Cousins at Shipstone very well Slept there

verso

on the 5th was at their meeting which began early
and a sitting with Friends theirin my minde was
refreshed and Comforted, after meeting walked to
Armscutt [Armscote] meeting with Cousin John, which was
very large of Friends and Neighbours and
sevral living Testimonies ware born, to direct the
People to wait upon their true teacher and be
obidient thereunto viz Jesus Christ the light in
man, which teacheth as nevver man Taught
and it appeared to be my duty to speak a few
words in the meeting, and I gave up and speak
them in humility and found inward peace af=
=terwards, after meeting walked to Charingworth
to se Cousins Slept there,
on the 8th after breackfast took my kinde leave of
Cousins and walked home, had a pretty long but
pleasent Journey and feeling a degree of Peace
in my poor minde at my return, I Remain
truly Thankfull to Kinde Providence for His
Love to me,
on the 14th this day was at meeting which was pretty
large and felt very comfortable to my minde it
appeared to be my duty to speak a few words amoungst
Friends I gave up and spake them tho in Humility under a

Page 69

sence of my own weakness
on the 15th took a walk to our Monthly meeting
held at Faringdon went from Witney with Friend
Barritt and some more friends a pretty comfortable
Meeting, after a time of solid Silence a testimonie
was born on Truths behalf after which friends
Proceeded upon the buisness which was held pretty long
there being a Deal to do, but it was gone through
in Love and Unity, after meeting walked back
again to Witney
on the 16th in the morning after going to see a few
friends walked Home,

on the 21st was at our meeting to day which felt pretty
Comfortabale to my minde and after Sitting in Silence
sometime waiting upon the Lord it appeared to be
my duty to speak a few words amoungst friends
and I gave up and speak them in Humility
and found peace of minde in so doing
on the 28th it being milton preparative meeting
and feeling a concearn upon my minde to be there
went to Burford to se Brother and Sistor and from
thence with them to Milton Meeting it was pretty

verso

large of Friends and Neighbours and a good meeting
it was I believe sevral Testimonies ware born
to arouse the mindes of the people to take heed
to the pure Light of truth in their own Mindes
and obey it, the buisness was conducted in Love
and Unity,
9mo 2nd was at our meeting today which felt pretty
satisfactory to my minde, it was also our pre=
=parative meeting at which the queries ware
answered to pretty good Satisfaction, and
the Buisness was gone through in Love
on the 9th took a walk to Milton a little meeting
about five miles distant, small meeting but as we sat
together in awefull Silence waiting upon the Lord
I trust we ware favoured with the springings up
of Devine Love amoungst us, and it appeared to be my
duty to speak a few words amoungst Friends
on the 10th was at our Monthly meeting held at Burford
a pretty large and good Meeting Sevral Testimonies ware
born on truths behalf and the people ware directed to
love fear and serve God, and keep their place
in the truth after=wards friends proceeded upon buis=
=ness which was gone through in Love and Unity

Page 70

1792

on the 15th 9mo [September] took a walk to Witney to friend Barritts and
on the 16th set out with friend Barritt for our quarterly
meeting to be held at Reading walked to Oxford to meeting
which began at Eleven, a largish meeting sevral testimo=
=nies ware born on Truths behalf to put the people in
minde to minde the pure witness of truth placed in them
by the Almighty and obey it in all its leadings if the
would Injoy happiness hear and hearafter and more to
that purpose after meeting walked with Friend Barritt
and friend May to streetly and some more friends,
on the morrow rose pretty early and walked with friend
Barritt and friend may to Reading found Cousin
Tutteys very well, the meeting began at ten which was
very Comfortable sevral Sober friends ware there and
sevral Living Testimonies ware born by sevral worthy
Friends wareby the people ware directed to turn their
mindes Inward to their true teacher Christ Jesus the
Light in them which would manifest to them what was
Right and what was rong and that they must obey it
if the would come to Injoy true peace of minde or words
to that purpose the after=noon Meeting also was pretty
large, sevral Living testimonies ware born by sevral
sevral solid Elderly friends and by some young friends

of Both sex and sevral pettions ware put up to the great
Creator of all things that He would be pleased to draw

verso

the people into awefull Silence that they might be made
sensible to His pure Will and Requireings and that He
would give them strength to do it or words to that purpose
on the Eighteenth the meeting for Buisness began at
nine a pretty large meeting sevral testimonies being born
by sevral worthy friends to stirup the pure mindes in
one another to minde their duty and that all should
retire inward and wait upon the Lord to know their
duty and to be Indowed with His pure power to do it
sevral friends ware appointed to visit the monthly=
=meetings and the buisness was gone through in Love
and Unity, sevral friends giving their Names freely
to labour for the Support of the pure Truth according
to their sevral Gifts and abilities which they had received
from the allwise Creator, after Dinner took my affec=
=tonate leave of Cousin Tutteys and other friends and walked
with friend Barritt and friend may to friend Mays
House at Henley, on 19th before meeting went to se friend
Mays son and wife and family was at their meeting[21]
which was Small their not being menny friends living there
after a time of solid Silence friend Barritt had a few
words to speak to the friends I also found it to be my duty
to speak a few words amoungst friends tho in much

Page 71

Humility being sensible of my own weakness and Unworthiness
and that without the help and assistance of Providence
I could do no good thing nothing to the Honnour of
His pure Everlasting Truth, after Meeting walked
with friend Barritt to Shillingford stoped with Friend
there that night, on the 21st walked before Meeting
walked to Warborough to friend Sawgoods about [illegible] who hath
one son and I believe the are very honest Friends
and they entertained us kindly, was at their meeting[22]
which was small there not being menny friends living
their abouts after a time of Retirement and stillness
a young woman Friend appeared in the meeting
by way of Testimonie which I believe had a good
effect after meeting took our leave of Friends and
went to Witney to friend Barritts and lodged at
his House, on the 22nd took my leave of Friend
Barritt and Called to see Cousins and some more friends
after which walked Home about 12 oclock having
had a pleasent Journey for which and all other
Mercies I remain in my minde truly thankfull to
kinde Providence,
on the 24th was at our meeting ware after a time of Re=
=tirement and waiting upon the Lord to know His pure
will a few words rose fresh in my minde which appeared

verso

to be my duty to speak in the meeting and I gave

21 Earliest recorded reference of meeting1668.

22 Earliest recorded reference of meeting1668.

up to what I believed to be my duty and speak
them in Humility and found peace to my poor
minde
in so doing and I have often found it a very awe=
=full thing to Speak a few words in an awefull
assembley or Meeting appointed for the Worship
of the Almighty and found great need to be
very Inward and still in my Minde and wait
upon Devine Providence long to know His pure
Will
and when he doethe require it of me to Speak
in a meeting and when He doth not,
the 27th was at Our weekday meeting
on the 30th was at our own Meeting
the 10mo [October] 4th was at our weekday
meeting which was smallish
on the 7th it being first day and feeling a little
drawings
in my minde to go to brails and be at their meet=
=ing asked leave of my parents and walked
thither to meeting which was a rather small
yet my minde was Comforted and I trust we
ware renewedly favoured with a fresh visitation
of Devine Love, and it appeared to be my duty
to speak a few words amoungst friends which I
did and found peace in so doing after meeting
walked Home,

Page 72

on the 8th it being our Monthly meeting it was
a pretty large Comfortable meeting and truth
appeared
to arise to the Uniteing Friends near one to
another
a Testimonie or two was born to Incourage all
that
had made some little progress in the pure Truth
not to be discouraged but to persevear in the
right
way and to wait in Stillness often upon the
Almighty
to know their duty the owe to Him and them to
do it
faithfully or word to that signification
the buisness was gone through in much Love
Friend Mintchen laid before the Meeting her
conc=
=earn she felt in her minde to visit some places
ware
no friends do live and have a few meetings
believeing
it would tend to the good of the Neighbours
friends
approved of Her concearn believeing it was right
on 21st was at our weekday meeting which was
smallish
yet it appeared to be my duty to speak a few
words
amoungst friends which I did in much Humility
being
often so very sensible of my own weakness and
in=
=ability to do any good that I am affraid to
speak men=
=ny times least I should Speak to the dishonnour
of the
pure truth instead of speaking to its Honnour
yet I
have often found peace to attend my poor minde
when I
have spake in much Humility and lonlyness of
minde

verso

---

on the 14th 10mo [October] was at our own
meeting and a sitting with Friends
my minde was refreshed,
on the 18th was at our weekday meeting
on the 19 went to Sibford on an arrand to fetch
a young woman to live with us, was at their
weekday
meeting which was Comfortable to my minde tho
I was made
greatly sensible of my own weakness and
nothingness
and Inability to do any thing that is good
without Devine
assistance, two friends appeard by bearing a
testimonie
on truths behalf and to stirup the pure mindes
of the peo=
=ple to a sence of their duty which they owe to
their
Creator and Love Him above all
on the 21st was at our meeting ware after sitting
some=
=time in awefull Silence a waiting upon the Lord
to know

His pure will it appeard to be my duty to speak a few
words amoungst friends but being greatly made sensible under a sence of my own
weakness
and unworthyness and inability of my self to do any
good without the Almightys assistance so sometime after waiting upon
Him for His help and assistance I speak what appeared
to be my duty and found inward peace to my minde in
so doing,
on the 29th it being first day feeling a little drawings
in my minde to go to Faringdon meeting took a walk thither small
meeting and the Life of Religion appeared to be

Page 73

very low amoungst them yet a sitting with them
few Friends my minde was Comforted a little
after meeting walked to Witney and Slept at
a friends house there,
the first of 11mo [November] was at our meeting which was
small some friends being from home yet a sitting theirin
my minde was refreshed and comforted
on the 4th it being first day took a walk to stow meeting
which was small yet my minde was comforted and
refreshed a sitting theirin and I believe
the Love and goodness of kinde Providence was
felt to arise amoungst us, it appeared to be my
duty to speak a few words amoungst friends and
I gave up and speak them and found peace to my
minde in so doing, after meeting walked home
on the 10th friend Barritt of Witney called to se us
on the 11 was at our meeting which was pretty
large and my minde was comforted under a
sence that Devine Love was felt to arise amoungst
us to the uniteing us near one to another
on the twelfth took a walk to our Monthly Meeting held
at Witney which in the meeting for worship before the

verso

the Buisness began was pretty comfortable two friends
appeared by way of Testimonie Indeavouring to put
the people in minde not to place their dependance on
man nor look to him for help to be lead and guided
by him in the straight path that leads to everlasting rest
but to the Lord alone, whose power is able to guide
and preserve them theirin if they put their trust in
Him faithfully, after which friends proceeded upon
buisness in much Love but friends ware greatly bur=
=thened by one man behaving in a very unbecoming
manner
on the fifteenth was at our own meeting which was smallish
on the eighteenth was at our own meeting which was pretty
full considering our Number of friends and the Devine
power appeard to me to be felt amoungst us to the com=
=forting our poor mindes,
on the twenty second was at our own Meeting and
a Sitting with Friends my Poor minde was a little
comforted and refreshed
on the twenty fourth father and brother set out in=
=tending to be at a meeting on the morrow at Broad=
=way a place ware no meeting of Friends is usualy
held but was appointed to be holden their by the
perticular desire of a Woman friend who felt a concearn

Page 74

upon Her minde to pay a visit to the neighbours their

on the twenty fifth was at our own Meeting and in sit=
=ting theirin my minde was a little refreshed and
Comforted tho made greatly sensible of my own
weakness and unworthyness to pertake of any good
thing
on 27th this day we ware favoured with the
good Company of two Women public Friends
viz Martha Howard and Priscilla Gurney
on whose account a meeting was held which
lasted near three ours and was very Com=
=fortable it was desired that the Neighbours
should be let know of the meeting which
was accordingly done and sevral came and
behaved very sober and quiet to what was
delivered to them
on the twenty eight having a desire to go to witney
weekday meeting and having a little buisness
to do took a walk thither a pretty comfortable
meeting and in sitting theirin my minde was
much refreshed and comforted sevral short

verso

Testimonies ware delivered on truths to Incourage
the faithfull ones
on the twenty ninth was at our weekday meeting
the 12mo the second was at our meeting and in
sitting theirin my minde was very low under
a sence of my own great weakness being
made sensible that without Devine help and
assistance I could do no good thing after our
meeting for Worship was over the the meeting
for discipline was adjourned till a half after
two A.N. [afternoon] which was conducted in Love and Unity
on the ninth it being first day took a walk to
Milton meeting about five miles of Small meeting
friends seem there very negligent in the attendance
of their meeting yet my minde was a little
refreshed and comforted a sitting with them
after meeting walked to Burford found Brother
and Sistor there pretty well, at Burford in
the evening a meeting was held by desire of friend
Mintchon she having a desire upon her minde to
have a meeting for the good of the Neighbours
the meeting began about six and was very full

Page 75

---

it was held to the honnour of the Almighty and His
Truth I believe
on the tenth was at the Monthly Meeting their
which was very comfortable sevral living testimonies
ware born on truths behalf and some of them by
young and Sober friends, afterwards friends
proceed upon the buisness which was gone through
in much Love and Unity, but was a little discom
=posed by man not worthy the name of a
friend behaving in a very unbecoming manner
after meeting took my leave of Brother and sistor
and walked Home with Brother,
on the thirteenth was at our meeting and a sitting
with friends my minde was a little refreshed and
Comforted
on the fifteenth was at witney called to se Friend Barritt
who was quite poorly
on the sixteenth was at our meeting and a sitting theirin
my minde was much comforted under a sence that
the Love of our good Creator was felt amoungst us
to the uniteing us near to each other

verso

---

first day the twenty third was at our own meeting
and in Sitting theirin my minde was a little refre=
=shed and comforted tho greatly made sensible of
my own weakness and Unworthyness of Injoying
any good thing and that I stood indebted to the
Almighty for every good thing I received from
Him and out of gratitude for them I could do no less than to
serve Him daily according to the very best
of my Understanding
on the twenty sevventh was at our weekday meeting

and in sitting theirin my minde was a little
refreshed and comforted under a sence that
the springings up of Devine Love was felt
amoungst us
on the thirtyeth was at meeting which was
pretty full and sevral strangers ware there
and after sitting a wile in awefull silence
a waiting upon the Almighty it appeared
to be my duty to speak a few words theirin

1793

1mo [January] 6th it being first day took a walk

to witney and was at both their morning

Page 76

and afternoon meetings which felt very
comfortable
to my minde, sevral young friends appeared
theirin by way of Testimonie to the honnour of
the Almighty and His Truth and it appeared to
be my duty to speak a few words in one of
the Meetings,
on the seventh took a walk to Burford to se
brother
and sistor who ware pretty well called to se
friend Mintchon found Her pretty well
on the thirteenth was at our meeting and after
sitting sometime in Solid silence a waiting upon
the Lord to know His pure will it appeared
to be my duty to speak a few words theirin
and I gave up to what I believed was required
of me and speak a few words with great
care and humility of minde and found In=
=ward peace in so doing
on the fourteenth it being our Monthly meeting
at
C[hipping] Norton took a walk thither with
Brother a pretty
large meeting sevral sober friends being their
from sevral other neighbouring meetings and
sevral
Testimonies ware born by sevral worthy Friends

verso

to the honnour of the great Almighty being I
believe afterwards friends proceeded upon
buisness
which was gone through in much Love and Unity
on the Nineteenth feeling a little drawings in my
minde
to take a walk to Faringdon Meeting and sett
with
the few friends their walked to Witney and rested
their on the morrow morning Fr'd Hankins was
so kinde as to bear me company which was very
axceptable to me, small Meeting yet in Sitting
theirin my minde was comforted and refreshed
under
a sence that Devine Love was felt amoungst us
walked to Witney witney with friend Hankins
and
on the morrow morning walked Home
on the twenty fourth was at our weekday Meeting
on the twenty seventh was at our Meeting and in
sit=
=ting theirin my minde was much comforted and
refreshed and it appeared to be my duty to speak
a few words theirin and I gave up and speak them
and found Inward peace in so doing
on the thirtyeth having a little buisness to do at
Witney
took a walk thither and stayed their weekday
meeting, called to se Ann Rich who was very
poorly

Page 77

on the second of the second month[February]
feeling it a
little my duty to go to Armscutt [Armscote]
Meeting acquainted
my Parents theirof and walked to Brails in the
afternoon found Cousins pretty well
on the third this morning walked from brails
to shipstone found Cousins there pretty well
walked with some of them to Armscutt
[Armscote] meeting
small meeting I believe on account of the
weather not being very good yet it appeared
a very good satisfactory meeting sevral good
Testimonies being born with an intent to put
the people in minde to wait upon their Creator
to know their duty to Him and then to do it,
after meeting walked with Cousins to Shipstone
and from thence with Cousin Wm Hemmings

to Brails Lodged their
on the fourth it being the monthly meeting for
that division
adjoining to banbury to be held at Banbury
and believing it to be in the line of my duty
to go thither walked thither called at Epwell
found my Relations there pretty well a pretty
comfortable
meeting yet the buisness went on heavily and

verso

---

it held long their being a deal to do and friends
appeared very backward to labour on Truths
behalf one testimonie was born wareby the
people ware directed to be obidient to their
Creator and please Him the buisness was
conducted in Love and Unity after meeting
walked to Epwell lodged the
on the fifth this morning after taking my
kinde leave of my Relations at Epwell walked
to sibford third day [Tuesday] meeting called to
se a few
friends before meeting with whome I ware
acquainted
small meeting yet I trust we ware renewedly
favoured with the springings up of Devine
Love to the Uniteing us near one to another
after meeting walked Home ware I found
my Friends pretty well was truly thankfull to
kinde Providence who did inable me to return
safe home again
on the seventh was at our fifth day [Thursday]
meeting
on the tenth was at our first day meeting
[Sunday] ware
we ware favoured with the Company of friend
Mintchon and her husband and it was a good
comfortable meeting I believe warein the Devine

Page 78

Power did arise amoungst us and flow from
Vessel to vessel to the comforting of menny
mindes
present and in the evening a meeting was held
by friend Mintchins desire intended for the good
of the neighbours, and a good meeting I believe
it was and held to the Honnour of the Almighty
being, sevral neighbours appeared pretty atten=
=time to what was delivered
on the Eleventh it being our monthly meeting
at Charlbury we ware favoured with the
company of Brother Henry and sevral
more friends it was a pretty large meeting
and it was recommended in meeting that
friends should wait upon the Lord that they
might witness their strength renewed by Him
and more to that Effect, after which friends
proceeded upon the buisness which held pretty
long there being a deal to do yet it was con=
ducted in Love and Unity,
on the fourteenth was at our own weekday
meeting
on the fifteenth having a little buisness to do
at Chipping=Norton took a walk thither and

verso

Stoped their six=day [Friday] Meeting
on the sevventeenth was at our First-day
[Sunday]
meeting which was pretty large and felt
very comfortable to my minde
and after a time of solid silence waiting
upon the Lord it appeared to be my duty
to speak a few words theirin and I gave up
theirunto and speak in humility and awe=
=fullness and found Inward peace in so doing
on the twenty fifth was at our own fifth
day [Thursday] meeting
on the twenty fourth having a desire to go
and be at Stow meeting asked my Parents
leave and walked thither small meeting
yet a sitting with them few friends my
poor minde was comforted and refreshed
being made sensible that Devine Love
was felt to arise amoungst us to the Uniteing
us near one to another after meeting took
my kinde leave of friends and walked Home
ware I found my friends pretty well

Page 78

---

for which and all other Mercies I remain
truly thankfull to kinde Providence
on the twenty eight was at our own fifthday
[Thursday]
meeting and in sitting theirin my poor
minde was a little refreshed and comforted

on the third of the third month [March] having
a desire
to go to Sibford meeting asked my Parents leave
and obtained their leave, walked thither in good
time fullish meeting and in sitting theirin my
minde was refreshed and Comforted under a
sence that Devine Love was felt to arise
amoungst us to the uniteing us near one to
another
on the fourth walked from Sibford to Adderbury
Monthly meeting fullish meeting sevral solid
Friends ware their and sevral good testimonies
ware born to the Honnour of the Devine being
and to the incouragement of the faithfull ones
the meeting of buisness was conducted in Love
and Unity, walked from thence to sibford and
slept
at Aunt Gilkes's , on the morrow took my kinde
leave of Aunt gilkes and Cousin Rebecca Gilkes
her Daughter Cousin Rebecca Gilkes I went to
see in hopes

verso

---

to have Her for a good companion and helpmeet
in this Life, if it should please kind Providence
to Unite us together in His Love as I humbly
followed
His Leadings and guideance in all things
walked from thence to southnewington meeting
which was small their being but very few
Friends living their abouts yet in Sitting theirin
my minde was comforted believein that Devine
Love was Extended towards us to the
Incouragment
of us to seek and wait upon Him often if we
would
Injoy his Love, after meeting took my leave
of friend Harris's and Grandmother and walked
to enstone found them pretty well spent a little
time with them in a friendly way and then bid
them farewell and walked Home ware I found
my Friends Indifrent well for which and all
other mercies I receive from Kinde Providence
I remain truly thankfull to Him,
on the sevventh was at our own weekday meeting
on the tenth was at our first day [Sunday]
meeting and
in sitting theirin my minde was refreshed and
comforted and it appeared to be my duty to
speak a few words amoungst friends and in so
doing I found Inward peace to my poor minde

Page 79

---

on the eleventh took a walk to our Monthly
meeting holden at Witney a pretty fullish
meeting and felt pretty comfortable to my minde
sevral mouths being opened to declare of the
Lords Love and goodness towards those that
in truth love Him, and that friends should
minde and remmember the covenant they
made with Him in the days of their affliction
that if He would be pleased to give them bread
to eat and water to drink then should He the
Lord be their God and more to that purpose
on the fourteenth was at our own fifth day
[Thursday] meeting
on the seventeenth feeling a little drawings in
my minde to go to Sibford meeting and se
Cousin Rebecca Gilkes and ask Her Mothers
leave to let me come to se her if she was willing
to become a kinde helpmeet to me and to axcept
of me for an helpmeet to she during Life if kinde
Providence was pleased in His Love to suffer it to
be, a large and comfortable meeting sevral sober
testimonies ware born to stir up the people to
minde
and be obidient to and serve their Creator
faithfully
if the would be loved by Him and more to that
purpose

verso

---

after meeting called to se a few friends and then
walked Home
on the twentyth took a walk to Witney and was
at
their weekday meeting which was small yet I
believe we ware favoured with the Springings up
of
Devine Love, and one youngish womanfriend
was drawn forth to speak a few words in prayer
to the Devine Being, found one woman friend
their
very poorly who had be so for sometime
on the twenty first was at our fifth day [Thursday]
meeting

on the twenty fourth was at our first day meeting
[Sunday]
and a sitting with friends my mind was a little
comforted tho greatly made sensible of my own
weakness
and the great need their was for me to wait pa=
=tiencly upon the Devine Being to be made
sensible
of His pure will and to ask of Him ability to
Inable
to Inable me to do it
on the twenty Eight was at our weekday
meeting
on the thirty first was at our own meeting at
which
a Strainger public Friends was present who had
a few words of Incouragement to the youth to
serve
the Lord faithfully or to that purpose,
to day our preparative meeting was held at

Page 80

which the Yearly Meeting Queries ware
answered in Love and Unity, afterwards
walked with Father to Burford to se Brother
and Sistor and with an Intent to be at the
Monthly meeting there in the morrow
4mo [April] 1st snow was at our Monthly
Meeting which
was small owing to the cold=ness of the weather
I believe yet it felt pretty comfortable to my
minde one friend speak by way of testimonie
to exhort friends to come up faithfully in the
discharge of their duty faithfully to the Devine
Being in what way soever He should be ple=
ased to make known to them to be their duty to
serve Him in and improve their gifts ac=
=cording to the best of their understanding and
more to that purpose, afterwards friends pro=
=ceeded upon the buisness which was gone
through
in much Love and Unity
2nd very cold with snow, this morning took my
kinde leave of Brother and Sistor and walked
home with friend Albright the weather proving
exceeding cold caused it to be a verry trying
Journey yet we ware Inabled to get Home safe

verso

for which mercy and favour I was very thankfull
in
my minde to Kinde Providence
on the forth took a walk to Witney to the Burial
of Friend Hill the meeting was large of Friends
and Neighbours, and sevral solid testimonies
ware born to stir-up the pure mindes of the
people
and put them in minde to prepare for their
latter end
on the 4th was at our own meeting
on the sixth having obtained my Parents leave
to take a walk to Sibford to se Aunt Gilkes
and Her Daughter Rebbecca walked thither
in the after=noon
on the seventh before meeting went to se a young
Woman Friend who was very ill not likely to
live long her illness was occasioned by swallowing
a pin as she thought or something which had
hurt her throat so that she could take nothing
but licquids for sometime, it had brought Her
so weak that she appeared in a deep Decline
was at their meeting which was pretty large
and felt pretty comfortable to my poor minde
after meeting walked Home with Joseph Gilkes

Page 81

1793

on the ninth took a walk to Witney to our Quar=
=terly Meeting a largish meeting, one very
worthy
Friend I believe was their in company with
another friend from America whose name was
Joseph or Job Scott, the buisness held pretty long
there
being a pretty deal to do but it was comducted
in much Love and Unity
on the eleventh was at our weekday meeting
which
was pretty large Friends being favoured
with the good company of William Marshall
from Southnewington and John Hall from
Hooknorton the Meeting felt very comfortable
and it was concluded by one of them with solem

Prayer to the Devine Being that He would be
pleased to Extend His Love to Friends
on the fourteenth was at our first day [Sunday]
meeting which
felt comfortable to my poor minde and after
a time of Solid Silence and waiting upon
the Lord it appeared to be my duty to speak
a few words amoungst Friends and in so
doing I found Inward Peace,
on the Eighteenth was at our own Weekday
meeting
on the Nineteenth took a walk to Chipping
norton

verso

---

and was at their weekday meeting, it felt very
comfortable to my poor minde I being made
sensible that the Devine Power was felt to
arise amoungst us, I believe to the Comforting
of the mindes of menny present
on the twenty first we ware favoured with
the company of Old Wm Barritt and Tho's
Smith from witney and one of them had a
few words to deliver to Exhort friends to examine
and know what they came to meetings for
even to profit to profit in that which would prove
for their Everlasting good
on the twenty fifth was at our own fifth day
[Thursday]
Meeting
on the twenty eight took a walk to Sibford and
was at both their morning and afternoon
Meeting
which felt very comfortable to my poor minde
sevral living Testimonies ware born to put the
people in minde to be diligent to wait upon their
Creator and minde His Inward teaching the light
of
Truth with them and obey it, after meeting
walked Home
on the fifth month [May] the first took a walk to
witney
and was at their fourth day [Wednesday] Meeting
which was
not very large yet it felt Comfortable to my poor

Page 82

---

minde and the Devine Power was felt to arise
amoungst
us to the uniteing us one to another
on the second was at our own fifth day [Thursday]
meeting
on the fourth feeling it to be my duty to be at
armscutt [Armscote]
meeting which is held on the fifth asked my
Parents
leave and obtained it, walked to Brails and rested
at Cousins, in the morning set out pretty early
for Shipstone and was at their mornig meeting
which felt very comfortable to my minde after
meeting walk with friends to Armscutt
[Armscote] Meeting it
was pretty large of Friends and Neighbours
sevral Public Friends ware their and sevral living
Testimonies ware born to turn and direct the
people
to minde the Light of Christ Jesus with them
and obey it which if they did it would teach
them what they ought to do and what they ought
to leave undone to please their Creator, the
meet=
=ing was Concluded with solem and awefull
prayer
after meeting walked with Cousins to Brails and
rested their and next morning took my kinde
leave
of them and walked home,
on the sevventh it being our Monthly Meeting at
Chipping
Norton took a walk thither, a pretty large
meeting
and it felt pretty comfortable to my minde the
Living
truth arose amoungst us to the uniteing us near
to
each other, the buisness was gone through in
much Love and Unity,

verso

---

on the ninth was at our own fifth day [Thursday]
meeting
on the twenty second was at our first day
[Sunday]
meeting and a sitting with friends my poor

minde was refreshed and comforted under a
sence that Devine Love was felt to arise
amoungst us,
on the sixteenth was at our fifth day [Thursday] meeting
on the nineteenth was at our first day [Sunday] meeting
which was small sevral friends being from Home
yet a sitting with them few my poor minde was
refreshed and comforted under a sence that our Heavenly
Fathers Love was renewedly felt amoungst us
on the twenty fifth believeing it to be my duty to
take a walk to Radway and be at Friends
Meeting[23] their asked my Parents leave
and they ware willing to let me go walked to
Epwell ware I found my Relations pretty well
slept their and in or on the morrow morning
walked with Uncle Gibbs to Radway called to se
Cousin John Malings who had lately met with a
great loss, that of an Affectionate Wife He was
bread up a friend but took to doing what he ought not
Drinking which caused friends to disown him
He seemed to be in a solid disposition of minde
and I hope so great and solem mourning would

Page 83

make him sensible of his undone and Miserable
state and cause Him to come to a sincear repentance
and ammendment of his ways
the meeting was pretty full considering the small
number of Friends being their the meeting felt pretty
comfortable to my minde two Women appeared by
way on in Testimonie in an affectionate and loving
manner, after meeting took my leave of Friends
and walked to sibford afternoon meeting, the meeting
felt pretty comfortable to my minde sevral friends
had a few words by way of exhortation to friends
to take up the cross freely if they would become the
true disciples of Jesus Christ, or words to that purpose
slept at Aunt and Cousin Rebbecca Gilkes's
and after breackfasting with them took my kinde
leave of them and walked Home,
on the thirtieth was at our fifth day [Thursday] meeting

6mo [June] 2nd 1793

was at our first day [Sunday] which which was smallish
yet in sitting theirin my poor minde was refreshed
and comforted and it appeared to by my duty to
speak a few words theirin and in so doing I found
Inward peace of minde
the sixth was at our own weekday meeting
the eight having felt it a degree of duty to my
Creator to take a walk to Faringdon meeting

verso

walked to Witney in the Evening and acquainted
Wm Harris of my Intention to visit Faringdon
Meeting and asked Him to go and take a walk
with me if after he had delibertly considered
thereof he found freedome in his minde to go, he considered
theirof and he was free to go with me, we set out
earlyish in the morning it being ten miles to
walk found friends pretty well the meeting
was small and in Sitting theirin my minde was
very poor and low which might be owing in some
degree to some friends their having their mindes
set more on earthly things than on Heavenly
things yet after my sitting sometime in Silence
a waiting upon the Lord it appeared to be my
duty to stand up and speak a few words amoungst
Friends which I did in much humility under
a sence of my own weakness and Inability without
Devine aid and assistance I found inward peace
to my poor minde in so doing, their was a young
man at meeting lately convinced of our principals
a very sober yound man and I believe he is truly
convinced of the truth and friends principals of

23 Earliest recorded reference of meeting 1668

he is willing to be obidient theirunto in the
afternoon
Wm and I walked back again to Witney ware

Page 84

we spent the evening solidly with some Friends
slept with Wm Harris and on the morrow
morning
took my leave of him and som more Friends
and walked Home, ware I found my Parents
tolerable well, for which mercy and blessing
and al others I remain truly thankfull to
Kinde Providence
on the thirteenth was at our fifth day [Thursday]
meeting
on the sixthteenth was at our first day [Sunday]
meeting
which was pretty full and after sitting sometime
in solid Silence a waiting upon my Creator it
appeared to be my duty in Obidience to Him to
stand up and speak a few words in meeting
on the Nineteenth a Commity of Friends
met who ware appointed sometime ago to attend
the monthly Meetings and held a select
meeting this Evening
on the nineteenth it being our Monthly
Meeting held at Charlbury by appointment
sevral Friends met more than usual I be=
=lieve on account of the committe of friends
that were expected to be there, the meeting
began at ten and felt very satisfactory

verso

to my poor exercised mind which longed
to pertake of Heavenly bread and
Heavenly water, sevral Living Testimonies
ware born by sevral Friends to direct
the People to turn their mindes Inward
to the pure light of Christ within them
and obey it, afterwards the friend
proceeded upon the buisness the met together
to do which was conducted in much Love
and Unity
on the twentieth was at our fifth day [Thursday]
meeting
which was small yet I trust we few that
ware present, ware made sensible of the
springings up of Devine Love amoungst
us to the comforting and refreshing our
Hungry and thirsty souls
the twenty first it being first Day [Sunday] this
morn
=ing set out on foot Intending to be at Ban=
=bury quarterly meeting walked to Shutford
meeting in the morning which was small
there being but few friends living there
abouts yet in sitting theirin my poor minde

Page 85

was refreshed and Comforted and it
appeared to be my duty to speak a few
words amoungst friends
walked from thence to Epwell ware I
found my Relations very well
walked from thence to Sibford afternoon
meeting which was very full
and in Sitting therein my poor minde
was refreshed and Comforted and I
trust Devine Love was felt to arise amoungst
us to the uniteing us near to each other
one friends had a few words to speak in the
meeting
to advise friens who ware once made sensible
of what was right for them to do to work
out their own Souls salvation not to be
Slothfull but to Improve it to their own
Souls Everlasting advantage or words
to that purpose
on the twenty fourth walked from little
Sibford to Banbury quarterly meeting which
was large and menny strangers public friends

verso

ware present and sevral friends appeared
by way of testimonie to direct the people
to turn their mindes inward and to minde
the pure light of Christ within them
and be Obidient unto it and not to look
outward towards man but to minde this
Inward teacher the true light which would
teach them better than any man could
teach them, was at their afternoon meeting
which was held in the Womens Meeting House
their being another held in the Mens as
usual that Meeting I sat in felt comfortable
to my minde sevral solid Friends appeared

by way of testimonie and opened to the
Neighbours that profess difrent to us in
the way of worshiping the Almight the
uselessness if their forms and the nescesiety
of mindeing the Light of Truth within them
which would bring them out of forms to the
substance of pure Religion, after meeting
walked with some friends to little Sibford
and went to se Joseph Harris who was

Page 86

very Poorly
on the twenty fifth walked with Friend
Hoton and his son from little sibford
to Richard Sconches at Netrup [Neithrop]
was at the meeting which began at nine
in the morning for buisness which was
gone through pretty soon the commity who
ware appointed sometime ago ware present
and the buisness was gone through in much
Love and Unity after meeting took my
kinde leave of Friend Sconch and some
more friends and walked Home with
Brother Robbert and young William Albright
I had a satisfactory Journey and was favoured
with peace of minde when I returned Home
and also found my Friends pretty well
for which mercy and Blessings and all
others I Remain truly thankfull to
Kinde Providence

verso

on the twenty sixth was at our fifth day
[Thursday] meeting
and a sitting with friends my poor
mind was a little refreshed and comforted
the thirtieth of the Sixth month [June] took a
walk
with William and James Albright to Barton
Meeting which was pretty full of Friends
and Neighbours who behaved very quiet
and appeared well satisfied with what
was Delivered as sevral living testi=
=monies ware born by sevral Friends
to advise the people to turn their mindes
Inward and minde the pure light of
Christ within them and obey it if they
would come to Injoy happiness and rest when
they had done with this World and
more words to that purpos, after meet=
=ing walked with Cousin Franklings
to their House at Ledal [Ledwell?] and from
thence
to Hooknorton to se friend Halls and
some more friends who ware pretty well
Lodged with Friend Hall
the seventh mo: the first got up pretty

Page 87

early and went to se friend Halls at
their work and some more friends before
Meeting time, was at their monthly meeting
which was pretty large and it appeared
to be over shadowed With that Devine
Power which refresheth and comforteth
them that truly hunger and thirst
after righteousness sevral living tes=
=timonies were born by sevral worthy
Friends and friends ware advised
to give up all and take up the Cross
freely to their own carnal inclinations
and mind the Heavenly manifestation
of pure Light and Truth within them and
obey its leadings and guidance in all
things or words to that meaning
afterwards friends proceeded upon the
buisness which was gone through in much
Love and Unity after meeting took my
leave of Friend Hall and some more
friends and walked Home ware I found
my friends pretty well for which I was

verso

Truly thankfull
5[May]=4 fine was at our fifth day [Thursday]
meeting and a
sitting with a few sober friends my poor
minde was refreshed and comforted
First day [Sunday] being the seventh of the
seventh month [July]
was at meeting to day and a sitting theirin
my poor minde was refreshed and Comforted
under a sence that Devine Love was felt
to arise amoungst us to the uniteing us
theirin near one to another, it was our
preparative meeting which was held in

much Love and Unity
the Eleventh was at our fifth day [Thursday]
meeting
which was small some Friends being
from home yet as I sat theirin my
poor minde was refreshed and
Comforted for I was made sensible
that Devine Love was felt amoungst
us to the Uniteing us near one to the
other

Page 88

on the thirteenth asked leave of my Parents to let
me take a walk to Stow meeting and
obtained it
on the fourteenth took a walk to stow
meeting called at Oddington to see friend
Hiden Kinde Providence was pleased
a few days ago to take away from Her her dear
brother
by Death but I trust it had been His
care not to offend Him in any thing
so it hath pleased Him to take him
out of this world of probation to Injoy
Everlasting rest, found Friend Hiden
tolerable well considering Her great loss
I was sorry to se so small a meeting
some friends seem neglectfull in comming to it
yet as I sat with them few my poor minde
was refreshed being made sensible of the
of the springings up of Devine Love
amoungst us to the Uniteing us near
one to the other, after meeting walked
to seasoncutt [Sezincote] to se Cousins and rested
there

verso

9mo [September] 1793

on the fifteenth walked from seasoncutt
[Sezincote]
with sevral Cousins to stow to the
funeral of Robert Hiden, the meeting
began about two it was very full of Friends
and Neighbours and a good solem meeting
sevral living testimonies ware born by
sevral friends and the people ware
advised to turn their mindes inward to the
pure light of Christ Jesus within them
and obey it if the would witness Him to be
Mercy full to them and forgive them
their sins and admit them into His Ever=
lasting Kingdom of Rest when they had
done with this World and more to the same
purpose
after meeting walked Home, found my
Friends very well
on the Eighteenth was at our fifth day [Thursday]
meeting
it felt comfortable to my minde
First day [Sunday] being the twenty first took a
walk to Witney and was at friends morning
meeting which felt pretty comfortable
to my poor minde after meeting took
a walk with friends from Witney to

Page 89

Brize=norton Meeting which was ap=
=pointed to beholden there at five in
the Evening, it was a very large meeting
of friends and Neighbours and sevral
living Testimonies was born by
sevral friends and it appeared to
be a renewed visitation to menny
present and the people ware directed
to minde the pure light and witness
of Truth within them which was given
to them in pure Love and came by
Jesus Christ and if the took heed
and minded its leadings it would
teach them better than any Man
could teach them after meeting
walked with Brother Henry to
Burford to se Sistor and Cousins
on the twenty second in the morning went
to se some friends afterwards took my
kinde leave of Brother and Sistor and

verso

walked home ware I found my friends
midling well
on the twenty fifth was at our fifth day
[Thursday]
meeting

on the twenty sixth feeling a little desire
to set with friends at Chipping Norton
meeting took a walk thither small meeting
yet as I sat with Friends my heart did rejoice
being made sensible that the renewed
visitation of the Lords Love and goodness
was felt amoungst us to the comforting
of sevral friends present,
on the 28th it being first day [Sunday] took a
walk to Milton meeting which was
not very large on account of their pre=
parative meeting being put of to be
holden their next first day [Sunday] if nothing
hindred it, I trust it was a good meeting
and we ware favoured with the Love
of our Great Creator to the refreshing
of the truly Hungry and thirsty souls
after meeting took a walk with sevral

Page 90

Friends to great Barington to a evening
meeting to be holden there by friend
Mintchons desire, it was a large
meeting of Friends and Neighbours
in which the Devine Power was renewedly
felt to arise amoungst us to the comforting
and refreshing menny mindes present
and a Friend was drawn forth in
awefull and solem Prayer to Kinde
Providence who is worthy to be prayed
unto and waited upon for His renewed
help and assistance to make known
our duty to us and to inable us to discharge
our duty to Him faithfully and with a
willing and chearfull minde,
walked to Burford and lodged at
Brothers and Sistors,
on the twenty=ninth this morning took my kinde
leave of Brother and sistor and walked
Home

verso

1793

8mo [August] 1st was at our own weekday meeting
on the third asked leave of my Father to let me
take a walk to Armscutt [Armscote] meeting and obtained his leave which was
to be on the fourth, walked to Sibford with
Thomas and Jn'o Gilkes slept at their mothers
who was very well
on the fourth set out early for Armscutt [Armscote] meeting
with four of Friend Gilkes sons called
at Brails to se Cousins there walked from
thence to Shipstone and was at their morning
meeting which was small yet the Devine
Power was felt to arise amoungst us to the
Refreshing of the flock of Christ
after meeting walked with Cousin Wells and
some more friends to Armscutt [Armscote] meeting which
was large, of Friends and Neighbours and
sevral good Testimonies was born by sevral
Friends to advise the people to minde the Light of
truth or the spirit of truth within them a measure
and manifestation of which all had received
and if they did but faithfully minde and obey it
it would teach them better than any man or

Page 91

woman could teach them, and an awefull prayer was
put up unto the great Creator of every good and
perfect thing praying to Him that He would be pleased to be good to His
Children after meeting walked with Cousin Wells's
and went to their House and stoped with them a
little wile walked from thence to Brails to se friends
and Cousins their, Lodged there
on the fifth took my kinde leave of Cousins and walked

Home, ware I found my friends Indifrent well for
which and all other Mercies I remain truly
Thankfull
to Kinde Providence
on the eight was at our fifth day [Thursday]
meeting
on the eleventh was at our first day [Sunday]
meeting and a
sitting with friends my minde was strengthened
and
refresh in the pure Truth being quite sensible that
the Love of our good Creator was extended to us
to the Uniteing us near one to another
on the twelfth it being our monthly Meeting
to be holden at Burford took a walk thither
fullish meeting and it felt very comfortable to
my poor minde I being made fully sensible of
the renewed overshadowings of Devine Love
amo=
=ungst us to the Uniteing us near to each other

verso

Friends went through the buisness in much
Love and Unity, after meeting waked home
with Brother and Phillip Gilkes
on the fifteenth was at our fifth day [Thursday]
meeting
on the eighteenth was at our first day [Sunday]
meeting
and after I had sat sometime in awefull
Silence waiting upon the Lord to know His pure
will appeared to be my duty to speak a few
words theirin which I did in Humility ad
care under a sence of my own great weakness
found Inward peace to my poor minde in so
doing
on the twenty second was at our fifth
day [Thursday] meeting and as I sat with friends
my poor minde was refreshed and comforted
first day [Sunday] being the twenty fifth believe=
=ing it to be in the faithfull discharge
of my duty to the Devine Being to take
a walk to Sibford meeting asked my
Parents leave and obtained their consent
reached meeting in good time it was a
largish meeting and felt very comfortable

Page 92

to my poor minde sevral Testimonies
ware born by sevral friends wareby
Friends ware advised to turn their
mindes Inward to the pure Light
and Spirit of truth within them
and obey it
was at their afternoon meeting also which
was a pretty large and good meeting
sevral Living Testimonies ware born
by sevral Friends by which the peo=
ple ware advised to wait for that true
and living power which comes from
the Great Creator of every good
Thing because their was no other
Power nor Name by which a Man
or woman could be saved but by the
Name and power of Jesus,
after meeting took my kinde leave of
Friends and walked Home

verso

9 [August]1793

on the twenty Ninth was at our fifth day
[Thursday]
meeting and as I sat with Friends my poor
minde was a little refreshed and comforted
with that living and everlasting power
which comes down from above
9mo [September] the first was at our first day
[Sunday] meeting
and a sitting theirin my minde was
Comforted with the Power of Truth,
our preparative meeting to day at which the
queries ware answered pretty near to what they
required and in much Love and Unity,
on the secon finding it to be my duty to
take a walk to Sibford Monthly Meeting
asked my Parents leave and obtained
it it was a large and comfortable meeting
and the Devine Power was felt to the over=
=shadowing it to the Uniteing friends
near one to another and sevral solid
Testimonies ware born to the honnour
of the Devine Being, afterwards friends

Proceeded upon buisness which was gone

Page 93

---

through in much Love and Unity,
the third after taking my leave of Cousin
and Aunt Gilkes and some more friends
walked to little Sibford to se some friends
their and from thence to Hooknorton to a
meeting appointed to be holden their by
Friend Mintchens desire it began at ten
and was a pretty large and Comfortable
meeting of Friends and Neighbours who
behaved very solid and attentive to what
was delivered sevral testimonies ware
born by which the People ware directed
to retire into awefull Silence that their
mindes might be brought into a good
situation to worship the Lord aright
after meeting took my leave of
Friends and walked Home,
on the fifth was at our weekday meeting
and as I sat with friends my minde was
very desireous to be brought into true
resignation
of minde to the Devine Will

verso

---

10 [September] 8. 1793

---

on the eight feeling a desire upon my
minde to take a walk to an evening meeting
at Adderbury in the morning walked
to Southnewington Meeting which was not
very large yet we ware favoured with
the overshadowing of Devine Love that
comforted and refreshed the hungry and
thirsty souls that Hungred and Thirsted
after Righteousness called to see Cousin
Harriss and afterwards walked with Friend
Marshall to Adderbury Meeting appointed
by friend Mintchins desire it was a
large meeting of Friends and Neighbours
who behaved very solid and appeared to
be much reached by the Power of Truth
which Overshadowed the Meeting, Friend
Mintchin was greatly favoured by
Kinde Providence to speak suiteable to
the states of the People
went to Adderbury to see some friends and rested
their
on the ninth set out early in the morning with
some friends for C[hipping] Norton monthly
Meeting

Page 94

---

it was a large Monthly Meeting
sevral friends being their that belonged
to other meetings, it was a good Satis=
=factory meeting in which sevral Living
Testimonies ware born by which the
poor dependant Children whose de=
=pendance was on the Lord alone
ware directed to look at Home and
take care of their own vineyards
before they took care of other Peoples
vineyards and more words to that
Purpose, the meeting of buisness
lasted long their being a great deal
to do, it was gone through in much Love
after meeting walked with some friends
home
on the twelfth was at our fifth day [Thursday]
meeting and as I sat with friends my
poor minde was Comforted and refres=
=ed being sensible that the Love of God
was felt amoungst us and it appeared
to be my duty to speak a few words in meeting

verso

9mo [September] 1793

---

on the fifteenth feeling a desire upon my
minde to go to Oxford Meeting which is
held on the first day [Sunday] before the
Quarterly
Meeting at Reading took a walk thither
with Brother, smallish meeting, I believe
sevral stayed at Home and neglected their
duty to the Devine Being on account of the
wetness of the weather which is cause of sorrow
to the truly upright hearted people and will be to
them when they

seriously consider that they have shunned the
cross and are in danger of loosing the true
Crown, the meeting felt comfortable to my
minde sevral living testimonies ware born
by sevral worthy friends wareby the people
ware directed to minde the true and inward
Teacher the Spirit of truth which if the minde
its leadings and guideance it would teach
them better than any man could teach
them after meeting took my leave of friends
and walked Home
on the nineteenth was at our fifth day [Thursday]
meeting

Page 95

on the twenty second was at our first day
[Sunday]
meeting and a sitting with friends my
poor minde was very much Comforted and
strengthened in the Truth being sensible of
the renewed visitation of Devine Love unto
us and the Widdow Squire who is lately returned
Home was drawn forth in solem Prayer to
the Devine Being praying that He would
be pleased to be near to his people and
strengthen them in the pure Truth
on the twenty sixth believeing it a discharging
my duty to Kind Providence to take a
walk to Campden Meeting asked my
Parents leave and obtained it on the twe=
=nty fifth walked to seasoncutt [Sezincote] found
cousins
there very well slept there and on the
morrow walked with a friend to the meeting
small meeting their being but few friends
living their abouts yet in our sitting together
we ware favoured with the overshadowing
of Devine Love to the comforting and uniteing

verso

our mindes near to each other in the truth
as we waited upon the Lord, walked with
friend Beavingtons to their House spent a
little time with them very comfortabley after=
=ward they ware so kind as to walk part
of the way with me to Charingworth spent
the evening with cousins at Charingworth
comfortabley,
on the 29th took my farewell of Cousins walked
from Charingworth to Shipstone
found Cousins and friends there very well
staid with them a little wile then took
my farewell of them and walked with
Friend Lamb she to a friends at Bason
and from thence to Brails to se some Relations
their and from thence to Sibford to se
Cousin Rebecca Gilkes in hopes to make
she my wife if it ware the will of Kinde
Providence it should be permited to be
on the thirtieth was at Sibford morning
meeting wich was pretty large in which
the Devine Power was felt to Overshadow
us to the Uniteing us near to each other

Page 96

sevral Testimonies ware born and friend
Joseph Harris had a few words in Prayer
to the Devine Being praing to Him
to strengthen His Children and Inable
them to live to His praise, was at the
afternoon meeting which felt Comfortable
to my poor minde and Friends ware
directed to wait upon the Lord and minde
His pure leadings and guidance in all
Things that they might be Inabled
to serve Him truly or words to that
purpose after meeting took my farewell
of friends and walked Home truly
thankfull to Kinde Providence in as
much as He was pleased to favour me
with Health and Inable me to Discharge
my duty to Him
on the second believeing it to be my duty to take
a walk to Witney meeting asked my parents
leave and walked thither smallish meeting
yet as I sat theirin my poor minde was
strengthened and Comforted with Devine

verso

Love and the good advice theirin given
on the third was at our fifth day [Thursday]
meeting and
as I sat with friends my poor minde was
strengthened in the truth
on the sixth was at our first day [Sunday] meeting
which was smallish yet as I sat theirin

my poor minde was comforted and refreshed
and it appeared to be my duty to speak
a few words theirin
In the afternoon took a walk to Chipping
Norton meeting and as I sat theirin my
minde was refreshed and Comforted I being
made fully sensible of the springings up
of Devine Love to the comforting of sevral
mindes present after meeting walked
to sibford to se Cousin Rebecca Gilkes and Her
Her Mother Aunt Gilkes,
on the sevventh took a walk to Adderbury
monthly meeting to which came menny friends
which felt very comfortable to my poor minde
sevral living Testimonies ware born which

Page 97

ware attended with that pure Devine Power
to the comforting and reffreshing menny
mindes present afterwards friends proceeded
upon the buisness which was gone through
in Love and Unity after meeting
walked to friend gilkes's at milton and
from thence to little Sibford to see friend
Joseph Harris, from thence to see Cousin
Rebbecca and Aunt Gilkes,
on the Eight took a walk to Shutford
third day meeting which was smallish yet
I trust in our sitting together the
saying of good Jesus was fullfilled
unto us that ware two or three are
met together in my Name their will
I be in the midst of them, after
Meeting walked Home
on the thirteenth was at our first day [Sunday]
meeting which was midling large considering
our small number we ware favoured with the
company of Friend Mintchon and and two of
Friend

verso

Huntleys who all sat in Silence during the
whole meeting yet I think we ware favoured
with the overshadowings of Devine Love as
much as wen menny words are Spoken
on the fourteenth Our monthly meeting was
held at Charlbury which was pretty large
and we ware favoured with the Company
of our friend Richard Sconce together
with sevral other public Friends and it
was recommended in our Meeting to be carefull
that our great Enemy did not hurt us
and that we might Injoy the blessing
of the Lord the buisness held pretty long
on account of some going out from the
Truth yet it was conducted in much love and
Unity
on the seventeenth was at our fifth day
[Thursday] meeting
and a sitting with friends my poor minde
was refreshed and comforted
on the twentyeth was at our first day [Sunday]
meeting
and a sitting with Friends my minde was
refreshed and Comforted and it appeared
to be my duty to speak a few words amoungst
them

Page 98

on the twenty fourth was at our fifth day
[Thursday]
meeting which was small yet a sitting with
friends
my poor minde was refreshed and Comforted
on the twenty fifth took a walk to
Sibford six day [Friday] meeting and a sitting
with Friends my poor minde was
refreshed with Devine Love and a
friend was drawn forth to exhort
friends to be truly faithfull rested
at friend Gilkes's on the morrow
morning took my leave of Friends
and walked to little sibford to see
friend Joseph Harris and from
thence Home ware I found my friends
tolerable well for for which mercy
and all others I remain truly thankfull
to Kinde Providence,
on the twenty seventh was at our first day
[Sunday]
meeting and after sitting theirin sometime
waiting upon the Lord it appeared to be
my duty to speak a few words theirin which
I did and found Inward peace of minde in so
doing

verso

On the thirty first of the 10mo [October] 1793
was at our fifth day [Thursday]
meeting
on the eleventh month the third believeing
it to be my duty to take a walk and be at
stow meeting asked my Parents leave and
walked thither, small meeting yet as I sat
amoungst friends waiting upon the Lord
I trust that Scripture was fullfilled unto
us which blessed Jesus expressed when He
was Personally upon Earth, that ware
two or three are met together in my Name
there I will be in the midst of them or
to that purpose after meeting took my leave
of Friends and walked to C[hipping] Norton to
se
Cousin Lambs and some more Friends
on the fourth believeing it to be my duty
to go to the Monthly meeting walked from
Chipping Norton to Sibford and from thence
to Shutford Monthly meeting with some
Friends, smallish meeting yet as I sat
with friends my poor minde was made
sensible of the renewed overshadowings
of Devine Love, to the Comforting of menny

Page 99

mindes present sevral Testimonies ware
born to Incourage friends to serve the
Lord faithfully and an awefull and Humble
Prayer was put up unto Him, afterwards
friends proceed upon buisness in much Love
and Unity, after meeting walked to Epwell
to see Uncles Aunts and Cousins
on the fifth this morning after takeing
my kinde leave of my Relations at Epwell
walked from thence to Sibford to se Cousin
Rebbecca Gilkes and Aunt and some more
friends took my leave of them and walked
from thence to little sibford to se some friends
there who ware very
well, and from thence home ware I arrived
safe and sound my Friends Indifrent
well, for which and all other mercies and
blessings I remain in my truly
thankfull to Kinde Providence,
on the sevventh was at our fifth day [Thursday]
meeting
which was quite small yet a sitting with
friends my poor minde was comforted with the
pure Power of Truth

verso

1793

on the tenth of the Eleventh month [November]
took a
walk to Witney preparative meeting the
meeting felt very comfortable to my minde
and Devine Goodness appeared to be af=
=fresh extended towards friends and a
renewed call unto them that they would
live up faithfully in true obidience unto
the Lord in answering His requireings
in all things after meeting call'd to
se some friends who ware loving
on the fourteenth was at our fifth day [Thursday]
meeting
and a sitting with friends my poor minde
was very low and very desireous to be made
sensible of what the Almighty would have
me to do and that I might receive strength
from Him to do it
on the seventeenth was at our first day [Sunday]
meeting
and in sitting with friends my minde was
favoured
with inward peace yet made so sensible of my
own
weakness that it appears to me that I ought to be
verry carefull
how I spend every moment of my time
to spend it carefully in the fear of the

Page 100

Lord as to be preserved in the straight and
narrow path that leads unto eternal Life and
to be preserved from the snares of my souls
Enemy
20th took a walk to witney and was
at friends weekday meeting and as I
sat with Friends my poor minde

was comforted and refreshed
being made sensible that Devine Love
was felt to overshadow us to the
uniteing is near to each other
after meeting walked Home
the twenty first was at our fifth
day [Thursday] meeting which was small and after
sitting in solid silence waiting upon the
Lord it appeared to be my duty to speak
a few words theirin
the eleventh month [November] the twenty fourth feeling
a concearn in my minde to go to Brails meeting
asked my Parents leave and walked thi=
ther small meeting there being but few friends

verso

living their abouts yet I trust we ware
renewedly favoured with the refreshing
overshadowings of Devine Goodness to the
refreshing and comforting of sevral
mindes present after meeting spent the
after=noon in a sweet and religious manner
with Cousins, Lodged at Cousins
on the twenty fifth this morning after taking
a walk up to Cousin Gilletts took my kinde
Farewell of Cousins and walked home having
had a Comfortable Journey for which mercy
and all others I remain truly thankfull to
Kinde Providence,
on the twenty eight was at our fifth day [Thursday]
meeting and a sitting with Friends my poor
minde was refreshed and comforted under a
sence that Devine Love was felt amoungst
us to the uniteing us near to each other
the twelfth month [December] the first was at our first
day meeting ware after sitting sometime
in solid Silence waiting upon the Lord it
appeared to be my duty to speak a few words

Page 101

amoungst friends which I did in much
humility of minde under a sence of my
own weakness and I found Inward
peace of minde in so doing
on the fourth took a walk to Milton Meeting
believeing it to be in the discharge of my
spiritial duty to Kinde Providence small
meeting yet we ware favoured with the
Devine Power to the uniteing us near to one another
on the fifth was at our fifth day [Thursday]
meeting which was midling large and it
felt quite comfortable to my poor minde
on the sixth believeing it to be in answering
the requireings of Kinde Providence to go to
Chipping Norton weekday meeting took a
walk thither and found inward sweetness
and refreshment in Sitting theirin
on the eight feeling it little drawings in my
poor minde to be at friends meeting at Burford
took a walk thither with my friends leave
a largish meeting sevral Scholars ware there
friends Children it appeared to be my duty

verso

to speak a few words theirin which I did
and found peace to my poor minde in so doing
after meeting walked up to friend Huntleys
and sat with friends and the scollars in
the school in which truth appeared to reign
it was a good comfortable meeting
on the ninth took a walk from Sistors
at burford to great Barington to Joseph
Cowdrys and spent sometime with Him in
a friendly loving manner he being formerly
a friendly good companion of mine afterwards
attended our monthly meeting at Burford
which was largish and felt comfortable to
my poor minde menny public Friends
ware ther and sevral good Testimonies ware
born to Incourage friends to serve the
Lord with more diligence and faithfullness
the buisness was gone through in much
Love altho truth appeared to be very low
in Meeting after meeting took my kinde
leave of Brother and Sistor and Friends
and walked Home ware I found my Friends
Indifrent well well

Page 102

on the thirteenth believeing it to be in answering
the requireings if Kinde Providence to walk

to friends Meeting at Sibford on six
day [Friday], took a walk thither a largish Meet
=ing and it felt comfortable to my poor
minde, sevral testimonies ware born
to direct the people to minde and be
obidient to their true teacher the spirit
or light of Christ Jesus within them
and the overshadowings of His Love was
felt amoungst is to the comforting of meny
meny mindes present, after meeting took
a walk to Joseph Harris of little Sibford
and some more friends to se them walked fro
thence
to Epwell to se my Relations their and spent
the evening very friendly with them
on the fourteenth took my kinde leave of my
Relations and walked Home safe and well
and found my Friends midling well for
which mercys and blessins and all others
I remain truly thankfull in my minde to

verso

---

to Kinde Providence
on the fifthteenth was at our first day [Sunday]
meeting and as I sat theirin my poor
minde was desireous to be brought into
such a state of true resignation to the
will of the Lord so as to be any thing
Just what he would have me to be and
in this state of pure resignation it appeared
to be my duty to speak a few words in
meeting which I did in humility of minde and
found Inward peace and satisfaction in so doing
on the eighteenth took a walk to witney and
was at friend fourth day [Wednesday] meeting
their
and in sitting theirin my minde was favoured
with inward peace and resignation to the will
of the Lord a friend spoke a few words
to advise friends to be carefull that they did
not cause truth to suffer through their wrong
conduct
on the nineteenth was at our fifth day [Thursday]
meeting
and in Sitting theirin my poor minde
was favoured to Injoy true peace and sweetness
of minde

Page 103

on the twenty second was at our first
day [Sunday] meeting in which my poor minde
was refreshed and Comforted tho greatly
made sensible of my own weakness and
that of my own self I could do no good
thing but that with Devine assistance
I could do whatsoever was pleasing
and axceptable unto Him
on the twenty sixth was at our fifth
day [Thursday] meeting, I finde there is great
need for one often to retire Inward
and wait upon the Lord to feel His
power to preserve one from the snares
and besetments of this World
on the twenty eight feeling a weight
upon my poor minde to take a walk
to faringdon meeting and sit with
friends their asked leave of my parents
and walked to witney found Friends
and Cousins there very well
The thirtyeth this morning set out early
with Friend Hankins and Wm Fardon

verso

---

for Faringdon found friends there
very well, small meeting the Life of
Truth felt to be very low theirin
after a time of solid Silence waiting upon
the Lord it appeared to be my duty to
speak a few words theirin which I did in
much humility and found Inward
peace to my poor minde in so doing
after meeting took my leave of Friends
and walked to Witney ware I spent the
evening comfortable
on the thirtyeth first took my leave of Friends
at witney and reached home about
ten in the morning safe and well having
had a Comfortable Journey for which
mercy and all others I remain truly Than=
=kfull to Kinde Providence
on the second of the first month [January] was
at our
fifth day [Thursday] meeting and in Sitting
theirin I was
sensible of my own weakness and without
Devine assistance I could do no good thing

Page 104

1794

the first month [January] the third feeling a desire
in my poor minde to go to Sibford six
day [Friday] meeting took a walk thither at
which there was a burial of a little
Child a fullish meeting and friends ware
very solid sevral Testimonies ware born
to direct the people to be very attentive
to the pure witness and light of truth
in them that they might become Innoscient
as a Little Child after meeting took my
kinde leave of Friends and walked
Home
on the fifth was at our first day [Sunday] meeting
and in Sitting theirin my poor minde
was much comforted and refreshed it
appeared to be my duty to speak a
few words theirin which I did in much
Humility of minde under a sence of my
own weakness and inability of myself
I found Inward peace of minde in Spe=
=aking

verso

afterwards when the meeting had sat
about two ours friends proceeded upon
the preparative meeting buisness at which
the quarterly meeting queries ware
answered to good satisfaction
on the sixth feeling a desire in my poor
minde to talk a walk to our monthly meeting
at C[hipping] Norton and also a monthly
meeting
at Eatington[24] [Ettington] walked there with
some
friends, our Monthly meeting was largish
two straingers ware there P.B. [public] friends
they both sat the whole meeting in
Silence yet it felt to be a good meeting
in which the devine Power was felt
amoungst us to the comforting of menny
mindes present, the buisness was gone
through in much Love, walked from
thence to shipstone to Cousin Wells rested
there on the sevventh took my kind leave
of Cousins and walked to Eatington Cousins
there ware very well the meeting was

Page 105

smallish yet I trust it was a good
satisfactory meeting sevral testimonies
ware born by sevral worthy friends
who testified of the Lords Love and
goodness to His Children, the meeting
of buisness was soon over after
meeting took my leave of Cousins and
walked to Brails Cousins there ware
very well
on the eight walked from Brails
to Radway to a Burial there the
meeting began about two sevral living
Testimonies ware born therein by which
the People ware recommended to minde
the pure Light of Christ within them
and be wholy obidient unto it which if
the ware it would Inable them when
they had done with the things of this
world to Injoy Everlasting Hapiness
after meeting took my kinde Leave
of Friends and waked to Broad Sibford

verso

with some friends rested there
on the ninth rose about seven and
walked home having had a satisfactory
Journey for which I remain truly thank
full to Kind Providence
at our meeting to day friends ware
favoured with the two Women Friends
who ware at our monthly meeting at C.[hipping]
Norton it felt to my minde to be a good
Comfortable meeting sevral Neighbours
ware present and one of the friends
was drawn forth in Public Testimonies
to the honnour of the great Creator of
all Things
on the tenth went with the two wommen
friends Who ware at our meeting to witney
to a meeting their which began about
three it was a good satisfactory meeting

24 Earliest recorded reference of meeting 1668

to some friends the friends ware drawn
forth in public testimonie to exhort friends
to keep their places in the truth
after meeting rode Home

Page 106

on the eleventh took a walk to Bur=
=ford to se Brother and Sistor who
ware very well heard that friends
there ware very well except one
on the twelfth believeing it to be my religious
duty to take a walk to Our Quarterly meeting
at Oxford I accordingly went, a large meeting
of Friends and Neighbours sevral Friends
appeared in Public directing the people
to be more sober and religious and be wholy
obidient to the pure Spirit of Truth within
them which if they war it would lead them
and guide them into all Truth
their was another meeting in the evening which
was very full of Friends and Neighbours
the people ware attentive to what was delivered
by sevral sober friends who spoke to menny
states and conditions it appeared to be a good
satisfactory Meeting, on the twelfth in
the morning took a walk down to Friend

verso

Jacksons's and spent sometime with them
in a loving and friendly manner, after
went to meeting which began at ten
it was midling large the friends sat sometime
to wait upon the Lord in Solid Silence
afterwards sevral mouths ware opened
to testify of the Lords Love to Mankind
afterwards friend went through the buis=
=ness in much Love and unity and advice
was given in the meeting that friends should
not suffer the things of this world nor even
lawfull things to hinder them from comming
up faithfully in the discharge of their duty
to the Lord, after meeting walked Home
with Brother I trust in this little Journey
I was Inabled with the Lords power to do
my duty to Him praises be to his worthy
name for Ever,
on the sixteenth was at our fifthday [Thursday]
meeting
on the nineteenth was at our first day [Sunday]
meeting
ware after sitting sometime in solid Silence
waiting upon the Lord to Know His

Page 107

pure will it appeared to be my duty to
speak a few words theirin which I did in
much Humility of minde under a sence of my
own weakness and Inability found peace to my
poor minde in so doing
on the twentieth as I sat in our Meeting
with friends my poor minde was Comforted
with the overshadowings of Devine Love
on the twenty fourth feeling a concearn in
my minde in Love to Kinde Providence to take
a walk to friends meeting at C,[hipping] Norton
went thither and as I sat with friends
in meeting I felt the incomes of Devine
Love which makes glad all the hearts of
the Children of God, after meeting walked
to Enstone to see Aunt and cousin Damaris
Jones who ware tolerable well and from thence
Home
on the twenty sixth feeling a concearn in my
minde to take a walk to stow meeting asked
my parents leave and walked thither
very small meeting friends there away
appear very cold in the attendance of Religious
meetings and want to be put in minde to

verso

be more diligent therein and to have
there mindes Brought of earthly things
and set on Heavenly things, after
meeting took my kinde leave of friends
and walked Home
on the thirtyeth was at our fifth day [Thursday]
meeting
ware after sitting sometime in solid silence
it appeared to be my duty to speak a few words
theirin which I did and found Inward peace to my
poor minde in so doing
the second month [February] the second feeling a
desire in my minde to take a walk to
the monthly meeting in Sibford devision
and also to sit with friends in their meeting
House at Shutford took a walk thither

but to my great disopointment when I
got thither I understood there was no meeting
intended to be held there that day which
was cause of sorrow to my minde and upon
consideration it appeared to be my duty to
desire friends to meet together which I did
and wee met together at a friends House
and as we sat together waiting upon the
Lord I felt that devine Power to flow amoungst

Page 108

us which comforts And refreshes the truly
Humble and contrite Hearted ones
after meeting walked to Epwell to se my
Relations there and from thence to little
Sibford to se Joseph Harris and some
more friends Joseph Harris is an old
Man and very weak and poorly his
days work appears to be near done I trust
He has been a diligent and faithfull
Labourer in the Lords vineyard and
will receive a reward of Everlasting rest
in the Kingdom of Heaven whe it shall
please the Lord to call Him out of this
world of Probation and that the Lord
will give so lasting a reward to all to all
who are faithfully given up to Labour diligently
in His vineyard according to the very best
of their Understanding
on the ninth took a walk with some friends
to a monthly meeting held at Banbury
it felt comfortable to my minde
sevral Living Testimonies ware born

verso

by which friends ware put in minde to
prepare to meet their great Creator as
they knew not how soon they might be called
upon the Lord to give an account how
they had spent their time and to receive
a reward according to their deeds done in
the body afterwards friends went through
the business in much Love
after meeting walked Home
on the sixth was at our fifth day [Thursday]
meeting
and in sitting theirin my poor minde was
refreshed and comforted

on the ninth was at our first day [Sunday]
meeting
and in sitting theirin my poor minde
was refreshed and comforted feeling that
devine Love to flow amoungst us which
refreshesh the Children of God, it ap=
=peared to be my duty to speak a few
words amoungst friends
on the tenth our Monthly meeting to day was
held at this place [Charlbury] it was pretty large
and
sevral good testimonies ware born theirin
by which friends ware advised to let their

Page 109

lights shine in them which the Lord hath
lighted least He should be angry with
them and one young friend was drawn
forth in solem prayer unto the Lord
besheetching Him that He would be pleased
to turn the mindes of the people unto
Him afterwards friend went through
the buisness in much Love and Unity
there was anaccount brought from one pre=
parative meeting concearning a young man who
had commited a very sinfull action which
was cause of great sorrow and trouble
to sincear hearted friends, it was Judged
right to disown Him without speaking
anymore to him
on the twelfth walked to Witney and was
at friends meeting their which was not
very large yet in felt comfortable to
my poor minde under a sence that
Devine Love was felt to flow amoungst us

verso

one friend was drawn forth in awe=
=full Prayer to the Devine
Being who nevver knew to
appear in prayer before
after meeting took my leave of
Friends and walked Home
on the thirteenth believeing it to be in
the doing my duty to kinde Providence
to take a walk to Hooknorton and
sit with Friends in their meeting
gave up to the Lords requireings and

went small meeting yet I trust the
gracious promise of blessed Jesus which
He promised when He was personaly on
Earth was fullfilled unto us that ware
but two or three are met together in
my Name their I will be in the midst
of them after meeting took my leave
of friends and walked to Enstone to
see Aunt and Cousin Damaris Jones
from thence home

Page 110

on the sixteenth was at our first day [Sunday]
meeting and after waiting upon the
Lord it appeared to be my duty to
speak a few words theirin which I
did in much humility, and it appears
to be my duty to live in much humility
and lowlyness of minde
on the twentieth was at our fifth day [Thursday]
meeting
and in sitting theirin my poor minde
was comforted and refreshed
on the twenty third feeling a desire in
my poor minde to take a walk to friends
meeting at Sibford too a burial of
an Elder and worthy friend Joseph
Harris of Little Sibford walked thi=
ther the meeting began about twelve
it was very large of Friends and
Neighbours Sevral Living Testimonies
ware born by sevral friends to put
the people in minde to minde the
pure light of Christ within them and

verso

be Obidient unto it in all things
and an awefull Prayer was put up
to the Almighty that He would be
pleased in His Infinite loving Kinde=
=ness to raise up faithfull Labourers
in His vineyard to Preach the Everlasting
Gospel of the Truth to the people
after meeting walked to Epwell and
spent the evening their in a loving
and an affectionate kindeness on to another
on the twenty fourth took my kinde
leave of my relations at Epwell and
walked to Sibford to see friend Haris's
who had lately lost their Affectionate
Husband and Parent spent sometime
with them then took my kinde farewell
of them and walked to Hooknorton
to a Meeting that was appointed
their in true Love to friends and
Neighbours it was a largeish gathering
on meeting Public Friend Barrit

Page 111

and sevral more friends it was a
good satisfactory meeting in which
the People ware recomended to become
acquainted with the Lamb of God
which taketh away the Sins of Man=
=kinde of they are truly and faithfully
Obidient unto Him in all Things
the People appeared well satisfyed
with what was delivered after meeting
took my kinde leave of friends and
walked Home ware I found my friends
tolerable well for which and all
other mercies I remain truly Thank=
=full to Kinde Providence
on the twenty sevventh feeling a desire
in my poor minde to take a walk to
friends meeting at Burford and
sit with them walked thither and
sat with friends At their meeting in
which I felt that Devine Power to

verso

overshadow us which unites us near
in Love one to another
on the second was at our first
day [Sunday] meeting and as I sat with friends
my poor minde was comforted under
a sence that Devine Love was felt
to flow amoungst us, believeing it
to be in disecharging my duty to
Kinde Providence to go to a monthly
meeting to be holden at Adderbury on
the morrow asked my parents leave
walked to Friend Tho's Harris's at Milton
Lodged there
on the third walked from Friend Harris's
to Adderbury to se some friends there

and from thence to the meeting it was
large and comfortable sevral living
Testimonies ware born by sevral Men
and Women Friends and an awefull
Prayer was put up unto the Lord
beeching Him that He would be pleased

Page 112

in His Love to turn the peoples mindes
unto Himself that the might be Inabled
to serve Him more faithfull who is
worthy to be Obeyed and served for
evermore, afterwards friends went
through the buisness in much Love
after meeting took my kinde farewell
of Friends and walked to cousin Franklings
at Ledal Lodged there
on the forth rose early took my kinde
Farewell of Cousin and walked Home
found my Friends tolerable well
for which mercies and all others I
remain truly Thankfull to Kinde Provi=
=dence
on the sixth was at our fifth day [Thursday]
meeting
and as I sat theirin my poor minde
was comforted under a sence that Devine
Love was felt amoungst us
on the ninth was at our first day [Sunday]
meeting
which was fullish and in sitting theirin

verso

my poor minde was favoured with
Inward peace and Comfort it appeared
to be my duty to speak a few words
theirin which I did in humility and
awefull care and found true peace
in so doing
on the tenth took a walk to our monthly meeting
held at Witney which was largish and held
longish their being a deal of buisness to do
we ware favoured with the overshadowings
of Devine Love that comforts the truly
Honest and upright Hearted ones their
was an Epistle that friend John Weal sent
to be read in the mens and Womens meeting
which was rote and sent in the Love of
Kinde Providence it was very comforting
to His Dear Children their was meny incouraging
sentances in it to incourage all friends to
live in the faithfull discharge of their duty
to Him after meeting walk Home
on the thirteenth was at our fifth day [Thursday]
meeting
as I sat theirin I was made sensible of my
own poorness and Unworthyness that without

Page 113

the Lords assistance I could do no good thing
on the fourteenth took a walk to Sibford
meeting believeing it to be obeying Kinde
Providence in the way of His pure
requireings it was a Comfortable Edifying
meeting sevral mouths ware opened to
Testify to the Lords Love and goodness
to His people who did meet together to
worship Him in Sincearity and in
Truth after meeting went to se sevral
friends found Philip Gilkes very poorly
took my kinde leave of them then walked
Home found my Friends tolerable well
on the sixteenth was at our first day [Sunday]
meeting and after sitting sometime in
Silence waiting upon the Lord it appeared
to be my duty to speak a few words theirin
which I did in humility and found Inward
peace in so doing
on the twentieth was at our fifth day [Thursday]
meeting
I am sensible friends ware made to pertaking
of that refreshment which comes down from

verso

above
on the twenty third feeling a little drawings
in my minde in being obidient to the pure
leadings of Truth within me to take a walk
to Chipping Norton meeting went to it
as I sat with friends theirin my poor
minde was refreshed and comforted being
made sensible that the renewed extendings
of Devine Love was felt amoungst us to
our great comfort after meeting walked Home
on the twenty seventh was at our fifth day
[Thursday]

meeting which was small yet I trust we
ware favoured with the renewed visitation
of Devine Love
on the thirtieth took a walk to Barton Meeting
which was large of Friends and Neigh=
=bours and felt to be a verry good meet
=ing in which the Devine Power was felt
to be extended towards the poor unworthy
sinners to call them to repentance that
they might Injoy the Love of God and it
was told them ware to finde the witness of Truth
which would lead and guide them into all
Truth in their own Hearts and mindes

Page 114

and an awefull prayer was put up to the
Devine Being beschecing Him that he would
be pleased to spare the People a little
longer in His Love, after meeting walked
Home
on the third of the fourth month [April] was
at our fifth day [Thursday] meeting in Sitting
theirin in minde was much Humbled
and in deep humility before the Lord
with desires of Him for His Help
and assistance to preserve me
from offending Him in any thing
on the sixth was at our first day [Sunday] meeting
and as I sat with friends my poor minde
was refreshed and comfortd yet greatly
made sensible of my own weaknesses
and that without Devine assistance I
could do no good thing, it was our
preparative meeting it was held in
Love and Unity
on the seventh took a walk to our monthly
meeting holden at Burford which was

verso

pretty large and comfortable the Devine
Power was felt to overshadow the meeting
so as to cause a degree of true livelyness
theirin some friends had to express
that the shout of a King was amoungst us
the buisness held long yet it was conducted
in much Love a Certivacate was drawn
up the meeting by friend minthchons
desire signifying friends unity with Her
of Intending to visit some meetings
on the ninth took a walk to friends
meeting at witney as I sat with them
my poor minde was favoured with spi=
=tial comfort and refreshment a friend
had to express that there was a nescessiety
for the people to come out of Babylon
after meeting walked Home
on the tenth was at our fifth day [Thursday]
meeting
in sitting theirin my poor minde was
made sensible of Devine Power being felt
theirin
on the eleventh was at a meeting at our meeting

Page 115

house which was appointed by the desire of
a Friend whose name I understood was stor
it was a meeting in which the Devine
Visitation was Extended to menny and menny
states ware spoken to by the Friend by the
apparition of Devine Power in him
was at our first day [Sunday] meeting which was
large it being before our quarterly meeting
sevral Living Testimonies ware born
theirin to direct the people unto their
true Teacher the Light of Christ in
them which would teach them better
than any man could teach them
on the thirteenth took a walk to our qua=
=rterly meeting held at witney it was
very large two strangers P.[ublic] friends viz
John Sto and George Dellwin the meet=
ing felt comfortable and the call of the
Lord went forth through his minister
to call the People to repent of their sins
and to amend their lives the meeting was
concluded
in awefull and Solem Prayer the after=

verso

=noon meeting was also large and the devine
Power was felt which would gather all
unto the true sheep foold if they would but
Improve the day of their visitation now wile
it was extended unto them, after meeting
walked Home
on the fifteenth took a walk to our quarterly

meeting at witney the meeting was very
comfortable the men and Women sat to=
=gether to wait upon the Lord before they
entered upon the buisness the Power of the
Lord went forth through His ministers
opening the states and conditions of the
people unto them and instructing them in
the way the should walk to obtain true
Peace and work Righteousness and that
all had receved one talent and the would
ceartainly be called upon to give anaccount
what they had made theirof and receive
a reward according to their deeds the buis=
=ness held long it was gone through in
much Love and unity two Testimonies

Page 116

from two monthly meetings ware delivered in
which ware
approved of Giving anaccount of two
public Friends Death Joseph Harris
late of little Sibford
on the seventeenth was at our fifth day [Thursday]
meeting as I sat theirin my minde was
very low under a sence of my own great
weakness being sensible without the Lords
assistance I could do no good thing
on the eighteenth feeling a little drawings
in my poor minde to take a walk to Sibford
meeting walked thither the meeting was
smallish one friend had a few words in
Testimonie yet the life of truth felt very
low to my poor minde which hungred and
thirsted after
Heavenly bread and Heavenly water of which
it pleased Kinde Providence to cause me
not to pertake of so liberaly as sometimes
He hath done in His mercy and goodness to
me after meeting walked Home

verso

on the twentyeth was at our first day [Sunday]
meeting
the meeting felt very comfortable to my
poor minde which is often afflicted with
sorrow under a sence of my own weakness
on the twenty fourth was at our fifth day
[Thursday]
meeting and as I sat theirin my poor minde
was favoured with a degree of Devine Love
which comforts and refreshes the truly
Humble and contrited Hearted ones
on the twenty seventh was at our first day
[Sunday]
meeting friend Wm Barritt of witney was
their the meeting felt comfortable to my poor
minde it appeared to be my duty to speak
a few words theirin which I did in much
humility under a sence of my own weakness
and Inability to speak in a meeting, found
Peace to my poor minde in Speaking a few words
5mo [May] the first was at our fifth day
[Thursday] meeting
as I sat theirin my poor minde was
favoured with a degree of true peace
which this world cannot give nither can
it take away

Page 117

5mo [May] 3rd 1793

having felt a religious concearn
in my minde to take a walk to Armscutt
[Armscote]
meeting with my parents leave I set out
and walked to Brails found Cousins
there very well, slept there
on the 5th walked with a friend from Brails
to Shipstone was at friends morning meeting
there which was not very large I think
on account of Armscutt [Armscote] meeting, yet
it
felt very comfortable to my mind afterwards
walked from thence to Armscutt [Armscote]
Meeting
which was very large of Friends and
Neighbours it felt very comfortable to
my minde sevral People appeared in
Testimonie directing the people not to
place their dependance on man but minde
the pure light of truth within themselves
and be obidient unto it and if the ware
it would lead and guide them into all
Truth the meeting concluded in Solem and

verso

awefull Prayer, after meeting
walked to shipstone to Cousin Wells's
spent a little time with them after took
my farewell of them and walked
to friend Petiphors spent a little time
with friends their, took my farewell
of them and walked to brails spent
the eveing with Cousins their very
comfortable slept at Cousins
on the 11th took my farewell of
Cousins at Brails and walked to Epwell
to see our relations there who ware
very well walked from thence
to shutford to the monthly meeting
there the meeting felt very comfortable
to my minde one Friend spake pretty
much on mixt marriages and the hurt=
=full tendency of them signifying that the
Spiritual Israel should dwell alone
the buisness was gone through in Love truth
appear'd to Reign altho the tender mindes of
some I thou=

Page 118

I thought ware very low
after meeting walked Home ware I found
my Friends tolerable well for which and
all other Mercies I am truly thankfull to
Kinde Providence
on the eight was at our fifth day [Thursday] meeting
on the eleventh was at our first day [Sunday] meeting
after sitting sometime in Solid and Humble
silence waiting upon the Lord I found it
to be my duty to speak a few words theirin
which I did in Humility and found a
degree of True Peace in so doing
on the thirteenth walk with Brother
and Sistor to our monthly meeting holden
at C[hipping] Norton it was largish sevral
straingers ware there Pub.[lic] Friends
and sevral good Testimonies ware born
by which Friends ware advised to be Obi=
=dient to the spirit of the Lord within them
and not to be much cast down but wait
His own good and appointed time and there
He would be Pleased to fill them with Heavenly
Oil and wine the buisness held long and

verso

it was very painfull to honest Hearted
friends on account of some disorderly
members yet it was gone through in much Love
three coupple Passed the meeting and
friends gave them leave to take each other
in Marriage
on the fifteenth was at our fifth day [Thursday] meeting
which was small yet I am sensible Devine
Love was felt to flow amoungst us
on the eighteenth was at our first day [Sunday]
meeting ware after sitting a wile in
solid Silence waiting upon the Lord it
appeared to be my duty to speak a few
words theirin which I did in much Humility
under a sence of my own weakness and
unworthyness to speak in a meeting found
true peace of minde in so doing
on the twenty first feeling a little drawings
in my minde to take a walk to friends meeting
at milton walked thither the meeting was small
truth appeared or felt very low theirin yet I felt a
little degree of Devine Love to overshadow us
after meeting walked Home

Page 119

on the twenty second was at our fifth
day [Thursday] meeting which was small yet my
minde was comforted being sensible that
Devine Love was felt amoungst us
on the twenty fifth was at our first
day [Sunday] meeting in sitting theirin my minde
was comforted and refreshed and in my
sitting in humble silence my minde was
very desireous to be made more sensible
of my Heavenly Fathers will and then that I might
be Inabled to do it
on the twenty eight it being fourth day [Wednesday] of
the week was at our meeting which was held
to day on account of a great number of people
being expected to be assembled in town on the
day in which our meeting is usualy held as I

sat with friends I felt that devine Love to
flow amoungst us which unites us near in
our spirits one to another
on the sixth month [June] the first feeling a
Desire in my minde in true love which
is superior to all earthly things to take
a walk to friends meeting at stow asked

verso

my parents leave and walked thither
small meeting the life of truth felt to
be low theirin yet I felt a degree of
Devine Love to overshadow us to the comforting
the sincear mindes and also in their going
through the Buisness of their meeting
after meeting took my leave of friends and
walked Home
on the sixth mo [June] 5th was at our fifth day
[Thursday] meeting
as I sat theirin my minde was refreshed and
comforted feeling Devine Goodness to be felt
amoungst us
on the sixth feeling a desire in my minde
in the love of pure unchaingable Truth
to take a walk to Sibford six day [Friday] meeting
walked thither at meeting I felt a Degree
of Devine goodness to be felt amoungst
us to the comforting the sincear and Honest
mindes and as I walked along I felt it to
flow in my minde it caused my Heart to
rejoice to feel that I was worthy to Injoy
Devine Goodness, after meeting walked
Home

Page 120

on the eight was at our first day [Sunday] meeting
after sitting a wile theirin in Solid Silence
waiting upon the Lord it appeared to be my
duty to speak a few words theirin which I
did in great Humility of minde under a
sence of my own weakness I found Spiritual
comfort in so doing
on the ninth took a walk to our monthly
meeting holden at Faringdon it was not
very large sevral Friends mouths ware
opened by the opperation of the Devine
Power within them to testify of the Lords
Love and goodness to His children that
Love and obey Him in all things, the
buisness was gone through in much love
after meeting walked to Witney with some
Friends spent the evening their in a very
agreable and loving way lodged their
on the tenth this morning walked home
found my Friends tolerable well
on the twelfth was at our fifth day [Thursday]
meeting
in sitting theirin my minde was retired
towards the Lord with fervent Breathings

verso

unto Him that I might be more and more
acquainted with His pure will and that
He would be pleased in His Love to Inable
me to do it
on the fifteenth was at our first day [Sunday]
meeting
the meeting felt pretty comfortable to my
minde my minde was earnestly Ingaged to
seek the Lord and to be more clearly sensible
of His pure will hopeing that He would
be pleased to Inable me to do it
on the nineteenth was at our fifth day [Thursday]
meeting in sitting theirin my minde was
very Low and poor for want of Devine
refreshement which I earnestly laboured for
on the twenty second was at our first
day meeting in sitting in meeting I was
quite willing to have sat the whole meeting
in Silence but it appeared to be my duty
to speak a few words theirin and I gave
up and speak them least I should loose
that true and sweet peace which I do Injoy
If I did not speak them
on the twenty sixth was at our fifth day
[Thursday]
meeting in sitting theirin my minde was very
desireous to be more and more acquainted with
the

Page 121

voice of the true shephard
on the twenty ninth took a walk to
Barton meeting it was large of
Friends and Neighbours and it
felt comfortable to my minde

the renewed visitation of the Lord
appea'rd to be a fresh extended to
the People through his sarvents
to put them in minde of the un=
=ceartainty of Death and the
great nescessiety their is to pre=
=pare for it walked from
thence to Cousin Franklings
and from thence to Cousin
Harris's Southnewington slept their
on the thirtieth walked to Banbury with
Friend Marshall, the Quarterly
meeting was large Devine Visitation
appeared to be a fresh extended towards
menny one Young Friend was drawn
forth in the spirit of Devine Love in
the fore part of the meeting in Sup=

verso

lication to the Lord on the Peoples behalf
and one Elderly Friend near the conclusion
of the Meeting and sevral Mouths ware
opened to testify how good the Lord is unto
those that Love and sarve Him before any
thing in this World, in the afternoon
there ware two meetings one in the mens and
one in the womens meeting House I was
at that at the Womens Meeting House it was
large and Devine Love was felt to the re=
=freshing of menny present, rested at
Friend Stones
on the fourteenth the Meeting for buisness began
at nine it was a large and comfortable
meeting, it held about six ours the Devine
Power was felt amoungst in an Extro=
arderny manner to the refreshing the
sincear and honest mindes I think Friends
mindes ware greatly strengthened in the pure
truth
after meeting walked with sevral Friends
Home and my minde being filled with a degree
of true peace I remain truly thankfull to Kinde
Providence, on the third was at our fifth day
[Thursday] Meeting
my minde was drawn to wait upon the Lord to
know His
pure will it appeared to be my duty to speak a few
words
theirin which I did with great care that I might
find true peace

Page 122

on the tenth was at our fifth day [Thursday]
meeting as I sat theirin my minde was
very low under a sence of my own weakness
on the thirteenth feeling a desire in my minde
in true Love to be at Friends preparative
meeting at Farindon walked thither small
meeting
it appeared clearly to me to be my duty to
speak a few words theirin, their preparative
meeting was cause of sorrow to my minde they
have but little desire to put Friends rules of
Descipline in practice, it is cause of sorrow to
to menny sincear Friends belonging to our
monthly Meeting, after meeting walked to
Witney spent the evening their very comfortabley
on the fourteenth our Monthly Meeting was
held at Witney it felt very comfortable to
my minde our Heavenly Father was pleased
to favour us with Devine refreshment to the
refreshing the Hungry and Thirsty souls
one young man appeared in the ministery
that I nevver heard before, the buisness was
gone through in much Love after meeting went
to se some truly honest hearted friends,
afterwards
walked Home, on the sevventeenth was at our
fifth day [Thursday] meeting

verso

on the twentieth was at our first day [Sunday]
meeting
it was largish after I had sat sometime theirin
waiting upon the Lord I felt a concearn
to speak a few words theirin and I spake
them in much Humility and felt true
peace by so doing, the yearly meeting Epistle
was read in meeting
on the twenty fourth was at our fifth day
[Thursday]
meeting
on the twenty fifth took walk to friends meeting
at Chipping=norton it was smallish in sitting
theirin I felt Devine Goodness to be near unto
us that would do us good if we would but be

obidient to the pure truth within us
after meeting walked Home
on the twenty sevventh was at our first day [Sunday]
meeting it felt very comfortabley to my minde
under a sence that Devine Love was felt
to flow amoungst us,
on the thirty first was at our fifth day [Thursday]
meeting it felt very comfortable to my
minde
on the eight mo, the second feeling a concearn
in my minde to take a walk to Shipstone
and Armscutt [Armscote] Meeting acquainted my

Page 123

Parents with what I believed to be my Religious
Duty, walked to Brails found Cousins
their very well Lodged their
on the third walked to Shipstone to Cousin
Wells they ware very well Except the
youngist Child was at friends morning
meeting it was not very large yet it ap=
=peared to me to be a good edifying Meeting
afterward walked with some friends to Armscutt [Armscote]
Meeting it was a largish Meeting Truth appeared
to Reign theirin, sevral Mouths ware opened
to testify of the Lords Love and goodness to them
that fear Him, after meeting walked to Cousin
Wells's and stoped a little then took my farewell
of them and walked to Chipping=norton Lodged their called
to see friend Harris's at Long Compton
on the second bid Cousins farewell and walked
Home found my friends tolerable well
on the sevventh was at our fifth day [Thursday] meeting
on the tenth was at our first day [Sunday] meeting
in sitting theirin my minde was Comforted being
sensible that Devine Love was felt amoungst us
after wards walked to Burford to friends Evening
meeting their it was largish sevral neighbours

verso

came in and we are favoured with a good
eddifying meeting, it was Concluded in Solem
and awefull Prayer, found Brother and Sistor
all very well Lodged their
on the Eleventh took a walk to great Barrington to
se Joseph Cowdry
afterwards went to the monthly Meeting
which was largish Devine Goodness was pleased
to own us with His Devine Presence one young
Man was Drawn forth in Solem and awefull
Prayer unto the Lord beeching Him in His
Love to conduct the people safe unto the
Heavenly Cannan, the Buisness was gone
through in much Love and Unity
after meeting bid friends farewell and walked Home
on the fourteenth was at our fifth day [Thursday] meeting
it was smallish yet I felt Devine Goodness
to be near unto us,
on the fifteenth took a walk to C.[hipping] Norton to
friends meeting their in Sitting theirin my
minde was comforted being made sensible that
the best of Teachers was near to us to teach us
on the 17th Having heard that friend Hall of Hooknorton
was very Ill not likely to live long took a walk
thither with an Intent to see Him but when

Page 124

I came their I understood by his son=in=law he
Died about two Days before and was to be buried
in the A.N. [afternoon] at Sibford He also informed me their
was to be no meeting held their that day so walked
to Sibford meeting in sitting theirin my minde
was Comforted and I trust I received some Heavenly
Instruction
the remains of Friend Hall was brough
from Hooknorton to Sibford, about three in
the A.N. [afternoon] it was decently Interd accompanied
by a great number of Friends and Neigh=
=bours He was Aged about seventy four
years a man well beloved Having for
menny years been favoured with a gift in
the ministery and traveled to menny meetings

on foot to Discharge His Duty theirin
He was taken Ill about one week before
He Departed this Life, bore His Affliction
patently signified to Friends He thought
he was near his End, a Solem meeting was
held at his Interment at Sibford the Devine
visitation appeared to be renewedly extended

verso

to menny through His Servants to put them
in minde of their latter end and warn them
to prepare for it, after meeting walked
with friend Barritt and Wm Fardon to
C.[hipping] Norton Lodged at friend Fardons, in the
morning being the eighteenth took our leave
of Friends and walked to Charlbury ware
I found my Friends Indifrent well
on the twenty first was at our fifth day [Thursday] meeting
on the twenty fourth feeling a concearn in
my minde to visit friends meeting at Farin
=gdon acquainted my parents with the feelings
of my minde and walked thither, small
meeting yet as I sat theirin my minde
was Comforted and refreshed being sensible
that Devine Love was present amoungst us,
after meeting walked to witney and spent
the evening with friends lovingly
in my Journey called to visit a young
woman a member of our society and to read
a Testimonie of disownment to Her on account
of her absenting Herself from friends meetings
and also finding a concearn to speak a few

Page 125

words to Her in the Love of God, I speak
to Her alone in a solid manner what rested
upon my mind so left Her feeling my minde easy
on the twenty fifth walked Home, ware
I found my Friends tolerable well
on the twenty eight was at our fifth day [Thursday] meeting in sitting
theirin I was desireous to be more acquainted with
mine Heavenly Shephards will
the ninth mo: [September] the first feeling a concearn in
my minde to be at Hooknorton Meeting walked
thither it was their preparative meeting
it appeared to be a good solid meeting in
which Devine Goodness was pleased to own
us with His Love their buisness was gone
through in Love, after meeting bad friends
Farewell then walked to Sibford to the
afternoon meeting their it was largish and
appeared to be a good Edifying Meeting
after meeting walked to Epwell Lodged at Uncle Gibb's
the second took my farewell of my Relations
at Epwell and walked to little Sibford
to see some friends and from thence to broad

verso

Sibford to see some friends was at the
Monthly Meeting their it was large and
felt comfortable to my minde sevral mouths
ware opened to advis friends to minde and
be obidient to their Heavenly Teacher within
them that they might witness a sitting under
their own Vine and Under their own fig
tree ware none might make them afraid
the buisness was gone through in much Love
after meeting waked Home ware I found
Father and Mother poorly the rest very well
on the fifth was at our fifth day [Thursday] meeting
in sitting theirin I was greatly made sensible
of my own weakness's and saw great need to wait
for Devine Help to Inable me to overcome them
on the sixth finding a concearn to rest upon my
minde to go and speak to a young man who
had been concearned in the Army to discourage
Him in the Fear of the Lord from Having
any hand in hurting his fellow Creatures, went
to His Fathers house and spake unto Him what
was made known to be my duty afterwards found
True Peace to flow in my minde

Page 126

on the sevventh was at our first day [Sunday]
meeting it felt Comfortable to my
minde sevral strangers being present
it was our preparative meeting the
buisness was gone through in much Love
after meeting walked with friend Hankins

to Enstone He being appointed with some
more friends to visit Cousin Damaris Jones
she having cept company with a young
man not of our society I could not finde
she was willing not to give the young
man her company yet the visit was to
the satisfaction of friends parted from
Aunt and Cousin in Love then walked with
friend Hankins to C.[hipping] Norton Lodged at
Jonathan Fardons, on the eight before the
monthly meeting began went to see some
friends they appeared glad to se me
the meeting was large sevral friends ware
present from a neighbouring monthly
meeting it felt comfortable to my minde

verso

---

and I think it was to meny the buisness
was conducted in much Love their was
one affair came before the Monthly meeting
it affected my minde with much sorrow
it was of a young man that menny took
to be a very good religious man as well as
my self he very hastily married a young
woman not of our Society and was maried
by a priest to the dishonour of the pure truth
and the great grief of honnest hearted
friends after meeting took my Farewell
of friends and walked Home ware I found
my friends tolerable will
on the Seventh feeling a desire in my
minde to take a walk to friends meeting
at Burford walked thither small meeting
yet I felt Devine Love to be present
amoungst us to the comforting of the true
sincear and upright mindes, called at
Friend Mintchons having a great
desire to se she but she was so very Ill
Her Husband thought it might be best for
me not to go to se she she having cept Her

Page 127

Bed for sevral days found Brother and
sistor and the rest very well after
meeting walked Home
on the thirteenth feeling it to be my duty
as I follow the leadings of Devine Providence
to take a walk to Oxford Meeting and from
thence to the quarterly Meeting at Reading
acquainted my Parents with my minde then
walked to Witney found friends there tolerable
well Lodged their
on the fourteenth walked with Friend
Barritt and Tho's Smith to Oxford meeting
it was smallish of friend but large of
Desenters and it felt to me to be a good
serviceable meeting in which the Lord was
Pleased in Love to visit menny Souls
and to make use of His humble Servants
as Instruments to put them in minde of
their true teacher the Spirit of Truth and
Grace of God within them which if they did
and ware faithfull Obidient unto it in all
things it would inable them to please the Lord

verso

---

after Meeting went with some friends to
friend Jacksons refreshed ourselves their them
walked to Shillingford with some friends Stoped
there a little wile then walked with Tho's Smith
to Streetly [Streatley] rested there with Friend
Smith
on the fifteenth walked with Tho's Smith from
Streetly [Streatley] to Reading found Cousins
Tutteys
very=well the morning meeting began at ten
in which Devine Goodness was pleased to appear
to hand fourth Heavenly refreshement to His
Obidient Children who truly hungred and
thirsted after Righteousness the Meeting was
concluded with solem Prayer, the Afternoon
Meeting began at three it felt very comfortable
also sevral mouths ware opened to advise the
People to wait upon our great Marster Jesus
Crist to know His pure will and then to do it
faithfully and with a willing minde or words to
that purpose, Spent the evening in a Solid and
agreeable manner at Cousin Tutties
slept at Friend Gilberts
on the sixteenth was at the quarterly Meeting of
buisness
it began at nine altho truth appeared to be low
and
by accounts brought in sevral little meetings
appeared to be in a decreasing state yet it
appeared

Page 128

to be a good Meeting in which Devine Goodness
was pleased to own us with His living power
and presence, Friends went through the
Buisness in a very condesending and loving
manner after meeting took my leave of friends
then walked with Edw'd May to Henley Lodged
there
on the seventeenth having felt a religious
concearn
in my Minde to be at friends meeting at Henley
and
also a friends meeting on the morrow at
Warborough
stay'd meeting which was small yet it appeared
to me that they that ware their ware sensible
Devine goodness was near to them to their
comfort
call'd to see sevral friends and took my leave of
them, after meeting walked to Shillingford
Lodged their
at cousin Ashby's there was a relation I
think Joseph Ashbys Mother she keeps her
room being very Infirm yet she appears to
be in a comfortable sweet frame of minde and
quite resigned to the Devine Will aged about 87
caled to se some friends afterward went to their
meeting as I sat theirin my minde was refreshed
and comforted after waiting upon he Lord in
Solid
Silence it appeared to be my duty to speak a few
words theirin which I did found true peace in so
doing after meeting bad friends Farewell, then

verso

walked Home call'd at friend Jacksons at Oxford
spent alittle time with them in a loving manner
found my friends at Home tolerable well for
which mercy and blessing and menny more
I remain Humbley thankfull to Devine
Providence
on the twenty first was at our first day [Sunday]
meeting
altho my minde was low theirin it felt
Comfortable
to my minde afterward feeling a desire in my
minde
in sincear Love to friends to take a walk to
friends
meeting at Burford and enquire how friend
Minchon
was walked thither the meeting was held in
Silence
Except a few words which I spake theirin as it
appeared to be my duty to speak them, found
true peace to my mind by speaking them heard
that friend Mintchon was a little recovered it
was cause of Joy to my minde found Broth'r and
his
family very well Lodged there
on the twenty second took my kinde leave of
them and walked Home
on the twenty fourth Having a desire in my minde
in true Love to go to a little Meeting at Milton
walked thither small Meeting truth appeared
very low
theirin yet after I had sat sometime in Solid
Silence
it appeared to be my duty to speak a few words
amoungst friends
after meeting bid friends farewell then walked
Home
on the twenty fifth was at our fifth day
[Thursday] meeting
on the twenty eight was at our first day [Sunday]
meeting

Page 129

at meeting wee ware favoured with the
company of Old Friend Barritt it appeared
to be a good satisfactory meeting in which
his mouth was opened to advise friends to be
very carefull and circumspect to follow Christ
in the way of self Denial I also felt it to be
my duty to speak a few words in meeting and
found true peace by so doing
the tenth mo, [October] the second was at our
fifth
day meeting as I sat with friends my
minde was refreshed and Comforted with
the Injoyment of Devine Love
after meeting feeling a desire in my minde
in true Love to attend friends six day [Friday]
meeting at
Campden walked to Charingworth found
Cousins

their very well Lodged their
on the third walked with Cousin Wm Cork
to Campden to friends meeting their it was
larger than I did expect and we ware
comforted with the renewed refreshment
of the devine Love to the comforting of our
feeble mindes whose mindes ware desirous
to be strengthened in the truth, after meeting
went with Cousin Wm to friend Beavingtons

verso

spent a little time with them Comfortable
afterward walked with Cousin Wm to their
house ware his sistor and we spent the
evening lovingly together Lodged their
on the fourth took leave of Cousin Corks
and walked from their House to their Re=
=lations at the Hill Farm Cousin John
haveing been Guilty of doing very rong
actions I advised Him in a very loving manner
to repent of them and amend his Life for
the future and do hope it will have a good
effect bear'd he and His family company
a little took leave of them then walked
to Cousin Ashby at uper Seasoncutt [Sezincote] staid
with them a little walked from thence to
Cousin Ashbys at Lower Seasoncutt [Sezincote] spent
the evening with them in a loving affectionate
manner Lodged there
on the fifth in the morning spent a little
time with Cousins then walked to Stow to friends
meeting there it was larger than I did ex=
=pect and Devine Goodness was near to us to
Instruct and comfort us with a renewed visitation
of His Love to the comforting our Souls their

Page 130

Preparative meeting was held in true Love
after meeting called to se Neighbour
Colletts and some friends in my way home
and some of Brother Roberts relations
reached home safe and well having had
a pleasent Journey for which and all
other mercies I remain truly thankfull
to Devine Providence
on the ninth was at our fifth day [Thursday]
meeting as I sat theirin I felt Devine
Love to flow amoungst us to the comforting
our mindes
on the tenth feeling a desire in my minde
in true Love to take a walk to friends
meeting at Stow appointed for the Mar=
=riage of Tho's Fardon and Jane Ashby
it was conducted orderly I think to the
honnour of the Truth menny friends
and Neighbours attended on the Occasion
and appeared very solid and attentive
to what was Delivered sevral Mouths
being opened to testify of the Lords Love
and Goodness to Mankind and Parents
war Exhorted to set good Examples to their

verso

Children and Sarvents that they
might come to Injoy Everlasting Happiness
after meeting went with friends to Dinner
then bid them farewell and walked
Home ware I found my Parents
Tolerable well
on the twelfth was at our first day [Sunday] meeting
in Sitting theirin my minde was refreshed
and Comforted with Devine Love it appeared
to be my duty to recomend to friends to be
willing to part with all that was near
and dear to ownself for Christ sake
on the thirteenth was at our Monthly
meeting it was held at Charlbury altho
truth appeared to reign yet I did not
feel the Lords power to flow so freely
from vessel to vessel as sometimes I have
felt it the Lord was Pleased to open my
mouth to recomend to friends not to forsake
Him because His commands might appear
hard and trying to our fleshly nature
but to give up all and follow Him faith=
=fully in that way which He should be pleased
to require them the buisness was gone through

Page 131

in true Love after meeting walked with
Friend Jacksons of Oxford part of
the way home
on the sixteenth was at our fifth day [Thursday]

meeting it felt comfortable to my minde
altho my minde was very low theirin under
a sence of my own weaknesses
on the nineteenth having heard that friend
Delwine Intended to be at a meeting at
Oxford felt a desire in my minde in
true Love to attend the meeting, walked
thither largish Meeting of Friends and
Neighbours it appeared to me to be a good
meeting in which Devine Goodness was
pleased to own us with His living presence
and to recomend to the people through His
servants to minde the pure Light of truth
with in them which would Inable them to
walk in the straight and narrow Path that
leadeth to Eternal Life friend Delwin
concluded the meeting with a Solem and awefull
Prayer, after meeting went to se friend
Jacksons's then took my leave of them and
walked Home Friend Delwin and His Wife
returning

verso

back to Charlbury
on the sevventeenth Friend Delwine having
a desire to have a meeting appointed
at Charlbury for friends only went to it
it was held much in Silence yet it ap=
=peared to be a good satisfactory meeting
the friend had to recomend to friends to In=
=deavour to be acquainted with Christ voice
and obey it
on the Eighteenth Friend Delwine having
a desire that a meeting should be appointed
at sixoclock in the evening and that
the sober Neighbours should be let know
of the meeting it was done according
to his Desire, it was a very large
meeting of friends and Neighbours
and a good comfortable meeting it was
in which Devine Goodness was pleased
to own us with a fresh visitation of His
Love to the Comforting of menny mindes
Present friend Delwine was favoured
with a fine time to open menny things
to the People that was nessescary for
them to understand that belonged to the
well being of their Immortal souls

Page 132

on the twentieth was at our fifth day [Thursday]
meeting it felt very comfortable to my
minde it was very low and humble during
my sitting theirin
on the twenty sixth was at our first
day [Sunday] meeting it felt very comfortable
to my minde my mouth was opened theirin
to speak a few words in much humility of minde
on the twenty sevventh having a little
buisness to do at Burford took a walk
thither found Brother and Sistor very
well called to se friend Minchon who
has been very Ill but is finely recovered
I had some solid conversation with she
concearning the Gospel Ministery and
she spoke very Incourageing and comfortable
to me afterward took my leave of She and
Brother and Sistor and walked Home
on the thirtieth was at our fifth day [Thursday]
meeting
as I sat with friends my minde was comforted
being sensible that Devine Love was
felt amoungst us
on the thirty first took a walk to Witney called
to see some friends found friend Hankins He and
some
of his family very poorly with the small pox

verso

1794

11mo [November] the first feeling a desire in my
minde
to attend Armscutt [Armscote] meeting
acquainted my
Parents with the feelings of my minde
walked to brails in the Afternoon found
cousins there very well slept their
on the second walked from Brails to Shipstone
to se Cousin Wells's who ware very well
and from thence with Cousin to Armscutt
[Armscote]
meeting it was not very large yet it felt
very comfortable to my minde Devine Goodness
being pleased to appear in His Love to the

renewed vissitting menny mindes, sevral
friends spake in Public Testimonie to recomend
to the People to attend to their true Teacher
the Grace of God and Spirit of Truth within
them
and be Obidient unto it which if they ware
they would be inabled to please God and ob=
=tain an Everlasting inheritance in the Kingdom
of heaven after meeting walked with a
friend to Shipstone took leave of Cousins
there walked from thence to se friend Pettiphers
and from thence to se from thence to se friends at
brails
slept their
on the third took leave of Cousins then walked
to Epwell to se our Relations there, walked from

Page 133

thence with Uncle Gibbs to Shutford to the
Monthly Meeting their it was not very
large altho Truth appeared very low yet
Devine Goodness was pleased to hand forth
of his Heavenly refreshment to the Comforting
some mindes present, altho the buisness
held long yet it was gone through in
Love and Unity after meeting walked
to Wigginton to see Cousins there and
from thence to Enstone to se Aunt and
Cousin had some agreeable conversation
with them concearning what belongs to
our Souls everlasting wellbeing rested
their, it being the fourth in the morning spent a
little time
with them, then took leave of them and walked
Home ware I arived very well and truly
Thankfull to Kinde Providence for His Love to
me
on the sixth was at our fifth day [Thursday]
meeting
as I sat theirin my minde was refreshed and
comforted and my spirit did rejoice being
sensible Devine Love was felt amoungst us
on the sevventh took a walk to C.[hipping]
Norton to
friends meeting there it was Small yet I
felt the Lords Power to arise to the refreshing

verso

---

and Comforting the Honest hearted
on the ninth was at our first day [Sunday]
meeting
after sitting sometime theirin in Solid Silence
it appeared to be my duty to speak a few
words theirin which I did in much Humility
of minde
on the tenth took a walk to our Monthly
meeting held at Witney it was largish
sevral Mouths ware opened in Public Tes=
=timonie to advise friends to be diligent in the
discharge
of their duties which the Lord required of
them Truth appeared to Reign and the
buisness was gone through in much Love
after meeting went to se some friends af=
=terwards walked Home
on the thirteenth was at our fifth day [Thursday]
meeting
it felt comfortable to my tried exercised minde
which is often very low
on the sixteenth was at our first day [Sunday]
meeting
in which Devine Goodness appeared to be
Present amoungst us to our comfort and
refreshment
on the nineteenth took a walk to friends meeting
at Witney it appeared to me to be a good
meeting in which Devine Goodness was
pleased to appear to the Comforting and
refreshing them mindes who did hunger and
thirst after Righteousness

Page 134

on the twentieth was at our fifth day [Thursday]
meeting
on the twenty third feeling a desire in my
minde in true Love to attend friends
meeting at Shutford walked thither smallish
meeting yet I felt the Devine Power
to be felt amoungst us to the comforting
and refreshing the true sincear and
honest Hearted children of the Lord
after a time of solid Silence it appeared
to be my duty to speak by way of Testimonie
in the meeting after meeting took my
Farewell of Friends then walked to Enstone

to se Aunt and Cousin Damaris Jones
spent the evening with them in a religious
and loving manner Lodged their
on the twenty fourth early in the morning walked
Home
on the twenty sevventh was at our fifth day
[Thursday]
meeting it appeared to me a comfortable
meeting true Love appeared to flow amoungst us
on the thirtieth feeling my minde drawn in
true Love to sit with friends at their preparative
meeting at Southnewington walked thither the
meeting appeared to bc a good meeting Devine
goodness was pleased to own us with His power

verso

---

to the refreshing our poor mindes and after
waiting upon Him in Solid Silence it appeared
to be my duty to speak amoungst friends
the buisness was gone through in much Love
after meeting walked with a friend near Bloxam
at Bloxam called see Aunt Minty who was
very poorly yet in a comfortable situation of
minde spend a little time with She and Cousins
very comfortabley afterwards walked to friend
Sconch's at Netrup [Neithrop], Lodged their
the twelfth mo. [December] the first went to see
some
friends and Aunt Jones before meeting Aunt Jones
was very poorly and in a lowly situation of minde
she having lately lost Her dear Husband by
Death, the meeting felt very comfortable to my
minde sevral mouths ware opened by the Lords
power to testify of the Lords love and Goodness
to
mankinde and to Incourage friends to fear and
obey
Him, the buisness was gone through in much
Love
after meeting took leave of Friends reach'd
C[hipping] Norton heard that friends
there ware very well Lodged their
on the second walked Home ware I found my
Friends tolerable well
on the fourth was at our fifth day [Thursday]
meeting
it felt comfortable and refreshing to my minde
on the fifth feeling a concearn in my minde
to take a walk to friends sixday [Friday] meeting
at

Page 135

---

sibford walked thither the meeting felt very
comfortable and refreshing to my minde it
appeard to be my duty to bear a Short testimonie
theirin which I hope will be instructing to
my minde and to others also, after meeting took
my leave of friends and walked Home
on the seventh was at our first day [Sunday]
meeting
in which I felt Devine Love to flow amoungst us
to the comforting them who truly hungred
and thirsted after Righteousness after meeting
took a walk to Burford too se brother and Sistor
their intending to be at our Monthly Meeting
on the morrow spent the evening with friends
in a very loving and kinde way Lodg'd at
Brothers
on the eight was at the monthly Meeting it was
Largish and it felt very comfortable to my minde
Devine Goodness was pleased to own us by
causeing
us to partake of His Heavenly Refreshment
not menny minutes to be considered of great
consequence the buisness was gone through in
Love and Unity after meeting took leave of
Brother and Sistor and walked Home
on the Seventh was at our fifth day [Thursday]
meeting
and altho it was smallish it felt very comfortable
to my minde
on the fourteenth feeling my minde drawn in
true Love to attend friends preparative meeting

verso

---

at Milton walked thither smallish meeting
some friends being from home the Life of
Truth appeared very low theirin yet after I
had sat sometime in Solid Silence a waiting
upon the Lord I spake a few words theirin
as it appeared to be my duty to Incourage
friends to give up all and sarve the Lord
faithfully according to the best of their
understanding
that they might be favoured to obtain the Crown
of Immortal Life, after meeting went to se

some friends and spent sometime with them very
lovingly then walked Home
on the Eighteenth was at our fifth day [Thursday] meeting
in sitting theirin my minde was strengthened
with Devine Goodness
on the nineteenth took a walk to friends
sixday meeting at C[hipping] Norton in Sitting
theirin my minde was comforted and
refreshed being made sensible that
Devine Love was felt amoungst us
after meeting went to se some friends
then walked Home
on the twenty first took a walk to friends
first day [Sunday] meeting at Witney the morning
meeting felt very comfortable and refreshing
to my minde one friend was drawn fourth in

Page 136

very solem and awefull Prayer
was at the Afternoon meeting it felt
to me a good satisfactory meeting and the Lord was
Pleased to make it known unto me that it
was my duty to speak a few words theirin
and I gave up and spake them and found
true peace in so doing after meeting took
leave of friends and walked Home
on the twenty fifth was at our fifth day [Thursday]
meeting it was a fullish meeting, it felt very
comfortable and refreshing to my minde
on the twenty sevventh feeling a desire in
my minde in true Love to attend our
Quarterly meeting to be held at Oxford
walked to Witney found friends their very well
Lodged at Friend Smiths
on the twenty Eight walked with friend
Smith and some more friends to Oxford
it was a largish Meeting of Friends and
Neighbours and a very good Solid meeting
one friend appeared in very solem Prayer
in the fore=part of the meeting and afterwards
sevral Living Testimonies ware born
to the honnour of the Lord and to Incourage

verso

the People to sarve and obey Him
after meeting spent a little time with some
friends that live their
the afternoon meeting or Evening meeting
began at Six it was very large the
Lord was pleased in His great Love to
visit the people a fresh with a renewed
visitation of His Love through His sarvents
to make them sensible what belonges to
their souls Everlasting well=being
on the twenty ninth the meeting for buisness
began at nine, it appeared to be a good
solid meeting Devine Providence was
Pleased to appear unto His Children and
feed them with Heavenly refreshment to their
Comfort and sevral friends appeared in
testimonie to Comfort the little ones, the
buisness was gone through in much Love
and Unity, after meeting bad friends
farewell and walked Home
on the second was at our fifth day [Thursday] meeting
as I sat theirin my minde was refreshed
with Heavenly refreshment
on the first mo: [January] the fourth feeling my minde
engaged in true Love to Discharge my

Page 137

Duty faithfully to Devine Providence
to take a walk to friends preparative
meeting at Stow and also to friends mon=
=thly meeting at Southnewington and
Eatington [Ettington] reached friends meeting at
Stow in good time it was very small
yet I felt Devine Love to be felt amoungst
us and that blessed Jesus did fullfill His
gracious promise unto us which He promiced
formerly that ware but two or three
are met together in my name there I
will be in the midst of them after
meeting walked to friend Hidens Spent a
little time with friends there in a truly
loving and profitable manner then took
leave of them and walked to C.[hipping] Norton
Lodged at Cousin Fardons
on the fifth walked from C.[hipping] Norton to Cousin
Harris's at Southnewington the monthly
meeting their felt very comfortable and refre=

=shing to my mind several Testimonies ware
born to the Honour of the Truth one friend was
drawn forth in very solem prayer unto the Lord
beeching Him to be near unto the Aged and also
unto

verso

---

the young people, the buisness was gone through
in much Love, after meeting walked with
some friends to little Sibford and from thence
to Cousin Hemmings at Brails, Lodged their
on the sixth walked from Brails with
Old friend Gillett to the monthly meeting
at Eatington [Ettington] the meeting was not
very
large and in the forepart before friends
enterd upon buisness it was held in
Solid Silence except a few words which I
spake amoungst friends believeing it to be
my religious duty so to do found true peace
of minde in faithfull dischargeing my
duty unto the Lord by speaking, the buisness
was soon gone through in much Love
after meeting walked near Shipstone with
some friends called at Shipstone to se Cousins
and some friends then walked from thence
to Long=compton to Tho's Harris's his Wife
was very poorly spent the evening their
very comfortabley Lodged their
on the sixth took leave of Friend Harris
walked from thence to C.[hipping] Norton
breackfasted at
Cousin Jon'n Fardons who ware very kinde

Page 138

---

and loving to me walked from thence Home
ware I found my friends tolerable well
for which mercie and blessings among meny
others I do Injoy I remain truly thankfull
to Devine Providence
on the eight took a walk to friends fifth
day [Thursday] meeting at Burford as I sat theirin
my
minde was Comforted and refreshed I was
fully sensible Devine Love was felt to flow
amoungst us to the refreshing and nourishing
the souls of those who truly hungred and thir=
sted after righteousness
after meeting walked up to friend Huntleys
spent the evening with them in a very solid
and Weighty manner we being truly concearned
for each others Everlasting wellfare and they
gave me some good Instruction in a very kinde
manner respecting my appearing in the Ministery
with tender advice to me to be carefull to attend
to the pure openings of the spirit of Christ when
I appeared in meetings and I hope it will prove
for my good as long as I live. Lodged at Brothers
on the ninth took my leave of Bror. and Sistor
then
walked Home

verso

---

on the Eleventh was at our first day [Sunday]
meeting at meeting we ware favoured
with the company of Friend Barritt
it appeared to me to be a good comfortable
meeting in which Devine Goodness was
Pleased to hand fourth good Instruction to His
Children
in the A.[after]Noon took a walk to C[hipping]
Norton with
an Intent to be at our monthly meeting at
at C[hipping] Norton on the morrow, slept at
Cousin Fardons
on the twelfth spent sometime with Cousins
and friends very agreeabley and Lovingly
the meeting was tolerable large sevral
Friends ware their from other neighbouring
meetings, sevral Living Testimonies ware born
to Incourage such as had begun in well=
=doing and ware travelling theirin to
Persevear theirin and not look back on
the pleasures and delights of this World
the buisness was gone through in much
Love after meeting took leave of friends
and walked home in company with some friends
on the fifteenth was at our fifth day [Thursday]
meeting
and as truth made it appear to my minde to
speak a few words theirin I spake them and
found true peace in so doing
on the eighteenth was at our first
day [Sunday]meeting as I sat theirin I felt

Page 139

Devine Love to be extended towards us
which felt to my minde sweeter than
the Honey comb and I think it did to meny
mindes present
on the twenty second was at our fifth day
[Thursday]
meeting and altho it was small yet as I sat theirin
it felt sweet and refreshing to my minde
on the twenty fifth was at our first day [Sunday]
meeting
it was comfortable and refreshing to my minde
it appeared to be my duty to advise friends to
set good examples to their Children that they
might be fitted and qualified to supply the
Places of faithfull Elders whome the Lord had
taken from works to rewards
on the twenty eight took a walk to
friends fourth day [Wednesday] meeting at Witney
it appeared to me to be a good meeting
and that Devine goodness was felt amoungst us
to our comfort and refreshment
it being a great flood part of Witney
street was fill'd with water which
caused the meeting to be a rather small
on the twenty ninth was at our fifth day
[Thursday]
meeting as I sat theirin my minde was com=
=forted and refreshed with the feelings of Devine
goodness

verso

on the thirtieth having felt drawings in my minde
as I take heed and am wholy obidient unto the
Spirit of Truth according to the very best of my
understanding to take a walk to friends six
[Friday]
day meeting at Sibford and to friends first day
[Sunday] meeting at Radway and also to
friends monthly
meeting at Banbury and friends third day
[Tuesday]
meeting at Southnewington walked to Sibford
to meeting after acquainting my parents
with the feelings of my minde after waiting
Solidly upon the Lord at Sibford meeting
as truth manifested it to me to be my duty
to advise friends to be very weighty in their
Spirits and attend the teachings of the
Lords Spirit within them and be obidient
unto it so I spake in meeting and felt true
peace to my minde after meeting went to
se some friends, walked from their to Bur=
=drope to se friend Grimes who was very poorly
and from thence to little Sibford to se some
friends found friend Holtoms son very poorly
with a Swelled leg Lodged their comfortabley
on the thirty=first spent a little time with friends
at little Sibford very comfortabley walked from
thence to Epwell spent sometime with our
Relations their in a very Religious and
Comfortable
manner especialy with Aunt Grace Hemmings

Page 140

concearning an affair of great Importance
Lodged at Uncle Gibbs
the second mo: [February] 1st walked with Uncle
Gibbs from
Epwell to friends meeting at Radway, the meeting
felt comfortable to my minde Devine goodness
was Pleased
to favour us with His living power, one
friend was drawn forth to suplicate the
Lord with solem and awefull Prayer their
Preparative meeting buisness was gone through
in true Love, after meeting spent a little
time with friends afterward walked with
Cousin Robt. Ashby to their House at Ticer
[Tysoe]
spent the evening with Cousins in a
very solid and Loving manner, Lodg'd their
on the second walked from ticer [Tysoe] to
Banbury
Cousin Robert accomping me Part of the
way was at the monthly meeting their it
felt comfortable and refreshing to my minde
the Monthly meeting felt very comfortable and
refreshing to my minde Devine Providence was
Pleased to own us with His Love and living
Power to our comfort the buisness was gone
through
in Love and Unity after meeting sent a letter
by a friend to acquaing my parents that I felt
it to be my religious duty to attend a few
meetings

verso

before I returned Home, afterwards went to se
our Relations and some friends Lodged at Cousin
Harris's Southnewing
on the third before meeting walked to Cousin
Wm. Jones at Wigginton He having married
one not of our Society and declined going to
our Meetings I was in hopes of Obtaining his
company to walk to the meeting but I could
not the meeting was small yet we ware favoured
to pertake of Devine Goodness after waiting in
Solid Silence upon the Lord I was led to pray
very solemly on my knees unto the Lord prayin that
in His Love He would be pleased to fullfill his gracious
promice unto us that ware but two or three ware
met together in His Name there He would be in
the midst of them, walked from thence to milton
to se some friends who ware very loving to me
and from thence to Adderbury to se some friends
with them I spent the evening very lovingly
Lodged at friend Plesters although His wife does not
Make profession with us yet she was very kind
And friendly and appears to be convinced of our
Princaples, before meeting went to se meny friends
the meeting felt very comfortable Divine Goodness
being Pleased to own us with His Love, one friend
concluded the meeting with solem Prayer, after
meeting walked from thence to Milton to se some friends
and from thence to Southnewington Lodged at Cousin Harris's
on the fifth took my Solem leave of friend Marshal
who was very Ill He is near 80 years of Age and has
been a harty Man, about a week ago He had beeing
at meeting and being a Smoking his pipe was taken suddenly

Page 141

Ill with the Palsy and fell down He was put to
bed, appeared to be very sensible which is a great blessin
walked from thence to Cousin Wm Jones and from
thence to friends meeting at Hooknorton before meeting
went to see sevral friends, the meeting felt very
comfortable and refreshing to my Soul after
speaking a few words theirin I was led to pray
unto the Lord very awefully, after meeting refreshed
my self at friend Mintchons, then took my leave
of them and walked to Sibford to se some friends
who ware very Poorly walked from thence to
Cousin Hemmings of Brails with them I spent
the Evening lovingly Lodged their
on the fifth in the morning went to Let sevral
friends know that I Intended to sit with them at
their meeting at meeting I felt it to be my duty
to speak a few words theirin and also to petition
the Lord on my knees Praing Him to draw our mindes
of Earthly things and Set them on Heavenly things
which belonged to our souls everlasting well=being
after meeting bid my friends farewell then walked
Home ware I found my friends tolerable well
in this little Journey I was favoured with good
Health and to go through menny trials and Difi=
culties better than I did expect for which blessings
and mercies and all other things my minde is bowed in
humble thankfullness unto the Lord who hath been very
good unto me
First day [Sunday] the 8th was at our first day [Sunday] meeting in which
I felt Devine Love to flow amoungst us to the uniteing us near one

verso

to another in true Love
on the ninth was at our monthly meeting held
at Charlbury it was not very large it being
not very good traveling but it felt comfortable
and refreshing to my minde sevral mouths ware

opened in Public Testimonie and it appeared to
be
my duty to speak a few words theirin to
Incourage
friends to wait solidly upon the Lord that they
might be Inabled to sarve Him faithfully
the buisness was gone through in Love and Unity
on the twelfth was at our fifth day [Thursday]
meeting in
sitting theirin my minde was favoured to Injoy
Devine Love to my comfort and refreshment
and I Trust sevral more did that ware present
on the thirteenth took a walk to friends six=
=day [Friday] meeting at C.[hipping] Norton in
Sitting theirin
my minde was comforted being quite sensible
that Devine Love was felt to flow amoungst us
after waiting sometime in Solid Silence
upon the Lord I felt it to be my duty to
Pray unto the Lord in a very Humble
and weighty frame of minde beetching Him
to make good the Gracious promice of His
Dear Son Jesus Christ unto us that ware
but two or three ware Met together in
His Name their He would be in the midst
of them found true peace to my minde by so
doing called to se Ann Stait she being
very poorly afterward walked Home

Page 142

on the fourteenth was at our first day [Sunday]
meeting as I sat theirin my minde was
comforted and refreshed under a sence that
Devine Love was near to us and it appe=
ared to be my duty in great humility of minde
to prey unto the Lord but all Friends
not Joining me in Solem Prayer it hath
brought a great exercise in my minde
on the nineteenth was at our fifth day [Thursday]
meeting
as I sat theirin I felt Devine Love to be present
amoungst us to the refreshing our Spirits
on the twenty second took a walk to friends
first day [Sunday] meeting at Burford the
morning
meeting felt comfortable and refreshing to my
soul, after waiting in Solid Silence upon the
Lord I felt a concearn in my minde to speak
a few words theirin and also in the Afternoon
meeting, my minde received some Instruction
theirin after meeting took a walk to Joseph
Cowdry's at Great Barington spent the
Evening with him in a very solid manner
on the twenty third after spending a little
time with my kind and affectionate friend walked
to Brothers and Sistors at Burford called to ask
how friend Marshall was he is an aged man about
70 was
a taken Ill of a palsy about 3 weeks ago he lay
in a dosing state and appeared to take very little
notice of any Body and to be near his end
afterward walked Home

verso

1795

on the twenty sixth was at our fifth
day [Thursday] meeting it felt truly refreshing to
my minde
the third mo: [March] the 1st was at our first day
[Sunday]
meeting after Sitting sometime in Solid Silence
waiting upon the Lord I spake a few words
theirin as truth manifested it to be my duty
to recomend friends to wait upon the Lord
patiently for His Heavenly Instruction
it was our preparative meeting the buisness
was gone through in true Love
1[st day, Sunday]=7th feeling a desire in my
minde in true
love to take a walk to friends preparative
meeting at Faringdon acquainted my parents
with the feelings of my minde, in the
evening walked to witney and acquainted
my friend Jn'o Hankins with the feelings
of my minde letting Him know if he found
freedom in his minde to go I should be pleased
with his Company and He soon consented
to go with me
F[irst] Day [Sunday] 8th friend Hankins and I
had a pleasent
comfortable walk to friends meeting at Far=
=ingdon Devine Goodness was pleased to own
us with his Heavenly Power both in the Journey
and also at the meeting to the refreshing of our

Page 143

Spirits, at meeting after waiting solidly
upon the Lord to know his pure will I felt
it to be my duty to speak a few words theirin
and also to petition the Almighty in Solem
Prayer becseeching Him to be pleased to
extend His Love unto us, it was their preparative
meeting yet it was held in such a manner
as to affect my Heart with sorrow after
meeting parted with friends in love and
walked with friend Hankins to Witney spent
the evening their comfortabley Lodged their
2[nd day, Monday]=9th before meeting went to se sevral
friends the monthly Meeting felt very
comfortable and refreshing to my mind
and I hope to all sincear honest Hearted
friends that ware present, the buisness
held long their being menny minutes to be
considered yet it was gone through in much Love
after meeting took leave of friends and walked
Home with Brother and another friend
5 [th day, Thursday] 12 was at our fifth day meeting as I sat
theirin my minde was comforted under a
sence that Devine Love was felt amoungst us
F[irst] Day [Sunday] = 15 was at our first day meeting
altho I felt most easy to sit the whole

verso

meeting in Solid Silence yet it appeared
to me to be a very good Comfortable
and lively Instructing meeting
=5[th day, Thursday]=19 was at our fifth day meeting in sitting
theirin my minde was comforted and refreshed
with the injoyment of Devine Love
6[th day, Friday]=20 feeling a desire in my minde in
true Love to take a walk to friends
meeting at Sibford acquainted my
parents with the feelings of my minde
walked thither it appeared to my
minde to be a refreshing Eddifying
meeting sevral men had to bear a Pub=
=lick Testimonie of the Lords love to His
Children and one friend was led to
supplicate the Lord in very solem
and awefull Prayer, after meeting
call's to se some friends who ware
Poorly, took my kinde leave of them
then walked Home
F[irst] Day [Sunday] 22 was at our first day meeting
and in Sitting theirin my minde was comf=
=orted and refreshed been made sensible of
the springings up of living water amoungst
us which nourisheth up the soul unto
Eternal Life
5[th day, Thursday]=26 was at our fifth day meeting

Page 144

F[irst] Day [Sunday] 29th took a walk with sevral
friends to Barton to a meeting their
which is held twice in the year in Order
that the People of other professions of
Religion may come and wait upon the Lord
with friends and feel taste and see how good
the Lord is to them that Love and fear Him
it appeared to be a very good comfortable
meeting in which Devine Goodness was pleased
to make use of His children as Instruments
to put the people in minde of their latter end
and the great nescessiety their was for them
to prepare for it After meeting took leave
of friends and walked Home,
4mo [April] 4th took a walk to Milton to friends
meeting their it was small yet we ware favoured
with the injoyment of Devine Goodness my spirit
was engaged to pray very solemly in a few words
and also to speak a few words in Testimonie
after meeting call'd to se a few friends afterward walked Home
5[th day, Thursday]=2 was at our fifth day meeting ware after
waiting upon the Lord in solid Silence as His pure
spirit manifested it to me to be my duty to speak a few
words theirin so I spake them

verso

1795

4mo [April] 5th F[irst] Day [Sunday] was at our first day
meeting, after waiting upon the Lord
for sometime in Solid Silence it appeared
to be my duty in humility to speak a
few words theirin, found true peace of
minde by so doing, it was our prepa=
=rative meeting Answers ware drawn
up to the quarterly meeting queries and
the other buisness gone through in much
Love, it having rested on my minde
very weighty for sometime respecting
a afternoon meeting being settled here
and believeing it to be my duty which
the Lord required of me to mention to
friends the feelings of my minde at our
Preparative meeting I mentioned it and
found true comfort by so doing
2[nd day, Monday]=6th took a walk to our Monthly Meeting
holden at Burford it was tolerable large
sevral solid Testimonies ware born
and one friend was engaged in very solem
Prayer, the meeting of Buisness was rather
labourious yet the Buisness was gone through
in much Love afterwards was holden an
evening meeting by friend Barritts desire
it appeared to me to be a good profitable
to menny Devine Love appeared to

Page 145

be afresh extended to the people
through His sarvents sevral living
testimonies ware born wareby the Lords
everlasting Love was set forth to the
Children of men how He strove with
them by His spirit of truth for their
sould everlasting good, but after meeting
my minde was very uneasy under a sence
that I had not kept watchfull enough
to the leadings and guidance of the Lords
spirit of Truth within my minde
Lodged at Brothers
3[rd day, Tuesday]=7 after takeing my kinde leave of
Brother and sistor and some more friends
walked Home pretty early
5[th day, Thursday]=9 was at our fifth day meeting it was pretty large
F[irst] Day [Sunday] 12th was at our first day meeting
it was pretty large sevral friends
being here on their Journey for our
quarterly meeting at witney the meeting
felt very comfortable to my minde Devine
goodness was felt amoungst us to the feeding
our souls with Heavenly refreshment
2[nd day, Monday]=13 took a walk to our Quarterly Meeting
holden at witney it was largish
and felt very comfortable to my minde Devine

verso

Love was felt amoungst us and it appeared
to be a renewed visitation of Devine Love
through the Lords Sarvents to menny present
one friend appeared in Solem Prayer
the A.N. [afternoon] meeting was very large of friends
and Neighbours and it also appeared to be
a good satisfactory Meeting sevral friends
appeared in Public Testimonie the Lord
Inabled them to speak to the spiritual states
and conditions of menny present, called to
see sevral friends, set my hand to three
wrightings called [rest of line left blank]
as trust with sevral more young friends who
also set their hands on the same account, after
meeting returned Home with sevral friends
3[rd day, Tuesday]=14 took a walk again to our Quarterly
meeting at witney it being the meeting at
which the buisness is gone through it felt to
my minde to be a very comfortable meeting
truth appeared to reign during the whole
meeting sevral Testimonies ware born with
a desire to stir up the luke warm and Indifrent
to a more steady attention and obidience to the
Devine principal within them, it also appeared
to be my duty to speak a few words theirin
in public Testimonie after meeting walked
home with some friends

Page 146

5 [April] 1795

4[th day, Wednesday]=15 took a walk to the Marriage of Wm
Barrits Daughter of Witney to Thos.
Skinner a convinced young man, it was
a large satisfactory meeting sevral liv=
=ing Testimonies ware born by sevral solid
Friends and two of them ware drawn
into very solem Prayer, after meeting
went up to friend Barrits with men=
=ny friends, spent the afternoon with them
in a very solid manner sevral Elderly
friends ware Inabled through devine
Goodness to speak to the states and con=
=ditions of some present afterward took
leave of friends and walked Home
5[th day, Thursday]=16 was at our fifth day meeting it was pretty large
7[th day, Saturday]=18 feeling a desire in my minde to
attend friends meeting at faringdon
walked to witney to friend Hankins's
Lodged there very comfortable
F[irst]D[ay] [Sunday] 19th walked with Jno Hankins to
the meeting at Faringdon it was
small and the life of Religion appeared
very low theirin yet I felt Devine
goodness to be felt amoungst us to the com=
=forting and refreshing our Souls

verso

after meeting went to se some friends
took leave of them & walk with friend
Hankins to witney Lodged at his house
on the morrow walked Home had a pleasent Journey
5[th day, Thursday]=23 was at our fifth day meeting and I was
very thankfull in my minde that I was
favoured to sit with Friends
F[irst]Day [Sunday] 26 was at our first day meeting it
was not very large yet it felt to my minde
to be an Instructing good meeting
5[th day, Thursday]=30 was at our fifth day meeting in sitting
theirin my minde was refreshed and comforted
been sensible Devine Love was felt to
flow amoungst us
7[th day, Saturday]=2nd of the fifth mo: [May] feeling drawings in
my minde towards Armscutt [Armscote] meeting ac=
=quainted my Parents with the feelings
of my minde, walked to Brails in the
A.[fter]Noon found Cousin there very well
Lodged at Cousin Hemmings
F[irst]Day [Sunday] 3rd took leave of Cousins then walked
with some friends to Shipstone to the morning
meeting their it was tolerable large Devine
Goodness was felt theirin to the comforting
and refreshing menny mindes present
after meeting walked with some friends to

Page 147

Armscutt [Armscote] Meeting, it appeared to
be a good instructing meeting Devine
Goodness was felt amoungst us to the
fresh visitation of menny present
and setting before them they way
of Life and Death through his Sarvents
with instructions that if they would
obtain Immortal life they must be
wholy obidient unto the manifestation
of Devine Light within them, walked
to Shipstone with some friends spent
a little time with friends their very comfor=
=tabley walked from thence with some
friends to Joseph Lambs at little sibford
called to se Michael petiphors family
spent a little time with them Lodged
at Joseph Lambs
2[nd day, Monday]=4th walked to Epwell pretty early to
se our Relations there spent a little
time with them very lovingly afterwards
had a pleasent walk with Uncle Gibbs to
the monthly meeting at Shutford it was largish

verso

and it felt very comfortable to my minde
Devine Goodness was felt amoungst us
to the comforting and refreshing the
truly contrited Hearted ones, the buisness
was gone through in much Love
after meeting went to cousin Ashby's
spent a little time with them in
a loving agreeable manner took leave
of them and walked Home called to see
Cousin Wm Jones and his wife and His
Mother and sistor found my friends
tolerable well for which and all other
mercies and blessing I remain truly
thankfull to kinde Providence
5[th day, Thursday]=7 was at our fifth day meeting
F[irst] Day [Sunday] 10th having heard that Cousin
Joseph Ashby of seasoncutt [Sezincote] was very
poorly not likely to live very long
took a walk to se Him and rest of
Cousins found him very Ill and ware
so Ill that he was obliged to sit up
night and day he to outward appearances
will not live long, was at friends meeting
at Stow it felt to my minde to be a good

Page 148

refreshing meeting, after waiting solidly
upon the Lord in Solid Silence, it appeared
to be required of me to Pray theirin in
a few words, after meeting walked
down to Seaconcutt [Sezincote] spent the afternoon
with Cousins and some more friends who
came to se them in a very loving and solem
manner Lodged their
2[nd day, Monday]=11 took my kinde leave of Cousins
and walked to our Monthly Meeting
at Chipping Norton it was largish
and it felt very refreshing and comforting
in the forepart of the meeting but the
latter part of the meeting felt not so comfortable altho the
buisness was gone through in much Love
after meeting walked home with some friends
4[th day, Wednesday]=13 was at an evening meeting at Cha=
=rlbury, appointed by friend Alexanders
who came from Needhams desire for friends only it appeared to be a
good profitable meeting the friends minde was
opend by the spirit of Truth and theirby He was
Inabled to speak to sevral states and Conditions
present as to Arouse some of the luke=warm

verso

that ware careless of the everlasting
wellbeing of their Souls and also to give
a word of Incouragement to some that
ware Spiritual Mourners
5[th day, Thursday]=14 was at our fifth day meeting it felt very
refreshing to my minde
F[irst] Day [Sunday] 17 was at our meeting in sitting theirin
my minde was much comforted and refreshed
and it appeared to be my duty to recomend
to friends to fear and sarve the Lord
who sees all of our thoughts and actions
3[rd day, Tuesday]=19 having heard of the Death of Cousin
Joseph Ashby of Seasoncutt [Sezincote] who died
of a dropsy aged about 61 took a walk
to the Funeral it was very large of
friends and Neighbours He was buried
in friends burying ground at Stow a
very large and solem meeting was held
on the Occation in the afternoon menny
Living Testimonies ware born by which
the people ware directed not to look to man
for spiritual help to [illegible] but unto the Lords spirit
of Truth within them which was able to
lead and guide them into all truth after meeting
walked down to seasoncutt [Sezincote] and spent the evening

Page 149

with Cousin in a very solid and Comfortable
manner Lodged their
4[th day, Wednesday]=20 spent a little time with cousins in a
solid agreeable manner after breackfasting

with them took leave of them and walked
Home called at stow and at some friends
and relations as I came along found my
friends tolerable well at home for which
mercy and menny more my minde is bowed in
humble thankfullness before the Lord
5[th day, Thursday]=21st was at our fifth day meeting
F[irst]Day [Sunday] 24 was at our first day meeting ware
after waiting in Solid Silence sometime
it appeared to be my duty in much humility
to bear a Testimonie theirin
5[th day, Thursday]=28 was at our fifth day meeting as
I sat theirin my soul was favoured
to pertake of Devine refreshment
F[irst] Day [Sunday] 31 took a walk to friends preparative
meeting at Stow, it felt to my minde to
be a good comfortable meeting in which
Devine Love was felt amoungst us to
our Spiritual refreshment, it appeared
to be my duty to recomend to friends to be
diligent to attend our religious meetings

verso

to wait upon the Lord and worship
Him their buisness was gone through
in Love after meeting walked to Cousins
at Seasoncutt [Sezincote] spent a little time with
them very lovingly, took my kinde
leave of them and walked Home found
my friends tolerable well
5[th day, Thursday]=4 was at our fifth day meeting
in Sitting theirin my minde was
comforted and refreshed
F[irst] Day [Sunday] 7th was at our Meeting it felt comfortable
to my minde, after waiting upon the
Lord it appeared to be my duty to speak
a few words theirin which I did and felt
great peace of minde in so doing it was
our preparative meeting at which the quarterly
meeting queries should have been answered
some friends ware not willing to answer
them on account of one of our members being
absent it to my minde appeared to be our duty to answer
them I Indeavoured what I could to have them
answered but could not prevail with friends to
answer them, afterwards felt myself clear

Page 150

6mo [June] 1795

2[nd day, Monday]=8th was at our Monthly meeting
holden here it was pretty large and
a good refreshing meeting wee
ware favoured with the refreshing
Power of our Heavenly Father
to the Incourageing us to sarve
Him faithfully, the buisness was
gone through in much Love
5[th day, Thursday]=11 was at our fifth day meeting as I sat
theirin my minde was much humbled under
a sence of my own weakness
F[irst] Day [Sunday] = 14 took a walk to friends
meeting at Southnewington it was
largish considering the small number
of friends living their, it felt to
be a good refreshing meeting to my minde
after meeting having heard of a fu=
=neral to be at Sibford walked thither
but was to late for the meeting call'd
to see some friends at L.Sibford
walked from thence Home
5[th day, Thursday]=18 was at our fifth day meeting
7[th day, Saturday]=19 walked to witney to se some friends

verso

7 [June]1795

F[irst] Day [Sunday] 21st walked with friend hankins
and some more friends to a friends meeting
at Faringdon it was largish and we

ware favoured with the visitation of Devine
Love to our comfort and through the
assistance thereof I was Inabled to bear
a Testimonie theirin after meeting spent
a little time with friends very lovingly
afterwards walked to witney Lodged their
5[th day, Thursday]=25 was at our fifth day
meeting
7[th day, Saturday]=27 believeing it to be my
duty to attend
a meeting appointed to be held at Oxfo=
and also the Quarterly Meeting at Banbury
acquainted my Parents with the feelings
of my minde walked to Witney Lodged
their
F[irst] Day [Sunday] 28 walked with Wm Fardon
to
the meeting at Oxford it was largish
and appeared to be a good edifying Meeting
in which Devine Goodness was pleased to
own His Children with His living power to
their great refreshment after meeting
walked with Jos. Sargood to Adderbury Lodged
at Friend Plesters very comfortabley

Page 151

2[nd day, Monday]=2 went to se Thos. Whichley
who was
very poorly took leave of Him and
some more friends walked from thence
with some friends to Banbury the
morning meeting was large and felt
very comfortable sevral Living testimonies
ware born and the meeting was concluded
in Solem Prayer, the afternoon meeting
was very large also sevral living Testimonies
ware born to Indeavour to turn the peoples
mindes Inward to their true teacher the
Light of Christ within them after meeting
went to se some friends spent the evening
with them very comfortabley Lodged at friend
Sconchs
3[rd day, Tuesday]=30 went to se some friends
afterwards
went to meeting it was largish sevral
elderly friends ware drawn forth in an
eminent manner to give good advice and
counsel unto friends in general and the
buisness was gone through in much Love
and Unity after meeting took my kinde
leave of Friends and walked Home with
Brother called to se Aunt Midwinter she
was very poorly called to se Aunt and Cousin

verso

Damaris Jones who ware tolerable well
Thankes and Praises be unto Devine Providence
who in this little Journey did favour me with
His Love and Inabled me to return safe Home
5[th day, Thursday]=2 was at our fifth day
meeting as I
sat theirin my minde was very low under
a sence of my own weakness's
6[th day, Friday]=3 took a walk to friends
meeting at
C[hipping] Norton it was smallish yet I felt
Devine Love amoungst us to our comfort
and refreshment after meeting walked Home
F[irst] Day [Sunday]=5 was at our first day
meeting as
I sat theirin my minde was very humble
and I was very desireous I might be kept
so Humble as not to do nor speak any
thing in mine own will but do and speak
Just what the Devine Principal within one
manifested to me to be my duty to do and speak
5[th day, Thursday]=9th was at our fifth day
meeting
F[irst] Day [Sunday] = 12 was at our first day
meeting
it felt comfortable and refreshing
to my minde after meeting walked with
Brother to witney spent the evening their
with some friends very lovingly Lodged at Fr.
Hankins
2[nd day, Monday]=13 walked with some friends
to our Monthly Meeting
at faringdon it appeared to my minde to be a
good
comfortable meeting sevral living solid
Testimonies

Page 152

ware born to the honnour of the Almighty
and His truth the buisness was gone through
in much Love, after meeting reach'd home

3[rd day, Tuesday]=14 walked with Cousin Robt. Ashby
to shutford meeting to the funeral of
his Brother it was a largish meeting
of Friends and Neighbours sevral
living Testimonies ware born it appeared
to my minde to be a good satisfactory
meeting in which Devine Love was felt
amoungst us to the fresh visitation of menny
mindes present, after meeting took my
leave of Cousins and walked to Adderbury
call'd to se Aunt Midwinter of Bloxham
she was very poorly called to se Tho's
Harris of Milton spent the evening
very friendly with some friends at adde=
=rbury Lodg'd at Tho's Whichleys
4[th day, Wednesday]=15 called to se some friends who ware loving
to me was at their meeting it felt comfortable
to my minde Devine Goodness being pleased
to own us by feeding us with Heavenly refreshment
after meeting spent a little time with fr. Harris
of Milton then walked Home having had a satisfactory Journey

verso

5[th day, Thursday]=16 was at our fifth day meeting as I sat
with friends my minde was comforted and
refreshed with Heavenly refreshment
F[irst] Day[Sunday]=19 was at our first day meeting it
felt very comfortable and refreshing to my
minde it was a fullish meeting sevral
strangers ware present
5[th day, Thursday]=23 was at our fifth day meeting
F[irst] Day [Sunday] 26th was at our first day meeting
at meeting we ware favoured with an American
friend Sarah Harrison and two other and it felt
to my minde to be a good comfortable meeting
by the friends desire an evening meeting
was held here and by their desire the Neighbours
ware let know it was a large full meeting
of friends and neighbours it felt comfortable
the American friend had a fine time to ease
her minde to the people to set before them
the way of Life and Death
2[nd day, Monday]=27 feeling my minde drawn by the love of
the truth to take a walk to friends monthly
meeting at Reading and also to friends fourth
day [Wednesday] meeting at Henly and friends fifth day [Thursday]
meeting at Warborough acquainted my Parents
with the feelings of my minde, set out early in
the morning and reach Reading about 8 at Night

Page 153

called to se fr'd Jacksons's and call'd at Cousins
at Shillingford and at some more friends
on the road the ware very kinde to me found
Cousins at Reading very well and they ware
pleased to se me Lodged there
3[rd day, Tuesday]=28 before meeting went to se sevral friends
they ware very loving to me their monthly meeting
was smallish It felt to my minde to be a
good comfortable meeting, it appeared to
be my duty to speak a few words theirin
the buisness was gone through in much love
after meeting spent sometime with Cousins
in a loving edifying manner bad them
farewell then walked to Henly found
friends their very well Lodg'd at Edwd. Mays
4[th day, Wednesday]=29 spent a little time before meeting
with friends very comfortabley the meeting
was small, yet my minde was refreshed
and comforted theirin stoped a little at
Jo's Coals then bad friends farewell and
walked to Shillingford spent the evening
with friends very comfortabley lodg'd at F. Ashbys
30 spent a little time with friends in an

verso

affectionate manner before meeting, it felt
to my minde to be a good Instructing meeting
Devine Love was felt amoungst us to our
comfort and it appeared to be my duty to bare
a Testimonie theirin, after meeting bad
friends farewell then walked Home called to
se friend Jacksons's she was very poorly
I was favoured in the Journey with Devine

Love to my great comfort for which mercy
and blessings and all others I remain truly
and Humbley thankfull to Kinde Providence
8mo [August] 1st feeling a desire in my minde in the
Love of the Gospel to take a walk to friends morning meeting
at Shipstone and a meeting at Armscutt [Armscote] acquainted
my Parents with the feelings of my minde they
ware willing I should go walked to Brails spent
the evening with Cousins and friends in a very
solid agreeable manner Lodged at Cous'n Gilletts
on the 2nd walked from Brails to Shipstone
to the morning meeting it was a largish
comfortable meeting Devine Love was felt
amoungst us to our comfort walked from
thence with some friends to the meeting at
Armscutt [Armscote] it was a larg meeting of friends
and Neighbours sevral P.[ublic] friends ware their
straingers one friend from America Sarah Harrison
sevral mouths ware opened to Invite the people to

Page 154

come taste and feel how good the Lord is
to them that Love and sarve Him after
meeting walked to Shipstone spent a
little time with friends their very lovingly
bad them farewell and walked to C.[hipping] Norton
Lodged at Cousin Fardons
on the 3rd rose early and walked Home
on the 6th was at our fifth day [Thursday] meeting
on the ninth was at our first day [Sunday] meeting
it was largish sevral Strangers ware
present wee ware favoured with the
visitation of Devine Love to our comfort
our preparative meeting buisness was
gone through in Love, after meeting
walked to Burford to the evening meeting
their sevral Neighbours came in, it felt
to my minde to be a good instructing meeting
sevral living Testimonies ware born theirin
Lodg'd at Joseph Cowdrys He is very loving to friends

on the tenth was at our monthly Meeting
their it was pretty largish and I think it
was a good profitable meeting in which
Devine Goodness was pleased to appear to the
a fresh visitation of menny mindes by puting
them in minde through His Sarvents to attend

verso

very carefully to the Instruction of His
holy spirit within them and be wholy obidient
unto it after meeting took leave of Bror. Sistor
Father and mother and friends then walked Home
on the 12th took a walk to friends fourth day [Wednesday]
meeting at witney it felt to my minde to
be a pretty comfortable meeting
on 13th took a walk to friends fifth
day [Thursday] meeting at Hooknorton it was
smallish yet I felt the devine Power
to flow amoungst us which refreshes
the humble contrited ones, it appeared
to be my duty to speak theirin after
meeting spent a little time Lovingly
with friends, walked from thence to
sibford found friends there tolerable
well Lodged at Joseph Lambs
on the fourteenth walked from thence
to Epwell to se our Relations before
meeting they ware tolerable well
the meeting was not very large
yet it felt to my minde to be a good
comfortable meeting it appeared

Page 155

to be my duty to speak a little theirin
after meeting went to friend Grimes's
spent a little time with them in a loving
manner afterwards walked Home
on the 16th was at our fifth day [Thursday]
meeting it was large sevral Strangers
ware their it felt to my minde to be a
tolerable comfortable meeting it appeared
to be my duty to advise friends to keep
clean from the spots of the world
on the 20th came home from Reaping
and went to meeting in my sitting theirin
my minde was refreshed and comforted

being sensible Devine goodness was
felt amoungst us
on 23rd took a walk to friends meeting
at Stow the meeting was very small their
being about three members present sevral
being removed by Death yet it felt to my
minde to be a good refreshing meeting
after meeting went to se some Neighbours
and friends spent a little time at friend
Hidens at Oddington very solidly and
comfortabley afterwards walked Home

verso

---

on the 27th was at our fifth day [Thursday] meeting
as I sat theirin my minde was comforted
and refreshed with Devine Love it appeared
to be my duty to speak a few words theirin
on the 30th took a walk to friends meeting
at Milton as I sat theirin my minde was
much comforted and refreshed, and it ap=
peared to be my duty to open my Mouth
in Prayer in a very solem manner
found true peace of minde by so doing
after meeting went to se some friends
walked from thence to Burford and found Mother
Brother and Sistor & the rest tolerable well
was at the Evening meeting their it felt
very comfortable and refreshing to my
minde and I hope to menny mindes present
after meeting took my kinde leave of Mother
and the rest of my relations then walked
Home being favoured with the Injoyment
of Devine Love in the Journey for which I
remain truly thankfull to Kinde Providence
on the third was at our fifth day [Thursday] meeting
F[irst] Day [Sunday] 6th was at our first day [Sunday] meeting
ware after waiting in Solid silence a pre=
=tty wile I spake a few words theirin

Page 156

---

as the spirit of truth manifested it to be
my duty so to do, the Writen Epistle was
read in our meeting, it was our prepa=
=rative meeting at which the Queries ware
answered pretty near to what they required
I again mentioned to friends what hath
remained on my minde with great weight
to have a first day [Sunday] afternoon meeting settled
here
on the 7th took a walk to our Monthly
meeting held at C.[hipping] Norton it felt to
my minde to be a good refreshing meeting
Friend Lambly was their from tredington
she had a Public Testimonie to bear
as also sevral other friends to the
honnour of the Devine Being, the
buisness was gone through in Love
three Meetings ware appointed to
be held at three places ware no friends
live altho friends have meeting Houses
their, and it was desired that the Nei=
=ghbours should be let know of the Meet=
ings after meeting walked Home
on the 10th it being our fifth day [Thursday]

verso

---

meeting their was a funeral at the
same time of Benjamin Holford
who died about two days ago of a
long and painfull Illness with
a Comer, I have a living hope
that He is removed out of his great
Affliction to Injoy a place of Everlasting
rest sevral friends ware Invited to the
Funeral and it felt to my minde to
be a very solid good Meeting sevral Nei=
=ghbours ware present as also Friends
Devine Goodness was pleased to own us by
visiting menny mindes with His eternal
Power and by the Testimonies of His
Sarvants wareby the People ware
Put in minde of the great nessecity their
was for them always to live as they would
wish to Die it fell to be my duty to leave
a Short Testimonie theirin the Meeting
was Concluded in Solem and awefull
Prayer
on the thirteenth feeling a concearn in my
minde to take a walk to our Quarterly

Page 157

---

meeting to be holden at Reading walked

thither with Brother it was a fullish
meeting of Friends and Neighbours
it appeared to my minde to be a good
instructing Meeting in which the Devine
Being was pleased to own us with His
Power and goodness to our great comfort
the Lord was Pleased to gratify sevral of
His Sarvants to bear living Testimonies
theirin after meeting walked in company
with sevral friends to Streatly Lodg'd their
on the 14 walked in Company with the
same friends to Reading with whose company
I was much comforted found cousin and friends
Tolerable well except one of friends tutteys
sons he appears to be a little in a Decline
the morning meeting felt to my minde to
be a good Instructing meeting after a time
of Solid Silence a friend appeared in Solem
Prayer afterwards sevral living Testimonies
ware born strangers P.B. [public] friends G
Dellwin
friend Townsend friend Pointer with menny
more I think the meeting in the afternoon

verso

was largish and felt very comfortable sevral
Living Testimonies ware born to the incou=
=ragement of the sincear and Honest hearted
People after meeting spent sometime with
cousins and friends in a loving and comfortable
manner Lodged at Tho's Stubbs
on the fifteenth spent sometime in a very solid
manner with Cousin Wm Tuttey who is poorly
before meeting the men and Women had
a comfortable sitting together before
they entered upon buisness the buisness
was gone through in much Love the
answers to the Queries ware read and
menny weighty remarks made theiron
and Instructions given to friends theiron
one P.B.[public friend] very strongly Desired
friends
to hold a womens Quarterly Meeting in
the winter as well as Mens as also a meeting
of Ministers and Elders after meeting
bid cousins and friends Farewell
walked from thence with sevral Kinde friends
Part of the way Home Lodged at Cous'n Ashbys
on the sixteenth being a little tired and friend

Page 158

Albrights being so kinde as to offer to
let me ride with them in their cart I
excepted their kindness and rode Home
in my way home called at the hospital
to see some acquaintance who ware poorly
their had a very comfortable Journey for
which mercy I am truly thankfull to
Kinde Providence
on the 17th was at our fifth day [Thursday]
Meeting
it felt very comfortable to my minde
on the nineteenth took a walk to Faringdon
towards two meetings appointed by our
Monthly Meeting one at Charl[t]on
and one at Uffington[25] called at witney
found friends there tolerable well as
also at Faringdon met sevral friends
there spent the evening with friends
very lovingly at Frd. Reynolds Lodg'd at Fr'd
Renolds
on the 20th went in company with
sevral Friends to the meeting at
Charl[t]on it was large of Friends
and Neighbours sevral P.[ublic] Friends
there two not belonging to our Monthly

verso

meeting viz Edwd. May from Henly
and Jo's Lamb from little Sibford
it felt to my minde to be a good Satis=
=factory Meeting in which Devine Love
was felt amoungst us to the comforting
of menny mindes and it appeared to be
a Devine Visitation to menny mindes present
sevral Living Testimonies ware born
to the honnour of the Devine Being
and a solem and awefull Prayer
was put up unto Him,
after meeting Friends went
to some friendly Neighbours to Dinner
the behaved kinde like unto Friends
walked with friends to the Meeting at
Uffington friends called at friend Potingers
ware we ware entertained friendly
the meeting appeared to be not quite

25 Earliest recorded reference of meeting 1668

so large as the Meeting at Charl[t]on
yet it felt to my minde to be a good
satisfactory Meeting in which Devine
Love was felt to our comfort sevral
Living Testimonies ware born theirin

Page 159

after Meeting went in company with
sevral friends back to Faringdon
spent the evening with friends at
Friend Renolds's very agreeably Lodg'd their
on the 21st some Friends having felt
a concearn in their mindes to have
a meeting at Faringdon and to have
the Neighbours acquainted theirof
stop't meeting it was not very
large yet I felt the Devine Power
to flow amoungst us to the comfort
of the sincear honest hearted People
sevral friends appeared in Pub=
lick Testimonie, after meeting spent
a little time at Friend Renolds's
then bid friends Farewell, walked
Home sevral friends going part of
the way with me whose company
was very comfortable to me found my
friends tolerable well at Home
on the 24th was at our fifth day [Thursday]
meeting
on the 26 feeling a concearn in my minde
to attend meeting appointed by our

verso

monthly meeting at Alverscott ware
no friends live on 27th walked to Witney
in the A.N. [afternoon] found friends in general
tolerable well Lodged at Fr'd Hankins
on the 27th walked with sevral Friends
to the Meeting at Alverscott it was
a largish Meeting of friends and
Neighbours it felt to my minde to be
a good comfortable meeting sevral living
Testimonies ware born to Indeavour to
turn the Peoples mindes inward to
their spiritual teacher that they
might have their mindes taken of
earthly things and set on Heavenly
things after meeting walked with
friends to Witney spent a little time
with friends there comfortabley after=
=ward walked Home
on the thirtieth took a walk to friends fourth
day [Wednesday] meeting at Milton, it was small
yet as I sat theirin I felt Devine
Goodness to flow amoungst us it appear'd
to be my duty to speak a few words
theirin after meeting went to see a few

Page 160

Friends bid them farewell and walked Home
10mo 1st was at our fifth day [Thursday] meeting
it felt comforting and refreshing
to my soul and body
on the 4th was at our first day [Sunday]
meeting it felt comforting and
refreshing to my minde, it appeared
to be my duty to speak a few words theirin
after meeting believeing it to be my
duty to take a walk to friends Monthly
Meeting at Adderbury acquainted my
Parents with the feelings of my minde
walked to milton call'd to see Cousins at Ledal
[Ledwell?]
spent the evening comfortable at Fr'd Pains
of Milton Lodg'd their
on the 5th walked to Adderbury call'd
to see sevral friends before meeting
found Tho's Harriss daughter Mary
very poorly some thinks she is in a
Decline she appeared to bare Her
Affliction patiently and much resigned
and in her minde given up to the Devine

verso

Will the Meeting felt very comforting
and refreshing to my minde it appeared
to be my duty to speak a few words
theirin by so doing I found peace
the buisness was gone through in much
Love after meeting walked to Milton to
se some friends and from thence to Ledal
[Ledwell?]
Cousins entertained me very kingly lodg'd their
on 6th rose early and walked home found
my friends tolerable well
8th was at our fifth day [Thursday] meeting it felt

comforting and refreshing to my minde
on 10th feeling a concearn in my minde to
take a walk to friends meeting at Stow
acquainted my Parents theirof, walked
to Stow in the afternoon to an acquaintance
their not of our society ware I was enter=
=tained kindly Lodg'd their
on 11th before meeting went to se some
acquaintance the meeting was small
Truth appeared to be very low theirin
yet we ware favoured with Heavenly
refreshment to the nourishing and refre=
shing our souls after meeting took leave
of Friends and acquaintance then walked Home

Page 161

on 12th it being our Monthly Meeting held
at Charlbury went to it the Life of
Truth appeared to be low theirin yet I felt
Devine goodness to be felt amoungst us
to our comfort and refreshment, it felt
to me to be my duty to speak a few
words theirin the buisness was gone through
in Love and Unity
on 15, was at our own fifth day [Thursday] meeting
In sitting theirin I was made sensible
of my own great weakness's and that without
Devine assistance I could do no good thing
on the sixteenth took a walk to friends
meeting at Sibford my minde was very low
as I sat theirin under a sence of my own
Weakness's and frailties being truly sensible
that without Devine Assistance i could do no good thing
after meeting went to se sevral friends
at little and broad Sibford walked from thence
to Epwell to see our Relations their spent the
evening at Uncle Gibbs in a loving solid
manner Lodg'd their
on the seventeenth took my Affectionate
farewell of Uncle Gibbs and the rest of
his family then walk Home

verso

1795 10mo [October]
on the 18th was at our first day [Sunday] meeting
at which my minde was comforted and refr=
=eshed, it appeared to be my duty to recomend
to friends to come out of the fashons costoms
and friendships of this World and spent the
time in a more solid manner
on 21st took a walk to friends meeting at
Witney as I sat theirin my minde was Comforted
and refreshed under a sence that Devine
Love was felt amoungst us, altho it was small
on the 22nd was at our fifth day [Thursday] meeting
it felt very comforting and refreshing to my minde
on the 25 was at our first day [Sunday] meeting as
I sat theirin my minde was refreshed and
comforted with Heavenly refreshment it
appeared to be my duty to speak a few words theirin
on 29th was at our fifth day [Thursday] meeting as I
sat theirin my minde was comforted and
refreshed being sensible that Devine
Love was felt amoungst us
on 30th took a walk to Friends meeting
at C.[hipping] Norton as I sat theirin my
minde was refreshed and comforted
being sensible that Devine Love was
felt amoungst us, it appeared to be my

Page 162

duty to bear a Testimonie theirin
after meeting went to se some friends
before I walked Home
11mo 1st was at our first day [Sunday] meeting it felt
to my minde to be a good satisfactory Meeting
it appeared to be my duty to put friends
in minde to be good examples amoungst mankinde
4th took a walk to friends meeting
at Witney the meeting was smallish
yet as I sat theirin I felt Devine
Love to flow amoungst us to our comfort
it appeared to be my duty in Humility
to speak a few words theirin after meet=
=ing walked Home
5th was at our fifth day [Thursday] meeting as I
sat with friends my spirit did rejoice
being sensible that the Love of God was felt amoungst us

11th feeling my minde drawn by the spirit
of Truth within me to take a walk to
Armscutt [Armscote] meeting acquainted my Parents
with the feelings of my minde walked to
Shipstone found cousin Mary Wells very
poorly spent the evening with friends
there comfortabley Lodg'd at Cousin Fardons

verso

11mo [November] 1795

8th spent the morning with Friends in
a very solid and Loving manner, walked
with some friends to Armscutt [Armscote] meeting
it was not very Large but few neighbours
comming in yet it felt to my minde to be
a good instructing meeting and a renew'd
visitation of Devine Love in Perticular
to the young friends sevral friends ap=
=peared in Testimonie after meeting
walked to Shipstone spent a little time
with our Relations their, took my leave
of them and friends, walked from thence
to C.[hipping] Norton spent the evening with
friends their very comfortabley Lodg'd
at Cousin Fardons
on 9th walked from C.[hipping] Norton to Witney
to our Monthly Meeting it was not very
large yet my minde was comforted and
refreshed theirin the buisness was gone
through in much Love after meeting went
to se some friends before I walked Home
on 12th was at our fifth day [Thursday] meeting it
felt comfortable to my minde
14 having felt drawings in my minde

Page 163

by the spirit of Truth to take a walk to
friends meeting at Faringdon acquainted
my parents with the feelings of my minde
walked to Witney in the A.N. [afternoon] to Friend
Hankins called to se some friends spent the evening comfortabley
15th walked to friends meeting at
Faringdon with fr'd Hankins it was
tolerable large and it felt comfortable
to my minde tho truth appeared to be
low theirin after speaking a few words
in Testimonie it appeared to be my
duty to pray in a few words found
true peace by so doing, my minde
was brought into a very low and Humble
situation after meeting spent a little
time with friends walked to witney
with fr'd Hankins spent the Evening
their with friends very comfortable
16th Breackfasted at fr'd Hankins's
afterwards called to se some friends
took leave of them and walked Home
19th was at our fifth day [Thursday] meeting it felt
comfortable to my minde and it appeared to be my

verso

---

duty to speak a few words theirin
22nd was at our first day [Sunday] meeting as I sat theirin
my minde was much refreshed and comforted and
it appeared to appeared to be my duty to recomend to friends
to attend to the teachings of the Lords spirit within them
26 was at our fifth day [Thursday] meeting it ap=
=peared to be my duty to recomend to frie=
=nds to be mercyfull
28th believing it to be my duty to take a
walk to friends meeting at Brails and a
few week day meetings acquainted my
Parents with the feelings of my minde
walked to brails found Cousins there
tolerable well, Lodg'd at Cousin Gillets
29 spent a little time with Cousins before
Meeting the meeting was tolerable large
it appeared to be my duty to leave a Testimonie
theirin their preparative meeting buisness
was concluded in much Love after meeting
walkd with Ric'd Fardon to little Sibford
to see the Widow Harris who was poorly after sitting with

she and some friends sometime in Silence
it fell to be my duty to speak a few words
of comfort and Incouragement to those who
Love the Truth call'd to see a few friends
Lodg'd at Cousin Fardons

Page 164

30th took leave of Cousins, and walked to
Brails spent sometime with Cousins and
friends their then walked to Michael
Petiphors spent a little time with them
very lovingly went from thence to Shipstone
spent the evening with friends their
very agreeabley Lodg'd at Tho's Hodgkins
12mo [December] 1st was at the Monthly
Meeting at Shipstone
it did not feel to my minde to be so comfortable
as some meetings I have been at it felt
to be my duty to speak a few words
theirin the buisness was gone through in
much Love, after meeting walked from
thence to Ticer [Tysoe] Cousin Ashleys
accompanying
me on Horseback spent the evening
with Cousins in a solid comfortable
manner Lodg'd their
2nd walked with Cousins to Radway to
meeting it felt to my minde to be a good
comfortable meeting it appeared to be my
duty to leave a Testimonie theirin after
meeting spent a little time at Cousin
Malings's walked back to Ticer [Tysoe] and from
thence to Brails spent the evening at Cousins

verso

Lodg'd at Cousin Gilletts
on the 3rd took leave to Cousins who ware
very kinde to me walked from thence to
Long compton was at their fifth day [Thursday]
meeting[26] it felt to my minde to be a good
satisfactory meeting it appeared to be my
duty to speak theirin after meeting spent
a little time at Friend Harris's who ware
very kinde to me walked from thence to
Shipstone stop'd with Cousins a little walked
from thence to Charingworth spent the
evening with Cousins their very agreeabley
Lodg'd their
4th walked to Campden to friends sixday [Friday]
meeting it was held at a friends House
one friend Jefry Beavington being blind
could not very well walk to the meeting
House Devine Goodness was felt to flow
amoungst us it appeared to be my duty to
speak theirin after meeting spent a little
time with friends took leave of them walked
from thence to Charingworth Lodg'd at Cousins
5th spent a little time with Cousins in a solid
manner took my kinde leave of them walked
from thence Home ware I found my friends
Tolerable well I was favoured with a comfortable
Journey for which and all other mercies I remain

Page 165

Truly Thankfull to Kind Providence
6th was at our first day [Sunday] meeting it felt
to
my minde to be a good meeting as Truth
manifested it to be my duty to speak a
few words theirin so I spake them the
Preparative meeting was gone
through in much Love the Quarterly
meeting queries ware Answered
10th was at our fifth day [Thursday] meeting it
felt
very comforting and refreshing to my minde
it felt to be my duty to speak theirin
13 was at our first day [Sunday] meeting it felt
very comforting and refreshing to my
minde it appeared to be my duty to speak theirin
14, walked to our Monthly Meeting at Burford
it felt to my minde to be a good Meeting
two friends appeared in Testimonie, the Buisness
was gone through in much Love after meeting
spent a little time with friends then took
leave of 'em and walked Home
17th was at our fifth day [Thursday] meeting
spake
a few words theirin
18 took a walk to Friends meeting at C.[hipping]
Norton as I sat theirin with a few friends my
minde was much comforted and refreshed

26 Earliest recorded reference of meeting 1668

verso

12mo [December] 20 took a walk to Our Quarterly
Meeting held at Oxford it was large of
friends and Neighbours and felt comfortable
to my minde sevral Mouths ware opened
to testify of the Lords great love unto
His children the meeting in the A.N. [afternoon]
was very large and crowded and disturbed
by some behaving in a very unbecoming
manner yet I felt the Lords power to
be over the meeting and menny friends
appeared in Testimonie to His Honnour
and Glory after meeting spent a little
time comfortabley with some friends
Lodg'd at Fr'd Horneymans
21st before meeting spent a little time
at Fr'd Jacksons's, the Meeting for buisness
began at nine in the morning it felt very
comfortable to my minde the Almighty
in His great Love was pleased to own us
with His living Power to our Spiritual
refreshment and comfort sevral both
Men and Women beared Testimonies to the
honnour of His great name the buisness
was gone through in much Love a Womens
Quarterly meeting was setteled their as also a
select meeting of Ministers and Elders after meeting

Page 166

23 took a walk to friends fourth day [Wednesday]
meeting at witney it was small yet
I felt Devine goodness to be near to the
comfort of the sincear Hearted friends
I spake a few words theirin after meeting
walked Home
24 was at our fifth day [Thursday] meeting it felt very
comfortable to my minde spake a few words theirin
27 was at our first day [Sunday] meeting it felt
very comfortable and refreshing to my
minde, spake a few words theirin
31, was at our fifth day [Thursday] meeting as
I sat theirin my minde was comforted
and refreshed spake a few words theirin

1796

1st mo: [January] 3rd believeing it to be my duty to
take a walk to stow meeting acquainted
my Parents with the feelings of my minde
the meeting was small yet as I sat the=
=irin I felt Devine Love to flow amoungst us
to our Spiritual refreshment and comfort
and I felt it to be my duty to speak a
few words and also to pray theirin, found
true peace by so doing, after meeting took leave
of Friends then walked Home

verso

1796 1st mo: [January]
7th took a walk to Burford was at friends
fifth day [Thursday] meeting, as I sat theirin
my minde was comforted and refreshed
being made sensible that Devine Love
was felt amoungst us to our Spiritual
comfort and refreshment, after meeting
took leave of Bror. and Sist'r then walked Home
10th was at our first day [Sunday] meeting it
felt to my minde to be a good comfortable
meeting, spake a few words theirin
11th took a walk to our monthly meeting
at C.[hipping] Norton it appeared to my minde to be a good comfortable meeting sevral Friends appeared
in testimonie and one young friend in Solem prayer
the Meeting of buisness held longish yet
it was gone through in much Love
after meeting went to se some friends took
leave of them and walked Home with some
friends
14 was at our fifth day [Thursday] meeting it felt to
my minde to be a profitable meeting spake
a few words theirin
on the 17th took a walk to a first days [Sunday] meeting
at Milton in sitting theirin my minde
was refreshed and Comforted being made
sensible that the visitation of Devine Love

Page 167

was extended unto us, spake theirin as
truth manifested unto me to be my duty so to do
21st was at our fifth day [Thursday] meeting,
spake a few words theirin
24 was at our first day [Sunday] meeting it was
comfortable to my minde spak a few words
theirin
28 was at our fifth day [Thursday] meeting it felt
comfortable and refreshing to my minde
31, took a walk to friends preparative meeting
at South
newington in sitting theirin I felt Devine
Love to flow amoungst us to our Spi=
=ritual comfort and refreshment, spake
a few words theirin and afterwards
my mouth was opened to speak a few
words in very solem prayer, after
meeting spent a little time with friends
walked from thence to Bloxham Aunt
Midwinter and the rest of our relations
their she was very poorly walked from
thence to Banbury spent the evening
with friends in a Solid comfortable
manner, Lodg'd at Fr'd Stones
2nd mo: [February] 1st went to se our Relations
and

verso

some friends was at friends monthly
meeting their the power of truth felt
to me to be low theirin yet according to
the feelings of my minde it reign'd, spake
a few words theirin the buisness was
gone through in Love after meeting
refresh'd myself at Rich'd Sconchs
took leave of fr'ds, walked with some
friends from thence to little Sibford spent
the evening with some friends in a solid
comfortable manner found the widow Harris
very poorly Lodg'd at Josh Lambs
2nd was at their third day meeting [Tuesday]
before
meeting went to se sevral friends at little
and Broad Sibford the meeting felt
comfortable to my minde I felt the Devine
Power to flow amoungst us which refreshed
the Hearts of the contrited ones, after
meeting took my leave of friends walked
from thence home ware I arrived about
six very well and found my friends as
well as i could expect for which blessings
I am very thankfull unto Kinde Providence
5 was at our fifth day [Thursday] meeting spake
a few words theirin one young Woman

Page 168

appeared in Meeting M, A, which
afforded me great comfort
6th took a walk to friends six day [Friday]
meeting
at C.[hipping] Norton it felt refreshing and
comfortable to my minde, spake theirin
after spent a little time with friends
bid them farewell then walked Home
7th was at our first day [Sunday] meeting it felt
comfortable to my minde, the preparative
meeting was gone through in Love
8th was at our monthly meeting held at this
Place it felt very comforting and refreshing
to my minde sevral living Testimonies ware
born to reminde friends to be diligent in
sarving the Lord, the buisness was gone
through in much Love
10 took a walk to friends fourth day [Wednesday]
meeting
at witney in sitting theirin my minde was
comforted feeling devine Love to flow
amoungst us to our spiritual refre=
shment speak a few words theirin
after meeting spent a little time comfortabley
with friends reach'd Home in good time
11th was at our fifth day [Thursday] meeting it
felt comfortable to my minde

verso

2mo [February]
spake a few words theirin
14th was at our first day [Sunday] meeting it
felt very comforting and refreshing to
my minde, spake a few words theirin
18 was at our fifth day [Thursday] meeting it felt
to my minde to be a good comfortable meeting
spake a few words theirin, ware favoured
with the Company of Fr'd Barritt
20 feeling drawings in my minde by the

spirit of Truth to take a walk
to faringdon meeting on the 21 acquainted
my Parents with the feelings of my minde
walked to witney in the evening found friends
their tolerable well Lodg'd at fr'd Hankins
21st walked with Fr'd Hankins to faringdon
meeting it was small Truth appeared
not to increase much theirin yet my minde
was comforted feeling Devine goodness to
be present amoungst us, spake theirin
after meeting call'd to se some friends
walked from thence to witney had a comfortable
walk with my kinde fr'd Hankins, walked
from Witney Home found my Father
very poorly he having been very poorly
for sometime so poorly as to keep his bed

Page 169

25th was at our fifth day [Thursday] meeting my
minde was refreshed theirin, spake theirin
27 feeling drawings in my minde by the
spirit of truth to take a walk to the
preparative meeting at Brails acquainted
my Parents with the feelings of my minde
walked to Brails in the A.N. [afternoon] spent
the evening with Cousins very comfortabley
Lodg'd at Cousin Gilletts
28 went to se some friends before meeting
the meeting felt very comfortable to my
minde Devine Goodness was felt amoungst us
to our comfort I was constrained by the
Power of Truth to appear in testimonie
and also in solem Prayer after meeting
took leave of Cousins then walked Home very
comfortabley
3mo [March] 3rd was at our fifth day [Thursday]
meeting, my
minde was refreshed theirin , spak theirin
6, was at our first day [Sunday] meeting my
minde was
comforted and refreshed theirin spake
a few word theirin
10 was at our fifth day [Thursday] meeting my
minde was refreshed theirin spake theirin
13 was at our first day [Sunday] meeting it felt

verso

---

comfortable and refreshing to my minde
spake theirin
14, took a walk to our monthly meeting
holden at witney it did not feel so refreshing
as some meetings have felt, yet truth ap=
=peared to reign theirin, the buisness was
gone through in much Love after meeting
went to se some friends then walked Home
17 was at our fifth day [Thursday] meeting it felt
very comforting and refreshing to my minde
20 took a walk to Milton to meeting
it was small truth appeared to be
low theirin yet I felt Devine Love to
flow amoungst us as truth manifested
it to be my duty to speak and Pray
theirin I was obidient theirunto found
Peace of minde by so doing after meeting
took leave of friends and walked Home
24 was at our fifth day [Thursday] meeting as I
sat theirin my minde was renewedly
refreshed with the Incomes of Devine Love
25 took a walk to C.[hipping] Norton to meeting
it was smallish yet it felt comfortable
and refreshing to my minde after meeting walked
Home
27th took a walk to Barton meeting it was
tolerable
large of Friends and Neighbours and I think a

Page 170

---

good comfortable meeting in which wee ware
favoured with Devine refreshment to our
Spiritual
strength sevral mouths ware opened to turn the
Peoples mindes inward unto their spiritual
teacher
it appeared to be my duty to pray in a few words
found true Peace by so doing after meeting
walked Home
Dear Father having been greatly Afflicted
for about 10 weeks past with a breaking out
which scab'd over his armes and body and
a Coughfing and spitting, this evening about
sevven oclock Departed this Life in a comfortable
manner being bolstered up in his Bed he spake
in a very comfortable manner about an hour
before he Died
to our family and sevral friends who ware
present in the Room, to this purpose, it would
be well for People to prise their time wile the

Almighty was pleased to favour them with Health
and strength by sarving Him in being obidient
unto His heavenly requireings and Indeavouring
to do their days work in the day time for he
found by expierence their was enoughf to do in
time
of sickness to bear the pains of the body and he
did not know he shoud be favoured with the like
oppertunity to spake his mind unto us, he
appeared
in a very comfortable frame of minde for
sometime
before he died sevral times signifying he had no

verso

desire to live but desired rather to leave this
world
if it ware the will of Devine Providence to re=
=move him but was contented to wait his good
and appointed time as it hath pleased the Lord
to remove him out of this troublesome World tho
the loss is dear Mothers who is left in a very
weakly
situation of body and ours his Children yet I have
a sence given me it is his Eternal Gain
Brother and Sistor Sessions on fifth
day [Thursday] morning last had their younest
son
removed by death after about half a years
Illness with fitts he went off very quietly
on the sevventh day [Saturday] following it
pleased
the Lord to remove their next younest son
by Death yet their is not the least doubt
but that they are called in a state of In=
=nosciency by Jesus Christ to Injoy ever=
=lasting rest the Almighty of late hath
seen meet in His Infinite wisdom
to try our Family with great and
bitter afflictions O! may we Indeavour to
bear then quite patiently and suffer them
to have a good effect on us so as to humble
us and bring us into much deep humility
of minde as to be content to suffer any thing

Page 171

and to be willing to be any thing Just what
the Lord would have us to be so that wee may
be favoured with His dear Love
28th spent this morning at wrighting letters
to our Relations
31st this day wee having appointed to Bury
Dear Father & Sistors & Brothers two Children
accordingly
the Corp's ware carried to meeting in a very
solem manner Father first and the two
Children after it was a large meeting of
Friends and Neighbours, sevral Pub.[lic] Friends
ware present, sevral mouths ware opened
to set forth the Awefullness of the sene
before them and to put the People in
minde to be obidient unto the spirit
of truth within them that the might
be inabled to live lives of holiness for
without Holiness none could se the Lord
I felt it also to be my duty to bear a
Testimonie theirin to put the People in
minde to prepare for their latter end
young and old as the prospect before
them set forth that the Lord was pleased to send
the messenger of Death to young as
well as old altho it was very trying to me

verso

on account of my Dear relations death
yet the Lords power was with
me and Inabled me to Discharge
wat I believed He required of me
faithfully and with a willing minde
the three Corps ware decently
Interd afterwards we ware favoured
with most of the Friends comp=
=any at our House, ware our Rela=
tions and friends had a comfortable sitting to=
=gether and friend Mintchon beared testimonie
that she had a sense that the Deceased
ware gone to Injon Everlasting Happi=
=ness our mindes ware comforted toge=
=ther under a sence that Devine Love was
felt amoungst us and altho our loss doth
appear very great my soul doth say
in Humility the Lord giveth and the Lord
taketh away for ever blessed be His Name
4mo [April] 3rd was at our first day [Sunday]
meeting it felt
to my minde to be a good meeting it appeared
to be my duty to bear a Short Testimonie

theirin, our Preparative meeting buisness
was gone through in much Love the Quarterly
meeting queries ware answered pretty near to
what the queries required

Page 172

4th took a walk to our Monthly meeting
held at burford with Brother it was largish
and felt very comfortable to my minde one
stranger there Ann Baker from Burmingham
P.[ublic] friend she appears to be a sincear honnourable
young Woman the buisness held not very
long, it was gone through in much love
after meeting spent a little time with Bro.r
and Sistor then walked Home
7th was at our fifth day [Thursday] meeting my minde
was comforted feeling Devine Love to be amoungst us
10th took a walk to a meeting appointed
to be held at Oxford [illegible] the quarterly meeting
Chiefly on friends account that live
their it was not very large of friends
but menny neighbours came in and behaved verry
well and appeared well satisfied with
what was delivered, it felt to my minde
to be a good satisfactory meeting after
meeting went to see some friends walked
from thence with sevral friends to witney
spent the evening with friends in a solid
agreeable manner, ann Elderly woman friend
a Minister gave me some very tender advice
concearning my appearing in the Ministery

verso

Lodg'd at friend Hankins
11th the morning I think was large and felt to
my minde to be a good Meeting in which
Devine Goodness was pleased to feed the
sincear in Heart with heavenly refreshment
sevral living Testimonies ware born
the A.[fter] Noon meeting was appointed at three
it was a large crowded meeting menny
neighbours being Present sevral testimonies
ware born to incourage the People to
minde the day of the Lords tender visitation
unto their Souls the meeting was concluded
in Solem Prayer the Neighbours appeared
well satisfied and I think it was a day
in which the Lord was pleased tenderly
to visit menny minde with His love
after meeting walked Home with some friends
12th took a walk with to our quarterly
meeting at witney it was largish and it
felt Pretty comfortable tho not so comfortable
as some meetings I have been at the queries
ware answered yet not to so good satisfaction
as menny could wish to my sorrow one meeting
house was order to be sold and Elder
David Bacon was present from America

Page 173

whose company was very axceptable
he traveling with a Certivacate
after meeting walked Home with sevral friends
14 was at our fifth day [Thursday] meeting altho it was
held in Silence it felt to my minde to be a good meeting
17 was at our first day [Sunday] meeting as I sat
theirin my minde was refreshed being
sensible Devine Love was felt amoungst us
spake a few words theirin
21 was at our fifth day [Thursday] meeting my minde
was refreshed one stranger young woman Pub.[lic]
friend she had a few words to speak to
Incourage friends to indeavour to lay up
treasure in Heaven
24, took a walk to friends meeting at Stow it
was small yet I felt Devine Love
to flow amoungst us to our Spiritual
comfort and refreshment ware favoured
at meeting with the company of Thos.
Huntley who was drawn forth in solem Prayer
after meeting call'd to see some acquaintance
and friends, also cousins at Kingham re=
=ached Home in good time

verso

4mo [April] 1796

28th was at our fifth day [Thursday] meeting it
felt comforting and refreshing to my minde
5mo [May] 1st took a walk to friends meeting at
Hooknorton it felt tolerable comforting
and refreshing to my minde beared a Tes=
=timonie theirin, their preparative meeting
buisness was gone through in Love after
meeting took leave of friends and walked
to sibford to the A.N. [afternoon] meeting it felt
comforting and refreshing to my minde
after meeting called to se some friends
spent a little time with them in a
very loving manner walked from
thence to Epwell to se our Relations
who ware very well Lodg'd at uncle Gibbs
2nd walked with uncle Gibbs to shutford
to the Monthly meeting their it was
largish and felt pretty comfortable to my minde
sevral Friends appeared in Testimonie
the buisness was gone through in much
Love friend Hannah Jarrot came into
the mens meeting and informed them

Page 174

that she had performed the visit
which she had laid before them sometime ago
and they signified their unity, and she
felt a degree of True peace to attend
Her minde after meeting called to see
some relations then walked Home
5, was at our fifth day [Thursday] meeting it was
small yet my minde was comforted and
refreshed theirin
7, feeling a desire raised in my minde
by the Spirit of Truth to take a walk
to Armscutt [Armscote] Meeting walked to Ships=
=tone found Cousin M Wells very poorly
and their young Child Dead, Lodg'd
at Tho's Hodgkins's
8, was at the morning meeting at Shipstone
it felt pretty comfortable to my minde
walked from thence to Armscutt [Armscote] Meeting
it was large of Friends and Neighbours
sevral living testimonies ware born which
appeared to have a good effect upon the
people returned back to Shipstone to
the burial of Cousin Wells's Child it was
a large satisfactory meeting spent the

verso

---

evening with Cousins in a verry loving
manner Lodg'd at Cousin Wells's
9, walked from Shipstone to C,[hipping] Norton
to our Monthly Meeting it felt very
comfortable and refreshing to my minde
menny living Testimonies ware born
by young friends the buisness was gone
through in much love after meeting
walked Home ware I found my friends
Tolerable well which caused my minde
to be bowed in humble thankfullness be=
=fore the Lord
12 was at our fifth day [Thursday] meeting in it my
minde was trully resign'd unto the Devine Will
15, was at our first day [Sunday] meeting it felt
comforting and refreshing to my minde
feeling Devine goodness to be amoungst us
after meeting took a walk to the evening
meeting at Burford it felt to my minde to be
a good satisfactory meeting my mouth was opened
to Incourage the Children to sarve the Lord in
their youth that He might be with them in the
time of tryals and Afflictions spent the evening
at Brothers comfortably Lodg'd their
16 took leave of my relations and walked Home
19, was at our fifth day [Thursday] meeting altho I have

Page 175

been very low and poor in my minde for sometime
yet my soul was comforted feeling Devine
Love to be amoungst us
22 was at our first day [Sunday] meeting as
I sat theirin I felt Devine Love to flow
amoungst us

25 took a walk to milton meeting in Sitting theirin
my minde was pained to see friends come in
so long after the time appointed & so few
yet after=ward I felt devine Love to flow
amoungst us, after meeting walked Home
29, took a walk to Witney to meeting
it felt to my minde to be a satis
=factory meeting, after meeting
went to Jno Hankins's to visit
Thos. Horneyman Wm Wood
& George Titterton of Oxfor
two of them having apply'd
to friends to be rec'd into mem=
=bership I was under appoin=
=tment with some more friends
wee ware owned in our visit
with Devine love, it felt

verso

[page left blank]

Page 176

[page left blank]

verso

to be a Satisfactory visit
after meeting bid friends fare=
=well and walked home
6mo [June] 2nd was at our fifth day [Thursday] meeting
it felt comforting and refreshing
to my minde
5th was at our first day [Sunday] meeting my
minde was comforted and refreshed
with Devine Goodness, spake theirin
9th was at our fifth day [Thursday] meeting my
minde was comforted and refreshed
feeling Devine Love to be present amoungst us
12, was at our first day [Sunday] meeting
it felt to my minde to be a good
refreshing meeting, spake theirin
our preparative meeting buisness
was gone through in love, the Quar=
=terly meeting queries ware answered
to good satisfaction
13. was at our monthly Meeting holden
at this place my minde was rather
uneasy on account of the meeting of

Page 177

Worship being broken up soonder
than it usualy is, the buisness was
gone through in Love it felt very
satisfactory to my minde, three young
men friends of Oxford ware received
into membership
16 was at our firth day [Thursday] meeting it
felt comforting and refreshing to my minde
18 feeling a little drawings in my minde
to walk to friends meeting at Faringdon
walked to witney in the evening Lodg'd
at fr'd Hankins's
19 after breackfasting at fr'd Hankins's
walked to Faringdon found friends
tolerable well, the meeting was not
very large yet it felt to my minde to be
a good meeting, it appeared to be my duty
to advise friends to take up the cross and
part with every thing that hindered them
from Injoying Devine Love after meeting
took leave of friends, walked to Witney

verso

spent the evening with friends their comfortabley
Lodg'd at fr'd Hankins
19 walked Home to breackfast
21, was at our fifth day [Thursday] meeting as I
sat theirin I was greatly sensible of my
own weakness's and the great need their
was for me to be very watchfull and wait
for Devine assistance to Inable me to
please the Almighty
26, took a walk with sistor and some more
friends to Barton meeting it was large
of Friends and neighbours and it felt
to my minde to be a good satisfactory
meeting in which Devine Goodness was
pleased to hand forth Heavenly re=
=freshment unto the souls of meny
present and to renew the tender
visitation of His Love unto them
after meeting walked with some
friends for Milton found Thos Harris
of Milton very low and Poorly Lodg'd
at Fr'd pains

27, took leave of friends at Milton
walked with some friends to Banbury

Page 178

the meeting began at nine my minde was
very low theirin yet menny appeared to
be comforted with Devine Love, menny
living testimonies ware born, sevral stra=
=ngers P.[ublic] Friends being their
the A.N. [afternoon] meeting was very large
of Friends and Neighbours, it felt
to my minde to be a good satisfactory
meeting in which the Lords Power pre=
=vailed to the opening menny mouths
to bear testimonie for His everlasting
Truth after meeting walked with a
friend to Fr'd Atkins of Northnewington
spent the Evening with them very
friendly Lodg'd their
28, walked with some friends to the
Quarterly meeting the men and women had a
sitting together before the enter'd uppon buisness
my minde was much comforted and refreshed
one friend
was drawn forth in very solem Prayer
and sevral in testimonie accompany'd
with Heavenly Power to the causing the
sincear in Heart to rejoice the buisness

verso

was gone through in Love some
meetings appeared to wand assistance
after meeting went to se Ric'd Sconce
who was Poorly took leave of Fr'ds
walked with Sist'r and some more
friends Home
30 was at our fifth day [Thursday] meeting my
minde was very low theirin under
a sense of my own weakness's and
the great need I stood in of Devine Assistance
7mo [July] 3rd feeling a little drawings
in my minde to take a walk to a
few meetings walked to stow to
meeting it was small yet I felt
Devine Goodness to be felt amoun=
=gst us, it appeared to be my duty
to Incourage Friends to be diligent
to attend all their religious mee=
=tings call'd to see some relations
walked from thence to Fr'd Heydons
she was very Friendly unto me
walked from thence to C.[hipping] norton found
Friends their mostly tolerable well

Page 179

Lodg'd at Cousin Fardons
4, took leave of Friends & walked
to Hooknorton to the Monthly meeting
my minde was very low theirin
the Life of Truth appeared to be
very low theirin speak a few words
theirin as truth manifested it to be
my duty so to do the buisness was
gone through in Love after meeting
took leave of friends and walked
to little sibford to se some friends
one being very poorly & from
thence to Broad Sibford to se some
friends and Aunt Minty, and from
thence to Brails to se Cousins
Lodg'd at Cousin Wm Gilletts
5 walked from thence to shipstone to se
Cousin M Wells and family she was
very poorly yet in a Comfortable
chearfull situation of minde walked
from thence to Charingworth found

verso

Cousins there very=well walked
from thence to Campden to the Monthly
meeting it was not very large yet
it felt very comfortable to my minde
sevral Testimonies ware born to Incourage
friends to minde and be obidient unto the
Heavenly teacher within them the
buisness was gone through in Love
after meeting walked to Charingworth
spent the Evening with Cousins Lovingly
Lodg'd at Cousin Wm Corks
6 after breackfasting with Cousins
took leave of them walked to Ship=
=stone to meeting it felt to my minde
to be a very comfortable meeting as
Truth manifested it to be my duty to
spake a few words theirin I spake
them, found true peace to flow in

my minde by so doing after meeting
spent a little time with Cousin
Wells's very comfortabley, I have a little
hopes she is a rather better she

Page 180

appeared Chearfull and in a sweet
disposition of minde took my farewell of Cousins and friends and set
out for Home call'd at C[hipping] Norton
spent a little time with friends very
friendly reach'd Home safe and well
found my friends tolerable well for
which mercies and blessings and all
others I remain truly thankfull unto
Devine Providence
7th was at our fifth day [Thursday] meeting as I
sat theirin my minde did rejoice feeling
Devine Love to flow amoungst us
10 was at our first day [Sunday] meeting at
which sevral strangers ware pre=
=sent, it felt refreshing and comforting
to my minde afterward walked to
witney spent the evening with friends
very comfortabley Lodg'd at Fr'd Hankins
11th walked with sevral Friends to
our Monthly meeting at Faringdon
sevral Neighbours came in, it felt

verso

to my minde to be a good satisfactory
meeting one Friend was led to speak in a
Perticular manner concearning the
vow made by those not of our society
at the Sprinkling of Infants, the
buisness was gone through in Love
took leave of Friends, walked with some
friends to Bampton & from thence with
Bror. to Burford found Bro'r & Sistor
Tolerable well Lodg'd their
12th took leave of Broth'r & Sistor walked Home
14, was at our fifth day [Thursday] meeting my
minde was very poor and low theirin
17, was at our first day [Sunday] meeting it felt
comfortable to my minde wee ware
favoured with the company of two
strangers, Mary Loyd & Shusanna Appelby
the meeting was held in Silence
Except I spake a few words as truth
manifested unto me to be m duty to do so
20, took a walk to friends fourth day meeting
at witney it was smallish yet I felt

Page 181

Devine Love to flow amoungst us, spake
a few words theirin as truth manifested it
to be my duty so to do
21 was at our fifth day [Thursday] meeting it felt
comforting and refreshing to my minde
24 was at our first day [Sunday] meeting it felt
comfortable to my minde spake a few
words theirin as truth Manifested it to be my
duty
26 feeling drawings in my minde
by the love of the truth to take a
walk to a few meetings call'd week
day meetings acquainted my friends
with the feelings of my minde, walked
to Southnewington to meeting it was
Small yet I felt Devine Love to
flow amoungst us to our Spiritual
comfort and refreshment after meeting
walked to milton to se Tho's Harris
who appeared to be poorly in His
minde and Body so that He keeps
very much at Home call'd to se friends

verso

at Milton walked from thence to
Adderbury spent the evening with
friends in a loving manner Lodg'd
at Tho's Whichleys
27 went to se sevral friends before
meeting it felt to my minde to be a
good refreshing meeting, it appeared
to be my duty to advise friends to be
very diligent to attend to the teachings
of the truth within them and be
wholy obidient unto it after Din'r
took leave of Friends and walked
to Netrup [Neithrop] to se Ric'd Sconce who
is very poorly with a Coughf ap=
=pears to be rather like a person
in a Decline yet quite given up
unto the will of Devine Providence
Live or Die spent the evening with

him very comfortabley Lodg'd their
28 walked from Ric'd Sconces to little
sibford refreshed my self at Jo's Lambs

Page 182

walked from thence to Hooknorton to
meeting call'd to se friends before
meeting the meeting was smallish yet
it felt to my minde to be a comfortable
meeting it appeared to be my duty to
advise friends to be diligent to attend meetings
after Dining at Wm Mintchins walked
to little Sibford call'd to se sevral friends
walked from thence to Epwell to se our
Relations Lodg'd at Uncle Gibbs
29 took leave of our Relations, walked
to Broad Sibford call'd to se sevral
friends before meeting, it was a large
meeting of Friends and Neighbours it
being the funeral of Tho's Harris, it felt
to my minde to be a good profitable meeting
in which Devine Goodness was Pleased to
Extend His gracious Visitation unto the Souls of
menny present, and through his Servants
call them to Repent of their sins and amend
their Lives, after Din'r took leave of friends

verso

walked to C.[hipping] Norton call'd to se sevral friends and Ann Stait she was very poorly
saw Aunt Edwin their, was much pleased
to se she, she being formerly a very a
greeable Intamate Relation of our family,
walked from thence Home ware I found my
friends tolerable well for which and all
other blessing I remain truly thankfull
to Kinde Providence
31 was at our first day [Sunday] meeting it felt to my
minde to be a Satisfactory meeting, feeling
Devine Love to flow amoungst us to the
refreshing of our Spirits
8mo [August] 4th was at our fifth day [Thursday] meeting it
felt to my minde Profitable and Instructing
I feeling Drawings in my minde to take a
walk to Armscutt [Armscote] meeting acquainted my friends
with the feelings of my minde walked to Brails
in the A.N. [afternoon] spent the evening with Cousins very
comfortabley Lodg'd at Cousin Gilletts
7th walked from thence to the morning meeting
at Shipstone it felt to my minde to be a comfortable
meeting found Cousin M. wells very poorly walked

Page 183

from thence with Friends to the meeting at Armscutt [Armscote]
it was very large of Friends and Neighbours
it felt to my minde to be a good profitable
meeting unto menny in which Devine Goodness
was pleased to renew His gracious visitation
of Love unto the souls of menny present sevral
mouths ware opened in testimonie to speak unto
the states of the People and the meeting was concluded
with Solem Prayer, after meeting walked to shipstone
spent some time their with cousins and friends
very comfortabley took leave of them then walked
from thence to C[hipping] Norton Lodg'd at Cousin Jona'an
Fardons, was taken very poorly with a sickness in the Night
8th through mercy in the morning I found
myself so well recover'd as to set out for
our monthly Meeting at Burford reach'd
their ab't meeting time went to meeting
but was so poorly could not set meeting
of Business continued very poorly near
all day Bro.r & Sistor waited upon me very kindly
9th was favoured with a good nights rest

verso

and so finely recover'd by morning as to
undertake to walk Home with Sistor
and some friends performed the Journey
very=well for which mercy and blessing
and menny more I do plentyfully Injoy
I rem'n truly thankfull to Kinde Providence
11. was at our fifth day [Thursday] meeting in Sitting

in Silence my minde Injoy'd sweet peace
14 was at our first day [Sunday] meeting as I
sat theirin my minde was greatly com=
=forted and refreshed we ware favoured
with the company of three Publick
friends viz Tho's Harris Joseph Lamb
& Sarah Lambly two of them spoke I
think very plain unto the states of Friends
signifying their was great nescessiety for
them to Labour to keep the vineyard of
their own Hearts clean and wholy to destroy
all that was displeasing unto the Almighty
and bring forth good fruits least He should
se meet to take away the fence from His vineyard
the friends ware upon a religious Visit to friends
Families and in the evening Paid us a Visit

Page 184

after sitting sometime in Solid Silence
each of them ware led to spake to
the states and conditions of our mindes
as plain as if the had received out=
=ward Information which is a true token
that they are the Children of the
Lord and that He did send them
and qualified them to speak in a
Profitable manner to the states and
condition of the people in a spiritual sence
18 was at our fifth day [Thursday] meeting it felt
comfortable and refreshing to my minde
21 was at our first day [Sunday] meeting as I sat
theirin I was greatly sensible of my own
weakness's but as I indeavoured to retire
to the pure witness of Truth within my
minde I received strength in a good degree
to overcome them
25 was at our fifth day [Thursday] meeting it felt
comfortable unto my minde
27 feeling a desire in my minde in the

verso

Love of the truth to take a walk to Brails
Meeting walked thither in the A.N. [afternoon] found
Cousins tolerable well spent the Evening
with them comfortabley Lodg'd at Cousin Gilletts
28 was at the meeting, it felt comfortable
to my minde it appeared to be my duty to
recomend to friends to be very diligent to
wait upon the Lord that they might witness
their Spiritual strength to be renewed
after meeting bid Cousins Farewell
then walked Home
9mo [September] 1st was at our fifth day [Thursday] meeting it
appeared to be a comfortable meeting it
felt to my minde to be my duty to sit in Silence
4th was at our first day [Sunday] meeting at it
sevral straingers ware present it felt
to my minde to be a good satisfactory
meeting it appeared to be my duty to
speak a few words theirin the preparative
meeting buisness was gone through in
much Love the queries ware answered
to the satisfaction of Friends

Page 185

8th was at our fifth day [Thursday] meeting it
felt to my minde to be a good Satisfa=
=ctory meeting ware favoured with
the Company of old Fr'd Barrit
11 was at our first day [Sunday] meeting it felt
comfortable to my minde it appeared to
be my duty to recomend to friends to be
weighty in their Spirits that they might
be taught by the spirit of Truth
12, walked with sevral friends to our monthly
meeting at C[hipping] Norton it was largish
it felt to my minde to be a good
satisfactory meeting it felt to my
minde to be my duty to sit in Silence
sevral appeared in public testimonie
accompanied with the Power of Truth
the buisness was gone through in
much Love after spent sometime
with friends comfortabley walked
home with sevral friends
15th was at our fifth day [Thursday] meeting it felt
comforting and refreshing to my minde
17, took a walk in the evening to witney Lodg'd at

verso

1796

Fr'd Hankins's
9mo [September] 18th walked with sevral friends to Oxford
meeting it was large of Friends and Neighbours
it felt to my minde to be a good edifying
meeting sevral Living testimonies ware born
theirin went to friend Jacksons's to refresh
my self walked from thence with sevral friends
to streetly call'd at Cousin Ashbys shillingford
they entertained us kindly Lodg'd at Streetly
19th walked from streetly to reading found
cousins their tolerable well considering the
Loss they have lately had of a Son who
died in a Decline about 21 years of age
in the morning meeting Truth appeared
to be very low one friend appeared in
solem Prayer after meeting went to see
some friends they ware very loving
the meeting in the A.N. [afternoon] felt to my minde
to be a Laborious meeting it was mostly
Held in Silence after meeting went to se
some friends spent the evening with them
in a Solid affectionate manner Lodg'd
at Fr'd Gilberts
20th the meeting began at Nine the men and
Women had a sitting together before the entered

Page 186

upon buisness an american friend was drawn
forth in testimonie very perticularly setting
forth menny tryals and exercises the righteous
meet with and Incouraging friends to love
the Lord and one another the buisness was
gone through in much love the American
friend was led to speak by way of testimonie
in a perticular manner against paying
tythe after meeting took leave of friends
then walked with Wm Mattocks to Henley
spent the evening with friends very
comfortabley Lodg'd at Joseph Mays
21 before meeting went to se some friends
the meeting was smallish yet I felt Devine
Love to flow amoungst us Frd. Barrit was
led to advise friends to Indeavour to part with
every thing which the truth manifested to
them was displeasing unto the Almighty
it appeared to be my duty to speak theirin
after meeting bid friends farewell, rode
with my Companion in a return'd Shaise to Benson
walked from thence to Shillingford to Cousin
jo's Ashbys met sevral friends who ware upon
a visit to friends families, walked to warborough

verso

---

was entertained kindly at Fr'd Sargoods Lodg'd their
22 before meeting went to se the friends
the meeting was smallish yet I felt Devine
Love to flow amoungst us to our great comfort
and Spiritual refreshment sevral living
Testimonies ware born theirin after meeting
spent a little time with friends very comfortabley
walked from thence to Oxford was entertained
kindly at Fr'd Jacksons's walked with Wm
Mattocks to witney Lodg'd at Jn'o Hankins's
23 called to se a few friends, walked Home
ware I found Mother and rest tolerable well
and I was Inabled to perform the Journey
comfortabley for which and all other mercies
my Soul is bow'd in humble thankfullness
before the Lord
25 was at our first day [Sunday] meeting as I sat
theirin my minde was greatly sensible of my
own weakness and that without Devine assistance
I could do no good thing Spake a few words
theirin as the Devine Power manifested it to
be my duty so to do
29, was at our fifth day [Thursday] meeting it
felt comfortable to my minde, spake a

Page 187

few words theirin
30th took a walk to Sibford, having
felt true Love to flow in my heart to=
=wards Sarah Gilks in hopes She may
become an help=meat unto me if the
Lord is pleased by His Devine power
to open a way for it, went to Sarah's
Parents asked their Consent truth felt

to my minde to be low in the meeting yet
i felt Devine Love to be present amoungst
us, spake a few words theirin after meeting
call'd to se some friends their company
was very comforting, walked from thence
to Epwell found our relations their tolerable
well Lodg'd at Uncle Gibbs's
10mo [October] 1st spent a little time with Uncle Gibbs
very comfortabley walked from thence Home
2nd took a walk to Stow meeting altho
it was small I felt the promise of
Blessed Jesus fullfilled unto us that ware
but two or three ware met together in
His Name their He would be in the midst
of them, spake a few words theirin call'd
to see some relations then walked to friend

verso

Hidens Oddington spent some time
with friends in a very comfortable
manner, walked from thence Home
6th was at our fifth day [Thursday] meeting
I felt Devine Goodness to be present
amoungst us to the refreshing the hearts
of the Humble contrite ones, spake theirin
9 was at our first day [Sunday] meeting it felt
comfortable to my minde it appeared to
be my duty to advise friends not to be
contented with a form of Religion with=
=out witnessing the Spirit of Christ
to dwell within them, the preparative
meeting buisness was gone through
in Love
13, was at our fifth day [Thursday] meeting it felt
comfortable to my minde, spake theirin
16, took a walk to a Preparative meeting
held at Milton sevral Neighbours came
in altho truth appeared to be low theirin
yet I think it appeared to be a good
satisfactory meeting sevral friends ap=
=peared in testimonie by which the peo=
=ple ware directed not to be contented with
the form of Religion without witness

Page 188

---

the Power within them, the buisness was gone
through in much Love, after meeting refre=
=shed myself at Friend Nortons took
leave of friends & walked Home
17 was at our Monthly meeting held at
Charlbury I think it was a good Satis=
=factory meeting we ware favoured with two
Straingers P.[ublic] friends Wm Crotch from Needham in Suffolk who
produced a Certivicate signifying friends
from whence he came had a good unity with
him as a Minister, the Womans Name Capen from Birmingham
Wm Crotch was led in testimonie to speak
to sevral States & conditions recomending
to friends to Indeavour to feel the Power
of Truth to arise in themselves and also
signified their ware some young friends
who if they ware faithfull unto the ma=
=nifestations of the Truth within them
would become valient for it, the buis=
=ness was gone through in much Love
19 took a walk to friends fourth day [Wednesday] meeting
at witney it felt to be a tolerable comfortable
meeting one friend appeared in solem prayer
called to see sevral friends spent some=
time with them very comfortabley and I Hope to

verso

---

the strengthening one anothers mindes in
the truth afterward walked Home
20th was at our fifth day [Thursday] meeting as I
sat theirin my minde was comforted, spake
a few words theirin
22nd took a walk to Sibford to Philip Gilks
to ask Philip and His Wifes consent to let
me come and See their Daughter Sarah
in order that she should become my Wife
if the Lord permit spent the evening
with them very comfortabley Lodg'd their
23 walked from Sibford to Shipstone
to Meeting it began at ten it did not
appear to be so comfortable a meeting
as some yet I felt the Lords power
to be near to some of us to our comfort
after meeting went to se cousin M Wells
she was very weak and poorly kept
Her bed yet appeared in a comfortable
frame of minde Devine Goodness was near
unto her I think to her great comfort and

to cause her spirit to rejoice the A.N. [afternoon] meeting felt pretty comfortable spake

Page 189

---

theirin after meeting went to cousin
Wells and refreshed my self, took my
solem farewell of Cousin M Wells
in a very affectionate manner nevver
expecting to se Her living any more
called to se friend Hodgkins she
was very poorly, walked to Cousin
Tho's Harriss's Long Compton spent
the evening their very comfortabley Lodg'd their
24 took leave of friends then walked Home
27 was at our fifth day [Thursday] meeting my
minde was low theirin yet my minde
was comforted yet it felt to be my duty
to sit Silent theirin
30 was at our first day [Sunday] meeting it felt
to m minde to be a good satisfactory
meeting in which Devine Goodness
was pleased to favour us with His Power
to our Spiritual comfort Fr'd S Squire
appeared in Solem Prayer it appeared
to be my duty to advise friends to be faith=
=full in little things that the Lord might com=
mit to their care greater

verso

1796

11mo [November] 3rd was at our fifth day
[Thursday] meeting
as I sat theirin my minde was refreshed
and comforted with Devine Goodness it
appeared to be my duty to sit in Silence
4th took a walk to the six day [Friday] meeting
at C[hipping] Norton it felt to my minde to
be a Satisfactory meeting spake a
few words theirin as truth manisted
unto me to be my duty so to do call'd
to se sevral friends they appeared
glad to se me done a little buisness
with some of them
5th took a walk to Witney spent the evening
with sevral Friends, heard that Jn'o Hankins
Wife was very poorly Lodg'd at Jn'o Hankins
6, walked to Faringdon alone Jn'o Hankins
proposed going with me sometime ago but his
Wife being so poorly he thought it was hard=
=ly prudent the meeting felt to be a good sa=
=tisfactory meeting, it appeared to be my duty
to recomend to friends to Indeavour to have
their mindes taken of Earthly things and
be more turned towards their Spiritual teacher
within them and be wholy Obidient unto it after
meeting spent sometime with friends very

Page 190

---

agreeabley took leave of them & walked to
witney a Convinced young man accompanying
me part of the way, spent the evening
comfortable with Cousins and friends
Lodg'd at Jn'o Hankins's
7th walked Home to breackfast
10, was at our fifth day [Thursday] meeting as I
sat theirin my Spirit rejoiced, feeling
Devine goodness to be amoungst us
12, took a walk to Sibford Call'd
to see Joseph Lambs Wife who was
in a comfortable frame of minde
and her leg which was broke about
12 weeks ago was so well that she could
walk about with assistance, spent
the evening at Philip Gilkes's very
comfortabley Lodg'd their
13, walked from thence to Brails
to Cousin Gilletts, Breackfasted
with them they ware very kinde
walked from thence to Cousin Jn'o
Wells's at Shipstone to the funeral
of his Wife she Died in a Decline

verso

Cousin Jn'o signified she was in a
comfortable frame of minde than
common a little before she died, sig=
=nified she should be relieved
out of her Affliction took her solem
farewell of them, shook hands with
him, desired her Love to her Child=
=ren, afterward went of comfortabley
it was a large comfortable meeting

according to the feelings of my minde of friends
and Neighbours it felt
to my minde to be a good Satisfactory
meeting, in which Devine Goodness
was pleased to extend the renewed
visitation of His tender Love unto
menny present, after meeting spent
sometime at Cousins with friends
very comfortable call'd to se friend
Jn'o Hodgkins's his Wife was very
poorly, took leave of Relations &
friends, waked from thence to C[hipping] Norton
Lodg'd at Cousin Jonathan Fardons
14, had a Comfortable walk with Wm Atkins
to Witney, our monthly meeting felt

Page 191

to be a good Satisfactory meeting
sevral short Testimonies ware born
be sevral young friends to the comfort
of the Meeting, the buisness was
gone through in much Love after
meeting spent sometime with
friends in a comfortable manner
walked from thence Home
15, feeling it to be a degree of duty
to attend the funeral of a Neighbour,
met with no molestation except having
my hat taken from me when I went
into the worship hous , it was gave
to me again when the people came
out, after their Worship was over at
the grave I felt it to be my duty
to speak a few words unto the people
in the fear of the Lord, felt true
Peace to fill my minde afterward
17, was at our fifth day [Thursday] meeting it ap=
=peared to be my duty to speak a few words theirin
20, was at our first day [Sunday] meeting it felt
refreshing to my minde it appeared

verso

to be my duty to recomend to friends
to Indeavour to live near to the Devine
Power that they might be able to with=
=stand and overcome every besetment
of the Enemy of our Souls hapiness
24 was at our fifth day [Thursday] meeting
as I sat theirin my minde was com=
=forted feeling Devine love to arise
amoungst us
27, was at our first day [Sunday] meeting it
felt to my minde to be a good comfortable
meeting, spak a few words theirin
12mo [December] 1st was at our fifth day [Thursday]
meeting sat in Silence theirin
3nd feeling a concearn in my minde to take
a walk to a few meetings, in the A.[fter]Noon walked
to milton, spent the evening with friends
their very comfortabley, Lodg'd at Fr'd pains
4th called to see tho's Harris who was poorly
walked from thence to adderbury before meeting
called to se some friends, the meeting appeared
to be a good satisfactory meeting it appeared
to be my duty to bear a Testimonie theirin

Page 192

the preparative meeting buisness was
gone through in Love, after meeting walked
with Cousin M. Witchley to Ayn[h]o, to se
Her Husband who appears rather disorder'd
in his Minde, found him rather better than
I expected had a little conversation
with Him, and his Understanding appear'd
tolerable good, in the Evening walked back again to
Adderbury Lodg'd at Tho's Witchleys
5th, walked with sevral friends to Ban=
=bury the monthly meeting felt to be a
good refreshing meeting after meeting
walked to little Sibford to see some
friends who appeared glad to se me
& from thence to broad Sibford to se
Philip Gilks who had been very Ill, found
him a little better, He signified he could
not perceive wether he might recover
or not yet he was quite given up unto
the Devine Will Live or die, Lodg'd their
6th stop'd their third day [Tuesday] meeting which felt
to be a very satisfactory meeting, took leave
of Fr'd Gilkes's leaving Philip in a very comfortable

verso

situation of minde, called to see some friends
at C.[hipping] norton in my way Home
8, was at our fifth day [Thursday] meeting as I sat
theirin my minde was comforted feeling
devine Love to flow amoungst us to our comfort
11, took a walk with Bror to the preparative
meeting at Milton it was small on account
of the coldness of the weather, yet I
felt the overshadowings of Devine
Love to flow amoungst us to our Spiritual
refreshment, it felt to my minde to be
my duty to Speak theirin, the buisness
was gone through in much Love, after
meeting walked to Burford, found Bror
H[enry] & the youngest Child very poorly,
spent the Evening with Bror & Sistor and
friends very comfortabley, Lodged at Bror
12, before the monthly meeting began
went to se a few friends, the meeting
did not feel as comfortable to my minde
as some meetings have, it was broke up
after friends had been gathered about
one hour which brought sorrow over my
minde, I feeling it to be my duty to speak
a few words theirin, after the Women ware

Page 193

seperated from the men the weight resting
on my minde, I spake a few words amoungst
the men by way of Testimonie, which
brought a little comfort to my minde
the buisness was gone through in Love
after meeting went to se a few friends
took leave of them & Bro.r & Sr & walked Home
14 took a walk to the fourth day meeting
at Witney, it was smallish, yet I felt
Devine Love to flow amoungst us, & it ap=
=peared to be my duty to advise the yound
Friends in perticular to be obidient unto
the manifestations of the truth within them,
after meeting went to se some friends be=
=fore I walked Home
15 was at our fifth day [Thursday] meeting, spake
a few words theirin
18, was at our first day [Sunday] meeting, altho it
was small some staying at home on ac=
=count of illness yet it felt to be a good com=
=fortable meeting, it felt to be my duty to speak
a few words theirin
19, feeling it to be my duty to pay a visit
to a Neighbour, not of our Society who was

verso

blessed with Plenty of the things of this world
she been
good to the poor also, went and sat with
she and her Family for sometime and spake
unto then what appeared to be my duty to
spake found true Peace to flow in my minde
be so doing
22, was at our fifth day [Thursday] meeting
it appeared to be a good refreshing meeting
25 took a walk to Stow it being a
very sharp frost caused me to feel the
cold a considerable deal, & it caused me
to feel for the poor who have but little
to comfort them, it felt to be a good sa=
=tisfactory meeting, it felt to be my duty
to bear a Testimonie theirin, after meeting
call'd to se a few friends & call'd to se
fr'd Hiden of Oddington, reach'd Home
in the evening
27, was very closely Imploy'd at sarving
out wood to about 100 Poor people it being
very cold weather, Friend Spendlove was
so Compasionate and tender towards them
as to give them about 5L worth of wood
like as he had done before in cold weather

Page 194

1796

29th 12mo [December] was at our fifth day
[Thursday] meeting, it felt
comfortable to my minde it appeared to be
my duty to speak a few words theirin

1797

1st mo: [January] 1st having felt drawings in

my minde to take a walk to a few meetings

acquainted my friends with the feelings
of my minde walked to the Preparative
meeting at Hooknorton, it felt to be
a good Satisfactory meeting, R Wagstaffs
Wife walked from C[hipping] Norton to the
meeting, she spake a few words theirin
which caused my spirit to rejoice. I felt
Devine Goodness attended what she spake
after meeting spent a little time with
Friends comfortabley, walked from thence
to P. Gilkes's found Philip very poorly
spent the Evening with friends their
very comfortabley, Lodg'd their
2nd walk with some friends to the monthly
meeting at Southnewington, it felt to be
my duty to advise the youth in perticular to be
very carefull to Obey the Instructions of

verso

---

the Truth within them, the meeting of
Buisness felt to be a very Labourious
meeting, and held long, after Din'r walk'd
to P. Gilkes Sibford, he appeard a rather
worse spent the Evening with them comfortabley L.[odged] their
3, walked to the monthly meeting at Eatington [Ettington]
it was not very large yet I think it was
a Satisfactory meeting, sevral Testimonies
ware born to the Honour of the Lord, the
buisness was gone through in Love, after
meeting refreshed my self at Jeffry Beavingtons
he appeared to be a very kind loving fr'd
walked with Tho's Hodgkins to shipstone
spent the evening with friends comfortabley
Lodg'd at Cousin Jn'o Wells's
4, before meeting went to se the Friends
I think it was a Satisfactory meeting I
felt it to be my duty to advise friends
to be diligent to attend meetings, near the time
appointed, after meeting bid relations & Friends
Farewell, walked to C[hipping] Norton spent the evening
with Friends lovingly, Lodg'd at Cousin Fardons
5, rose early & walked Home, found my Fr'ds tolerable well
8. took a walk with Brother to Our Quar=
=terly meeting held at Oxford it was large

Page 195

of Friends and Neighbours and I
think a good satisfactory meeting
two Strangers their, Rebecca Young
and Deborah Darby one of them
was drawn forth very notabley in
testimonie, in the A.N. [afternoon] friends had
a Solid Sitting togeth at an Inn
and sevral States & conditions ware
spoken unto, in the evening had a
comfortable sitting with Fr'd Jacksons
and some more friends, Lodg'd their
9, the Men and Women friends had a
sitting together before they enter'd upon
buisness the women friends ware largely
drawn forth in Testimonie & one of
them in very Solem Prayer, the buisness
was gone through in much Love, after
meeting took leave of friends, and walked Home
12, was at our fifth day [Thursday] meeting it felt
comforting and refreshing to my minde
15, was at our first day [Sunday] meeting as I sat
theirin my minde was comforted feeling
Devine Love to be present amoungst us

verso

1797 1mo [January] 16th took a walk to our Monthly
meeting at C.[hipping] Norton, it appeared to be
a Satisfactory meeting sevral Living
Testimonies ware born by sevral young
Friends the buisness was gone through
in Love after meeting spent sometime with
friends very agreeabley at R. Wagstaffs
I was led to speak in a perticular manner
to a young man that has lately took to going
to meetings, walked from thence to Philip
Gilkes Sibford found Him a little better
spent the evening with them comfortabley
Lodg'd their
17, took leave of Friend Gilkes's and walked
Home ware I found Dear Mother very
Poorly she having been very Poorly for
sevral days, rest was tolerable well
19 was at our fifth day [Thursday] meeting as I sat
in Silence my minde was comforted with
Devine refreshment

22. was at our first day [Sunday] meeting, according
to the feelings of my minde it was a good
meeting spake a few words theirin

Page 196

26 was at our fifth day [Thursday] meeting in which
my minde was strengthened with Devine Goodness
29, took a walk to Brails to meeting it
was small their being but a few friends
living their abouts yet I think it was
a good satisfactory meeting, after
meeting spent sometime with Cousins
and friends very comfortabley walked
from thence to P. Gilkes Sibford found
Philip a little better but Aunt Midwinter
a rather worse spent the evening their
very comfortabley Lodg'd their
30, after spending a little time at
Philips very agreeabley took leave
of them & walked Home ware I found
Mother very poorly she having been
so poorly as to keep to her room for sometime
2mo [Februuary] 1st took a walk to Witney to the fourth
day [Wednesday] meeting, i think it was a good Satis=
=factory meeting, after meeting spent sometime
with Cousins and friends, afterwards walked Home
2. was at our fifth day [Thursday] meeting it felt re=
=freshing to my minde

verso

2mo [February] 1797

5th was at our first day [Sunday] meeting, it appeared
to be my duty to put friends in minde to do
their days work Spiritualy in the day time
the preparative meeting buisness was gone
through in Love

9, was at our own fifth day [Thursday] meeting, in it my
soul was refreshed
11, in the A.N. [afternoon] took a walk to Sibford
to see P. Gilkes & Family found him
and Aunt Midwinter very Poorly spent
the evening their very comfortabley Lodg'd their
12 before meeting I was taken very
poorly with a Sickness & head Ake, but
through Devine Mercy I was so well recovered
before meeting as to go and Injoy the
meeting comfortabley, and I felt it to be
a degree of duty to speak a few words
theirin after meeting took leave of Friends
& walked Home ware I found Mother as
well as she has been for sometime and Un=
=der a sence of the menny blessings I daily
receive from the Lord my minde is bow'd in
Humble thankfullness before Him
13 was at our Monthly meeting held at this place
it felt to my minde to be a good Satisfactory
meeting sevral living Testimonies ware born

Page 197

The buisness was gone through in much Love
16 was at our fifth day [Thursday] meeting
19 was at our first day [Sunday] meeting it felt
comforting and refreshing to my soul
spake theirin
23, was at our fifth day [Thursday] meeting I felt
it to be my duty to speak theirin
24, took a walk to the sixday meeting
at C.[hipping] Norton it felt to my minde
to be a good satisfactory meeting
it felt to be my duty to speak theirin
25 took a walk to Milton, call'd at
Cousin Franklings little Barverd [Barford St. John]
found them tolerable well as also Friends
at Milton Lodg'd at Robt Pains
26 before Meeting went to se some
friends at Adderbury they ware loving
the Meeting felt to be a good Satisfactory
meeting, I felt it to be my duty to speak
theirin, Din'd at Robt Pains Call'd to se
Tho's Harris & Sistor they ware very poorly
walked from thence to P. Gilkes Sibford found

Philip rather worse & Aunt Minty & Midwinter very poorly

verso

---

spent the Evening with Philip & his
Family in a very solid comfortable
manner Lodg'd their
27 spent sometime at Philips comfortabley
call'd to se some friends, took leave
of them, walked to Fr'd Minchons
Hooknorton, spent sometime with them
in a very solid manner, bid them farewell
then walked Home
3mo [March] 1st it haven fallen to my lot to be drawn
as a militia Man I was summonds to ap=
=pear at the Wite Hart in C[hipping] Norton, I ac=
=cordingly went with tender breathings
and Cries in my minde unto the Lord that
I might be preserved from offending Him
in either Thought Word or Deed and also
that He would be pleased to Inable me to
bear a faithfull Testimonie against
War and Fighting altho I might suffer
greatly for so doing. Wm Atkins was so
kind as to go with me before the Officers
I Indeavoured to make them sensible that
blessed Jesus had Taught me to love mine
Enemies to do good to them that hate me &
to pray for them that despitefully use
me and Persecute me and on that account
I could neither go nor hire one to go, they

Page 198

signified the Law was if I had no property
to suffer Imprisonment, if I had pro=
=perty to have it taken from me, after=
=wards spent a little time with Friends
they ware loving to me, took leave
of them and walked Home with tender
breathins in mine Heart unto the
Lord that He would be pleased
to Inable me to discharge my duty
unto Him Faithfully according to
the very best of my Understanding
and ability He should give me
2nd was at our fifth day [Thursday] meeting I felt
it to be a Satisfactory meeting
I been invited to the funeral of a Neighbour
felt most easy to go, when I was seated in
the Worship House a Neighbour came and
took of my Hatt, I keept silent, when the
serimony was over at the Grave He put
it on, I being much Grieved at their Singing
could not feel quite easy without speaking
a few words to the people at the Grave,
theirfore I took of my Hatt & speak in
the fear of the Lord the people heard me
very quietly, felt true Peace in my minde
by speaking

verso

1797

3mo [March] 4th in the Evening took a walk to Witney
Heard of a young man that had given way
to drinking & had an Inclination to go for
a Soldier upon which I felt it to be a
degree of duty to Advise Him Solidly
in the fear of the Lord to forsake such
bad thoughts & Actions, spent the evening
with friends comfortabley Lodg'd at Jn'o Hankings
5, walked with Jn'o Hankins to the Meeting
at Faringdon it felt to my minde to
be a good Satisfactory meeting, after
meeting spent sometime with friends in
a very affectionate manner, walked
with Jn'o Hankins to Witney spent the
evening Lovingly with Cousins & Friends Lodg'd at Jn'o Hankins
6, after Breackfasting at jn'o Hankins walk'd Home
9, was at our own fifth day [Thursday] Meeting
12, took a walk to Milton to Meeting
as I sat theirin my Minde was refreshed
and it felt to my minde to be my duty to
speak theirin, spent a little time with friends
& walked to the A.N. [afternoon] meeting at Burford
it felt to be a good refreshing meeting found
Sistor Betty very poorly spent the evening

with them and friends lovingly Lodg'd at
Brothers
13, took leave of Bro.r & Sr. and walked from
thence
to our Monthly Meeting at Witney, it felt to be a

Page 199

time of good Instruction unto some through
the Lords Servants, the buisness was
gone through in Love. I think it was
cause of sorrow unto some to see some who
ware at liberty & appeared qualified for
sarvices in the Church, backwards & unwilling
to axcept of Appointments; spent a little
time with friends before I walk'd Home
16, was at our meeting, spake a few words theirin
19, took a walk to Sibford to meeting
it felt to my minde to be a good refres=
=hing meeting, spake theirin feeling it
to be my duty so to do spent the A.N. [afternoon]
at P. Gilks's except going to visit some
friends, found P. Gilks very poorly
& Aunt Midwinter very Ill so as to
keep her bed, Lodg'd at P. Gilks's
20, spent sometime with P. Gilks & Family
and some friends very comfortabley,
afterwards walked Home
22 this day Sistor M[argaret] was safely Delivered
of a Daughter, named Hh [Hannah?]
23 was at our fifth day [Thursday] meeting it felt
com=
=fortable to my minde
26 took a walk to Barton to Meeting
it was large of Friends & Neighbo=
=urs & I think it was a good Satisfactory

verso

meeting in which Devine Goodness
was pleased to visit the People
with His Heavenly Power to put
them in minde what they should
do and what they should leave un=
=done to please Him, sevral living
testimonies ware born theirin
after meeting went to Fr'd Jarvices
to Diner walked from thence Home
30, was at our fifth day [Thursday] meeting it felt
comfortable to my minde George Waford
came from Sibford to let us know of
Aunt Midwinters Death, Died yesterday
in the afternoon walked with George to P. Gilks's
found
Philip a little better rest Tolerable well
Lodged their
31 before meeting went to see some friends,
I think it was a tolerable full meeting
on account of the burial of Aunt mid=
=winter & a good Satisfactory meeting it ap=
=peared to be my duty to warn the People
not to put of the work of Repentance untill
another day afterward spent sometime at
Philips with our Relations & friends com=
=fortabley, took leave of them and walk'd Home
Inside of back cover
ware born to the Honnour of the Almighty
and His truth the buisness was gone through
in much Love and Unity, after meeting
reached Home having had a very comfortable
Journey

Journal B

Page 1

1797 4mo [April] 2nd took a walk to Stow to
meeting, it was Small their being
but few Friends belonging to it
yet I felt Devine Love to flow
amoungst us, Spake theirin as truth
manifested unto me to be my duty so to
do in the A.[fter]N.[oon] spent sometime with
some friends very comfortabley
walked from thence to Burford Lodg'd
at Bro.rs
3rd before the Monthly meeting began
went to se some friends, I think it was
a Satisfactory meeting, sevral Short
testimonies ware born theirin, the buisness
was gone through in Love, after meeting
took leave of Bro.r & S'r & walk'd Home
6: was at our fifth day [Thursday] meeting, it
was comforting to my minde
9: was at our first day [Sunday] meeting, it
felt comforting to my minde, it fell
to be my duty to speak theirin after=
ward walked to Witney, spent the
Evening with friends lovingly Lodg'd
at Jn'o Hankins's
10, before meeting began spent sometime
with friends in a good Instructing manner

verso

altho in the morning I think truth ap=
=peared low yet I think it was a Satis=
=factory meeting, sevral friends appeared
in Testimonie, in the A.[fter]N.[oon] meeting I think
truth arose with more dominion, sevral
Living Testimonies ware born theirin
after meeting walked home with a friend
11th walked to our Quarterly Meeting at
witney it was a large & I think a Satis=
=factory meeting the Men & Women
had a Comfortable Sitting together be=
=fore they Proceeded upon buisness, it
appeared by the answers to the Queries that
Love & Unity was generaly preserved
Except in the Monthly Meeting at
Reading on which account a Committy
was appointed to attend the monthly Meeting
at Reading and Join friends to visit the
disorderly Members, after meeting walked Home
13, was at our fifth day [Thursday] meeting it felt
comfortable to my minde ware favoured
with the company Ann Craly P.B. [public friend]
15th took a walk to Sibford to se Philip Gilkes
and his Family found Philip very poorly Lodg'd
their

Page 2

16th before meeting went to se sevral
friends who ware poorly I think it was
a Satisfactory meeting, Spake a little
theirin in the A.[fter]N.[oon] meeting I think we
ware favoured with the overshadowings
of Devine Love after meeting took leave
of friends & walked to C.[hipping]Norton spent
the evening at R. Wagstaffs comfortabley
Lodg'd at Cousin Fardons
17, rose early and walked Home to Breackfast
20 was at our fifth day [Thursday] meeting I
think it was a comfortable meeting sat in Silence
23. was at our first day [Sunday] meeting in it
my minde was comforted, but sorry at a
friend or two indeavouring to break up
the meeting quite early, I feeling a
few words to arise in my minde to speak
informed friends of the feelings of my
minde friends sat down, I spake what
appeared to be my duty to speak & felt
a degree of Peace to flow in my minde
27 was at our fifth day [Thursday] meeting spake
a few words theirin
30 took a walk to the preparative meeting
at Hooknorton I think it was a good Satis=

verso

=factory meeting, felt most easy to Incourage
Friends to labour faithfully according to
the Manifestations of the Truth within them
that their days work might go on with the
day time, after meeting went to se some
friends, walked from thence to the A.[fter]N.[oon] meet'g

at Sibford, it felt pretty comfortable to
my minde, spent the evening with some friends
Lodg'd at P. Gilks's, Philip continues very poorly
6 [May] 1st took a walk with sevral friends
to a Monthly Meeting at Shutford I
think it was a Satisfactory meeting
I pass'd with my Fr'd Sarah Gilks in
order for Marriage, after meeting walked
to Sibford with sevral friends spent the
evening with Fr'd Gilks's & some other
friends very comfortabley, Lodg'd at Philips
2nd in the morning took leave of Fr'd Gilks's
then walked Home, found my Mother very
Poorly she has been a weakly Woman for
menny years, and of late has been afflicted
with the palsy,
4, was at our fifth day [Thursday] meeting
6, took a walk to Cousin Harris's Long Com=
=pton with Jn'o Rutter of Witney Lodg'd their

Page 3

1797

7th walked from thence to Shipstone to
the Morning Meeting it was Small
which was cause of sorrow to my minde
yet my spirit was a little refreshed as I
sat theirin, walked from thence with some
friends to Armscutt [Armscote] Meeting, it was not very
large yet I felt Devine Love to flow
amoungst us, Sevral Public Fr'ds ware
their & menny Short living Testimonies
ware born, after meeting walked to friend
Lamblys Tredington, spent a little time
their very comfortabley, walked with menny friends to Shipstone
stop'd with friends a little, walked to
Michael Petiphors they ware very kinde
to me, Lodg'd their
8, walked to our Monthly Meeting at C.[hipping] Norton
I think it was a good refreshing meeting
in which Devine Goodness was pleased
to make use of some of His Children to convey
His Will unto others, the buisness was gone through in Love,

after meeting spent about two ours with
friends took leave of them & walked Home
11, was at our fifth day [Thursday] meeting, in it my
minde was comforted
14, took a walk with Bro.r to Witney to meeting

verso

---

the morning meeting I think was a Satis=
=factory meeting, Spake theirin what
the Truth manifested unto me to be
my duty to speak, the A.[fter]N.[oon] meeting
felt pretty comfortable, spake a few
words theirin, call'd to see sevral Friends
in affliction, & I think their company
(or our meeting together) was comforting to me and them, in the
Evening walked Home
18, was at our fifth day [Thursday] meeting, it felt
comforting &refreshing to my minde
21, took a walk to Brails to Meeting
I think it was a Comfortable meeting
I found it to be my duty to speak
theirin, spent a little time at Cousins
comfortabley, walked from thence
to the A.[fter]N.[oon] meeting at Sibford
my minde was refreshed theirin
spent the Evening at Philip Gilks's
lovingly Lodg'd their
22, spent sometime at Philips comfortabley
went to se a few friends, walked from
thence to C.[hipping]Norton, called to se a few

Page 4

---

friends, one in perticular who was
very poorly, could not feel easy
without calling to se she, walked
from thence Home
25 was at our fifth day [Thursday] meeting felt
most easy to sit in Silence
28, was at our first day [Sunday] meeting, it felt
comforting and refreshing to my minde,
felt most easy to speak a few words theirin
6mo [June] 1st took a walk to Burford to the fifth
day [Thursday] meeting, it felt comforting & refreshing
to my minde, found Sistor Betty & Han.h

Huntley very poorly, walked Home in the Evening
4th took a walk with Bro.r Rob.t to Sibford
to meeting it felt comforting and refreshing to
my minde felt most easy to sit in Solid Silence,
the Preparative meeting buisness was gone through in Love,
found P. Gilks very poorly, the A.[fter]N.[oon] meeting
felt comforting to my minde, felt east to sit
in Silence, after meeting spent the Evening at
Philips & with some other friends Lovingly, Lodg'd at Philips
5th took a walk with Sarah Gilks to the Monthly
meeting at adderbury, I think it was a pretty
large Comfortable meeting, altho held in Silence,
the buisness was gone through in Love, Sarah

verso

Gilks & I pass'd the second time in order
for Marriage, after meeting called to se sevral
Friends families, walked with Bro.r R & Philip
Gilke's Daughters & some more friends to Sib=
=ford spent a little time at Philips very
comfortabley Lodg'd their
6 being the day appointed for I and Sarah
Gilks to take each other in Marriage a
Meeting was appointed for that purpose to
begin at 10 oclock it was a large meeting of
Friends and Neighbours, my minde was much
exercised & fervent breathings and desires ware
begotten in my minde, unto the Lord, that I
might be preserved in His Fear so as not to
neglect my duty unto Him in the least degree
by seeking to pleasure & gratify myself, & as my
minde was bowed in humility before the Lord
He was mercifull unto me, and Inabled me to bear
a Testimonie for His Honnour and the truth, before I took my
Friend Sarah Gilks to be my Wife, afterwards
I and Sarah took each other in Marriage in
a very solid manner, Joseph Lamb was pretty

Page 5

---

much drawn forth in Living Testimonie, the Neigh=
=bours behaved well & appeared well satisfied with
the Meeting, Spent the A.[fter]N.[oon] mostly at Fathers
& Mothers in a Religious Chearfull & Loving
manner with Friends, Lodg'd their
7, spent part of the day with my Wife &
new Sistors very agreeabley in visiting some
friends Lodg'd at Fathers
8, took a walk to Hooknorton to the fifth day [Thursday] meeting & altho
it was small it felt refreshing to my minde &
I felt it to be my duty to advise friends to be
diligent in attending meetings to wait upon the
Lord & Worship Him, after spending a little
time with friends walked back to fathers
& prepared to return Home, Lodg'd their
9, very early took leave of Father & Mother
& returned Home with my Wife, ware we arived
safe & well & found our friends much the
same as the had been for sometime, for which
mercy and blessings my minde is bowed in Humble
thankfullness before the Lord,
10. I & my Wife ware very buisy a putting our goods
in place at our new habitation
11th was at our first day [Sunday] meeting ware favoured
with the Company of our friend Jn'o Hodgkins, he

verso

---

was led in Testimonie to speak very comfortabley
to friends, spent some of the A.[fter]N.[oon] at Home
with some friends who came to se us very comfortabley
12, was at our Monthly Meeting held at this place
I think it was a large Comfortable Meeting
in it sevral Testimonies ware born,
the buisness was gone through in Love
after meeting we ware favoured with the
Company of menny friends who came to
visit us at Our new Habitation & Friend
Mintchon was led to advise us to keep our
Places in the Truth to live in Love & Unity
together to bear & forbear with one another
15th went with my Wife to our fifth day [Thursday] meeting,

felt most easy to sit in Silence
18, was at our first day [Sunday] meeting felt most easy
to speak theirin, I think it was a Satisfactory meeting
22 was at our fifth day [Thursday] meeting, felt most
easy to sit in Silence
25. walked with some friends to Barton
meeting it was pretty large I think
it was a good Satisfactory meeting
& what Friends had to speak in Tes=
timonie I think reach'd the pure witness in some

Page 6

walked after meeting to Sibford, found my
Father in Law very poorly, Lodg'd their
26 took leave of Father & Mother
in Law walked from thence with some
friends to our quarterly Meeting at Banbury
it was large of Friends & Neighbours
& I think a good Satisfactory meeting one
Public Fr'd from America David
Lands, who appeared pretty long in Tes=
timonie in a very perticular manner,
and afterwards in very Solem prayer,
the A.[fter]N.[oon] meeting was large & I think
the Lord owned us with His Everlasting
Power, after meeting went to se some
friends spent the Evening with them in a
Solid loving manner
27, the Men and Women had a comfortable
sitting together before the entered upon
the buisness the American friend was
led to speak to sevral States, & in a
perticular manner to advise friends not to set

verso

1797

their Hearts upon Money or the things
of this world, the buisness was gone through
in much Love, after meeting took leave
of friends & walked Home, found my Dear
wife very poorly
29, was at our fifth day [Thursday] meeting it felt refreshing
to my minde, spake theirin
7mo [July] 1st my Wife being poorly & her Father
being very poorly not like to continue
long in this World, took her on Horse=back
to se her Father, found him very weak
& poorly yet in a comfortable frame
of minde he appearing to be quite
willing to die when it should please
the Almighty to remove him hence,
found Mother & sistors tolerable well
2nd spent the morning very solidly &
lovingly before meeting at Fathers, the meeting felt
to my minde to be very comforting & refreshing
the Preparative meeting buisness was gone
through in Love, the meeting in the A.[fter] N.[oon]
felt comforting and it was tolerable large
after meeting spent a little time at fathers

Page 7

in a very Solid & Affectionate manner father
& I being ready to think wee should nevver
se one anothers Faces in this world any
more, yet a Degree of Faith sprang
in my minde that if we continue to live
in faithfull & true Obidience unto the
Heavenly power within us, unto the end
of our Days, we shall be inabled to
meet in the Kingdom of Everlasting
Happiness ware we shall nevver be
seperated more
took leave of my Wife Mother & Sistors
then returned Home
6, took a walk to Hooknorton to meet'g
it was small yet it felt comforting
& refreshing to my minde I felt it
to be my duty in a perticular manner
to advise friends to be very carefull
to Improve the Talents and Gifts that
the Lord had committed to their Trust
walked from thence to Sibford found
Father very weak, rest Tolerable well
Lodg'd at Fathers

verso

1797

7mo [July] 7th took my Solem & I think last Farewell
of my Father=in=Law, left my Wife
to help nurse him, walked from thence
to C.[hipping]Norton to meeting, it felt refreshing
to my minde, went to see Cousin Lambs
she was very poorly and low in her minde
after spending sometime with them in a
loving & Affectionate manner, took leave
of friends & walked Home
9, took a walk to the Preparative
meeting at Witney, I think it was a good
satisfactory meeting sevral Living Testimonies
ware born theirin, and one friend was drawn
forth in Solem Prayer, after meeting walked
with some friends to Faringdon, found friends
their tolerable well & very loving Lodg'd at fr'd Reynolds
10th ware favoured with the Company of
David Sands an American Fr'd He appeared
pretty long in Testimonie, it also after the Fr'd
had done speaking, felt to my minde to be my
duty to let friends know that the Visitation of
the Lords Love was afresh extended unto their
Souls, and it was their duty to make good use theirof

Page 8

1797

so as to profit theirby or words to that purpose,
ware also favoured with the company of another
P.F. [public friend] [blank] of [blank] the buisness was gone
through in much love, after meeting took leave
of Friends and walked Home
13, ware favoured at our Meeting with the
company of David Sands & his Companion
I think it was a good meeting in which
Devine Love was felt to flow amoungst
us in an extroardernary manner David
was led to spak tenderly to menny states
and in a perticular manner to such as had
strayed from their fathers house and had
spent their portion of Riteous living
he set forth that if they would Obey
the truth within them repent of their
wrong doings and amend their lives & return
to their Heavenly Father in Sincearity
He would have mercy on them and love
them, the Friends desired to have a
meeting in the evening & desired to have

verso

the Neighbours acquainted of it it was
Pretty large & I think a very Satisfactory
meeting, David Sands in the fore=part
of the meeting was drawn forth in very
solem Prayer, & afterward in a living Tes=
=timonie, & near the conclusion of the Meeting
I could not feel easy without letting the
People know that wee could be led but by
two Spirits the Spirit of Christ & the
Spirit of Satan & to inform them how they
might know by which Spirit they ware led
by, & to Incourage them to be led by the good
Spirit that they might come to Injoy Eter=
=nal happiness when time to them in this
world should be no more
16 took a walk to the first day [Sunday] meeting at Brails,
in the fore=part of the meeting my minde
was very low, under a sence of my own
weakness, but after=ward truth arose to
our great comfort & to the Uniteing us

Page 9

near one unto another, & I was Inabled
to bear a Testimonie theirin, after refreshing
myself at Cousins walked to Sibford
found Father very weak and poorly,
the A.[fter]N.[oon] meeting felt refreshing to my minde,
spent the evening mostly at Fathers comfortabley
17. went to se a few friends, afterwards took
my solem farewell of father, not much
expecting ever to se him Living any more
walked from thence with my Wife Home

20. went with my Wife to our fifth
day [Thursday] meeting my minde was comforted
and refreshed theirin
22 having felt drawings for Sometime
to take a walk to friends first day [Sunday]
meetings at Reading
and also their monthly Meeting acquainted
my Wife and some friends with the feelings
of my minde, walked to Reading reach'd their
about sun set call'd to see some friends in
my Journey they ware very loving and
Entertained

verso

me kindly, Lodg'd at Cousin Tutteys they ware
very kinde to me all the time I was their
23 the morning Meeting began at ten, it felt
to my minde to be a Satisfactory meeting,
spake theirin as the truth manifested unto
me to be my duty so to do, the A.[fter]N.[oon] meeting
also felt refreshing to my minde, after meeting
went to see some friends, spent the evening
with them very lovingly
24 spent most of the day a visiting friend
they ware loving as I sat with them in a Solid
manner, when I felt my minde Influenced by
Devine Love to speak a few words amoungst
them, speak them, found sweet peace to flow
in my minde by so doing
25, before the monthly Meeting began went
to se some friends the monthly Meeting
felt very comforting to my minde sevral
straingers ware their Public Friends,
the Buisness was gone through in much
Love and I think much to friends Satisfaction

Page 10

after meeting spent a little time with
friends then bid them farewell walked
from thence with John Horn & E. May to
Henly Lodg'd at E Mays
26 before meeting went to se some friends
they ware loving the meeting felt very
comforting & I think it was a fresh
visitation of Devine Love unto some young
mindes present after meeting stop'd
a little with friends walked from thence
to Cousin Ashbys Shillingford Lodg'd their
27 before meeting, went to se some
friends, they ware loving, the meeting
felt very comfortable, it appeared to
by my duty to advise friends to
be very carefull to Improve their
Gifts and Talents wich the Lord had
Intrusted them with, after meeting
took leave of friends and walked
Home, safe and well found my Wife
& friends Tolerable well for which

verso

blessing and all others my minde
is bow'd in humble Thankfullness
before the Lord
30 was at our first day [Sunday] meeting I
think it was a very comforting &
refreshing season to some
8mo [August] 3rd was at our fifth day [Thursday] meeting
as I sat theirin m minde was much
oppress'd, on account of some giving
way to their own weakness's
6, took a walk to Sibford to se Father
& Mother, found Father very weak
and poorly yet he appeared easy and
comfortable in his minde, the morning
meeting felt comforting to my minde,
felt most easy to speak theirin, the pre=
=parative meeting buisness was gone
through in Love. I thin the A.[fter]N.[oon]
meeting was a Satisfactory meeting
after meeting took leave of Father Mother
& friends and walked Home

Page 11

8mo [August] 1797

10 was at our fifth day [Thursday] meeting it
felt comforting and refreshing to my
minde, felt most easy to speak a few
words theirin,
13 took a walk with my Wife to milton
to meeting, I think it was a good meeting
it appeared to be my duty to Incourage

Friends to be willing to part with
any Earthly Injoyments to Injoy Devine
Love, after meeting spent a little time
with friends then bid them farewell &
walked to the Evening meeting at Burford
it felt comfortable to my minde two
friends appeared in Testimonie, I felt
easy to sit in Silence, spent the rest
of the Evening at Bro.s Lovingly Lodg'd their
14th before the Monthly meeting began went with
my Wife to see some friends they appeared
Loving, the meeting appeared very
comforting and refreshing to my minde,
sevral Living Testimonies ware born
theirin, and one friend appeared in Solem

verso

Prayer, the Buisness was gone through
in Love, & Unity after meeting spent
a little time with Bro.r Sistor & some
friends, bid them Farewell & walked
with my Wife & some friends Home
17 went with my Wife to our fifth day [Thursday] meeting, altho my minde was low under
a sence of my own Weakness's, yet my
minde was comforted and refreshed theirin
20, was at our first day [Sunday] meeting, felt
most easy to speak a few words theirin
24 I & my Wife came Home from
reaping & went to meeting could not
feel quite easy without speaking a
few words theirin
27 was at our first day [Sunday] meeting it felt comforting
and refreshing unto my Soul, could not feel
easy without speaking a few words theirin,
31 went with my Wife to our fifth day [Thursday] meeting
it felt comforting to my minde
9mo [September] 3rd took a walk with my Wife to Sib=
=ford found my father=in=law Dead he was

Page 11

---

long Afflicted with an Inward complaint
& it was so sevear for about three quarters
of a year before he died that he often
cried out very loud he gradualy decayed
as his Strength decayed so his pain seemed
to decrease he died very quietly he was one
who delighted to minde the teachings of
the spirit of Christ within him, and to
obey it and quite carefull to Instruct his
Children to do the same, and also con=
=cearned for the good of Friends Especialy
such who he thought did not live such good
lives as they ought to do, he would admonish
them to Indeavour to minde the Teachings
of the Almighty power within them and obey
it with more carefullness & diligence & was
a Serviceable Member in the Church, and
altho menny may Mourn for the Loss of his
good company, they having felt at times
Devine Love to flow through him unto them,
yet I think his days work was done, and the Lord
has been pleased to remove him from this World
of Affliction & Probation, into His Everlasting

verso

Kingdom of Rest & Joy ware all tears are
wiped away and sorrows are known no more
His Wife appeared to bear the loss of her
Dear Husband with true patience and contentedness
of minde and also his Children the loss
of their tender & Loving Father
was at both the morning and after=noon
meetings the felt pretty comfortable to
my minde felt most easy to speak a
few words in the A.[fter]N.[oon] meeting spent
the evening with Mother Sistors & friends
lovingly Logd'g at Mothers
4 was at the Monthly Meeting at
Sibford I think truth was rather
low theirin the buisness was gone
through in Love, one Woman & three
men friends ware appointed Elders
if the Quarterly Meet'g approv'd of them
went to see some loving friends after
meeting
5th being the day appointed for the funeral
of my Father=in=law a Meeting was

Page 12

---

held on the occasion a pretty menny

friends attended the Funeral I think
it was a solem Meeting in which
Devine Providence was pleased to
renew the tender Visitation of His Love
unto menny Present & to call them
to repent of their Sins and amend
their Lives sevral Testimonies ware
born and one Friends was drawn fourth
in Solem Prayer, after meeting
friends had a Solid comfortable sitting
together at Mothers, & some friends
through the opperation of the Devine
Power ware engaged to speak Comfortabley
to Mother Sistors & other friends
afterward bid Mother my Wife Sis=
=tors & friends Farewell, I leaving
my Wife to bare Mother company
a day or two, reach'd Home about nine
at Nigh safe & well for which blessing
and all others my minde is bowed in Hum=
=ble thankfullness before the Lord

verso

1797

9mo [September] 7th was at our fifth day [Thursday] meeting could not
feel quite easy without speaking a few words theirin
10 took a walk to stow to meeting, met with
Fr'd Tho's Huntley & his Wife, the meeting
was larger than I have sometimes seen
it, their appears to be a little convincement
that way, could not feel quite easy without
speaking a few words theirin, after meeting
spent sometime in a Solid and loving
manner with some who have lately took
to going to our meetings, Lodg'd at Wm
Coulings Oddington
11, walked to C.[hipping] Norton, the Monthly
meeting was smallish, it being a Rainy
morning, the meeting felt pretty comfortable
to my minde, I felt it to be my duty by
way of Testimonie to advise friends to keep
near to their Devine Guide, and spake as it
directed them, & not in their own wills that
the Lord alone migh have the Honour, by
their going through the buisness that might
come before them, the buisness was gone through
in Love, after meeting spent sometime with
Friends loving, walked Home in the Evening

Page 13

14, went with my Wife to our fifth day [Thursday] meeting
17, took a walk to Oxford to meeting, it
was large of Friends & Neighbours
and I think a Satisfactory meeting
two strangers P.[ublic] Frds ware their one Sarah Line
a young friend, appeared very remarckable
in Testimonie, I felt it to be my duty
to speak a few words theirin, walked
from thence with Edwd May & some friends,
to Wallingford, Lodg'd at Frd Greens,
18, rose early & walked with some friends
to Reading, the Morning Meeting did
not feel very lively, I felt it to be my
duty to speak a few words theirin
I think the A.[fter]N.[oon] meeting felt more lively
S.L. was pretty much drawn fourth
in Testimonie, and one friend was drawn
fourth in solem Prayer, in the Evening
went to see some friends who ware very
loving, Lodg'd at Tho's Honeymans
19 the Quarterly meeting began at nine the

verso

Men & Women had a very solid sitting
together before the entered upon buisness
the buisness was gone through in a Weighty
manner & in Love, in the Evening
spent sometime with friends in a
solid & loving manner, Lodg'd at F. Stubbs
20 walked with my Brother=in=Law Home
except riding about ten Miles
21, went with my Wife to our fifth day [Thursday]
meeting, it felt refreshing to my minde
24, went with my Wife to our first day [Sunday]
meeting, as I sat theirin my minde was
much oppressed on account of my being
reproached for my Indeavouring to keep my
Contience quite clean and void of Offence
towards God and all mankinde, by one

whose duty I think it was to Incourage and
to Indeavour to strengthen me to perform
that duty which I believed the Lord required
of me to do, a young Woman spake a few words
theirin & I think they ware attended with Devine

Page 14

Power which caused my Heart to rejoice
28, went with my Wife to our fifth day [Thursday] meeting, it felt comforting to my minde
10mo [October] 1st went with my Wife to our first day [Sunday]
meeting, it was largish sevral friends strangers
ware present & I think wee ware favoured
with the overshadowings of Devine Love to the
comforting and refreshing the truly honest Hearted
5th went with my Wife to our fifth day [Thursday] meeting
my minde was comforted and refreshed theirin,
altho my minde has been much Exercised and
afflicted of late
7, took a walk to little Barverd [Barford St. John] to see
Cousin Franklings heard that Cousin
Mary was dead, she was a Loving
agreeable Friend, died in a decline,
spent the Evening with Cousin Wm
& his Daughter very loving Lodg'd their
8, took leave of Cousins, walked to Wm
Barrits at Adderbury, Breackfasted
with them before meeting went to se
sevral Friends they ware very Loving,

verso

the meeting was pretty large, sevral
Strangers ware their, my minde was
comforted and refreshed theirin, could
not feel easy without speaking theirin,
& in a perticular manner to advise friends to
be very diligent to attend their religious
meetings, after meeting walked to Robt
Pains of Milton to Din'r, they ware
very friendly, walked from thence Home
9 was at our Monthly Meeting held at
Charlbury, I think it was a very good
refreshing Meeting, unto sincear friends,
sevral short Testimonies ware born by which
Friends ware advised not to be contented with
a Profession of Religion without Injoying
the substance, the buisness was gone through in
a weighty and loving manner,
11, took a walk to Witney, was at their
fourth day [Wednesday] meeting, altho I was sorry
to see such a small Number yet my
minde was comforted as I sat theirin,
feeling Devine Love to flow amoungst us,
after meeting spent a little time with some

Page 15

Friends very comfortabley, walked from thence Home
12th was at our fifth day [Thursday] meeting, and my
Wife, it felt comforting to my minde
15, went with my Wife to our first day [Sunday]
meeting, I think it was a good refreshing meeting
19, went with my Wife to our fifth
day meeting, felt easy to sit in Silence
22 went with my Wife to our first day [Sunday]
meeting, my minde was refreshed theirin,
I felt it to be my duty to advise friends
always to Indeavour to be prepared for Death,
26, went with my Wife to our fifth day [Thursday]
meeting, felt most easy to speak a few words theirin
29 went with my Wife to our first day [Sunday]
meeting, it felt comforting and refreshing
to my soul, spake a few words theirin
11mo 2nd went with my wife to our fifth day [Thursday]
meeting, felt most easy to sit in Silence
4, took a walk to Sibford to see Mother
& Sistor, found them very well, Lodg'd their
5, before meeting spent sometime with
Mother & Sistor very agreeably, I think
it was a good Meeting in which Devine
Goodness was pleased to appear to the comforting

verso

menny mindes Present, after the Prepa=
=rative meeting buisness was gone through
walked to Hooknorton, call'd to se Garick
Phipps & his Family, found his Wife

very low & Poorly with a Coughf, a little
like one in a Decline, walked from
thence Home
6, this day a meeting was held on account
of the Burial of Grace Fell, she was
Sistor to Sarah Squire, it was a large
meeting of Friends & Neighbours and I
think it was a good Satisfactory Meeting
in which the Lord was Pleased to bless
us with His Life giving Power & Presence
sevral Mouths ware opened to testify of
His Love and Good ness unto all mankind
and to warn the People to prepare for
their later=end
9. went with my Wife to our fifth day [Thursday]
meeting, it felt comforting to my minde
10. took a walk to Norton, was at the sixday
[Friday] meeting
my minde was comforted as I sat theirin
I found it to be a degree of duty to speak
theirin, calld to se some friends in the Evening
walked Home

Page 16

1797

12. took a walk with my Wife to Witney
it was their parative meeting it felt Tolerable
comfortable to my minde spent the A.[fter]
N.[oon] with
Cousins & Friends very lovingly Lodg'd at
Cousins
13, the Monthly Meeting was pretty
large & it felt pretty comfortable to my
minde was favoured with the company of Sarah
Line and another Friend, Sarah altho
yound appears to have a large Gift in
the Ministery, she has a loudish voice
and through Devine Assistance is Inab
=led to Speak to the States and Conditions of
menny
with an Undaunted Minde, not fearing
Man, nor respecting Person, & is much
led amoungst People not of our Society,
the Buisness was gone through in Love
After meeting I and my Wife spent a
little time with Friends very agreeabley,
and in the Evening walked Home
16. went with my Wife to our fifth day [Thursday]
meeting wee ware favoured with the Company
of Sarah Line & Hank Huntley, the advised
Friends to beware of a lukewarm Indifrent
state of minde, & Incouraged to labour to have

verso

Devine Love dwell within them, in the
Evening, a meeting was held by the
Friends desire, & the Neighbours ware
let know by the Friends desire, it was
a very large Satisfactory meeting Devine
Goodness was wonderfully felt theirin
and Sarah Line was filled with Strength
and boldness to Preach the Everlasting
Gospel, unto the people, & to tell them
plainly that they must minde the Tea=
=chings of the Spirit of Crist within
them and obey it, if ever they came to In=
Joy everlasting Happiness, she concluded
the Meeting in Solem Prayer
19, went with my Wife to our first
day [Sunday] meeting, I think it was a good
meeting, my Mouth was opened to advise
friends to make good use of the menny
blessings they receive of the Lord,
23. went with my Wife to our fifth day [Thursday]
meeting, it felt refreshing to my Exercised minde

Page 17

25th in the A.[fter]N.[oon] took a walk to Brails
found
Cousins tolerable well, spent the Evening with
them Lovingly Lodg'd at Cous'n Wm Gilletts
26 before meeting went to se some friends
the Meeting was small yet I think the gracious
pro=
=mice of blessed Jesus was fulfilled unto us,
ware but two or three are met together in
my Name their I will be in the midst of
them, after meeting spent a little time with
cousins bid them Farewell, walked from
thence to Sibford found Mother & Sistor
Pretty well, spent the Evening with them &
some friends very agreeabley Lodg'd at Mothers
27 after breackfasting at Mothers took leave

of them & walked to C.[hipping] Norton, stop'd with
friends a little, walked from thence Home
30. went with my Wife to our fifth day [Thursday] meeting
felt most easy to sit in Silence
12mo [December] 3rd went with my Wife to our first day [Sunday]
meeting, it felt comforting and refreshing to
my Exercised minde, the Preparative meeting
buisness was gone through in Love
6th took a walk to the fourth day [Wednesday] meeting at Witney
it was small yet it felt comforting to my minde

verso

---

after meeting spent a little time with Friends
Lovingly, afterward walked Home
7. went with my Wife to our fifth day [Thursday] Meeting
I think we ware favoured with the Injoyment of Devine Love
10, took a walk to the Preparative meeting
at Burford it felt pretty comfortable to
my minde the buisness was gone through
in Love, spent the A.[fter]N.[oon] at Brors & with
some more friends very comfortabley
Lodg'd at Brothers
11th it was a largish monthly meeting &
I think friends ware much favoured
with the overshadowings of Devine Love,
the buisness was gone through in Love,
after meeting spent a little time with
friends & Bror & Sistor, bid them Farewell
& walked Home with Bror Robt.
14, went with my Wife to our fifth
day [Thursday] meeting, it felt refreshing to my
soul and body
17 went with my Wife to our first day [Sunday]
meeting, my minde was comforted as I sat
theirin, felt east to sit in Silence
21, went with my Wife to our fifth day [Thursday] meeting

Page 18

1797

12mo [December] 23rd in the A.[fter]N.[oon] took a walk to Witney
spent the evening with some friends
in a Solid loving manner, Lodg'd at Jno Hankins
24 walked with Jno Hankins to Farringdon
to Meeting, it was small yet it felt
pretty comfortable. I felt it to be my
duty to Advise friends to minde & be
very carefull to acknowledge the Lord in
every Thought Word & Deed, that they might
feel His Power to flow amoungst them
as from vessel to vessel, after meeting
spent a little time with friends loving,
bid them Farewell & walked with Jno
Hankins to His House, Lodg'd their
25, took leave of my kinde friends Jn'o
Hankins & Family, & call'd to see some
more friends whose Company was comforting, walked
from thence Home
28, went with my Wife to our fifth
day [Thursday] meeting, it felt very comforting
to my exercised minde
31, took a walk to Oxford to meeting it
was pretty large menny Neighbours

verso

---

comming in, & behaved pretty orderly
yet I think Truth did not arise
with so great dominion as I have
sometimes felt it, sevral Friends ap=
=peared in Testimonie I felt easy to
sit in Silence, spent the A.[fter]N.[oon] with
menny friends in a Solid agreeable
manner, Lodg'd at George Tittertons

1798

1mo [January] 1st Breackfasted at George Tittertons
the Quarterly Meeting was not very
large yet Sevral Strangers ware

their Pub.[lic] Friends, & I think it was
an Extroardernary favoured Meeting in
which menny ware blessed to feed on the
Bread & Water of Life, to their great
Comfort, & to the Inableing them to Labour
Chearfully in the Lords Vineyard, Se=
=veral Living Testimonies ware born &
sevral good advices ware given, to Incourage
Friends to keep near to the Spirit of
the Truth in all their proceedings, the
Buisness was gone through in much
Love, after meeting took leave of Friends
& walked Home with two Friends

Page 19

1798 1mo [January] 4th went with my Wife to our
fifth day [Thursday] meeting I was very low in my
minde, under a sence of my own Weakness's
7, took a walk to Brails to meeting, found
Cousins Tolerable well I think it was a
satisfactory meeting two friends ware
their on a Religious Visit, viz Wm Alex=
=eander & Wife, walked from Brails to
Sibford to see Mother & Aunt, found
Aunt in a very weak state, took leave
of them and walked to Longcompton to
an Evening meeting appointed by the
desire of the above mentioned friends,
it was a very full meeting of Neigh=
=bours and I think a Satisfactory one
walked from thence to R. Fowlers little
Rolewright [Rollright] Lodged their
8, walked from thence to our Monthly
meeting at C.[hipping]Norton, at the Meeting
friends ware favoured with the Company
of the friends above mentioned & Tho's
Shelito, Tho's had to express that there was

verso

a great nescessiety for Friends to have
their mindes weaned more and more from
the things of this world, and to have their
affections set more on things above,
the buisness was gone through in
much Love, after meeting went to se
some friends, bid then Farewell &
walked Home with my Wife

10, this day a meeting was appointed for
the Marriage of Robt. Ashby of Stains
to M Albright, it was pretty large
of Friends, three straingers ware their viz Wm
Alexander & Wife from [blank]
and Tho's Shelito, I think it was a good
refreshing meeting, in which Devine
Love was felt to flow amoungst us, menny
Friends & other set their Hands to the
Marriage Certivicate. after meeting friends
spent the A.[fter]N.[oon] in a loving & Solid
manner, sevral Friends gave good advice
by way of Testimonie,
11, took a walk to Burford found Bror
& Sistor tolerable well, was at the

Page 20

Marriage of Cousin Jn'o Gibbs, who
took to Wife Abigail Tims, it was
a Pretty full meeting & I think a Satisfactory
meeting, Tho's Shelito, was pretty much
drawn forth in Testimonie after meeting
I went with Uncle Gibbs and Cousins
to Tainton [Taynton], spent a little time with
them in a Solid weighty manner then
bid them Farewell & walked Home
14, went with my Wife to our first
day [Sunday] meeting, it felt comforting & refreshing
to my minde, felt most easy to speak a
few words theirin
18, went with my Wife to our fifth day [Thursday]
meeting I think it was a low time with some
21, went with my Wife to our first day [Sunday]
meeting, as I sat theirin my minde was Comforted
I think Devine Love was felt to flow amoungst us
25. went with my Wife to our fifth day [Thursday]
meeting, it felt comforting and refreshing
to my exercised minde
28, took a walk to witney was at the morning
meeting it felt pretty comforting and refreshing
to my minde

verso

as also the A.[fter] Noon meeting did, spake a few
words in each meeting, felt Satisfaction to my
minde by so doing, after meeting went to se
some friends, spent the Evening with them

in a Solid and loving manner, Lodg'd at Jn'o Hangs
29 took leave of Cousins Barritts & Fr'ds, & walk'd Home
2mo [February] 1st went with my Wife to our fifth
day [Thursday] meeting, having been poorly for
sevral weeks, it felt comforting & refreshing
to my minde and body
4th having felt drawings in my minde for
sometime to take a walk to the Preparative
meeting at Southnewington and to the Monthly
meeting at Banbury, walked to Southnewington
to meeting it was small which was cause of
sorrow to my minde, it appeared to be my
duty to put friends in minde to Incourage
oneanother to be diligent in attending Meetings
and to set good Examples one unto another
after meeting spent a little time with friends
at Wm Harris's very comfortabley, walked from
thence to Banbury spent the Evening with
Friends in a loving agreeable manner Lodg'd at
Edw'd Stones
5th before meeting went to se some friends and
some acquaintances the all appeard very loving

Page 21

I think it was a good Satisfactory meeting
in which Devine Love was felt to flow
in some degree as from vessel to vessel,
the Buisness was gone through in Love
after meeting took leave of Sistor & Friends
& walked with some friends to Sibford Lodg'd
at Cousin Jn'o Hennocks
6th spent most of the morning with Mother
Aunt Archer & Cousin Harris, Aunt &
Cousin ware very poorly, Mother was
tolerable well, took leave of them & walk'd
to C.[hipping]Norton to se some friends who ware
poorly, walked from thence Home
8, went with my Wife to our fifth day [Thursday]
meeting, felt easy to sit in Silence
11, went with my Wife to our first day [Sunday]
meeting I think it was a good refreshing
meeting, felt easy to sit in Silence
12, went with my Wife to our Monthly
meeting held at this place, I think
it was a large satisfactory meeting
wee ware favoured with sevral Straingers
Wm Crutch was one, he was Inabled to

verso

Speak to the conditions of sevral Present
the buisness was gone through in Love,
after meeting menny Friends call'd to
se us, of whose Company we ware very glad
15th, went with my Wife to our fifth day [Thursday]
meeting, felt most easy to speak a few words theirin
18 went with my Wife to our first
day [Sunday] meeting, felt easy to sit in
Silence, I think Devine Love was
felt to flow amoungst us, to the unite
ing us near to each other
2=22 went with my Wife to our fifth
day [Thursday] meeting
F'day 25, took a walk to Stow to meeting
it was larger than I have sometimes
seen it, several ware their who are
under convincement, and I think if
they are truly faithfull unto the
manifestations of the Truth within them,
and Obey its Devine Instructions in
all things, they will become valueable

Page 22

Friends, I think it was a Satisfactory
meeting Devine Love being felt to
flow amoungst us to the Uniteing us
near to each other, spent most of the
Afternoon with friends in a Solid
and loving manner, Lodg'd at Fenmer
Peglers of Maughsbury they ware
very kinde to me
26, rose early & walked to Wm Couldings
Oddington to Breackfast, & from
thence Home
28, took a walk to Witney, was at the
fourth day [Wednesday] meeting, altho it was smallish
yet it felt pretty comfortable to my
minde, after meeting spent a little
time with friends in a loving & weighty
manner, walked Home in the Evening
3mo [March] 1st went with my Wife to Our

fifth day [Thursday] meeting, it felt very
comforting to my minde
3, took a walk with my Wife to C.[hipping] Norton
call'd to se some friends who ware Poorly af=
=terward returned Home, my Wife going
on for Sibford

verso

3mo [March] 1798

4th took a walk to Sibford to meeting
it was pretty large yet I think Devine
Power was felt to flow so plentifully
from vessel to vessel as I have
sometimes felt it, the preparative
meeting buisness was gone through
in much Love, after meeting I and
my Wife spent a little time at my
Wives mothers pretty comfortabley
afterward walked Home
8th went with my Wife to our fifth
day [Thursday] meeting in Sitting theirin my
Poor exercised minde was Comforted
felt easy to sit in Silence
11th took a walk to the Preparative meeting
at Witney, it felt pretty comfortable to my
minde, the buisness was gone through in Love,
spen the A.[fter]Noon with Cousins and some friends
very Comfortabley, had a Perticular Solid op=
=pertunity with one friends Family ware
my Mouth was opened to speak Comfortabley
to them, Lodg'd at Jno Hankins's
12th our Monthly Meeting was Tolerable large

Page 23

and I think a good Satisfactory Meeting
the buisness was gone through in Love,
after meeting spent a little time with
Friends agreeabley, walked Home with my
Wife and Sistor in the Evening
15th went with my Wife to our fifth day [Thursday]
meeting, felt most easy to sit in Silence
18, went with my Wife to our first day [Sunday]
meeting, it felt comforting and refreshing
to my minde
22, went with my Wife to our fifth
day [Thursday] meeting
25, took a walk to Milton to Meeting
altho it was small, yet according to the feel=
ings of my minde, the gracious promise of
blessed Jesus was fulfilled unto us, that ware
but two or three are met together in my
Name there I will be in the midst of them,
after meeting spent a little time with friends
in a Weighty and loving manner, and I
felt most easy to speak a little amoungst
them by way of Testimonie took leave of
them and walked Home

verso

1798

3mo [March] 29th went with my Wife to our
fifth day [Thursday] meeting
4mo [April] 1st took a walk to Barton to
meeting, it was smallish of Friends
but large of Neighbours, they I
think behaved tolerable well, I
felt most easy to advise the People
at seasonable oppertunities to Retire into Solid
Silence, that they might Expiearence
a being taught by the best of
teachers as teacheth as nevver Man
Taught, after meeting went to
Jarvices to Dinner, spent a little
time with them in Solid & Loving
manner, walked from thence to Enstone
to se Aunt Jones & Her Children,
& from thence Home
3. took a walk to our Monthly Meeting held
at Burford, it was largish, wee ware
favoured with the Company of Tho's Shelito
of Totenham, who is on a Religious Visit

Page 24

in these parts, In his Testimonie he desired
young Friends in a Perticular manner to sarve
the Lord quite Faithfully according to
the Knowledge they had received from

Him, least He should see meet to with=
draw His Power from them and nevver
vissit them with it any more
the Buisness was gone through in
Love, after Dining at Brors took
leave of them, walked from thence
with my Wife Sistor and another Friend Home
5, went with my Wife to our fifth day [Thursday] meeting
8, went with my Wife to our first day [Sunday]
meeting, it felt comforting and refreshing
to my minde, wee ware favoured with the
Company of Hanh Jarrot, she was Inabled
to bear a Comforting Testimonie theirin
9, took a walk with my Wife and
several Friends to our Quarterly
meeting held at Witney, both morning
and A.[fter]N.[oon] Meeting was very large of
Friends and Neighbours, the Neighbours I

verso

think ware well satisfied with the Meetings,
my minde was very low theirin, being sensible
of my own great Weakness's, and I also trully
see a great nescessiety for me to keep very
near to my Heavenly Guide, and Obey its
Instructions in all things not only in meeting
but out of Meeting, that I might be In=
=abled to overcome my Weakness's, and live
more to the Honnour of the Lord, Tho's Shelito
I think was Inabled to speak pretty Plainly
to the states and Conditions of menny present
after the Last meeting walked Home
10.walked to the Quarterly Meeting with
some relations, I think it was pretty
large, the Men and Women had a comfor=
=table sitting together before they enter'd
upon Buisness, the Buisness was gone
through in Love altho it held long, after
meeting my Wife I and sevral more friends
walked to Charlbury
12 went with my Wife to our fifth day [Thursday] meeting
15 went with my Wife to our first day [Sunday] meeting
I felt most easy to advise Friends to Indeavour

Page 25

always to have their mindes preserved in a
quiet comfortable state, by the opperation of
Devine Love within them
19, went with my Wife to our fifth day [Thursday] Meeting
22. went with my Wife to our first
day [Sunday] meeting, wee ware favoured with the
Company of sevral Friends, and I think
it was a good refreshing meeting, two Tes=
=timonies ware born theirin
I and my Wife ware Invited to the Fune=
=ral of a Neighbour not of our Society,
I thinking it to be a little degree of
my duty to go, I and my Wife went, it
was a very large Funeral, could not
feel easy without going into the Worship
House, tho some Friends I think object
against going any further than the Porch,
lest they should give Offence by Keeping
on their hats, I solidly considered wether I had
best go in or stay without I thought if I
staid without it would be because I would
shun the Cross and fear man which I knew I ought not and as to giveing

verso

Offence by keeping on my hat I felt it was
no Just cause of Offence, therefore I felt
most easy to go in, but their way of Worship
was so much in forms and Cerimonies, that
I could not feel qite easy without bearing
a Testimonie against it, I stop't till their
Cerimonies ware over at the grave, and then
I spake what I felt to be my duty to speak,
felt sweet Peace by so doing
26, went with my Wife to our fifth day [Thursday] meeting
as I sat theirin I mourned under a sence of my
own Weakness's, and great desires ware revised in
my minde unto the Lord that in His Love He would
be Pleased to favour me with Devine Power to over=
=come them
29 went with my Wife to our first day [Sunday] meeting

my minde was very low theirin. I seemed to be
such an Unworthy Mortal, as to be unworth of almost
any good thing
5mo [May] 3rd went with my Wife to our fifth
day [Thursday] meeting, felt most easy to sit in Silence
5th, took a walk to Longcompton Lodg'd

Page 26

with Cousin Bissel, who was Tolerable well
6th, got up early and walked to Shipstone
to Cousin Wells's to Breackfast, found
them and Friends Tolerable well,
was at their morning Meeting it was
Small yet it felt pretty comfortable,
walked from thence with Cousins and
some friends to Armscutt [Armscote]Meeting,
it was Large of Friends and Neigh=
bours I think it was a good meeting in
which Devine Goodness was pleased to
favour us with the Overshadowings of
His Heavenly Power, sevral Living Testimonies
ware born theirin, I could not finde Freedom to
open my Mouth, because of the sence I
had of my own Weakness, after meeting
walked to Cousin Fardons Treddington, spent
a little time with Cousins and Friends in
a loving and comfortable manner walked
from thence to Shipstone took leave of
Friends and Walked to Sibford with Jno Stone,
Lodg'd at Michael Petiphors

verso

7th of the 5mo [May] 1798 went pretty Early to se my
Mother=in=Law Aunt & Cousin spent a little
time their very Comfortabley, took leave
of them Except Mother who walked to
the Monthly Meeting, I walked with
some friends their, according to the feelings
of my minde Truth was low theirin,
the buisness was gone through in Love,
their was one thing that came under friends
consideration which required very Solid & deliberate
consideration, it was respecting putting down a
meeting held at Barton twice in a year
Chiefly on account of the Neighbours, I let
friends know the feelings of my minde which
was the Neighbours menny of them came, & I
thought if but two or three did meet together
in the Name of blessed Jesus, He would condescend
to be in the midst of them, their was no Nescessiety
for such friends to go as did not feel easy, let them
go as did, & if their was but one Sinner turned
from Darkness to Light and from the Power of
Satan to the Power of God, by the Workings of

Page 27

Devine Love, I thought the Meetings would
be pleasing in the Almightys Sight, but
friends concluded to put them down I thought
in to hasty manner, without giveing themselves
time Solidly to consider of so very weighty
affair, for I thought it was like Shutting the
Door against their Neighbours who ware willing
to come, and withdrawing their Love from them,
and as the had agreed to shut the Door it would
not be easily oppened again if their was a
nescessiety for it, my minde was much affected
with sorrow on account of the Meetings being
put down for I have been at menny very
good comforting meetings their
after meeting walked Home ware I found my
dear Wife pretty well, and feeling Devine Love
to cover our Mindes, my Minde was bowed in Humble
thankfullness before the Lord, and a thought was
brought to my Remmemberance which I had upon
the Road as I returned Home, on considering of my
menny great weaknesses and that without Devine
Assistance I could do no Good, it was this be very
carefull what thou dost, and ware thou dost go,

verso

5mo [May] 1798

10th went with my Wife to our fifth day [Thursday] Meeting

felt easy to sit in Silence
11 wee had an Evening Meeting appointed
by the desire of two Women Friends,
who ware on a Religious Visit from
America viz, Mary Sweat and Charity
Cook, they desired the Neighbours should
be let know of the Meeting, the accor=
=dingly ware, and a pretty menny
came, I think it was a large Satisfactory meet=
=ing, Devine Goodness was please to
Inable one Friend to bear an arrouseing
Testimonie to the lukewarm & such as
ware careless about the Salvation of
their Immortal Souls, of which I think
there ware menny in the Meeting, she also
was drawn forth in Solem Prayer
13. went with my Wife to our first day [Sunday]
meeting, it felt very comforting to my poor Minde
could not feel quite easy without speaking a
few Words theirin
14th I and my Wife went to our Monthly Meeting
held at C.[hipping] Norton, I think it was a good re=

Page 28

=freshing Meeting, one friend appeard in
Testimonie, the buisness was gone through in
Love, after meeting went to se some friends
they ware very Loving, in the Evening walked Home
16. took a walk to Witney, found Friends
Tolerable well, was at their fourth day [Wednesday]
meeting it was small yet it felt pretty
comfortable to my minde
17 went with my Wife to our fifth day [Thursday] meeting
19 this day the Constable and Tytheing men
came with a Warrant and took away our goods,
to the value of [blank] on account of my being
drawn as a Militia man more than a year agoe, I had been
sumonds sevral times to appear before the Justices's,
I appeared and let them know I could not do the least
thing to Incourage War and Fighting if I knew it, but
I clearly knew it had to be my duty to discourage it, and I
knew it to be my duty to Love my Enemies and do good to
them that hated me, and more to that purpose, but nothing
would satisfy them without causeing our goods to be taken
from us. I was much exercised in my minde and I prayed
in secret unto the Lord that He would be pleased to favour
me with His Life giveing Power that I might not offend Him
in Either Thought Word and Deed, what ever our Sufferings might

verso

be, and that I might be Inabled to bear all Tryals &
afflictions patiently for His great Names sake,
and Praises Praises be unto the Lord for Ever and for
Evermore saith my Soul, for His great mercy to me
and my dear Wife, because He was pleased to favour
us with His Life giving Power, in such a manner that
our mindes ware preserved still and quiet, altho the Tears
at times would run down our Cheeks and His Love caused
us to rejoice and breathe fourth thankfullness unto
Him, for His great Mercy unto us poor unworthy
Creatures, and altho we are reduced to have but very
little in this World yet wee have faith that if wee
Love the Lord in Sincerity and in Truth, and Obey His
Heavenly Power in all Things, He in His Everlasting
Love will give us Bread to Eate and Raiment
to Put on, and also feed us with the Bread and Water
of Life to the Comforting Refreshing and Nourishing
up our Souls unto Eternal Life

20 went with my Wife to our first day [Sunday] meeting altho
it was smallish five friends being gone to the Yearly
Meeting, yet I felt Devine Love to flow amoungst
us, to our Comfort and refreshment, and my Mouth
was Opened to testify of the Lords great love to His
Children,
24, went with my Wife to our fifth day [Thursday] meet=
=ing, it felt Comforting to my minde, felt easy to sit
in Silence

Page 29

27 went with my Wife to our first day [Sunday] meeting,
my minde was low theirin, and I was greatly sensible
of my own Weakness's, felt most easy to sit in Silence
31 went with my Wife to our fifth day [Thursday]
meeting, my minde was very low, felt most
easy to sit in Silence
3. took a walk to the Preparative meeting at
Southnewington, my Exercised minde was com=
=forted and refreshed, could not fall easy
without Advising Friends to be very carefull
of their Words & Actions that the might set
such good Examples unto others, as to be as
Lights in the World and as a City that is set
upon a hill which cannot be hid
their Preparative meeting buisness was gone
through in Love after refreshing my self at
Wm Harris's walked to the A.[fter]Noon meeting at
Sibford, it felt pretty comfortable to my minde
after meeting call'd to see some Relations & friends
walked from thence Home
7th went with my Wife to our fifth day [Thursday] meeting

verso

1798

6mo [June] 10th went with my Wife to our first day [Sunday] meeting
I was much sensible of my own Weakness's & the
want of Devine Power to refresh and comfort my
exercised minde which caused me to mourn, felt
most easy to sit in Silence, the Preparative
meeting buisness was gone through in Love
-11, went to our Monthly Meeting held at this place
I think it was pretty large and Comfortable
one Strainger Public Friend , she appeared in
Solem Prayer, in her Prayer she desired of the
Almighty that if He should be pleased to
try His People with much greater Triales
that they had been tried with, He would be
with them and Inable them to bear them Patiently
the buisness was gone through in Love
14, went with my Wife to our fifth day [Thursday] meeting
15, a Meeting was appointed to begin at
seven in the Evening by the desire of two
Friends in the Ministery, Joseph Nicolson from
Ireland, & John Abbot [blank] the Neighbours
ware let know according to the Friends
desire, a pretty menny came, I think it
was a good Satisfactory meeting, one friend

Page 30

was Inabled to speak pretty much concearning
the unprofitableness of Prayer, unless the
first felt the Almighty by His power to
prepare an Offering in them, I felt
it to be my duty to speak a few words,
which I did in Humility and fear under
a sence of my own weakness, felt Peace
to flow in my minde by so doing
17 rode before my Mother=in=law to her
Home at Sibford, was at the morning and
afternoon meeting, in both I mourned under
a sence of my own Weakness's and the
want of Devine Power to overcome them,
I found it to be very nesseceary for me to be

more carefull of my Words and Actions and
to be more attentive to the Instructions of the
Devine Power & Indeavour to Obey it more
Diligently and Carefully for the future,
after meeting took leave of my Relations
and rode Home
20, took a walk to Witney, was at the fourth
day [Wednesday] meeting, it felt comforting and
refreshing

verso

---

to my minde, spake a few words theirin,
after meeting went to se Cousins & some
friends, spent a little time with them
comfortabley, walked Home in the Evening
21, went with my Wife to our fifth day [Thursday]
meeting I sat in a lowly mournfull state,
under a sence of the menny trials and Exercises
that attend me and are likely to attend me,
I felt most easy to keep Silent
24, set out with my Wife towards our quarterly
meeting
to be held at Banbury, call'd at Jno Jarvices's
Barton, they ware very kind to us, and let my
Wife
Ride from their House to Adderbury as I sat in
Meeting I was very low and Sorrowfull under a
sence of my own Weakness's and the want of
Devine
Goodness, yet I think this was not the Situation
of menny Present, after meeting went to se some
friends. I felt it to be my duty to advise one
Friend that had fricquented Public Houses, to
be very
carefull of his Conduct, and indeavour for the
future
in Every Thought Word and deed to Acknowledge
the
Lord, that he might find Mercy of Him, before
the
things which belonged to his Everlasting
Hapiness ware
hid from his Eyes, walked to Milton, spend about
an
hour at Rob.t Pains and another friends in a
Solid and

Page 31

Loving manner. afterward walked to Banbury,
found
Sistors and friends Tolerable well, Lodg'd at
Tho.s Beesleys
25th was at Both the Public Meetings they ware
very
large a pretty menny People ware present not
of our Society, the behaved Tolerable well and
ap=
=peared to be well satisfied with the meetings,
and I think the ware very comfortable, Devine
Goodness was pleased to own us by causeing
His Everlasting Power to be felt amoungst us, to
the greatly comforting and refreshing menny
Present, and to make use of His poor
Instruments
to testify of His Loveing Kindness to the
Workmanship
of His Hands, and to advise the People not to
rest
contented with Religious forms and Ceremonies
without
Witnessing the Living Eternal Power, so to
operate
Within them, as to Cleanse them from all Sin and
Inicquity, after meeting spent the Evening in a
very Thoughtfull solid manner, Lodg'd at a
Neighbours
26, the Men and Women had a very comfortable
siting together before they Entered upon
buisness,
the American Friend was drawn forth in Prayer
in a Perticular manner at the forepart of
the Meeting, ware favoured with the Company of
Phebe Speakman from America, & Tho.s Cash
from
Cheshire, the buisness was gone through in Love,

verso

---

one Minute took up a pretty deal of time, it was
Concearning dropping the Public Meetings held
on Second day [Monday], some ware of the
minde they
should be kept up, some ware of the Minde the
had better be droped, I think as well as menny
Friends do the ware set up by the Direction of
best

Wisdom, the People are very desireous to come
and do flock to them and if Friends will In=
=deavour to live in Perfect obidience to the
mani=
=festations of the Truth within them, I think
the will be good and profitable meetings, and
will be held to the Honnour and Praise of the
Lord, after meeting walked Home with Bro.r,
had a Comfortable satisfactory Journey having
felt
Devine Love to be with me and my Wife to the
comforting and refreshing our Souls, and to the
Inableing us to bear tryals and Exercises
Patiently
for which mercies and Blessings and menny
others,
which we Injoy and are unworthy of our Souls
are
bowed in Humility and Humble Thankfullness
before the Lord,
27, yesterday my Wife walked with her Mother
to Sibford, and this day in the A.[fter]N.[oon] I
walked
to C.[hipping] Norton ware I met my Wife, and
walked
with she Home

Page 32

6mo [June] 1798

28th, went with my Wife to our fifth day
[Thursday] Meeting
7mo [July] 1st took a walk with my Wife to a
meeting held at Barton, Thos Cash out of
Cheshire was their, & several more stra=
=ngers Public Friends, It was a large
meeting a pretty Neighbours ware
their, I think it was a very refreshing
Satisfactory Meeting, Thos Cash was
greatly favoured to speak to the states
of menny present, & to speak to their
Conditions so as to reach the pure Witness
in them, & make then sensible that that it
was very rong for them to spend the
precious time which the Almighty giveth
them in a light careless & Thoughtless
manner and much more to Instruct them
concearning the Things which belonged
to their Eternal Happiness, after meet'g
went to John Jarvices to Dinner, spent a
little time with them in a Loving and agreeable
manner, took leave of them and walked to
Enstone, to se Aunt Jones & Cousins, & from
thence Home
5th went with my Wife to our fifth day
[Thursday] meeting sat in a

verso

7mo [July]: 1798

---

sorrowfull mournfull Situation being greatly
sensible of the want of Devine Power & Comfort
8th walked to Witney to the Preparative meeting
ware my minde was low under a sence of the want
of Devine Comfort and refreshment, felt most
easy
to sit in Silence, spent the A.[fter]N.[oon] with
Friends
in a Solid and agreeable manner, Lodg'd at Jno
Hankins
9 walked to our Monthly Meeting at Faringdon
ware I met my Wife she Riding with some
Friends in a Cart, from Charlbury, I think it was
a Satisfactory meeting altho my minde was low
and
poor being sensible of menny weakness's, I could
not
feel quite easy without adviseing the People to
minde
very carefully the Teaching of the Spirit of Truth
within them the Comforter, and be obidient unto
all
its Heavenly Instructions, that they might be lead
and
guided into all Truth, the buisness was gone
through
in Love, after meeting spent a little time with
friends
very agreeabley, Din'd at Robt Reynolds's,
afterwards
took leave of Friends and walked Home, my Wife
Return=
=ing in a Cart

12th went with my Wife to our fifth day [Thursday] meeting
it felt comforting to my minde felt most easy to sit in

Page 33

Silence, wee ware favoured with the Company
of Thos Huntley from Burford, and another
Friend in the Ministery from London, they
Both appeared in Public to Friends Incouragement
and Comfort
14 this day wee had a meeting by the desire
of two Women Friends in the Ministery, viz
Phebe Speakman from America, & Ann Crawly
from Uxbridge, it began at 10 oclock the Friends
ware wholy silent, I could not feel quite easy
without speaking a few words theirin
15, I went to our first day [Sunday] meeting, I was very
low and Sorrowfull theirin under a sence of the
menny Weakness's that attended me, and Strong
desires ware begotten in my minde, that the
Lord would be Mercyfull unto me and give me
Strength to overcome my Weakness's, and also to do
His Pure Will quite faithfully , and the Lord in His
great Love was Pleased so to Visit me With
His Power, as to bring my Heart into a State
of great tenderness and Contrition, to the causeing
mee to shed menny Tears, I felt most easy to sit
in Silence, at the latter Part of the meeting the Yearly
meeting Epistle was Read, which I think was very comfort=
=ing to menny

verso

7mo [July] 1798

19th went with my Wife to our fifth day [Thursday] meeting,
was low and Sorrowfull, for I see myself to be a
Poor weak mortal. Sat in Silence.

22, went with my Wife to our first day [Sunday] Meeting
it felt pretty comfortable and refreshing to my minde,
could not feel quite easy without speaking a
few words theirin, walk to C[hipping] Norton with
Cousin M. Bissel was at the Evening
Meeting it began at five, it felt comforting
and refreshing to my minde & I think it was
a Edifying and comforting Season, walked
Home after meeting
26 took a walk to Burford was at their
fifth day [Thursday] Meeting, as I sat theirin
my minde was oppress'd, been sensible
of great Weakness and the want of Devine
Power to Comfort me, and Inable me
to overcome my Weakness, found Brors
Family pretty well except Sistor, and Sistor as well
as could be expected, she having been
Delivered of a Son, last third Day [Tuesday],
spent a little time with them very
agreeabley, in the Evening walked Home
29, went with my wife to our first day [Sunday]

Page 34

Meeting, I felt poor and low in the fore=
part of the meeting, but afterward I think
Devine Power & Goodness arose and spread
over friends, & by the Power theirof I was
Inabled to speak a few words amoungst them,
8mo [August] 2nd went with my Wife to our fifth day [Thursday]
meeting, still continues in a low and mournfull
state yet the meeting felt a little comforting
4, In the A.[fter]N.[oon] took a walk to Brails
found Cousins there Tolerable well
spent the Evening with them comfortabley
Lodg'd at Cousin Wm Gillets
5, walked from Brails with Jno Gillett
to the morning meeting at Shipstone,
it was small which was cause of
sorrow to my minde, yet I felt a
little of the refreshing goodness of
the Almighty, walked from thence
with sevral Friends to Armscutt [Armscote]
meeting, it was pretty large of
Friends & Neighbours, and I think a

good Satisfactory Meeting, sevral

verso

Living Testimonies ware born theirin,
and I think the Pure witness was
reached in menny, and they ware
directed how and ware to finde the
unering teacher, as Teacheth better than
any Man or Woman could teach them,
spent a little time with Cousins
& Friends thereabouts very loving,
went from thence to Richd Fowlers
little Rowlright [Rollright], they ware very
kinde to me, Lodg'd there
6. after Breackfasting there walk'd Home
9, went with my Wife to our fifth day [Thursday]
meeting, it felt comforting and refreshing
to my minde, & I think to menny we ware
favoured with the
company of Tho's Speakman from
Reading, and Ann Ashby
10. went with Tho's Speakman and
Ann Ashby to C.[hipping] Norton, was at the
Meeting their, sevral Friends appeared
in Testimonie, but my minde was so low
under a sence of my own Weakness's that
I felt but little Comfort there from,

Page 35

went to Friend Atkins and spent a
bout an Our with them and some more
friends very comfortabley, sevral friends
through Devine Assistance ware In=
abled to speak Instructingly and Comfortabley
afterward took leave of Friends and
return'd Home
12, went with my Wife to our first day [Sunday]
meeting, it felt very comforting and refreshing
to my minde could not feel quite easy
without Speaking a few words theirin,
in the A.[fter]N.[oon] walked with my Wife and
some friends to Burford, found Bror &
Sistor & rest pretty midling, was at the
Evening meeting it felt comforting &
refreshing to my minde, ware favoured with the Com=
=pany of Tho's Speakman and Ann Ashby the Meeting was
concluded in Solem Prayer, Lodg'd at Bror
13, before meeting I an my Wife went to
se some friends they ware kinde, the
Monthly Meeting was large and I think
an Extroarderny favoured Meeting Sevral
living Comforting and Instructing Testimo=
=nies ware born theirin, the buisness was gone

verso

---

through in Love, and I think Truth Reign'd
throughout the whole Meeting, after
meeting spent a little time with Bror
& Sistor & Friends very agreeabley, in
the Evening had a comfortable walk Home
16, went with my Wife to our fifth day [Thursday]
meeting, I felt it to be my duty to seek
after a lowly Humble state of minde
19 walked to Milton with my Wife to the
Preparative Meeting, altho it was not
very large yet it felt pretty comfortable
to my minde, spake a few words theirin,
thinking it to be my duty so to do, the
buisness was gone through in a comfortable
manner, after meeting spent a little
time with friends in a loving Solid manner, in
the Evening I and my Wife walked Home
23, went with my Wife to our fifth day [Thursday]
meeting, my Exercised minde was a little
comforted theirin, & altho held in Silence I
think it was an Instructing Profitable meeting
26 went with my Wife to our first day [Sunday]
meeting it
was a little comforting to my poor Exercised
minde, one
friend spake a few words theirin

Page 36

1798

8mo [August] 30th went with my Wife to our fifth
day [Thursday] meeting, it felt a little comforting
to my
Exercised minde
9mo [September] 2nd went with my Wife to our
first day [Sunday] Meeting
it was held in Silence, my minde was comforted

and refreshed theirin, the preparative meeting
buisness was gone through in Love, in the A.[fter]
N.[oon]
walked with my Wife to C,[hipping] Norton, was
at the
evening meeting, it felt comforting & refreshing
to my minde, spake a few words theirin,
after meeting went to se some friends with
them we had some Solid agreeable Conversation
Lodg'd at Hanh Fardons
3 walked with my Wife to Sibford found
my Wives Mother Tolerable well we ware at
the monthly Meeting their it felt pretty
comfortable, yet I think it would have been
more Satisfactory if Friends had sat a little
longer before the had ented upon buisness,
sevral Women Friends appeared, their
Testimonies
ware short yet much to the purpose, the buisness
was gone through in Love, after meeting stop't
a little at My Motherinlaws, their company
was pleasent, took leave of them and my Wife
walked from
thence to Hook=Norton, drank Tea at the
Widow
walfords, she is Old and quite feeble, and altho
she is

verso

---

not Received a member, yet she goes to meetings
&
is kind and loving, and I think the Almighty doth
bless her at times with the Injoyment of His Love
to her great Comfort, took leave of her and
walked Home
5, went to C.[hipping] Norton in the A.[fter]
N.[oon] to meet my
Wife she staying behind me at her Mothers,
she and I spent a little time with Friends very
agreeabley
Returned Home afterward
6, went with my Wife to our fifth day [Thursday]
meeting, altho it was held in Silence it
felt comforting to my much Exercised minde,
9, went with my Wife to our first day [Sunday]
meeting,
my minde was much comforted theirin, I felt
most easy to advise friends to Indeavour to know
the Spirit of Supplication to be begotten within
them
10 took a walk with my Wife and
Brother=in=law
to our Monthly Meeting at C.[hipping] Norton,
towards
the latter part of the meeting Devine Good=
=ness was in great Mercy pleased to own us
with His Heavenly Power to our Spiritual
Comfort and refreshment, and to Inable some
to bear living Testimonies, the Buisness was
gone through in a Comfortable manner,
after meeting I and my Wife went to see
some friends and it being rainy stop'd all
Night, Lodg'd at our kind friends H. Fardons

Page 37

11th took leave of Friends and in the morning
walked Home
12, took a walk to Witney was at the fourth
day [Wednesday] Meeting, altho it was smallish
yet it
felt pretty comfortable, spake a little by
way of Testimonie, after meeting call'd
to se Cousins & some friends in the A.[fter]
N.[oon]
walked Home
13, went with my Wife to our fifth day [Thursday]
Meeting
it felt refreshing, it seemed to be my duty to
advise the young Friends to sarve the Lord
willing and with delight
16 walked to Oxford to Meeting it was very small
of Friends which was cause of sorrow to my
much
exercised minde, I think there was no friend in
the Ministery, except Jno Hankins's Wife &
myself
I could not feel easy without advising the People
to wait in Silence that they might be acquainted
and taught by the Unering teacher as teacheth
as nevver Man Taught Fr'd Hankins had also
a few words to Speak theirin, after meeting went
to Frd Jacksons's with some friends ware wee re=
=freshed ourselves, walked from thence to
Cousin Jos
Ashbys Shillingford, stoped a little & drank Tea
with menny friends walked from thence to
streetly

to Lodge

verso

9mo [September] 1798

17th rose Early and walked with some friends
to Reading found Cousn Tutteys tolerable well,
was at the morning Meet'g, it was quite small of
Friends, I think friends ware much comforted
with
the Power and Presence of the Lord, some ware
Inabled to bear living Testimonies, the afternoon
meeting altho larger was rath heavy and not so
lively,
owing in some degree I think to its being held
soonish
after Dinner, spent the evening a going to se some
friends, their company was pleasent and in some
degree
Edifying Lodg'd at Thos Stubbs's
18 the Quarterly Meet'g was not very large, the
Men
and Women sat together before they entered upon
buisness, it was a comforting refreshing time,
one frd
was drawn fourth in Solem Prayer, & good
Instruction
was given by way of Testimonie, the meeting of
Buis=
=ness I think was not a near so comfortable, &
Truth
did not arise into Dominion, their ware three
strangers
their viz Saml Southal & Ann Cristy & M Stacy
from London
I think all friends in the Ministery, the two
Women
Friends felt a concearn to pay the Men a visit
which the Men willingly consented to, Ann Cristy
express'd
that she though the public Meetings on second
day [Monday]
ware a rather a hurt to the Quarterly Meeting
buisness on third day [Tuesday], and she thought
it might
be best to have the Quarterly Meeting held on
second day [Monday], the other friend I think
express'd that

Page 38

---

she thought it would be best to dropt them
or make some alteration, and she desired friends
to take it weighty under their consideration,
and not be to hasty in concluding on it, Friends
considered of it and in a little wile one proposed
their being drop't, it did not feel easy to my
minde on account of People of other societies
who had Flocked to our Meetings some in a
solid manner with longing desires I think
to receive Devine Instruction & comfort to their
Poor souls, I told Friends I thought if they
ware to have the Select Meeting in the
morning on Second day [Monday] and to have an
Evening
meeting to begin at five, at which time I
thought friends would be got into town, it
might be very well, and better than to drop
them all at once, but no Friend makeing
any reply, a Minute was made to drop them
wholy, which was cause of sorrow and great
morning to my minde, afterward the other
minutes ware gone through tho not to much
Satis=
=faction, after meeting took leave of friends and
walked with some friends to Shillingford Lodg'd
at Cousin Jos Ashbys
19 after Breackfasting with Cous'ns who ware

verso

---

very kinde & loving to friends, took leave
of them and friends and Walked Home, some
friends accompanying me Part of the way
20. went with my Wife to our fifth day [Thursday]
meet'g
it felt comforting and refreshing to my Low
and sorrowfull minde, I could not feel quite
easy without adviseing friends to live agreeable
to their Holy Proffessions
22, took a walk to Jno Peglers Maughsbury
they ware pretty well and ware very kinde
to me, Lodg'd their
23 after breakfasting with Jno Pegler & His Wife
walked to Stow, call'd to se some friends
before meeting, their ware about fourteen

People at meet'g most of them not members, yet sevral
under Convincement and if they live in true Obidience to the Instructions of the Truth, I think they will become Usefull Members, amoungst us. Tho's Huntly was their from Burford, He was Inabled to speak Instruc= =tingly in Testimonie, and was drawn forth in very Solem Prayer, I think it was a very comfortable meeting, Devine Goodness being felt to flow from Vessel to Vessel, to our Great Comfort

Page 39

after Meeting stop'd a little with friends their company was pleasent, had a little com= =pany with Jno Pegler & Wife by them selves, was Inabled to speak unto them concearning the Trials and Exercises they ware likely to meet with if they Indeavoured to live in true Obidience unto the Instructions of the Truth, (they having been for sometime under Convin= =cement) also to Incourage them to trust in the Lord & be of good courage & He would strengthen their Hearts, Jno Pegler walked with me to Wm Coulings Odington, stop'd their a little
and drank Tea, took leave of them, walked from thence Home
27 went with my Wife to our fifth day [Thursday] meeting
it felt comforting, felt easy to sit in Silence
30 went with my Wife to our first day [Sunday] meeting,
altho my minde was low under a sence of menny Trials and Exercises that I have met with of late, yet my minde was comforted, it appeared to be my
duty to advise Friends to bear Trials and Afflictions
Patiently for the Truth's sake
10mo [October] [illegible] went with my Wife to our fifth day [Thursday] meeting
it felt comforting to my minde, it was held in Silence
7, went with my Wife to our first day [Sunday] meeting
ware Favoured with the Company of old Frd Barritt

verso

he Signified he Hoped to have felt the spring of Life to have flowed comfortabley amoungst us but was quite disapointed feeling a cloud to be over the
meeting, he thought it was caused through Friends
Inatention to the Devine Instructer
8, was at our Monthly Meeting, it was tolerable large and I think a pretty com= =fortable Meeting, sevral short Testimonies ware born theirin, to Incourage Friends to more Faithfullness, & to advise Friends to take care that the things of this World did not hurt their mindes, nor hinder their groth in the Truth, the buisness was gone through in Love, and I think we ware favoured with the Injoyment of Devine Love
11 went with my Wife to our fifth day [Thursday] meeting
it felt pretty comfortable, it was held in Silence
14. went with my Wife to our fifth day [Thursday] meeting,
I think Friends ware blessed with the Injoyment of Devine Refreshment, to the comforting and Strength
=ening them, spake a few words towards the latter
Part of the meeting
18 went with my Wife to our fifth day [Thursday] Meeting
I was sensible of my own weakness and the great need their was for me to patiently wait and seek for Devine Comfort

Page 40

21 went with my Wife to our first day [Sunday] Meeting,
felt easy to sit in Silence
25 went I and my Wife to our fifth day [Thursday] meeting, I think it was a low time with some
27, in the A.[fter]N.[oon] took a walk to Witney call'd to se Tho's Smith & his Family found three of his Children very poorly, two of them have been poorly for a long time, it is I think a great Affliction to the Parents, yet I think the bear it Patiently, believeing all Things will work together for their good if they love God in

sincearity and in Truth, went to Jn'o Hankins
ware I lodg'd and was kindly entertained.
28, before Meeting went to se Cousins and some
friends, the morning meeting felt pretty
comfortable, I was concearned to desire friends
to make good use of the precious time which
the Almighty see meet to give them & to Ex=
=piearence their Days work to go on with the
day time, Din'd at Cousin Barritts, the
A.[fter]N.[oon] meeting was small and felt not quite
so comfortable, after meeting had some refreshment
at Frd Diers, walked Home in the Evening
11mo [November] 1st went with my Wife to our fifth day [Thursday] meeting
Sistor Margarett was Safely Delivered of a
Daughter abt 3 in the Afternoon

verso

11mo [November] 4th took a walk to the Preparative
meeting at Hook=norton, it felt pretty
comfortable to my minde, I felt a concearn
to advise friends to Indeavour to become
acquainted with true Silent Worship that
the might Expiearence a being taught by
the Spiritual Teacher, as teacheth as nevver
man taught and that the might have a sence
that their days Work did go on with the day
time, after meeting went to see some friends
spent a little time with them in a Solid agree=
=able manner, walk Home afterward
6, took a walk to a monthly meeting held at
Stow, altho it was small yet I think it was
a pretty comfortable meeting, I spake theirin
by way of Testimonie as did also another Friend,
to Incourage Friends to be more diligent and care
=full to obey Devine Instructions, the Buisness was
gone through in a pretty comfortable manner, after
meeting spent a little time with Friends comfortabley
took leave of them and Walked Home
8, went with my Wife to our fifth day [Thursday] meeting
my minde was sorrowfull under a sence of my
own weakness's, and the want of Devine Comfort
11th, went with my Wife to our first day [Sunday] meeting, my
minde was low theirin, felt comfortable to sit in Silence
in the A,[fter]N,[oon] I and my Wife took a walk to Witney

Page 41

spent the Evening with some friends and Cousins
in a Solid and loving manner Lodg'd at Cousin Barritts
12 before the Monthly Meeting began went to see
some friends, the Meeting felt pretty comfortable
two of our Elder Friends appeared in Testimonie,
the Buisness was gone through in Love, after meeting
spent a little time at Frd Smiths, they are much
afflicted sevral of their Children have been poorly
for a longish wile & she is very poorly, which
caused me to Sympathise with them & in some
degree to mourn with them, call'd to se some more
friends, afterwards walked Home with some young Friends
15. went with my Wife to our fifth day [Thursday]
meeting, felt easy to sit in Silence
16, took a walk to C.[hipping]Norton, was at the Meeting
there, altho. it was small yet it felt com=
=fortable, & I think Devine Love was felt
to flow amoungst us, to the Uniteing one unto
the other, could not feel easy without speaking
theirin, after meeting spent a little time
with friends in a weighty agreeable manner,
afterwards walked Home
18, went with my Wife to our first day [Sunday] meeting
I think wee ware favoured with the flowings of
Devine Goodness amoungst us, it appeared rite for me
to advise the youth in a perticular manner to
sarve the Lord and Love the Truth

verso

[PAGE LEFT BLANK]

Page 42

[PAGE LEFT BLANK]

verso

1798

11mo 21st took a Walk to Milton, was at the fourth
day [Wednesday] meeting, it was very small which was
cause of Sorrow to my Minde, only a few Elder
=ly friends, except myself & one more, I felt a
little nescessiety to advise the Aged to be diligent
to Incourage others by Example and Precept
to be diligent in a tending meetings, and to
discharge their duties to the Almighty, after
meeting went to see some friends who ware
Poorly, afterwards walk'd Home
22, went with my Wife to our fifth day [Thursday] meeting,
sat in a low mournfull state
25, went with my Wife to our first day [Sunday] meeting
it felt pretty comfortable, Advised friends to
Labour to be possed with Charity,
Neighbour Cobb who is call'd Docter of [blank]
having rote to me desireing me to set out the
Tythe in our Garden, I being sorry, wrote
a paper and sent to him, Signifying it was
Contrary to Christ & His Desciples Doctrine to
pay Tythe, therefore for Conscience sakes
could not do it, I also made him a present of a
little Book which gave anaccount of the Reason
why the People Called Quakers do not pay Tythe
29 went with my Wife to our fifth day [Thursday] Meeting,
12mo [December] 2nd went with my Wife to our first day [Sunday] meeting,

Page 43

12mo [December] 1798

it felt Comforting to my minde, I thought a
Remant ware favoured to pertake of Devine Refreshment
to their Comfort, and to the renewing their Spiritual Strength,
the Preparative meeting buisness was gone through in Love,
5, took a walk to Witney was at the
fourth day [Wednesday] Meeting, two Strangers
both friends in the Ministery ware
at Meeting, Samuel Dier from Bristol
and Joseph Clerk from Street in Sumersetshire and the both appeared in Testimonie,
to arose the Careless ones, and Put them
in minde to sarve the Lord in Sincearity
and in Truth, also to Comfort and Incourage
the Mournfull Travelers Zion ward to hold
on their way without looking back
after meeting went to see Cousins and some
friends, Stop'd with them a little wile after=wards walked Home
6. went with my Wife to our fifth day [Thursday] Meeting,
Friends ware favoured with the Company of the two friends who
ware at Witney yesterday, I think it was a good
refreshing Time, the Friends ware led in a perticular
manner to advise friends to take care that a spirit
of bitterness did not getinamoungst any, but to
Indeavour to be truly Loving one towards another,
and indeavour to have their own wills Brought into True
subjection to the Devine Will, one Friend was drawn
fourth in Solem Prayer

verso

1798

12mo [December] 9th went with my Wife to our first day [Sunday]
meeting, my minde was refreshed and Comforted
theirin, Spake a few words to advise friends to
Indeavour to make the best use of the Lords blessings

and Favours, in the A,[fter]N,[oon] walked with
 Bror
and another friend to Burford, found Bror Sistor
& rest tolerable well, was at the Evening
meeting appointed by the two friends desire
who ware lately at Charlbury, it was a very
large meeting, menny Neighbours being Present,
and I think it was a Comfortable Satisfac=
=tory meeting, Sevral Living Testimonies ware
born theirin, and Samuel was drawn fourth
in Solem prayer, Lodg'd at Bros
10th before meeting went to see some friends,
the Monthly Meeting was pretty large and
Comfortable, Samuel in his Testimonie put
friends in minde how greatly friends Suffered
formerly in bearing faithfull Testimonies for
the truth, and Signified it was nescessary for us
to be truly greatfull for the liberties we do
Injoy, and Indeavour to bear Faithfull
 Testimonies
against all Unrighteousness, the buisness was
 gone
through in a loving Comfortable manner, after
meeting stop't a little at Bros took leave of them

Page 44

and walked with some friends Home, my Wife
Returning in the Cart
18th went with my Wife to our fifth day
 [Thursday] Meeting,
my minde was low being greatly sensible of the
 want
of Devine Comfort
15, in the A.[fter]N.[oon] took a walk with Bror
Robert to Witney spent the evening with
Cousins and friends very lovingly Lodg'd
to Jn'o Hankins's
16, took a walk to Oxford with some
friends to our Quarterly Meeting,
the publick meeting this day was not
very large yet it felt Comfortable,
the Lords Power was felt amoungst us,
and His Power Qualified & Inabled His
Sarvents to Spake to the States and
Conditions of the People, & to Incourage
them to depend on the Teachings of the
Spirit of Crist for Salvation, and
not to depend to much on Mans Teaching
after Meeting felt a Concearn to go and
se a Man & his Wife who have went to
Meetings sometimes, they appeared in Loving

verso

Tender frame of Mindes, I spake to them
what I believed Truth pointed out to me
to be my duty to speak I was much
Comforted by sitting with them & I think
the are Convinced in some degree of our
Principals, if the truly are Sincearly
Obey the Instructions of the Comforter
the Spirit of Truth within them, the
will become solid Friends, afterwards
went to se Jn'o Jacksons and His Family
he has lately lost his beloved Wife, she
was removed by Death very suddainly as
in the Prime of Life, which I think was
a great Affliction to him and his Family
yet the seem pretty comfortable and to bear
their Affliction quite Patiently, Lodg'd their
17, the Quarterly Meeting began at Nine I
think it was a pretty comfortable meeting
menny mouths ware opened to advise friends
not to be contented with the form of Religion
but Indeavour to Expiearence the pure Life
to arise in them, that their Labour might tend
to the Honnour of the Truth and to the
 Edification
and comfort of one another, friends ware put in
minde that it would be well for them to shut up

Page 45

their Shops to attend meetings, the buisness
was gone through in a pretty comfortable
manner towards the conclusion Samuel Dier
Expressed he felt a Concearn to have a
Public meeting in the Evening, which was
consented to, after meeting took leave of
some friends, walked Home with my Bror
in Law, had a Comfortable Journey my
minde is humbled and Contrited before the
Lord for His Love and Mercy unto me a poor
unworthy Creature praises be unto Him sayeth
my Soul for ever more
20 went with my Wife to our fifth day [Thursday]
 meeting
23 went with my Wife to our first day [Sunday]
 meeting,

it felt comforting and refreshing to my minde,
and I trust Devine Goodness was felt to flow
as from vessel to vessel, to the Uniteing us to=
=gether in Love
27 went with my Wife to our fifth day [Thursday] meet'g
30, went with my Wife to our first day [Sunday] meeting
my minde was Comforted and refreshed

1799 1mo [January] 3rd went with my Wife to our fifth day [Thursday]

meeting, it felt comforting to my minde
5th, took a walk to Sibford found Mother

verso

tolerable well, spent a little time with Mother
Aunt and rest comfortabley, Lodg'd at my
kinde friends Michael Petiphors
6th was at the Preparative meeting at Sibford
it felt pretty comfortable, found a concearn
to advise friends to Indeavour to be possess'd
with Charity, spent the A,[fter]N,[oon] with my Rela=
tions and some friends very comfortabley, went
to se Mary Gilks, who appears to be in a Decline,
I think she appears resigned unto the Devine
Will and to be in a comfortable state of Minde,
Lodg'd at M. petiphors, he and his Family
ware very kinde to me
7th, walked with sevral Friends to the Monthly
meeting at Southnewington I think it was
largish and pretty comfortable, felt a Concearn
to advise friends to Indeavour to be possess'd
with Charity and Incourage one another to sarve
the Lord, the buisness was gone through in a con=
=descending Loving manner after meeting walk'd Home
10th went with my Wife to our fifth day [Thursday] Meeting
my minde was refreshed and comforted
13 went with my Wife to our first day [Sunday] meeting
it felt comforting and refreshing to my Exercised minde
in the A,[fter]N,[oon] walked with my Wife and

Page 46

another friend to C.[hipping]Norton, spent
the Evening with some friends Love=
-ingly, Lodg'd at Hanh Fardons
14, before the monthly Meeting began
I and my Wife went to se some
friends, the Monthly Meeting I think
was tolerable large and comfortable
we ware favoured with the Company
of our friend Eliz. Mintchon who
hath been from Home a pretty wile
on a Religious visit, She Expressed
in Testimonie that Friends should be
very carefull not to set their Hearts
on the things of this World, nor covet them,
and also that they should set good Examples
unto others and be very carefull to keep
within the limits of Truth, in their Dealings,
the buisness was gone through in Love,
Eliz: Mintchon came into the mens Meeting and expressed that she
had performed Her Visit through Devine Assistance
to her Satisfaction and sweet Peace, she
Signified she had Public Meetings much to her
comfort and Perticularly at one Island, ware at

verso

on near the Conclusion of one Meeting, a
Woman stood up not of our Society, and Ex=
=pressed in the French Language her Satis=
=faction of the Meeting, and She perceived
she spoke through the Assistance of the
same Spirit and Power by which she went
to visit the People in, after Meeting I
and my Wife walked Home with some friends
17. went with my Wife to our fifth day [Thursday] Meeting
18, took a walk to Witney to the Funeral
of John Fardon a Solem Meeting
was held on the Occasion, of Friends
and Neighbours, sevral Living Testimonies
ware born to put the People in minde
of the Unceartainty of Life and ceartainty

of Death, as also of the nescessiety there
was for them to live Righteous and Holy
lives that the might be always ready without
fear to meet the Messenger of Death, who will
not be denied by any not even the very Healthyst
and Strongest, but all must submit to him
when ever it shall please the Almighty to send
him, and then the must receive a reward according
to the Deeds done in the body, after meeting went
to see some friends and the Children of the deceased
who ware Poorly, and appeared to have their mindes

Page 47

covered with a degree of awefull solemness
for the Loss of their dear Father,
walked Home with Bror Robert.
20. went with my Wife to our first day [Sunday] meeting,
it felt refreshing to my much exercised minde,
could not feel quite easy with out Incouraging
friends to Indeavour to love Solid Silence, that they
might be become acquainted with the Will of the Lord,
and also receive strength from Him to do it,
24 went with my Wife to our fifth day [Thursday] meeting
was greatly sensible of my own Weakness's and the
nescessiety for me to Patiently wait & Earnestly
Labour, for Devine Instruction and Refreshment
27, went with my Wife to our first day [Sunday] Meeting
it felt comfortable, and I think we ware favoured
to pertake of Heavenly refreshment to our great
comfort and Incouragement, to Indeavour always
to walk in the way of true Peace
31, went with my Wife to our fifth day [Thursday]
meeting, my minde was refreshed and Comforted
2mo [February] 3rd went with my Wife to our first
day meeting, it felt comforting, Sat in
Silence, it was our Preparative meet'g,
7, went with my Wife to our fifth day [Thursday] meeting,
it felt refreshing and Comforting

verso

2mo [February] 1799

10th I went to our first day [Sunday] meeting, my Wife
staid at Home, she having sat up last night
with Dear Mother who is very poorly, the meeting
felt refreshing to my much Exercised Minde,
spake a few words to Incourage Friends to Indeavour
to feel True Peace of Minde,
11th went with my Wife to our monthly Meet'g
it was very small on account of the Weather,
it was held in Silence yet I trust we ware
favoured with the flowings of Devine Love
to our Spiritual Refreshment and Strength,
and to the Uniteing us near to each other,
the buisness was gone through in a Loving Manner
14 went with my Wife to our fifth day [Thursday]
meeting, it felt comfortable, felt easy to sit in Silence
17 went with my Wife to our first day [Sunday]
meeting, felt easy to sit in Silence
21. went with my Wife to our fifth day [Thursday] Meet'g
it was a low time with me. sat in Silence
24 went with my Wife to our first day [Sunday] Meeting
my minde was much exercised and very sorrowfull
on account of the exercises and trials I have met
with, yet my minde was comforted with the Injoyment
of Devine Love, at the latter part of the Meeting
spake a few Words
27th took a walk to Witney was at their week day
meeting, it felt pretty comfortable altho small

Page 48

28th went with my Wife to our fifth day [Thursday] meeting,
it felt refreshing, sat in Silence
3mo [March] 1st took a walk to C.[hipping] Norton was at the
sixth day [Friday] meeting, it felt comforting

spake a few words towards the
Conclusion of the Meeting
3. took a walk to Burford found Bror
poorly, Sistor & rest tolerable well,
was at the preparative Meeting, it
felt pretty comfortable, Frd Mintchon
was perticularly drawn forth in Tes=
=timonie towards the Scollars, I could not
feel easy without speaking a few words
towards the latter part of the Meeting,
spent the A.[fter]N.[oon] with Bror & Sistor and
in visiting some friends in a loving com=
=forting manner, Lodg'd at Brors
4 took leave of Bro'r & Sistor pretty Early
and walk'd Home
7 went with my Wife to our fifth day [Thursday]
Meeting,
10, went with my Wife to our first day [Sunday]
Meet'g
it felt pretty comfortable, spake a few
words to advise friends to feel after a state of
sweet Innosciency
11, took a walk to our Monthly Meeting at

verso

Witney, it felt Tolerable comfortable,
I could not feel quite easy without adviseing
friends to Labour diligently for true Peace
of minde, the buisness was conducted in love,
I think this is a very Exerciseing time with
sincear Honest hearted friends in some degree
on account of a tax lately put upon In=
=come, on purpose to Support War. I being
much exercised concearning it, thinking Friends
could not pay it and bear a faithfull and
Christian Testimonie against War and Oppressing
our fellow Mortals, towards the Conclusion
of the Meeting I stood up, and expressed what
I felt concearning it, wishing Friends to solidly
Consider
of it and not do any thing that might disturb
the peace of their Mindes, after meeting spent
about two ours with friends agreeabley, walk
Home with my Wife and sevral Friends
14, went with my Wife to our fifth day [Thursday]
Meeting
17, went with my Wife to our first day [Sunday]
Meeting, my minde was very low under a
a sence of the menny Trials & Exercises
I meet with and are likely to meet with,
felt easy to sit in Silence

Page 49

3mo [March] 1799

21st went with my Wife to our fifth day
[Thursday]
meeting, it felt refreshing and Comforting
23, took a walk to Sibford call'd to
se some friends found Mother & Sistor
tolerable well, but Aunt very poorly
walked from thence to Brails, found
Cousins pretty well, Lodg'd at Cousn Wm
Hemmings
24 before Meeting spent the time with
Cousins and some friends in a Comfortable
Edifying manner, altho the Meeting
was small yet I think there is a
degree of Increase of late, it felt
pretty comfortable, I had a pretty
comfortable time in Testimonie, warein
I was led to Incourage them to persevear
in the way of well doing, and in a perti=
=cular manner to Incourage the youth
to Join in with the gracious Visitation
of Devine Love which I thought was
Mercyfull extended towards them,
Dind at Cousin Wm Gilletts who ware very
kinde to me took leave of Cousins and
walked Home
28 went with my Wife to our fifth day [Thursday]
Meeting

verso

[page left blank]

Page 50

[page left blank]

verso

3mo [March] 1799

31st went to our first day [Sunday] Meeting it felt
pretty comfortable felt easy to sit in Silence
it was our Preparative Meeting
in the A.[fter]N.[oon] took a walk to Burford,
4mo [April] 1st before meeting went to se some friends,
the Meeting before the enter'd upon buisness
felt very comfortable, sevral living Testimo=
=nies ware born, I felt a Concearn to speak
a few words but was afraid of moving before
the right time and friends standing up pretty
soon one after another I put it of till near
the conclusion of the meeting, and then I was
ready to say in my minde their has been a deal
said it may not be nescessary for me to Speak,
but upon considering if I did not I might
go away with a Burden on my minde, I con=
=cluded it would be best to speak what rested
with weight upon my minde, theirfore I spake
in Humility and with much care being fearfull
least I should take up too much time in the Meet'g
the Buisness was gone through in Love, the
yearly meeting Queries ware answered and an
account of Friends Sufferings Brought in,
after meet'g took leave of Bror Sistor & Friends
& walked with my Wife Home
2nd went with my Wife to our fifth day [Thursday] meeting
7th went with my Wife to our first day [Sunday] Meeting,
it felt comforting and refreshing

Page 51

8th in the A.[fter]N.[oon] took a walk to Witney found Cousins &
Friends tolerable well, Lodg'd at Cousin Wm Barritts
9th before our Quarterly Meeting began went to se
some friends, the Meeting I think was Tolerable large
& it felt pretty comfortable sevral Living Testimonies
ware born, wareby Friends ware advise to be more
Carefull to attend to devine Instructions and to be more diligent to
obey them, I felt easy to sit in Silence, afterward
the Men and Woman seperated for to go through the
Buisness. the Answers to the Queries gave accounts that
Friends ware in a low Situation, when they came to
that Query, are friends Faithfull in our Testimonie
against bearing Arms &et I could not feel quite
easy without expressing I thought if Friends
paid a New Tax which is Said to be on purpose
to Inable the King to carry on a War, they could not
clearly say, We do not know but friends bear
a faithfull & Christian Testimonie against
bearing Arms, Sevral Friends signifyed they
thought it was not right to pay it or something
to that purpose after meeting I and my Wife
walked Home with some more Friends
11 went with my Wife to our fifth day [Thursday] meeting
we ware favoured with the Company of Edwd
May and Hannah Jarrot, I think it was a
good refreshing Meeting, sevral mouths ware opened

verso

4mo [April] 1799

to testify of the Mercy and goodness of God to such
as put their whole Trust and Confidence in Him,
14, went with my Wife to our first day [Sunday] meeting
18, went with my Wife to our fifth day [Thursday] Meet'g
it was a low season with me, I being sen=
=sible of the want of Devine Comfort
21 went with my Wife to our first day [Sunday] meeting

my minde was refreshed and comforted, feeling
Devine Love to flow amoungst us,
25. went with my Wife to our fifth day [Thursday]
meeting, it felt comforting to my poor Minde
28 went with my Wife to our first day [Sunday]
meeting
it felt quite comforting, held in Silence
5mo [May] 1st a Public Meeting was appointed
to be
held in the Evening by the desire of two
Women Friends from America, viz Hanh
Barned and Elizth Cogshall, it was a large
& comfortable meeting, menny Neighbours came
and behaved
tolerable well, one Friend appeared in
Testimonie, she Signified in a perticular manner
their was a great
Nescessiety for the People to amend their
ways and their doings, for if they did not,
she was a fraid they would feel the Judgement
of the Lord more than they had felt them,

Page 52

1799

5mo [May] 2nd went with my Wife to our fifth
day [Thursday]
meeting, wee ware favoured with the Company
of the American Friends, one of them
was drawn forth in an arouseing Testimonie
to the luke=warm and Indifrent, she also
Incouraged the Sincear Honest Hearted to put
their trust in the Lord and Sarve Him
Faithfull, she was also drawn forth
in Solem Prayer
5th went with my Wife to our first day [Sunday]
meeting
it felt comforting, spake a few words theirin
7, took a walk to our monthly meeting
at C.[hipping]Norton it felt pretty comfortable,
towards the conclusion of the Meeting sevral
youngish Friends appeared in Testimonie to
the comfort and Incouragement of the sincear
Honest Hearted mindes, as also to arouse
the lukewarm & Indifrent ones and to put
them in minde of their Duty,
the buisness was gone through in a comfortable
manner
after meeting went to see some friends,
in the Evening walked Home,
9 went with my Wife to our fifth day [Thursday]
meeting
12. took a walk to Burford found Bror &
sistor tolerable well, the Meeting felt pretty

verso

Comfortable, after meeting spent a little time
with friends, Elizth Mintchin was poorly,
Drank tea at Brors in the Evening walked Home
15th took a walk to Witney, was at the fourth
day [Wednesday] meeting. spent a little time with
Friends
comfortabley, afterward walked Home
16 was at our fifth day [Thursday] meeting, it felt
comforting, felt easy to sit in Silence
19 went with my Wife to our first day [Sunday]
Meet'g
it felt refreshing, it was held in Silence
23, went with my Wife to our first day [Sunday]
meeting, I was low and poor in my Spirit,
but after sitting a wile in Solid Silence
the Lord was please to arise to my Comfort
all Praises be unto Him, felt easy to sit in Silence
30. went with my Wife to our fifth day [Thursday]
Meet'g
2nd took a walk to Sibford found Mother
& sistor tolerable well, was at the Prepa=
=rative meet'g, my minde was refreshed therein
felt a concearn to advise the youth to be
more Obidient to Devine Instructions, spent
the A.[fter]N.[oon] with Mother and friends
Comfortabley
Lodg'd at Michael Petiphors

Page 53

6mo [June] 1799

3rd walk'd with a friend to the Monthly
Meet'g at Adderbury, my minde was
refreshed being sensible Devine Love
was felt amoungst us to the Comforting
of Friends, the Buisness was gone through

in Love, after meeting walked to Milton
Spent a little time with friends agreeabley
walked from Milton Home
6. went with my Wife to our fifth day [Thursday] Meet'g
9, went with my Wife to our first day [Sunday] Meet'g
it felt very refreshing, Some Mouths ware
opened to testify of the Lords Mercy and
goodness, to such as truly Obeyed the teachings
of His Spirit within them
10 went with my Wife to our Monthly Meet'g
held at this Place, it felt comforting, sevral
living Testimonies ware born, the buisness
was gone through in Love
13. went with my Wife to our fifth day [Thursday]
meeting, we ware favoured with the
Company of Thos Huntly. He appeared
in a Comforting manner
F[irst] Day [Sunday] 16 went with my Wife to meeting, it
felt quite comforting, I Hope we ware favoured
to Injoy that Love which comforteth the Poor and Contrited

verso

6mo [June] 1799

20 went to our fifth day [Thursday] meeting, my
Wife stay'd at Home on account of being
with my Dear Mother in the Night
23, last night my Dear Mother Departed
this Life, after a long time of Illness,
she went through much Bodily weakness
for menny years before she Died, which
she bore I trust with Patience and Re=
=signation, she was a loving and affectionate
Parent, and Industerous according to the little
strength she was favoured with, she laboured
to have her Children grow up in the Truth
and walk agreeable theirunto, she gradualy
got weaker, her weakness towards the Last was
so great that she was not able to feed nor
turn herself in the Bed for menny weeks
before she Died, she was favoured to Depart
quietly and I do not doubt but that the
Lord in His Everlasting Love has removed
her Soul out of a State of great Affliction
and Probation, into His glorious Kingdom
their to praise Him and Injoy Everlasting Happiness

Page 54

I went to our first day [Sunday] meeting and was favoured
to pertake of Devine Refreshment,
24 took a walk to Milton Lodgd at Robt Pains
they behaved very friendly and kinde
25, walked to our quarterly Meeting at Banbury,
I think it was largish, the men and Women
sat together before the entered upon buisness,
and the Neighbours ware suffered to come in,
sevral Friends appeared in Testimonie, one stranger
Thos Cash, by answers to the Queries
Account was receive as hath been the case generaly, that
some friends ware neglectfull in the Attendance
of Meetings on first day [Sunday] afternoons and those
call'd week days, and also drowsy ness appeared,
Friends ware much advised to be very diligent in
the attendance of our Meetings for if their greatest
Love was to live to the Praise and Honnour of the
Lord and to se truth reighn over all, or to that purpose
the could not be easy to neglect Meetings, and when their
to give way to a Drowsy careless disposition,
I think it is a great Mercy and Blessing for which
Friends ought to be very Thankfull, that they are
favoured with oppertunities often to meet together without

verso

---

being molested, to Wait upon the Lord to receive Devine
Instruction and Spiritual refreshment, and also rest
and Refreshment to their Bodies, I think such as
slight such Blessings, Reject the tender Mercies
of the Lord, and Neglect to do their Days Work in

the day time, O! that such might be aroused and
put in Remembearance to work wile it is day, to
work out their own Souls Salvation with fear and
Trembling before the Lord, wile He is favouring them
with assistance strength and Oppertunity, for the
Night cometh warein no Man can Work, and we
know not how soon,
after meeting bid friends Farewell and walked Home
27th this being the day appointed for the Burial
of Dear Mother who Died in the [blank] year of her
Age, after a long time of Affliction and Bodily
Weakness which I Hope she bore with Patience &
Resignation, a pretty menny Friends and Neighbours
attended the Meeting, & I think it was a good Comforting
Edifying meeting, in which Devine Providence
was Pleased to extend His Love and His Goodness
unto menny, sevral Living Testimonies ware
born to put the People in minde of their duty
unto the Almighty and of the nescessiety their was

Page 55

for them to prepare for their latter end,
I wished I might be easy to keep Silence,
but feeling a Concearn in my minde to advise
the people to be more obidient to the Instructions
of the Truth within, that the might Expear=
=ence their days work to go on with the
day time, I spake what rested upon my
minde, felt easy in so doing, after meeting
spent the A.[fter]N.[oon] with Relations and Friends
Comfortabley
30. went with my Wife to our first day [Sunday] Meeting
it felt very comforting and refreshing to
my much Exercised minde, spake theirin,
7mo [July] 4th went with my Wife to our fifth day [Thursday] Meet'g
-7 went with my Wife to our first day [Sunday] meet'g
I was greatly sensible of my own Weakness,
and the want of Devine Assistance and
Comfort after meet'g walked to Witney spent
the evening with Friends I Hope to our
Edification and Comfort Lodg'd at my Kinde friends Jno Hankins's
8 walked to our Monthly Meet'g at Faringdon
it was largeish sevral Neighbours came in,
two Strangers their Wm Crutch and David Dent,
sevral Testimonies ware born, I Hope to the Instruction

verso

Edifycation and comfort of the People, Stop'd
a little after meet'g with Friends, observed some
young friends to light and airy, which was cause of Sorrow
in the A.[fter]N.[oon] Friends gathered together at R.
Reynolds's ware the ware favoured to Draw into
Stillness and Retiredness and I Hope to seek unto the
Lord for His Instruction Help and Comfort,
I trust He was pleased to own us, sevral States
ware spoken unto, in the Evening took leave of
Friends and walked with Bror R. to Witney Lodg'd at JH
9th Breackfasted at Jn'o Hankin's & spent a little
time with them very comfortable, felt a little
concearn to visit Wm Fardon being one of our
Society a young man who has neglected Meet'gs and been very
Disorderly in his Conduct other ways,
I Indeavoured to be quite plain with him and Spake
what I believed was my duty to speak, felt
Satisfaction by so doing, he appeared reach'd
and tendered, expressed he took my visit kindly,
reach'd Home about one Oclock
11 went with my Wife to our fifth day [Thursday] Meet'g
12 went with my Wife to our first day [Sunday]
meeting, it felt very comforting which caused
my Heart to rejoice with Fear under a sence
of my own Weakness, speak a few words
16, went to our fifth day [Thursday] meeting

Page 56

7mo [July] 21st went with my Wife to our first
day meeting, it felt very Comforting

and refreshing, we ware favoured with
the Company of two Friends in the
Ministery, viz Sarah Talbot from
America, & Sarah Shackelton from
Ireland, one of them appeared in
Testimonie, I trust to the Comfort
Instruction & Edifycation of menny
in the Eving a meeting was held
by the appointment or desire of the
two strangers the Neighbours ware
let know of the Meet'g and menny
came I think the behaved tolerable
well, and it was a good meeting in which
Devine Providence was Pleased to cause
His Power to be felt amoungst us,
sevral Testimonies ware born and sevral
states spoken unto, and menny I trust ware
comforted Edifyed and Instructed how they
might walk in the way of true Peace
22nd went to C[hipping] Norton with some friends
on Horse=back, and the Friends who visited
us, ware a meeting was held by their desire

verso

I trust it was a good Satisfactory Meet'g
in which the Sincear Honest Hearted ware
comforted and refreshed, and the Lukewarm
and Indifrent ware Instructed to be more
diligent in sarveing the Lord, that they might
be prepared with Oil in their Lamps that
when the Bride Groom came they might be ad=
=mited in With Him, after meeting spent a
little time with the Friends and Other
Friends Comfortabley, took leave of them
and Rode Home before my Wife, who walked
yesterday with her Mother
25. went with my Wife to our fifth day [Thursday] Meet'g
28, went with my Wife to our first day [Sunday] Meeting
it felt comforting, felt easy to sit in Silence
8mo [August] 1st went with my Wife to our fifth day [Thursday] Meet'g
3rd took a walk to Shipstone with Cous'n
Wm Cork & his Sistor, Lodg'd at Cous'n Widow Ashbys
4th was at the morning Meeting at Shipstone,
it was Small truth appeared low amoungst
friends their, which was cause of Sorrow to my
minde, my Mouth was opened theirin, their was one
young Man, George Wills, who I think latelyish came
amoungst Friends, he appeared greatly Exercised even
to such a degree as to tremble very much, afterwards
he appeared in a few Words, I felt pretty much for

Page 57

---

the Young Man, and had some conversation with him
afterwards, I think he told me he was nevver
Exercised in any meeting before in such a manner, afterwards
walked with sevral friends to Armscutt [Armscote]Meet'g,
it was large of Neighbours, I do not know that
their was any Frds or the Ministery beside Thos Harris & Myself, I think it was
a Comfortable Satisfactory Meeting, after meeting
walked to Frd Lamblys Tredington to Din'r,
took leave of Frds and walked to Shipstone, spent
a little time with Friends their agreeabley. took
leave of them and walked to Richd Fowlers RoleWright [Rollright]
ware I was kindely Entertained,
5 walked to C.[hipping]Norton, stop'd with Frds there a little,
& afterward walk'd Home
8, went with my Wife to our fifth day [Thursday] Meeting
11 went to our first day [Sunday] meeting, it felt
comfortable, spake a few words theirin
12 took a walk to our Monthly Meeting
held at Burford, it felt comforting, sevral
Friends appeared in Testimonie, I felt easy to sit in
Silence, and was very desireous for to feel a Nes=
=cessiety laid upon me to speak if it was my
duty to Speak, the buisness was gone through in
a comfortable manner, after meeting went to

verso

se some friends spent a little time with them
and Bror & Sistor comfortabley, took leave of
them and walked Home, my Wife rode Home
15th went with my Wife to our fifth day
[Thursday] Meet'g
18, went with my Wife to our first day [Sunday]
meeting,
I think Devine Providence was pleased to
manifest
Himself amoungst us, to our Comfort and
refresh=
=ment, it was held in Silence
22 went with my Wife to our fifth day [Thursday]
Meeting
24 sometime ago I felt a concearn to speak to a
young
man I understood it was Intended he should be
Instructed for to
be a Parson, so call'd I thought in some degree
he was
of a good Disposition, on that account was the
more
desireous to speak with him to Incourage him to
be very
carefull to minde the Instructions of the Truth in
his own minde and
Diligently Obey them, and also to let him know
that it was
out of the Power of men with all their Teachings
and Wisdom
to Prepare & Qualify any Person to be a true
Gospel
Minister, for that did belong to the Lord, I
Indeavoured
to get an Oppertunity to speak with him several
times
but could not, on that account I wrote what I
felt a
concearn to speak to him, and delivered it to his
Mother
to give to him, felt comfort to my minde by so
doing,
25 went with my Wife to our first day [Sunday]
meeting, my Minde
was refreshed and comforted, speak theirin
29, went with my Wife to our fifth day [Thursday]
meeting, it was
held in Silence

Page 58

1799

9mo [September] 1st went with my Wife to our
first day [Sunday] Meeting,
it was held in Silence, I was greatly sensible of
my own Weaknesses's, and of the Necessiety their
is
for me to Wait in Humility for Devine
Refreshment,
our Preparative meet'g buisness was gone
through in Love,
5th went with my Wife to our fifth day
[Thursday] meet'g
felt easy to sit in Silence, it felt comforting
8 went with my Wife to our first day [Sunday]
meet'g, I think
Devine Goodness was pleased to comfort &
refresh us
with His Life-giveing Power, Wm Lawton of
London
appeared in Testimonie, I also felt a Concearn to
speak,
9, took a walk to our Monthly Meeting at
C,[hipping]Norton, my Wife Rode, I
think it was a good refreshing meeting, sevral
Friends
appeared in Testimonie, the young Friends ware
advised
in a perticular manner to be quite faithfull unto
Devine Instructions & Requireings, that they
might be
Prepared and Qualified to supply the Places's of
the
Elders, the buisness was gone through in Love
after meet'g I and my Wife spent a little time with
Friends and walked Home
12, took a walk to our fifth day [Thursday]
meet'g with my Wife
it felt comforting I hope to menny, praises &
Honnours
be unto the Lord
15, took a walk to Oxford with Bror R, the
meeting was small of Friends & Neighbours,
one friend appeared in Testimonie, I was greatly
sensible of my own Weakness and the wants of
Devine Comfort,

verso

Dined at George Tittertons, walk'd afterward with some
friends to Shillingford , found Cousin Ashbys tolerable
well, went to Warborough to se Joseph Sargood
who is lately Maried, Lodg'd at Jno Sargoods,
16 walked with some friends to Reading, found Friends tolerable well, went to see our
Relations and some friends, their Company was
Comforting, Lodg'd at Cousin Tutteys,
17 Call'd to se some friends before the Quarterly meeting began,
the men and Women sat together before the
entered upon buisness, sevral living Testimonies
ware born, I also felt a Concearn to speak a few
sentances, the buisness was gone through pretty comfortabley,
after meet'g took leave of Friends and walk'd
to Shillingford ware I was kindly entertained with
other friends, at Cous'n Jo.s Ashbys, Lodg'd their,
18. after Breackfast walk'd to Oxford, spent a
little time with friends their, I trust in a Comforting
Eddifying manner, walked from thence with Bror R. Home
19 went with my Wife to our fifth day [Thursday] meet'g
my minde was comforted, it was held in Silence
22 walked to Brails to meeting it felt pretty comfortable
spent the A.[fter]N.[oon] with Cousins and some Friends
in a Solid manner, giveing through Devine Assistance
some Instructions ware I thought it to be my duty so to do,
Lodg'd at Cousin Wm Gilletts they ware very kinde
23 walked with friends to the Quarterly Meeting at Shipstone
I think it was a Satisfactory Meet'g, T. Shelito was there from

Page 59

sevral Friends appeared in Testimonie,
I thought menny friends had to much love for the
things of this World, and set their Hearts to much upon
them, which hindred them from dischargeing their
duty unto the Lord faithfully, and from being
good Bright Examples to others,
after meet'g went to se some Relations and friends
took leave of them and walked to Rich'd Fowlers
Wrolewright [Rollright], the ware kinde, Lodgd their
24 after Breackfast walked Home
26 went with my Wife to our fifth day [Thursday] meet'g,
it felt comforting, sat in Silence
29 went with my Wife to our first day [Sunday] meeting,
it felt comforting, spake a few words to advise
friends to attend constantly unto their Heavenly Guide
and Faithfully Obey its Instructions
10mo [October]3, went with my Wife to our fifth day [Thursday] meet'g
5th took a walked to John Peglers Maughsbury
found John very Ill in Bed, I went to see
him, he appeared in a low humble frame of
minde, and I hope Devine Providence is at
work by His Almighty Power within him,
to fit and prepare him to labour in
His vineyard, if he will but be truly Obidient
and faithfull unto all His Devine Instructions,
spent the Evening there in a loving agreeable
manner Lodg'd their

verso

10mo [October] 1799

6th before meeting call'd to see some Relations
and Friends, had some Solid conversation with
them, the meeting felt pretty comfortable,
felt a Concearn to speak theirin, Parted with friends
lovingly, walked down to Jno Peglers to Dinner,
spent a little time with them Comfortabley,
took leave of them in an affectionate manner,
walked from thence Home,

9, went with my Wife to our fifth day [Thursday] Meet'g
it felt comforting, it was held in Silence
13, went with my Wife to our first day [Sunday] meeting,
it felt comforting & I trust the good Presence
and Power of the Lord was felt amoungst us,
to the strengthening of a remnant and bowing
their mindes in a Contrited Humble Thankfullness
before the Lord, under a sence of His great Love and
Mercy to such as fear and Sarve Him in Sincearity & in Truth
14 went with my Wife to our Monthly Meeting held
at this place, it felt comforting, sevral Friends
appeared in Testimonie, the buisness was gone through in Love
17 went with my Wife to our fifth day [Thursday] meet'g
20, went with my Wife to our first day [Sunday] meet'g
my minde was refreshed, felt easy to sit in Silence
24 went with my Wife to our fifth day [Thursday] Meet'g
27 took a walk to Milton to meeting
felt pretty comfortable and I hope the

Page 60

Almighty's Power was felt amoungst us, to our
Comfort, felt a Concearn in a Perticular manner
to Exhort the Elders to set good Examples unto
others, and to be Faithfull in the discharge of
their dutys unto the Almighty, so that if they
had sliped and fallen short in their duty unto
the Lord through His Assistance they might be
Inabled for the time to come to make up for all,
after meeting spent a little time with Friends
in a Solid comfortable manner, walked Home afterwards
31 went with my Wife to fifth day [Thursday] meeting
11mo 3rd went with my Wife to our first day [Sunday]
meeting, my minde was Comforted under a sence
that Devine Goodness was near unto us, felt easy to sit in Silence
7, went with my Wife to our fifth day [Thursday] meet'g
10, I and my Wife went to our first day [Sunday] meet'g, it felt comfortable,
my minde was tendered and Contrited I Hope by Devine
Love, and fervent desires ware begotten in me that I might
be more carefull of my Thoughts Words and Actions
that I might Injoy more Devine Comfort, sat in Silence,
in the after=noon walked with my Wife & sistor M,
to Witney spent the Evening with Relations &
Friends Comfortabley Lodg'd at Jno Hankins's
11th before the Monthly meeting began went with my Wife
to see some friends, the meet'g felt Pretty comfortable, sevral
living Testimonies ware born, the Lukewarm and Indifrent
ware in a Perticular manner aroused and put in minde to
be very diligent to discharge their Duty's unto the Almighty

verso

the Buisness was gone through in Love, after meeting
I walked Home with Bror R, my wife staid at Witney
with Sistor M, on account of the Weather
14, went with my Wife to our fifth day [Thursday] meeting
my minde was low and poor theirin, and I think it
was a low time with friends for want of Devine
refreshment and Comfort, it was held in Silence
15 took a walk to C.[hipping]Norton, was at their
six=day [Friday] meeting, it felt comforting, I hope
Devine Love was felt to flow from vessel
to vessel, felt a concearn to speak a little theirin
17, I went to our first day [Sunday] meeting, it felt a little
comforting, felt a Concearn to advise Friends
to discharge their duties wile they ware favoured

with time and ability one towards another, and also
towards their Neighbours , yesterday my wife went
to Burford to be a little with Bror & Sistor, Sistor
B having lately Lay in on the 11mo [November] 14th with a Son who is named Samuel
21, I went to our fifth day [Thursday] meeting, felt easy
to sit in Silence
24, took a walk to Burfor found Bror
Sistor & rest tolerable well, was at the
meeting it felt comforting, spake a few
words theirin in a carefull humble manner
being sensible of great weakness and the Neces=
siety their was for me not to lean to my own
understanding, after meeting took leave of Bror
sistor and rest & walked with my Wife Home
28, went with my Wife to our fifth day [Thursday] meet'g, Wm Lawton
appeared in Testimonie by way of Incouragement to the feeble ones

Page 61

12mo [December] 1st went with my Wife to our first day [Sunday] meeting,
it felt comforting & refreshing I hope a Remnant
ware made sensible that Devine Comfort and Instruction
was extended towards them in Solem Silence, spake a
little towards to the conclusion of the meet'g, it was our Preparative meet'g
5, went with my Wife to our fifth day [Thursday] meeting,
8, went with my Wife to our first day [Sunday] meet'g
it felt refreshing, felt a concearn to speak a few words theirin
in the A.[fter]N.[oon] my Wife went to Burford with some Frds
9, walked to our Monthly Meet'g at Burford
with Bror Robt I think it was a pretty
comfortable meet'g, it was held mostly in Silence
before Friends entered upon buisness, the buis=
=ness was gone through in a pretty agreeable
loving manner, what made it more Comfortable
was I think on account of being favoured with
the Company of Jos Lamb & Ricd Holtom from Sibford
after meet'g I and my Wife returned Home
12. went with my Wife to our fifth day [Thursday] meeting,
15. went with my Wife to our first day [Sunday] meet'g
it felt comforting, it was held in Silence,
19, went with my Wife to our fifth day [Thursday] meet'g
felt easy to sit in Silence
22 went with my Wife to our first day [Sunday] meeting
my minde was Comforted, it was held in Silence
23rd I having been much concearned and
grieved for a long time on account of some

verso

People Swearing dreadfully I purchased
some Papers giving anaccount how great
a Sin it was and also a Warning to
Swearers to Repent Speedily and turn to
the Lord that they might finde Mercy
I felt a Concearn to go round to the Public
Houses and desire the People belonging to
them to give me leave to stick a paper
up in their Houses that People might have
an Oppertunity to read them, most of them
gave me leave and behaved friendly,
found Comfort to my minde by so doing
26 went with my Wife to our fifth day [Thursday] meet'g
it was held in Silence
29 went with my Wife to our first day [Sunday] meeting my
minde was refresh'd, I was Concearned to speak a few words theirin
it having been very cold weather of late
and things very dear, Bread but a little
more than 4lb for one Shilling, on which
account I was much concearned for the Poor
and felt a Concearn to go to some Neighbours
who ware of ability to help the poor to In=
=courage them to be good to the poor and also desire
them to Incourage others to be good to the poor
I went to my Neighbours and spake what rested upon my minde,

they took it friendly, found comfort to my minde
by so doing

1800

1mo [January] 2nd went with my Wife to our fifth day [Thursday]

meet'g, it felt comforting

Page 62

1800

1mo [January] 4th set out in the A.[fter]N.[oon] for our Quarterly
meeting, walked to Witney, spent the Evening
with friends comfortabley, Lodg'd at Jno Hankins's
5. walked to Oxford, the Meeting felt pretty
comfortable a pretty menny Neighbours
came in, I think Wm Barritt had a good
oppertunity with them, I also was concearned
to direct the People to the Teachings of
the spirit of Truth within them,
spent the A.[fter]N.[oon] with friends comfortabley
went to se a Man and his Wife who I
think pretty generaly comes to meetings
when there is any at Oxford, I had a good
Opertunity with them, they appeared tender
and loving, the man I think is under con=
=vincement, parted from them in Love,
spent a little time at Jno. Jacksons's agreeabley, Lodg'd their
6. the Quarterly meeting I think was pretty
large, Strangers in the ministery, Wm Crutch
David Dent & Ann Crawley, Friends
had a Comfortable sitting together before
the entered upon buisness, menny friends
appeared in Testimonie, Wm Crutch spoke
pretty much concearning the seed being in a
Suffering state, and that there was a nescesiety

verso

for Friends to be willing to suffer, if the
would become vessels fitted for the great
Masters use, the buisness was gone through
in Love, altho I think it was a low
time with some on account of the weak
Situation that some meetings appeared to
be in, after meeting took leave of Friends
and walked Home
9, went with my Wife to our fifth day [Thursday] meet'g
12. went with my Wife to our first day [Sunday] meeting
I think the spring of Devine Love was felt
to flow amoungst us, I was concearned to advise
the youth to be diligent in reading the Scriptures,
and to Indeavour to live in the fear of the Lord,
13, took a walk to our Monthly meeting
held at C.[hipping]Norton I think it was pretty large
and comfortable, sevral Friends appeared in
Testimonie, the meeting of buisness held pretty
long their being a deal of buisness to go through
yet I think it was gone through in an Harmonious
manner, after meeting spent a little time with
friends and walk'd Home
16, went with my Wife to Burford to the Bu=
=rial of Bror Henrys youngist Child,
Samuel, he was about eight weeks old when
he Died, found Bro'r & Sistor very poorly
I think it was a good refreshing meeting
two Friends appeared in Testimonie I felt
easy to keep Silence, after meeting spent a little time

Page 63

at Brors took leave of them and returnd Home
19, went to our first day [Sunday] meeting, my minde
was comforted, I was concearned to advise friends
to live daily in Obidience to the Spirit of truth
within them so as to feel true Peace of minde
was refreshed
26, Went to Burford to fetch my Wife home
Bro'r & Sistor beeing poorly my Wife went
and Stay'd with them a wile I was at
their first day [Sunday] meeting, it felt comforting
and I trust the Lords Power was felt amoungst
us, to the comforting of menny Present,
I felt a concearn to speak a little theirin

30, went with my Wife to our fifth day [Thursday] meeting
my minde was refreshed, felt easy to sit in Silence
2mo [February] 2nd went with my Wife to our first day [Sunday]
meeting, I trust the Lords Power was felt
amoungst us to our comfort and refreshment
spake a few words theirin
in the A.[fter]N.[oon] walk'd to Banbury call'd
to se some Relations & Friends by the
way, Lodg'd at Edwd Stones they ware
very kinde & loving
3, Breackfasted at E. Stones, before the
Monthly Meet'g began went to se some
friends & Relations, I think the meeting

verso

---

was comforting & refreshing to menny
and that Devine Love was felt to flow
amoungst us to our comfort, sevral
Testimonies ware born to put friends
in minde to be diligent to discharge
their duty as there appeared a great
nescessiety for their comming up in their
Places which Devine Providence had
allotted them, the buisness was gone through
in love, after meet'g took leave of Sistor
& friends and walk'd Home
6, went with my Wife to our fifth day [Thursday] meeting
felt easy to sit in Silence
7, took a walk to C.[hipping]Norton, was at their
sixth day [Friday] meeting it felt comforting, I
was Concearned to advise Friends not to
rest contented untill they had witnessed such a
state as the Scripture Testifieth viz, there
is no Condemnation to them that are in Christ
Jesus, after meeting went to se some friends &
walked Home
9, went with my Wife to our first day [Sunday] meet'g
it was pretty large on account I think that our
monthly meet'g is to be held here to morrow
I think it was a pretty comforting season, we
ware favour'd with the Company of Jos: Lamb
and Jos: Huntley from Sibford, I was concearn'd
to advise friends to Labour to be Indow'd with pure Wisdom

Page 64

2mo [February]=10th went with my Wife to our Monthly Meet'g
held at this place, we ware favoured with the
Company of Jos.h Lamb & Jos.h Huntley who are
on a Religious visit to the meetings within
the Compass of our Quarterly Meeting, I think
it was a Comfortable meeting altho truth felt
to be low amoungst us, Sevral living Testimonies
ware born by which Friends expressed that
some of our Society ware in a Declineing state
yet if such would return walk lowly and
Humbley for the future and Indeavour to
discharge their duty, the Lord would be gracious
to them, the buisness was gone through in
Love Elizh Mintchon laid before us a Con=
-cearn that had rested upon her minde for
sometime to visit the monthly and Preparative
meetings within the Compass of our Quarterly
meeting, Friends express'd their Unity with
her and granted her a Coppy of a minute
which was made on account of her laying
her Concearn before the meeting,
13 went with my Wife to our fifth day [Thursday] meeting
16, went with my Wife to our first day [Sunday]
meeting, altho it is a low Exersiseing
time with the truly religious, it felt com=
=forting, spake theirin
it being of late a very trying time with
the poor, things being very dear, and the weather

verso

Cold Bread being three pound and a half
for the Shilling, I felt a concearn to go
round to the Overseers of this place and
two more towns, I laid before them the
distressed situations of the poor according to
what I felt, Signifying that I thought
menny wanted Bread, I much desired they would
be kind and tender towards them and do what
they could to help them to food and Raiment,
they appeared to take my visit kindely
and Signified they ware sensible it must
be very trying with the poor and they would
indeavour to be kinde to them, I felt satis=
=faction and Comfort to my minde by going

to speak to them, it was yesterday and
the day before that I went and spoke to them
20, went with my Wife to our fifth day [Thursday] meet'g
23, went with my Wife to our first day [Sunday]
meeting, it felt pretty comfortable, felt
easy to sit in Silence
27, went to our fifth day [Thursday] meet'g, altho our number was
small yet it felt refreshing, spake a few words theirin
3mo [March] 1st Having felt a concearn for sometime,
to be at Shipstone first day [Sunday] meeting, and
also the Monthly Meeting to which Shipstone
belongs, I set out in the A.[fter]N.[oon] walk'd to
Long=compton spent a little time at T. Harris

Page 65

very comfortabley, Lodg'd with Cousin J. Bissell
2nd walked to Shipstone to meet'g, it began
at ten, friends ware a pretty wile a gathering
some comming in late which is I think a
hurt to a meeting, and setteth forth that
such are in an Indifrent careless state of
minde respecting the things wich belongs
to their Peace, altho truth appeard to be
low amoungst friends, yet I think it arose
into dominion, and it was a very comforting
meeting, Sarah Lambley appeared in Tes=
=timonie which was very Instructing and
Comforting, I was concearned to speak theirin,
the A.[fter]N.[oon] meeting felt pretty comforting,
it was their preparative meeting, spent the
Evening with some Friends and relations, in a Loving & weighty manner
Lodg'd at Cousin Ashbys
3, walked to Campden, found Cousin Jno
Corks wife and some more of the Family
very poorly spent a little time with them
in a Solid weighty manner, I was In=
=abled to Incourage them to put their trust
in the Lord the physician of value and In=
=deavour to sarve Him Faithfully, in the A.[fter] N.[oon]
Went to see the Friends they ware Loving and
kind to me and their company was quite com=
forting, Lodg'd at Cous'n Sarah & Mary Corks

verso

1800

3mo [March] 4th walk'd to Shipstone with my Relations
before meet'g went to se some friends, the
Monthly Meeting I thought was pretty com=
=fortable, I was concearned to advise friends
to Indeavour to come to meetings and sit down
under the government of the Prince of Peace,
in which there would be no Strife nor contention
but their Labours would be in Love Indeavouring to
Incourage one another to discarge their duties faith=
=fully unto the Lord, the buisness was gone through
in a pretty comfortable manner after meet'g
took leave of Cousins & some friends and walk
home
6, went with my Wife to our fifth day [Thursday] meeting it
was held in Silence
9, went with my Wife to our first day [Sunday] meet'g
it felt quite comforting, I was concearned to speak a little theirin
10, took a walk to our Monthly Meeting held at Witney
sevral Friends appeared in Testimonie, I trust to
the Comfort Eddification and Instruction of Friends,
one Strainger in the Ministery there viz Ann Baker
altho the buisness was gone through in Love yet it did
not feel very comfortable, sevral minutes ware con=
=tunied & I thought friends ware pretty much be=
=hinde hand in their buisness after meeting I & my Wife spent
a little time with our Relations and Friends, walk
Home in the Evening
13. went with my Wife to our fifth day [Thursday] meeting, it
felt pretty comfortable, felt easy to sit in Silence,

16 went with my Wife to our first day [Sunday] meeting

Page 66

Altho of late it has been a lowly Humbling
time with menny both Spiritually and Temporaly
yet I trust Devine goodness and mercy was Exten=
=ded towards us and under a sence thereof we ware
refreshed and Comforted, I was concearned to speak theirin
20 went with my Wife to our fifth day [Thursday] meet'g
23, went with my Wife to our first day [Sunday] meeting,
felt easy to sit in Silence, my minde was pretty
much Exercised and concearned for the good and
Everlasting Happiness of the souls of the
people of other societies, and I felt love
to flow in my Heart towards them
27 went with my Wife to our fifth day [Thursday] meeting
it was held in Silence
30, took a walk with my Wife and some
Relations to C.[hipping]Norton my Wife intending to
go to Sibford to se her Mother & Relations
their, I, my Wife, & Relations was at the
morning meeting at C.[hipping] Norton, in Sitting
theirin I was greatly sensible of my own
weakness, the A.[fter]N.[oon] meeting felt more
comforting, I felt a concearn to speak
theirin, call'd to se some friends their com=
=pany was comforting in the Evening walk'd Home
I was lately Invited to the Funerals of some
Relations a woman and her Son who died of a
Fever she left a Husband & sevral yound Children

verso

I was pretty much consearned for their Relations
and was led to sympathise with them, in their
Affliction, something preventing my attending
the Funerals, I was concearned to write letters
to them, sent them by a friend

3rd went with my Wife to our fifth day [Thursday] meeting
6, went with my Wife to our first day [Sunday] meeting
it felt comforting, I was concearned to advise friends
to Indeavour always to keep their Consciences clear
and void of Offence towards God and all Mankinde
in the A.[fter]N.[oon] took a walk with some friends
to Burford spent the Evening with Bror Sistor
& some friends in an agreeable manner Lodg'd at Brors
7th before meeting went to se some friends, the meeting
felt pretty comfortable, sevral friends appeared
in Testimonie, I felt a concearn to speak theirin
the Buisness was gone through in a Comfortable
manner after meet'g spent a little time at
Brors & went to se some friends, walked Home
with Bro'r & another friend in the Evening
10, went with my Wife to our fifth day [Thursday] meeting
felt easy to sit in Silence
13, went with my Wife to our first day [Sunday] meeting, my
minde was refreshed, I was concearned to advise friends
to Indeavour to live humbley and lowly before the Lord
15th took a walk to our quarterly Meeting held
at Witney my Walked to Witney with sistor yesterday

Page 67

I think it was a pretty large & Comfortable
meeting the Men and Women sat together be=
=fore the enter'd upon buisness as is the usual
way, the buisness was gone through in a
loving manner, by answers to the Queries
from the monthly Meetings, affairs appear'd
to be in a poor low Situation which was
cause of sorrow, and friends ware advised
to live more in Obidience to the Truth within,
and lay their Foundation upon that Rock
which is Immoveable, that they might be
able to stand fast if times of greater tryals

and Exercises should be permited to come upon
them, after meeting walked Home with some
friends
17, went with my Wife to our fifth day [Thursday]
meet'g
20, went with my Wife to our first day [Sunday]
meeting,
it felt comforting, we ware favoured with the
company of our friend Edwd May, he was drawn
forth in Testimonie in a perticular manner to the
young friends, to Incourage them to turn their
mindes
Inward and minde the Lords teachings within
them and faithfully
obey them, that they might be favoured to Injoy
Devine
blessings wilest here, and also be Inabled to work
out their
Souls Salvation, I felt easy to sit in Silence
Things of late have been very dear Bread but
about

verso

3lb for one shilling Bacon Eleven pence pr Pound
I have been led to simpathise and feel for the poor
and I have been Concearned to go round to some
who
are blessed with plenty and Incourage them to be
good to the poor and Indeavour to make a
Colection
for them, felt comfort to my minde by so doing,
since a Collection has been made for the poor
& I think it will be thankfully rec'd, some being
much distress'd by the dearness of Provision and
other things
lately I felt a Concearn to go and speak to a
young man
a Doctor, who has been guilty of Drinking to
Excess, which rendered him as I heard unfit to
attend his
Patients, I went and spoke to him what rested
upon my minde found satisfaction to my minde
by so doing
24, went with my Wife to our fifth day [Thursday]
meet'g
27, went with my Wife to our first day [Sunday]
meet'g
my minde was refreshed, spake a little theirin
29, this day a meeting was held by the Desire
of David Sands an American Friend, the sober
Neighbours ware Informed of the meeting, some
came, I think it was a very Satisfactory meeting
David was drawn forth in a long Solem Prayer,
and afterwards in Testimonie which was Instruc=
ting to the Ignorant concearning the way of Life
Incourageing to such whose Hearts panted after
the
living God, and very Incourageing to the young
friends
to be truly Obidient to the truth within,
signifying if
Page 68
they ware, they would be preachers of
Righteousness
unto others, In the A.[fter]N.[oon] we ware
favoured a little
with the Company of David Sands & another Frd
who came with him to Charlbury
5mo [May] 1st took a walk to Burford to the
Funeral
of Elizth Mintchon who Died after a Short
Illness, I think she was aged about 50 years,
& the Loss of she will be greatly felt
by menny, she was much beloved was favoured
with a pretty large gift in the Ministery
and laboured diligently to Improve it, she
Travel'd pretty much at times menny miles
from Home, in the work of the Ministery
there was a large meeting at the Funeral
of Friends & Neighbours, sevral strangers
ware there Ministering friends, it was a
highly Favoured Meeting sevral living
Testimonies
ware born and one friend appear'd in Solem
Prayer after Dinner friends had a Comfortable
sitting together at the Widowers it was a Solem
refreshing time & friends parted in much Love
in the Evening walk'd Home
3, in the A.[fter]N.[oon] walk'd to Brails, spent
the Evening
with Cousins comfortabley Lodg'd at Cousin Wm
Gilletts
4 walked to the morn'g meeting at Shipstone, &
from
thence with some friends to Armscutt [Armscote]
Meeting, it was

verso

large of Neighbours, I think it was a good
Satisfactory
meeting, Sarah Lambly was Inabled to Preach
the Gospel to them very powerfully wareby
I trust the witness was reach'd in menny mindes
I also was Inabled to put them in minde that
the light and Spirit of Christ within them
was the Unering Teacher which if they would
but faithfully minde its Instructions and Obey
them they would be Inabled to walk in the
straight
and narrow way which leadeth unto Life, after
meeting spent a little time at S. Lambleys &
Cous'n
Tho's Fardons, walked from thence to Brails,
Lodg'd at Cousin Wm Gilletts
5, walked from Brails to Shutford to the Monthly
meeting, it felt pretty comforting, I was con=
=cearn'd to appear in Testimonie as did also some
more friends, the buisness was gone through in a
comfortable manner, walk'd from thence to
Sibford spent a little time with Mother Aunt
&et after ward went to see some friends, Lodg'd
at Mothers
6, walk'd from Sibford to Brails, having felt a
concearn to speak to a relative
who for a long time past had behav'd in
a very disrespectfull manner to her Husband,
I Indeavoured to speak to her what rested upon
my minde, she was unwilling to hear, so that I
could say but little, yet I spoke to her so as to
ease my minde, was at the monthly Meeting, it
felt refreshing, I was concearn'd to speak theirin

Page 69

as was the case with another friend, the Buisness
was gone through in Love, after meeting
spent a little time at Cousin Wm Hemmings,
took leave of them and some friends, walked
from thence Home
8, went with my Wife to our fifth day [Thursday]
meet'g,
felt easy to sit in Silence
11 I and my Wife ware at our first day [Sunday]
meeting,
it felt refreshing, spake a little theirin,
13 walked to our Monthly Meeting at
C.[hipping]Norton
it felt comforting and I hope menny
mindes ware refreshed, Comforted, Instructed,
and Incouraged to persevear in the way of
well doing, sevral living Testimonies ware
born theirin, the buisness was gone through in
Live, after
meeting call'd to se a poor old Friend who is
weakly, she was pleased with my Company
also call'd to se some more friends, in the
Evening walk'd Home with my Wife and sevral
friends
15 went with my Wife to our fifth day [Thursday]
meeting
18, went with my Wife to our first day [Sunday]
meeting, it
was comforting to my poor Exercised minde,
spake a little theirin
21 I have been much grieved for a long time
to perceive danceing to be Incouraged knowing
it to be a Sin, and menny Evel concequencies
attending it, I felt a concearn to go and speak
to a Clergyman, who I though might Incourage

verso

it before his Door, I went to his House and
informed him of the feelings of my minde
and advised him not to suffer it to be before
his Door, felt ease to my minde by so doing
22 went with my Wife to our fifth day [Thursday]
meet'g
felt easy to sit in Silence
25. went with my Wife to our first day [Sunday]
meet'g
it felt very comforting, I was concearned to ad=
=vise friends to Labour earnestly to know the
Almightys
Will, and also be concearned to do it Faithfully
29. went with my Wife to our fifth day [Thursday]
meet'g
felt easy to sit in Silence
6mo [June] 1st I and my Wife ware at our first day
[Sunday] meet'g
it felt comforting and I trust the Almighty Power
was felt amoungst us to teach and Instruct us in
our duty
4, took a walk to Witney, was at their fourth day
[Wednesday]

meeting, in the A.[fter]Noon went to se a Religious Woman
not of our Society had some Religious & weighty Con=
=versation with she, spent sometime with some friends
very comfortabley, return'd Home in the Evening
5, went with my Wife to our fifth day [Thursday] meeting, sat in Silence
7, in the A.[fter]N.[oon] walk'd to Maughsbury to Jno Peglers
spent the evening their in a comfortable weighty manner also
went to se some of their neighbours had some religious
conversation with them, Lodg'd at Jno Peglers,
8, first day [Sunday] of the week walked up to stow, Breackfasted with
the Neighbour Colletts, with them I was well acquainted,
had some Religious Conversation with them before

Page 70

meeting went to se some Relations who ware very
Poor and in Distress, I was much concerned to Labour
with some people for their Relief, the meeting felt
Pretty comfortable, I was concearn'd to speak theirin
felt comfort to my minde by so doing, I trust friends
in general ware comforted and refreshed with Devine
Goodness after meeting call'd to se some friends,
walk'd down to Jno Peglers to dinner they ware very
friendly and kinde, spent some time with friends their
in a solid weighty manner, walked from thence Home
9, our Monthly Meeting was held at this place it felt
pretty comfortable, sevral friends appear'd in Testimonie,
I also felt a concearn to speak by way of Testimonie,
by which friends ware advised to Labour for the Lords
Presence to attend them, and not to spend any time to gra=
=tify themselves but to Indeavour to spend it all to the
honnour of the Lord to whome it doth belong, friends ware
also advised to keep low and humble, which was the onely
way to receive Honnour of the Lord
the buisness was gone through pretty comfortabley
12, went with my Wife to our fifth day [Thursday] meet'g,
was very poor and sorrowfull, under a sence of the
want of Devine Comfort
15 went with my Wife to our first day [Sunday] meeting I
trust Devine Love and goodness was felt to flow
amoungst us, I was concerned to advise friends to
Labour to feel it to flow from one unto another not
onely in Meetings but when at Home, and also towards their Neighbours

verso

this A.[fter]N.[oon] went to se a man who I understood was
given to drinking to much, and to wrideing in a resulute
Passionate manner, altho he had been much warned
not to ride in Such a manner, he was thrown from
his Horse as he was rideing in a hasty manner & hurt
in Such a manner that it was thought he would not
have liv'd, but through Mercy his Life as yet has been
spar'd, I was concerned to advise him and his Wife to
be truly gratefull and thankfull unto the Lord for His
Mercy and goodness to them in preserveing his Life and
Inableing him to get so well, and I advised them to Indeavour

to sarve the Lord with Perfect and Upright Hearts and
in all their ways to give Him the praise to whome it doth belong
19 went with my Wife to our fifth day [Thursday] meeting
22, took a walk to Milton to meeting it was small
there being but few friends belonging to it and
Jno Norton & his Wife have lately been remov'd by
Death out of it, I understood they ware about 50
years Old each of them and died after about a weeks
Illness, my minde was oppress'd in the meeting feeling
the want of Devine Refreshment to comfort me, I
was concearned to advise friends to be diligent to attend their
meetings altho their number was small, after meeting went
to se the friends spent a little time solidly with them
reach'd Home about five A.[fter]N.[oon]
26, went with my Wife to our fifth day [Thursday] meeting, my minde was refreshed
28 in the Evening set out for our Quarterly Meet'g to be held at Banb'[ur]y
walked to Barton to Thos Jarvices spent a little time with them
in a Solid weighty manner. Lodg'd there
29th walk'd with T. Jarvis to Adderbury meeting, it felt pretty comfortable

Page 71

1800

I was concearn'd to speak theirin, was led to Incourage
the youth to sarve the Lord faithfully and chuse Him for
their Portion, which if they did I hoped they would be good
Examples unto others and be Inabled to Instruct others to walk
in the way which leadeth unto Eternal Life,
went to se some friends at adderbury and theirabouts Lodg'd at T. Witchleys
30, spent a little time at Adderbury in a Solid and I
hope Instructing manner walked from thence to Wm
Franklings Barverd [Barford St. John], I was concearned to Incourage him
and his Daughter to be diligent in attending Meetings
and to Obey the Instructions of the Comforter the Spirit of
Truth Faithfully, walked from thence to milton spent
a little time with friends there afterward walk'd to
Banbury found my Wives Mother at Edw'd Stones Lodg'd there
7mo [July] 1st I think the Quarterly Meeting felt very comforting
ware favour'd with the company of Wm Hickman from otchester in Kent
several Friends men & women appeared in Testimonie & I trust
the Almighties Love & goodness was felt to the comfort
of menny, the buisness was gone through in a weighty
manner sevral minutes ware rec'd from the Yearly Meet'g
and ordered to be Weightily considered, after meet'g walked with Bror R Home
3, went with my Wife to our fifth day [Thursday] meet'g, felt poor & low
6, went with my Wife to our first day [Sunday] meet'g it felt
very comforting I was concearned to advise friends to
labour diligently to be acquainted with solem Silent Worship,
I was Concearned to write to a Neighbour in pretty
much buisness to desire him not to seek to much after
the things of this World but after such things which be=
=longed to his souls Everlasting Happiness, also desired
him to set a good Example to others by Indeavouring to sell
things at reasonable Prises

verso

1800

7mo [July] 10th went with my Wife to our fifth day [Thursday] meetg it felt comforting
11, a meeting was appointed to begin this day at Ten, by
the desire of Thos Speakman from Reading, & Wm
Hickman from [blank] it was a very comforting Meet'g
Devine mercy and Visitation appeared to be a fresh
extended, several Living Testimonies ware born,
the youth ware advised in a perticular manner not to
rest contended with hearing tell of the Messias and of
His great goodness unto His followers, but Labour to
know Him for themselves and to taste see and feel
how good He is to them that love Him, for to hear
tell of the Lords love and Mercy would do nothing
for them without they felt it for themselves
13, went with my Wife to our first day [Sunday] meet'g, my minde
was low theirin, sat in Silence, in the A.[fter] N.[oon] set out
for our monthly meeting, to be held at Faringdon,
walked to Witney, spent the evening with Friends in
a loving agreeable manner, Lodg'd at Jno Hankings's
14, walked with a friend to Faringdon, the Monthly
Meet'g was not very large but I trust it was a Solid
good Eddifying meeting, Wm Hickman & Thos Speakman
ware their, their Testimonies was to Sound an allarm in Israels
Camp, for friends to put away wrong things from amoungst
them, not to set their Hearts upon the things of this World, and
to Incourage all friends to live in Obidience to the Truth
within them, the buisness was conducted in Love after meetg
spent a little time with friends and walk'd with some
friends to Witney, Lodg'd at my kinde friends Jno Hankins
15, rose early and walk'd Home, ware I found my Wife well
felt sweet peace of minde, & Satisfaction in performing the
Journey, all Praise and Honnour be given unto the Lord for without

Page 72

his Assistance we can do no good thing who was pleased to favour
me with His Love and living Power and Inabled
me to perform what I believed to be my duty with a degree of Joy
17 went with my Wife to our fifth day [Thursday] meet'g
20, went with my Wife to our first day [Sunday] meet'g,
sat in Silence except after the yearly Meet'g
Epistle was read, I felt a concearn to stand up
and advise friends to let it have due place in their
mindes and not lay it by without reading it pretty
much, that through Devine Mercy the labour of
our dear Friends might prove fruitfull
22 went with my Wife to meeting, it was appointed at
this place by the desire of Mary Watson from Ireland and
Mary Alexander from Essex the Neighbours ware acquainted with the
meeting, who ware thought would like to come, several
Neighbours came and behaved Solid, I was concearned to
advise the people to be Obidient to the light of Christ
within themselves and Indeavour to know an Inward
acquaintance with Christ as that was the only way to

obtain Everlasting Happiness to their Immortal Souls,
one of the friends had a fine oppertunity with the
People to declare the Truth amoungst them, and was
I trust Inabled to reach the pure witness in menny
to the convinceing them how they might become ac=
=quainted with God and be at Peace,
24, went with my Wife to our fifth day [Thursday] meeting
27, went with my Wife to our first day [Sunday] meet'g it was
largish sevral straingers ware there, I trust the good
Power and Presence of the Almighty was felt amoungst us,
spake a little theirin

verso

1800

7mo [July] 31st went with my Wife to our fifth day [Thursday] meet'g
I was greatly sensible of my Weakness's and that
the Spirit was willing but the Flesh was
weak, therefore there was great need for me
always to attend to the pure light within minde
its Devine Instructions and Faithfully Obey them
8mo [August] 3rd went with my Wife to our first day [Sunday]
meet'g, it was held in Silence it was our Preparative meeting
7. went with my Wife to our fifth day [Thursday] meet'g
10. went with my Wife to our first day [Sunday] meeting,
of late I have met with menny tryals and Exercises,
and I have been favoured to see my self a Poor
weak unworthy Creature, and that without Devine
assistance I can do no good thing, therefore there is
great need for me often to wait for Devine Assistance
and very carefull to minde the Instructions of the Truth,
and faithfully obey them, that I may be preserved from
doing the least thing to displease the Almight, and may be
Inabled to discharge my duty unto Him,
having perceived some Neighbours to attend a public House,
and I think they ware their most of the Night till morning
I felt a Concearn to go to their Houses and Inform them
how very rong it was, and such doings lead in the broad way
which leadeth to Distruction, they acknowledged such doings
to be rong and behaved Neighbourly, I felt comfort by
speaking what rested upon my minde to them, in the A.[fter]N.[oon]
walk'd with my Wife to Burford intending to be at the

Page 73

1800

Monthly Meeting there, found Bro'r Sistor & rest
tolerable well, we lodg'd their,
before the Monthly Meeting began went to se
some friends the meeting felt pretty comfortable,
sevral friends appear'd in Testimonie to the
Comfort Eddification and Instruction of the
upright Hearted I trust, & Perticularly to the
youth, the buisness was gone through in a com=
=fortable manner, after meeting spent sometime
comfortabley with Relations and friends, in the
Evening walked Home,
14 came home from Reap'g, & went with my Wife to
our fifth day [Thursday] meeting
17, went with my Wife to our first day [Sunday] meet'g, sat in silence
21, went with my Wife to our fifth day [Thursday] meeting,
sat in a mournfull state, being greatly sensible
of the want of Devine Comfort,

24, went with my Wife to our first day [Sunday] Meet'g, it
felt comforting, I was concearned to advise
friends to be very diligent to sarve the Lord, that they might
be favoured with an Evidence at the close of the
day that their days Work was done,
28, went with my Wife to our fifth day [Thursday] meeting sat in Silence
31, went with my Wife to our first day [Sunday] meet'g, felt easy to
sit in Silence, altho it was mostly held in Silence yet I trust
menny ware sensible of being taught by the Unering Teacher,
9mo [September] 3rd took a walk to Witney found Cousin Barretts poorly,
was at the fourth day [Wednesday] meet'g, it felt comforting, spake a few words theirin

verso

9mo [September] 4th I went to our fifth day [Thursday] meet'g, it felt pretty
comforting, felt easy to sit in Silence. My Wife
stay'd at Home on acct of sitting up last night with a Child that was Ill
7. went with my Wife to our first day [Sunday] Meet'g, it
felt comfortable, one Friend appeard, I felt easy
to sit in Silence, our preparative meetg buisness was gone throughin Love
8 took a walk with my Wife to our Monthly Meet'g
at C[hipping]Norton, I think it was a good Edifying
meet'g we ware favoured with the Company
of two Women Friends in the Ministery, viz M
Caper & Mary Beesley, they both appear'd their
Testimonies ware Comforting to the poor Exercised
Contrited ones, but very arouseing to the Lukewarm
& such as appeared outwardly Religious but wanted
the substance, I felt easy to sit in Silence, the buis=
=ness was gone through in Love, after Meet'g spent
a little time in going to se some friends, in the Evening
I and my Wife walk'd Home,
11. this being our Weekday meet'g their was a Funeral,
it was Wm Albrights Daughters Child, it died in its
Infancy, I and my Wife went, the meet'g felt com=
=fortable and refreshing, my Mouth was Opened as
was also another friends, to speak concearning the
solemness of the Ocasion and how nessecary it is
for us to indeavour to be alwayes prepared for Death,
14, walk'd to Oxford to meeting, it was small of Friends
and not very menny Neighbours, I was concearned
to advise the People to Indeavour to be acquainted
with stillness, that they might know the ariseing
of the Power and Spirit of Christ within them
to teach them and to Inable them, to Walk in the Straight

Page 74

and narrow Path which leadeth unto Etearnal
Life, another friend appeared, and I Hope the
Power of the Lord was felt over the Meeting to
the Comforting menny present, Refresh'd myself
with some more Friends at Jno Jacksons's,
walked with Wm Padbury & Wm Mintchin to
Reading, call'd to se Cousin Josh Ashby at Shilling=
=ford they behaved very kinde to me Stop'd at Jno
sargoods to Lodge
15, reach'd Reading in the Afternoon spent the A.[fter]N.[oon] comfortabley
in going to se some friends and stoping with them
a little, Lodg'd at Cousin Jonathan Fardons
16, went to se some friends before the Quarterly
Meet'g began, the Meeting was small & things felt rather low and discourageing
yet I trust Devine Mercy and refreshment was
pertaken of to the comforting and refreshing menny poor

mindes, I was concearned to appear in Testimonie
as was also another Friend, and one friend appeard
in Solem Prayer, the Buisness was gone through
pretty lovingly, yet the pure Life seem'd to be low amoungst us,
one Public Meet'g which has been usualy held on the
first Day before this Quarterly Meeting was drop't,
it was cause of Mourning to my minde, I Labour'd
hard to have it not droped as yet, desireing Friends
not to be to hasty in such a Weight affair, but to
take a little more time to consider of it, felt satis=
=faction in Speaking my minde, concearning it after
meeting took leave of Relations and Friends, walk'd
with some friends to Shillingford Lodg'd at Cousin Ashbys
17, took leave of Friends at Shillingford & warborough and
walk'd with Bror Home

verso

1800

9mo [September] 18th went with my Wife to our fifth day [Thursday] meet'g, it felt pretty
comfortable, it was held in Silence
21. went with my Wife to our first day [Sunday] meet'g it felt comforting
to my poor Exercised minde I was concerned to advise
Friends to Indeavour to live lowly and Humbley before
the Lord, and to have their mindes taken of the things of
this World and to have their dependance on the Lord,
another friend also appear'd to friends Comfort & Incouragement,
encourageing them to Labour to get down to the Living Fountain,
that they might be refreshed Inabled to live to the Praise
of the Lord and feel His Light to shine upon them in these dark times,
25, went with my Wife to our fifth day [Thursday] meetg, it
felt comforting, felt easy to sit in Silence
28, went with my Wife to our first day [Sunday] meet'g, it was
mostly held in Silence, it felt refreshing and Comforting,
10mo [October] 2st went with my Wife to our fifth day [Thursday] meet'g
it felt comforting, it was held mostly in Silence
5th took a walk with my Wife and some Relations
to the burial of Thos Smiths son, Aged about
Eight years, was at the Morning Meet'g it
felt comforting, the Funeral was at the A.[fter] N.[oon]
meet'g it was pretty large of Friends and Neighbours
and I trust a Comforting refreshing season unto
menny, warein Devine Visitation was renewedly
Extended, sevral Mouths ware opened to testify
of the Lords great Love and Mercy to the People
& to Instruct them how to know their Unering Teacher and
ware to finde Him viz, within themselves Christ
within the hope of Glory & without the carefully Obeyed
His Devine Directions the could not Injoy true peace
wile in this World, nor Obtain an Everlasting Inheritance
for their Immortal Souls in the Kingdom of Heaven

Page 75

the Power of the Lord appear'd to be much felt
and menny mindes to be tenderd theirby, after
meeting I and my Wife took leave of Friends and
walked Home with Comfort & Thankfullness
in our own Hearts, under a Sence of the Lords
love and Mercy being renewedly extended unto us,
8, took a walk to Witney, was at their Fourth
day [Wednesday] meet'g, it felt comforting, after Meet'g walked home

9, went with my Wife to our fifth day [Thursday] meet'g,
my minde was comforted, being sensible Devine
Goodness was felt to flow amoungst us,
12, took a walk to Milton to meet'g, it was Small,
some of late has been removed by Death, and them
that attend it appear to be in a feeble State, yet I
trust we ware favour'd to feel the mercy and Good=
=ness of the Almighty to flow amoungst us to our Comfort,
after meet'g called to se some friends and walk'd Home
13 went with my Wife to our Monthly meet'g it was
smallish and the pure Life felt to be low amoungst us
sevral friends appeared in Testimonie and one friend
in Solem Prayer, the Buisness was gone through in Love
16 went with my Wife to our fifth day [Thursday] meetg, it felt Comforting
19, went with my Wife to our first day [Sunday] meet'g, I
trust it was a good refreshing meet'g, felt easy to
sit in Silence, one young Woman appeard with a
few Words by way of Testimonie, that has letelyish
fricquented our Meet'gs
23. went with my Wife to our fifth day [Thursday] meet'g, I
felt poor & low, felt easy to sit in Silence
26 I went to our first day [Sunday] meet'g, it felt pretty comfortable, my Wife being
gone to Burford to be with Bro.r & Sistor a little wile

verso

Sistor Betty being Deliver'd of a Daughter
30 went to our fifth day [Thursday] meet'g it felt Comforting
felt easy to sit in Silence
11mo 2nd took a walk to Burford to see our Re=
lations, Bro'r Henrys youngest Daughter
was born 10mo [October] 19th 1800 & she is called Reb[blank] [Rebecca?]
I and my Wife was at the first day [Sunday] meet'g , it
felt Comforting, I was concearn'd to Incourage
friends to Indeavour patiently to pattern after
blessed Jesus, who came not to do His own Will
but the Will of His Heavenly Father, another
Friend appear'd in Testimonie, it was their Pre=
=parative Meeting, after meet'g spent a little
time at Brors Comfortabley took leave of them & walk'd
Home with my Wife
6 went with my Wife & her Sistor M to our
fifth day [Thursday] meet'g, it felt comforting, spake a
few Words theirin, as did another Friend
7. went with my Wives Sistor M, to C[hipping] Norton she intending to go from thence
after meet'g Home, she & I was at their six=day [Friday] meet'g
it felt to my minde to be a Comfortable meet'g, I
was Concearned to speak theirin to Incourage
friends always to Labour to keep their Conciences's
clear and void of Offence towards God and all Mankinde,
after meet'g spent a little time with Frds and walk'd Home
9, went with my Wife to our first day [Sunday] meet'g, it
felt comforting and refreshing, two friends appear'd
in Testimonie which was Instructing & Comforting, I felt
easy to sit in Silence, in the A.[fter]N.[oon] walked to Witney
spent the Evening with some friends in a Solid

Page 76

Comforting manner, Lodg'd at Jno Hankins's,
16, the Monthly Meet'g before the friends enter'd
upon Buisness felt pretty comfortable, I could not
feel easy without expressing when friends in
their Silent waiting upon the Lord ware favour'd
to see their duties pointed out to them, the way
to Injoy true Peace of minde was faithfully to
discharge them, I also incouraged friends to Simpathise
with the Afflicted, sevral more friends appear'd
in Testimonie, some part of the Meet'g of buis=

=ness was cause of deep mourning to my minde it
was as floweth our friend Hanh Smith who a pretty
wile ago had felt a Concearn to have a Public meet'g appointed
at Barton, felt a Concern to come into the mens
meet'g and Signify'd she felt not quite clear of that
Place, and she should like to have another meet'g at that
Place if it was agreeable to friends, friends consented she should afterward
express'd I felt tenderness in my minde towards the peo=
=ple of that place in a perticular manner & I should
be pleased to be left at Liberty to attend the meet'g,
some friends ware appointed to attend the meet'g, one
of the Friends express'd if any friend that appear'd in
the ministery that was not recommended to the Meet'g
of Ministers & Elders was left at Liberty to go, he
did not know that he should consent to be under appointment or he was not willing or Words to
that purpose, afterwards friends ware not willing
I should attend the Meeting I sopose rather on ac=
=count of what the friend said & some friend or friends spoke
against my speaking sometimes in meet'g which was cause of
sorrow to my minde, after meet'g went to se some friends
and walk'd Home

I felt easy to sit in Silence
16, went with my Wife to our first day [Sunday] meet'g
my poor Exercised minde, was a little refresh'd
and Comforted, felt easy to sit in Silence
20, went with my Wife to our fifth day [Thursday] meet'g
my minde was refresh'd, felt easy to sit in Silence
23. went with my Wife to our first day [Sunday] meet'g, it felt
comforting felt easy to sit in Silence
26, took a walk to Witney, was at their
week day meet'g, it felt pretty comforting
to my poor Exercised minde, felt easy to sit in silence
27 took a walk to the Burial of Uncle Wm
Gibbs, who Died after a Short Illness of
about 3 Days, he was a hearty strong
looking man, which sets fourth their is no
Ceartainty of Life for any time even to the strong & Healthy
I was Concearned to speak theirin, to put the
People in minde how nesseceary it was for them
always to live in Obidience to the Comforter the
spirit of Truth within them, that they might be
prepared to Injoy a place of everlasting rest,
when ever the Lord should se meet to call them from
works to Rewards, after meet'g spent a little time
at my Motherinlaws with the Relation of the
Deceased Comfortabley, took leave of them and walked Home
30. took a walk to the Preparative Meet'g at
Banbury, it felt pretty comfortable, I was concearned
to speak theirin which relieved in some degree my much
Exercised minde, the buisness was gone through in a loving manner,

verso

Page 77

11mo 1800

13, went with my Wife to our fifth day [Thursday] Meet'g, my
Poor exercised tested minde was a little comforted,

1800

spent the A.[fter]N.[oon] with Friends in a solid comforting
manner, Lodg'd at Edw'd Stones who was very loving to Friends

12mo [December] 1st before meet'g went to se
some friends &
Relations, the Monthly meet'g felt Tolerable
comfortable
I was concearned to advise friends to dwell in
Love
and be tender towards one another,
the buisness was gone through in a pretty
agreeable
manner, altho it was Exercising and Labourious
to
the honest Hearted, after meet'g refresh'd
my=self
at Edw'd Stones, took leave of Friends & walk'd
Home
4, went to Burford with Sistor Margt to the
Burial of Sistor Bettys youngest Child,
Aged abt six weeks, the meet'g felt comforting
Devine Goodness was pleased to own us with
His Power, sevral Mouths ware opened to
speak concearning the solemnity of Death,
& how Nesseceary it was for us always to live
in Obidience to the Truth, that we might be al=
=ways prepared for Death, after meet'g spent
a little time with Bror & Sistor Comfortabley
took leave of them & returned Home with Sistor,
7, went with my Wife to our first day [Sunday]
meetg, my
minde was refresh'd, felt easy to sit in Silence
in the A.[fter]N.[oon] walk'd with Jos: Albt to
Burford found
Bror Henry & Sistor tolerable well, spent the
Even'g
with them and some friends Comfortabley,
Lodg'd at Brors
8, before meet'g went to se some friends, the
Mon=
=thly meet'g felt tolerable comfortable I was
Inabled
to bear a Short Testimonie theirin, as ware also
sevral
others, the buisness was gone through pretty
comfortable
after meet'g took leave of Relations & Frds &
walk'd Home

verso

12mo [December] 1800

11th, went with my Wife to our fifth day
[Thursday] meet'g,
my minde was mournfull under a sence of my
own Weakness's, felt easy to sit in Silence
14, went with my Wife to our first day [Sunday]
meet'g
it felt comforting and refreshing, I could not
feel quite easy without expressing how necessary
it was for Friends daily to Expiearence a state
of no condemnation, as their is no
Condemnation
to them that are in Christ Jesus,
18. went with my Wife to our fifth day [Thursday]
meet'g,
it felt refreshing, felt easy to sit in Silence
21, went with my Wife to our first day [Sunday]
meet'g,
it felt comforting & I trust some ware
favoured to pertake of Heavenly refreshment,
to the comforting and strengthing their Souls &
causeing them to rejoice, the meet'g was held in
Silence
25, went with my Wife to our fifth day [Thursday]
meet'g,
my minde was comforted, spake a little to
Incourage the youth to Indeavour to live in
the Fear of the Lord
28. took a walk with Bror R. to Oxford to
Meet'g, a
pretty menny Friends ware their, & I trust it
was a good refreshing meet'g, a pretty menny
friends appear'd in Testimonie which was to
menny's
Comfort and Instruction, & I trust menny ware
made
sensible that the best of Teachers was within
themselves, they ware also much Incouraged to
hearken theirunto and obey its Devine
Instructions,
I spake a little theirin Under an apprehention
that
it was my duty so to do, the Neighbours as well as
Friends ware much reach'd & tender'd by the
Power

of the Gospel, spent the A.[fter]N.[oon] with Friends &

Page 78

in visiting the friends which lives at Oxford
in a solid agreeable manner
29, Breackfasted at Jno Jacksons's, the Quarterly
meet'g I think was pretty large and felt comforting,
& I trust the Power of the Lord was felt to the
Comfort and refreshment of menny, the Buisness
was gone through in a tender loving Weighty
manner, it was proposed sometime ago to drop the
meet'g on first day [Sunday] preceeding this meet'g, and a
Minute was made Concearning it, but at this
meet'g it was drop't, it haveing been a good meet'g
yesterday and menny Weighty friends Expressed that they thought
it would be better to Continue it, which was cause of Joy to my minde, after meet took leave
of some friends & walked Home, had a Comfortable
Journey & was favour'd to pertake of Devine Refreshment
to the renewing of my Spiritual Strength, Praises
Obidience and Thanksgiveing be unto the Lord sayeth
my Soul who is Worthy of it for Ever,
31, went with my Wife to our Meet'g, it was held on
this day on acct of a Fair being to be to morrow,
the meet'g felt comforting spake a few words theirin
1800 1mo [January] 4th went with my Wife to our first day [Sunday] meet'g, it
felt comforting, I felt my Spiritual Strength renew'd
under a sence that the mercy and Goodness of the
Lord was extended, felt easy to sit in Silence
8, went with my Wife to our fifth day [Thursday] Meet'g
my minde was Comforted, felt easy to sit in Silence
11 went with my Wife to our first day [Sunday] meet'g, it felt
comforting, I felt a concearn to speak a few words theirin
afterwards walk'd to Enstone to se Aunt Jones & Cousins
spent a little time with them agreeabley, walk from thence

verso

to C.[hipping] Norton ware I unexpectedly met with Sarah
Lines & Mary Stacey from London, they had appointed
a Public Meeting to begin at six, I got there Just on time
to be at the meet'g, it was a large meet'g menny Nei=
=ghbours ware present, I trust it was a good Edifying
meet'g, Sarah Lynes was favour'd with a fine Opper=
=tunity a mongst them, to declare that there was a
Necessiety for them to come out of Lifeless forms &
Ceremonies, to a firm reliance & Faithfull Obidience
to the Devine Light Truth & Spirit of Christ within them,
that they might be inabled to walk in the way of
Life & true Peace, after meet spent a little time
with the straingers and other friends, Lodg'd at J. Kings
12, before our Monthly Meet'g began went to see some
friends, the Meet'g felt comfortable, we ware favour'd
with the Company of S. Lynes & M. Stacy, they ware
favour'd to declare Truth and to speak pretty closely to
menny present, I felt easy to sit in Silence, altho
in the meet'g of buisness the pure life felt low amoungst us
yet the buisness was gone through in Love , after
meet'g spent a little time with friends comfortabley in the Ev'ing walk'd Home
15 went with my Wife to our fifth day [Thursday] meet'g my minde was refreshed

18, went with my Wife to our first day [Sunday] meet'g my minde
was refresh'd, spake a little theirin, to Incourage
friends to feel & Labour after a State of sweet Innosciency
22, went with my Wife to our fifth day [Thursday] meet'g
25, went with my Wife to our first day [Sunday] meet'g, it felt
Comforting, we ware favour'd with the Company
of sevral Strangers, Sarah Hankins from Witney
appeard I trust to the Comfort and Incourage of
Friends to persevear in the line of their duty, I felt easy to sit in Silence
29, went with my Wife to our fifth day [Thursday] meet'g,
it was held in Silence, my minde was Comforted,

Page 79

1801

2mo [February] 1st went with my Wife to our first day [Sunday]
meet'g, my minde was Comforted it was held in Silence
5, went with my Wife to our fifth day [Thursday] meet'g, it was held in Silence
8. I & my Wife ware at our first day [Sunday] meet'g, my
my minde was refresh'd, it was held in Silence
9. went with my Wife to our Monthly Meet'g held
at this place, it felt pretty comfortable, sevral
women friends appear'd in Testimonie to Incourage
friends diligently to persevear in the way of
well doing, I felt easy to sit in Silence,
the buisness was gone through in Love,
12. went with my Wife to our fifth day [Thursday] meet'g
15. went with my Wife to our first day [Sunday] meet'g, my
minde was Comforted and refresh'd under a
sence that Devine Power was felt amoungst us,
spake a little theirin,
I lately procured some paper wrote by a frd
setting fourth the great sin of Swearing
taking the Sacred Name in Vain Drunck=
=enness &et I felt a Concearn to go to some
little Towns as well as this Place & distribute
some of the papers, & I was Concearned to Incou=
=rage such People that had it in their Power to be good to the
Poor to be good to them & relieve such as ware
in Distress, for it was the way to obtain mercy
of the Lord, as I was sensible menny wanted
relief & I was afraid menny suffered for want
of the Nessecaries of Life, Provisions & things in general
being dearer I sopose than ever was known by the
oldest Parson Living, felt peace & Comfort by so doing & People
appeard to take my visits kindly,

verso

1801

2mo [February] 18th took a walk to Witney, was at their
fourth day [Wednesday] meet'g, it felt Pretty comfortable,
I trust there ware present a little Living
remnant who ware sensible that ware but
two or three are met together in Jesus's
Name, there He would be in the midst
of them, I was Concearned to advise Friends
to be diligent in waiting upon the Lord,
19, went with my Wife to our fifth day [Thursday] meet'g, my
minde was refresh'd, it was held in Silence
20, took a walk to C.[hipping]Norton, was at their six-day [Friday]
meet'g, it felt pretty comfortable, I was concearned
to speak theirin felt satisfaction by so doing, after
meet'g went to se some friends in Affliction, the
appeard to take my visit Kindly, return'd Home in the Even'g
22, went with my Wife to our first day [Sunday] meet'g it
felt comforting, and I trust Devine Power and
goodness was felt to flow amoungst us to our
Spiritual refreshment, I was concearn'd to speak therein

26 went with my Wife to our fifth day [Thursday] meet'g,
my minde was refresh'd, felt easy to sit in Silence
3mo [March] 1st took a walk to Brails to the Preparative Meet'g it felt pretty
comfortable, I was concearn'd to advise friends to be
very diligent in attending Meetings, and labour to In=
=Joy sweet peace of minde, after meet'g spent a little
time with Cousins Comfortabley, walk from thence
to Sibford found my Mother=in=law & some of our Relations very Poorly, spent
a little time with them agreeabley, Lodg'd at my kinde
friend M. Petiphers
2 walk'd to the Monthly Meet'g at adderbury it felt
tolerable comfortable, I was concearn'd to speak theirin
the buisness was gone through comfortabley, after

Page 80

---

meet'g walk'd to Milton to Din'r, stop'd a little
with friends, walk'd from thence to Sibford & from
thence to Cous'n Wm Gilletts of Brails who ware very kind Lodg'd there
3, took leave of Cousins at Brails & walk'd to
the Monthly Meet'g at Shipstone, before meet'g
went to se some friends, found Rich'd Tyler
in a very weak state of Body, he appears to
be in a decline & near his end, spent a little
time with him in a Solid manner, he express'd
that he was easy in his minde & Resign'd unto the
Devine Will which was Comforting, took leave of
him Expecting nevver to se him more
the meet'g did not feel very refreshing, it hath ap=
=pear'd unto me that some friends have set their
mindes on the love of Earthly Treasure which is
an hindrance to them from Labouring to lay up Tre=
=asures in Heaven & shuts up their Bowels from
being tender and Compassionate towards the Poor
distress'd ones, I was Concearn'd to advise friends
to make good use of the Lords blessings that when
they ware call'd to give anaccount of what use they
had made of them they might have a good account
to give, the buisness was gone through pretty lovingly,
after meet'g took leave of friends & Relations & walk'd Home
5. went with my Wife to our fifth day [Thursday] Meet'g, felt easy to sit in Silence
8. took a walk with my Wife to Sibford to se her
Mother, found her weak & poorly, was at their first
day meet'g, my minde was refresh'd, it was held
in Silence, after meet'g took leave of my Wife
and Relations & walk'd Home
9, took a walk to our Monthly Meetg held at Witney

verso

---

it did not feel very comforting, the pure Life
felt to be low theirin, speak a little in Testimonie
the buisness was not gone through in a very
lively Comforting manner, there appeard
a pretty deal of work that should be done
but not sufficient strength to do it, after meet'g visited
some friends in affliction their Company was Comforting
call'd to se some other Frds, in the Evening walk'd Home
12, I went to our fifth day [Thursday] meet'g, my minde was refresh'd
it was held in Silence
15, took a walk to Hooknorton to meeting, it was
small, the Truth felt to be low amoungst
them, yet I trust the Love & Mercy of the
Almighty was Extended, and I was Inabled
to speak to the states of sevral present
in an extroarderny manner, after meet'g walk'd
to Sibford found my Wives Mother better, walk'd
from thence with my Wife to C.[hipping] Norton Lodg'd
at Josh Kings

16, rose pretty early, took our leave of Frds & walk'd Home
19, went with my Wife to our fifth day [Thursday] meet'g
it felt to be a refreshing meet'g altho held in Silence
22. went with my Wife to our first day [Sunday] meet'g
it felt refreshing & Comforting, spake a little theirin, to Incourage friends not onely to be willing but also to desire to be fed with food convinient for them, and as they indeavoured to bear every alottment of Devine Providence with Patience & Resignation
to His will, I trusted it would all work together for their good
26, I went to our fifth day [Thursday] meet'g, my minde
was refresh'd, it was held in Silence
29, took a walk to Barton to visit Thos Jarvis

Page 81

and his Family, found his Wife & Oldest Daughter very Ill, I had a pretty comfortable oppertunity with them, to Incourage the Afflicted to Indeavour
to bear their Affliction patiently and to look and seek to the Phisician of Value for help and Comfort, and also to Instruct the Children to love the Truth and live in Obidience their= =unto, went from thence with T. Jarvis & one of his Children to the meet'g at Adderbury, there ware a pretty menny young friends there, Truth felt to be low amoungst them, I was Concearn'd to Advise the young friends in a perticular manner carefully to attend to Devine Instructions & Indeavour faithfully to Obey them, which if they did they would be fitted a qualified to become Labourers in the Lords Vineyard, after meet'g spent a little time with friends at Adderbury, returnd from thence with T. Jarvis to Barton, stop'd with them a little they ware kind and loving appeard glad of my visit, walk'd from thence Home
4mo [April] 2nd went with my Wife to our fifth day [Thursday] meet'g
my minde was refresh'd, it was held in Silence
5, went with my Wife to our first day [Sunday] Meetg
it felt comforting, it was held in Silence
our Preparative Meet'g buisness was gone through in Love
in the A.[fter]N.[oon] walk'd to Burford spent the Evening
with Bror Sistor & some friends Comfortabley
6, Before our Monthly Meet'g began went to se some friends the meet'g felt pretty comfortable

verso

Sevral Living Testimonies was born & one friend appeard in Solem Prayer,
altho in going through the Buisness things felt very low and friends got but little forward, yet I trust the pure Life was kept to so as for it to Reighn, *a Testimonie which was drawn up by a Commity of Friends*
was Approved and sign'd on behalf
of Eliz^h Mintchin late of Burford, who died
abt a year agoe, She was a Valueable Ministering Frd & often inabled to speak to the States
& Conditions of menny, was much belov'd & Laboured hard in the Work of the Ministery, after meet'g spend a little time with Bror Sistor & some friends & walk'd with sevral friends Home
9, went with my Wife to our fifth day [Thursday] meet'g
it was held in Silence
12 went with my Wife to our first day [Sunday] meet'g, my minde
was Comforted, & I trust Devine Love was felt to flow amoungst us, it was held in Silence, we ware favourd with the Company of Hanh Jarrot
14, walk'd with my Wife & some friends, to our Quarterly Meet'g
at Witney, it was pretty large & I think a much Favour'd Meet'g, we ware favourd with the Company
of a Ministering Fr'd from Tukesbury, viz Ann Low
Menny Friend appear'd in Testimonie, & I Trust sevral states ware spoken closely unto, the Luke= =warm & Indif'rent ware aroused, even such as had

been much Visited with the Loving=kindeness
of the
Lord, & their rong doings had been clearly
pointed
out unto them, & they had slited the tender
Mercies
of the Lord time after time, & they ware put in
minde that if they did not Join in with the Tender

Page 82

Mercy & Visitation of the Lord & yield faithfull
Obidience theirunto, their was a danger of their
being ever visited again, two friends appear'd in
Solem prayer, the meet'g of Buisness held
long, friends appeard to be in a low weak state,
& the Travellers Zion ward Mourned Under a
sence that there was a deal of work to do, &
but few labourers willing to do it, after meet'g
I & my Wife walk'd Home with some friends
16, went with my Wife to our fifth day [Thursday]
meet'g
it felt comforting, we ware favourd with the
Company of Ann Low, she was favour'd to
speak Instructingly, & to Incourage us to give
up all as into the Lords Hands, & be willing to
part with all that the Truth Manifested to
us to be our Duty to part with for His Sake,
19, I went to our first day [Sunday] meet'g my
Wife being
with my Sistor she being very poorly, the meet'g
felt comforting, we ware favour'd with the
Company
of sevral strangers who ware appointed by our
Monthly Meetg to pay Ann Coleman a Visit, she
having made Application to be Rec'd into
Member=
ship with us, sevral mouths ware oppen'd to
testify
of the Lords Love & goodness to such as love &
fear Hime, & to Incourage the youth in a
perticular
manner to live in His Fear & be wholy Obidient
unto His Devine Instructions within them, as
that
was the only way to become truly Wise & to be
bless'd
both Spiritualy & Temporaly & to be preserved
from
menny sorrows Troubles of minde, I felt easy to
sit in silence
23, went with my Wife to our fifth day [Thursday]
meet'g, my minde was
refresh'd, it was held in Silence

verso

1801

4mo [April] 26th went with my Wife to our first
day [Sunday] meet'g
it felt comforting to my poor Exercised minde,
speak a little theirin, felt Satisfaction by so doing
I have been poorly of late & I have been brought
into a low
Situation of minde, I have been favour'd to see
the Nescessiety there is for such as would finde
axceptance with the Lord, to live a lowly humble
selfdenying Life, & to very carefull to attend unto
the Instructions of the Truth within & live daily
in Obidience to its Devine Instructions,
30, went with my Wife to our fifth day [Thursday]
meet'g, my
minde was refresh'd, it was held in Silence
5mo [May] 2nd took a walk to Sibford found
Mother pretty midling
walked from thence to Brails, found Cous'ns
tolerable well
spent the Evening with them and friends
comfortabley Lodg'd at Wm Gilletts
3 after breackfasting at Cous'n Wm Gilletts
walk'd to the morn'g
meet'g at Shipstone, sevral strangers ware there,
who came
out of Love & goodwill towards friends, but
there ware
but very few there, which was I believe cause of
mourning
to the Honest Hearted Friends to percieve friends
to be so
neglectfull in so great a duty as that of attending
Meetings,
walk'd from thence with some friends to the
Meet'g at
Armscutt [Armscote], it was very large of
Friends & Neighbours,

and I trust the Lords love and Mercifull Visitation was
Extended to menny, sevral friends appear'd in Testimonie,
& I hope they ware Inabled to reach the pure witness in
menny mindes, so as to make them sensible that the True
Teacher was within them, vis Christ the light in Man, and
if they would live in a State of Axceptance with the Lord,
they must live daily in Obidience to the Light within and In=
=deavour to do nothing that the Devine Teacher disaprov'd of,
Ann Low was there who appeard in Solem Prayer, I was
concearnd to speak theirin, it was much exercising so to do,

Page 83

under a Sence of my own Weakness, the weightiness of
the work, yet it afforded my minde Comfort, after meet'g
walk'd to Thos Farthings Tredington, spent a little time
with friends there Comfortabley, Walk'd from thence with
Thos Harris to his House at Longcompton, Lodg'd there,
4, took leave of Fr'd Harris's, and walk'd Home in the Morn'g
7, went with my Wife to our fifth day [Thursday] meet'g, my minde
was refresh'd
10, went with my Wife to our first day [Sunday] meet'g, it felt
comforting & I trust we ware favour'd with the un=
=erring Teacher, as Teacheth as nevver man Taught,
speak a little theirin, in the A.[fter]N.[oon] I and my
Wife walk'd with some friends to C.[hipping] Norton spent
the Evening Comfortabley with some friends Lodg'd at Jos Kings
11, before our Monthly Meet'g began I and my
Wife went to se some friends, the meet'g was
largish & I trust we ware favour'd with the
overshadowings of Devine Goodness to our
comfort and Refreshment, sevral Friends
appear'd in Testimonie which was Instructing
and Comforting & Perticularly to the youth, I was
concearn'd to speak theirin, the buisness was
gone through Pretty comfortabley, after meetg
spent sometime in visiting some friends in Afflic=
=tion, & some other friends, I & my Wife walk'd
Home in the Even'g with some friends
12, this Evening we ware favour'd with the Company
of Deborah Darby of Colebrook Dale, who desired to have
a meeting appointed to begin at six in the Even'g
& to have the Neighbours let know, which was accord=
=ingly done, it was a large and Comfortable meet'g
menny Neighbours came and behaved quiet, Deborah
was much favour'd to declare Truth amoungst the
People, She was led pretty much to Speak concearning

verso

true Spiritual Prayer & the great Necessiety there
was for them to Consider their latter end also to know
a Death unto sin & a new Birth unto Righteous=
=ness, that they might be inabled to live to praise
the Lord and obtain an Inheritance in his Glorious
Kingdom, when time to them in this World should
be no more, I think she was upon her feet
about an hour, She Concluded the meeting
with solem awefull Prayer
14, went with my Wife to our fifth day [Thursday] meet'g I
had much to do to struggle with my Weakness's, it was held in Silence
17, went with my Wife to our first day [Sunday] meet'g it felt com=
=forting, & I trust Devine Goodness was felt amoungst us

to our Refreshment, speak a little theirin,
20, took a walk to Witney, was at their fourth day [Wednesday]
meet'g, it felt comforting & refreshing, it was held
in Silence, in the A.[fter]N.[oon] Ann Oldaker walked with me to Charlbury
21, went with my Wife to our fifth day [Thursday] meet'g, I felt
to be a poor Creature, it was held in Silence
24, went with my Wife to our first day [Sunday] meet'g, it appear'd
to me to be a time in which there was a Necessiety for
Friends diligently to Labour for Lowlyness and Humility,
my minde was refresh'd, it was held in Silence,
28 went with my Wife to our fifth day [Thursday] meet'g
was sensible of great weakness and poorness
31, went with my Wife to our first day [Sunday] meet'g, it felt
comforting, spake a little theirin, was led to Incourage
the youth to labour earnestly to Injoy Innoscient meek states of minde
I have been much Exercised and grieved of late
on account of People Dancing & following such vain
Amusements, & I was concearn'd to go to some Houses &

Page 84

and Advise the Heads of the Families, not to suffer
such things to be at their houses or before there
Doors also to do what they could to discourage such
Practices, they appear to receive my advice friendly
and promis'd they would discourage it, I felt comfort
by so doing
4th went with my Wife to our fifth day [Thursday] meet'g, felt poor
and unworthy of the blessings I daily receive, it was held in silence
7, went with my Wife to our first day [Sunday] meet'g, it felt com=
=forting, I trust we ware favourd with the power of the Lord
to our Comfort & Spiritual refreshment, I was concearn'd
to advise friends to Labour to be rightly acquainted with pure Silent
Worship, in which the minde is favoured to receive teaching
and Comfort from the Unering Teacher
8th went with my Wife to our Monthly Meet'g held at
this Place, it felt to be a Tolerable comfortable Meet'g,
sevral friends appear in Testimonie, as for me I
felt low and poor and in a moornfull State, yet I
was a little comforted, feeling Devine goodness to be
administered, felt easy to sit in Silence, the buisness
was gone through pretty Lovingly
11, went with my Wife to our fifth day [Thursday] meet'g, it was
held in Silence
12, took a walk to C.[hipping]Norton with my Wives Sistor H,
who has been to pay us a visit, was at their sixday [Friday]
meet'g, my minde was Comforted, it was held in Silence,
14, went with my Wife to our first day [Sunday] meet'g, it was
a little Comforting to poor Exercised minde, felt easy to sit in Silence
18, went with my Wife to our fifth day [Thursday] meet'g, it felt
refreshing, it was held in Silence
21, went with my Wife to our first day [Sunday] meet'g my minde
was poor and low theirin, & I thought there was a nescessiety
for Friends to labour Earnestly for Devine Refreshment

verso

25, went with my Wife to our fifth day [Thursday] meet'g, it was held in Silence
28, this morning my Wife set out with Ann Oldaker,
Intending for the Quarterly Meet'g at Banbury,

I went to our first day [Sunday] meet'g, it felt comforting
altho I felt to be a very poor Creature, I was
concearned to Incourage friends to Labour earnestly
for that Meat wich nourisheth up the Soul unto Eternal Life
and not to be Anxious to Provide things for the
support of the Earthly Bodies which soon must return to the Dust
29, walk'd to Banbury with Bro'r Robt in order to
be at our Quarterly Meet'g to be held at Banbury,
I & my Wife Quarter'd at E. stones, who ware very kinde to us,
30, the Quarterly Meet'g I think was tolerable large
and Comfortable, five Friends in the Ministery there
with Certivicates, viz Charity Cook & Mary Sweat
from America, Ann Bird, Sarah Rudd, Sarah Luckett, sevral
friends appeard in Testimonie & one in Prayer, which
felt to be attended with Life & Power, & I Trust was Incourageing
& Comforting to menny, a pretty menny minutes ware
rec'd from the Yearly Meet'g, which ware weightily
consider'd, the buisness was gone through pretty Comfortabley
after Meet'g Din'd at T. Beesleys, took leave of Friends
and walk'd Home with my Wife & Bro'r Robt
7mo [July] 2nd went with my Wife to our fifth day [Thursday] meet'g, it was held in Silence
5 went with my Wife to our first day [Sunday] meet'g, I sat Com=
=fortable theirin, and it felt refreshing, felt Easy to Sit
in Silence, it was our Preparative meet'g
9, went with my Wife to our fifth day [Thursday] meet'g, very
Poorly & much exercised in minde it was held in Silence
12 went with my Wife to our first day [Sunday] meet'g, it felt
comforting to my minde, I thought a rement
ware concearnd in pure Silence to seek after the Lord
for themselves and to be more acquainted with His Love, spake theirin

Page 85

in the A.[fter]N.[oon] walk'd with Ann oldaker to Witney spent
the Even'g Comfortabley in visiting some friends &
relations, Lodg'd at Jno Hankins's
13, rose Early & Walk'd with some friends to our Monthly
meet'g at faringdon, it felt pretty comfortable
sevral friends appear'd in Testimonie, the Yearly
Epistle was read, sevral printed Minutes ware rec'd
from the Yearly meet'g read & consider'd & the other Buisness
was gone through pretty agreeabley, after meet'g spent a few hours at Robt
Reynolds's & his Sons pretty comfortabley, in the Eving
walk'd with a fr'd to Witney, Lodg'd at Jno Hankins's
14th in the morn spen a little time with some friends at
Witney in a solid lov'g & agreeable manner & walk'd with Bror R Home
16, went with my Wife to our fifth day [Thursday] meet'g, my minde
was refresh'd, it was held in Silence
19, went with my Wife to our first day [Sunday] meet'g, sat
comfortabley, my minde was refresh'd, it was held in
Silence Except the Yearly Epistle was read, and I was concearnd
to put friends in minde of the good and weighty advices
it contain'd, & how very neseceary it was for Friends to let
them have a proper weight upon their mindes,
21, took a walk to Burford with my Nephew, found Bror
Sistor & Family pretty tolerable, was at the
Third day [Tuesday] meet'g, my minde was refresh'd, it was held in Silence

after meet'g spent a little time with Bro'r & Sistor &
in going to se some friends, in the Even'g walk'd Home
23, went with my Wife to our fifth day [Thursday] meet'g, my minde
was refresh'd, altho the pure Life felt to be low amoungst
us, it was held in Silence
26, went with my Wife to our first day [Sunday] meet'g, it felt
refreshing & comforting, I was Concearn'd to put friends
in minde to Indeavour so to live in Humility & the Fear
of the Lord as to have their minds loosen'd from the Things
of this World, that [illegible] they ware call'd from Works to rewards the
Prospect might appear glorious, another friend appear'd in Testimonie

verso

1801

7mo [July] 30th went with my Wife to our fifth day [Thursday] meet'g, my minde
was refresh'd, it was held in Silence
8mo [August] 2nd went with my Wife to our first day [Sunday] meet'g
sat comfortabley, my minde was refresh'd as I
trust the mindes of most present ware, it was held in Silence
9, went with my Wife to our first day [Sunday] meet'g I felt
to be a very poor Creature, it was held in Silence
in the A.[fter]N.[oon] I my Wife and another woman Frd walk'd
to Burford, found Bro'r & Sistor tolerable well spent
the Even'g with them and some friends comfortabley, Lodg'd at Bro'rs
10, before our Monthly Meet'g began, went to se some
friends, I think the Meet'g was pretty large and felt
pretty comfortable, sevral Mouths ware opened to tes=
=tify of the Lords Love and goodness to such as love
Him & delight to live in His fear, much Incourage=
=ment was given to the youth for them to diligently
minde the Instructions of the Truth within them and
Faithfully to obey it, one friend appear'd in Prayer,
the Buisness was gone through in a pretty agreeable
manner, after meet'g spent a little time in going
to se some friends & with our Relations, in the
Even'g walked Home with my Wife and the Fr'd
13, went with my Wife to our fifth day [Thursday] meet'g
16, took a walk with Bro'r to a meet'g at Barton ap=
=pointed at our last Monthly Meet'g by the desire of
Hanh Smith of Witney, who felt a concearn to have a
Public meet'g there, it began at ten, it was not very
large, sevral friends ware their in the Ministery besides
H. Smith, Menny mouths ware open'd to testify of the
Lords love and goodness to them that fear Him and I
think they ware Inabled to reach the pure witness in menny
and it felt to be a renew'd Visitation of the Lord to menny

Page 86

I felt a Concearn to put the People in mind
not to put of the work of Repentance untill another
day, but to use all Diligence to make their calling
and election sure, wile the mercy of the Lord was
extended towards them, after meet'g went to Thos
Jarvis's to Din'r, spent a little time with them
and some friends in a solid Comfortable manner,
walk'd from thence with Bro'r Home

23, went with my Wife to our first day [Sunday] meet'g, it felt pretty
comfortable, we had the Company of Wm Lewton of London who is
on a visit to his Relations, two Frds appear'd in Testimonie
which was Incourageing to the poor Exercised mourners who ware
concearn'd to Travel Zion Ward, I felt easy to sit in Silence
27, went with my Wife to our fifth day [Thursday] meet'g, my minde was
refresh'd, felt easy to sit in Silence
30, went with my Wife to our first day [Sunday] meet'g, it felt com=
=fortable and I trust we ware favour'd to be drawn into
a degree of Solid Silence, and ware favour'd to feel
the best of Teachers to arise in us, whose teaching is best
felt and understood in Stillness when our mindes are depending on the Lord alone
for help & Comfort, spake a little theirin to Incourage friends
to Indeavour to live lowly & humbley & daily wait patiently
upon the Lord,
9mo [September] 2nd took a walk to Witney was at their fourth day [Wednesday] meet'g,
at which was a Funeral, a Child of about 7 years
of Age, it felt pretty comfortable sevral Mouths
ware open'd to direct the people to minde the Law
of God writen in the Hearts, & advise them not to sin
against it, that they might be prepared to leave this
World, when ever the Almighty should see meet to remove
them with a well ground'd hopes that they should be favour'd
with an Everlasting Inheritance with the Righteous, I spake a little
theirin, after meet'g call'd to se some fr'ds & return'd Home

verso

1801

9mo [September] 3rd went with my Wife to our fifth day [Thursday] meet'g my
minde was refresh'd, & I was concearn'd to advise friends
to Labour earnestly to Obtain that living water which
nourisheth up the Soul unto Eternal Life
6 went with my Wife to our first day [Sunday] meet'g, it felt
comforting, two Friends appear'd in Testimonie, I
felt easy to sit in Silence, it was our Preparative
meet'g, the buisness was gone through in Love, in the
A.[fter]N.[oon] walk'd to C.[hipping]Norton spent a little time in going
to se some friends whose company was comforting
Lodg'd at Jos Kings
7 before our Monthly Meet'g began went to se some
friends, the monthly Meet'g felt pretty comfortable
one fr'd appear'd in Prayer in the forepart of the
Meet'g, & sevral in Testimonie which was Instructing
& Comforting & sharp to the Indifrent & lookewarm,
the buisness was gone through pretty agreeabley, after
meet'g spent a little time in going to se some friends,
took leave of them & walk'd with my Wife & some friends Home
10, went with my Wife to our fifth day [Thursday] meet'g, my minde
was refresh'd, felt easy to sit in Silence
12th in the afternoon set out for our Quarterly Meet'g at Reading,
walk'd to Oxford, spent the Even'g at Jn'o Jacksons's
Comfortabley, Lodg'd at Jn'o Jacksons's
13. walk'd to Warborough to meet'g it felt pretty
comfortable, spake theirin, spent the after=noon

with Frds at Warborough & Shillingford I trust in
an agreeable Edifying manner, Lodg'd at Cous'n J. Ashbys
14, set out in the morning with Jn'o Sargood for
Read'g, reach'd there abt 3 oclock, spent the Even'g
agreeabley at Relations & Frds, Lodg'd at T. Stubbs

Page 87

9mo [September] 15th before the Quarterly Meet'g began went to
se a pretty menny friends, being desireous to pay
most of them a visit before I left Reading, the
meet'g felt pretty comfortable, one friend appear'd
in Prayer & sevral in Testimonie, two Strangers
there on a Religious visit, viz Edwd May & Richd
Gilks of Devises, the Buisness was gone through
pretty agreeabley, after meet'g took leave of Relations
& Frds & walk'd with Jn'o Sargood to his House at
Warborough, he is a free agreeable Frd & one I trust
who loves to se friends grow up in the Truth and Con=
=duct themselves agreeable to our Holy Profession,
also is concearn'd to labour for its Honnour, Lodg'd at his House
16 walk'd up to Cousin Jos Ashbys to breackfast with
them & some friends who Lodg'd there being on there
return from the Quar. Meet'g, walk'd from thence to
Jno Jacksons Oxford, spent a little time there comfortabley
walk'd from thence Home, ware I found my Wife well
I was favour'd to feel a degree of Peace in my minde,
having Indeavour'd to Labour Faithfully to discharge my
duty unto the Lord, & in as much as He is pleased at times
to break in upon my Soul with his Life giveing
Power & goodness, my Heart Breaths forth Praises
unto Him, & it is my sincear desire that I may so live
in His Fear & in faithfully answering His requireings
as to be truly Gratefull for the menny Favours & bless=
=ings we daily receive, Poor unworthy Creatures
16, I & my Wife ware at our fifth day [Thursday] meet'g
20, I went with my Wife to our first day [Sunday] meet'g, it felt pretty comfortable
24, I 7 my Wife ware at our fifth day [Thursday] meet'g, my minde was
refresh'd, felt easy to sit in Silence
27, went with my Wife to our first day [Sunday] meet'g, altho our meet'g
was Smallish, yet I trust we ware favour'd with the Overshadow=
=ings of Devine Love to our Comfort & spiritual refreshment,
felt easy to sit in Silence,
10mo [October] 1st went with my Wife to our fifth day [Thursday] meet'g, we ware
with the Company of Edwd May from Holton & Richd Gilks

verso

1801

from Devises who are on a religious visit, the Meet'g
felt Comforting, both of them appear'd in Public
which was Instructing Comforting & Incourageing for
us to keep moving forward towards the Land of Rest
10mo [October] 4th went with my Wife to our first day [Sunday] meet'g,
sat pretty comfortabley, altho my minde has been
much in a Clouded situation of late, one Frd
appear'd in Testimonie, I felt easy to sit in Silence,
5, went with my Wife to our Monthly Meet'g held at
this place, the pure Life felt to be low amoungst us,

two Frds appear'd in Testimonie, one of them in a very arouseing manner to the Careless & lukewarm,
and Incourageing to the youth in perticular,
to come up in obidience to the Truth
also one of them appear'd in very solem Prayer, the buisness
was gone through pretty comfortabley,
8, went with my Wife to our fifth day [Thursday] meet'g, I
felt weak poor & low, both inwardly & outwardly
11, went with my Wife to our first day [Sunday] meet'g,
sevral strangers ware there, it felt refreshing
spake a little theirin to recomend friends to be
obidient to the Light of Christ within, which
preserves from all Sin,
15, went with my Wife to our fifth day [Thursday] meetg, it
felt comforting, it was held in Silence
18. took a walk to Milton to Meet'g, altho it was
a Small meet'g, yet I trust Kinde Providence
was pleased to manifest His love and Mercy
unto us, I was concearn'd to speak theirin to
Incourage friends to be diligent in attending
meet'gs, & in being obidient to Devine Requireings,
after meet'g went to se the Friends, spent a little
time with them in a solid manner, afterward walk'd Home

Page 88

10mo [October] 22nd went with my Wife to our fifth day [Thursday] meet'g, my
minde was refresh'd, sat in Silence
25, went with my Wife to our first day [Sunday] meet'g,
my minde was refresh'd as I trust menny
present ware, one Frd appear'd, I felt easy to
sit in Silence
29 went with my Wife to our fifth day [Thursday] meet'g,
it felt comforting, my minde was refresh'd, sat in Silence
11mo 1st went with my Wife to our first day [Sunday]
meet'g, we ware favour'd with the Company
of Josh Huntley and Ann Ashby, who came on a
Religious Visit to friends Families, it felt
pretty comfortable, held in Silence except Josh
Huntley had a few words to Incourage friends
to Indeavour to Expiearence what bless'd Jesus
did, vis to Overcome the World,
5, went with my Wife to our fifth day [Thursday] meet'g, my
minde was refresh'd, felt easy to sit in Silence
8, went with my Wife to our first day [Sunday] meet'g, it
felt pretty comforting, one friend appear'd, I felt
easy to sit in Silence, in the A.[fter]N.[oon] walk'd with
my Wife & Sistor M to Witney, spent the Evening
with Frds their comfortabley, Lodg'd at Wm Barrits [illegible]
9, our Monthly Meet'g I think was pretty large,
there being a Committy of friends there, who ware
appointed by the Quarterly Meet'g to Join a Com=
=mitty of our Monthly Meet'g, to consider of what
Friends they thought ware proper to be appointed
Elders, the Meet'g felt comfortable, & I trust Devine
Providence was pleased to favour us with his living
Power to the comforting & refreshing menny Present,

verso

sevral living Testimonies ware born & one
friend appeard in Solem Prayer in which he
had to Express, We ask not for Richs nor
honnour nor length of days, but that thy
living Power & Presence may attend us in our
labours for the prosperity of the Everlasting
Truth or to that Import, & I think it would be
a great comfort if menny would labour to Injoy
after such a manner, the buisness was gone
through in Love, one woman friend, viz Ann Coleman was receiv'd into
membership, she has come to meet'gs a pretty wile,
and friends ware appointed to visit her, (she having
made application to be rec'd into membership)
which they did, and brought in a report that they

believed she was worthy of Friends Notice,
after meet'g spent a little time with some friends
& walk'd with my Wife & Sistor Home
12, went with my Wife to our fifth day [Thursday] meet'g, it
felt refreshing to my poor exercised minde, felt easy to sit in Silence
15, went with my Wife to our first day [Sunday] meet'g
my minde was refresh'd, altho Truth felt to be
low amoungst us, I felt easy to sit in Silence
one friend spake a few words which was comforting
& Incourageing to us, to live daily in pure obidience
to the Eternal Word and Power of God,
19 went with my Wife to our fifth day [Thursday] meet'g, my minde
was refresh'd felt easy to sit in Silence
22 went with my Wife to our first day [Sunday] meet'g, it
felt comforting altho held in Silence & I trust
a remant ware favour'd to receive Heavenly Food
26, went with my Wife to our fifth day [Thursday] meet'g, my minde
was refresh'd, felt easy to sit in Silence

Page 89

11mo 29th went with my Wife to our first day [Sunday] meet'g,
I felt poor & low in minde, yet it felt a little
comforting, felt easy to sit in Silence
12mo [December] 3rd went with my Wife to our fifth day [Thursday] meet'g,
my minde was refresh'd, it was held in Silence
6, went with my Wife to our first day [Sunday] meet'g,
it felt comforting, it was held in Silence
10. went with my Wife to our fifth day [Thursday] meet'g, my
minde was refresh'd, it was held in Silence
13. went with my Wife to our first day [Sunday] meet'g,
my minde was refresh'd, it was held in Silence
in the A.[fter]N.[oon] walk'd with my Wife & some friends
to Burford, spent most of the Eving at Bro'rs Comfortabley, Lodgd their
14 before meet'g began went to se some friends, the
meet'g felt pretty comfortable, some friends appear'd
in Testimonie which was Comforting & Incourage
=ing to friends to persevear in the way of welldoing,
I felt a Concearn to speak theirin, but having
met with great discouragement from some in
that work, it was much in the Cross for me to
appear, yet I found if I would sarve the Lord in
sincearity & in Truth & Injoy his Living Power, I
must live daily in Faithfull Obidience to all
His requireings, felt comfort by giveing up to what
I believed was required of me & speaking the feelings
of my minde, the Buisness was gone through in Love
after refreshing ourselves at Bro'rs, I and my Wife walk'd Home with some friends
17, went with my Wife to our fifth day [Thursday] meet'g, my
minde was refresh'd, it was held in Silence
19, took a walk to Maughsbury Lodg'd at Jn'o Peglers
found him & his Wife poorly

verso

12mo [December] 1801

20th walk'd to stow & before meet'g went to se some friends also
some Relations in Affliction, & I was led to feel
for them & Simpathise with them, being sensible
some of them ware in want of the Nesearies of
Life, the meet'g was very small yet I hope
there was a little degree of Life felt to arise therein,
spake a few words theirin, after meet'g stop'd a little
at Stow with Relations & friends, afterward walk'd
down to Jn'o Peglers spent most of the Evening
their pretty comfortabley, Lodg'd their
21, rose pretty Early walk'd to Oddington, breack=

=fasted with Wm Colding, spent a little time with
him in a solid manner, walk from thence Home
24th went with my Wife to our fifth day [Thursday] meet'g,
my minde was refresh'd, it was held in Silence
27, went with my Wife to our first day [Sunday] meet'g
it felt comforting, spake theirin, was concearned
to Incourage the youth to seek an acquaintance
with the truth and love it,
31, went with my Wife to our fifth day [Thursday] meet'g, it
felt comforting, it was held in Silence,

1802

1mo [January] 3rd went with my Wife to our first day [Sunday] meet'g,

it felt comforting, it was held in Silence,
7, went with my Wife to our fifth day [Thursday] meet'g, my
minde was refresh'd, it was held in Silence
F[irst] Day [Sunday], 10th took a walk to the Public Meet'g at
Oxford, which is usualy held on the first day be=
=fore the quarterly Meet'g, it was not very large
of Friends, but a pretty menny Neighbours came in
who behaved pretty well, & seem'd to be reach'd & affected

Page 90

with what was deliver'd, spent the A[fter] Noon
mostly at George Tittertons & Jno Jacksons's
with Friends pretty comfortabley, Lodg'd at Jno Jacksons's
11, Breackfasted with some friends at Jno Jacksons's
who behaved very kinde to friends, the Q[uarterly] Meet'g
began at 9 oclock, it felt pretty comfortable,
sevral friends appear'd in Testimonie, one
was led in a perticular manner to such as had
met with menny Tryals & deep Baptiseing seasons, In=
=courageing them to hold on their way and not to be un=
=easy because they seem'd to have greater Tryals &
Proving seasons aloted them than others, (signifying
the Lord knew what Food was best for us to be fed
with) but as they had known that the Lord had been
with them in Six Troubles, so he would be with
them in the sevventh, if they did but truly Trust
in him and sarve him Faithfully & Incouraged
friends to be valient in the Truth, I felt a concearn
to speak theirin, but I haveing met with menny
discouragements it was much in the cross for me to
speak what rested on my minde, & I have thought
through fear of offending some, and for want of
Patiently attending to that Power which qualifies & In=
=ables to Speak with Devine Athority , I have some=
=times spoke to little & sometime to much, & sometimes
in such a fearfull manner as not to be distinctly
understood by some, & I do think such as have a Gift
in the Ministery, should keep close to that Power which
removes the Fear of man, & when they speak they should
speak what they believe is their duty to speak & no more, not

verso

regarding wether it is pleasing to them that hear them,
but takeing great care that it be sound Doctrine
and axceptable unto the Lord, the buisness ap=
=peard to be gone through pretty comfortabley,
after meet'g took leave of some friends & walk'd Home
14, went with my Wife to our fifth day [Thursday] meet'g, my
minde was refresh'd, I was concearn'd to Incourage
Friends to be very gratefull, for the menny bless=
=ings and Favours they receive,

17, went with my Wife to our first day [Sunday] meet'g
it felt to be a low time amoungst us, it was held in Silence
in the A.[fter]N.[oon] took a walk with my Wife to
C.[hipping] Norton spent the Evening with some friends
comfortabley, Lodg'd at Josh Kings
18, before meet'g went to se some friends, the
meet'g felt pretty comfortable sevral Soldiers
came in and behaved I think solid, some friends ap=
=pear'd in Testimonie, the Buisness was gone through
in Love, after meet'g spent a little time with friends
& visited some in Affliction, afterwards return'd Home,
My Wife stopping she Intending to go to her Mothers
at Sibford we having heard of Aunt Hh Archers Death
21. went to our fifth day [Thursday] meet'g, afterward took
a walk to sibford found Mother pretty Tolerable
considering she having so lately lost her Sistor, I was
very weary with the Journey, I having been very
Poorly for several days with a cold, found my
Wife poorly with a Cold, Lodg'd at Mothers,
22, this being the day appointed for the burial of Aunt

=tain His blessings, after meet'g spent the A.[fter]N.[oon] with
Relations & friends pretty comfortabley, Lodg'd at Mothers
23, I and my Wife after spending a little time with
our Relations took leave of them & walk Home,
24 was at our first day [Sunday] meeting, it felt pretty
comfortable, I was concearn'd to advise friends to
keep to plainness in Speetch behaviour & apparel
like as our fore Fathers did, & build upon the same
Rock, not mindeing what men should say of them
but indeavouring to feel an Evidence within themselves
that God Axcepted their Works,
28, went with my Wife to our fifth day [Thursday] meet'g,
my minde was refresh'd, it was held in Silence
31, went with my Wife to our first day [Sunday] meet'g, it felt
comforting, it was held in Silence,
2mo [February] 3rd took a walk to Witney was at their fourth
day [Wednesday] meet'g, it felt pretty comfortable altho small,
4 went with my Wife to our fifth day [Thursday] meet'g, my
minde was refresh'd, it was held in Silence
7 went with my Wife to our first day [Sunday] meet'g, I finde

Page 91

Hanh Archer, who died in the 69 year of her
Age, A Meet'g was held on the occation which
was attended by Neighbours & Friends I trust
to good Satisfaction, sevral friends appear'd in
Testimonie, in order to turn the mindes of the Peo=
=ple to their Unering Teacher, the Light & Truth within
their own Hearts, which if they would but carefully
& Diligently minde it & obey it, it would Inable them
to do the Will of the Lord, by which they would Ob=

verso

there is great need for me to Labour for Devine
Counsel & Asistance, to preserve me in the way
of true Peace, it was held in Silence
2mo [February] 8th went with my Wife to our Monthly Meet'g
held at this place, one friend appear'd in Solem
Prayer, I felt a concearn to speak a little theirin
but was prevented by the Meet'g being broke up
early, which was cause of sorrow to my minde, & I
think friends should be very carefull not to break
up meet'gs to soon, the buisness was gone through in Love

11 went with my Wife to our fifth day [Thursday] meet'g, it felt
comforting, I trust a Remant ware favour'd to feel
the Influence of Devine Love
14 went with my Wife to our first day [Sunday] meet'g, it felt
pretty comfortable, it was held in Silence, in the
A.[fter]Noon took a walk with Sister Margt to Burford
found Sistor B very Ill & some of the rest of the
Family poorly, Lodg'd at J. Cowdrys who ware kinde & loving
15, took leave of Bror Sistor & rest, & walk'd Home,
17, took a walk to Burford with my Wife found Sistor
B very Ill, left my Wife & walk'd Home in the A.[fter]N.[oon] with Sistor M
18. I went to our fifth day [Thursday] meet'g, it felt pretty com=
=fortable, it was held in Silence
21, I went to our first day [Sunday] meet'g, my Wife being from Home, my minde was refresh'd
it was held in Silence
25, I went to our fifth day [Thursday] meet'g,
my minde was refresh'd, it was held in Silence
28. took a walk to Burford found Sistor B
a little better tho very weak, was at the first
day meet'g, it felt comforting, spake theirin, after meet'g took leave
of Bror Sistor & rest & return'd Home with my Wife

Page 92

3mo [March] 4th went with my Wife to our fifth day [Thursday] meet'g,
came away comforted, it was held in Silence,
-7 went with my Wife to our first day [Sunday] meet'g,
my minde was refresh'd, it was held in Silence,
after meet'g I and my Wife walk'd to Witney,
I felt a Concearn to go and visit Wm Harris & Wife,
he was disown'd for Marrying out but hath since
come to meet'gs & sometimes his Wife, he applyed to
be rec'd again into Membership, but has not been
receiv'd as yet, I & my Wife had a Comfortable Oppertunity
with them, I was led to Incourage them to come to
meetings & to live in Obidience to the Truth within,
Lodg'd at our kinde Friends J. Hankins's,
8th before the monthly Meet'g began went to se
some friends, I think the meet'g was smallish,
sevral Testimonies ware born theirin, I also was
Concearn'd to advise Friends to Labour earnestly
to be true Iseraelites Indeed in whome is no Guile,
the buisness was soon gone through their being but
little to do, after meet'g spent about 2 ours with
Friends walk'd Home in the Evening
11, went with my Wife to our fifth day [Thursday] meet'g, my poor
Exercised minde was comforted, it was held in Silence
13. in the A.[fter]N.[oon] took a walk to Brails found
Cousins their pretty well, Lodg'd at Cousin Wm Gilletts
14, before Meet'g went to se some friends who
ware Loving the Meet'g felt pretty comfortable
altho their is but few members belonging to it to what
their be at some places, yet I Hope their is a living
Remant left I felt a Concearn to speak theirin and

verso

---

had a good Oppertunity to relieve my minde,
after Dineing at Cousin Gilletts & spending
a little time with them, bid them Farewell &
walk'd to Sibford found Mother & Sistor M
tolerable well heard a very sorrowfull account of
a Child that was burned in such a manner that
its life seem's doubtfull I understood it happened
in the following manner, after the Parents returned from
meet'g one of them made a Firer afterwards they
both went out to se after their Victuals and left the
Children in the House, the Cloths of one of them took firer
and the Child ran out the Mother being thoughtfull
about her Children soon return'd and met her Dau=

=ghter who was about years old her Cloths ware in a flame she Indeavoured to help her poor Child what she could the Parents appear'd much troubled to see their poor Child in such an afflicted
state it twill I think be a warning to menny to be very carefull of Firer & Especialy to take care how they trust Children by it alone Lodg'd at M. Petiphors
15, spent the Morning at Mothers & some friends pretty
agreeabley, in the A.[fter]N.[oon] took leave of them & walk'd Home
18, went with my Wife to our fifth day [Thursday] meet'g my
much Exercised minde was refresh'd, it was held in Silence
21, went with my Wife to our first day [Sunday] meet'g, it seem'd
to be a low time amoungst us yet my minde was refresh'd
felt no Concearn to speak theirin,
25, went with my Wife to our fifth day [Thursday] meet'g
28, took a walk to Witney, was at their morning and A.[fter]N.[oon] meet'g which felt pretty comfortable, I was concearn'd

Page 93

to speak in the A.[fter]N.[oon] meet'g, I signifyed that Words was not wanting amoungst us, but a more diligent attention to the teachings of the Comforter the Spirit of Truth with us and Obidience theirunto, after meet'g stop'd a little with some friends, in the Evening walk'd Home
4mo [April] 1st went with my Wife to our fifth day [Thursday] meet'g,
it was held in Silence
4 went with my Wife to our first day [Sunday] meet'g,
it was held in Silence, our Preparative meet'g buisness was gone through in Love, walk'd to Burford in the A.[fter]N.[oon] with my Wife and Sistor M found Sistor B better, Lodg'd at JC
5 before the M meet'g began went to se some friends, the meet'g felt pretty comfortable, sevral friends appear'd in Testimonie, & the Almighty Power I trust was felt amoungst us to the tendering menny mindes, I felt easy to sit in Silence, the buisness was gone through in Love
8, went with my Wife to our fifth day [Thursday] meet'g, it was
held in Silence
11, went with my Wife to our first day [Sunday] meet'g, my
minde
felt poor & low & it appeared verry necessary for me to keep close to the Opperation of the Truth in my own heart, & very carefully to obey its Devine direction, if I would Injoy true Peace of minde, it was held in Silence
13, took a walk with sevral Friends to Our Quarterly Meet'g at Witney, it felt comforting & I trust the tender visitation of the Lord was re=newedly Extended to menny, sevral Living Testimonies

verso

ware born, I was much Exercised and concearnd in my minde, that I might be faithfull in the discharge of my duty according to the Mani= =festations of the Truth within me, without fear=
=ing man, being desireous to be any thing or Just
what the Lord would have me to be, and the Lord was gracious unto me and Inabled me to speak to the relief of my own minde, both by way of Testimonie, and concearning the buisness, so that I came way with comfort, praises and true Obidience be given unto Him for His very great Mearcies , unto me a poor Unworthy creature, the buisness was gone through in Love, after meet'g spent a little time in going to se some friends, In the Evening walk Home with my Wife & some friends
15, went with my Wife to our fifth day [Thursday] meet'g,
was sensible of much Weakness & great need of watchfullness, it was held in Silence
18, went with my Wife to our first day [Sunday] meet'g,
it felt pretty comforting, could not feel quite easy without speaking a little theirin
22. went with my Wife to our fifth day [Thursday] meet'g, poor

and low under a sence of my own Weakness's and the want of Devine Comfort, However I hope
I shall Learn this, there is great need to gard against
my own Weakness's and Indulgeing self, and it is very
nesseceary to be always attentive to the Truth within and
Indeavour to live in Faithfull Obidience theirunto,

Page 94

4mo [April] 25th went with my Wife to our first day [Sunday] meet'g,
it was held in Silence, which felt comforting & refreshing
29, I went to our fifth day [Thursday] meeting, (my Wife being
gone out with Sistor Margt to Campden &et
to se some Relations) sat in a low Mournfull
state, it was held in Silence
5mo [May] 2. I went to our first day [Sunday] meet'g, it felt comforting
and I trust we ware favoured with the re=
=newings of Devine Love, spake theirin,
-6 I went to our fifth day [Thursday] meet'g, felt the
Heart tendering Power of the Lord, to the
refreshing and Comforting my poor minde, it was held in Silence
7 My Wife return'd Home with Sistor Margt
from her visit to Campden Shipstone Brails
Sibford &et was favour'd with a comfortable Journey
9 I went with my Wife to our first day [Sunday] meet'g,
sat comfortabley & felt refreshment, it was
held in Silence
10th took a walk with my Wife and some friends
to our monthly meet'g held at C,[hipping] Norton, it
felt pretty comfortable, and I trust the Crook
of the Fathers Love was a fresh Extend to menny,
sevral Living Testimonies ware born, the
buisness was gone through comfortabley, ware
favour'd with the Company of a Public Frd from
a Neighbouring Monthly Meet'g which was a
comfort to ours, after meet'g I and my Wife went
to se some friends in Affliction, in the Evening walk'd Home
13. went with my Wife to our fifth day [Thursday] meet'g, it
felt pretty comfortable, it was held in Silence

verso

1802

5mo [May] 16th took a walk with my Wife to C.[hipping]Norton
was at their morning & Afternoon meet'gs, at
the first was the Funeral of Richd Wagstaff
it felt to be a good Satisfactory meet'g,
a pretty menny Neighbours ware Present, sevral
Friends appear'd in Testimonie to turn their
mindes Inward to their true Teacher the Light
& Spirit of Truth within them, I was con=
=cearn'd to speak theirin, felt comfort by so
doing, between meet'gs we went to see R. Wag=
staffs Widow & her Children, & sevral friends
the A.[fter]N.[oon] meetg felt pretty comfortable, it was
held in Silence, after Meet'g we walk'd Home
20, went with my Wife to our fifth day [Thursday] meet'g,
I think it was a low time, it was held in Silence
23, went with my Wife to our first day [Sunday] meet'g
sat comfortabley it was held in Silence altho my minde is much Ex=
=ercised to know what to do for the best or
how I shall conduct my self most to the honnour
of the Truth, and to feel quite accepted of the Lord,
and my minde is bowed in humility before Him
under a sence of my own Weakness's and my
desires is that He will be pleased to Inable
me to do his Will with a willing minde, that I
may Injoy a midst the various Exercises & Proving
Seasons, that Peace which this World cannot give
neither can it take away,
26, took a walk to Witney, was at their fourth day [Wednesday]
meet'g my minde was refresh'd, sat in Silence

27, I & my Wife was at our fifth day [Thursday] meet'g, it was held in Silence
28, went to the Burial of a Neighbour, was much op=
=press'd and grieved in minde on account of the Lightness and

Page 95

the Worldly mindedness of menny of the Neighbours
that attended it they discoursed of Worldly affairs
more like being at an Ale House than attending
such a solem Ocasion
30, went with my Wife to our first day [Sunday] meet'g, sat
comfortabley, it was held in Silence
6mo [June] 3rd went with my Wife to our fifth day [Thursday]
meet'g it was held in Silence
6, went with my Wife to our first day [Sunday] meet'g,
it felt pretty comfortable, it was held in Silence
9, went with my Wife to our fifth day [Thursday] meet'g, it
was held in Silence, felt spiritualy poor, and low,
13 went with my Wife to our first day [Sunday] meet'g, sat
pretty comfortabley altho poor in minde, it was held in Silence
14, went with my Wife to our Monthly Meet'g held at
this place, it felt pretty comfortable ware favourd
with the Company of one Stranger, Jacob Bell from
[blank] who appeard in Testimonie in which he Signified
it was good for Friends to be diligent in attending
meetings of Discipline, but much more so to attend
to the Discipline of the Cross of Christ,
17 went with my Wife to our fifth day [Thursday] meet'g, sat
pretty comfortabley, it was held in Silence
20th went with my Wife to our first day [Sunday] meet'g, sat
Comfortabley, I was concearned to speak a few words theirin
24, went with my Wife to our fifth day [Thursday] meet'g,
it was a low time with me, it was held in Silence
27, went with my Wife to our first day [Sunday] meet'g, sat
comfortabley, I trust in some degree, we ware favour'd
with Devine Goodness to flow as from vessel to vessel, it was held in Silence
28 took a walk with my Wife to milton near Adderbury

verso

call'd at sevral Friends Houses in our Journey,
Friends ware kinde to us and I hope our meet'g to=
=gether was comforting and Incourageing to one another
to persevear in the way of our duty, Lodg'd at R.
Pains Milton, they ware very kinde
28, walk'd to our Quarterly Meet'g at Banbury,
the Meet'g felt pretty comforting before friends
enter'd upon buisness, one friend appeard in Prayer,
and sevral living Testimonies ware born, the buisness
was gone through in Love, after meet'g spent a
little time with Friends, took leave of them & walk'd Home
7mo [July] 1st went to our fifth day [Thursday] meet'g it was held in Silence
-2, went to Sibford for my Wife whome I left be=
=hinde at the Quarterly Meet'g, she went with her
sistor to her Mothers at Sibford, I was at their
sixday [Friday] meet'g, I felt poor & weak in Spirit, sat in
Silence, one friend appeard in Testimonie which was Instructing,
after meet'g return'd Home with my Wife & Motherinlaw
-4 I and my Wife went to our first day [Sunday] meet'g, it felt
a little comforting, I was concearn'd to advise friends
always to Labour to keep their Conciences's clear &
void of Offence, towards God and allmankinde ,

8, went with my Wife to our fifth day [Thursday] meet'g, it was held in Silence
11, went with my Wife to our first day [Sunday] meet'g, it was
a low time with me, it was held in Silence
in the A.[fter]Noon set out for our Monthly Meet'g to be
held at Faringdon walk'd to Burford. was at
the Evening Meet'g it felt comforting, Lodg'd at Bro'rs H,
12, walk'd with Bro'r R to Faringdon, the Meet'g was small
yet it felt comforting, sevral friends appear'd in Testimonie,
I was concearn'd to speak a little theirin, the buisness was gone
through pretty agreeabley, spent a little time with Friends

Page 96

after Meet'g, in an agreeable manner, took leave of them
& walk'd with some Friends to Witney Lodg'd at Wm Barritts
13 in the morn'g walk Home
15, went with my Wife to our fifth day [Thursday] meet'g
16, took a walk to C,[hipping]Norton was at their six day [Friday] meet'g
I was concearnd to speak a little theirin, in the Ev'g walkd Home
18, walkd to Milton to the first day [Sunday] meet'g it was small and felt to be in
a poor state, yet I was favour'd to come away a little
comforted, went to se Wm Green who appear'd to be very weak= [illegible]
& rather Childish through Old age, walk'd from thence
to the Ev'g meet'g at Burford, it felt pretty comforting,
Lodg'd at Bro'r Henrys, 19th walk'd Home
22. went with my Wife to our fifth day [Thursday] meet'g, it was held in Silence
24, took my Motherinlaw on Horse=back to her
Home at Sibford, call'd at C.[hipping]Norton, stop't a wile
and went to se some friends, whose Company was comforting, reach'd Sibford in the Evening, took a
walk with Sistor M. up to the grounds, Lodg'd at M. Petiphors
25, before meet'g went to se some friends, was a
little comforted at meet'g altho I felt poor & low,
sat in Silence, one friend appear'd in Testimonie,
after meeting took leave of Relations & return'd to
C.[hipping]Norton, stop't the Even'g Meet'g, it felt very
comfortable, it was held in Silence, after meet'g return'd H[ome]
29, went with my Wife to our fifth day [Thursday] meet'g, it
was held in Silence
8mo [August] 1st went with my Wife to our first day [Sunday] meet'g, my Soul was
refresh'd felt easy to sit in Silence, Wm Lewton
appear'd, who is come from London on a visit to his Relations
5, went with my Wife to our fifth day [Thursday] meet'g, was sensible of great Weakness

verso

8mo [August] 7th set out on foot for Armscutt [Armscote]Meetg, call'd at
Thos Harris's Longcompton there I was entertained
kindly reache John Wells's Shipstone Lodg'd their, they Enteartained me kindly
8th, was at the morning Meeting at Shipstone which small
some friends seeming cold in their love for Truth,
walk'd from thence to the meet'g at Armscutt [armscote], it was large
and felt pretty comfortable Sevral Friends ware drawn
fourth in Testimonie, to the Instruction Edifycation & Comfort,
of menny present I trust, I felt a concearn to speak a little
theirin, came a way greatly comforted under a sence that the
Almightys Love was graciously extended unto menny not
of our Society & Truth felt to Reighn , Praises Living

Praises unto Zions King, call'd to se some friends in my
way Home who ware loving, Lodg'd at T. Gilks C[hipping] Norton
9, walked from thence to our monthly Meet'g at Burford,
it was pretty Large, sevral appeard in Testimonie I also
could not feel Quite easy without speaking a little, in the mens
meet'g H. Smith laid a Concearn before Friends, that
had rested upon Her minde for sometime to have meet'gs ap=
=pointed at Dedington,
Friends had Unity with her, and Pretty soon concluded
to leave her at liberty to proceed as Truth Opened
the way, and some friends ware appointed to attend the
meet'gs, after meet'g took leave of Relations and walk'd
Home, with my Wife and Sevral Friends
12, went with my Wife to our fifth day [Thursday] meet'g, sat in Silence pretty Comfortably
15, took a walk to Dedington to a Public Meet'g ap=
=pointed by the desire of Hanh Smith, of Witney, Friends
ware disapointed of a Place to meet in, therefore
met under some Warlnutt Treese near the Town,
there was a very Lusty Man whose name was
a Lawer, who behaved in a very Wicked manner running

Page 97

against Friends, and to Indeavour to distirb
the meetg, he sent a man up in a tree which
was near over H. Smiths head and menny more,
and ordered him to Lop it, the man seemd a poor
Ignorant Wretch seem'd Rejoiced to be Imploy'd
to disturb the Righteous, began to cut, but on
Friends with drawing a little distance, the man
did not go on, Friends held their Meet'g standing,
the People mostly appear'd to behave well, and
to be attending to what was Deliver'd, & I trust
Hanh Smith was favour'd to Discharge her Duty,
some other friends appear'd in Testimonie, I also
felt a concearn to speak, & was favour'd to
relieve my minde, when the meet'g was over the Peo=
=ple departed quietly, after meet'g stop'd a little
with Friends whose Company was Comforting, also
call'd to se some Relations, & a yound Man who is
an Exciseman, he appear'd to be a sensible young
man, and one who love'd the Truth in Sincearity, & to
be Convinced, I was favour'd to speak Instructingly
to him and I believe he receiv'd it in Love, took leave
of him & Friends and return'd Home
19, went with my Wife to our fifth day [Thursday] meet'g,
felt very poor & great need to seek for Devine
mercy and help, it was held in Silence
22 went with my Wife to our first day [Sunday] meet'g, it felt
comforting, after sitting a pretty wile in Silence, I was
concearn'd to Speak theirin, as was also another friends ,
29, went with my Wife to our first day [Sunday] meet'g
came way refresh'd altho sensible of great Weakness
& Nescessiety to Labour for Devine Help, it was held in Silence,

verso

9mo [September] 2nd I & my Wife came Home from Field & went
to our fifth day [Thursday] meet'g, it felt comforting,
5 went with my Wife to our first day [Sunday] meet'g, it felt
Pretty comforting, I felt easy to sit in Silence
7 I walked with my Wife and some more friends to
our Monthly Meet'g held at C[hipping] Norton, it felt quite
comforting, we ware favour'd with the Company
of Tho's Cash out of Cheshire, he had been out
on a religious visit, & was on his way Home,
he was Inabled to bear a Comfortable Testimonie

to the sincear honest Hearted, but close & sharp
to
the Luke=warm Indif'rent ones, after meet'g
call'd to se some friends, in the Even'g walk'd
Home
12, set out for our Quarterly Meet'g to be held at
Reading, In the Morning walk'd to Oxford, had
a Sitting with the friends, who meet on first
days & hold a little meet'g at Jno Jacksons, it
felt a little comforting, spake theirin to
Incourage
them to persevear in the way of their duty, after
dining at Jno Jacksons's walk'd to Shillingford
to Jos. Ashbys who was very kinde, walk'd down
to
Jno Sargoods to Lodge,
13, walk'd with Jno Sargood & Wm Mintchin to
Henly, was at the Monthly Meet'g there, it felt
to be a low time amoungst friends, walked from
thence with the friends above mentioned to
Reading,
in the Evening went to se some friends, who ware

Page 98

kinde, Lodg'd at Jno Tuttey's the Elder,
14, before meet'g went to se some friends & Re=
=lations, the Meet'g felt Tolerable comfortable
sevral friends appear'd in Testimonie, I could
not feel quite easy without appearing theirin,
the buisness was gone through in Love, yet
it felt to be a low mournfull time, after dining
at Cous'n Tutteys, I and J, Sargood and W.M.
walk'd
to Warborough, Lodg'd at Jno Sargoods who
Entertained us kindly,
15 after Breackfasting at J. sargoods, took leave
of them, and walk'd with Wm Mintchin,
untill the roads part, ware we took leave of
each other, he taking the road for his Home,
and I, that for mine, ware I arive'd in good
time, & found my Wife Well, having had a
comfortable
Journey, & being favour'd at time to feel Devine
Goodness near, my minde is bow'd in Humble
Thankfullness before the Lord, for His Great
Mercies, which I and my Wife Pertake of,
16 went with my Wife to our fifth day [Thursday]
meet'g, it felt
comforting altho smallish, it was held in Silence
18, took a walk with my Wife to Sibford to see
my
Wives Mother, who has been very poorly for
sevral
weeks, found she very poorly, she & Sistor M
ware glad to se us, Lodg'd there
19, was at the First day meet'g, which was large,
sevral Straingers being present, it felt pretty

verso

comforting, I was concearn'd to speak theirin, it
was pretty much in the cross, being sensible of
my
own great weakness, yet by giveing up &
Indeavouring
to speak no more than to relieve my minde, I felt
easy, spent the A.[fter]Noon mostly at Mothers
comfort=
abley, in the Eveng took a walk with my Wife and
sistor to se some friends, Lodg'd at Mothers,
20, after a solem oppertunity at Mothers which I
hope refresh'd our mindes, took our leaves, and
walk'd Home, call'd to se a friend at Hoock=
norton who seem'd to be in a Decline, it seem'd
comforting to she, to se us and have a little of
our Company, & I hope it was good for us,
23, went with my Wife to our fifth day [Thursday]
meet'g
felt poor & weak in a Spiritual sence, it was held
in Silence
26, I went with my Wife to our first day [Sunday]
meet'g,
it felt comfortable & I trust a remnant ware
drawn into a patient waiting upon the Lord,
I was concearn'd to speak theirin, to set fourth
how
necessary it was for us to be found doing our own
Buisness
30, went with my Wife to our fifth day [Thursday]
meet'g, sat
as under a Cloud, it was held in Silence
10mo [October] 3rd was at our first day [Sunday]
meet'g, it felt comfortable
5, went with my Wife to our monthly Meetg held
at this Place, it felt pretty comfortable, I was
con=
cearn'd to speak a little theirin, when I feel
concearn

to speak in meet'g, I am very much desirous to speak
just as much as to relieve my minde, and no more
lest I should bring trouble to my minde & Burden the
meeting, instead of bringing comfort & Peace to my minde, &
being Instrimental to do good to the meet'g, some more friends
appeard which felt Edifying, the buisness was gone through in Love
H Smith express'd she felt Comfort & Peace in Her Indeavours to Discharge her Duties at the Public Meetings [part of previous line]

Journal C

Page 1

1802

10mo[October] 7th went with my Wife to our fifth day [Thursday] meet'g
it felt comforting, it was held in Silence
-10, took a ride to Burford to fetch Sistor B, M
was at the first day [Sunday] meet'g, it felt comforting
one friend appear'd, she express how very neseceary
it was for us to know a being as the wise Virgins
& not only to know our Lamps to be once lighted but
to them to be kept continualy Burning,
I was also concearn'd to speak a little towds the Conclusion
of the meet'g, in the A.[fter]N.[oon] return'd with Sistor,
17, took a walk to Witney, was at the first day [Sunday]
morning & A,[fter]noon meeting, could not feel quite
easy without speaking a little theirin, one more
friend also appeard, after meet'g spent a little
time with some Religious Friends, their Company
was Comforting, return'd Home in the Evening,
21, went with my Wife to our fifth day [Thursday] meet'g, it
felt refreshing to my Clouded minde, sat in Silence,
one friend appeard, whose Testimonie was comforting to
the Sincear in heart & Incourageing to them to press forward
24 went with my Wife to our first day [Sunday] meet'g, I thought
it was a Solem time, in which friends ware concern'd to get
down deep, to Obtain that food with refresheth the
soul, one friend appear'd I also was concearn'd to speak a little theirin
28, I went to our fifth day [Thursday] meet'g, my Wife being poorly
staid at Home, my minde was comforted, it was held in Silence
31, I went to our first day [Sunday] meet'g (my Wife stay'd at
Home being poorly) it felt comfortable, spake a little theirin
a man & horse came from Sibford, & brough a letter
giveing anacct of my Wives Mother being quite Ill,
& would like to have my Wife go to see them, accordingly

verso

1802

my Wife went on horseback, altho she was weak and poorly
11mo [November] 4th I went to our fifth day [Thursday] meet'g it felt comforting
to my poor minde, it was held in Silence
I went to our first day [Sunday] meet'g it felt pretty comfortable
it was held in Silence, in the A.[fter]N.[oon] took a walk to
Witney, spent the evening there with some friends
& realations comfortabley. Lodg'd at our kinde friends Jno Hankins's
8, before our Monthly Meet'g began call'd to se some
friends, the meet'g felt comforting, sevral friends
appear in Testimonie, which was comforting & Incourageing
to the sincear Honest hearted friends to hold on their
way, but sharp to such as refused to receive the Truth
in the Love of the Gospel, one appear'd in Prayer,
after meet'g spent a little time with friends in a loving
manner, in the Evening walk'd Home,

10 went to Sibford for my Wife. found Mother very
poorly, spent a little time with them comfortable, in the
A.[fter]N.[oon] return'd Home with my Wife,
11, went with my Wife to our fifth day [Thursday] meet'g, I think
it was a low time, it was held in Silence
12, took a walk to C.[hipping] Norton on Buisness, was at
their six day [Friday] meet'g, it felt to be a low time,
14, I and my Wife went to our first day [Sunday] meet'g, it was a
time of mourning with me, Under a sence of my
unwatchfullness & unsteady attention to the pure Light,
yet my minde was favour'd to be brought into a degree
of humble contritedness, & I return'd refresh'd, it was held in Silence
18, went with my Wife to our fifth day [Thursday] meet'g, felt a
little refresh'd, it was held in Silence
21, went with my Wife to our first day [Sunday] meet'g, my minde was
humbled under a sence of my own weakness, it was held in Silence

Page 2

---

22 this day we ware favourd with the company of a
Woman Fr.d, Chairman from Rygate in Surrey, who is on a religious visit, her husband
travels with her, a meet'g was appointed on their
acct it began at 11 oclock, she appeard sevral
times in Testimonie, & once in Prayer,
my concearn was to get into solid Silence, felt easy to keep
silent, in the A.[fter]N.[oon] went to C.[hipping] Norton to Inform friends
that the friend desired to have a Public Meet'g their this Evening
25 went with my Wife to our fifth day [Thursday] meet'g,
it was held in Silence, came away refresh'd
28, went with my Wife to our first day [Sunday] meet'g, it felt a little
comforting altho I felt very poor, spake a little theirin,
12mo [December] 1st took a walk to Witney, was at the fourth day [Wednesday]
meet'g, felt poor, & great need earnestly to Labour
for Devine help, felt easy to sit in Silence,
2, went with my Wife to our fifth day [Thursday] meet'g, felt
a little refresh'd, it was held in Silence
4, took a walk to Sibford, found my Wives Mother
quite poorly, spent the Evening with Mother & Sistor
M. Comfortabley, Lodg'd their
5, sometime ago I understood that the Person who
Married Cousin Rebecca G. had behav'd very ill
to her sevral times, therefore could feel quite
easy without going & adviseing her Husband not
to give way to passion nor abuse his Wife, for if
he did, he would have it to answer for, as he ought
faithfully to fulfill his Marriage Promis, after
speaking what rested upon my minde I felt easy &
left him, was at Sibford Meet'g, I felt my minde
a little comforted, I was concearnd to appear theirin,
in the A.[fter]N.[oon] went to see some friends at little Sibford,
spent most of the evening at Mothers, Lodgd their

verso

1802

12mo [December] 5th took a walk with Sistor M & another friends
to Banbury to the Monthly meet'g their, I felt
poor & low theirin, sat in Silence, went to Edwd
Stones to Dinner, who had the company of menny
friends, & he was very kinde to them, after Din'r
return'd back to Mothers Lodg'd their
7, spent a little time with Moth'r and Sistor in a loving

weighty manner, took leave of them & return'd Home
9, went with my Wife to our fifth day [Thursday] meet'g, it
felt pretty comforting, it was held in Silence
12, went with my Wife to our first day [Sunday] meet'g, my minde was
favour'd to feel Devine Comfort, it was held in Silence,
in the A.[fter]Noon took a walk with Bror to Burford,
found Bror H very poorly with a Coughf, Lodgd at Bro,rs
before the monthly meet'g began went to se some friends,
I think it was a pretty comfortable meet'g, Sevral
friends appear'd in Testimonie, I also spake a little,
believeing a Necessiety was laid upon me so to do,
the buisness was gone through pretty comfortabley,
pretty soon after meeting took leave of friends & walk Home,
16, went with my Wife to our fifth day [Thursday] meet'g, felt a
little refresh'd, it was held in Silence
19 went with my Wife to our first day [Sunday] meet'g, it felt to be a
low mournfull time, it was held in Silence
23, went with my Wife to our fifth day [Thursday] meet'g, it felt refreshing,
26, went with my Wife to our first day [Sunday] meet'g, felt Devine goodness
to tender & contrite my minde, I was Concearn'd to speak a little theirin,
30, went with my Wife to our fifth day [Thursday] meet'g, felt a
little refresh'd, it was held in Silence,

1803,

1mo[January] 2st took a walk with Bror Robt to Oxford,

it being first day [Sunday], there was a meeting held as usual,

Page 3

1803

we ware favour'd with the Company of Deborah
Darby from Colebrook Deal who felt a Concearn to attend our Quarterly
meet'g, I trust it was a good precious meet'g, in
which Deborah was much favour'd to preach
the Gospel of glad tidings, "Peace on Earth & good=
=will towards men", the people appear'd to be well
satisfied with the meet'g, another public meet'g was
held in the Evening by Deborahs desire, which
was a favour'd meet'g, spent most of the time between
meet'g with the friends who live at Oxford,
3, the Quarterly Meet'g began at 9 oclock, which felt
very comforting & Deborah I hope was Inabled to
speak plainly to the states of some, & to relieve her
minde so as to feel the comfortable evidence that her
Labours ware axcepted by the Lord, after they
men and women seperated they enter'd upon the buis=
=ness, which was gone through pretty comfortabley,
after meet'g took of Friends & walk'd Home
6. went with my Wife to our fifth day [Thursday] meet'g, it felt
to be a low time with us, O! that we may keep low
& wait the Lords time & power to Exalt us, it was held in Silence
9, went with my Wife to our first day [Sunday] meet'g it again
felt to be a low time, it was held in Silence
in the A.[fter]Noon I & my Wife walk to C,[hipping]Norton, spent the
evening there with some friends in a comforting Edifying
manner, Lodg'd at Jos. Kings
10th felt comforted at meet'g, I was concearn'd to speak

theirin as was also another friend, the buisness was gone
through pretty agreeabley, after meet'g visited some friends
in Affliction, afterward walk'd Home with my Wife
13, went with my Wife to our fifth day [Thursday] meet'g, it was held in Silence
16, went with my Wife to our first day [Sunday] meet'g, it felt

verso

1803

refreshing altho a low time, speak a little theirin,
1mo [January] 20th went with my Wife to our fifth day [Thursday] meet'g, it was held in Silence
21, took a walk to C,[hipping]Norton, was at their six day [Friday]
meet'g, it was held in Silence, call'd to se sevral
Friends in affliction with whome I was led to simpathise
23, went with my Wife to our first day [Sunday] meet'g, it felt
comforting, I was concearn'd to advise Frds to labour
after a more Inward acquaintance with the Lord,
27, went with my Wife to our fifth day [Thursday] meet'g, felt a
little refresh'd, it was held in Silence
29, took a walk to Sibford, call'd at Jos Lambs & had
some refreshment, & their company was pleasent, found
my Motherinlaw much as she has been a pretty wile, Lodg'd at Mo:
30, was at their first day [Sunday] meet'g, felt a little comforted
I was concearned to speak a little theirin, spent the A.[fter]Noon
mostly at Mothers in a comfortable manner, Lodg'd their
31, spent a little time agreeabley at Mothers, afterwards walk'd Home
2mo[February] 3rd went with my Wife to our fifth day [Thursday] meet'g
-6. went with my Wife to our first day [Sunday] meet'g, it felt
pretty comforting, it was held in Silence
10. went with my Wife to our fifth day [Thursday] meet'g, it felt a
little comforting, it was held in Silence
13. went with my Wife to our first day [Sunday] meet'g, felt low
and poor theirin, it was held in Silence
14, I & my Wife went to our Monthly meet'g held at this place,
some friends appear'd in Testimonie, and two in Prayer,
it felt comforting, & I trust some sincear mindes ware
made to rejoice, under a sence that the Almighty is still pleas'd
to Manifest his power amoungst us, altho menny appear to
slight Devine Admonitions,
17, went with my Wife to our fifth day [Thursday] meet'g, it felt comforting
one friend appear'd whose Testimonie was instructing & comforting

Page 4

20, took a walk to Burford found Bror Henry very
poorly seems pretty much like one in a decline,
was at Both morning & A.[fter]Noon meetings, which
felt pretty comfortable, I was concearn'd to speak a
little in the last, spent the evening mostly at Brors in
an agreeable solid manner Lodg'd their
21, after spending a little time at Brors comfortabley, took an
affectionate leave of them and walk'd Home,
24, went with my Wife to our fifth day [Thursday] meet'g, it felt
to be a low time with us, it was held in Silence
27, went with my Wife to our first day [Sunday] meet'g, I was
concearn'd to speak a little theirin, to express what a Solem
thing it is to die, & how necessary it is to be prepared for Death

3mo[March] 2nd, went on foot to Witney was at their fourth day [Wednesday] Meet'g
-3, I went to our fifth day [Thursday] meet'g, felt a little refresh'd, it was held in Silence
-6, went with my Wife to our first day [Sunday] meet'g, it
felt to be a low time, it was held in silence"there is
a great Necessiety for Friends to walk humbly
in the fear of the Lord,"
-10, went with my Wife to our fifth day [Thursday] meet'g felt poor & low, it was held in Silence
-13. went with my Wife to our first day [Sunday] meet'g, it felt
a little comforting, a Woman friend appear'd in a few words
14, walk'd with my Wife to Witney to our Monthly meet'g,
I think it was a comforting edifying meet'g, sevral
Friends appear'd in Testimonie, & the youth ware much
Incouraged to live in Obidience to the Truth, the buisness
was gone through pretty agreeabley, after meet'g spent
a little time with Frds, in the evening walk'd Home
17. went with my Wife to our fifth day [Thursday] meet'g, it felt to
be a very low time, it was held in Silence
20. walk'd with my Wife to C.[hipping]Norton, found sevral friends
quite poorly, Din'd at Jno Lambs he was very weak, & seems

verso

---

nearly worn out by Old Age, was at their morning & A[fter]noon
meeting, I was concearn'd to speak a little in the morn'g meet'g,
in the Even'g we walked Home,
24, I went to our fifth day [Thursday] meet'g, felt poor, it was held in Silence
27, went with my Wife to our first day [Sunday] meet'g it felt
pretty comforting, I was concearn'd to speak a little theirin
31, went to our fifth day [Thursday] meet'g altho poor & low yet
felt a little refreshed, it was held in Silence
4mo[April] 3rd took a walk with my Wife to C[hipping] Norton, to the Burial
of Jno Lamb, who appear'd to be worn out with Old Age,
Aged about 86 Years, the meet'g was pretty large of Frds
and others who ware pretty still, I was concearn'd to advise
the people to Indeavour to be acquainted with stillness, & to turn
their mindes to the light within, & indeavour to be acquainted
with Devine Instructions in their own Hearts, I also was con=
=cearn'd to speak a little at the grave, after meet'g call'd
to se some friends, afterward we walk'd to Burford, found
Bro'r Henry very poorly I lodg'd there
4th before meet'g took a walk to se some friends, the meet'g
felt pretty comfortable one friend appeard in Testimonie,
the buisness was gone through pretty agreeabley, in the
Evening walk'd Home
7, went to our fifth day [Thursday] meet'g, continues to be a low time with
us, it was held in Silence,
10, went with my Wife to our first day [Sunday] meet'g, it felt to be a
exerciseing time, & a time in which they that are desireous of
help & strength must seek unto the Lord alone & know him to
administer it to them, it was held in Silence
12, took a walk to our Quarterly meet'g held at Witney, the
meet'g before they enter'd upon buisness felt quite comfortable,
sevral friends appear'd in Testimonie I also was concearn'd
to speak a little theirin, the meet'g of Buisness did not
feel so comfortable in the Even'g I & my Wife walk'd Home with
a pretty menny frds

Page 5

1803

4mo[April] 14th went with my Wife to our fifth day [Thursday] meet'g, felt low &
Spiritualy poor, it was held in Silence
17, went with my Wife to our first day [Sunday] meet'g, it felt a little comforting
I was concearn'd to speak theirin, to advise friends to indeavour
always to live agreeable to our great and Holy profession, for
if they did that which might cause others to stumble at the
Truth, I believed they would be call'd to an account for so doing
21. went with my Wife to our fifth day [Thursday] meet'g, felt very
poor, & great need of walking Humbley, to obtain Devine Comfort
24 I went to our first day [Sunday] meet'g (my Wife being gone to
Sibford to se her Mother)
28. went with my Wife to our fifth day [Thursday] meet'g, felt
poor & low, it was held in Silence,
5mo[May] 1st went on foot to Hooknorton was at the first day [Sunday] meet'g
I was concearn'd to speak theirin, it felt pretty comforting,
after meet'g went to se a friend who had lately lost his
Wife, he seem'd brought into a pretty humble tender state of
minde, went from their to Sibford found my Motherinlaw
poorly, Lodg'd at Mothers
=2 went to the monthly meet'g held at Shutford, it felt pretty
Comfortable, after meet'g return'd back to Sibford, went
to se some young friends who have set up a bording
school, had some solid convearsation with them, in the
Evening Joseph Lamb came to my Motherinlaws to pay
a visit & we had a verry comfortable sitting together,
(Mother being in Bed) in Mothers Chamber & Joseph was
favourd to speak comfortingly, and also Incourageingly, for
us to Labour earnestly in the faithfull discharge of our
duty, Devine Love united us near one unto another, Lodg'd at M's
=3 took leave of Mo: & Sistor & walk'd to Brails, found Cousins pretty
well, was at the monthly meet'g their which felt comforting,
sevral friends appear'd in Testimonie the buisness was gone
through in Love, after meet'g Din'd at Cousin Gilletts, took leave
of them & friends and return'd Home

verso

5mo[May] 1803

8th, went with my Wife to our first day [Sunday] meetg, Thos Smith & Hanh his wife ware
their, it felt pretty comfortable, it was held in Silence,
in the A,[fter]noon I and my Wife walk with a friend to C[hipping]Norton spent
the Evening with friends their comfortabley, Lodg'd at Jos: Kings
9, before the monthly Meet'g began went to se some friends, at
meet'g we ware favour'd with the Company of Two strangers, viz,
Susanna Horn, from Totnam, & [blank] Hack from Chicester,
they appear'd in Testimonie, which was comforting Edifying
and much Incouraging to such whome the Lord should se meet
to try & prove greatly, to put their trust & Confidence in
Him & Indeavour to persevear in the way of their duty, &
then He would be their support, & give them to Injoy

that Peace which the World cannot give, one appd in Prayer,
after meet'g we spent a little time with frds and walk'd Home,
12. went with my Wife to our fifth day [Thursday] meet'g, felt great
poverty, it was held in Silence
15, went with my Wife to our first day [Sunday] meet'g, it felt pretty
comfortable, it was held in Silence
a week ago I was concearn'd to go to a Neighbours, (ware
sevral had met together the day befor & drank to Excess)
and read a paper setting forth the great Sin of Drunkness,
most of them ware present when I read the paper (which I took
to be rather a Providecial thing) they appear'd to be sensible of
their bad conduct & acknowledg'd what I read to be true, I also
spoke a few words to them signifying the great Danger they
ware in, if they persisted in such a wicked course of Life,
19, went with my Wife to our fifth day [Thursday] meet'g, it was held in Silence
22, went with my Wife to our first day [Sunday] meet'g, it felt com=
=forting, I was concearn'd to speak theirin, signifying it
was very necessary for us to know a being Inwardly taught
by the spirit of the Lord,
26, went with my Wife to our fifth day [Thursday] meet'g, felt a great
need to Labour Earnestly for Devine help, it was held in Silence,

Page 6

1803

5mo[May] 29th took a walk to stow to meet'g, it was small, and it felt to
me that there was a want of warmth & Zeal amoungst
them for the cause of Truth, was concearn'd to speak
theirin, in the A,[fter]noon spent a little with friends also
visited some Neighbours & Relations, in the Evening walk'd Home
6mo[June] 2nd went with my Wife to our fifth day [Thursday] meet'g it was held in Silence
Having been much grieved on account of people Incouraging Dancing
I was concearn'd to go to some as Incouraged it, and manifest
to them its Evel tendancy, & warn them not to Incourage it,
5th went with my Wife to our first day [Sunday] meet'g, it felt comforting, it was held in Silence
9, went with my Wife to our fifth day [Thursday] meet'g, it was held in Silence
12, went with my Wife to our first day [Sunday] meet'g, it was held in
silence, It hath appeared to me very necessary for us Earnestly
to Labour in Stillness, to be more acquainted with the Devine
Teacher within ourselves, & also more Faithfully to Obey
its Teachings
13, went with my Wife to our monthly meet'g held at this place,
it was pretty large and felt pretty comfortable, some friends
appear'd in Testimonie, I also speak a little theirin to Incourage
friends to Persevear faithfull in the discharge of their
duty, one friend appear'd in Prayer, the Buisness was gone
through pretty agreeabley,
16, went with my Wife to our fifth day [Thursday] meet'g, we ware favoured
with the Company of two women friends who are on a Religious
visit, *viz N [illegible] from Gurnsey & [blank] Sanderson from London, the meet'g felt comforting both of them appear'd, the*
Testimonie of one was much comforting and Incouraging to
such as has met with discouragements and ware much cast down

to have faith in the Almighty Power trust in God, and persevear
in the way of their duty, and then He would be near unto them
and cause them to rejoice in Him, the meet'g concluded in Prayer,
19, went with my Wife to our first day [Sunday] meet'g and altho
held in Silence it felt comforting & I trust we ware favoured
with the best of Teaching,

verso

6mo[June] 23rd 1803

went with my Wife to our fifth day [Thursday] meet'g, it was held in Silence
26, I went to our first day [Sunday] meet'g (my Wife being gone
for Sibford with Bro'r R), it felt pretty comforting
I was concearn'd to speak theirin, to advise the youth
to minde the Light of Christ in the Consciences,
and wait for its ariseing, and Indeavour to bring
their deeds unto it, that they might be made manifest
wether they ware good or wether they ware evel,
27, I set out for our Quarterly Meet'g to be held at Banbury
call'd to se some of our Relation on the way, found
Edw'd Stone of Banbury finely recovver'd, heard of a man
that lately had a very Bad Axcident, slipt down
near or behind a Horse in a cart, the Horse kick'd
him very bad on the head, and the Wheel of the cart
I understand went over his Thigh and broke it, the
Relation of it affected me much and I could not feel easy
without paying him a visit he and his Wife appear'd
to take it kindly, I spake to them what I believed
to be my duty, felt comfort in so doing,

28 I think the Quarterly Meet'g was pretty large & comfortable,
sevral friends appear'd in Testimonie, I also was concearn'd
to speak theirin, the buisness was soon gone through, after meet'g
spent a little time with friends in a Solid comforting manner,
I and my Wife return'd Home at Night,
30, went with my Wife to our fifth day [Thursday] meet'g
7mo[July] 3rd went with my Wife to our first day [Sunday] meet'g felt spiritualy poor & weak,
6, went with my Wife to our fifth day [Thursday] meet'g felt poor & low
9th took a walk with my Wife to Witney to the first day [Sunday] meet'g after
dinner I & my Wife walk'd to Faringdon had a Comfortable
walk, Lodg'd at friend Reynolds, who entertaind us Kindly

Page 7

10th spent the morning Comfortable with friends ware
favour'd with the Company of M Story from London
who was on a religious visit. the Monthly Meet'g felt
Pretty comfortable, M.S. was enabled to speak to
the states of the People & to some in a close manner,
I was concearn'd to speak theirin, the buisness was
gone through pretty agreeabley, after meet'g took leave
of Friends, my Wife returning in the Evening to Witney & I Home,
14, went with my Wife to our fifth day [Thursday] meet'g
17, went with my Wife to our first day [Sunday] meet'g, it was held in Silence
21, went with my Wife to our fifth day [Thursday] meet'g, it was held in Silence
24, went with my Wife to our first day [Sunday] meeting it felt pretty
comfortable, I was concearn'd to speak theirin
28, went with my Wife to our fifth day [Thursday] meet'g, it was held in Silence

30, took a walk to Sibford (went through C[hipping]Norton, went
to se some friends as was drawn as Militiamen, I was
concearn'd to advise them to faithfullness in their Testimonie
against such things,) found my Wives Mother poorly, Lodg'd there
31, was at the first day [Sunday] meet'g at Sibford, I was concearn'd
to speak a little theirin, spent a little time at Mothers
comfortabley, in the evening walk to North=newton Lodg'd
at Jno Atkins's who ware kind & Friendly,
8mo[August] 1st walk'd to the Monthly meet'g held at Banbury, which felt
pretty comfortable, spent a little time after meet'g with friends,
in the evening return'd to Sibford call'd at North=newington
& spent a little time with some convinc'd friends agreeabley, Lodg'd at Mothers
2, after spending a little time with Mother & Sistor in weighty
manner took leave of them & walk'd Home
3, took a walk to witney was at the fourth day [Wednesday] meet'g their
4, went with my Wife to our fifth day [Thursday] meet'g, it was held in Silence
7, went with my Wife to our first day [Sunday] meet'g, it felt pretty com=
=fortable, it was held in Silence
8, walk'd to Burford to our Monthly meet'g it felt pretty
comfortable. One friend appeard, after meet'g spent a little time

verso

---

at Bro'rs & with some friends agreeabley, in the even'g
I and my Wife return'd Home with some friends,
11, went with my Wife to our fifth day [Thursday] meet'g felt
very poor & weak, it was held in Silence
14, went with my Wife to our first day [Sunday] meet'g, it
felt pretty comfortable, had the company of Wm Lenton
of London, (who is on a visit to his relations) he appear'd,
I also was concearn'd to speak theirin,
21, went with my Wife to our first day [Sunday] meet'g, was greatly sensible
of my own weakness and of the necessiety of Labouring earnestly for
Devine Help & Counsel, one friend appear'd Incourageing friends
to double their diligence to Labour to do the Almightys Will,
28, went with my Wife to our first day [Sunday] meet'g, was much
exercised in minde, felt easy to sit in Silence, one friend appear'd
9mo[September] 1st went with my Wife to our fifth day [Thursday] meet'g
-4, went with my Wife to our first day [Sunday] meet'g, one friend
appear'd, whose Testimonie was sharp to the Lukewarm
& such as contented themselves in a fawlse rest, but com=
=forting to the Honest Hearted, another frd also appear'd
8, went with my Wife to our fifth day [Thursday] meet'g, my
minde was refresh'd, felt easy to sit in Silence
11, went with my Wife to our first day [Sunday] meet'g I was concearn'd
to speak a little theirin, another frd also appear'd
12, took a walk with my Wife & some friends to our M. Meet'g
held at C,[hipping]Norton it was pretty large, two friends appear'd
in Testimonie, the meet'g of buisness held pretty long, after meet'g
went to se some friends, in the evening return'd Home,
15 went with my Wife to our fifth day [Thursday] meet'g, it was a low
time with me altho I felt refresh'd, one frd appear'd in Testimonie,
17, set out on foot for our quarterly meet'g to be held at Read'g
stop'd a little at Jn'o Jacksons's Oxford and had some
refreshment, reach'd Shillingford about 8 oclock at

Night, went to Jos Sargoods to Lod'g who
entertaind me kindly

Page 8

9mo[September] 1803

18th stop'd at Warborough & Shillingford all day,
was at the Warborough Meet'g (& sevral more Strangers
ware there from distand places on their Journey
to the quarterly meet'g) I was concearn'd to speak
theirin, to Incourage them to live in Love, another
friend also appear'd, Din'd with a pretty menny
friends at Joseph Ashbys Shillingford who was
very kinde to friends, he has a pretty deal of this
worlds goods, I believe he is of a generous Heart
& desireous to do good theirwith, not only to friends
but to the poor, & his Heart and House is Open
to entertain Friends, call'd to se some more friends,
had a little solid conversation with a religious young Woman,
who it was thought had been in a Decline, but
now she appear'd finely recover'd, I hope the
Lord in Mercy has visited her and Preserved her
Life, in order that she may be an Instrument
in His Hand to Instruct others in the way of Righteousness
Lodg'd again at Jos: Sargoods,
19, walk'd with Jno Sargood and another friend to
Read'g, reach'd their about 3, A.[fter]Noon, went to se
some friends and Relations in the Even'g,
Lodg'd at Cousin Jno Tutteys who gets old and feeble,
yet appeard Loving and cheerfull & glad to se friends,
19 , the Quarterly Meet'g began at nine, and I think it
was pretty large sevral friends appear'd in Testimonie
I also was concearn'd to speak a little theirin, I think it
was a Comfortable time to menny, Friends ware
much exercised with respect to going through their buisness

verso

on acct of one Person who had been Disowned refuseing
to leave the meeting when friends enter'd upon buis=
=ness, sevral friends tenderly desired him to with=
=draw, but he Obstinately refused, therefore friends
adjourn'd the meet'g from time to time untill they had got an Oppertunity
to meet without him, and then they went through the
buisness pretty comfortabley, Lodg'd again at Jno Tutteys
21, having had a perticular desire for some time to
go to stains to se Robt Ashby & his family (who
married Wm Albrights Daughter of this Town) and
their Relations, the way appear'd open for me
to pay them a visit: set out on foot pretty early
reach'd Stains about 3 oclock A.[fter]N.[oon] found friends
pretty well, they appear'd glad to se me, & I believe
we rejoiced in the Spirit to se one another under a sence
that Devine Love was felt amoungst us, spent the
A.[fter]N.[oon] with friends comfortabley, Lodg'd at Robt Ashbys
22, was at the week-day meet'g at Stains, which was
not very large, I was concearn'd to speak theirin,
spent the A.[fter]Noon in an agreeable loving manner
amoungst the friends. I was much Exercised under
a sense of my own Weakness's & was desireous that I might very care=
fully attend unto the pure Light with & live in
Obidience theirunto, that through my conduct no
Dishonnour might be brought on the Truth,
Lodg'd at Robt Ashbys

23, took my leave of friends at Stains, some friends being comming
in a Shaise as far as Maidenhead they ware so kind as to let
me ride with them afterward went on foot to Shillingford, stop'd
a little at Henly to se the friends, reach'd Shillingford about 7 oclock

Page 9

at Night, Lodg'd at Jos Ashbys, was very poorly in the Night,
24, in the morning been better, took leave of Friends after Breack=
=fasting with them, & walk'd Home, stop'd a little at Jno
Jacksons's Oxford they ware Loving, reach'd Home abt 5 in the Evening
25 went with my Wife to our first day [Sunday] meet'g felt comforted,
after meet'g went on foot with my Wife to Burford Lodg'd at Bror H
26, I return'd Home my Wife stop'd till the fourth day [Wednesday] following
29, was at our fifth day [Thursday] meet'g
10mo[October] 2, went with my Wife to our first day [Sunday] meet'g, felt comforted,
4, my Wives Sistor Hanh came to se us from Warwick, who lives at Wm Evans,
5, took a walk to Witney with Sistor H, was at their fourth
day [Wednesday] meet'g it felt comforting, One friend appear'd setting
forth the difference there was between true Humility and lowly=
=ness of minde, and a State of Dispare, as the first being
the work of the Lords power, the second being by the Power
of the Enemy, who seeks to take away mans Peace,
O that none might give way to the Suggestions & Insinuations
of the Enemy, but Trust wholy in the Lord, & confide in
the Everlasting Truth, and do their utmost Indeavours to
live in Obedience theirunto, & then I Trust they would know
the Injoyment of that precious Peace, which the World nor all the things that are theirin cannot
give neither can they take it away,
after meet'g we went to se some friends, in the Even'g return'd Home
6, went with my Wife to our fifth day [Thursday] meet'g, it was held in Silence
8, went with Sistor Hanh to Mothers at Sibford, found Mother
Poorly, spent a little time at Mothers comfortabley, Lodg'd at M. Petiphors
9 before meet'g went to se some friends who had had their
Goods seiz'd and taken away on acct of being drawn, I simpa=
with them, & was led to Incourage them to be faithfull & to bear a faith=
=full Testimonie against such Things, which if they did I believed they
would feel great Satisfaction, the meet'g felt pretty comfortable
I was concearn'd to speak theirin, to advise Friends to Build upon the sure

verso

Foundation that Rock which is Immoveable, that should
the Windes and Rains be suffer'd to beat upon them, should
Tryals & proving seasons be permitted to come upon them they might
be Inabled to stand safe, after Dining with Mother &
Sistors bid them Farewell, & return'd Home on foot,
13. went with my Wife to our fifth day [Thursday] meet'g
it was held in Silence, felt Spiritualy poor & weak
16, went with my Wife to our first day [Sunday] meet'g, I
think it was a time that the living ware favour'd
to feel Devine Refreshment, it was held in Silence,
17 went with my Wife to our Monthly meet'g held
at this place the meet'g for Worship felt comforting
some friends appear'd in Testimonie and Prayer,
which was attended with Devine Power and Solemnity,

20, went with my Wife to our fifth day [Thursday] meet'g
23 went with my Wife & her Sistor Mary (who came
from Sibford yesterday to se us) to our first day [Sunday]
meet'g, I felt refresh'd, it was held in Silence
27, went with my Wife to our fifth day [Thursday] meet'g, it was
a low time with me, it was held in Silence
30, went with my Wife to our first day [Sunday] meet'g, it felt
to be a low time amoungst us, a time in which
their is great need for us in stillness to Labour
for Devine Counsel support & Power, to Direct & Inable
us to persevear in the right way, it was held in Silence
11mo [November] 3rd I and my Wife went to our fifth day [Thursday] meet'g, it was
held in Silence I have felt there is a great necessiety
for me to walk Humbley in the fear of the Lord
-6 went with my Wife to our first day [Sunday] meet'g, it felt to be a
low time for us, it was held in Silence
10 went with my Wife to our fifth day [Thursday] meet'g, it felt a little comforting
& was held in Silence

Page 10

13th went with my Wife to our first day [Sunday] meet'g, it was
held in Silence, was favour'd to feel the Heart tendering
Power of Providence, which bow'd my minde in humble Thankfullness
14 took a walk to Witney to our Monthly meet'g, it felt
pretty comfortable, sevral friends appear'd in Tes=
=timonie which was attended with Life & Power, I also
felt a concearn to speak theirin, spake what I be=
=lieved was my duty to speak, found satisfaction by
so doing, the buisness was gone through in Love,
after meet'g call'd to se some friends, & walk'd Home

17, went with my Wife to our fifth day [Thursday] meet'g, it felt a little refreshing
20, went with my Wife to our first day [Sunday] meet'g, it felt com=
=forting, it was held in Silence
24, went with my Wife to our fifth day [Thursday] meeting, it was held in Silence
27, went with my Wife to our first day [Sunday] meet'g, it felt comforting
I was concearn'd to advise friends to seek the Lord for our fellow
mortals in Distress,
12mo [December] 1st went with my Wife to our fifth day [Thursday] meet'g, it was held in Silence
-4 went with my Wife to our first day [Sunday] meet'g, my minde
felt refresh'd, it was held in Silence
-7 took a walk to Witney, was at the fourthday [Wednesday] meet'g
altho it was small yet my minde was refresh'd
-8 went with my Wife to our fifth day [Thursday] meet'g, it was held in Silence
11 went with my Wife to our first day [Sunday] meet'g, it
felt comforting altho a low time with us, it was held in Silence
in the A,[fter]Noon walk to Burford found Bro'r H
poorly, spent the Even'g mostly at Bro'r, Lodg'd their
12, the Monthly meet'g was not very large, the pure
Life feels to me to be low amoungst us, two
friends appear'd in Testimonie, after meet'g I & my Wife
took leave of Relations & return'd Home

verso

1803

15th went with my Wife to our fifth day [Thursday] meet'g, it felt
a little refreshing, it was held in Silence
18 went with my Wife to our first day [Sunday] meet'g, it

felt to be a low time with us, it was held in Silence
22, went to our fifth day [Thursday] meet'g it was held in Silence
23, took a walk to C[hipping]Norton, was at the Funeral of
Hannah Fardon who was took amiss suddainly the last
first day [Sunday] at meet'g, and died quietly about 2 ours after,
it felt to be a quiet comforting meeting, several friends
appear'd in Testimonie, after meet'g had a comfortable
sitting with friends at Jno Gilkes, afterward walk'd Home,
24 walk'd to Oxford with Bro'r to our Quarterly meet'g,
the first day [Sunday] meet'g was smallish, yet it felt comforting,
spent the A[fter]Noon, mostly at Jno Jacksons's comfortabley, Lodg'd their
25, Quarterly Meet'g began at 9 oclock it felt comforting,
sevral friends appear'd in Testimonie, the buisness was
gone through in love, a woman friend felt a concearn
to come into the mens meet'g, & I trust her visit was to good
satisfaction, after meet'g took leave of some friends & return'd Home
29, went with my Wife to our fifth day [Thursday] meet'g, it was held in Silence

1804

1mo[January] 1st went with my Wife to our first day [Sunday] meet'g, it felt to

---

be a low time, a time of Affliction, it was held in Silence,
3, a Neighbour ours dying a rather suddainly & I
being invited to attend the Funeral went did not
feel easy to Into the Worship therefore walk round the
graveyard till the people came out, & then stood
with them at the grave
5 I went to our fifth day [Thursday] meet'g my minde was refresh'd
I earnestly Breath'd to the Almighty for Devine Comfort,

Page 11

1804

1mo[January] 8th went with my Wife to our fifth day [Thursday] meet'g, it
felt refreshing, it was held in Silence
in the A.[fter]Noon I my Wife & another fr'd walk'd
to C[hipping]Norton, spent the even'g with friends comfortabley
9, Breackfasted at J. Kings, ware we Lodg'd, be=
=fore the monthly meet'g began call'd to se
some friends, hear'd of the Death of
Padbury's Wife of Burford, who Died suddainly last first
day, at meet'g felt a little refresh'd, was made
sensible of the great necessiety their is to attend to
the Instructions of the Light within, & to be very diligent
in living in Obidience theirunto, after meet'g
spent a little time with Fr'ds & walk'd Home
12, went with my Wife to our fifth day [Thursday] meet'g
felt a little refresh'd it was held in Silence
13, took a walk to Burford was at the Funeral
of Matthias Padbury's Wife, Tho's Speakman
from Reading & sevral other friends in the Minis=
=try ware there, it was a pretty full meet'g of friends,
and others not of our Society, it felt to be a solid
good meet'g, sevral Living Testimonies ware born
wareby the people ware advised to live in the
fear of the Lord and sarve him in sincerity &
in Truth that might be prepared for Death,
after meet'g spent a little time with Bro'r & sistor
in a solid manner took leave of them & walk'd Home,
15, went with my Wife to our first day [Sunday] meet'g, it was a

I believe a time in which friends mindes ware bowed
in humility before the Lord, I was concearn'd to speak
theirin, to Incourage the youth in perticular to sarve the Lord faithfully

verso

1804

1mo[January] 19th went with my Wife to our fifth day [Thursday] meeting
we also went again to meet'g in the Even'g,
it was a meet'g appointed by the desire of Joseph
Cloud, who is on a Religious Visit, it was held in Silence
22, I went to our first day [Sunday] meet'g (my Wife being poorly
did not go) ware again favour'd with the Company
of Jos: Cloud he was drawn pretty much in Testimonie
which I think was close and powerfull he
Desired another meet'g to be appointed in the Even'g
a Public meet'g which was accordingly done,
and a very full meet'g it was, but very soon
after the Friend began to speak the floor of the meet'g
house gave way which caused such a Disturbance
that some feared the meet'g House was a going
to fall, in the hurry to get out menny ware hurt
tho not very much, some lost one thing some another
and the meet'g was quite broke up, menny ware
sorry that such an axcident should happen,
I think friends should be very carefull at such solem
occasions, to feel for the friend or friends, who desires
to have a meet'g appointed, & to se that the meet'g House
is in good order and the seats also, Friends should mix
with the People to keep them in awe direct them
ware to sit, & to Indeavour to keep them as still as
possible, that all things may be conducted orderly
agreeabley to the weightyness of the Occasion,
29 I and my Wife went to our first day [Sunday] meet'g, which felt
comforting, we ware again favour'd with the Company of
Joseph Cloud, (he appear'd in Testimonie) he return'd hear

Page 12

last fifth day [Thursday], I believe he could not feel
easy without Indeavouring to have another
Public meet'g, as he stop'd here wile our meet'g house
was a Repairing, he desired to have a Public
meet'g appointed to begin at 6 oclock this Evening, which was
accordingly done, it was a very throng'd meet'g,
and some appeard to be disposed to disturb,
but the Lords Power appear'd to be over
all, Praises Obidience & Honnour be given unto
Him for Evermore. Joseph appear'd a pretty
wile in Testimonie wareby the pure witness
I trust was reach'd in menny mindes
31 took a walk about 3 miles to Chadlington to
meet some friends, Joseph Cloud having signified his desire to
have a meet'g their, I and Wm Albt. met some friends
of C.[hipping]Norton, and after some consultation about
a meet'g, we procured a large Barn & some forms,
also sent a man round to Inform the Inhabitance
that a meet'g was appointed to begin at 3 oclock
A,[fter]noon. a pretty menny Neighbours came to the
meet'g and behaved pretty well, about 7 friends
came from C[hipping] Norton to the meet'g, Joseph was
pretty much concearn'd to turn the peoples mindes inward
to the Grace of God & Instructions of the Spirit
of Truth within them, & to desire them to live in
obidience thereunto, as the only means appointed for them
to Expierience their souls salvation, after meet'g I return'd Home

verso

1804

2mo[February] 1st took a walk to Witney was at the fourth day [Wednesday]
meet'g, it felt pretty comfortable
2, was at our fifth day [Thursday] meet'g, it felt to me as a Cloudy time
5. went with my Wife to our first day [Sunday] meet'g, it felt com=
=forting, it was held in Silence
9, went with my Wife to our fifth day [Thursday] meet'g
this day we Remov'd to Wm Albrights House near
their dwelling House, on acct of our Landlord giving
us notice to quit the House we live'd in sometime ago,
12, went with my Wife to our first day [Sunday] meet'g it was
held in Silence, have felt of late much exercised in
Body & minde, and have been made often sensible of
my own weakness's & of the great necessiety there is
often to retire Inward into stillness and Wait upon the
Lord, to Labour after His mercy & his Power to support
my minde a midst the menny Exercises that I meet
with, and as I have patiently waited upon the Lord
I have felt my minde comforted and strengthened, & I have
seen a great necessiety to be always upon the Watch
& not to lean to my own understanding, but in all my
ways to Acknowledge the Lord, if I would be preserv'd
in that way in which true & sweet peace of minde is Injoyed
13, I and my Wife went to our Monthly meet'g held at
Charlbury, one friend appear'd in Testimonie, signifying
how necessary it is to be diligent in a Spiritual sence, in
Labouring in the Lords work, it being the way to become
Rich with the Lords good things, the buisness was gone through in Love
16 went with my Wife to our fifth day [Thursday] meet'g, it was
held in Silence

Page 13

19th went with my Wife to our first day [Sunday] meet'g, it
felt pretty comforting, altho held in Silence
23, went with my Wife to our fifth day [Thursday] meet'g, it was held in Silence
26, went with my Wife to our first day [Sunday] meet'g, it
felt pretty comforting, I was concearn'd to speak theirin, to
Incourage friends always to live so in obidience
to the Lords power, as to know a being cleansed of all sin
29 took a walk to Sibford to se my Motherinlaw
my Wife being sent for (on second day [Monday] last) on
acct of She being very Ill, found she very weak,
but seem'd to be a little better left my Wife with Mo:
and return'd Home at Night
3mo[March] 1st I went to our fifth day [Thursday] meet'g
-4 I went to our first day [Sunday] meet'g, it felt comforting
it was held in Silence
8 my Wife being from Home, I went to our fifth
day meet'g, it felt refreshing, it was held in Silence
11, took a walk to Sibford found Mother in
a very weak state, was at their first day [Sunday]
meet'g, it felt Comforting, & I believe the
Loving=kindness and Mercy of the Lord was
renewedly Extended to menny, a friend appeard in a
Powerfull manner in Prayer and Testimonie,
I also was Concearn'd to speak theirin
after meet'g spent a little time comfortabley at Mothers

took our leave of them and my Wife & I return'd Home
12 took a walk with my Wife & some friends to our monthly meet'g at Witney it felt pretty com= =fortable sevral friends appear'd in Testimonie the buisness was gone through pretty comfortabley
after meet'g we call'd to se some friends & walk Home

verso

1804

3mo[March] 15th went with my Wife to our fifth day [Thursday] meet'g, it was held in Silence
-18, went with my Wife to our first day [Sunday] meet'g,
it appear'd to be my duty to speak a little matter theirin
altho it was very little I gave up and spake it, found
satisfaction by so doing
22 went with my Wife to our fifth day [Thursday] meet'g, felt a
little refresh'd, it was held in Silence,
25, went with my Wife to our first day [Sunday] meet'g, it
was held in Silence, it felt refreshing
28, went to Witney on some buisness, was at their fourth
day meet'g, wich felt comfortable, it was held in Silence
29 went with my Wife to our fifth day [Thursday] meet'g, it was held in Silence
4mo[April] 1st went with my Wife to our first day [Sunday] meet'g,
I felt poor & to stand in need of Devine help,
it was held in Silence, in the A.[fter]Noon I walk'd
to Burford with my Wife spent the Evening
mostly at Brors comfortabley, Lodg'd at S. Lockeys,
2nd the Mo: Meetg mostly felt pretty comfortable,
several friends appear'd in Testimonie, I also
was concearn'd to speak theirin.
by the Answers to the Queries the Life of Religion
appears to be low amoungst us, pretty soon after meet'g
took leave of Relations & walk'd Home
5, went with my Wife to our fifth day [Thursday] meetg, it was held in Silence
8. went with my Wife to our first day [Sunday] meet'g, a largish
meet'g, several friends being their on their way to
the Quarterly Meet'g, I was concearn'd to speak a
little theirin,
10, walk'd with some Relations to Witney to our Quarterly meet'g,
it was pretty large & felt Tolerable comfortable, several
friends appear'd in Testimonie & one in Solem Prayer,

Page 14

after meet'g stop'd a little with Relations & friends took
leave of them and walk'd Home with my Wife,
12, went with my Wife to our fifth day [Thursday] meet'g, it
felt refreshing, it was held in Silence
15, went with my Wife to our first day [Sunday] meet'g, it
felt to be a low time, was concearn'd to speak a little theirin,
19, went with my Wife to our fifth day [Thursday] meet'g, it was held in held in Silence
22, went with my Wife to our first day [Sunday] meet'g, felt a little
refresh'd, it was held in Silence,
26, went with my Wife to our fifth day [Thursday] meet'g, it felt
a little comforting, Susanna Coales of Henly, was at
meet'g & spake a few words theirin
29 I went to our first day [Sunday] meet'g, felt a little re=
fresh'd, it was held in Silence
5mo[May] 3rd my Wife being from Home I went to our
fifth day [Thursday] meet'g, it was held in Silence
-5, having felt some drawings in my minde to attend Armscutt [Armscote]

meet'g in the Afternoon walk'd to Shipstone was kindly enter=
tain'd at Jno Wells's, Lodg'd their,
-6 was at the morning meet'g at Shipstone which was small
afterward walk'd with some friends to Armscutt [Armscote] meet'g which
was large and felt comfortable menny of appearing sollid
& attentive to what was Deliver'd I spake a little theirin to
advise the People not to rely on forms but to labour to come
unto the Light & Power of Christ within & live in Obidience
thereunto that they might know a being made free from Sin,
Sarrah Lambley was drawn fourth pretty largely in Testimonie
after meet'g call'd to se friend Lambleys & some more friends,
& walk'd with Sistor M.G. to Sibford, found Mother Poorly,
7, walk'd to the monthly meet'g at Shutford, felt a little refresh'd
return'd to Rich'd Holtoms to Din'r afterwards call'd to se some
friends, Lodg'd at Mothers,
8, took leave of Mo: & Sistor & walk'd Home with the Comfortable Injoyment of Peace,
10, was at our fifth day [Thursday] meet'g & on the morrow took [blank]

verso

1804

5mo[May] 13th I went with my Wife to our first day [Sunday] meet'g, felt
great need to Labour for Devine help under a sence of
great weakness, it was held in Silence,
-14, too a walk with my Wife to our Monthly meet'g held
at C,[hipping]Norton, ware favour'd with the Company of two
Strangers P[ublic],F[riends], viz: Deborah Darby & Mary Loyd, both ap=
=pear'd in Testimonie & one in Prayer, I trust it was a
comfortable meet'g, after meet'g went to se some friends in the
Even'g walk'd Home,
17, went with my Wife to our fifth day [Thursday] meet'g, it was held in Silence
20, went with my Wife to our first day [Sunday] meet'g, felt a little
refresh'd, I was concearn'd to speak a little theirin, to ad=
=vise friends to examine themselves & se if the work of their
souls Salvation went forward with the daytime
24 went with my Wife to our fifth day [Thursday] meet'g it was held in S,
27, went with my Wife to our first day [Sunday] meet'g it was
held in Silence felt very poor & to feel the want of
Devine Comfort,
31, went with my Wife to our fifth day [Thursday] meet'g, it was held in Silence
6mo[June] 3rd was at the first day [Sunday] meetg at Burford, felt very poor
theirin, it was held in Silence, went to se Thos Huntly
who was taken abt a month agoe very Ill, found him
comfortable yet poorly, in the Even'g walk'd Home
-7, went with my Wife to our fifth day [Thursday] meet'g
-10, went with my Wife to our first day [Sunday] meet'g it felt a little
comforting, it was held in Silence
-11, went with my Wife to our monthly meet'g held at this place, I felt
very poor & my minde oppress'd, two friends appear'd in Testimonie
felt oppress'd in the meet'g of Buisness,
14, went with my Wife to our fifth day [Thursday] meet'g, felt very low
and the want of Devine Comfort,
17, went with my Wife to our first day [Sunday] meet'g, felt Devine
Goodness to tender, humble & Contrite my minde, which is cause
of humble thankfullness unto the Lord,

21st I & my Wife went to our fifth day [Thursday] meet'g

Page 15

24, went with my Wife to our first day [Sunday] meet'g, sat in a
low state yet it hath appear'd best for me to Indeavour
not to give way to discouragment, but to keep striveing
on having faith in Devine Goodness,
25, went on foot with my Wife & Sistor to near Banbury they going
to Banbury, and I to North-newington, to Thos Rileys a Convinced
young man, had some solid Conversation with him concearning Religion
also went to se some more friends in that Place. Lodg'd at T. Rileys,
26 walk'd to Edwd Stones (Banbury) to Breackfast, the Quarterly
meet'g as usual began at 9 oclock I think in the whole it was pretty
comfortable, a pretty menny friends appear'd in Testimonie,
after meet'g Din'd at Widow Beesley's took leave of Friends & return'd Home,
28 went to our fifth day [Thursday] meet'g. Joseph Russel call'd to see me,
7mo[July] 1st went with my Wife to our first day [Sunday] meet'g it was held in Silence
5, went with my Wife to our fifth day [Thursday] meet'g, it was held in Silence
-8, walk'd to Witney to their first day [Sunday] meet'g, one friend appear'd, in
the Even'g walk'd from thence to Faringdon Lodg'd at Rt Rey=
=nolds's who entertain'd me kindly
-9, the monthly Meet'g began at 10 we ware favour'd with the
company of two strangers viz: *John Kirk out of Esex & John Wilk*
from High Wickam in Buckinghamshire
The both appear'd in Testimonie
which was attended with Life and Power, the yearly Epistle
was read, and afterwards friends went through the buisness,
after meet'g spent sometime with friends pretty comfortabley at
Reynolds's, in the Eveng some friends ware so kind as to let me
ride with them to Witney, Lodg'd at Cousin Wm Barritts,
10, in the morn'g spent a little time with some friends & return'd Home,
12, went with my Wife to our fifth day [Thursday] meet'g, it was held in S,
13, we ware favour'd with the Company of the two above mention'd
friends at a meet'g this Even'g which was appointed
by their desire, one of them appear'd in Testimonie in
which he signify'd he believ'd there ware in the meet'g
some visited mindes & he advised friends to be faithfull unto
Death that they might be favour'd to Injoy a Crown of Life,
15, was at our first day [Sunday] meet'g ware again favour'd with the Company of
John Kirkham & Jno Wilkin It felt a favour'd meet'g & both men ware drawn fourth in Testimonie

verso

in the A[fter] Noon John Kirkam was concearn'd to have a Public meet'g,
according to his desire a meet'g was appointed to begin at 6 oclock in the even'g,
the Neighbours ware acquainted theirwith and a pretty menny came,
I trust it was a Satisfactory meet'g, a time in which the mercifull
visitation of the Lord was extended unto the people. I think it
was an Exerciseing time with friends, & Jno Kirkham Labour'd very
hard in Testimonie the other friend also appear'd, I think there ware menny
loose Religious People in the meet'g, but truth arose over all and
the ware put in minde of their dangerous situation & warn'd to repent
of their Iniquieties turn unto the Lord and minde the reproofs of his Spirit

which smites them in seacreet for so doing and indeavour to live in obidience
thereunto in the day of the Lords mercy that it might be well with them,
19th went with my Wife to our fifth day [Thursday] meet'g (oppress'd in minde)
22 went with my Wife to our first day [Sunday] meet'g, felt a little re=
=fresh'd, it was held in Silence except the yearly meet'g
Epistle being read, it was a comfort to my minde to feel
that friends of the Early meet'g ware led to feel for and
be much concearn'd for the good and growth in the Truth of
their Brethren & Sistors
26 went with my Wife to our fifth day [Thursday] meet'g. Silent Meet'g
29 I went to our first day [Sunday] meet'g, (my Wife being very poorly did not
go,) felt a little refresh'd, it was held in Silence
8mo[August] 2nd went with my Wife to our fifth day [Thursday] meet'g, it was held in Silence
-5, went with my Wife to our first day [Sunday] meet'g felt very
poor & low,
-12, went with my Wife to our first day [Sunday] meet'g, felt a little
refresh'd, it was held in Silence
-13 took a walk to our Monthly meet'g at Burford (my Wife
going the night before) I believe it was a pretty comfortable meet'g,
was again favour'd with the Company of Jno Kirkham who was
very lately at Charlbury, he was drawn forth pretty longly
in Testimonie, the buseness was gone through pretty comfortabley,
in the Ev'ing return'd Home
-16, I & my Wife went to our fifth day [Thursday] meet'g it was held in Silence
-19, went with my Wife to our first day [Sunday] meet'g, felt a little refresh'd, it was held in S,
-26, went with my Wife to our first day [Sunday] meet'g, felt a little refresh'd,
it was held in Silence

Page 16

9[August] 1804

30th went with my wife to our fifth day [Thursday] meet'g, it was held in Silence,
9mo[September] 2nd went with my Wife to our first day [Sunday] meet'g, it felt pretty
comfortable, it was held in Silence, in the A,[fter] noon walk'd
to Sibford, found my Wives mother Poorly, Lodg'd at Mothers
-3rd was at the Mo: Meet'g at Sibford, it felt pretty comfortable,
after meet'g went to se some friends & spent sometime at Mo: comfortabley, Lodg'd their
-4, took leave of Mother & Sistor & walk'd Home
-6 went with my Wife to our fifth day [Thursday] meet'g we ware favour'd
with the Company of Jos Huntley & Ann Ashby, it felt
to be a refreshing time, even a renew'd Visitation of the Lords
goodness, both appear'd in Testimonie which was much Incourageing
to the try'd Exersised mindes to keep striveing to get forward, but
somewhat sharp to shuch whose mindes ware not clean signifying
the rubbish must be done away before they could feel a state
of axceptance with the Lord – in the afternoon went
with the friends to Milton to a meet'g appointed to begin at
five in the Even'g, which I hope was to Satisfaction,
9, went with my Wife to our first day [Sunday] meet'g, it felt re=
=freshing, it was held in Silence, in the A[fter] Noon my Wife walked
to C[hipping] Norton
10th I went to C[hipping] Norton to our Monthly meet'g (it was held in
House belonging to Jos King the New Meet'g H[ouse], which has been
building being not quite finish'd) Jos Huntley & Ann Ashby

ware there and appear'd theirin, it felt pretty comfortable
after meet'g I & my Wife went to se some friends, in the Ev'g return'd Home
13 went with my Wife to our fifth day [Thursday] meet'g, felt a little refresh'd
16 set out on foot towards our Quarterly Meet'g, walk'd to Jno
Jacksons's to meet'g, there ware three besides their family
I trust we ware favour'd to feel a little of Devine Refreshment
after Dining at J. Jacksons's walk'd to Shillingford. Lodg'd at
Joseph Ashbys ware I was entertained kindly, call'd to se friends at Shillingford
17, rose early and walk'd with Jno Sargood to Henly was
at the Monthly Meet'g there, the Power of truth seem'd
to be low amoungst friends, after Meetg walk'd with Jno Sargood
to Reading, reach'd their abt five in the Even'g, went to se some friends
went to see Henry Finch a Disowned Person who troubled us much
at the last Quarterly meet'g which was held at Read'g last year,
I got an oppertunity to speak with him concearning his Behaviour

verso

I Indeavoured to make him sensible how rong it was for him
to hinder friends in their buisness at the Quarterly Meet'g, signifying
it was not doing as he would like to be done unto, & if he thought
he had been used rong by friends he should Indeavour to overcome
evel with good, and if we wish to have our Labours tend to good,
they should be in weakness and through the Assistance of the Power
of Him, who is the way the Truth and the Life, he heard me
pretty Patiently, I signify'd I spoke to him in Love, separted
Friendly – sup'd with friends at Jno Tutteys the Elder. Lodg'd at H. Smiths
18, before meet'g went to se some friends, according to what I felt at
meet'g it was a low exerciseing time with sincear friends, sevral
friends appear'd in Testimonie - (Rich'd Gilkes from Deviz=
=es was their) the Buisness was gone through in Love altho it appear'd
by the answers to the queries there was great need for friends to be
stirred up to Diligence in the attendance of Religious meet'gs & other
religious Duties, H. Finch was not their, after meet'g return'd in a one Horse=Carriage
with two friends to Shillingford Lodg'd at Jos Ashbys, as did also sevral other friends
-19, after breackfasting with friends, took leave of them and return'd Home
-20, I went with my Wife to out fifth day [Thursday] meet'g, it felt a little comforting, silent
-23, I & my Wife went to our first day [Sunday] meet'g, it was held in Silence
-27, went with my Wife to our fifth day [Thursday] meet'g, I felt a little refreshed (silent)
-30, went with my Wife to our first day [Sunday] meet'g I trust in our sitting
in Silence we ware favour'd to pertake of Devine Refreshment
10mo[October] 4th went with my Wife to our fifth day [Thursday] meet'g, I felt a little refresh'd
-7, went with my Wife to our first day [Sunday] meet'g it felt a little refreshing
-8, I and my Wife went to our Monthly meet'g held at this place it was
not very large & to me it felt to be a Cloudy time – it was held in silence
-10, went with my Wife to our meet'g felt a little refresh'd, it was held in silence
-14, Borrow'd Wm Albt Horse & Rode before my Wife to Sibford
to se Mother & Sistors, found Mo: poorly, rest pretty well, was at
the first day [Sunday] meet'g, felt a little refresh'd, it was held in Silence

spent most of the A.[fter]N.[oon] at Mo: pretty comfortabley, we lodg'd their
15, this morning I and my Wife took leave of Mo: & Sistors & return'd Home
18, went with my Wife to our fifth day [Thursday] meet'g, it was held in silence
21, went with my Wife to our first day [Sunday] meet'g, it felt refreshing held in silence
25, went with my Wife to our fifth day [Thursday] meet'g, it was held in Silence
28, went with my Wife to our first day [Sunday] meet'g, it felt a little comforting, held in Silence

Page 17

1804

11mo [November] 1st went with my Wife to our fifth day [Thursday] meet'g, held in Silence
-4, went with my Wife to our first day [Sunday] meet'g, it felt refreshing, silent
8, went with my Wife to our fifth day [Thursday] meet'g, held in Silence
-11, went with my Wife to our first day [Sunday] meet'g it felt refreshing. Silent
-12, took a walk to the monthly Meet'g held at Witney, Silent before
before friends enter'd upon Buisness, - return'd Home in the Ev'ing
-15 went with my Wife to our fifth day [Thursday] meet'g, felt a
little refresh'd, it was held in Silence
17, took a walk to Dedington, visited several Persons
who of late have attend Friends meetings had a pre=
=ty comfortable visit Lodg'd with one of them
18, took a walk with some of them to adderbury to meet=
=ing, had some Religious coversation with them which I
hope was Edefying, felt pretty comfortable at meet'g,
spake theirin, after meetg walk to milton to Robt Pains to
Din'r, went from thence to Sibford (Thos Mall accompanying
me as far as Bloxam) found Mother poorly, Lodg'd there
19, it being rainy stop'd at Sibford, spent most of the day at Mothers agreeabley
20, bid Mother & Sistor farewell & walk'd Home
22, went with my Wife to our fifth day [Thursday] meet'g, felt a little refresh'd
25, went with my Wife to our first day [Sunday] meet'g, it felt a little refreshing, silent
29, went with with my Wife to our fifth day [Thursday] meet'g, felt a
little refresh'd it was held in Silence
12[December], 2, went with my Wife to our first day [Sunday] meet'g felt a little refresh'd S
-6, went to our fifth day [Thursday] meet'g (my wife being out) held in Sil:
-9 went with my Wife to our first day [Sunday] meet'g, it felt refreshing
altho held in Silence, in the afternoon went to burford found
Bro'r H very poorly, spent most of the Even'g at Bror's comfortabley, Lodg'd their
-10, before the Monthly meet'g began went to se some friends, the
meet'g felt pretty comfortable, sevral friends appear'd in Testi=
=monie, the buisness was gone through in Love, after meet'g walk'd Home
-13, went with my Wife to our fifth day [Thursday] meet'g, felt refresh'd. Silent
-16, went with my Wife to our first day [Sunday] meet'g, felt refresh'd Silent
-20, went with my Wife to our fifth day [Thursday] meeting, felt refresh'd. Silent

verso

1804

12mo [December] 22nd went with my Wife to our first day [Sunday] meet'g, it felt refreshing, silent
-26, went to our fifth day [Thursday] meet'g, held in Silence,
-28 I went to our first day [Sunday] meetg, (my Wife did not go
on account of sitting up with sistors youngest Child who

was Ill, it felt refreshing, held in Silence

1805

1mo[January] 3rd I and my Wife went to our fifth day [Thursday] meet'g
-6, I and my Wife was at our first day [Sunday] meet'g at which was
a Funeral (of Sarah Busby who liv'd at this town,)
it was a Pretty large meet'g of Friends & Neighbours
it felt to be a refreshing meet'g several friends appear'd
in Testimonie viz Wm Barritt Thos Huntley s.quire after meet'g spent sometime with friends comfortabley
-10, went with my Wife to our fifth day [Thursday] meet'g
-13, went with my Wife to our first day [Sunday] meet'g, it was held in Silence
in the afternoon walk'd to Oxford our Quarterly Meet'g being
to be held there spent the evening at Jno Jacksons's Lodg'd their
14 the Qua: meet'g began at 9 oclock as usual and I trust it was
a good refreshing meet'g, Pub: friends, Ann Crawley, Shusanna
Horn, Wm Barritt, Tho. Spikeman and sevral others sevral
of them appear'd in Testimonie, one friend had to reminde
friends not to remove the antient Land=mark, signifying
they should keep to the plainness and Innosciency which Truth
leadeth into, the meet'g of Buisness held not long – after meet'g
spent a little time with friends comfortabley, and return'd Home
17, went with my Wife to our fifth day [Thursday] meeting, it was held in Silence
20 went with my Wife to our first day [Sunday] meet'g it felt a little
refreshing, spake a few words theirin
21, I and my Wife went to C,[hipping] Norton to the monthly meet'g
it was not very large, but felt pretty comfortable,
I was concearn'd to speak a little theirin as was also another
friend, the buisness was gone through in Love, and meet=
=ing we call'd to se some friends & return'd Home
24 went with my Wife to our fifth day [Thursday] meet'g, silent
27 went with my wife to our first day [Sunday] meet'g, Silent

Page 18

1805

1mo[January] 31st went with my Wife to our fifth day [Thursday] meet'g (silent)
2"[February] 1, took a walk to C[hipping] Norton to the Burial of Ann Stait,
who was much afflicted for menny years, she was so
drawn together that it was affecting to se her, her Fingers
ware so drawn in towards her hands, that they put a
little something soft to her hand to prevent her fingers
drawing into the flesh of her hand. the Meetg felt
pretty comfortable, Thos Harris of Longcompton was
their who appeard in Testimonie, I also was concearn'd
to speak a little theirin, after meet'g spent a little time
with friends & return'd Home
3, went with my Wife to our first day [Sunday] meet'g, it felt refreshing, silent
7, went with my Wife to our fifth day [Thursday] meet'g, (silent)
10, went with my Wife to our first day [Sunday] meet'g, it felt a
little refreshing, altho it feels to me to be a low time
amoungst us (Silent)
11 I and my Wife attended our monthly meet'g at this place
I felt poor & weak two friends appear'd in Testimonie

14, I went to our fifth day [Thursday] meet'g, my Wife being very
poorly, staid at Home (silent)
17, went with my Wife to our first day [Sunday] meet'g, it felt refre=
shing, one fr'd appeard theirin
21, went with my Wife to our fifth day [Thursday] meetg (silent)
24, went with my Wife to our first day [Sunday] meet'g (silent)
28, went with my Wife to our fifth day [Thursday] meet'g (silent)
3mo[March] 2nd in the A.[fter]Noon walk'd to Sibford found my Wives Mother
very weak met with William Jackson at Jos Huntleys
an American Frd who is on a Religious visit in this Nation Lodg'd at M:
3, was at Sibford meet'g Wm Jackson was their, it was a
largish meeting and I hope to good satisfaction W. Jackson
was drawn forth in Testimonie in which he express'd how
dangerous it was to have the minde set on Earthly Things,

verso

---

and things of this World but how very Necessary it was to
seek first of all the Kingdom of Heaven and it Righteous=
=ness, spent about 2 hours at Mothers pretty comfortabley
after meet'g in the Evening walked to milton Lodg'd at R. Pains
4, before meet'g walk'd to adderbury to se some friends,
the monthly meet'g felt pretty comfortable Wm Jacksons was
their, appear'd in Testimonie, I also was concearn'd to speak theirin
W Jackson was concearn'd to speak pretty much as to the
buisness signified friends should be very carefull what they
said respecting the buisness and be very weighty in their Spirits
that they might speak to the purpose – after meet'g Din'd
at _ Malls Milton, and walk'd from thence with some friends
back to sibford, Lodg'd at Mothers
5 after Breackfast took leave of Mother & sistor Mother
appear'd [illegible] and concearn'd about her latter end, reach'd Home in the Ev'ing
7, went with my Wife to our fifth day [Thursday] meet'g
10, went with my Wife to our first day [Sunday] meet'g (silent)
11, took a walk to Witney to our monthly meet'g it felt pretty
comfortable, sevral Friends appear'd in Testimonie
which felt edifying, & was to stir up friends to a diligent
attention to the Inward teachings of the Spirit of Christ
in their own Souls, and a faithfull Obidience theirunto,
"to do this is comming to the substance of Pure Religion"
after meet'g call'd to se some friends in the Ev'g walk'd Home
14. went with my Wife to our fifth day [Thursday] meet'g, silent
17, I went to our first day [Sunday] meet'g, my Wife being very
poorly staid at Home, it was held in silence
21, went with my Wife to our fifth day [Thursday] meet'g (silent)
24 I went to our first day [Sunday] meet'g, felt a little refresh'd,
it was held in silence, yesterday my Wife set out
for Sibford to se her Mother
28, went to our fifth day [Thursday] meet'g with my Wife, silent

Page 19

3mo[March] 31st went with my Wife to our first day [Sunday] meet'g
it was held in Silence
4[April], 1st I and my Wife ware at the monthly Meet'g at
Burford, it felt pretty comfortable, sevral friends

appear'd in Testimonie, after meet'g Din'd at Bro'r
Manders we return'd Home in the Evening
4, went with my Wife to our fifth day [Thursday] meet'g (silent)
7 went with my Wife to our first day [Sunday] meet'g, ware
favour'd with the company of Hannah Jarrot of
Netrup [Neithrop], who is on a religious visit, it was held in Silence
8, I and my Wife walk with some friends to our Quarterly
meet'g held at Witney, it felt pretty comforting sevral frds appear'd in Testimonie which was somewhat sharp to the Careless & Indifrent walkers, but
comforting and edifying to the Sincear hearted mindes,
the meet'g of Buisness held long & it felt hard labour to get
forward, after meet'g spent sometime with fr'ds, in the Ev'g return'd Home
11, went with my Wife to our fifth day [Thursday] meet'g, it was held in Silence
14, went with my Wife to our first day [Sunday] meetg (silent) it felt to
be a low time with friends, as it has done for a pretty wile past
18, went with my Wife to our fifth day [Thursday] meet'g (silent)
21, went with my Wife to our first day [Sunday] meet'g, in sitting theirin
my minde was humbled under a sence of the Love of God &
his goodness to me, and thereby I trust I was constrained to
speak a little theirin, to Incourage friends to be diligent in
doing their duty,
25, went with my Wife to our fifth day [Thursday] meet'g (silent)
28, went with my Wife to our first day [Sunday] meet'g (silent)
29, went to take Wm Albrights Horse to Water, it kick'd & Pranced
about till it got me of wareby my right foot was much hurt, I
sopose she kick'd it after I was down, the mare was young & it liv'd
well & work'd but little, which I think might be the cause of its being so unruly,
the hurt & Fright caused me to take very poorly for sometime, but through

verso

1805

Devine Mercy in about a week (with taking good care and applying suitable
things to my Wounds & Bruses) I was favour'd to be finely recover'd
I think People should be carefull not to keep Horses above their work,
& riders should be very carefull how they ride
5mo[May] 2nd my Wife went to meetg, but I did not go, being poorly
-5, I went with my Wife to our first day [Sunday] meet'g, felt a little refresh'd
9, went with my Wife to our fifth day [Thursday] meet'g, it felt a little refreshing (silent)
12, went with my Wife to our first day [Sunday] meet'g, my minde
was humbled under a sence of the Necessiety to Live an
upright holy Life, felt a little comforted, spake a little
theirin, being a fraid I should fall short of my duty if I did not,
15, this day we had a Public meet'g by the desire of
two Strangers viz Deborah Darby and Rebecca Bird,
(the meet'g began at 10 in the morning it was I trust a
solid good meet'g in which the renew'd Visitation of
Devine Love, I trust was felt by menny mindes)
they ware Led pretty much in Testimonie & one of them
in Solem Prayer, I was concearn'd to speak a little
theirin, to Incourage the People to minde the Devine
Teacher within themselves to love it and live daily in
obidience thereunto – pretty soon after meetg the friends set out

for Oxford, an Evening meet'g being appointed to be held their
16, I went to our fifth day [Thursday] meet'g, my Wife being poorly
staid at Home
19, went with my Wife to our first day [Sunday] meet'g, was poorly so that
it felt trying to me to get to meet'g, yet it felt comforting
and refreshing, I think I may say it was good for I to be
their, one stranger spake a few words theirin
23 went with my Wife to our fifth day [Thursday] meet'g felt poor both
spiritualy and Temporaly, indeavoured to Labour in Patience after
Devine Refreshment,

Page 20

6mo[June] 1805

26th went with my Wife to our first day [Sunday] meet'g, it was
held in Silence which felt comforting
6mo[June] 2nd went with my Wife & Sistor M. Gilks (who came yester=
=day to se us) to our first day [Sunday] meet'g it felt a little refreshing
spake a little theirin
6 went with my Wife to our fifth day [Thursday] meet'g, it felt a little refreshing (silent)
9 went with my Wife to our first day [Sunday] meet'g (silent)
10 went with my Wife to our Monthly meet'g held at this place
it felt to be a pretty comfortable meet'g sevral friends
appear'd in Testimonie which was comforting & edifying
13. went with my Wife to our fifth day [Thursday] meet'g (silent)
16, went with my Wife to our first day [Sunday] meet'g (silent)
20 went with my Wife to our fifth day [Thursday] meet'g was favour'd
to feel Devine Goodness to tender and refresh my Spirit,
23, went to our first day [Sunday] meet'g with my Wife (silent)
24 our Quarterly meet'g being to be held to morrow at
Banbury my Wife walked thither with Bro'r Robt my foot
been so lately hurt & I been but poorly I staid at Home
I understood it was a pretty large meet'g and Jno Kirkham
was there after meetg Wife went to Sibford to se Mother & Sistor
27 went with my Wife to our fifth day [Thursday] meet'g (silent)
30 went with my Wife to our first day [Sunday] meet'g felt a little refresh'd (silent)
7[July]-4 I went to our fifth day [Thursday] meetg (silent)
6, being pretty well recover'd of my lameness & a little better in
health to what I have lately been set out for our Monthly meet'g to be held at Far=
=ingdon, walk'd to witney in the Evening Lodg'd at Jno Hankings
7 was at the first day [Sunday] meet'g at Witney, it felt refreshing
after Din'r walked to Faringdon was kindly Entertained
at Robt Reynolds's with other friends, Lodg'd their
8, the monthly meet'g felt pretty comfortable, sevral
friends appear'd in Testimonie which felt comforting In=
=structing & Edifying, after Dining at Frd Reynolds's Return'd Home

verso

7mo[July] 9th we ware favour'd with the Company of a friend who
is on a Religious visit, Benjm Middletons Wife from [blank]
a meet'g was appointed to begin at 10 oclock in the morn'g
I believe it was a satisfactory meetg, & I trust she was
Inabled to speak to sevral states present
-11 went with my Wife to our fifth day [Thursday] meet'g (silent)

-14 went with my Wife to our first day [Sunday] meet'g (silent)
16 this Evening we had a meeting, it began at six, by
the Desire of James Howarth from [blank] who is on a
Religious visit in these parts it was held in Silence
17, went with James Howarth to Witney as Guide, was at
their weekday meet'g, it felt a pretty comfortable meet'g,
James was led to speak in an arouseing close manner, put=
=ting them in minde to be Jealous over themselves, lest by
giveing way to Indiferency and carelessness with respect to
Religion, they should be rejected and others call'd in in their
room, after meet'g Din'd at Jno Hankins took leave of Frds & return'd Home
-18, went with my Wife to our fifth day [Thursday] meet'g, Silent, it felt a little refreshing
-21, went with my Wife to our first day [Sunday] meet'g, felt a little refresh'd (silent)
-25, went with my Wife to our fifth day [Thursday] meet'g (silent)
-28, went with my Wife to our first day [Sunday] meet'g, silent except the
Yearly Epistle being read, which was comforting Instructing & edifying
8[August],1, went with my Wife to our fifth day [Thursday] meet'g (silent)
-3, set out for Armscutt [Armscote] meet'g on foot reach'd Shipstone about
nine at Night, Lodg'd at Cousin Jno Wells's
-4, was at the meet'g at Shipstone which was held in the morning
before friends went to Armscutt [Armscote] after meet'g walk'd to the meet'g
at Armscutt [Armscote], it was large, James Howarth was there (who had
been at Charlbury) sevral friends appear'd in Testimonie J.H.
had a pretty favourable oppertunity with the People
after meet'g Din'd with menny friends at the Widow Lambleys Tredington
ware we had a comfortable sitting together, in the Even'g walk'd to Sibford
Mother being gone to Bed Lodg'd at my kinde friend, M Petiphors

Page 21

1805

8mo[August] 5th walk'd to the monthly meet'g at Banbury call'd at Thos
Rileys a convinced friend, who was an Exciseman but when
he came amoungst friends he left that Imploy
and took to schooling, he has now got a pretty large school
he appear'd to have a Gift for teaching Children they appeard
to be treated with tenderness, to be Instructed to be cleanly, to behave
orderly as well as minde their Learning in the School,
Inasmuch as he has took up the Cross to follow or to be Obidient
to the pure leadings of Truth in his Own Heart I trust
the Lord hath blessed his Honnest Indeavours, walk'd with
him and some of His Scolars to the meet'g, sevral friends appeard
theirin, I also was concearn'd to speak a little theirin, to Incourage
friends to live in Obidience to Devine Requireings, signifying
their Happiness stood in their Obidience to the Lords Requireings,
afterward friends enter'd upon the buisness which towards the conclusion felt painfull,
after meet'g Din'd at E. Stones with menny friends walk'd
from thence to Sibford found Mother much as she has been of
late Lodg'd there
-6 spent the day at Mothers and in going to se some friends, Lodg'd at Mo:
-7 spent a little time in a solid manner with Mother, took leave
of she and friends & return'd Home

-8 I and my Wife went to our fifth day [Thursday] meet'g we ware favour'd
with the Company of [blank] Chairman & his Wife from [blank]
she is a Friend in the Ministery, appear'd in our meet'g
-11 went with my Wife to our first day [Sunday] meet'g, it felt a little refreshing (silent)
-12, took a walk to our monthly meeting at Burford sevral friends ap=
pear'd theirin, after meet'g I and my Wife took leave of our Relations & return'd Home
-15, went with my Wife to our fifth day [Thursday] meet'g
-18, went with my Wife to our first day [Sunday] meet'g (silent)
-22, went with my Wife to our fifth day [Thursday] meet'g, (silent)
-25, went with my Wife to our first day [Sunday] meet'g, felt a little refresh'd (silent)
-29, came home from Reap'g & went with my Wife to our fifth day [Thursday] meeting
9[September],1st went with my Wife to our first day [Sunday] meet'g one friend appear'd theirin I was [part of previous line]
silent feeling poor & Low
-8 went with my Wife to our first day [Sunday] meet'g ware we ware again

verso

Favour'd with the company of James Howarth, who was here
about 3 weeks ago, it felt to be a comforting meet'g, James Hth
was led to speak concearning the necessiety of friends being witness's
for Christ, signifying they could not be true witness's for Christ
without knowing Him feeling his Power to operate in their Hearts
causeing them to bring forth good fruits
9mo[September] 9th I and my Wife took a walk with some more friends
to our monthly meetg at C[hipping] Norton, J Howarth was there
who appear'd in Testimonie as also another friend
we met in the new Meet'g House
after meet'g we call'd to se some friends & return'd Home,

12, went with my Wife to our fifth day [Thursday] meet'g, one friend appeard
15, set our pretty early towards our Quarterly Meet'g to be held
at Reading, reach'd Oxford about eleven, sat with Jno Jacksons
& his Wife (and two persons more) it being their practise to hold a
little meet'g on a first day [Sunday] – after Dineing with them walk'd
to Shillingford, quarterd at Josh Ashbys who is very kinde and loving
to friends, walk'd down to Warborough to the Widow Sargood who has
lately lost her Husband he being remov'd by Death, Lodg'd at J.A.
16, this morn'g Jos Ashby was so kind as to let me ride with him to
Reading reach'd there about 10 oclock, was at their monthly Meet'g which
was adjourn'd to this day on account of a Commity being appointed
to attend it from our last Qua: Meetg, it did not feel very comfortable
after meet'g call'd to se some friends & Relations who ware Loving Lodg'd at Jno Tutteys
17, the Quarterly meet'g having been lately appointed to begin at ten friends
met accordingly, the Meet'g felt comfortable, straingers in the ministery
James Howarth & Jno Wilkinson, sevral friends appeard in Testimonie
afterwards friends enter'd upon buisness which altho it went on slowly yet
it felt pretty satisfactory, Ann Ashby laid a concearn which she felt be
fore the meet'g to have a public even'g meet'g which after solid consideration
was granted her, I did not stop, but after Din'r took leave of Relations

Page 22

---

and friends, & Return'd to Shillingford with Jos: Ashby, who again was so kinde
as to let me ride with him, Lodg'd at Shillingford
18 after Breackfasting with sevral friends at Jos: Ashbys we
took leave of our kinde friends, and oneanother and set out for

our Homes, I was pretty much fatagued when I reach'd Home
it being a very hot Day, was favoured to feel a degree of Peace in my minde
19, went with my Wife to our fifth day [Thursday] meet'g (silent)
22 went with my Wife to our first day [Sunday] meet'g (silent)
26 went with my Wife to our fifth day [Thursday] meet'g (silent)
29 went with my Wife to our first day [Sunday] meet'g, we ware favour'd
with the Company of Samuel Alexander he appeard in testimonie, which
was much to the youth, signifying that the visitation of the
Lord was extended towards them, & they should be faithfull in
the discharge of their duty even in little matters, if they would know
an advancement in the truth, also that friends should prise the
priviledge which they now Injoy of meeting together quietly,
10mo[October] 3, was at our fifth day [Thursday] meet'g (silent)
-6 took a walk to the first day [Sunday] meet'g at milton, it was
small yet it felt a little refreshing, I was concearn'd
to speak theirin, after meet'g return'd Home
-10, went with my Wife to our fifth day [Thursday] meet'g (silent)
-13, went with my Wife to our first day [Sunday] meet'g (silent)
-14, went with my Wife to our monthly meet'g held at this Place
-17, went with my Wife to our fifth day [Thursday] meet'g (silent)
-20, went to our first day [Sunday] meet'g felt a little refresh'd (silent)
-24, went with my Wife to our fifth day [Thursday] meet'g (silent)
-27, took a walk to Burford to se Bror & Sistor & their Children,
was at the first day [Sunday] meet'g, it felt to be a low time (silent)
after meet'g spent a little time at Bror's Comfortabley, cousin
Hanh being a going from Home I was concearn'd to advise she to
Indeavour to live in the fear of the Lord which is the way to be truely
wise and love the Truth, about 3 oclock took leave of them & returnd Home
31 went with my Wife to our fifth day [Thursday] meet'g, felt a little refresh'd

verso

1805

11mo [November] 3rd went with my Wife to our first day [Sunday] meet'g, it felt a little refreshing, silent
8, went with my Wife to our fifth day [Thursday] meet'g, Silent
-10 went with my Wife to our first day [Sunday] meet'g, felt a little refresh'd,
altho greatly sensible of my own weakness's and of the great necessiety
for me to Labour for Devine Mercy and help (silent)
in the A.[fter]Noon walk'd to Witney spent the Even'g with friends Agreeabley
-11, was at the monthly meet'g, it felt pretty comfortabley, sevral
friends appear'd in Testimonie, Din'd up at Old Wm Barritts with
Tho's Huntley & Wife, Tho's is so cumbersome and feeble that he cannot
get out from Home much to meet'gs very well, took leave of fr'ds and walk'd Home
14, went with my Wife to our fifth day [Thursday] meet'g (silent)
17, went with my Wife to our first day [Sunday] meet'g, spake a little theirin
as believing it to be my duty to advise friends to feel after the Devine
Teacher in their own selves,
21, I went to our fifth day [Thursday] meet'g, felt a little refresh'd, (silent)
24, took a walk to Burford to se Bro'r & Sistor they
being booth poorly, Sistor with a bad leg (which its

thought proceeded from a Fever) so that she is confin'd
to her Bed, Bro'r with a bad finger, altho their Afflic=
=tion is great, yet, I think they seem'd to be pretty much re=
=sign'd, was at the first day [Sunday] meet'g, I was concearn'd to speak
a little theirin to advise friends to keep close to the Truth and
Indeavour to feel it to approve of all that they did
in the A=noon I & my Wife took leave of our Relations & walk'd Home
28, went with my Wife to our fifth day [Thursday] meet'g
12mo [December] 1st went with my Wife to our first day [Sunday] meet'g, felt a little
refresh'd, it was held in Silence
-5, went with my Wife to our fifth day [Thursday] meet'g
-8, went with my Wife to our first day [Sunday] meet'g, felt a little refresh'd, silent
in the A-noon walk'd with Bro'r Robt to burford found Sistor
better rest tolerable well spent the Evening at Bror's comfortabley, Lodg'd their
9, the monthly meet'g felt comfortabley & I trust it was a refreshing time,
sevral friends appeard in Testimonie and two in Prayer, I was concearn'd

Page 23

to speak a little theirin, signifying the great nessciety there is
to follow the leadings of him, who was meek and low in Heart,
in the afternoon took leave of Relations & walk'd Home
12, went with my Wife to our fifth day [Thursday] meet'g (silent)
14 took a walk to sibford, found Mother & Sistor poorly, Lodg'd their
15 was at their first day [Sunday] meet'g, I was concearn'd to speak theirin,
spent the A[fter] Noon comfortabley at mothers with some friends, Lodg'd at Mo.
16, after spending a little time with Mother & sistor in a Loving manner, walk'd Home
19, went with my Wife to our fifth day [Thursday] meet'g (silent)
22 went with my Wife to our first day [Sunday] meet'g, sat as in a beclouded state of minde
26 went with my Wife to our fifth day [Thursday] meet'g (silent)
29 walk'd to Oxford to our Quarterly Meet'g, sevral strangers
their in the ministery, vis Deborah Darby, Mary Loyd, Jacob
Bell, Wm Simons, & other friends, there ware two Public meet'gs
on first day [Sunday], I think the Neighbours behaved orderly & the meet'gs ware
to good satisfaction, Deborah, I trust had a Pretty good opper=
=tunity amoungst the People, and also sevral other friends
30, the meet'g began at 10 oclock friends ware favour'd with
a pretty comfortable sitting together before the seperated to
go through the buisness, which was gone through in Love,
after meet'g walk'd Home with Bro'r Robt

1806

1mo[January] 2nd went with my Wife to our fifth day [Thursday] meet'g (silent)
-4, this morn'g we had a meet'g by the Desire of Jacob Bell who is on a
Religious Visit, it felt refreshing – in the Evening was a
Public meet'g by the Desire of the afore=said friend, which felt
Pretty satisfactory & Jacob I hope had a pretty good oppertunity to relieve his minde
5 went with my Wife to our first day [Sunday] meet'g (silent)
9, went with my Wife to our fifth day [Thursday] meet'g (silent)
12, went with my Wife to our first day [Sunday] meet'g, it felt to be a
cloudy time, silent meet'g
13, took a walk with some friends to C.[hipping] Norton to our Monthly Meet'g
it was smallish & held not very long there being but little buisness to do,

after meet'g call'd to se some friends & walk'd Home
16, went with my Wife to our fifth day [Thursday] meet'g, felt a little refresh'd

verso

1mo[January] 19th went with my Wife to our first day [Sunday] meet'g, it felt
refreshing, and I trust we ware refresh'd in our Spirits, silent
-23, went with my Wife to our fifth day [Thursday] meet'g (silent)
-26, went with my Wife to our first day [Sunday] meet'g, I was concearn'd
to speak a little theirin, felt a little refresh'd
-30, went with my Wife to our fifth day [Thursday] meet'g (silent)
2.2 went with my Wife to our first day [Sunday] meet'g (silent)
-6 went with my Wife to our fifth day [Thursday] meet'g (silent)
-9 went with my Wife to our first day [Sunday] meet'g (silent)
-10 went with my Wife to our monthly meet'g held at this place
I trust it was a refreshing meet'g sevral mouths ware open'd
to testify of the Lords love and mercy toward the People
13 was at our fifth day [Thursday] meet'g
16, went with my Wife to sibford was at the meet'g their which
was held in Silence after meet'g spent about one hour at Mo:
with Mo: & Sistors (sistor Hanh been come from her place at
Mansfiel to se them) agreeabley then took leave of 'em & return'd Home
20 went with my Wife to our fifth day [Thursday] meet'g
23 went with my Wife to our first day [Sunday] meet'g (silent meet'g)
3mo 2nd went with my Wife to our first day [Sunday] meet'g, felt a little refresh'd
-6, went to our fifth day [Thursday] meet'g (silent)
-9, went with my Wife to our first day [Sunday] meet'g (silent)
-10, walk'd to Witney to our monthly Meet'g, small meet'g it being
a very snowy & windy Morn'g, it felt a little refreshing, held
in Silence before friends proceeded upon buisness, in the A.[fter]N.[oon] return'd Home
-13, went with my Wife to our fifth day [Thursday] meet'g (silent)
-16, went with my Wife to our first day [Sunday] meet'g, it felt a
little refreshing, (silent)
-20, went with my Wife to our fifth day [Thursday] meet'g (silent)
-23, went with my Wife to our first day [Sunday] meet'g, I was concearn'd
to speak a little theirin,
-27, went with my Wife to our fifth day [Thursday] meet'g (silent)
-30, went with my Wife to our first day [Sunday] meet'g, felt a little refresh'd (silent)

Page 24

1806

4mo 6th went with my Wife to our first day [Sunday] meet'g, felt a little
refresh'd, silent, in the A.[fter]N.[oon] my Wife walk'd to Burford
-7 I walk'd to Burford to our Monthly meet'g ware favourd
with the Company of Thos Speakman from Reading, and
Sarah Lambley from Treadington, Both being on a
Religious Visit, two friends appear'd in Testimonie
the meeting of Buisness held long their being a Pretty deal
to do, after meet'g spent a little time at Bro'rs agreeabley
& went up to Thos Huntleys found young Thos poorly tho
I believe much better than what he had been – walk'd Home in the Evening
10, went with my Wife to our fifth day [Thursday] meet'g, felt poor &
weak (silent)

13, went with my Wife to our first day [Sunday] meet'g, felt spiritually
Poor (silent)
15, took a walk with my Wife and some friends to witney
to the Quarterly meet'g held their, it was pretty large
considering the weather, Sarah Lambley was their who
is on a religious visit, sevral friends appear'd in Testimonie
after which friends separated and proceded on buisness, the work I
think went on heavily – after meet'g spent a little time
with friends agreeabley and returnd Home –
17, went with my Wife to our fifth day [Thursday] meet'g
20, went with my Wife to our first day [Sunday] meet'g, under a sence of
my own Weakness, felt great need to Labour for Devine help
24, went with my Wife to our fifth day [Thursday] meet'g
26 this day Sarah Lambley paid us a visit, who is on a
Religious Visit to the meet'gs & friends families
27 went with my Wife to our first day [Sunday] meet'g ware favourd
with the Company of S, Lambley, I felt a little refresh'd,
this Evening a Public meeting was held by the desire of
Sarah Lambley the meeting was large and I trust to good
satisfaction sarah was drawn forth pretty much in Testimonie
wareby she advised the People to prepare for their latter end,

verso

4mo 28th Sarah Lambley having Express'd a concearn'd to
have a Public meet'g at Enstone I and some other
friends went there and procured a place to meet in
I and another friend went round to Inform the neighbours
the meet'g was apointed to be held in the Evening
it was pretty large, Sarah appear'd in Testimonie a pretty wile
5mo 1st went with my Wife to our fifth day [Thursday] meet'g
-4 a Public meet'g being appointed to be held at
Barton by the desire of S Lambley, took a walk
there with a relation, it was appointed to begin at 11 oclock
it was pretty large, sevral friends appeard in Tes=
=timonie, much of which was to direct the People to
turn their mindes Inward and indeavour to feel after
the devine Teacher within their own Hearts, & minde it
be obidient unto it, which if they ware it would lead them
in the way that is pleaseing to the Almighty
after meeting Din'd at T. Jarvis's with a pretty menny others
walk'd from thence Home,
-8, went with my Wife to our fifth day [Thursday] meet'g (silent)
-11, went with my Wife to our first day [Sunday] meet'g, my poor
exercised minde felt a little refresh'd, silent
13, walked to C.[hipping] Norton to our monthly meeting it felt
pretty comfortable, ware favour'd with the Company
of Samuel Rundell from [blank] , who is on a Religious
visit, he appear'd in Testimonie as did also some other
friends, after meeting call'd to see some friends & walk'd
Home with my Wife
15, went with my Wife to our fifth day [Thursday] meet'g, was
favour'd with the Company of S. Rundell & his companion
silent meeting, in the afternoon went as Guide with Saml
Rundell and his frd to Oxford, Saml being poorly Lodg'd their
16, went with Saml and his frd to Shillingford to Jos: Ashbys left them

Page 25

their, after going to see some friends and Dining at Jos: Ashbys,
took leave of Friends & Return'd Home, much tir'd not being used to
travel so long a Journey on Horseback –
18, went with my Wife to our first day [Sunday] meet'g felt a little refresh'd, silent
22, went with my Wife to our fifth felt a very poor Creature (silent)
25 went with my Wife to our first day [Sunday] meet'g, it felt a little refreshing
29, went with my Wife to our fifth day [Thursday] meet'g (silent)
6:1. went with my Wife and her two sistors (who are
come to se us) to our first day [Sunday] meet'g, (Silent)
-6, walk'd with my Sistors=in=law to Chipping Norton was at
the weekday meeting, silent meeting – there being a friend
in good sircumstances who did not attend the meeting nor none
of his family, I was concearn'd after meeting to go and
speak to him concearning it, and let him know that I thought
it was setting a bad example to others, felt peace by so doing –
after Din'r walk'd with sistors to Sibford found Mother poorly Lodg'd at Mo:
-7, spent the day at Mo: excep going to se some
friends & Relations - - Lodg'd at Mothers
-8, was at the first day [Sunday] meet'g at sibford it felt refreshing
sevral Testimonies ware born, I felt easy to sit in silence
O! how much good Instruction we are favoured with
but how little it seems to be regarded or the spirit
of Truth attended unto, unto which it Directs
in the A.[fter]Noon took leave of my Relations and walk'd Home
9, it being our Monthly meet'g was held at this place it did
not feel very lively, some friends appear'd, I also was concearn'd
to speak a little theirin, in meeting of Buisness my minde was
oppress'd on account of friends speaking so thick as to hurt the
solemnity of the meeting, I do not think in meetings of buisness friends
should labour to be weighty in their spirits, not speak in their own
wills, but as the Spirit of Truth shall Instruct them & but one at a time,
if this was to be the case, I believe it would much conduce to keep down a
rong spirit and causing the good to arise into dominion, which is I think often oppress'd

verso

1806

6mo 12th was at our fifth day [Thursday] meeting (silent)
-15, went with my Wife to our first day [Sunday] meet'g, silent
-19, went with my Wife to our fifth day [Thursday] meet'g, silent
-22, went with my Wife to our first day [Sunday] meet'g, felt a little tender'd
and refreshed, under a sence that Devine Goodness was near, (silent)
-26 went with my Wife to our fifth day [Thursday] meet'g, felt more
comforted & refresh'd than at sometimes (silent)
29 went with my Wife to our first day [Sunday] meet'g, felt a little
refresh'd, altho under exercise of minde, (silent)
in the A.[fter]N.[oon] set out towards our quarterly meet'g to be held
at Banbury reach'd dedington in the Evening ware I
had a little conversation with the convinsed friends to
satisfaction & comfort, Lodg'd with Wm East
30, spent a little time in the morning with the Convinsed friends
the Wife of one of them having been much against her Husband going
to meet'g I had an oppertunity to speak to her a little on the

subject which I hope had some good effect upon her –
walk'd from thence to Ayno, to se James Wycherley his Wife & Family
they ware kinde, in the Evening took leave of them & walk'd to
Adderbury to se some friends and from thence to Milton, was kindly
entertain'd at Thos Malls Lodgd their
7mo 1st walk'd from thence to Banbury, the Quarterly Meet'g I think was
pretty large the Meet'g for Worship felt tolerable or good comforting
meet'g (ware favour'd with the Company of Thos Cash
who is on a religious visit) the meet'g for buisness did not feel
so lively and comforting, after meet'g Din'd at E. Stones took leave
of friends & return'd Home
-3, took a walk to C.[hipping]Norton to the Funeral of Wm Atkinss son
John, who died after a short Illness, which I think was a
great affliction to his Parents & relations I understood his Afflic=
=tion was very heavy at times yet was favoured with a sence
that his sins ware or would be forgiven Him that he should Die and be happy

Page 26

it was a large meeting on the occasion menny friends
& Neighbours being present, Thos Cash who is on a Religious
visit was their, & was drawn forth in Testimonie attended
with life and Power, the Bro'r of the deceased appear'd
in Testimonie in a Perticular manner in which he mention'd
sevral of the Expressions which his Bro'r utter'd in the
time of his Illness,
pretty soon after meeting I return'd Home
6, I and my Wife ware at our first day [Sunday] meet'g
10, went to our fifth day [Thursday] meeting
13 went with my Nephew to Witney to meet'g (there was a funeral) it felt
to be a good satisfactory meet'g, some friends appear'd at the grave,
and several in the meeting House which I hope had a good effect,
after meeting went to se the Widow Putter (who about three or four
weeks agoe as she was a comming down some steps into the shop she
step'd on something which lay on one of the stairs, which caused her to
slip so as to break her Leg, by which she was confin'd to her bed &
since has been so Ill as her Life to be despair'd of, after sitting a little
time in Silence with she and her Daughter, I was concearn'd to utter a few words
in Prayer, altho she was very weak she seem'd pretty comfortable
& I trust Devine Goodness was near to support her in Affliction,
in the Afternoon walk with my Nephew to Farington was kindly
entertaind at Robt Reynolds's Lodg'd their as did also sevral more friends
14 it being our Monthly Meet'g at Faringdon, it felt to be a pretty good
refreshing meeting, sevral Neighbours came in who appear'd to be reach'd with
the power of Truth, the Buisness was gone through pretty agreeabley,
after Dinner walk'd back to Witney Lodg'd at my kinde friends Jno Hankins's
15 after breackfasting with them walk'd Home –
20. went with my Wife to our first day [Sunday] meet'g, Life did not feel much
to arise amoungst us, (silent)
24 went with my Wife to our fifth day [Thursday] meet'g spake a few
words theirin being afraid if I did not I should neglect my Duty
27 took a walk to Milton to meeting it was small I was conce=
arned to advise them not to be discouraged from attending their
meetings altho they might feel poorness of spirit at times but wait

verso

1806

Patiently upon the Lord and then I hoped they would reap if they fainted
not, after meeting spent a little time with friends agreeable, and returned Home
7mo 30th went with my Wife to our fifth day [Thursday] meet'g, felt oppress'd
8, 3, went with my Wife to our first day [Sunday] meet'g, it felt a little
refreshing spake a little theirin setting fourth the great value of
Injoying a clean Heart,
-10, went with my Wife to our first day [Sunday] meeting, it felt a little
refreshing, silent – Bro'r Mander came and fetch'd Sistor
Margarett & my Wife over to burford
11, set out with Bro'r Sessions to Burford reach'd their in good time,
the Monthly Meet'g felt pretty comfortable, was favour'd with the
company of Ann Low who is on a religious visit, she appear'd in
Testimonie which felt Instructing and Edifying, after Dining at
Bro'r Manders went to se some friends and walk'd Home
17, went with my Wife to our first day [Sunday] meet'g it felt pretty com=
=fortable ware favour'd with the company of Ann Low, she ap=
=pear'd in Testimonie she signify'd it was very necessary for us to
keep to our Devine Leader and obey his commands, which if we did
should be Inabled to stand before our Enemies,
21, went with my Wife to our fifth day [Thursday] meet'g (silent)
24 went with my Wife to our first day [Sunday] meet'g, I was concearn'd to
advise friends to be very carefull not to offend the Lord,
28 went with my Wife to our fifth day [Thursday] meeting
-31, went with my Wife to our first day [Sunday] meeting, I was concearn'd to speak
a little theirin respecting the necessiety of being constantly upon our
watch, even to watch unto Prayer
9[September]=4 I & my Wife went to our fifth day [Thursday] meet'g felt a little refresh'd
Jno Hiden came from Sibford to fetch my Wife to se her Mother
she being very Ill, they set of about 4 oclock
-7 I went to our first day [Sunday] meet'g, felt a little refresh'd (silent)
-8, took a walk to our Monthly Meeting held at C.[hipping]Norton it was smallish

Page 27

I was concearn'd to speak a little theirin as was also another
friend, the meeting of Buisness did not feel very comfortable,
friends being hasty in speaking so as to Interupt one another
which removes the solemnity of a meeting, after return'd Home
9mo 11th I went to our fifth day [Thursday] meet'g (silent)
14 it being first day [Sunday], set out for our Q. Meet'g to be holden at
Reading, walk'd to Jno Jacksons's Oxford & sat with them, they
being used to sit together on first days [Sunday] & hold a little meet'g,
after dining with them walk'd to Shillingford Lodg'd at J Ashbys
15, walk'd from thence to Reading, found Relations & friends pretty
well went to se most of our Relations whose company was
agreeable & Comforting, Lodg'd at Cous'n Jno Tutteys,
16 the Q Meet'g began at ten which was not very large, sevral
appear'd I also was concearn'd to appear theirin, to advise the
People not to slight their day of Visitation
the meet'g of buisness felt pretty comfortable, after meet'g
Din'd at Jno Tutteys the Elder, took affectionate farewell of

Relations, & rode with Cous'n Jos: Ashby in his Carriage to
Wallingford, from thence walk'd with a fr'd to shillingford. Lodg'd at J Wests
=17, pretty early went down to Jno Sargoods to Breackfast,
who ware very kinde, walk'd from thence with a friend
untill we came to ware the road parted, he taking that which
led for his Home, & I that which led for mine Home, ware I
arrive about five in the Evening, being favour'd to feel a
degree of Peace, & Comfort, which bows my minde in Humble thankfullness
-18, went with my Wife to our fifth day [Thursday] meeting, silent, felt a little refresh'd
-21, went with my Wife to our first day [Sunday] meet'g, felt refresh'd, (silent)
28, went with my Wife to our first day [Sunday] meet'g it felt refreshing
altho mostly held in Silence & I think when our mindes
are favour'd to be brought into solid Silence, we are also favour'd
to know our Spiritual strength to be renewed
10mo 2.n went with my Wife to our fifth day [Thursday] meet'g, it felt a little refreshing,
took a walk to sibford found my Motherinlaw very weak & poorly
yet through mercy pretty chearfull Lodgd at Mothers

verso

1806

10mo 5th was at the first day [Sunday] meet'g, it was held in Silence,
spent the A.[fter]Noon mostly at mothers – Lodgd their
6, took leave of Mother & Sistor and walk'd Home
10, went with my Wife to our fifth day [Thursday] meeting, silent
12, went with my Wife to our first day [Sunday] meet'g, silent, yet it
felt pretty comfortable – this morn'g I went to se a Neighbour
who seems to be in a Decline, he has been a man that
has given way much to drinking bad Company and such
Like, I advised him to Indeavour to repent, amend his Life
& seek the Lord Earnestly for Mercy, he appear'd to take
my visit kind,
-13, I & my Wife went to our Mo: Meet'g held here (viz Charlbury) I was
concearn'd to speak theirin, as I had nothing in view but a desire to
to be found in the discharge of my duty, I spake in the fear
of the Lord, as his Power I trust Instructed & Inabled me, felt a
degree of Comfort by so doing, another friend also appeard –
the Buisness was gone through pretty agreeabley –
16 I went to our fifth day [Thursday] meet'g, silent
19 walk'd to Burford, found Bro'r weak & poorly, was at
the first day [Sunday] meeting at which my spirit was refresh'd,
feeling Devine Goodness to the tendering & refreshing
the Living amoungst us, in the after=noon walk'd Home with my Wife
23, went to our fifth day [Thursday] meet'g it felt refreshing, silent
26, went with my Wife to our first day [Sunday] meet'g (silent)
29, went to witney was at their fourth day [Wednesday] meet'g
30, went with my Wife to our fifth day [Thursday] meet'g (silent)
11, 2, went with my Wife to our first day [Sunday] meet'g, it felt refreshing (silent)
-6, went with my Wife to our fifth day [Thursday] meet'g (silent)
-9, went with my Wife to our first day [Sunday] meet'g silent
-10, I & my Wife went to Witney to our M. Meet'g, it felt a little refreshing

a little matter arose in my minde with some degree of weight
which I thought might be right for me to speak, but through
fear I put it off till it was to late, felt a little uneasy afterwards,
the buisness was gone through pretty agreeabley

Page 28

after meeting feeling a little concearn to speak to a
Relation that is underdealing for misconduct, I went
to his house & spoke to him & his Wife what what ap=
=peard to be my duty, felt satisfaction by so doing –
call'd to se some more friend & returnd Home in Evening
-13, went with my Wife to our fifth day [Thursday] meet'g, it felt a little refreshing
-16, went with my Wife to our first day [Sunday] meet'g (silent)
-20, went with my Wife to our fifth day [Thursday] meet'g
-23 went with my Wife to our first day [Sunday] meet'g, felt a little
refresh'd, sevral strangers ware there, I was concearnd to speak
a little theirin, to advise friends to retire to, and minde
the Teaching of the spirit of Truth in their own Hearts,
-27, went with my Wife to our fifth day [Thursday] meet'g silent
-30, went with my Wife to our first day [Sunday] meet'g, it felt
to be a weight good meeting, altho held in Silence
12=4, went with my Wife to our fifth day [Thursday] meet'g
-7 went with my Wife to our first day [Sunday] meet'g one friend
appear'd, felt a little refresh'd – 11th went to our fifth day [Thursday] meet'g
-14, went with my Wife to our first day [Sunday] meet'g it felt a little
refreshing, I feel a little uneasy for not speaking a little
matter which arose in my minde,
-18, went with my Wife to our fifth day [Thursday] meet'g, felt refresh'd, altho silent
-21, went with my Wife to our first day [Sunday] meet'g,
it felt refreshing, held in Silence,
-25, went with my Wife to our fifth day [Thursday] meet'g, it felt refreshing silent
-31, went with my Wife to our weekday meeting it was held in Silence

1807

1[January]=4 went with my Wife to our first day [Sunday] meet'g, I believe
it right for me to speak a little theirin, concearning
worship in which state the Devine Teacher is known,
-8, went to our fifth day [Thursday] meet'g – 10th walked to Sibford
found Mother very weak, sistor tolerable well Lodg'd at Mothers
-11 was at the first day [Sunday] meeting at Sibford it felt pretty comfortable

verso

1807

I was concearn'd to speak theirin, after meet'g was pretty
much with Mother & sistor as my visit seemd to be mostly to them,
12, took leave of sistor having bid mother farewell the night be=
=fore and walk'd to our Monthly meet'g at C.[hipping]Norton it
(I think) was a low time amoungst us, yet I trust there ware
some exercised mindes present and my spirit felt near to them
I was concearn'd to speak by way of Testimonie to Incourage
friends to faithfullness it being the only way to be favour'd
with the Injoyment of True Peace

after meeting call'd to se some friends call'd to se Wm Atkins's
whose Servant (this day) was remov'd by Death I understood a young
woman of about 19 years of age who was so well but 2
days before as to go about her Buisness, her Death might
be as a warning to others, In time of Health through
Devine assistance indeavour to be prepared for Death,
walk'd Home, with some Relations in the Evening
15, went with my Wife to our fifth day [Thursday] meet'g
18, went with my Wife to our first day [Sunday] meet'g, I was con=
=cearn'd to advise friends not to lean to their own Understandings
but in all their ways to aknowledge the Lord, and he
would direct their Paths,
-22, went with my Wife to our fifth day [Thursday] meet'g (silent)
-25 took a walk to Witney was at the morning and After=
noon meetings, they felt pretty comfortable altho small,
sevral friends appear'd in Testimonie I also appeard
a little in the morning meeting, which was much to
the young friends advising them to chuse to live in
the fear of the Lord and to love Devine Instructions
which if they did I believed the Lord would preserve
them in the time of Tryal – returned Home in the Evening
29 went to our fifth day [Thursday] meet'g
2mo 1st I went to our first day [Sunday] meeting it felt refreshing,

Page 29

2mo 5th went with my Wife to our fifth day [Thursday] meet'g, I felt
a little refreshed in Sitting in Silence, altho pretty
much exercised in minde,
-8, went with my Wife to our first day [Sunday] meet'g,
it felt a little refreshing, to my Exercised minde (silent)
-9 went with my Wife to our monthly meet'g held at this
place, (Charlbury) after sitting a pretty wile in Silence
I was concearn'd to speak theirin as was also another
friend, the meeting of Buisness felt exerciseing & my minde was oppress'd
11, took a walk to Witney was at fourth day [Wednesday] meet'g
12, went with my Wife to our fifth day [Thursday] meet'g it felt
refreshing, I was concearn'd to speak a little theirin,
as was also another friend, setting fourth the mercies
and goodness of the Lord unto his People,
14 went to Burford with Sistor M Sessions found Bro'r
Henry quite Ill, appears in a Decline and not likely
to live very long, sistor was also poorly, so that it is
an Exerciseing time with them, we ware led to simpathise
with them, and to Labour together for Devine Mercy, Lodg'd at Bro'rs
15, was at their first day [Sunday] meet'g it was held in Silence,
after meeting Sistor M & I spent a little time at Bro'r
Manders with them, in a solid weighty manner, took
our Affectionate leave of them and return'd Home,
22 went with my Wife to our first day [Sunday] meet'g, it felt re=
=freshing, I was concearn'd to advise friends to Labour
after a state of Perfection
26, went with my Wife to our fifth day [Thursday] meet'g (silent)
3[March]=1, went with my Wife to our first day [Sunday] meet'g, it felt a little
refreshing, I was concearnd to speak theirin

verso

1807

3mo 5th went with my Wife to our fifth day [Thursday] meet'g (silent)
-8, went with my Wife to our first day [Sunday] meet'g, it felt
to be a low time with us (silent)
-12 went with my Wife to our fifth day [Thursday] meet'g (silent)
-15, went with my Wife to our first day [Sunday] meet'g (silent)
-19, went with my Wife to our fifth day [Thursday] meet'g (silent)
-21, took a walk to Sibford, found Mo: & Sistor poorly Lodg'd at Mo:
-22 went to Brails to Meet'g, it is a small meet'g, yet it felt tolerable
comfortable, I was concearn'd to speak theirin, after meet'g Din'd at
cousin Wm Gilletts, spent a few hours with them & some other Frds
comfortabley, in the Evening returnd to Sibford Lodg'd at Mo:
-23 after spending a little time agreeabley at Mo: took leave of
Mo: & Sistor & return'd Home,
26, I went to our weekday meet'g (silent)
-29, went with my Wife to our first day [Sunday] meet'g, it felt
refreshing, I was concearn'd to speak a little theirin,
to advise friends to Labour after the Injoyment of true Peace
4-2, went with my Wife to our fifth day [Thursday] meet'g I felt great
need for me to walk humbley and circumspectly in the fear
of the Lord,
-5 went with my Wife to our first day [Sunday] meet'g, I was concearn'd
to appear theirin, it was our Preparative meet'g, the buisness
was gone through in Love – in the A.[fter]Noon walk'd with Bro'r
R to Burford found Bror H a little better altho very weak
& Poorly, spent the Evening at Bro'rs in a solid comfortable manner lodg'd their
-6, the monthly meet'g began at 10 oclock it was pretty large
& I trust a pretty good refreshing meet'g, ware favoured with
the Company of Jno Abbot & Wife (friends in the Ministry)
sevral friends Appeard in Testimonie & one friend in Prayer,
after meet'g spent a little time at Bro'r H in a comfortable manner
In the Evening return'd Home, with some friends,
-9, went with my Wife to our fifth day [Thursday] meet'g (silent)

Page 30

4[April]=12 went with my Wife to our first day [Sunday] meet'g (silent)
14, walk'd to our quarterly held at Witney it felt pretty comfortable,
sevral friends appear'd in Testimonie & one in Prayer –
after meeting spent a little time with friends agreeabley, also
went to see some Relations whose conduct hath not been agreeable
to our Proffession, I was favour'd to give them some Advise –
afterward return'd Home with my Wife –
-16, went with my Wife to our fifth day [Thursday] meet'g
-19, went with my Wife to our first day [Sunday] meet'g
-23, I went to our fifth day [Thursday] meet'g, my Wife being poorly, staid at Home,
-26, went with my Wife to our first day [Sunday] meet'g (silent)
its a time of Affliction, a pretty menny friends are poorly,
which appears to humble the minds of Friends, O that
they may be brought down into a state of deep humility,
brokenness & contritedness of Hart before the Lord, that they
may be Inabled to offer an offering unto the Lord that is
pleasing and Acceptable in His sight,

-30 went with my Wife to our fifth day [Thursday] meet'g, at meet'g ware
favour'd with the company of Susanna Horn, who is on
a religious visit, she appear'd pretty much in Testimonie
by which Incourage=ment & comfort was administered to the
upright Hearted that go mourning on their way, all ware
advised to be found Improveing their Talent or Talents, that
they might have the Answer of well=done –
5,3 went with my Wife to our first day [Sunday] meet'g, it felt a little
refreshing, (silent)
-7 went with my Wife to our fifth day [Thursday] meet'g I felt to be a poor
Creature
-10, went with my Wife to our first day [Sunday] meet'g silent still much exer=
=cised in my minde, and my Earnest breathing of Spirit is unto the
Almighty that He will be pleased to forgive me mine Offences,

verso

1807

5mo 11 I & my Wife went to our Monthly Meet'g held at C[hipping] Norton
it felt to be a favour'd meeting & in some degree a watering
time, a time of consolation to them that go mourning on their way,
friends ware much advised to be faithfull unto Devine
requireings I also was concearn'd to appear theirin –
altho I have appear'd in Meetings for a number of years at
times, it is now quite Exerciseing to me to appear theirin, under
a sence of my own weakness, and least I should speak in
my own Zeal without feeling a right Necessiety, so bring
a Cloud or be a burden to the meeting, and sorrow to my
own minde – and when the concearn in right their is great
need of Humility and watchfullness in speaking to keep to
the pure Guide, to speak what it points out to us to relieve
our mindes and no more – return'd Home pretty soon
after Dinner
-14 went with my Wife to our fifth day [Thursday] meet'g, felt pretty much Exercised
-17, went with my Wife to our first day [Sunday] meet'g, felt a little
refresh'd, I was concearn'd to speak a little, to Incourage friends to faithfullness,
-21, went with my Wife to our fifth day [Thursday] meet'g, it felt a little refreshing
-24, went with my Wife to our first day [Sunday] meet'g, it felt refreshing (silent)
-28, went with my Wife to our fifth day [Thursday] meeting, felt a poor Creature Indeed
-31, went with my Wife to our first day [Sunday] meet'g (silent)
6-3, was at the Marriage of Jos: Hankins of Witney to Hanh Mid=
=winter which was at friends meeting House at adderbury,
it felt to be a satisfactory meeting sevral friends
appear'd in Testimonie, which was much to young friends,
adviseing them to live in the fear of the Lord and sarve
him, that they might be qualified to supply the places of
the Elders, which ware removed from Works to Rewards,
one friend appeard in Prayer, after meeting friends went
to Bloxam to Din'r – in the Evening the Married coupple
went to Witney

Page 31

1807

I with my Nephew return'd Home – as did also the Relations and friends
4, was at our fifth day [Thursday] meet'g
7 went with my Wife to our first day [Sunday] meet'g (silent)
8 I & my Wife went to our monthly meet'g held at this place viz Charlbury
it felt comforting & I trust the Love and Mercy of the Lord was extended
towards us, to the refreshing & strengthening menny, some friends appear'd
in Testimonie, the buisness was gone through in Love, -
-9, I went to Sibford to the Marriage of William Corks to Hanh
Gilks, my Wives Sistor I trust it was a Satisfactory Meet'g
some friends appear'd in Testimonie, after meet'g the married Coupple
with menny others Din'd at Mothers ware things was conducted orderly
after Tea friends seperated & went for their Homes –
10, I & my Wife return'd Home, -
11, I went with my Wife to our fifth day [Thursday] meet'g, felt a little refresh'd
14, went with my Wife to our first day [Sunday] meet'g, much exer=
=cised in my minde under a sence of my own weakness's
& Inability to do my duty unto the Lord without his help &
assistance, for which I am much concearn'd to Labour Diligently,
18 this day Bro'r & Sistor session's Child (about 9nths old) was
Inter'd who died a few days ago, it being our week day meet'g
went to meeting with the Corps at eleven meeting time, my minde
was much exercised, time appear'd to be precious I was con=
=cearn'd to speak theirin, to advise the Children to minde the
teachings of the Devine Power, which reproves for Sin,
& teaches to do good, & to advise the Parents also to be found
in the discharge of their Duty to their Children, & to live in
the fear of the Lord that they might know his Power to preserve them from
sin, I trust it was a time in which Devine Mercy was Extended
21, went with my Wife to our first day [Sunday] meet'g ware favour'd with
the Company of Sushanna Horn (her sistor accompany's Martha
accompanies her) it felt to be a favour'd meet'g susanna was drawn
fourth pretty much in Testimonie being Inabled to speak to several states,

verso

I was concearn'd to speak a little theirin to set forth the Love &
goodness of God towards the People universally who desireth not the Death
of one Sinner but would rather that all should come to the knowledge
of the Truth and be saved –
-25, I went to our fifth day [Thursday] meet'g (silent)
-28, went with my Wife to our first day [Sunday] meetg I trust it was
a refreshing meeting in which friends mindes ware turn'd
to feel after the Devine Teacher within themselves also
ware favour'd to feel its Teachings, I was concearn'd to
advise the youth to chuse the Lord for their Portion &
to give up unto his call be concearn'd to Labour faithfully
be willing and obidient & then I trust they would eat the good of the Land
-29, walk'd with Bro'r to Enstone to se Aunt Jones who had
been quite Ill, found her a little better, walk'd from thence to
Bloxam, call'd to se cousin Midwinter who has been afflicted with

a Stroke of the Palsy, found she so helpless as not to be able to
get about much, stopt a little being led to simpathise with the Afflicted,
walk'd from thence to Milton Lodg'd at T Malls –
30, walk to Edwd Stones (Banbury) to Breackfast, the Quarterly=
=meet'g began at 10, which was large & felt pretty comfortable,
Susanna Horn was there & other friends in the Ministery sevral
Testimonies ware born, Din'd at E Stones in the Evening walk'd to Sibford,
7[July]=1, took leave of Mother who was very weak and return'd Home –
-2, went with my Wife to our fifth day [Thursday] meet'g (silent)
-5, went with my Wife to our first day [Sunday] meet'g (silent)
-9, went with my Wife to our fifth day [Thursday] meet'g (silent)
-12, walk'd with my Wife & Sistor to Witney to their first day [Sunday]
meet'g, some friends appear'd theirin, I was Silent, I return'd
Home in the Evening my Wife & Sistor stop'd intending to go
to our Monthly meeting to be held at Faringdon to morrow
-16 I my Wife went to our fifth day [Thursday] meet'g (silent)
-19, went with my Wife to our first day [Sunday] meet'g, it feels an Exer=

Page 32

ciseing time, a time of morning rather than rejoiceing (silent)
having felt a Concearn to go and pay a visit to a Person
[blank] I Indeavoured to visit her but could not agreeabley
obtain it, therefore I wrote the feelings of my Minde & sent it signifying
my desire was that she would be concearn'd to wait upon
the Lord and seek unto him for the Assistance of His
Devine Power that she might be favour'd to know her
own state, & Examine herself thereby that she might
se how things stood between god and her nevver dying
soul, & might be Inabled to use all Diligence to make her Calling & Election
sure & also signified she should Indeavour to be of a
Charitable mercifull & forgiveing Disposition that
She might be favour'd to obtain Mercy and forgiveness
of the Lord
-23, went with my Wife to our fifth day [Thursday] meet'g (silent)
-26, went with my Wife to our first day [Sunday] meet'g, it felt a
little refreshing, the yearly Meeting Epistle was read, it
felt comforting, & Incourageing to friends to hold on their way,
-30, went with my Wife to our fifth day [Thursday] meet'g (silent)
8[August]=2, went with my Wife to our first day [Sunday] meet'g it felt a little
refreshing, I was concearned to speak a little theirin –
-6, sent a letter to some relations (who have went on in a
Disreputeable manner) to put them in minde of their rong
doings, & to desire them to humble themselves before the
Lord, wait upon him for the help and assistance of his
Power & Spirit, and Indeavour to live in Obidience thereunto
that they might be favour to Obtain Mercy
I & my Wife went to our fifth day [Thursday] meet'g, (Silent)
-9 went with my Wife to our first day [Sunday] meet'g, it is an Exerciseing
time to my minde, (silent) in the A.[fter]N.[oon] walk'd to Burford found Bro'r H
a little better

verso

1807

8mo 10th was at our Monthly meeting held at Burford, it felt
to be an exerciseing time, two friend appear'd in Prayer,
after meet'g spent a little time with some friends at Bro'rs agreeabley
in the Evening walk'd Home with Bro'r Robt
-16 went with my Wife to our first day [Sunday] meet'g, it felt a little refreshing (silent)
-20 went with my Wife to our fifth day [Thursday] meet'g
-23 went with my Wife to our first day [Sunday] meet'g, a pretty full
meeting & it felt comforting & refreshing, I was concearn'd
to speak a little theirin
-26, took a walk to witney was at their weekday meet'g, silent
-27, went with my Wife to our fifth day [Thursday] meet'g (silent)
-30, went with my Wife to our first day [Sunday] meet'g (silent)
9-3 I went to our fifth day [Thursday] meet'g (my Wife being gone to Sibford)
-6 I went to our first day [Sunday] meet'g (silent)
-8, took a walk to our Monthly Meeting held at C[hipping]Norton
it felt to be a time of Poverty in which the want
of Devine Refreshment was known, the meeting of
Buisness felt Exerciseing & rather painfull, after meet'g
went with my Wife to se some friends, in the Even'g return'd Home
-10 went with my Wife to our fifth day [Thursday] meet'g, it felt a little
refreshing, I was concearn'd to advise friends to strive to
walk in that way which leadeth unto Life,
-12, set out for our Quarterly Meet'g to be held at Reading, walk'd to
Oxford, stop'd a little time at Jno Jacksons's walk from thence to Shilling=
Lodg'd at Joseph Ashbys who is a good open hearted friend,
-13 stop'd friends meeting it was small sevral friends being out,
I was concearn'd to speak theirin, Din'd at Wm Sanders's, in the A[fter]Noon
walk'd to Reading, found friends there pretty well, Lodg'd at Cous'n Jno Tutteys
-14 was at a meeting which was held on account of a Committy who attend'd it,
appointed by the Quarterly Meeting, after meet'g went to se some Relations
and friends who ware Loving and free, Lodg'd at J Tuteys

Page 33

9[September]=15th this morning the Quarterly Meet'g began at 10 oclock it was
not very large but I think pretty comfortable some friend
appear'd in Testimonie – pretty soon after Dining at
Cousin Tutteys set out on foot with two friends for Shillingford
reach'd their about nine at Night, Lodg'd at Jos: Ashbys
=16 walk'd Home was favour'd with a pretty comfortable Journey & visit
James Howarth was at the Quarterly Meet'g who is on a Religious visit
=17 went with my Wife to our fifth day [Thursday] meet'g (silent)
=20 went with my Wife to our first day [Sunday] meet'g it felt
refreshing, it was held in Silence,
=24 went with my Wife to our fifth day [Thursday] meet'g, it felt a little refreshing
-27 went with my Wife to our first day [Sunday] meet'g, it felt a
little refreshing
10[October]=1, went with my Wife to our fifth day [Thursday] meet'g
-4 went with my Wife to our first day [Sunday] meet'g, it felt
a little refreshing, I was favour'd with a sence of
my own weakness's and slippings and a desire was
raised in my minde, that I might be brought nearer unto the

Lord & through a more watchfull & diligent attention
unto the pure Devine Principal of Light & Life in my
soul come to know a more perfect & Peaceful state,
and the Breathings of my Spirit unto the Lord is that
that this may be my happy Experience, -
-5th went to our Monthly Meet'g held at Charlbury, I felt a little
refresh'd, altho the pure Life seemd to be oppress'd by a to forward buisy Spirit,
-7, took a walk to Witney, was at friends fourth
day meet'g it felt a little refreshing,
-8, went with my Wife to our fifth day [Thursday] meet'g
-11, went with my Wife to our first day [Sunday] meeting, it felt a little
refreshing to a poor unworthy creature, - silent meet'g

verso

1807

10mo=15th our meet'g House being a Repairing, we held our meet'g
at a friends house, it felt refreshing - -
-18 met at our meet'g house in Silent waiting upon the
Lord, my minde was pretty much exercised under a
sence of my own weakness's and my cries ware unto the
Lord that he would be pleased to make clean my Heart,
it felt refreshing to my Exercised minde, silent
22, went with my Wife to our fifth day [Thursday] meet'g (Silent)
25, went with my Wife to our first day [Sunday] meet'g, it felt a little refreshing, (silent)
29, went with my Wife to our fifth day [Thursday] meet'g, (silent)
1[November]=1 went with my Wife to our first day [Sunday] meet'g, (silent)
-5, went with my Wife to our fifth day [Thursday] meet'g, silent
-8, went with my Wife to our first day [Sunday] meet'g, it felt
refreshing, silent, in the A.[fter]Noon my Wife walked
with Sistor Margt to Witney in order to be at our Monthly meeting
-9 I walk with some friends to Witney, the monthly meet'g
was not very large yet it felt pretty comfortable & as a
renewed visitation of Devine Mercy unto some, sevral friends
appeard in Testimonie, friends ware advise to Indeavour
through Devine Assistance to be prepared for Death
there seems to be a want of more true Life and Power
in our meetings of Buisness, which goes on heavily,
walk'd Home with my Wife sistor & sevral others in the Evening
12, went with my Wife to our fifth day [Thursday] meet'g, silent
15, went with my Wife to our first day [Sunday] meet'g, silent
it felt a little refreshing to my Exercised minde,
19, went with my Wife to our fifth day [Thursday] meet'g, silent
22, went with my Wife to our first day [Sunday] meet'g, (silent)
26, went with my Wife to our fifth day [Thursday] meeting, silent
29, went with my Wife to our first day [Sunday] meet'g, it felt re=
=freshing, one friend appear'd in Testimonie which felt Edifying,

Page 34

1807

12mo [December],3rd went with my Wife to our fifth day [Thursday] meet'g, it felt
a little refreshing, altho held in Silence,
-6 went with my Wife to our first day [Sunday] meetg, it felt comforting

-10 went with my Wife to our fifth day [Thursday] meet'g
-12 went with my Wife to Sibford to se her Mother who
has been very Ill found her a little better, tho very
weak, I return'd Home at Night much tir'd
-13 was at our first day [Sunday] meeting, silent
-14 walk'd with my Nephew to our Monthly Meet'g at
Burford the meeting for worship felt pretty comfortable,
sevral friends appeard theirin, one also in Prayer,
after meet'g Din'd at Bro'rs spent a little time with
them & some friends in a loving agreeable manner,
also call'd to se a friend who was poorly, reach'd Home
in the Evening
17, went to our fifth day [Thursday] meet'g it felt refreshing,
20 I went to our first day [Sunday] meet'g, it felt refreshing,
some friends appear'd, I felt easy to sit in Silence
24, went with my Wife to our fifth day [Thursday] meet'g,
one friend appear'd – it felt refreshing
27 went with my Wife to our first day [Sunday] meet'g, I trust
it was a good meet'g, altho held in Silence –
31, went with my Wife to our fifth day [Thursday] meeting, it
felt refreshing, I was concearn'd to advise friends
to Indeavour above all things to do the will of the
Lord, it being the way to Injoy true peace of minde,

verso

1808

1mo[January] 3rd went on foot to Sibford found Mother in a
very weak state, was at the first day [Sunday] meeting
it felt refreshing, I trust devine goodness was
felt to be near, & ready to do menny good & Inable them
to forsake their evel ways & to turn unto the Lord repent
& live, if the would accept of Devine Mercy,
Hear and Obey the Instructions of the Spirit of the
Lord & thy soul shall live - - after meeting
spent a little time at Mothers agreeabley Lodg'd their
-4 walked with some friends to the monthly meet'g held
at Southnewington, which was not very large yet felt
pretty comfortable, after meeting return'd to Sibford
-5, took leave of Mo: & Sistor and walk to C[hipping]Norton, being
poorly & it raining stop their all night, on the morrow reach Home
7, was at our fifth day [Thursday] meet'g - -
10, set of early for our Quarterly Meetg to be held at Oxford,
was at the Meeting on first day [Sunday] which began at eleven
I trust Devine Goodness was please to be near & to Inable
his Sarvents to speak to the Instructing of the People to minde the
Devine Teacher with in them, that they might be Inabled to forsake
their evel ways & how they might know the true Teacher
& be brought out of a state of Disobidience into a state of
axceptance & favour'd with God, after meeting spent
the afternoon mostly with friends –
11, the Quarterly meeting began at ten, the meet'g for Worship
felt pretty comfortable, sevral friends appeard in testimonie,
the meeting of Buisness did not feel so comfortable, it was

Page 35

---

agreed to drop the meet'g for Worship on first day [Sunday] and to hold the

Quarterly Meetg on third day [Tuesday] for the future,
after meeting I walk'd Home, ware I was favour'd to arive safe
14, went with my Wife to our fifth day [Thursday] meet'g, silent
17, went with my Wife to our first day [Sunday] meet'g, it felt refreshing
18, walk'd with my Wife to C.[hipping]Norton, to our monthly Meet=
=ing, it was small yet I trust Devine Goodness
was pleas'd in mercy to own us, I was concearn'd to
speak a little theirin, - the buisness was gone
through pretty agreeabley, after meeting call'd to se
some friends & return'd Home,
21, went with my Wife to our fifth day [Thursday] meet'g,
24 went with my Wife to our fifth day meet'g, felt refreshing
28 went with my Wife to our fifth day [Thursday] meet'g, one
friend appear'd, the meeting felt comforting and refreshing
31, went with my Wife to our first day [Sunday] meeting, it felt
refreshing, I was concearn'd to speak theirin signifying
it would be well pleasing unto the Lord, for friends
to be Zealous in Labouring to the Honnour of the
Lord, & for the spreading of the Everlasting Truth
2[February]=4 went with my Wife to our fifth day [Thursday] meeting it felt refreshing
-7 felt my strength renewed in sitting in Silence at
meeting, altho I though we sat as under a Cloud
8, went with my Wife to our Monthly Meet'g held at
this place (Charlbury) my minde was pretty much
Exercised, it was my desire to Indeavour to be faithfull
in the discharge of my duty, & as I Indeavoured to Labour
theirin according to what I believed was required of me, I felt a degree of satisfaction

verso

1808

2mo[February] 11th went with my Wife to our fifth day [Thursday] meet'g,
-12 a very cold winde with frost, I was out in the
morning a little before breackfast the cold affected
me very much, I had a kinde of a fainting fitt –
but after takeing a little something I was favoured
to recover, it was rather alarming to me and put
me in minde of the unceartainty of Life, also of
the necessiety their is for us to Indeavour to be
always Prepared for Death, Happy for them
who do always Indeavour to live in obidience to
the Instructions & requireings of the Truth, and
to be continualy upon their watch, as blessed are
those servants whom the Lord when he commeth
shall finde watching, - -
-14 went with my Wife to our first day [Sunday] meet'g, silent
-18, went to our fifth day [Thursday] meeting my minde low &
much exercised,
-21, went with my Wife to our first day [Sunday] meet'g (silent)
yet it felt refreshing
-25, went with my Wife to our fifth day [Thursday] meet'g, much
exercised in minde,
-28, went with my Wife to our first day [Sunday] meet'g (silent)
3-3, went to our fifth day [Thursday] meet'g, felt poor & Exercised (silent)
-5, went on foot to Sibford to se Mother found she
very poorly on the morrow was at their first day [Sunday]
meeting, it felt to be a good meeting, spent most of
the A.[fter]Noon at Mothers in a weighty manner sympathising

Page 36

1808

with them in their affliction, in the evening walk'd
to milton, spent the rest of the Evening at T. Malls
in a free agreeable manner Lodg'd their,
3[March]=7 was at the monthly meeting at adderbury, my minde
was much exercised theirin, I Indeavoured to relieve my
minde by speaking a little which I believed to be my
duty to speak, yet came away oppress'd, return'd
to milton to Din'r afterwards return'd Home, -
10, went with my Wife to our fifth day [Thursday] meet'g - -
13, went with my Wife to our first day [Sunday] meetg,
it felt comforting & refreshing, the visitation of
Devine Love felt to be a fresh extended, some
friends appear'd setting fourth the Love & goodness
of the Lord unto them that fear Him - -
=14 took a walk to our monthly meet'g held at Witney,
it felt to be a dull meeting one friend appear'd
in Testimonie, Din'd at Hh Rutters in the Evening returnd Home
=17, I went to our fifth day [Thursday] meet'g (silent)
=20, I went to our first day [Sunday] meet'g (my Wife being
gone to Sibford) one friend appear'd, my minde
was pretty much oppress'd, yet the meet'g felt refreshing
24, went with my Wife to our fifth day [Thursday] meeting
27, went with my Wife to our first day [Sunday] meet'g my minde
felt a little tender & I hope in some degree was con=
=trited and humbled before the Lord, 31st was at our fifth day [Thursday] meet'g
4[April]=3 went with my Wife to our first day [Sunday] meet'g, it felt re=
freshing to much Exercised minde (sat in Silence),

verso

1808

4mo[April]=4th was at our Monthly Meting held at Burford, it
felt pretty comfortable as a renewal of Devine
visitation unto some, sevral Mouths ware opened
in Testimonie, Prayer also was put up unto the
Lord for his mercies, - Din'd at Bro'rs, who continues poorly
in the Evening return'd Home, - -
-5 went on foot to Sibford found Mother very weak &
poorly – was at the Burial of Thos French, a pretty large
meeting was held on the occasion, some friends appear'd in
Testimonie, the People ware put in minde of the solemnity of
Death and of the necessiety there was through Devine assistance
to know a Preparation for Death, spent most of the
afternoon at mothers agreeabley Lodg'd their, - -
-6, was at the Wedding of Cousin Wm Gibbs, a meeting was
held on the occasion, it was pretty large and I trust the
Power of the Lord was felt amoungst us to the tendering
menny mindes, (especially the youth) sevral friends appear'd in Testimonie
-7 rose early after breckfast took leave of Mother & Sistor& returnd Home
-10, was at our first day [Sunday] meeting, it felt Exerciseing, yet a little refreshing
-12 went with my Wife to Witney to our quarterly Meet'g
one Stranger their (in the ministery) who is on a religious visit
viz Jno Kensey of London, who appear'd in Testimonie &
some other friends, it felt to be a good refreshing meeting,

after meeting din'd with menny friends at Jno Hankins's in the
Evening we return'd Home, - -
=14 was at our fifth day [Thursday] meeting, ware favour'd with the Company
of Jno Kensey he was drawn fourth in Testimonie I trust to the
relief of his own minde & to the Instruction Eddifycation and
Instruction of friends after meetg he call'd to se us – was favour'd

Page 37

with a few words of Instruction to us, signifying it was good
for us to be content in our alotment & to be fed with that
food which the Lord was Please to afford us, without coveting
great things, it was not the lot of all to be rich – riches
had done great hurt amoungst us, - he went in the A,[fter]noon to C[hipping] Norton
4[April]=17 went with my Wife to our first day [Sunday] meetg my minde was made
tender theirin and refresh'd (silent)
-21 went with my Wife to our fifth day [Thursday] meet'g (silent)
-24 went with my Wife to our first day [Sunday] meeting, it
felt a little refreshing and I sincearly desire
I may through Devine Assistance be preserved from all
Evel, that it may not grieve me, - 28th was at our fifth day [Thursday] meet'g
5[May]=1, went with my Wife to our first day [Sunday] meet'g, it
felt to be a refreshing meet'g, O that friends
may Labour to keep humble and lowly, under a
sence of the Lords great Love and mercy & their
own unworthyness, 5th was at our fifth day [Thursday] meetg
-8 went with my Wife to our first day [Sunday] meet'g, it
felt to be a good refreshing meet'g, (nearly Silent)
-9 walk'd with my Wife & some friends to C.[hipping]Norton to our
monthly meet'g, felt easy to sit in Silence, - after
meet'g went to visit some friends in affliction, the ap=
=pear'd to take my visit kindly, through Devine Assistance
I trust I was Inabled to speak to their Comfort & Edifycation
after=ward return'd Home, -
12, went with my Wife to our fifth day [Thursday] meet'g, felt
very poor & need, [illegible] to stand greatly in need of
Devine mercy & refreshment

verso

1808

5mo[May] 15th went with my Wife to our first day [Sunday] meet'g,
it felt refreshing, 19th was at our fifth day [Thursday] meet'g
=22 went with my Wife to our first day [Sunday] meet'g, it
refreshing I was concearn'd to speak a little
theirin to Incourage friends to minde the teachings
of the Lords Power & spirit above all things,
26, went with my Wife to our fifth day [Thursday] meet'g
29, went with my Wife to our first day [Sunday] meet'g (silent)
6[June]=2, went with my Wife to our fifth day [Thursday] meeting
-5, went with my Wife to our first day [Sunday] meet'g I belived
it right for me to speak a little theirin to set fourth
how the Lord was pleased to appear unto some formerly
by His Power and make them sensible of their states &
Conditions & how the stood in need of a Saviour & Redeemer
& was please to fit and Prepare them through menny
tryals & Exercises to be Instruments in His hand to

turn menny from Darkness to Light & from the Power
of Satan unto the Power of God, - 9th was at our fifth
day meet'g, 10th took a walk to C[hipping] Norton was at the
sixth day [Friday] meet'g also visited some friends in Affliction,
12, went with my Wife to our first day [Sunday] meet'g it felt
to be a refreshing meeting, in which we ware favour'd
to feel the Devine Teacher within us I trust to teach &
Instruct us in our Duty, altho a Silent Meeting –
13, I & my Wife went to our Monthly meet'g held at this place,
it felt pretty comfortable one friend appear'd theirin a pretty=

Page 38

=wile, afterwards friends proceeded upon business which
was gone through pretty agreeabley, 16th was at our fifth day [Thursday] meet'g
19, went with my Wife to our first day [Sunday] meet'g, it felt refreshing
23, went with my Wife to our fifth day [Thursday] meet'g (silent)
25, in the afternoon set out for our Quarterly meeting to be
held at Banbury, reach'd Milton & Lodg'd at Thos Malls
26, was at adderbury meet'g it felt to be a pretty comfort=
able meeting I trust the Crook of the Heavenly Fathers
Love is graciously extended towards menny belonging to that
meeting and such as do attend it, O that they may be con=
=cearn'd to retire inward and wait upon the Lord to feel
after the Devine Teacher in their own Hearts, and be Obidient
theirunto in all things, if they are, I trust they will be
good Examples unto others wich will have this Inviteing
Language, come taste and feel how good the Lord is to
them that Love and sarve Him, I was concearn'd to
appear in the meeting, after meeting went to adderbury
to se some friends, walked from thence to sibford found
Mother very weak yet seem'd pretty comfortable Lodg'd their
27, in the Afternoon took leave of Mother & Sistor and walk'd
to North=newington call'd to se the friends their, Lodg'd at Jno Atkins's
28, befor meeting walk'd to Banbury, at the Q Meeting ware
favour'd with the Company of our Loving friend Thos Cash,
it felt to be a favour'd meeting, T. Cash was led to speak in
an Incouraging manner to such as ware much tried and
exercised, signified altho a woman might be so void of Compassion
as to forget her Sucking Child, yet the Lord would nevver forget

verso

His poor Exercised Contrited Children, - the Buisness was
gone through in a weighty loving manner, after meeting return'd Home
-30 was at our fifth day [Thursday] meeting
7[July]=3 was at our first day [Sunday] meeting 7th was at our fifth day [Thursday] meet'g
-10, walk'd to Witney to meet'g it seem'd to me their was a want
of Devine power & of the Pure Life to be felt amoungst
them, which animates and causes zeal & love in them to
Incourage one another to be Diligent in the attendance
of their meetings I was concearn'd to speak a little theirin
after Din'r walk to faringdon found friends tolerable
well they ware Loving & kinde to friends Lodg'd at R Reynolds

-11, was at the Monthly meet'g at Faringdon it felt to be a re=
=freshing good meeting in which Devine mercy was felt to be extended
unto the People sevral friends Appeard in Testimonie
after meet'g Din'd at James Reynolds's, after Dinr ware
favour'd as friends sat with them to feel Devine Goodness to be
near to the comfort I trust of some mindes, afterwards return Home
17 went with my Wife to our first day [Sunday] meet'g it felt a
little refreshing, the Epistle from the Early meeting
was read, which was both Instructing & comforting,
20, this morning a very moornfull Accidence happend, as Joseph
Albright was leading a young Horse out into a two Wheel'd Carriage
the Horse seem'd unwilling to go forward but on its being
touch'd with the Wip, it set out & run with such violence
by the quine of a House, that it appeard Joseph Head
was between the Wall & the Wheel of the Carriage wareby
his Head was so much hurt & it is believed he spoke no more,
He Died about three hours afterwards, was favour'd to go of quietly,

Page 39

7mo[July] 21st was at our fifth day [Thursday] meet'g this Afternoon I help put the
body of Jos: Albt into his Coffin, the Weather being warm
the Coffin was made near 1 Inch think & the same
Evening a under lid put on and sorder'd down to prevent
it from smelling disagreeable,
-24, this being the day appointed for the Burial of J,A,
Menny friends and Neighbours attended it, it was a
very large & I trust solid good meeting sevral friends
appear'd in Testimonie – after meeting friends went to
the Parents of the Deceased to Din'r, after Din'r friends
ware drawn into Stillness, two friends spoke by way of Testimonie
it was a solem time menny being much affected, he being as
in the bloom of youth like a flower cut down in full bloom
-28, was at our fifth day [Thursday] meeting
-31, went with my Wife to our first day [Sunday] meet'g (silent)
8[August]=4 went with my Wife to our first day meet'g,
-7 went with my Wife to our first day [Sunday] meet'g, it was an
Exerciseing time me altho held in Silence,
-11 went with my Wife to our fifth day [Thursday] meet'g silent it
remains to be with me in meeting an Exerciseing time, also out of Meeting,
=14, went with my Wife to our first day [Sunday] meet'g was favour'd
to feel a little more Joy & Comfort, feel as tho I must walk by
faith, as I believ'd it to be my duty to speak a little matter in
meet'g, so I gave up and spake, feeling my minde brought in to a
degree of Resignation unto the Devine Will,

verso

1808

8mo[August] 18th was at our fifth day [Thursday] meet'g-
-21 was at our first day [Sunday] meeting, it was pretty large of
young friends & it felt comforting, I was concearn'd to
speak a little theirin, to advise young friends to be throughly given
up to sarve the Lord in the way of his Requireings,-

-25 was at our fifth day [Thursday] meet'g
-28, took a walk to sibford to se Mother, she continues
in a very weak state, to appearance not likely to
live but a little wile, was at the first day [Sunday] meeting,
spent about 3 ours at Mothers in a weighty manner
afterwards walk'd Home,
9[September]=1 was at our fifth day [Thursday] meet'g
4, was at our first day [Sunday] meeting, it felt refreshing held in silence
8, was at our fifth day [Thursday] meet'g
=10, having understood that Cousin Jno Wells of Shipstone
has been in a poor state of Health for sevral months
past, I felt a desire to go and se him, this day
went on foot thither, found Him poorly rest of the
family tolerable well by the account he gave me of Inward
weakness of Body, he seems to be in a rather dangerous
state of Health, altho their seem'd to be some hopes he might
be favour'd to get better, on the morrow being first day [Sunday] was
at the morning and afternoon meetings, spent most of
the rest of the day at Cousin Wells's in a loving agreeable
& weighty manner, after tea took leave of them and walk'd
to longcompton Lodg'd at Thos Harris's they entertaind me kindly
-12, walk'd to C,[hipping]Norton to our monthly meet'g, my minde was
pretty much exercised yet felt a little refresh'd, after meet'g
call'd to se Jno King who is in a poor low afflicted state, appear'd

Page 40

1808

to take my visit kind: call'd to se some more friends walk'd Home in the Even'g
9[September]=15 was at our fifth day [Thursday] meeting,
=17 set out for our Quarterly meet'g to be holden
at Reading, reach'd Jos: Ashbys shillingford Lodg'd their
=18, stop't friends meet'g which is holden at Woborough [Warborough] ,
meeting was smallish, a pretty menny friends being
gone out, it was held in Silence, after meeting Din'd at
Robt Greens, they are kind Religious friends, walkd from
thence to Reading, Lodg'd at Cousin Jno Tutteys,-
-19, it being Monthly meet'g at Reading, I was their, it held
long and did not feel very comfortable, they seem so
weak as to be hardly able to keep the Discipline in good
order, after meeting went to se some Relations they ware
very loving, spent the Evening with them agreeabley Lodg'd at Cousins
-20, before the quarterly meet'g began call'd to se some friends
the meeting was small, one friend appeard in Testimonie
which was Instructing and Edifying, the meeting of buis=
=ness did not feel very comforting, after meeting Din'd at
Cousin Jno Tutteys, bid them, farewell, and walk'd to Shillingford Lodg'd at J.A.
-21, after Breackfasting at our kinde friend Jos: Ashbys with
several more friends who Lodg'd their, took leave of them
& return'd Home
-22 was at our fifth day [Thursday] meet'g

-25, went with my Wife to our first day [Sunday] meetg, (silent)
-29, was at our fifth day [Thursday] meet'g, my much Exercised minde
being concearn'd to wait upon the Lord for his help, I was favour'd
to feel refreshment

verso

1808

10mo[October] 2nd went with my Wife to our first day [Sunday] meet'g
was pretty much exercised in minde apprehending it to
be a Degree of my duty to speak a little theirin
I gave up and spake a little that rested upon my minde
-6 was at our fifth day [Thursday] meeting
-9 went with my Wife to our first day [Sunday] meeting, silent,
yet it felt a little refreshing to my poor exercised minde
10 was at our Monthly meeting held at this place
(Charlbury) it felt a little refreshing, felt easy
to sit in Silence, two friends appear'd –
after which friends proceeded upon the buisness
which was gone through pretty comfortabley,
-13 was at our weekday meetg
-16 took a walk to milton to meeting, small
meeting, as my trust and dependance was in
the Lord alone I was favourd to feel a little re=
=fresh'd, after meeting din'd at T. Perkinss & returnd Home
-20 was at our fifth day [Thursday] meeting
-23, went with my Wife to our first day [Sunday] meet'g (silent)
I think we ware favour'd to feel our Strength renew'd
-27, was at our fifth day [Thursday] meeting
-30, went with my Wife to our first day [Sunday] meet'g it was Silent
yet I hope it was a profitable meeting
11[November]=3 was at our fifth day [Thursday] meeting
-6, took a walk to sibford was at the first day [Sunday] meet'g
I was concearn'd to speak theirin another frd appear'd
spent the A.[fter]N.[oon] at Mo: and with some friends Lodg'd at Mo:

Page 41

1808

11mo[November] 7th was at the Monthly meeting at Sibford I was
under a Concearn of minde believeing it to be my
duty to appear theirin but under a sence of my own
weakness I put it of till the meeting of Worship broke
up which was cause of sorrow to my minde – Lodg'd at Mo:
=8 after spending sometime at Mothers and Dining their
took my solem farewell of Mother not much Expecting
to se her living any more – in the afternoon walk'd
to Milton was kindly entertaind by friends their Lodg'd at T. Malls
=9 was at friends weekday meeting at Adderbury at
which was a Marriage viz: Henry Stone & Eliz: Wicheley
Ann Ashby appear'd in Testimonie, I also spake a little
theirin, after meeting return'd to milton to Din'r, and from milton Home
-10 was at our fifth day [Thursday] meet'g
-13, was at our first day [Sunday] meeting, it felt a little refreshing,
I was concearn'd to speak a little theirin, to advise
friends to be faithfull in answering the Lords requireings,
-14 I & my Wife went to our monthly Meet'g holden at Witney,
it felt pretty comfortable, sevral friends appeard in
Testimonie, which was Instructing comforting & Edifying,

the buisness was gone through pretty agreeabley, in the Even'g return'd Home
-15, rec'd an account of the Death of my Wives Mother who had
been in a very weak state for a pretty wile so weak as to
keep her bed, she appeard to bare her affliction patiently and
to be resign'd unto the Devine Will, was favour'd to go of very
quietly

verso

1808

11mo [November] 20th walk'd to Sibford to the Funeral of my motherinlaw
it was a pretty large Meeting menny of the Neighbours
being present, I trust it was a solid good meet'g in which
the renew'd visitation of Devine Goodness was felt, sevral
friends appear'd theirin, I was concearn'd to speak theirin, setting
fourth the awfullness of Death and the great necessiety their
was for us to be prepared for such a solem time, altho their might
be them who had sinned against God, yet I believed his mercy
was Extended and if they did sincearly repent of their rong doings
amend their ways and ask for forgiveness in the Name of
Jesus, they would be favourd to obtain it, after meeting we
Relations ware favourd with the Company of a pretty menny
friends and we had a comfortable sitting together, and I trust
Devine Love was felt which nearly united us one to another Lodg'd at Mo:
=21st took leave of Relations in an affectionate manner and return'd Home
-27, went with my Wife to our first day [Sunday] meet'g, it felt
refreshing, it was held in Silence
12[December]=4 went with my Wife to our first day [Sunday] meet'g, it felt to be
a refreshing edifying meeting altho held in Silence
-11, went with my Wife to our first day [Sunday] meet'g, it felt
refreshing, my minde was humbled under a sence of
my own weakness, & I was desireous to feel a state of
greater acceptance with the Lord
in the A.[fter]Noon walk'd to Burford found Bro'r Henry
very poorly Lodg'd there
-12 was at the monthly meet'g held at Burford, it felt re=
freshing and Comforting, one friend appear'd in Testimonie, return'd Home at Night

Page 42

12mo [December] 15th was at our fifth day [Thursday] meet'g, speak a little theirin
being afraid if I did not I should not quite discharge my duty
unto the Lord,
=18, was at our first day [Sunday] meeting, held in Silence, yet
I trust we ware favour'd to feel the Love of Devine
Goodness to be near, to the refreshing our Spirits
& to the uniteing us near one unto another,
=25 was at our first day [Sunday] meet'g, I trust it was a refresh=
=ing meet'g, held in Silence

1809

1mo[January] 1st went with my Wife to our first day [Sunday] meet'g it felt a little refreshing, silent meeting
-5, was at our fifth day [Thursday] meet'g
-8, was at our first day [Sunday] meet'g felt a little refresh'd, silent
-9, I and my Wife went to our Monthly meet'g
held at Norton, my minde was pretty much exercised,

and I was very desirous I might do nothing against
the truth, If I could not do anything for its advancement
after meet'g went to se a friend in Affliction, was
led to simpathy with him and to Incourage him to
Labour to be resign'd unto the Devine Will, and to In=
deavour to bear his affliction Patiently, after Dining
at Wm Atkinss returnd Home,
-15, went to our first day [Sunday] meeting it felt refreshing, (silent)
-22, went with my Wife to our first day [Sunday] meet'g (silent)
-27, took a walk to C,[hipping]Norton to the Burial of Jno King,
it was a pretty large meeting a pretty menny Neighbours
being present, Sarah Lambley was their, she appear'd
in Testimonie & also in solem Prayer, it felt to be a good
refreshing meeting, after meet'g call'd to se some friends in
the Evening return'd Home

verso

1809

1mo[January] 29th went with my Wife & Sistor M Gilks to our
first day [Sunday] meet'g, my minde was pretty much exercised,
being desireous that the Lord would be pleased to In=
=able me so to be found in the discharge of my duty
as that I might Injoy true peace of minde,
2[February]=5, went with my Wife to our first day [Sunday] meet'g
my minde was Humbled & I much desired I might
be found doing the will of the Lord, I was concearn'd
to speak a little theirin, under an apprehention
that it was my duty so to do,
=12, went with my Wife to our first day [Sunday] meet'g it felt
refreshing I was concearn'd to speak a little theirin
=19 went with my Wife to our first day [Sunday] meeting, it was a
little refreshing, I was concearn'd to advise friends
to feel after the Power of God, which cleanses & purifies
the Consciences, and Inables us to sarve the living God in
newness of Life
26 went with my Wife to our first day [Sunday] meet'g, it felt refreshing
I was concearn'd to speak a little theirin,
3[March]=4 walk'd towards Brails & next morning went to
Brails & from thence to their preparative meet'g held at
Shipstone friends thereaway seem to be in a low state on
the morrow was at the Monthly meeting in Banbury
in my Journey call to se some friends in Affliction
I was led to sympathise with them and spake a little I
hope to their Comfort, on the seventh was at the monthly
meeting held at Shipstone, after meeting stop'd at Cousin Jno

Page 43

Wells's & Lodg'd their, he has been very Poorly for a
pretty wile with an Inward complaint, I was led
into near simpathy with him and our Conversation I
hope was to Edification & Comfort, He I trust is a
sincear honest Hearted friend and has been very
usefull amoundst friends & is a good Example
amoungst his Neighbours, I had hopes he might be
spared a little longer, for his Family & the Church's sake,
3mo[March] 8th took an affectionate farewell of them & return'd Home

=12 went with my Wife to our first day [Sunday] meet'g
am in a low exercised state of minde
-19 went with my Wife to our first day [Sunday] meet'g
ware favour'd with the Company of Joseph
Lamb & Joseph Huntley, I was concearn'd to
speak a little theirin,
-26 went with my Wife to our first day [Sunday] meet'g
it felt refreshing, altho held in Silence
4[April]=2 went with my Wife to our first day [Sunday] meet'g
it felt refreshing altho held in Silence, in
the afternoon walk'd to Burford with Bro'r Robt
found Bro'r Henry very weak & poorly appears to
get weaker, he appears to bear his affliction Patiently
and to be pretty much resigned unto the Will of Devine
Providence whose Power I trust is as an ancor to his
Soul, took a walk to se some young friends, I was led
to advise them to set good examples unto others & Indeavour
to keep low and humble in their mindes and then I believed

verso

1809

they would increase in Love and in favour with
God and his People, Lodg'd at Bro'rs,
4[April]=3 was at the Monthly meet'g the meeting for worship
felt pretty comfortable two friends appear'd theirin
the meeting of Buisness felt dull and Exerciseing –
after meeting Din'd at Bro'r Henrys spent a
little time with them, in an agreeable solid man=
=ner, took leave of them and walk'd Home
-9, went with my Wife to our first day [Sunday] meeting
my minde was pretty much exercised with
respect to my being found faithfull in the dis=
=charge of my duty, but as I Indeavourd to give
up freely unto the Devine Will I felt resignation
of minde, & in that state I stood up and spake
a little that rested upon my minde – altho I
feel my own weakness's & Inability to do any good of
my self, yet I feel it safest for me through Devine Assistance in Humility
for to be found Indeavouring to discharge that duty
which I believe is required at my Hands,
11, took a walk to our Quarterly Meeting held at Witney
a pretty large meeting sevral friends appear'd in Testimo=
=nie the buisness was gone through pretty agreeabley, after
meeting stop'd a little with friends, & went to se some in Af=
fliction, in the Evening return'd Home,
-16, was at our first day [Sunday] meeting, it felt refreshing, I
trust menny ware concearned to draw near unto the Lord in
their Spirits, with Desires to be taught & Instructed thereby,
I was concearn'd to speak a little theirin

Page 44

1809

4mo[April] 23rd was at our first day [Sunday] meeting I was very
desirous to draw near unto the Lord in my Spirit
under a sence of my own weaknesss , as believeing
it to be the only way to obtain healing virtue
from Him, the meetg felt a little refreshing
-29 took a walk to Campden to se our Relations their
-30, was at the first day [Sunday] meeting at Campden, it was
small there being but few friends living thereabouts yet
it felt refreshing, I was concearned to Incourage
friends to give up freely and sarve the Lord faith=

-fully – spent the A[fter]noon & the morrow with relations and
friends in an agreeable manner, Lodg'd at Bro: W Corks
5[May]=2, walk'd from Campden to stow to the monthly
meeting there, I trust friends ware favour'd to
feel Devine Goodness to be near to their comfort & refreshment
went down to maughsbury to Jno Peglers and Din'd there
with a pretty menny friends, Lodg'd there, on the morrow return'd Home
-7 was at our first day [Sunday] meeting, it felt a little refreshing,
-8, took a walk with my Wife to our monthly meet'g
held at C,[hipping]Norton, it felt refreshing sevral friends
appear'd in Testimonie Old Wm Barritt was
their aged about 82 years old, in the Eveng we return'd Home
-14, was at our first day [Sunday] meetg, much reduced under a
sence of my own weakness and unworthyness, yet my
Spirit is concearned to keep wrestelling and breathing unto
the Lord for mercy and for power to preserve me that I
may not faint and I may not bring any dishonnour
on the Everlasting Truth, if I am unable to Labour for
its Honnour

verso

1809

5mo[May] 21st took a walk to Witney having felt a little con=
=cearn to be at their first day [Sunday] meetings, was at
both the meetings, which felt not very lively, yet
I trust we ware favour'd to feel [illegible] pertake a little
of Devine nourishment, I was concearn'd to advise
friends not to be discourag'd from attending meetings altho their
meetings ware small, for I believe if their ware
but two or three met together in the Name of Jesus
their he would be in the midst of them, teaching and
Instructing them by his Spirit which I much de=
=sired they might come unto & not to lean to their own
understandings but Indeavour in all their ways to
acknowledge the Lord and then he would direct their paths,
call'd to se some friend who ware poorly, in the
Evening returnd Home,
-23. recd anacot of Bro'r Henry Manders Death (of Burford)
who has been afflicted a long time with a Coughf,
which appeard to affect his lungs wareby he was much
reduced untill he could breathe no more, left a Wife
& 5 Children to mourn for the loss of a Religious &
Tender Husband & Parent,
-28, went to the funeral of Bro'r Henry it being first day [Sunday] was
took to meeting at 11oclock (usual meeting time) I trust
it was a good meeting in which Devine Goodness was pleas'd
to own us with his Living Power, sevral Mouths ware
open'd to testify of the Loving kindness to the Children of
of men, & to set fourth the Blessed Death of the Righteous
signifying if we would Die the Death of the Righteous

Page 45

---

we must minde the pure witness of Truth wich is
afforded us through the Love of Christ, which as it is
loved and Obey'd leadeth its Children out of all Evel &

into all Truth O! that all would love & live in
Obidience always
unto this Devine Guide Comforter feeder &
Keeper, then I trust
they would be blessed & happy wile here, and to
all Eternity,
Din'd at Sistors with relations & friends, after
Dinner
we ware favour'd with a refreshing time some
friends
ware favour'd to administer Counsel &
Consolation to the
afflicted, in the Evening walk'd Home with Bro'r
Robt
6[June]=4 was at our first day [Sunday] meeting,
held in Silence, yet I
trust as we waited in patience upon the Lord we
ware favoured to feel our Spiritual Strength
renewed
-11, was at our first day [Sunday] meeting, felt a
little refreshed
altho in a low situation of minde, finding a great
necessiety to be Watchfull, & to keep in a Humble
watchfull state, depending on the Lord for help &
Preservation
-12, was at our monthly Meet'g held here
(Charlbury) it was
not very large, held in Silence, except I was
concearned
to speak theirin, to advise friends so to live in
Obidience
unto the Devine Teacher, as to expiearence a state
in
which their is no Condemnation, the meeting of
Buisness
was conducted in Love,
-18, was at our first day [Sunday] meeting it felt
refreshing
I was concearn'd to speak theirin to set forth that
Man was Created in a state of Innosciencey, but
through
disobeying his Creator, he fell from a state of In=
=nosciency & happiness, but the Lord in great
Loving
kindness was pleased to order a way for mankinde
to be

verso

---

redeemed out of a State of Transgression into a
state of Happiness (or favour with the Lord, by
sending
his Beloved son into the World that whoso
believeth in him
should not perish but have Everlasting Life,
6[June]=24 set out for our Quarterly Meeting to
be held at Banb'y
walk'd in the A=noon to Thos Jarviss Barton
ware
I was favour'd with an Oppertunity with the
Children, to Incourage them to live in the fear of
the Lord & sarve him in their youth – walk'd
from
thence to Dedington call'd to se some convinced
friends
I was led to Incourage them to hold on their way
and
be faithfull unto Devine Instructions the Spirit
of Truth
in their own Hearts, Lodg'd with a young man
under
convincement, who lives with his Mother she
appears to be a Religious Woman
-25 rose pretty Early and walk to Adderbury at
Wm Barritts met
with two Women friends who are on a religious
visit in
these parts, in being first day [Sunday], was at
friends
meeting, the afore mentioned Women friends
ware
their they both appear'd I trust to the Edification
and comfort of friends after meeting din'd with
them
at Wm Barritts after calling to se some friends
walk'd
to Banbury to the Evening meeting, the
aforementioned
Woman friends ware there & I trust it was a
refreshing
meeting, after meeting walk'd to Milton Lodg'd
at T Malls
-26 walk'd from thence to Sibford found Sistor
M.G. very
poorly, on the morrow morning walk'd to
Banbury to

Page 46

1809

the Quarterly Meeting, several friends appear'd in Tes=
=timonie which was Instructing comforting & Incouraging unto
such as ware desire to walk in the straigh & narrow way
which leads to Blessedness, or in which true Peace is Injoy'd
after Dining at Jno Adkins's took leave of friends & walk'd to sibford
6[June]=28 spent a little time with sistor MG, in a Solid &
affectionate manner she being very poorly about noon
took my leave of her & return'd Home
7[July]=2 was at our first day [Sunday] meeting, my minde was pretty
much exercised I thought it my duty to speak a little
theirin but I neglected to speak untill the right time
appeard gone by, so I perceive it is a great matter to
know how to speak when to speak & what,
-5, this day we had a meeting appointed it began at 11 oclock
by the desire of the two Woman friends viz Mary Gessop
& Hanh Evans, they both appear'd, express'd it was very
necessary to be obidient to the Instructions of the Lords
spirit as Obidience was better than Sacrifise, & when
their duty was manifested to them then was the time
to work, work wile it is day, - - - in the Evening
went Gide with the friends to Burford –
-9 was at our first day [Sunday] meeting it felt to be a good
refreshing meeting, held in Silence
10 I & my Wife ware at our monthly meeting held at Faringdon, the
women friends above mentioned ware their they both appeard
in Testimonie I trust it was a good favour'd meeting in
which friends ware favour'd to feel the renewed visitation
of Devine Love to be extended, after meeting spent a little
time with friends, took leave of them and walk'd to Witney

verso

1809

7mo[July] 16th was at our first day [Sunday] meeting
-23, was at our first day [Sunday] meeting, it felt refreshing
I was concearn'd to speak a little theirin
-30 was at our first day [Sunday] meeting my minde was
much exercised, & much desireous to be found doing
the Will of the Lord, that I might be as the Clay
and He the Potter, -
8mo[August] 5th set out for Armscutt [Armscote] meeting, walk to Thos Harris's
Longcompton, it being rainy Lodg'd their
-6 set out pretty early in the morning for Shipstone,
found Cousin Jno Wells very poorly Breackfasted there,
after spending a little time with them in a weighty
manner, walk'd with some friends to the Meeting at
Armscutt [Armscote], it felt to be pretty comfortable sevral friends
Appear'd in Testimonie I was led to advise the People not
to trust in forms & ceremonies but Labour to be acquainted
with the substance of Religion, which is to be acquainted
with the Power of Christ within & live in Obidience to the

guidance of his Spirit, who came to put an end to sin and
finish transgression & in the room thereof to bring in
Everlasting Righteousness which I desired they might ex=
pearance for themselves, - after meeting Din'd at Cousin Thos
Fardons & spent sometime with friends there agreeabley –
in the Evening walk'd to Campden, Lodg'd at Bro'r Wm Corks
-7 spent a little time agreeabley at Bro'rs & in going to se relations
& friends, after Din'r walk'd with Bro'r to Sibford call'd
again to se cousin Jno Wells who at first appear'd very poorly &

Page 47

low, but before we left him, his spirits seem'd to revive –
He signified he was given up and resined to the will of the Lord
& altho at times his affliction of body was great, yet he was
favour'd to feel peace of minde and Devine Goodness to be
near to comfort him and be his support,
8[August]=8 having some buisness to do at Sibford spent the day there,
& Bro'r Wm & I ware favour'd to do the buisness we went
about to Satisfaction, on the morrow took leave of Sistor MG & return'd Home
=13, was at our first day [Sunday] meeting after meeting took a walk with
Bro'r Robt to burford found Sistor poorly, was at the Evening
meeting, it was small yet it felt a little refreshing, Lodg'd at Siss
=14, before the monthly Meeting began call'd to se some friends
also some Neighbours that I was acquainted with who,
had lost a near Relation by Death, he was a young man,
died in a Decline, they seem'd much affected with their
loss, their mindes being tender, I had some discourse with
them concearning the work of Religion in man, which I
trust was to Eddification & Comfort, - the meeting
felt refreshing, sevral friends appear'd in testimonie – according
to what I feel the Lords love and Mercy is great towards
the youth & He beareth long with the backslideing & Dis=
=obidience of some & yet they appear not willing to give
up all Deny themselves take up their daily cross and follow
the leadings of the Spirit of Jesus in all things, altho He hath
declared that whoso loveth any thing more than Him is not
worthy of Him, the buisness was conducted in Love, after Dining
at Sistors took my leave of them and friends & walk'd Home

1809

8mo[August] 20th was at our first day [Sunday] meeting, it felt refreshing
-27 was at our first day [Sunday] meeting, it felt refreshing
I was concearn'd to speak theirin
9[September]=3 was at our first day [Sunday] meeting, it felt refreshing
I was concearn'd to speak theirin – its a poorly time
amoungst people, which appears to humble them O! that
it may bring them down into true Humility before the Lord
-10, was at our first day [Sunday] meeting, it felt refreshing
altho held in Silence, yet I trust we ware favour'd
to feel the Divine Teacher within us, which leadeth
& Guideth its followers into all Truth, -
=17, was at our first day [Sunday] meeting it felt refreshing,
I was concearn to speak a little theirin

=24 was at our first day [Sunday] meeting, it felt refreshing
it appear'd to me to be right to speak a little matter altho
I could willingly have kept it & Injoyed the opening to my=
self, but if I did I was afraid (if I kept it back)
I should withold that which was for the good of others
therefore I gave up and spake
10mo[October] 1st was at our first day [Sunday] meeting it felt to be a
good meeting, altho held in Silence
=8, was at our first day [Sunday] meetg held in Silence
=9 was at our Monthly meeting held at Charlbury
the Life of truth felt to be low amoungst us sev=
=ral Elderly Ministers being hardly capable to attend
I was concearn'd to speak a little theirin to advise

Page 48

friends to Exercise themselves daily to keep
their Consciences void of Offence towards God
and towards man, to take care not to do
any thing that might hurt any tender seeking
mindes after the Truth but to be concearn'd
above all to Labour for its honnour –
the buisness was gone through pretty agreeabley
=13 I & my Wife ware at the six day [Friday] meeting
at Sibford it felt a little refreshing after
dining at Sistors took our farewell of she & return'd Home
=15, walk'd to Witney to the Burial of Jno
Hankins's Wife who was poorly a pretty
wile before she Died, seem'd like a Decline
the meeting was large a pretty menny Neigh's
ware present she being a Woman well
respected, I trust it was a good Satisfactory
meeting – after meeting a pretty menny
friends Din'd at Jno Hankins's and afterward
they had a verry solem sitting with the family
& some more friends some friends ware led to speak com=
=fortabley & incouragingly unto them signif=
=ing that if they would but live in the fear of
the Lord and delight to please him, He would
be pleased to be with them & by his power Preserve in trying
and proving seasons & lead them safely in the way

verso

1809

that is cast up for the ransomed & redeem'd
to walk in, afterwards I call'd to some
friends who appeard glad to se me, & I trust
we ware favour'd to comfort & Edify one another,
Lodg'd at Jno Hankins's, on the morrow returned Home
10mo[October] 22 was at our first day [Sunday] meeting, it felt re=
=freshing, I was concearn'd to advise friends to
walk humbley & lowly before the Lord signifying it was a happy state
=29 I was at the first day [Sunday] meeting at Sibford, in
the afternoon I went over to Epwell to se my relation
they appear'd glad to se me, and I trust we ware
comforted and edified together under a sence that
Devine Love was felt amoungst us,
=30 took leave of Sistor & return'd Home - -
=31, walk'd to Burford was at their third day [Tuesday] meeting
it was small, some friends being poorly –
in the Evening I went up to se old friend Huntleys
they lately heard of the Death of a near Relations which
affected them pretty much, had a comfortable sitting
with them and they young woman whose sistor
was Dead, spent the remainder of the Evening at
my Sistors agreeabley, on the morrow return'd Home
11[November]=5 was at our first day [Sunday] meeting it felt to be a good
refreshing meeting altho held in Silence –
this morning the young people being gather'd to=
=gather (it being call'd fifth of Nov:) making a racket

Page 49

and letting of Gunpowder, I was concearn'd
to go and admonish them not to sin against
God, but to Indeavour to repent of their rong
doings and seek for forgiveness of the Lord,
felt peace in so doing,
=11 went with sistor M. Gilks to Sibford Lodg'd at sistors
=12, went before meeting went to se a friend
who was Ill, appeard to be in Decline
I was concearn'd to pray – the meeting
was pretty large I was concearn'd to speak theirin
to set fourth the Love of God unto mankind
in sending his beloved son into the world that whoso be=
=lieved in him should not perish but have
Everlasting, who laid down his Life for
our sakes, that we might be favour'd with
the teachings of His Spirit which as we come
to live in Obidience theirunto it would re=
=deem us out of a fawlen state into a
state of favour and axceptance with the Lord
after meeting Din'd at Sistors, bid she farewell
and return'd Home,
=13th walk to our Monthly meeting held at witney
it was rather small yet felt a little refreshing
I was concearn'd to speak a little theirin

verso

another friend also appear'd – the buisness
was gone through pretty agreeabley, after
meeting call'd to se some friends, in the Evening
return'd Home,
11mo [November] 19th was at our first day [Sunday] meeting I was
concearn'd to advise friends to Indeavour
to be more acquainted with the true Spirit
of Supplication as believeing it would be
a means of obtaining favour of the Lord &
witnessing their strength to be renewed that
that they might know a ceasing to do evel
=20 we ware favour'd with the company
of Sarah Lambley & Elizabeth Townsend
who are on a Religious Visit a Public
Meeting was appointed on their acct the
meeting began at six in the Evening it was
large, I trust it was a renewed visitation
of Devine Mercy, to menny present, sarah
& her companion ware led to set fourth the
unceartainty of Life & the ceartainty of Death
and the great Necessiety there was to prepare for
it, the call was also extended to the Sinners
they ware warned of their dangerous state &
Invited to return to the Lord through sincear
repentance and amendment of Life

Page 50

and those that had run well for a time and
had not given way to great Evels like some,
ware advised not to grow slack and think there
was not so great need of watchfullness as formerly
but, let them that think they stand take heed,
least they fall (I believe a Necessary caution)
signifying they should be constantly upon
their watch and Indeavour to get forward &
know an advancement in a Religious Life –
as the only way to know a getting forward in
the path that leadeth to the crown of Life Immortal
=26 was at our first day [Sunday] meeting it was held in
Silence, yet it felt to be a good refresh=
=ing meeting, in which friends ware favourd
to feel the unering Teacher within themselves,
even the Comforter the Spirit of Truth,
which leadeth & guideth into all Truth such as live
wholy in Obidience thereunto
12[December], 1, was at our first day [Sunday] meeting, it felt refreshing
I was concearn'd to speak a little theirin, to Incourage
friends to minde the anointing which they have
receiv'd, & to know it to abide in them to be their Teacher,
in the afternoon walk'd to Burford found Sistor
and the Children tolerable Lodg'd at Sistors –
=11 was at our Monthly meeting held at Burford,

verso

1809

the meeting was smallish yet Devine Goodness
felt to be near & I think He waiteth to be gra=
=cious unto such as do freely give themselves up
and are devoted in Heart to sarve him faithfully
in the way of his requireings – after dinner
bid relations and friends farewell & walk'd Home
12mo [December] 17 was at our first day
[Sunday] meeting, it felt refreshing
=24 was at our first day [Sunday] meeting it felt
refreshing
I was concearn'd to speak a little theirin,
=31, was at our first day [Sunday] meetg I trust
it
was a good refreshing meeting, held in Silence

1810

1mo[January] 7th was at our first day [Sunday]
meeting it felt refreshing
I was concearn'd to advise friends to be faith=
=full in answering the Lords requireings as
it was the only way to be accepted of him,
-8, walk'd to our monthly meeting held at
C.[hipping]
Norton, the Power of Truth seems to be low
amoungst us, and I feel a very poor Creature
at times, & great Necessiety for me to wait and
seek unto the Lord for his Power to strengthen
me, and preserve me in the way of true Peace
after meeting Din'd at S. Atkin's, took leave of
friends and return'd Home
-14 was at our first day [Sunday] meeting it felt
re=
freshing & comforting, held in Silence

Page 51

1810

1mo[January] 16th went to our Quarterly
Meeting held
at Oxford, it felt pretty comfortable
a friend appear'd solem Prayer afterward
another friend apear'd in Testimonie
he signified it was very necessary for friends
to hearken to the voice of the Lord and be
obidient to his requireings, as to obey was
better than Sacrifise and to hearken to the
Voice of the Lord than the fatt of rams
also signified when Israel had enter'd
the promis'd land their enemies prevaild
against them because one amoungst them
had taken of what was forbidden, of
the Babalonish Garment & wedg of Gold,
therefore signified friends should indeavour
to search them selves and put away
whatsoever they found to be rong, and turn
to the Lord & sarve him with their whole
Hearts and then he would be near to them
and Inable them to overcome their Enemies
and get forward in the work and duty which was
appointed them to do – another friend appeard
in Prayer – the buisness was gone through

verso

1810

pretty comfortabley, after meet'g walk'd Home
1mo[January]21, was at our first day [Sunday]
meet'g, held in Silence
having observ'd the Evel Tendency of Ringing
bells, how it caused lightness of minde and
led such as practised it into bad Company
to Drink to Excess &et lately I was concearnd
to advise such to leave of Ringing & such
things as they knew to be rong that they might
be favour'd to obtain mercy of the Lord,
I also Rote some papers & put them up at some
places ware I thought People would be like
to read them, signifying Ringing of Bells
tended to vain mirth & lightness of minde by
which God was Dishonour'd therefore ought
not to be put in places appointed for the
Worship of Almighty God – and such of prac=
tis'd Ringing ware led into bad Company to
Drink to Excess &et with a warning to such
to forsake sin and Transgressions lest they draw
down the Judgements of the Lord upon them &et

-28, was at our first day [Sunday] meeting it was held in Silence, yet it felt refreshing
2[February]=3 walk'd to Banbury, call'd on the way to se Aunt

Page 52

Jones and some more friends who ware Poorly one friend was very weak appeard in a Decline I was concearnd to Instruct her to Labour to be resign'd unto the Devine Will wether to Live or Die – I went to Henry Stones
he and his Wife ware very kinde Lodg'd their
2mo[February] 4th before meeting call'd to se some friends,
the meeting felt refreshing I was concearn'd to speak theirin, Din'd at the Widow Beesleys she & her Children ware tender and affectionate afterward call'd to se some friends, towards evening went to Overthrup and paid Thos Riley & his scholars a visit, was favour'd with a little oppertunity with the scholars to Instruct them to minde & attend to the pure Principal of Truth in their own Hearts, that they might be inabled to sarve the Lord and grow up in his favour – spent the remainder of the Even'g with some friends at Banbury, Lodg'd at H Stones
=5, was at the monthly meeting held at Banbury, Hannah Jarrot laid before the Monthly Meeting a Concearn that had rested weightily upon her minde for sometime to visit friends meetings in sevral Countys, - after meeting spent a little time

verso

1810

with friends Comfortabley took leave of them & walk'd with same friends to Sibford. Lodg'd at Sistors
2mo[February] 6th in the morning part call'd to se some friends
& one who was very Ill I sat with him some= =time I signified it was good to labour to be resigned and given up unto the Devine Will, after Dining with Sistor took my leave of she and walk'd Home - -

=11, was at our first day [Sunday] meeting it felt refreshing
-12, was at our monthly held at Charlbury I was concearn'd to speak theirin, signifying friends should awake unto righteousness & sin not, for we might by loving the World & having our mindes set on earthly things get into a sleepy dull state as to the spiritual Life, yet the Lord was Mercifull & friquently calling us by his Spirit to come away and leave those hindering things, with respect to the buisness some friends are
sometimes not weighty enough in their spirits giving way to speak more than one at a time, which is unsavoury and hurtfull –
=18, was at our first day [Sunday] meeting, it felt refreshing
=25, was at our first day [Sunday] meeting my minde
was Humbled before the Lord and I much desired I might be preserved from offending Him,
=28, took a walk to Witney & was at friends fourth day [Wednesday] meeting which felt a little refreshing

Page 53

1810

3mo[March]=2nd took a walk to C.[hipping] Norton, was at the sixday [Friday]
meeting – after meeting call'd to se some friends, to some of them I was concearn'd to give advise, respecting their giveing up to sarve the Lord in the way of his requireings, felt peace in so doing – in the Evening walk'd Home
=4 was at our first day [Sunday] meeting it felt a little refreshing
=11, was at our first day [Sunday] meeting it felt to be
a low exerciseing time, may friends abide in Patience under the Exerciseing & proving Hand of the Lord & seek unto Him for sup= =port for help & Instruction, & then I trust they will be Inabled to persevear in they way of true Peace & Expearence these seasons to work together for their good,

=12, walk'd to our Monthly held at Witney it was
small it felt to be a low time, a time of much
Exercise of Spirit to the truly Religious mindes,
the buisness went on heavily – after meeting
call'd to se some friends, in the Even'g returnd home
=18 was our first day [Sunday] meet'g it was held in Silence
yet felt refreshing,

verso

1810

3mo[March] 25th was at our first day [Sunday] meet'g it
felt a little refreshing, my minde was
much exercised being desireous to be found
faithfull in the Discharge of my duty
that I might be favour'd to Injoy true Peace,
and I was concearn'd to Express that it was
only as we minded the good Spirit & Law
of God written in our Hearts that we could be
helpfull one unto another & strengthen one
another in the Living faith &et
4[April]=1, was at our first day [Sunday] meet'g it felt a little re=
freshing, held in Silence, our preparative
meet'g, in which I was concearn'd to advise
the youth to give up and sarve the Lord in the
way of his requireings, which if they did I
believed it would be an acceptable offering
unto the Lord –
-2 was at our monthly meet'g held at Burford
A friend appear'd in Solem Prayer afterward
I was concearn'd to speak a little theirin –
the meeting of buisness was Exerciseing to my minde
on account of some buisness that came before
the Meeting, however I Indeavour to speak my
minde respecting it, one thing that was before
the meet'g was respecting a meeting House at

Page 54

Alvescot[27], it being out of repair, some friends
ware for having it repaired thinking it
might be of service for friends to hold a meet'g
there sometime, on the Neighbours acct,
others seem'd to think much of the Expence of
Repairing it, & ware for having it pull'd down,
it was concluded to take it down, I was sorry
as believeing there was a little oppening for
friends to hold a meeting there sometimes, &
if they would have given up chearfully & willingly
so to do I think a Blessing would have attended it,
after meet'g spent a little time at sistors & with
some friends – in the Evening walk'd Home
-8, was at our first day [Sunday] meeting, it felt a little
refreshing I was concearn'd to speak a little
theirin, signified friends should Earnest Labour
after Purity of Heart, Blessed are the pure in
Heart for they shall se God,
-10, walk'd to witney to our Quarterly meeting held
their, it was smallish it being very rainy, it felt
to be a good refreshing meeting, my minde was
tender'd and contrited before the Lord under a
a sence of his Mercy being renewedly Extended, two
friends appear'd in Testimonie and one in solem Prayer

verso

1810

after meeting spent a little time with friends
in a loving agreeable manner in the Eveng walk'd Home
4mo[April]=15th, was at our first day [Sunday] meeting at which
their was a Burial of Wm Albrights youngest
Child, it was a time of exercise to my minde
but as mine Eye was single unto the Lord Tender
breathings ware begotten in me that I might

---

27 Earliest recorded reference of meeting 1677

be inabled to do his Will, and under an appre=
=hention of Duty I stood up and spake unto
the People sevral Neighbours being present what
rested upon
my minde, felt a degree of Peace in so doing,
in the afternoon I and my Wife vissited some
friends in affliction, in sitting with them
in a solid weighty manner I was led to sym=
=pathise with them & to wait upon the Lord
with them for help and Comfort & I trust we
ware favour'd to feel a little renewal of strength
-22 was at our first day [Sunday] meet'g sat in a
mourn=
=ful state yet felt a little refresh'd
-29 went with my Wife to our first day [Sunday]
meet'g
it was silent, yet felt a little refreshing
to my poor exercised minde
5[May]=6 went with my Wife to our first day
[Sunday] meet'g
it felt a little refreshing, altho it is a time of
exercise & mourning

Page 55

5mo[May] 13th was at our first day [Sunday]
meeting was in
a state of mourning under a sence of my
own weakness's & slippings aside, and fervent
breathings ware begotten in my minde unto
the Lord for mercy, and forgivness – in the after=
=noon my Wife walk with some friends
to C[hipping]Norton to be at our monthly
meeting
=14, went on foot to our monthly meetg
held at C[hipping] Norton, I believe it is an
exercise=
=ing mournfull time, to the truly religious
mindes whose great Concearn is for the
prosperity of Zion – after meeting
call'd to se some friends, in the Evening
walk Home with my Wife and some friends
=19 as I have nevver been at the Yearly meeting
altho I have thought pretty much of going
thither sometime this year I believ'd it right
If I ware favour'd to be tolerable well to In=
deavour to attend it, accordingly this morning
I set out thither=ward, reach'd shillingford by
Dinner time, Din'd at Joseph Ashbys and
Lodg'd their He as usual was very kinde He
is a generous Open Hearted friend not only
towards
friends but towards his Neighbours, being
Charitable

verso

1810

and loving towards them Indeavouring to do
them
good and I do believe his Labours are & will be
blessed
5[May]=20 stop'd friends meeting, before
meeting
call'd to se some friends who appeard glad to
se me, after dining at Joseph Ashbys took leave
of friends & went to Joseph Mays Henly found
Joseph May poorly they ware very kinde Lodg'd
their
=21 rode with Josh Mays son in their Carriage to
Maden Head, stop'd with Nicolas and Hanh Albt
till
after Tea their company way comforting, walk'd
from maiden=head to stains in the Evening
found friends pretty well except Mary Ashby
who was poorly Lodg'd at Robt Ashbys –
=22 spent the day pretty comfortabley at Robt
Ashbys & in visiting his Father Mother &
relations
=23, rose early & went with Wm Ashby by Coach
to London (being afraid if I went alone by
my self on foot I could not very well finde my
way through the town to Meeting) W. Ashby
went with me to meeting menny friends from
Divers
Parts ware present, the A[fter]Noon meeting
began at 4
oclock friends heard the Answers to the Queries &
menny weighty remarks ware made theiron
=24 was at morning and A[fter]Noon meetings
=25 was the Peel meeting which was comforting
& refreshing
sevral friends in Testimonie I was concearnd to
speak a

Page 56

little theirin after meeting went with Stephen Mathews
Dind with him & his family saw Hanh tyler who
look poorly yet I believe was glad to se me and
my Bror in law in our meeting together I trust we ware
favour'd with the Injoyment of Devine Goodness,
in the A[fter] Noon was at the meeting for Buisness
=26 was at the meeting for Buisness
=27 was at the Burrow meeting both morning & A[fter]Noon
which ware large and favour'd meetings sevral
friends appeard theirin whose Testimonies felt edifying
and comforting before and after the meetings spent
most of the time at Cousin Thos Sherwells ware I Lodg'd
=28 & 29th attended the meetings for Buisness
=30, the meetings being open for Worship I attend
Ratclif meeting which felt comforting sevral
friends appeard theirin after meeting went to Jno
Harris's to Dinner spent a little time with friends
there in a loving agreeable manner, in the A[fter] Noon
attended the meeting for buisness & also on the morrow
attended the meeting for Buisness in the Evening which began at 5 there being
no meeting for buisness in the morning excep for the
Commities to meet I walk'd down to Wm Dartons Plaisto[w]
to se James Albright, who I found weak & poorly
yet much better than what he had been he appeard
glad to se me I was led to speak a little to him con=
=cearning his affliction signifying I believed it was a
time of the Lords visitation & thought he might have

verso

1810

been led to Covenant with the Lord that if he would
be pleased to spare his Life & show mercy he would
Indeavour to live more carefully & live in his fear
for the future and as he had been favour'd to finde
mercy I wish'd him to remember to be gratefull for
Devine Favours, in the A[fter] Noon took leave of him his
wife and there relations and return'd with some friends to london
was at the meeting for Buisness in the Evening
6[June]=1, was at the meeting for Buisness which at
was Concluded I thought it was one of
the best meetings during the whole sittings
Epistles that had been drawn up by the Com=
=mities ware read being as answers to those
that came from difrent Parts of America
scotland &et also the general Epistle was read
for this Nation, all approv'd of and Sign'd
& the meeting concluded in Brotherly Love
-2 after Breackfasting at Cousins had an
oppertunity to mention a little what I
felt respecting their future happiness
and also present, parted in much
Love Cousin Thos & his Wife taking a
walk with me to conduct me on the road
call'd at Saml Harris, they ware kind
staid Din'r & Tea – bid them farewell & walkd
to stains Lodg'd & was kindly Entertaind at Robt Ashbys

Page 57

1810

6[June]=3 was at the first day [Sunday] meetings at stains the
morning meeting felt pretty comfortable I
was concearnd to speak theirin the afternoon

meeting was held in Silence Lodg'd at R Ashbys
4, took leave of friends at stains & walked to
maden=
Head call'd at Wm Batts Din'd their spake a
little to them to Incourage them to be diligent
in the attendance of their meetings, spent most
of the remainder of the day comfortable at
Nicholas
Albrights with him & his sister Hannah pretty
comfortabley was also concearn'd to advise them
to be Diligent in the attendance of their
meetings
to wait upon the Lord and worship Him, Lodg'd
their
-5 rose pretty early after Breackfasting with them
bid them farewell & walk'd to henly was kindly
entertain'd at Joh Mays, after Din'r walk'd to
shillingford drank Tea at Wm Sanders's spent a
little time with them comfortabley Lodg'd at J
Ashbys
6, after Breackfasting with Josh Ashby & his
House=
=keeper who ware loving and tender bid them
farewell
walk from thence Home. Was favour'd to finde
my Wife pretty well & things comfortable at
Home
in the before mentioned Journey I have been
favourd
to se my own Weakness's & great necessity to be
Watchfull

verso

1810

---

and have my dependance on the Lord as the alone
way to live to his Praises, as it is his own Works
that Praise Him
6[June]=10, was at our first day [Sunday]
meeting
=16 sistor M. Gilks went for Home who had
been a paying
us a visit, whose Company was Comforting
=17 having heard that my kinde friend John
Hankins
was very poorly took a walk to Witney to se him
found him Poorly He told me he had been pretty
much
Exercis'd in his minde concearning his Souls
Salvation
being almost ready to dispare of Mercy, but
hoped if his Life was spar'd a little longer he
should live a better life than he had heretofore
done
He signified that no form how fine soever as to
Religion, would stand in stead or be accepted
of the Almighty, nothing would be accepted with
him but the Substance of Pure Religion –
was at friends morning and afternoon meetings
they felt a little comforting, - the Widow Rutter
was in a low mournfull state, having lately
slipt down and put her Hip out, & it seem'd not
likely to be set again, what seem'd to make it
more trying was that she had met with sevral
afflicting falls before, she appeard in her minde
tender humble & Contrited before the Lord, & I
have a
Hope she will be favoured to feel him mercy and
Injoy his
Love, know Devine Power to her support in her
great
Affliction

Page 58

1810

6mo[June] 17th my Wife & Sistor M.S. set out
intending to
be at our Quarterly Meeting to be held at
Banbury
=24 was at our first day [Sunday] meeting it felt
pretty
comfortable after meeting call'd to se friend
Bright
and friends their was favour'd to speak a little
to the newly Married Copple Adviseing them to
be
Plain even in the furniture of their House and to
keep near to the Truth and minde its leadings in
all things, Not to lean to their own
understandings
but in all their ways to acknowledge the Lord
then

he would direct their Paths, Inable them to walk in
the way of true Peace.
7mo[July]=1st was at first day [Sunday] meeting it felt pretty comfortable
held in Silence
-8, was at our first day [Sunday] meeting I was
concearnd to advise friends to seek an acquaintance
with God that they might be favour'd to
feel Peace, in the A[fter] Noon set out for
our Monthly Meet'g to be held at Faringdon
walk'd to Witney, call'd to se some friends
who ware poorly, Lodg'd at Jno Hankins's
=9 rose early after Breackfasting at Jno Hankins's
walk'd to Faringdon to our Monthly Meeting
it was small some friends appeard theirin the
buisness was gone through pretty comfortabley after
meeting spent a little time with friends agreeabley –

verso

1810

in the Evening walk'd to Witney Lodg'd at J Hankins
7mo[July] 10 spent a little time with friends agreeabley aftwards return'd Home
-15, was at our first day [Sunday] meet'g silent I was
desireous to draw near unto the Lord in Spirit
and that I might be strengthen'd so to live in Obi=
=dience to his Spirit & have my minde staid on
the Lord as to be keep't in perfect Peace –
-22, was at our first day [Sunday] meet'g it felt refreshing
spake a little theirin, setting fourth that
the Dear Redeemer when he was personally
upon Earth to such as had faith in him and came
to be healed he was pleased to heal them so
in his Inward & Spiritual appearance
such as have Faith in His Power and come to live
in Obidience thereunto, I believed he will be
Pleased to Heal them of their Spiritual Diseases
-23, having heard that a Public meeting was appointed
to be held at Enstone by Wm Fosters desire I
took a walk thither it was held in a roomy
Barn, began about 6 in the Evening a pretty
menny Neighbours ware there and some friends
attended from C[hipping] Norton & Charlbury the Neigh=
=bours behaved well, I trust it was a good satis
=factory meeting, a renewed Visitation of Devine Love
& mercy to menny present Wm Foster spake a

Page 59

---

pretty wile Instructing the People, & the call
was unto the sinners to Repent & believe the
Gospel, I was concearn'd to speak a little theirin
Desireing that none might content themselves with
a form of Religion without comming to
witness the Substance, even of attending unto
the Inward and Spiritual appearance of
Christ, which reproved them for sin, & Instructed
and Inabled them to do well, as they livd in
Obidience thereunto would Inable them to be
true worshipers, even to Worship the father
in Spirit & In truth, after meeting spent
about quarter of an Hour with friends, took leave
of them & walk'd Home,
27, this day in the evening a Public meeting was held
began about 6 oclock by the desire of Wm
Foster from near London I think it was a
good meeting, a renewed visitation of Devine
mercy unto menny present W.F. was led to spake
to the states of menny I believe & the Neighbours
ware affected and well satisfied,
-29 was at our first day [Sunday] meet'g, ware favour'd with
the Company of Wm Foster & John Willis who
bares him Company, it felt to be a refreshing
meeting in which William was drawn forth in
Testimonie,

verso

7[July]=29 took a walk to Burford to a Evening meet'g
appointed by Wm Fosters desire, menny
Neighbours Present, it felt to be a good
meeting in which William had good service
8[August]=5 was at our first day [Sunday] meet'g it felt refresh=
=ing, altho my minde is pretty much exercised
in great exercises this scripture is a little Incouraging
to persevear in the way of duty, all things work
together for good to them that Love God,
8, took a walk to Witney was at friends fourth day [Wednesday]
meeting, the visiting friends ware their viz Wm
Foster & Jno Willis I think it was a good re=
=freshing meeting, W.F. I believe was led to
speak to the states of sevral present through
Devine mercy to the tendering & contriting their
Spirits, Dind with the friends at Jno Hankings's
by the desire of Wm Foster a Public meeting was
held in the evening at ensham it appeard to be to good
satisfaction, return'd to Witney Lodg'd at T. Smiths
-9 walk'd to Oxford ware by the desire of the
friend, in the Evening a Public meeting was held
it was pretty large & I trust to good satisfaction,
stop'd with friends at Oxford & Lodg'd their,
-10, Wm Foster having a desire to have a meeting
at Islip about six miles from Oxford, friends
went thither & Indeavourd to get a place but could
not it appear'd the Dean was very much against
it & the People ware so much under him as not to
spare their Places lest they should offend him,

Page 60

---

at Islip took leave of friends they returning
to Oxford intending to have another Public meet'g
their in the Evening, & I returnd Home –
=12, was at our first day [Sunday] meetg it felt to be
a good meeting altho held in Silence
19, was at our first day [Sunday] meet'g it was held
in Silence,
-26 was at our first day [Sunday] meeting it felt a little
refreshing I was concearn'd to speak a little theirin
I being afraid to withold what I thought was
given to me for others good, lest I should return
from meeting with a degree of Condemnation
9[September]=2nd walk to Sibford to the preparative meeting
the meeting was large & felt pretty comfortable
some friends appear'd theirin, after meeting spent
sometime at Sistors comfortabley toward Evening
went to se some friends at little sibford heard
that Cousin Jno Gibbs's Wife was dead, - Lodg'd at Sis:s
-10th was at the monthly Meeting held at Sibford, I was
concearn'd to speak theirin signifying the time was
come spoken of by the Prophet Joel 2 Cha, 28 verse
another friend appear'd theirin, the meeting of Buisness
held long their being a pretty deal to do after meeting
spent a little time with some friends at little sibford
agreeabley, in the Evening took leave of Sistor &
walk'd to brails with Cousin M Cork, Lodg'd at Wm Gilletts
3 walk'd with a friend to Shipstone to the monthly meeting

verso

---

it was small, I believed it my duty to speak theirin
Thos Harris also appear'd theirin – Din'd at the Widow
Wells, spent the rest of the afternoon with friends and
relations at Shipstone pretty comfortable, Lodg'd at Cous'n Wells
-4 stop friends fourth day [Wednesday] meeting at Shipstone
before meeting was favour'd with an oppertunity with
the Widow and Children of the late Jno Wells
I was led to give them good advice and spake Comfortabley

to them, signified that if they would live in the fear of
the Lord and be Obidient to the Teachings of his spirit
I believed they would be qualified for sarvice in his
Church, and the Lord would be with them, be as a Husband
to the Widow, and a Father to the fatherless –
the meeting was small, I was concearned to advise
friends to be diligent in the attendance of their
Religious meetings, and not to let in discouragements
for if they did I thought it was the way for their meet'gs
to become smaller, but I wishd them to Incourage
oneanother to Diligence as that would be the way
to have their meetings become larger for I believ'd
the Lord was near and willing to do them good
and to gather them near unto himself –
after meeting Din'd at Cous'n Wells took leave
of them, and walk'd to Thos Harris Longcompton
spent about one hour (and Drank tea) with
them comfortabley walk from thence Home

Page 61

1810

9mo[September] 9th was at our first day [Sunday] meeting it felt
comfortable, towards the latter part of
the meeting I was concearn'd to speak a little
concearning how bow'd in Humility before
the Lord as I believed some present ware
and their Spirits drawn near to the Lord
which was true Worship, and as they ware
concearn'd to live in Obidience to his spirit
the would know an Inheriting substance,
even the Life of true religion –
=15 set out for our Quarterly Meeting to be holden
at Reading walk'd to Shillingford, met
with some friends on the way who accompanied
me to Shillingford met with sevral friends at Joseph
Ashbys we ware kindly entertaind Lodg'd their
=16 it being first day [Sunday] before meeting call'd to se
some friends, the meeting felt a little refreshing
I was concearn'd to speak a little theirin, Din'd
at Wm Sanders's who ware Loving in the A.[fter] N.[oon]
went to reading found Cousins Tolerable well
Lodg'd at Cousin Jno Tutteys, the Elder's
-16 was at the monthly meet'g held at Reading, it
held long their being a pretty deal of buisness to
go through, after meet'g dind at Jno Tutteys Jun'r called
afterwards to se some other friends held a little sitting
with Jonathan Fardons Children was favour'd to give them

verso

good advice and Instruction, they appeard tender
9mo[September]=17th the Quarterly Meeting began at 10 oclock it
felt to my minde very comforting sevral friends
appear'd theirin amoungst which ware two young
friends I think their names ware (Tucket) one
friend appear'd in solem Prayer, - the meeting
of buisness held long, tho I believe it would have
been gone through pretty soon and comfortabley, had it
not been for an appeal concearning the settelment of
some friends, the Case appeard so difficult to
the Quarterly meeting, that it was agreed to write
to the Yearly Meeting, to desire that meeting to
give their Judgement to deside the matter –
the meeting held so late that I stopt at Readig
all Night as menny others did, friends menny
of them ware kindly entertaind at Jno Tutteys
and their Relations, friends Company felt comforting
18, after breackfasting with menny friends at
Jno Tutteys took an affectionate farewell
of Relations and friends, & rode with Joseph
Ashby in his Carriage to his House at Shillingford
Dind there then took leave of friends and walk'd
with four friends to Oxford refresh'd ourselves there
then set out for our Homes, took leave of each other

upon the road, I reachd Home about 10 at Night

Page 62

1810

9mo[September] 23rd was at our first day
[Sunday] meet'g in an humble
frame of minde I spake signifying that when
we are brought into an Humble contrited
state before the Lord, their is great of
Watchfull=
=ness and attention to Devine Power to be
preservd
in such a state, becaus of menny things that are
likely to draw us aside on the right hand and
on the left out of the straight and narrow
way which leadeth unto Life, without we
are very watchfull
=30 felt a great desire this morning that I
might spend the day in the fear of the Lord
and in Obidience to his power, so carefully
as to have my minde preserved in Peace –
was at our first day [Sunday] meeting, it was held
in silence
10[October]=7 was at our first day [Sunday]
meeting, it was held in silence
-8, was at our Monthly held at Charlbury
the meeting for worship felt pretty comfortable
the meeting of Buisness was Exerciseing yet I
think in the whole it was pretty satisfactory,
=14, was at our first day [Sunday] meeting, it
was held in silence
=21, was at our first day [Sunday] meeting my
minde
was in a Humble frame, and I was very
desireous so to live in the fear of the Lord
as to be preserved from offending Him,
=28 was at our first day [Sunday] meeting: I was
very desire=
=ous to be Preserved in the fear of the Lord
which is

verso

1810

a fountain of Life,
11mo [November] 4th I went to our first day
[Sunday] meeting (my Wife
gone to Sibford) it felt refreshing,
-11 was at our first day [Sunday] meeting, held
in Silence
-12, took a walk to our Monthly Meeting
held at Witney I was very desireous
I might so carefully attend to the Guideance
of Truth and be obidient theirunto as to return
with Peace – which I was favoured to
Expearence, thanks be unto the Lord for
his mercy the Meeting of Buisness was
exerciseing yet it was gone through pretty
comfortabley – Din'd at Jno Hankins's after=
=ward call'd to se some friends, in the Evening
return'd Home,
=18, was at our first day [Sunday] meeting I was
led to
consider how acceptable is the Prayer of the
Righteous,
& to speak a little concearning Prayer, signifying
we should Labour to put up our pettions unto
the
Lord with a perfect & upright Heart, & then I
be=
=lieved we should finde acceptance with the Lord
and obtain Mercy
=22 this morning Sarah Squires's sistor Lucas
Died, being
poorly a pretty wile & about a week ago was
afflicted
with a stroke of the Palsy,
-25 was at our first day [Sunday] meet'g silent
-29 this day Margt Lucas was Inter a large

Page 63

meeting was held on the occation a pretty
menny Neighbours ware present it felt
to be a good meeting Sarah Lambley had a
pretty good oppertunity in Testimonie H
smith also appear'd S Lambley was also
drawn forth in Supplication, I also at

the Grave was Concearned a little in
Supplication, after meeting the friends
went to S. Squires in the Evening and sat with
friends, there S Lambley had a fine oppertunity
with friends setting forth the mercies and
Favours of the Lord to friends & Incouraging them to
faithfullness as the onely way to be blessed
12[December] 2st was at our first day [Sunday] meeting silent yet it
felt refreshing
-9, was at our first day [Sunday] meeting it was
smallish some friends being poorly it felt refreshing
-16, was at our first day [Sunday] meeting, felt a little
renewal of Devine Goodness which tender'd and
contrited my Heart, & I was concearned to In=
=courage friends to give up to the all shearching
Power of the Lord that they might know their Hearts

verso

1810

to be cleansed and purified and made Temples for
the Lord to dwell in
12mo [December]=23 went with my Wife to our first day [Sunday]
meeting, it felt refreshing, my minde much Exercised
under a Sence of my own weakness and
liableness to slip aside as on the right Hand
and on the left without a continual watchfullness
and Circumspect walking in the fear of
the Lord, waiting upon & seeking unto Him
daily for a renewal of Strength
=30 went to our first day [Sunday] meeting, held in Silence

1811

1mo[January] 6st was at our first day [Sunday] meeting it felt a
little refreshing
-7, went to our Quarterly Meeting held at
Oxford, rather small meeting, truth felt
to be low and it to be a time of mourning,
under a sense of our weak and feeble state,
-13 was at our first day [Sunday] meeting, it felt a
little refreshing, altho a time of mourning –
=14, was at our monthly meeting held at C.
Norton, small meeting, yet I trust Devine
goodness was felt amoungst us, -
=20, went with my Wife to our first day [Sunday] meet'g
it felt refreshing, I was concearnd to speak a
little theirin to Incourage friends to Labour to have

Page 64

Obidience keep pace with Devine Knowledge
1mo [January]=27th was at our first day [Sunday] meeting my minde
was Humbled and Contrited before the Lord
I trust through the Influence of His Power
and I was very desireous to be as Clay in
the Hand of the Potter, to be what the
Lord would have me to be, O that this desire
may continue and remain with me to the
end of my days, that it may be well with my soul
2mo[February] 3rd took a walk to Witney to the Burial of
old Wm Barritts Wife who was afflicted pretty
much with the Palsy sometime before she
died, I thought it was a pretty comfortable
meeting, H. Smith was drawn fourth in Tes=
=timonie to the turning of the mindes of the People
Inward to their true unering Teacher Christ
Jesus who Inligtheneth every man that cometh into
the World, incouraging them to live in Obidience
thereunto, as the only way by which they could
come to Witness the Salvation of their Souls
I also was concearned to speak pretty much to the
same Import signifying that no form of Religion
how fine in appearance soever it might be would
not do, without comming to Expiearence the substance
of Pure undefiled Religion before God and the Father,

verso

1811

2mo[February] 10th was at our first day [Sunday] meeting my minde felt
a little refresh'd. altho sensible of much Spiritual
weakness, and of the Necessiety to Labour for devine
help and renewal of Strength –
=11, was at our monthly meeting held at Charlbury
it felt pretty comfortable I was Concearnd
to speak theirin to Incourage friends to
be faithfull in little things signifying it
was the way to know a groth in the Truth,
=17 was at our first day [Sunday] meetg
=24, was at our first day [Sunday] meeting, held in
silence, it feels to be a time of Mourning
and Probation amoungst friends
3mo[March] 3rd was at our first day [Sunday] meeting my minde was Humbled
under a sence of own unworthyness & I Labour'd to
know contritedness of Spirit, ware favourd with the
company of Sarah Squire at meeting to day, who has
been so poorly as not to attend meeting for menny weeks
=10, was at our first day [Sunday] meeting felt myself to
be a very poor Creature, yet very desireous I
might so carefully attend unto the Teachings of
Devine Power within me and be obidient unto its
leadings as to feel no Condemnation,
=16, walk'd to sibford found sistor tolerable well Lodg'd there
=17, was at the first day [Sunday] meet'g at Sibford
it felt to be a good refreshing meeting, in which
Devine Power was felt to the tendering & Contriting

Page 65

---

the Spirits of some before the Lord, after meetg
Din'd at sistors, took leave of she and some
friends & returnd Home, -
24 was at our first day [Sunday] meeting it was held in Silence
=28, at our meeting to day was favour'd
to feel Devine Goodness to be near to the
causing me to rejoice in Spirit, & I was
Inabled to speak a little to Incourage friends
to Labour for an Inward stillness and re=
=tiredness of minde that the might be fav'd
to know an acquaintance with God and be
at peace sistor H & Cousins from Campden,
at meeting who are come to pay us a visit –
31 was at our first day [Sunday] meeting it felt a little re=
=freshing spake a little theirin to Incourage the
Elders to watch over the youth for good and be
concearn'd to give them good Instruction, also advised
the youth to minde the good Instruction that was
given them and not turn a deaf ear unto it, but
esteem it as the mercy of the Lord –
4[April]=1 was at our monthly Meeting held at Burford
it felt a little refreshing
=7 was at our first day [Sunday] Meeting it felt comforting
I was concearn'd to advise friends to wait upon the
Lord & in all their trails & Exercises to seek unto
Him who knows our states & Conditions for help, whose
tender regard is towards them that fear Him

verso

1811

4mo[April] 9th walk'd with my Wife and some friends to
Witney to our Quarterly Meet'g it felt pretty
Comfortable Josh Lamb was drawn fourth in
a perticular manner to the youth signifying how
graciously he had been visited in his youth and the
Judgements of the Lord he had felt for Disobidience

unto the Instructions and requireings of his
Spirit,
Warning others not to slight the tender
visitations
of the Lord nor be Disobidient unto his Devine
Instructions, but give up wholy to sarve the
Lord, for that was the only way to be favour'd
with the Injoyment of True Peace
H Smith also appear'd & I was concearn'd to
advise friends to faithfullness – the buisness
was gone through pretty agreeabley –
=14 was at our first day [Sunday] meeting it felt
to be a
good Comforting meeting, S. Squire appeard
in Testimonie which was Comforting and
Edifying
=21, was at our first day [Sunday] meeting it felt
refreshing
I was concearn'd to advise friends to minde and
be obidient unto the pointings and Instructions
of the Living Power within them, that the might
Witness a growth in the Everlasting Truth,
=28, Went with my Wife to our first day [Sunday]
meet'g it
felt refreshing, held in Silence
5[May]=5 was at our first day [Sunday] meet'g it
felt a little
refreshing, my minde was humbled before the
Lord

Page 66

O it is the Breathing of my spirit, that I may
be preserved in true Humility & lowlyness of
minde before the Lord
5[May]=12 was at our first day [Sunday] meeting
tender breathings
ware begotten in my minde that I might be
found sarving the Lord in faithfullness –
=19, was at our first day [Sunday] meeting I was
Concearn'd
to advise friends to minde the seasons &
oppertunities which the
Lord is please to favour us with to do his Will
and do it faithfully that being the way to finde
acceptance with the Lord –
the young men being very much given to
spend their time in Revelling & rediculing
People &et as they pass about their buisness
especialy on a first day [Sunday] of the week
I was Concearn'd to write a paper to such a
solemn warning
of their dangerous state with advise
unto them to turn unto the Lord speedily &et
lest in his Anger He withdraw his
mercy for Ever put up a paper in a barbers shop
and another in another place,
=26 was at our first day [Sunday] meet'g it felt
refreshing
6[June]=1, I having felt a little Concearn to
attend a few
meetings from Home, in the A.[fter]Noon walk'd
to
Milton in the Evening call'd to se the friends their
who ware pleas'd to se me, Lodg'd at my kind frd
T. Malls

verso

6mo[June] 2nd was at the first day [Sunday]
meeting at adderbury
I was Concearn'd to speak theirin, after meet'g
went with the widow Wycheley & her Children
to ayn[h]o, spent the A[fter] noon with she & her
family
in a solid agreeable manner Lodgd their
=3, after Breackfasting with Cousin Wycherleys
walk'd
to the monthly meeting at adderbury it was
largish
but did not feel very comfortable after meeting I
return'd to Thos Malls to Din'r in the evening
walk'd
to Sibford Lodg'd at Sistors M Gilks's
=4, after breackfast took leave of Sistor &
walk'd to the
monthly meeting held at Shipstone it felt to be
a heavy meet'g as tho there was a want of
faithfull
Labourers in the Lords vineyard, in the Evening
went to
Cous'n T. Fardons, spent a little time with them
in a loving agreeable manner Lodgd their
=5 after breackfast walk'd to shipstone was at
their
fourth day [Wednesday] meet'g, I was Concearn'd
to speak theirin
I trust we ware favourd to feel the slowings of
Devine

Love to our Spiritual refreshment – Dind at Cousin
Wells's afterwards was Inabled to advise them to seek
after Devine Love that they might know it to preserve
them in unity & Love one with another & cause them to
Labour for one anothers spiritual & temporal good
in the A.[fter]Noon walk'd to Campden found our Relations
there tolerable well Lodg'd at Bro'r Wm Corks
=5 spent the day with Relations & friends in a

Page 67

solid agreeable manner was Concearn'd to give them
some good advise – I hope it will through the devine
blessing have some good Effect
7, was at friends sixday [Friday] meeting at Campden it was
small, I was led to feel & simpathise with friends
who are in a mournfull tried situation, & to Incourage
them to be Diligent in the attendance of their Religious
meetings, for I did believe the visitation of the Lord
was extended & if they ware but two or three met to=
=gether in blessed Jesus his Name, there he would
be in the midst of them teaching & Instructing them
by his good Spirit, which leads & guides into all Truth
after meeting bid Relations & friends farewell & walk'd Home,
=9 was at our first day [Sunday] meeting it felt to be a little refreshing
=10 was at our monthly meeting held at Charlbury
it felt a little refreshing, the meeting of
buisness was exercising yet I Indeavoured to labour
faithfully in the Discharge of my duty,
I finde that is the only way to Injoy Peace
=16 was at our first day [Sunday] meeting, silent
my minde has been much exercised of late
& have been greatly sensible of my own
weakness's under a sence thereof I do breathe
unto the Almighty for his good power to preserve
me from doing any thing against the Truth
if I am not able to do any thing for it yet it
is my desire that I may be Inabled to Labour for

verso

1811

its Honnour & the Honnour of the Lord
also to Incourage others so to do,
6mo[June] 21st this Evening a meeting was held by
by the Desire of two Women friends
who are on a Religious visit
it felt to be a Comforting refreshing
meeting both the friends appeard in
Testimonie and one in Solem Prayer,
-22 went to se the friends and had a Com=
=fortable oppertunity with them at
Wm Albts I trust Devine Love & mercy
was extended, O that friends may be truly
gratefull unto the Lord for all his mercie
they friends went away about 11 oclock
-23 was at our first day [Sunday] meeting –
-24, set out for our Quarterly meeting to be held
at Banbury, call'd to se some Relations
on the way who ware poorly Lodg'd at Jos: Harris North
-25, walk to Banbury to Cousin M Corks, (who is
newly set up in Buisness their) Breackfasted
their with a pretty menny friends, I think the
Quarterly meeting was pretty large and Comfortable
sevral friends appeard in Testimonie and two in
Prayer – after Dining at Henry Stones took leave

Page 68

1811

of friends and walk'd Home with Bro'r R.S.

6mo[June]=30th was at our first day [Sunday] meeting, held in Silence
I have been very desireous that I may so carefully
attend unto Devine Instructions & live in Obidience
thereunto as to feel true Peace to attend my minde
as I step along through Exercises Tryals and
proving seasons, which poor mortals are subject
to wile they have a being in this unceartain
World – this is the Peace which Christ giveth to his
Followers and is an anchor to their Souls
7[July] 7 was at our first day [Sunday] meeting it was held in Silence
in the A[fter] Noon walk with Bror to Witney call'd
to se some of the friends in the Evening Lodg'd at Jno Hankins's
8 set out pretty early for our monthly meeting to be held
at Faringdon, the m. meeting was small, after sitting a
wile in Silence I was concearn'd to speak theirin
to advise friends to Labour to know a being cloath'd
with humility & the spirit of Meekness walking
in the fear of the Lord that they might know
Pride and high mindedness brought down & to
become as Clay in the hand of the Potter to be
formed by the Lord into vessels for his use,
to be inabled to shew forth his Praise, - the Yearly
Epistle was read afterwards friends proceeded upon
buisness which was gone through pretty agreeabley
Din'd at Robt Reynolds afterward call'd to se the other
friends took leave of them and return'd to Witney –

verso

1811

6mo[June] 9 spent a little time with friends agreeabley at
Witney bid them farewell & return'd Home to Dinr
=14, was at our first day [Sunday] meeting it felt refresh=
=ing, at the close or latter end of the meeting
the yearly meet'g Epistle was read which was
Comforting to feel that friends are still concearn'd
to Incourage their Bretheren & sistors to faithfull=
=ness that they may know the work of the Lords
Salvation to go forward and a being begotten into
the likeness of the Dear Redeemer
=19 took a walk to the sixth day [Friday] meeting at
C.[hipping]Norton felt satisfaction in attending it,
=21, was at our first day [Sunday] meeting, I was
much concearn'd to labour after the pure
Power & Word of Life & feel it to arise into
Dominion, over that which opposeth it, -
=28 was at our first day [Sunday] meeting felt a little re=
=freshment, this morning was favour'd to feel
a little of Devine mercy extended, O! that I may
walk so Humbley & lowly before the Lord as always
to live under a sence theirof
8[August]=2 took a walk to the sixth day [Friday] meet'g at sibford
at which was 2 funerals viz the Widow of Jno Lamb
as went from C[hipping]Norton & Jno Hall of Hooknorton, it was
a Solemn time the People ware put in minde to prepare

Page 69

---

for Death as they knew not who might be call'd
away next therefore it was good always to live in
Obidience to the pure Power & Spirit of Truth that they might
know a being inabled thereby to cease from Sin & be
Inabled to work the works of Righteousness that they
might be prepared to enter the Glorious Kingdom

ware any unclean thing, must never enter, I think it
was a satisfactory meeting, Dind with the friends
at Jno Henocks, - drank Tea at sistors –
=3 walk'd to shipstone Din'd at Cousin Wells's in
evening walk'd to Cousin Thos Fardons Tredington Lodgd their
4, call'd to se friend Lambly's Children (she being from
Home & had been a pretty wile on a religious visit)
they appear Chearfull & comfortable so I think the
Mother being out in the Lords service, & the Children
being inclined to fear the Lord & sarve him, his blessing
rested upon them to their Joy & Comfort, was at Armscutt [Armscote]
meeting which began at 11 a Pretty large meeting of
friends and Neighbours who behav'd quiet and Commendable
it appear'd to be a good satisfactory meet'g & to be favourd
with the Lords living Power, through which his servants
ware Inabled to Instruct them how they might through
Devine assistance be inabled to walk in the way of Life & Salvation
two friends appear'd in Solem Prayer –
after meeting went to T Fardons to Din'r who ware very
kinde to friends had a Comfortable sitting with friends
after Din'r took leave of them & return'd to shipstone

verso

1811

Drank tea at Cousin Wells's I was Concearn'd to
advise the Widow & Children to love the truth &
Indeavour to be led & guided by it in all things that
they might be inabled to live in Love and be inabled to
Labour for oneanothers good booth spiritual & Temporal
walked from thence to Sibford Lodgd at Sistors
8[August]=5, walk'd to Banbury was at the monthly meet'g
their one friend appeard in Testimonie after which
friends Proceeded upon buisness which was dull and
the buisness went on heavily it being very Exercising
to the truly religious mindes, yet I hope truth
was preserved over mans Judgements & Wisdom which
leads from the pure Living power, into Contentions
after meeting call'd to se some of the friends, and
had an Oppertunity with some friends before &
after meet'g who had had some Difrence, advised
them to be tender and of a forgiving disposition one
towards another wishing they might labour through
Divine assistance to be reconciled one towards another
toward evening took leave of friends and walkd Home
-11, was at our first day [Sunday] meet'g it felt refreshing
Devine Mercy I trust was Extended, I was
Concearn'd to Incourage friends to Breathe
unto the Lord and put up their Supplications
unto Him in secreet, that He would be pleas'd
to preserve them from doing any thing against
the Truth but rather that He would Inable them

Page 70

---

to Labour for its Honour
8mo[August] 12th walk'd to our Monthly meet'g held at Burford, it
felt a little refreshing two friends appeard in
Testimonie the buisness was gone through pretty
comfortabley – after din'r walk'd Home
16, took a walk to C.[hipping]Norton to the Funeral of Wm
Coles's Wife, who died after a short illness except
she had been a little poorly before it was a

pretty large meeting of friend and Neighbours
sevral mouths ware open'd to signify the solemnness of
Death & the Necessiety to be prepared for it,
as time was precious, there being no ceartainty of
Life to the youth nor aged therefore all ware
advised to live in the fear of the Lord and love his
Power and be obidient to it in all things which work's
by Love to the purifying of the Soul –
at the grave I thought it to be my duty to pray, which I did
in a poor feeble manner, it was a humbling
Exercise to my minde, after meeting had a comfortable
sitting with friends at Wm Coles's took leave of friends
in the evening walk'd Home
18 was at our first day [Sunday] meeting it was held in silence yet
felt to be a good edifying meeting to those who ware
concearn'd to gather inward and Labour in their
own Vineyards after spiritual refreshment
-25, was at our first day [Sunday] meetg it was held in Silence

verso

9mo[September] 1 was at our first day [Sunday] meet'g, it was
held in Silence yet I hope a profitable meet'g
-8, was at our first day [Sunday] meet'g it felt re=
freshing, held in Silence,
-9 walk with my Wife & some more friends to
our M Meet'g held at C,[hipping] Norton I was concearn'd
to speak a little theirin, to Incourage friends to
faithfullness, adviseing them to be carefull not
to set their Hearts & affections upon the things
of this World so as to hinder them from comming
up in their duty to the Lord, not to love any
thing more than Him for he must have the
pre-eminence in our Hearts if we would be his
Dear Children, after meet'g I and my Wife call'd to se some
friends and spent a little time with them in an
agreeable friendly manner, in the evening walkd Home

-14, went with a friend to Reading walk'd part of
the way & rode part of the way, found Relations
& friends tolerable well Lodg'd at Jno Tutteys Sen'r
-5, was at their first day [Sunday] meetings both morning
and afternoon, in Evening call'd to se some friends
-16, was at friends monthly meeting held at Reading
after meetg Din'd at Jno Tutteys Jun'r spent a little
time with friends their agreeabley, Drank Tea at
Joseph Huntleys (who is lately remov'd to Reaging) spent
sometime with friends their agreeabley, - sup'd with

Page 71

1811

---

sevral friends at Jos Lambs, Son to the late Wm Lamb of
Adderbury he & his sistor being lately setteld their,
I was Inabled to give them a little matter of advise
signifying it was good for them to live in the fear
of the Lord and feel the approbation of truth in their undertakings
and keep to the plainness & simplicity of the Truth in their furniture
Joseph lamb of Sibford was also favourd to give
them some good advise, Lodg'd at Cousin Jno
Tutteys seinr they and their Children ware very
kinde to friends I Hope they will Injoy the
blessing of the Lord –
17, the Quarterly meeting for worship did not feel very
comfortable the buisness was gone through
pretty agreeabley, our Quarterly meet'g
agreed to contribute to the school at
[blank] near London, that they might have
the privilage to send Children there, the
terms being the same as ackworth school
after meeting Din'd at John Tutteys sein'r
took leave of them & other Relations & friends

in the Evening walk'd to Henley, was kindly
entertaind at Joseph Mays, Lodg'd their
18, before meeting call'd to se some friends
they appear'd glad to se me, the meeting was
smallish there being but few friends living their,
yet it felt pretty comfortable I was concearn'd to
speak theirin

verso

1811

Din'r at E. Swains, spent a little time there
in a religious friendly manner, afterward took
leave of friends & walk'd to Shillingford, Joseph
May was so kinde as to walk a little way with
me, with whome I had some agreable
conversation,
found Jos: Ashby and his Housekeeper as usual
very friendly & kinde Lodgd their, -
9[September]=19, was at the weekday meet'g,
(called to se some
friends before meet'g) it felt refreshing
I was concearn'd to advise friends to Labour
for Devine assistance, that they might be
Inabled to walk in the way of Peace in which
there is no Condemnation, - Din'd at Jos:
Ashbys took my Farewell of him and his
Housekeeper, he was so kinde as to send his
Nephew with his Carriage to take me
part of the way towards home, was Inabled
to reach Home about nine at night found
my Wife tolerable well, thanks be unto the
Lord for his Mercies & blessing which
we are favour'd to pertake of –
=22 was at our first day [Sunday] meet'g
=29 was at our first day [Sunday] meet'g
10[October]=2 I & my Wife went to the Burial of
Jos: Hankins
of Witney who died of a hurt he recd in his
forehead at his Eye, he liv'd about 3 Days after

Page 72

---

his wound was not thought by some to be
dangerous,
I think it might turn to a mortification,
he left a Wife and one Child, he and his
wife I believe liv'd very comfortabley together
ware married about 4 years & ware favour'd
to be comfortabley setteld in Buisness, it was
a great tryal to the Wife to loose a dear
and affectionate Husband in so suddain a
manner, & caused her to mourn deeply & shed
menny tears, I hope the Lord hath heard her
cried & if she lives in his fear & truly loves
him he will be mercifull & will be a suppor
& comfort to she & her Child,
the meeting felt pretty comfortable some
friends appeard theirin I appeard in
Prayer, believeing it to be my duty so to do,
it was an Exercise that bowed my minde in
Humility before the Lord, O! that I may
be favourd to walk in a truly humbled &
contrited state of minde before the Lord,
10mo[October] 6th was at our first day [Sunday]
meeting sevral straingers
ware their, it felt refreshing, I was con=
cearned to speak a little theirin
=13, was at our first day [Sunday] meeting it felt
refreshing
=14, was at our monthly meeting held at
Charlbury
I thought it felt as a Cloudy time & I was con=

verso

=cearned to speak a little theirin to Incourage
friends to seek an acquaintance with the
Lord that they might be favour'd with Peace
also was concearn'd to mention, let him that
thinketh he standeth take heed lest he fall
there being no safety, without we keep upon
our watch & near to the Devine Power
10mo[October]=20th was at our first day
[Sunday] meet'g silent
=27, was at our first day [Sunday] meet'g, my
minde
was pretty much exercised, & I much desired
to be found in the way of my duty
11[November]=2 took a walk to sibford found
sistor tolerable
well, spent the evening there comfortabley Lodg'd
their
=3, was at the first day [Sunday] meeting at
Sibford
it felt pretty comfortable – in the A[fter] Noon
went to little sibford to se some friends. saw a

friend in a poor low state of minde I was
concearn'd to advise her not to give way to being
cast down but to seek to the Lord for help who is
mercifull unto them that fear Him, -
-4 was at the monthly meet'g at Sibford I was
concearn'd to advise friends to Love oneanother
mentioning that Scripture"we know we are
passed from Death unto Life because we love
the Bretheren", another frd appeard

Page 73

the meeting of Buisness held long on acct
of a Difrence between two friends a Com=
=mity had been appointed to Indeavour to
get the Difrence made up, but could not
& the monthly meet'g seemd at a loss to know
how to settle it
11 was at our first day [Sunday] meet'g & on the morrow at our
monthly meet'g at witney
=17, was at our first day [Sunday] meeting it was
held in Silence, yet I trust it was a
good meeting to such as ware concearned
to be Inward & weighty in their Spirits,
& to seek after an acquaintance with the
spirit of the Dear Redeemer & to be
Taught by it,
=24 was at our first day [Sunday] meet'g it felt refreshing
I was concearn'd to advise friends not
to trust in a form of Religion with com=
=ming to expearance the substance thereof
12[December]=1, was at our first day [Sunday] meet'g it felt a little
refreshing, it was held in Silence
-15 was at our first day [Sunday] meet'g it us a low
mournfull season amoungst us yet I was
concearned to advise friends not to be discouraged
as all things work together for good to them

verso

1811

that love god in sincerity & in Truth

12mo [December]=19th attended the Burial of the Widow
Bright who Died after having been poorly
a pretty wile aged about 80 years
she was of a tender loving & quiet spirit
feeling for the Poor & Afflicted, & Charitable
to them, and a lover of Religious good friends
therefore I think she is releas'd out of
a state of Probation, into a Glorious King=
=dom, ware Love Joy & Peace will abound
for Ever – it was a large solem meet=
=ing on the occation of friends & Neigh'rs
sevral friends appeard in Testimonie & I
hope their Labours will be Blessed & have
a good effect upon the People –
after meeting the friends went to R Spendloves
to Din'r
-22, was at our first day [Sunday] meeting, held in Silence
it is a low and mournfull time, or a time
of Mourning amoungst us,
I wish it may cause us to look to our own
standing, and see if our feet are firmly
established upon the Immoveable rock
Christ Jesus, If we finde they are not
I desire we may earnestly Labour through Devine

Page 74

assistance they may be so, then I trust these
Exercises and proving seasons will work
together for our good, -
12[December]=29 was at our first day [Sunday] meeting, held in Silence
my spirit bow'd in humility & reverence
before the Lord under a sence of the
Tryals & Afflictions some of us meet with
and of the great need we stand in of
Devine help & Comfort to sopport us
under them –
O that the Lord may be pleased to arise
for the Cries of the Poor & sighing of the needy
to the scattering of their enemies, and to be
unto them strength in weakness, riches in
Poverty, and a Present help in every need=
=full time, that they may set fourth his Praise
and magnifie him amoung the People –

1812

1mo[January] 5th was at our first day [Sunday] meet'g it felt
refreshing, altho it is a humbling season
I was concearn'd to Incourage friends to waight
upon the Lord that they might feel their
strength renewed –
12 was at our first day [Sunday] meet'g my minde
was pretty much Exercised theirin,

verso

1812

1mo[January] 12th walk'd to our monthly meeting held at
C[hipping] Norton it felt pretty comfortable I was concearnd
to speak a little theirin, after meet'g
call'd to se some friends who had been pretty
much Afflicted felt I trust Devine good=
=ness to refresh us as I sat with them
=19, was at our first day [Sunday] meet'g I was
much exercised feeling something of a
Concearn rest upon my minde to appear
in Prayer, but under a sence of my weak=
=ness and the solem weightyness of the
work, I was desireous that the Lord would
lay the matter more weightily upon me
before I proceeded theirin, so put it of,
yet the Exercise rests weightily upon my
minde and I hope if it be of the Lords requireings
in mercy he will be pleas'd to open the way
and give me strength to perform His
will –
=25, took a walk to Jno Peglers maughsbury
the sight of me Perticularly affected them
as they had understood I was dead, spent
the evening agreeabley with them Lodg'd their
26, after breackfasting at J. peglers walk'd up

Page 75

to stow call'd to se some acquaintance before
meeting, the meeting was as it usualy is very
small, which is cause of mourning –
spent the afternoon at Jno Peglers pretty
comfortable in religious communication –
in the evening went to stow to se Harry
Collett and Family who ware pretty
well, they are religious People, before
supper they all neeled down & he pray'd
in a solemn manner a pretty wile
our discourse was chiefly concearning religion
I hope it tended to our eddification & comfort
27, after breackfasting with Neigh'r Collett,
had a little conversation on the weightiness of
Prayer – took leave of them and walk'd
to Burford found sistor & the Children
tolerable well went up to se Tho's Huntly
& family he gets very Infirm Lodgd at Sisrs
-28, was at friends third day [Tuesday] meeting it felt
a little refreshing I was concearn'd to speak
a little theirin, after meeting Din'd at sistors
bid them farewell & return'd Home
2[February]=2 was at our first day [Sunday] meeting it felt refreshing
-9, was at our first day [Sunday] meet'g it felt

verso

1812

refreshing I was concearn'd to speak
theirin signifying as in the outward so
in the Inward, their ware winterly
seasons Expearenced but if there
was but abideing these seasons with
Patience & cleaving to the Lord, I believed he would be pleas'd to water
us with Heavenley Rain, to the causing
us to bring forth Fruit to His Honnour,
2[February]=10, was at our monthly meet'g held
at Charlbury altho it is a low time amoungst
us, & a time of mourning yet the meet=
=ing felt refreshing & I believe the Lords
mercy is extended & he is willing to do us
good if we will but fear him and walk
in his ways I was concearn'd to appear
in Prayer, it was an Exercise to me
to give up, but being very desireous
to be found sarving & to be in the discharge
of my duty to the Lord that I might be

favourd to Injoy his Love, I gave up
and was favoured to feel it tended to my
Peace & relief of my minde
the buisness was gone through Pretty com=
=fortabley,

Page 76

2[February]=16 was at our first day [Sunday] meeting
it felt comforting & refreshing, it
was held in silence
-23 was at our first day [Sunday] meeting I was con=
=cearned to advise friends to seek after
the covering of the Spirit & Power of
the Lord that they will know his Enemies
to be scattered, & their mindes to be preserv'd
in Peace,
3[March]=1 I was at our first day [Sunday] meet'g it felt
refreshing, altho held in Silence –
=8, was at our first day [Sunday] meet'g, it was
held in Silence
=15, was at our first day [Sunday] meet'g it felt
refreshing I was concearn'd to speak a
little theirin,
=22 was at our first day [Sunday] meeting it felt
refreshing, as I was concearned to
draw near in Spirit unto the Lord,
I was desireous that I might not only
know the new Birth brought forth
but also to know a groth in the unchaingable
Truth
-29 was at our first day [Sunday] meet'g it felt refreshing
altho held in Silence I was very desireous

verso

I might follow Christ, who said whoso follow=
=eth me, shall not walk in Darkness but
shall have the Light of life,
4[April]=5, was at our first day [Sunday] meet'g it felt refresh=
=ing, - Wife gone for Burford with Bro'r & sistor
-10, took a walk to C[hipping] Norton to the
funeral of Shusanna Hatwood,
it was their sixday [Friday] meeting, & a Comfortable
refreshing oppertunity it was, menny Neigh'rs
being present after meeting call'd to se some
friends, afterwards returnd Home,
=12 was at our first day [Sunday] meeting, - in the
Evening we ware favour'd with a large
Public meeting by the desire of Henry Hull
from America, a friend in the Ministry, who
hath been from Home on a religious visit
about two years, menny Neighbours came
to the meeting & behav'd well H, Hull was
favour'd with a fine oppertunity in Testimonie
he express'd it was a pity any one should miss
of being happy when it was in their Power
to be so, then he oppened to them ther way sig=
=nifying that Christ was the way twas through the assistance
of his Power and by living in obedience theirunto
that man might know a being redeemed out of a
sinfull state, be preserv'd from sin, and in=

Page 77

abled to sarve god acceptabley, as help was laid
upon one that was mighty and able to Deliver,
all them that come unto him and have faith
in his Power which Living faith works by Love,
to the purifying of the soul – he was upon
his feet a pretty wile, I trust the witness was
reach'd in menny mindes through the power of
the Gospel, which made a deep Impression on
them O! that it may prove as seed sown on good
ground that may spring up grow and Increase
bringing fourth fruit to the Praise of the Lord,
=14 I and my Wife walked to Witney to the Quarterly
meeting it was a large and Comforting meeting
sevral Straingers ware their as Henry Hull,
Thos Clark &et sevral friend appeard in
Testimonie & one in solem prayer,
the buisness held long, yet was gone through
pretty comfortabley, after meet'g spent a littel
time with some friends took leave of them &
walk'd Home, Thankfull in my minde to Kinde
Providence for his Mercies that I and menny
more ware favour'd to pertake of,
=16, at our meet'g was favourd with the Company of Thos
Clark a ministering friend from Bristol way
the meet'g felt comforting the friend was

drawn fourth in solem Prayer, as well as Testimonie
=17, I went as guide with T. Clark to C[hipping] Norton, stopd

verso

1812

their week=day meet'g, T. Clark was drawn in Testimonie, after meeting stop'd a little with friends, took leave of them & return'd Home
=19 was at our first day [Sunday] meet'g it felt refreshing –
=26, was at our first day [Sunday] meeting, I was concearnd
to speak a little concearning the seed of the Kingdom, wishing friends might know their Hearts (by attending to the Power of God) cleansed
& kept clean theirby, that they might know the good seed to grow up & bring forth fruit to perfection, that they might know a growing up to a state of Perfection
5[May]=3 was at our first day [Sunday] meeting it felt refreshing
I was concearn'd to advise friends to keep to the Devine Law written in the Heart for by so doing we by our conduct & conversation are Inabled to bear our Testimonies against the follies & vanities that are in the world and by keeping near to the Devine Power is the way to be preserved from the sorrows & Miseries of the World
=10 was at our first day [Sunday] meet'g I trust it
was a refreshing season to some & that their mindes ware bowed in Humility & reverence before the Lord
=11, walked to our monthly meeting held at C[hipping]Norton

Page 78

I was concearned to speak a little theirin, signifying the necessiety there was for us to Labour after the ariseing of the word of Life to quicken and make us alive unto god –
after meeting Din'd at Saml Atkins's he was poorly I signified it was good in Affliction to labour after resignation to the Devine Will Indeavour not to be to much cast sown but put our trust in the Lord be of good comfort & he would strengthen our Hearts and inable us to put up our Supplications unto him so as to finde acceptance, as he was the Physician of value to whome we should seek unto for help, call'd to se some more friends, in the evening return'd Home
-17, was at our first day [Sunday] meet'g, it was held in Silence, yet I trust friends ware refresh'd and favour'd to feel the teachings of the pure enlivening quick'ning Word of Life, that speaks in Silence & whose voice is most distinctly & Instructingly felt in the silence of all flesh,
=19 this morning my Wife set out with sistor & her
son & Kathrine Morgan for the yearly meeting held in London sent a Letter to Cous'n Kewells & one to Cous'n Wm Barritts

verso

1812

5mo[May] 24th was at our first day [Sunday] meet'g, my
minde doth expiearence a low exercised state, yet through mercy was favour'd with willingness to be any thing Just what the Lord would have me to be
=31, was at our first day [Sunday] meet'g it felt refreshing
6[June]=5 my Wife with Sistor & her son return'd Home from the yearly meet'g they having had a Pretty comfortable Journey
-7, was at our first day [Sunday] meeting it felt refreshing, I was concearned to speak a little concearning the Devine Principal in man, which shows unto us our duty, but it is only as we have Faith in it & live in obidience to its pure Instruction that it will avail us, so as to Inable us to work out our souls Salvation before the Lord –
=8, was at our Monthly meet'g held at Charlbury

we ware favour'd with the Compan of Saml
Rundal out of the Carnal being in his return
from the Yearly meeting, it felt to be a com=
=fortable edifying meeting, S. Rundal was drawn
forth in Testimonie and one friend in solem
Prayer
=14 was at our first day [Sunday] meet'g a pretty
full

Page 79

meeting & I trust profitable to those whose
mindes
ware concearned to feel the ariseings of the pure
Power and word of Life in their own Hearts,
which is quick & Powerfull sharper than any
two edged sword piecing even to the dividing
asunder
of soul & spirit, Joint & marrow & is a dis=
=cearner of the thoughts and intents of the
Heart,
=21, was at our first day [Sunday] meet'g my
minde
pretty much exercised being very desireous
that Truth might arise and have the
Dominion amoungst us, yet feel as tho:
it was oppress'd and I suffer through it,
may I be willing to suffer Patiently as
Crist did, believeing that they that suffer for
his namesake will come to Reighn with Him
=27 set out for our Quarterly meeting walk'd to
sibford found our Relations tolerable well
=28, was at the first day [Sunday] morning &
Afternoon meetings
in the morning meeting I was concearned to
speak a little theirin signifying how necessary
it was to feel the Power of the Lamb of God
which taketh away the sin of the world –
in the A.[fter]Noon Jos: Lamb appeard in
Testimonie and Prayer,
after meeting call'd to see some friends I hope to
Edification

verso

6mo[June] 29th after calling to se some friends
took leave
of my Relations & walk'd to Aunt Hemmings
Epwell Drank tea their bid them farewell &
walk'd
to Banbury to Cousin Mary Corks found them
tolerable well – Lodgd their,
=30 Q meeting began at 10 oclock – it felt to
be a good refreshing meeting in which I
trust menny hearts ware bowed in con=
=tritedness before the Lord under a sence
of his mercy sevral strangers there ministers
as Ann Burges
and sevral appear'd in Testimonie & one in
solem prayer, I was concearned to speak
a little theirin, signifying it was necessary
for the youth to come to expiearence, Not to
lean on their own understandings but in all
their ways to acknowledge the Lord, and
that friends should be carefull not to trust in
unceartain Riches but in the Living God,
a woman friend found a concearn to come into
the mens meeting, she signified friends must be
a distinct People and not mix with other societies
therefore call'd to bear a Testimon against things
which others did not, and wish'd friends might

Page 80

Indeavour to be faithfull and not desire to con=
=form to the world in any thing, wish'd they
might be faithfull in their Testimonie agains
an hireling ministery, and also against war:
as the Gospel Power led from those things,
after meeting Dind at Wm Brights they ware kind
& loving to friends, afterward bid Realations &
friends farewell & walk'd Home with Bro'r
7mo[July] 5, was at our first day [Sunday]
meeting was very
desirous to feel the Injoyment of Devine
Power and to feel it to preserve my minde
in a calm serene state, because of my own
weakness and the things that we poor
creatures meet with in this world that is
apt to discomepose the minde & unsettel
it, compareable to storms & tempests
unless favoured to be preserved therefrom by
Devine goodness, -
12, was at our first day [Sunday] meeting, it felt
a little
refreshing, held in Silence – in the A[fter] Noon
walk'd with Bro'r to Witney drank tea at my
Kinde friend J. Hankins's afterward went to se
some friends who ware Poorly, Lodgd at J
Hankins's

verso

1812

7mo[July] 13th walk'd with Bro'r to our monthly meeting
held at Faringdon, it was small yet felt tolerable
comfortable I believed it my duty to speak a little
theirin to Incourage friends to strive to walk in the
straight and narrow way which leadeth unto
Life, another friend also appeared, the buisness was
gone through pretty comfortabley after meeting call'd
to se the friends, in the evening return'd to Witney
=14, Breackfasted at Jno Hankins's took leave of friends
and return'd Home,
=19, was at our first day [Sunday] meet'g, I was con=
=cearned to Exhort friends to Faithfullness
=26, was at our first day [Sunday] meeting held in
silence, yet I trust we ware favoured
to feel the living Power which humbles
and contrites the heart before the Lord
& Inables to worship God in Spirit and in Truth
-30, at our fifth day [Thursday] meeting felt a little
refresh'd, was very desireous that nothing
might hinder the flowings of Devine Love
in our Hearts to our Comfort & spiritual refreshment
8mo[August] 1 set our for Armscutt [Armscote] meet'g walk'd to
C[hipping] Norton, call'd to se some of the friends
their and rested a little walk'd from thence

Page 81

to Thos Harris's Longcompton found them
tolerable well drank Tea their, walk'd
from thence to shipstone Lodg'd at Cousin Wells's
=2, walk'd with some friends to Armscutt [Armscote]
meeting which was a large favour'd
meeting, the Neighbours ware still &
quiet, appear'd attentive to what was
deliver'd after meeting dind at Sarah Lamb=
=leys with other friends, ware we had a
Comfortable sitting together after dinner
Drank tea at Cousin Jnan Fardons took leave
of friends & walk'd to Sibford Lodgd at Brors
-3 walk to Banbury to the monthly meeting
I was concearn'd to speak a little theirin
the meeting of buisness felt rather painfull
for want of friends not enoughf getting down
to the pure witness and being led by it, which
preserves in Love and tenderness one to wards
another, and Inables friends to keep the unity
of the spirit in the bond of Peace,
after meeting went to se Hannah Jarrot who was
poorly, having sometime ago had a stroke of the
Palsy, she appeard pretty chearfull & Comfortable
Spent part of the Evening at Cousn M Corks & Lodgd their

verso

8mo[August] 4th walk'd from Banbury to Radway
to the monthly meeting it felt refreshing
and comforting & Divine Love prevailed
to unite friends in an harmonious Labour
for the honnour of truth and preservation
one of another, - after dining with friends
had a comfortable sitting together before we
Parted, which I hope through the Divine
blessing prov'd incouraging and strengthening
to oneanother in the truth, walked from
thence to Sibford, call'd to se my Relations
at Epwell, - Lodg'd at Bro: J Gibbs's
=5, took leave of Relations & friends & walk'd Home
9 was at our first day [Sunday] meeting, - in the A[fter]Noon
walk'd to Burford, was at the evening meet'g
their, it was held in silence, afterward went
with sistors up to old Thos Huntleys he ap=
=peard in a very weak feeble state Lodgd at sistors
=10, was at our monthly meeting held at Burford
sevral friends appeard in testimonie wareby

the youth ware much incouraged to hold on
their way in faithfullness, din'd at sistors & drank
Tea, in the Evening walk'd Home with sistor
Margt and her son James
16, was at our first day [Sunday] meeting it felt a
little refreshing

Page 82

18, took a walk up in the fields to se the corn
it appears to be fine crops, & good altho later by
about a month than what it has been sometimes,
I think it behoves people to be very thankfull for
good crops of corn, as Bread is now at 1,6d the
quartern Loaf & meat also dear, -
hearing the bells ring I understood it was to
signify
a rejoicing on accont of menny of the French
People being slain by the English, it grieved
me much to think that People should rejoice
at the Destruction of their fellow Mortals, and
I was concearned to go and speak to some who I
believed ware leading men theirin, I Laboured
with them, Indeavouring to convince them of
such
sinfull practises, & how contrary it was to the
Christian Nature & Gospel Dispensation,
& the command of Christ to Love our Enemies
&et
they seem'd to take it pretty well & I felt peace
by Indeavouring to relieve my minde –
I have menny times (when People have come
to Charlbury to act plays, shows, and such vain
amusements, & sinfull Practises ware by the
youth
& others are led into vanity their Hearts
corrupted
they incouraged to gratify the flesh & give way to
the lust of the Eye which is not of the Father
but of the world which lieth in wickedness)

verso

been concearned to go to the People as have kept
Public
Houses, & Indeavoured to Perswade them not to
harbour such People, Indeavouring through
Devine Assistance to make them sensible of the
sinfullness of such things and how it led people
from the fear of God into vanity to hearken to
lies Idle words &et, also I have been concearn'd to
go and speak to the Justice & men as I thought
ware in Athority to hinder such things, desireing
them to discourage or not to suffer such things,
but to use their Power & Athority to supress
them,
I now feel a degree of Peace & comfort in as=
=much as I have Labourd to discharge
my duty concearning such things, and am
thankfull that the Lord hath Inabled me
to bear a Testimonie against the Works
of Satan & his Instruments –
O! that the Lord in mercy may be pleased
to raise up menny more to bear their Tes=
=timonie against the snares & Temptations
of the Devil, that the People may be brought
of from sin & Iniquiety which in this age
doth much abound, to sarve the Living God
in reverence & fear, -

Page 83

1812

8mo[August] 23rd was at our first day [Sunday]
meet'g, I was concearn'd
to speak theirin, signifying the great trouble
and distress Disobidience to the Instructions of
the Lords spirit brought people into,
mentioning a little respecting Jonah, when he
disobey'd the command of the Lord and fled
from his presence, the Lord did not leave
him but brought trouble & Distress upon
him but when he prayed to the Lord and
repented he found mercy,
-30, was at our first day [Sunday] meeting was
in a low situation as to the state of my
minde, may I contine low enoughf as at
the footstool of Jesus, untill by his Living
Power He is pleased to raise me up and cause me
to re=
joice under a sence of his mercy
9[September]=6, was at our first day [Sunday]
meet'g, it was held in Silence
I trust I was given up to speak if I believed it
was realy my duty
=10 I was led at meeting to speak a little
concearning

our setting forth our Love to God by keeping our Dear Reedemers commandments,
12 set out for our Quarter meeting to be held at Reading
walk to Shillingford to Robert Greens who lives at

verso

---

the House ware Joseph Ashby Liv'd (who Died about a quarter of a year ago after a short Illness he was a kind open hearted man towards friends and Neighbours one that feard the Lord and sarvd
him in sincerity and uprightness of heart I trust was
favourd with the Injoyment of Devine Love which
flowed through him to his friends & Neighbours to
their Joy & Comfort, altho the Loss of him is felt by menny yet I trust he is enter'd into the Joy of his Lord,) he and his Wife entertain'd me kindly some of the family ware poorly Lodg'd their
13, before meeting call'd to se some friends, the meeting at warborough felt pretty comfortable I was concearn'd to speak theirin to Incourage friends
to faithfullness in answering the Lords requireings
spent the Afternoon with friends in a loving agreeable manner, Lodg'd at Robt Greens –
-14 set out pretty early & walk to Reading reach'd
Jno Tutteys J, about 2 oclock, found old Jno Tutty Poorly appears to break pretty much, spent the afternoon with friends agreeabley Lodgd at Old Jno Tutteys
=15 before the meeting began call'd to se some friends
the Quarterly meeting was not large yet it felt pretty comfortable I was concearn'd to speak theirin
Page 84
sevral friends appear'd in Testimonie
the buisness was gone through pretty comfortabley
after Dinner took my farewell of Relations & friends
and walk'd with two friends to Shillingford Lodg'd at R Greens
=after breackfasting at R. Greens with sevral other
friends took leave of friends and return'd Home
=20, was at our first day [Sunday] meeting it felt a little
refreshing
=27 took a walk to C[hipping] Norton (to walk Home with my Wife who walked
there yesterday) was at the first
day [Sunday] meeting, it felt a little refreshing
I was concearned to speak a little
theirin, in the A[fter]Noon call'd to see
a friend in affliction, was led a little
to simpathise with her & her Husband
and to Incourage them to trust in
the Lord & seek unto him for help &
Comfort, afterward we walked Home
10[October]=4 was at our first day [Sunday] meeting, it felt re=
=freshing, I was concearn'd to speak a little
theirin signifying all have receiv'd gifts sufficient

verso

---

as we are found through Divine assistance
Improving them to live daily to the praise
of the Lord, and as we are thus doing
it is we increase in his Favour
-5, was at our monthly meeting held at Charlbury
it felt pretty comfortable, one friend
Ester Atkins appear'd in Prayer who
I nevver heard before in Prayer –
I was concearn'd to appear a little theirin
the buisness was gone through pretty com=
=fortabley Truth appear'd to have the Dominion
=8, was at our fifth day [Thursday] meet'g I am
greatly sensible of my own weakness's In=
=wardly and outwardly and I am concearn'd
to breath & to pray unto the Lord for help & for
for His healing virtue to strengthen virtue to re=
=fresh comfort & strengthen me both Inward=
ly and outwardly if it pleaseth him, that I
may yet live to praise him upon the banks
of Deliverance a very poor creature as I
feel myself to be –
=11, was at our first day [Sunday] meeting, in a very

Page 85

low situation, being poorly in body
and exercised in my minde, yet my
dependance & trust is in the Lord and
unto him will I seek for refreshment
& Comfort, also for Deliverance from
all my Enemies Spiritual & temporal
=18, was at our first day [Sunday] meet'g it was
held in Silence, I was concearn'd to wait
Patiently upon the Lord for Devine
refreshment
=25, took a walk to milton (near Burford) to
meet=
=ing it was small only three friends
their besides my self, yet I trust
Devine mercy was extended towards us,
I was concearned to advise them to wait
upon the Lord and feel the teachings
of the spirit of the Dear Redeemer,
it is the spirit that quickeneth & giveth
Life to them that live in Obidience their=
=unto, return'd Home to tea,

verso

1812

10mo[October] 28th took a walk to Witney was
at their
fourth day [Wednesday] meeting it felt a little
refreshing
=31 took a walk to Sibford found Bro'r &
sistor tolerable well Lodg'd their –
11[November]=1, was at the first day [Sunday]
meeting at sibford
it was pretty large it being their pre=
=parative meeting I was concearned to
speak a little theirin, in the afternoon
call'd to se some friends and spent a
little time with them in a loving agree=
=able manner
=2 was at the monthly meet'g at sibford
I was concearned to speak a little theirin
setting forth, by shewing mercy it was
the way to obtain mercy of the Lord &
be forgiving others their trespases, it was
was the way to obtain forgivness of our
Heavenly Father, mentioning that scrip=
=ture, if thou bring thy Gift to the Alter
& there rememberst that they Bro'r hath
ought against thee leave there thy Gift
before the alter and go thy way first be
reconciled to thy Brother and then come &
offer thy Gift, - another friend appeard in

Page 86

Testimonie the meeting of Buisness felt rather
painfull, the work seem'd to go on heavily
their seemed to be something amoungst them
that hinderd the stream of Devine Love
from flowing as from vessel to vessel, to
the uniteing them in an harmonious Labour
together for the exhaltation of the everlasting
Truth, and the Prosperity of it amoungst
them, Din'd at Bro'rs and spent sometime
there in an agreable manner, -
=3, after Breakfasting with Bro'r & Sistor bid
them farewell
and walked Home, -
=8, was at our first day [Sunday] meeting it felt
a little
refreshing, it was held in Silence,
-9 took a walk to Witney (my Wife went
yesterday) to our monthly meeting, altho
truth appears low amoungst us yet it
felt pretty comfortable H. Smith appear'd
in Testimonie – the buisness was gone
through pretty comfortabley, after meeting
call'd to se some friends & return'd Home
=15, was at our first day [Sunday] meet'g, it felt
a little refreshing, it was held in silence
=22, was at our first day [Sunday] meet'g it was
held
in silence it was the desire of my minde

verso

1812

that I might be fervent in spirit
sarving the Lord,
11mo [November] 29, was at our first day
[Sunday] meet'g
felt my own weakness & great neces=

siety to be diligent in Labouring for
Divine support & refreshment –
12[December]=6 was at our first day [Sunday] meeting felt easy
to sit in silence, it felt a little refreshing
=13, was at our first day [Sunday] meeting I
felt a poor Creature, may I wait
Patiently for the Lords Power to streng
=then me, and Inable me to his Will
14, walk to Burford to our monthly
meeting it felt refreshing, sevral mouths
ware opened to testify of the Lords love and
goodness to such as love & fear him also to
incourage them to watchfullness,
after meeting din'd at sistors took leave of
them and walk home, with my Wife Bro: & Sistor
=20, was at our first day [Sunday] meeting, I trust we
ware favour'd with the Injoyment of Divine
Love, & I was led to speak of the Preciousness thereof

Page 87

12mo [December] 27th was at our first day [Sunday] meeting, it was
held in Silence yet I trust we ware
favour'd to feel the unering teacher amoungst
us, to our edification and comfort,
=31 was at our fifth day [Thursday] meet'g as it is
the Practice of me and my Wife constantly
to attend, except any thing very perticular
happens, am in a Mournfull state of minde
under a sence of unwatchfullness
& slippings aside, yet my trust and Depend=
=ance is in the Lord who hath all power in
heaven and Earth, & unto him will I seek
and breathe for mercy forgiveness & com=
=fort, that I may know sorrow & sighing to cease
and Joy & Gladness to spring in my Heart
with Praises unto the Lord for his mercy's

1813

1mo[January]:3 was at our first day [Sunday] meeting felt easy
to sit in Silence I trust it was a satis=
=factory meeting & friends mindes ware turned
inward to feel the Devine unering Teacher within themselves

verso

1813

1mo[January] 11th took a walk with Bro'r to Ox=
=ford (our Quarterly meeting being to
be held there on the morrow) spent
the Evening agreeabley with friends
at an Inn, Lodg'd their –
-12, the Quarterly meeting felt tolerable
comfortable, the Lord was please to
own us with his Power, sevral friends
appear'd in testimonie, to turn the Peo=
=ples mindes inward to the light of Christ
who Inlighteneth every man, that the might
be favour'd to see their own states & con=
=ditions altho man & woman may deceive
oneanother yet they cannot deceive the
Lord and as he is pleas'd to show then their
duty they ware Incouraged to do it faithfully
that they might answer the great end for
which they ware created, viz: to Glorify
God, the buisness was gone through pretty
comfortabley, after meeting Din'd with friends
at the Inn, & walk'd Home –
=17 was at our first day [Sunday] meeting it felt re=
=freshing & comforting, & I trust the hunger's

Page 88

& thirsters after Righteousness ware favoured
to pertake of Devine refreshment, -
-20 took a walk to witney was at their
fourth day [Wednesday] meeting it was smallish yet
felt a little refreshing – after meeting
call'd to se some friends, had a little sit=
=ting with Jno Hankins & his Daughters
I was concearn'd to give his Daughters
some good advise, I signified the day
of their visitation was extended & they
had had the call of the Lord, & I wished
they would live in obidience to the Power

of the Dear Redeemer as to be the chosen
of the Lord – return'd Home in the Evening
=24 was at our first day [Sunday] meeting it
was held in silence, yet felt to be a
refreshing meeting
-31, was at our first day [Sunday] meeting it
was held in Silence, yet I trust
friends ware favour'd to feel the
Teachings of the Comforter the Spirit
of Truth, wich leadeth & guideth
into all Truth
2[February]=4 as my minde was exercised at our fifth day [Thursday]

verso

1813

meeting I thought I had nothing to give
to others, but was in need of help myself
& I was concearn'd to Labour for mercy and
refreshment of the Lord, who feedeth them
that hungereth and thirsteth after Righte=
=ousness with his good things, even he
doth give Power to the faint and to them
that have no might he Increaseth
strength to them that trust in the Lord
with all their Hearts and fear to offend Him
in any thing
2[February]=7 was at our first day [Sunday] meeting, I was concearn'd
to speak a little towards the conclusion of the
meeting signifying Christ Jesus was the vine of
Life & it is only as we abide in Him and are
concearn'd to Labour to receive Nourishment from
him that we are Inabled to bring fourth fruit
to his praise, in the A[fter]Noon went to se a friend
affliction was concearn'd to speak a few word to Incourage
her to trust in the Lord Labour after Patience &
resignation unto the Will of the Lord whose mercy I
believed was extended –
-8 was at our Monthly held at Charlbury one friend
appear'd in Testimonie I felt poor & low as to my spiritu
=al state, yet my trust is in the Lord, who is riches in
Poverty to those as wholy trust in Him –

Page 89

2mo[February] 14th was at our first day [Sunday] meeting I
was concearned to draw near in Spirit
unto the Lord with desires that the
Lord by his spirit might draw near
unto me and manifest my duty clearly,
and also strengthen me to do it to his
praise and my peace
-18, was at our fifth day [Thursday] meeting it felt a
little strengthening to my minde and the
breathing of my Spirit is unto the Lord that
he may be pleased to forgive my Transgressions
which are menny from my youth up, and that
in the way of his Judgements He will be pleased
to remmember mercy, and shew mercy unto a
very poor Creature
=21 was at our first day [Sunday] meeting it was held
in Silence – as I am concearn'd to drawn near
in Spirit unto the Lord it appears to be my
duty to keep near to his power and to Indeavour
in all things to acknowledge the Lord, then I
trust by his Spirit He will direct and Inable
me to walk in the way of Peace & Joy, whose
ways are ways of Pleasentness and all his Paths Peace

verso

1813

2mo[February] 28th was at our first day [Sunday] meeting, my Exer=
cised minde was comforted under a sence
that Divine Goodness was near and I was
concearn'd to speak a little theirin –
3[March]=7 walk'd to milton to meeting (distributed some papers

concearning a Christian duty as I went along) small
meeting yet it felt a little refreshing, went from thence
to burford found Relations pretty well Except sistor
who had a soar foot, call'd to se Thos Huntly who gets
very helpless, spent sometime with him his Wife & son
in a solid tender manner, spent the evening at sistors
in an agreeable manner & I trust to our edification & Comfort
=8, after breackfast took leave of relations & walk'd Home
=9 walk'd to our monthly meeting held at Witney
it felt refreshing, I was concerned to speak
theirin to Incourage friends to be lowly &
humble & learn of him who was meek &
lowly in Heart two women friends also appeard
whose Testimonie was edifying & comforting
after Din'r call'd to se Wm Barritt (who keeps
his Bed yet appear'd sensible) & some other friends
in the evening I and my Wife return'd Home
=14, was at our first day [Sunday] meeting, it was held in
silence, yet I trust it was a good Edifying meet'g
=21, was at our first day [Sunday] meeting, I was very
desirous to Labour for Devine Instruction, that

Page 90

I might be favoured to be sensible of my duty
and also be Inabled to do it so as to feel
acceptance of the Lord
=28, was at our first day [Sunday] meeting, felt
poor & weak, However I Indeavoured
to have my minde turned inward to feel
the ariseing of Heavenly Power which
giveth strength in weakness to them that
love the Lord, did not feel my way open
to communicate any thing by Precept –
4[April]=4, was at our first day [Sunday] meeting, I was
concerned to speak a little of the new birth,
signifying it was necessary for us to know a
Child like state of Innoscency, before we
could become Heirs of the Kingdom of Heaven
=5, walk'd to our monthly meet'g held at
Burford, Devine Goodness felt to be near,
by his Power to refresh comfort strengthen
and Incourage friends to persevear in the
way of their duty, the buisness was gone
through pretty comfortabley after meeting call'd
to se some friends, afterward returned Home
with my Wife and relations, -

verso

1813

4mo[April] 11th was at our first day [Sunday] meeting a pretty
full meeting, some friends who have been
poorly a pretty wile ware inabled to get
to meeting, I was concearn'd to speak a little theirin
=13, took a walk to witney to our Quarterly meet'g
it felt to be a refreshing satisfactory meeting
sevral friends appeard in Testimonie & one in
awefull prayer two strangers strangers their viz
[blank] Powell & his Wife out of [blank] she being a
ministering friend on a religious visit, her Husband
accompanying her, a short Testimonie was brought
in (from the monthly meeting of Banbury Devision)
concearning Hannah Jarrot Deceas'd, but it not being
sign'd by the monthly Meet'g at large it was re=
=turn'd in order to be properly sign'd after meet'g
Din'd the Widow Rutters with menny friends, call'd
to se some more friends in the evening return'd Home
with my Wife Bro'r sistor &et –
=15, at our weekday meeting ware favour'd with the
company of [blank] Powell & his Wife she appeard in Tes=
timonie to friends Edification & Comfort –

Page 91

1813

4mo[April] 18th was at our first day [Sunday] meeting I was
led to consider the great Happiness those
Injoy who are quite given up to sarve the
Lord in the way of his requireings such
are favourd with the Injoyment of the
Lords Power & life giving Presence, which
maketh hard things easy and sweeteneth
the bitter cups that they have to drink of,
and such are formed into vessels of use &
service in the Lords House, - For a day
in thy court is better than a thousand
I had rather be a Doorkeeper in the House of
my God than to dwell in the tents of Wickedness,
for the Lord God is a Sun & Shield: the Lord
will give grace & Glory: no good thing will He
withold from them that walk uprightly
=22 was at our fifth day [Thursday] meeting, I feel as a
very poor Creature in a Spiritual state
& temporal also I know its good for me to
seek unto the Lord for help & strength
believeing if I Love and fear him and sarve Him in the way

verso

1813

that his holy Spirit leads & Instructs me,
I shall be favoured to Injoy his blessings
which maketh truly rich wareunto no
sorrow is added, - O pure & happy state
4mo[April] 25 was at our first day [Sunday] meeting it was
held in Silence
=29, was at our fifth day [Thursday] meeting we ware
favour'd with the Company of Stephen
Grillett from America a frenchman born the meeting was
held in Silence except I spake a little
towards the conclusion of the meeting, fearing
I should not be favoured with the injoyment
of Peace if I did not, -
5[May]=2 was at our first day [Sunday] meeting it was
held in Silence
=9, was at our first day [Sunday] meeting it was held in
silence I feel myself a poor Creature the
cares & Concerns of this Life so croud into my
minde as to cause an Exercise, yet it is the
breathing of my Spirit unto the Lord that he
will be pleased to Inable me by his Power to
aspire get above & overcome them
=10, I and my Wife walk'd to our monthly meetg
Held at C[hipping] Norton it felt pretty comfortable

Page 92

I and my Wife din'd with some more friends at J,
Atkins's, they are favour'd with much of the things
of this world, it will be well for them if they don't
take up their attention to much, so as to cause them
to overlook & neglect their duty to the Creator,
I was concerned to speak to them signifying they ware
bless'd with plenty of the things of this wourld it would
be well for them mot to trust in uncertain riches but
in the Living God, and indeavour to good with them
and Honnour the Lord with their substance and the
first fruits of all their Increase then I believed the
Lord would bless them, - afterward call'd to se some
other friends, in the evening walk'd Home –
15 set out early in the morning for the Yearly
meeting held in London rode to Oxford
breackfasted their, then walked to Warborough
Din'd at Jno Sargoods, drank tea at R Greens
shillingford (friends Company felt comforting)
afterward walk'd to Henly reach'd Henly about
9 oclock much tired, was favourd with the

company of Loving & kinde friends Lodg'd at E
Swains
16, was at the first day [Sunday] meet'g at Henly
it
felt pretty comfortable Din'd at J Mays, after=
dinr Joseph May Jun'r was so kinde as to take me

verso

1813

in his Fathers Carriage to Maidenhead reach'd
there by meeting time, it began at 4 A[fter]
N[oon]
it felt pretty comfortable I was concearn'd
to speak theirin, spent the evening at Nichos
Albrights & Wm Butts, with some other friends
in an agreeable comfortable manner Lodg'd
at N. Albrights as did Edmund Hatcher & Wife,
6[June]=17 walk'd from Maidenhead to stains
(Din'd
in my way thither at Thos Wooleys whose Wife
was
poorly a little like one in a Decline)
found Mary Ashby in a weak & poorly state
other friends tolerable well was kindly enter=
taind at Robt Ashbys. call'd to se his mother
who apper'd in a comfortable resing'd state,
Her Husband having been lately removed by
Death Lodg'd at R Ashby –
-18, call'd to se some of the friends at stains, after
Dining at Robt Ashby's walk to Saml Harris's
Brenford they ware gone London way, except
the servants, Lodgd their
=19, rose Early & walk'd to London to Cousin
Kewells
to Breackfast, at 10 oclock mew with friends
at the Opening of the Yearly meeting which felt
comforting one friend appear'd in Prayer and
sevral

Page 93

in Testimonie, Ann Burgess felt a Concern to
to visit the mens meeting, according to he
desire she was admitted she appear'd a pretty
wile in Testimonie Incouraging friends to
faithfullness in answering the Lords requireings
two Testimonies concearning Deceas'd friends was
Deliver'd & read viz: Jno Abbot [blank] & Frances
Fox [blank] – in the A[fter] Noon the answers to
the Queries ware read & remarks made thereon
another Testimonie was Delivd & read of a
Deceas'd
friend vis [blank]
5mo[May]:26 y.m. met at 10 answers to the
Queries continued to be
read & menny weighty remarks made thereon
a Testimonie Deliv'd & read concerning Thos
Colley Deceas'd also a short acct of Ann
Priestman
deceas'd Delv'd & read, A[fter] noon, answers to
the
Queries finish'd a Testimonie read Concerning
Ann Jacksons Deceas'd the Epistle from Ireland
Dermount &et read which ware comforting a
Commity
was appointed to draw up answers to the Epistles
for the approbation of the meet'g, meet'g
Concluded in Prayer
21 was at the Peel meet'g ware the Children of
Islington school attend, a favour'd meet'g sevral
Living Testimonies born, after meet'g call'd at the
school se the Children abt 100 went to Stephen

verso

1813

Mathews to din'r se H. Tyler who kept her bed
appeard glad to se me
5mo[May] 22 meet'g began at 11 oclock minute
read concer=
=ning Corespondants sevral dead more ap=
=pointed in their room menny remarks made
on the uncertainty of Life & the neccessiety
their was for all to be found in the discharge
of their duty that they might be favour'd to have
a good account to give of
their Stewardship, when reqiured so to do,
=23 was at the first day [Sunday] morning &
A[fter] noon meet'gs
which ware much favourd with the renew'd
visttation of Devine Love & mercy menny
friends appeard in Testimonie Din'd at Thos
Sturges's

=24 met y.m. met at 11 oclock felt pretty comfortable
the Women requested of the men friends that
Part of a Querie might be ommited to be an=
swer'd to the yearly meet'g for the future, the
men accordingly agreed to it
afternoon meet'g a letter was read recd from
[blank] – signifying altho through the Infirmities
of old age he was unable to attend yet Love
had drawn his minde towards them and he
was concearn'd for their Prosperity, desireing
they might be preserv'd in that Love which first

Page 94

formed them to be a society, and would be
their Preservation when other things would fail
=25 one meeting for buisness in the A,[fter]noon, a
Commity was appointed to visit the Quarterly
meetings in this Nation to Indeavour to be dipped
a little into their state, & to be inform'd wether
some alteration could be made to advantage with
respect to laying them more compact together –
one Epistle read & agreed to
=26 took a walk with some relations to Radcliff
meeting a pretty comfortable a stranger their which
spoke a pretty deal in Testimonie Din'd at Jno Harris's
and Drank tea at Saml Harris's son=in=laws
afterwards return'd to meet'g for buisness
=27, met at 11 oclock an Epistle of advise & Counsel to
friends of [blank] concluded on, a friend remark'd
as we ware concern'd to give good advise unto others
it ware good for us to look well to ourselves & Indeavour
to be Examplery in our Conduct & Conversation agreeable
to our advise given to others
Din'd at Daniel Rutters, Tea'd at Wm Dartons spent a
little time there with friends agreeabley
28, wrote a Letter to m Wife, meet'g at 11, a Commity brot
in the acct they had concluded on concerning appeals,
after some alterations it was agreed to
-29, met at 11, the Epistle to america & to the Quarterly

verso

1813

Meetings in Great Britain &et with some alterations approv'd & agreed to
the meeting felt comfortable the Lord being pleas'd to
own us with his Life giving Power, sevral friends
towards the Conclusion of the meeting appear'd in Testimonie
Incouraging friends to live in Love Indeavour to live
under the Influence of Devine Love & be faithfull
in sarving the Lord in the way of his requireings
it being the only was to obtain Peace & true Happiness
30, was at Gracechurch=street morning meeting there was
a funeral of Joseph Gurney Beavons Wife, the
Corps was Inter'd at [blank] it felt to be a
good satisfactory meeting, sevral friends ap=
=pear'd in Testimonie Stephen Gillett was
their & had a fine oppertunity in Testimonie
I was concearned to spake a little theirin,
in the A.[fter]Noon was at the Burrow meeting
which was large & Comfortable, having been
at sevral good meetings & through Divine assistance
menny mouths being opened to Publish the glad
tidings of the Everlasting Gospel, which is
Peace on Earth and goodwill towards men
it appears to be a Day of the Lords renewed
visitation unto the Children of men friends are
Perticularly called upon to be attentive & Obidient

Page 95

to the Teachings of the holy Spirit and Labour
after a state of purity & holyness of Life, in which

state with the high & low Rich & Poor there is
acceptance with the Lord and such will let
their lights shine before men, & others seeing
their good works will have cause to glorify
their Heavenly Father, -
31, after Breackfasting at Cousin Kewells who
entertain'd me kindly took leave of them in a
weighty tender manner & walked to stains, call'd
to se the Widow Chandler whose Husband when
I went
was well, I understood he set out on third day
[Tuesday] afternoon before
the Yearly meeting began intending to be at it
call'd at Wansworth to se a Niece
when he went into the House found him=
self poorly, after takeing a glass of Wine
sunk down in the Chaire and Died next
morning about 4 oclock,
a striking Instance of the uncertainty of
Life & the danger their is of putting of the
work & buisness of the present day untill
another, not knowing that we may be favour'd
with the like oppertunity because the Night may

verso

1813

---

come in which no man can work, (it may
be not altogether as to the outward day
or time, but as to the spiritual Day) before
we are aware or at an our we think not,
quarter'd at R. Ashbys Stains he & his wife
entertain'd me very kindly call'd to se their
relations
6mo[June] 1st after breackfast took my leave of
R Ashby
& family & walk'd most of the way to Maiden
=Head, stoped with friends their till after Tea
took leave of them & walk to Henly Lodgd at J.
Mays
=2, Breackfasted at Joseph may's before meetg
call'd to se some friends whose Company was
comforting, was at their fourth day [Wednesday]
meet'g at which ware
present other strangers it felt a little refreshing
Din'r at Edwd Swains, his Wives Sistor was their
on a visit, her husband & she has the
mannagement
of the Retreat at York she gave us some acct how
the afflicted ware treated, took leave of friends
& walk'd to shillingford in the A,[fter]noon call'd
to
se some of the friends their Lodg'd at R. Greens
who kindly Entertaind me
=3, was at their fifth day [Thursday] meet'g at
which we ware
I trust favour'd with Divine refreshment, after
Dining at Robt Greens bid friends farewell &
walk Home
was favour'd to finde my Wife Relations &et
pretty well, had
a pretty comfortable Journey thanks be unto the
Lord for

Page 96

---

his mercies and blessings, may I ever remember to
be truly gratefull for them,
6mo[June] 6th took a walk to Milton to meeting,
was concern'd
to speak theirin, return'd Home to tea
=13, was at our first day [Sunday] meet'g
=14, was at our Monthly meet'g it felt pretty
comfortable
=20 was at our first day [Sunday] meeting it felt
comfortable
=27, was at the funeral of old Thos Huntley of
Burford
who Died near a week ago, being about 80 year
of
age very weak & appear'd like one in dropsy for
a pretty wile before he died he was of a bold
disposition & spirit but was often I trust tender'd
& Contrited by the opperation of Divine Power
in his Heart, was favour'd with a Gift in the
Ministery, I trust he Labour'd to Discharge his
duty theirin, his appearances was attended with
Life and Power to the refreshing & tendering
the upright in Heart, I believe the Lord in
mercy hath removed him out of a state of
of Affliction, to Injoy a Crown of Righteousness,
in his Everlasting Kingdom of Joy & Peace,
wile I was in London heard of the Death of old
Wm Barritt of Witney who Died through
Infirmitie

of old age being about 86 years old He was favour'd
with a Gift in the ministery a man well beloved

verso

---

and respected by his friends & Neighbours
travel'd mostly on foot wile capable, sociable
& agreeable in Company, in his Ministery was pretty
much led to speak to the states & conditions
of such as did not profess with friends, &
Inabled to reach the pure witness in them
to the Convincing them of sin & the error
of their ways also Instructing them in their
duty, setting forth that the grace of God which
bringeth salvation hath appear'd unto all
men Teaching us to deny all ungodliness &
Wordly lust we should live soberly righteously
& Godly in this present World looking for that
blessed hope and the glorious appearing of the great
God & our Saviour Jesus Christ, who gave him=
=self for us that he might redeem us all
Inicquity and Purify unto himself a peculiar
People zealous of good Works, &et now I trust he is
favoured to Injoy an Inheritance Incoruptable
undefiled and that fadeth not away
menny of the friends in the Ministery & Elders
lately & of late years have been removed from
amoungst us and I doubt not but it is in unerring
Wisdom and who shall say unto God what dost
thou but Patiently submit to every Dispensation
of Divine Providence who doth all things well,

Page 97

may we Labour after such resignation of
minde, as to say in humble submition to his
pure will the Lord giveth & the Lord taketh
away Blessed be the Name of the Lord,
truly the Harvest appears great & the
Labourers few, O! that it may be our great
concern to Pray unto the Lord of the Harvest
that he will be pleased to send fourth more
Labourers into his Harvest, for his Power
is the same and he is able now as ever he was to
raise up Children unto Abraham & I trust
he will do it, if there is but a looking and breathing
unto him for help & truly submitting our
Necks to the Yoke of Christ Jesus, then will
He be pleased to carry on his own Work
& cause friends (as well as menny more not in
society with us) to be Instruments in his Hands
to Labour to His Honnour & Praise to the spreading
& Exaltation of the Everlasting truth in the
Earth to the turning People from Darkness
to Light and from the Power of Satan unto
the Power of God & to the Power of Jesus Christ
which as it is believed in and loved also Obey'd is the
Hope of Glory and Produceth Glory to God in
the highest Peace on Earth & good will amoungst mankinde

verso

1813

6mo[June] 29th walk'd to Banbury to our Quarterly meet'g
held their (my Wife went yesterday with her
relations) I trust we ware favour'd with
the renewed Influence of Divine Power to
our comfort & spiritual refreshment,
one friend appear'd in Prayer & some in
Testimonie the Buisness was gone through pretty
comfortably Din'd at Jno Heads, he maried
Cousin My Cork, call'd to se some of the friends
after tea walk'd Home
7[July]=1 was at our fifth day [Thursday] meet'g, in the Evening
my Wife Sistor &et returned Home
=4 was at our first day [Sunday] meet'g it felt to be a
good refreshing meeting I was concerned to speak
theirin, signifying it is the Lords good Power
& Presence which quickeneth giveth Life
& Inableth us to deny ourselves take up our
daily cross, follow and Obey the leadings of
the spirit of the Dear Redeemer, which
such as wait upon the Lord are favoured to feel
and He is so gracious as to strengthen and abilit
his People according to the work & duty he is

pleased to point out & require at their Hands

Page 98

1813

7mo[July]=8th was at our fifth day [Thursday]
meeting felt poor
& weak was concern'd to labour for that food
which nourishes up the soul unto Eternal Life
=11, was at our first day [Sunday] meet'g my
minde
was comforted under a sence that the Lords
Power was felt, and his spirit is striving with us,
in order to bring us nearer to himself and
cleans us from all unwrigtheousness if we will
but submit in all things to his Will
I was concern'd to speak a little theirin
in the A.[fter]Noon walk'd to Witney drank tea
at frd Hanh Rutters was comforted with
friends there under a sence that Divine
Love was felt amoungst us Lodgd at
my kinde friends Jno Hankins's
=13, rose early after Breackfasting at J Hank's
walk'd with Daniel Rutter & another
friend to Faringdon to our Monthly Meet'g
not very large two strangers their viz
Wm Bird & Rebecca his Wife it felt pretty
comfortable W. Bird appeard in Testimonie
in the Evening a meeting was held by the
desire of W & R Bird the Neighbours ware
let know & menny came, it was a comfortable

verso

---

meeting, Wm & his Wife appear'd pretty
much in Testimonie which felt to be
attended with Life & Power & to reach
the witness in menny mindes to convince
them of the errors of their ways & Instruct them
in their duty, turning their mindes Inward
towards the Divine Power & light of Christ,
which Inlighteneth every man that cometh into
the world that through living in obidience
thereunto they might be Inabled to walk in the
straight and narrow way which leadeth unto
Life, sup'd at J Rennolds's & Lodgd at Rich'ds
-13, Wm Bird & his Wife intending to be at the
weekday meeting at Burford I walk'd
thither in my way Home it felt a satisfactory
good meeting, Wm Bird & his Wife appear'd in
Testimonie I Din'd at Sistor Manders spent
a little time there comfortabley in the A[fter]
Noon return'd home
=15, Wm Bird & his Wife attended our weekday
meeting, it felt to be a time of renew'd visitation
of Devine Mercy, the friends both appear'd, they
ware I trust Inabled to speak to the states of
friends present,

Page 99

1813

7mo[July]=18th was at our first day [Sunday]
meeting it felt comfortable
it was held in Silence except at the conclusion
of the meeting the Yearly meet'g Epistle was
read,
=22, was at our fifth day [Thursday] meeting it
was held
in silence a comfortable meet'g believing that the
true Light shined amoungst us, which lets
us se our own states & conditions which is
a favour
25, was at our first day [Sunday] meeting it felt
com=
=forting & refreshing, I was concerned to
advise young friends to give up all &
sarve the Lord faithfull in the morning
of their day, & then I believed the Lord would
be with them and be their support & comfort
in tryals Exercises & Afflictions, & they
would be Inabled to rejoice under a sence of his
Love –
=29 was at our fifth day [Thursday] meet'g a
trying meet'g
=31 in the A[fter] Noon walk'd to Shipstone
drank
Tea at Thos Harris's Longcompton his wife
was poorly Lodg'd at Cousin Wells's shipstone
8[August]=1 after breackfasting with Cousin
Wells's was
Inabled to give them some good advise, call'd to

verso

se some friends at Shipstone, walk from
thence to Armscutt [Armscote] to meeting not very
large but it felt pretty comfortable
sevral friends appear'd in Testimonie
I was concerned to appear in Prayer in a
few words, - Din'd with menny friends at
Cous'n Jnan Fardons Tredington & drank
Tea at Sarah Lambleys she was out from
Home on a Religious visit, her Children
appear to be Religious friendly young men
& Women, I believe they love the Lord his Truth
& People are a Blessing to their Mother
and an Incouragement to her to give up all
to sarve the Lord & labour in his Sarvice,
in the evening walked with Sistor Cork to
Campden found Bro'r Wm & Relations tolerable
well lodg'd at Bro'rs
=2, visited my Relations & friends it was short
but I trust to our Edification & comfort after
Tea walk'd with Bro'r Cork & Cous'n Jno Bissel
to Shipstone (they being on their way for their
monthly meeting) their I took my leave of them
and walk'd to Thos Harris's Longcompton Lodgd there
=3 after breakfasting with Thos Harris & family bid
them farewell and return'd Home, call'd at C[hipping]Norton

Page 100

1813

to se some friends, was at a meeting of the
Bible society
8mo[August]8th walk'd with some Relations to milton to
meeting, from thence we walk'd to sistors Burford
to Din'r, they ware tolerable well except
my Nephew Wm Mander who was poorly –
was at friends Evening meeting, it felt refreshing
=9, was at our monthly meeting held at Burford
at which we ware favour'd with the Company
of two friends on a Religious visit Joseph Metford
& Joseph Clark from Somersetshire they appear'd in Testimonie
and one of them in Prayer I trust it was a good
meeting Divine Goodness being Pleased to own
us with his Life giving Power, - the buisness
was gone through pretty comfortabley, Robt Huntley
& [illegible] Renolds pass'd the meet'g in order for Mar:
=10, last evening the friends Joseph Metford & Jo:
Clark came to Charlbury, on whose acct a meet'g
was held for friends began at 11 oclock – it felt com:
fortable (the friends both appear'd in Testimonie)
and in the Evening a Public meeting was held
it began at six, a pretty menny Neighbours ware
Present, who ware quiet & attentive to what was
deliver'd the friends appear'd a pretty wile in
Testimonie and one of them in Solem Prayer,

verso

I trust it was a good meeting & the witness
was reached in menny mindes and they ware
favoured to se the sinfullness of sin & the danger
there was of their loosing the Love and favour
of the Lord for Ever if they persisted theirin
also to see the necessiety there was for them to for=
=sake sin turn to the Lord with their whole
Hearts and live lives of Righteousness if they
would Injoy his favour and finde acceptance
with him,
15, was at our first day [Sunday] meet'g, it felt refreshing
altho held in Silence, & I trust we ware
favour'd to pertake of Divine refreshment
to the renewing of our Spiritual Strength
22, was at our first day [Sunday] meet'g felt a poor
creature, felt strong desires raised in my minde
that I might keep close to the truth (the Divine
Teacher) & so live in Obidience to its leadings
as to feel sweet Peace to attend my minde,
a midst the various tryals and Exercises that
I may have to go through,
29 was at our first day [Sunday] meeting a pretty full
meeting sevral Strangers ware present I

was concearn'd to draw near in Spirit unto the Lord
and breathe unto him that I might be preserv'd

Page 101

in the way of my duty being very desirous
to Injoy true Peace which this world nor all
the things thereof cannot give neither can
they take it away from the Children of the
Lord, whose chiefest Joy is to be found walking
in the Truth,
=30 having heard that Jos: Lamb of Sibford had
for sometime been very ill of a fever, wrote a few
lines & sent him by a friends, signifying my
simpathy with him& his family on acct of his
Illness, with Incouragement for them to trust in the Lord
9mo[September]=5th was at our first day [Sunday] meet'g it felt refreshing
a Silent meet'g, it was our preparative meet'g,
in the afternoon my Wife walk'd with Bro'r &
sistor to C[hipping] Norton in order to be at the monthly
meet'g to be held their on the morrow –
=6, very wett morning, I walk'd to C[hipping] Norton
to our monthly meetg it felt pretty comfortable
some friends appear'd in Testimonie I also was
concern'd to speak theirin, the buisness was gone
through agreeabley, after meet'g call'd to se
some friends, drank tea at Wm Atkins Jun'r he
& his Wife ware friendly and kinde, in the Even'g walk'd Home

verso

1813

9mo[September] 12th set out early for our Quarterly
meeting to be held at Reading Wm Albt
was so kinde as to let me ride with him
to shillingford reach'd warborough
meet'g which began at 11 oclock, it was
held in Silence Din'd at Robt Greens
in the afternoon visited some of the friends
who appear'd glad to se me, Lodgd at R. Greens
13, walk'd to Reading, call'd to se some
Relations & friends, our meeting together
I trust through Divine mercy was to
our Edification & Comfort Lodgd at Cousin Tutteys
-14, call'd to se some friends before meet'g
sevral strangers ware at the Quarterly
meeting, three friends of the Yearly meetg
commity appointed to visit Quarterly meet'gs
also Jno Sim & Jno Wilkinson ministering
friends sevral friends appeard in Testi=
=monie signifying the day of the Lords
visitation was Extended, Incouraging friends
to be quite faithfull in Sarving the Lord in
the way of his requireings, then would He

Page 102

cause their Lights to shine before men
& they would be as a City set upon an
Hill that could not be hid, the meet'g
concluded in Prayer, the buisness was
gone through Pretty comfortabley –
after meet'g Din'd at Cousin Jnan Fardons
bid friends farewell, & walk'd with
Jno Enock to Shillingford Lodgd at Robt Greens
=15 set out early and walk'd Home –
found my Wife tolerable well, having
had a pretty comfortable Journey, for
which favours and menny more my minde
is bowed in Humble thankfullness
before the Lord, -
-19 was at our first day [Sunday] meet'g I trust it
was a good meeting altho held in Silence
in which the Truly Religious mindes ware
drawn near to him who is the Fountain of
life, from whence all our mercies & good things
spring, who is pleased to administer to his People
(as they are concerned to draw near to him) food
and refreshment suitable to their states & Con=
=ditions without the help of man –

verso

1813

9mo[September] 26th was at our first day [Sunday] meeting, it felt

to be a refreshing meeting, I was concern'd
to Incourage friends to wait Patiently for
the arising of the Power of Life, that
they might be a living People, and be
Inabled to shew fourth the Praise of the
Lord
10[October]=3 took a walk to milton to meet'g,
I trust
we ware favoured to pertake of Divine
refreshment
=4 was at our monthly meet'g held here
(at Charlbury) it felt a little refreshing
I was Concearn'd to speak a little theiring
to Incourage friends to labour after a
state of true Silence, in which they might
be favour'd to know their true Teacher Christ
Jesus the Light within, the hope of Glory
and have their dependance on the Lord by
which they would be preserv'd from the be=
=setments of the Enemy – the meeting of buis=
=ness did not feel very lively I feel so weak
as not to be able to Labour in such a vigiours
manner as to obtain my minde relived from
oppresion, the meeting at milton was drop't

Page 103

10mo[October] 10th was at our first day [Sunday]
meet'g I was
very much concern'd to feel a renewal of
strength being much sensible of Spiritual
weakness & Inability to Labour on Truths
behalf without Divine assistance, one
friend appear'd to Incourage friends to
Faithfullness in answering Divine
Instructions, in the Afternoon attended a
Commity appointed by our monthly meeting to
draw
up minutes or Testimonies, concerning Wm
Barritt & Thos Huntley ministering friends
lately deceased, a Testimonie was drawn up
concerning Wm Barritt, & the Commity
appointed
to meet next first day [Sunday] to draw up a Tes=
=timonie concerning Thos Huntley, it felt to be
a refreshing season,
=17, was at our first day [Sunday] meeting spake
a little theirin, to Incourage friends to
dwell near to the Divine Power that
they might be favoured to se their Duty
with desires, that they would be faithfull
in the discharge thereof, in the Afternoon
attended Part of a Commity who met to

verso

1813

to draw up a Testimonie (as was agreed
upon last first day [Sunday]) concerning Thos
Huntley Deceased a testimonie was
drawn up but not finish'd sevral of the
commity not being present –
10mo[October] 24th was at our first day [Sunday]
meeting,
my earnest desire & Labour of Spirit
was to draw near in Spirit unto the
Lord that I might be favoured to
feel my spiritual strength renewed,
being sensible of much weakness,
7 that of my ownself I could do nothing
=25, this morning friends ware favour'd
with the Company of Jos Wood from
[blank] who is on a Religious visit (Wm Midg=
ley accompanying him) he appeared pretty
much in Testimonie he very much desired that
friends might be concerned to present
by the mercies of God their bodies a Living
sacrifise Holy acceptable unto God, which is
our reasonable service
10[October]=30 having felt drawings in my
minde to
be at adderbury first day [Sunday] meetg &
monthly
meeting at Sibford

Page 104

set out about one oclock walk'd to Dedington
to Thos Fardons, he & his Sistor in law ware
friendly & kinde had some Religious con=
versation with them call'd to se the other
friends who live their - -
=31 after breackfasting at Thos Fardons
walked with him to Adderbury mill,
Thos Fardon & some of his family being
lately come from Tredington to reside
their before meeting call'd to se some

of the friends of Adderbury, the meeting
felt pretty comfortable I was concearn'd
to speak their=in to Incourage friends to
faithfullness, signifying the Lord had
begun a good work in them & he would
carry it on to his own Praise if they ware
but willing & obidient in answering his
requireings, after meeting din'd at Thos Malls
milton, walk'd from thence to Hooknorton
to an evening meeting apointed by the desire
of Joseph Wood, at the meeting a pretty
menny Neighbours ware present Joseph
was pretty much drawn fourth in Testimonie
the People behaved solid and attentive and I

verso

1813

trust it was a good satisfactory meeting
after meeting walk'd to little sibford Lodg'd at
Jos Harris
11mo [November] 1st , went to Bro'r Gibbs's
found them
Tolerable well was at the monthly meet'g
held at Sibford Joseph Wood & his Companion
ware there the meeting was held in Silence
except one friend spake a few words –
the Buisness was gone through pretty com=
=fortabley, Din'd at Bro'rs, afterwards
walk'd to little Sibford to se Jos Lamb who
is finely Recover'd Drank tea with him his
Wife & friends, I trust friends ware com=
=forted & thankfull unto the Lord under a
sence of his mercy in Raising up Jos Lamb as
from the brink of the Grave, he having
been a usefull member in the Church &
concerned to Labour to the honour of the Lord
& to
the Edification and comfort of his People
=2, after breackfast tooke leave of Relations &
friends & walk'd Home, Bro'r Gibbs Daugh'r
yesterday rode in Edwd Hopkins cart to
C[hipping] Norton, and to day walk with me to
Charl=
bury altho not quite nine years old –
=7 was at our first day [Sunday] meet'g

Page 105

11mo [November] 8th m Wife & I went to our
monthly
meet'g held at Witney it was rather
small but felt pretty comfortable
after meet'g call'd to friends & walk'd Home
=14 was at our first day [Sunday] meeting
=21, was at our first day [Sunday] meeting it felt
re=
freshing, was Inabled to speak Incouraging
to the youth signifying it is the day of the Lords
visitation
to their souls, wishing them to yield obidience
to Divine Instructions give up all that
the Lord is calling for at their Hands &
sarve him in the morning of their day
& then I trust he would favour them with
the Injoyment of his Love give them
Bread to eat & Raiment to put on be
with them in the way that they should go,
enable them to se the baits and snares of
the Enemy of their Souls & refuse them
=28, was at our first day [Sunday] meeting, it
was held in silence, yet I trust Divine
Love was felt to be present amoungst us,
12[December]=5 was at our first day [Sunday]
meeting I was
concern'd to speak theirin, to Incourage

verso

1813

friends to live in the fear of the Lord
which is a Fountain of Life which
preserves from the snares of Death
Bro'r J Gibbs & Cousin W Gibbs came
from Sibford to se us to day, -
12mo[December]=12th was at our first day
[Sunday] meeting, it felt
refreshing altho held in Silence, &
I trust Divine Goodness was felt to
the tendering & Contriting the Spirits
of the Humble – 13th was at our monthly meet'g
held at Burford at which the two Testimonies
Concerning T Huntley
& Wm Barritt ware sign'd

=19 was at our first day [Sunday] meet'g, I felt
in a low Situation sensible of
weakness yet I am concerned to wait Patiently
and labour after the Injoyment of
the Power of him who is the Physician
of soul & Body that I may feel Inward
& outwardly refreshed & strengthened
=26 was at our first day [Sunday] meeting, I was con=
=cerned to speak a little theirin, to Incourage
friends to wait Patiently upon the Lord that
they might know their Hearts prepared and
they might be Inabled to offer such offerings
as would be accepted of the Lord, the meeting
felt a little refreshing,

Page 106

1814

1mo[January] 2nd was at our first day [Sunday] meeting we
ware favoured with the company of
George Withey, a friend in the ministery
it was a Comforting refreshing meeting
George was favour'd pretty much in Testimo=
=nie signifying it was the day of the Lords
mercy, Incouraging friends to persevear
in the way of Truth & Righteousness,
the meeting was Concluded with solem
Prayer
=4 I & my Wife went to our Quarterly Meet'g
held at Oxford, I trust it was a satisfactory
good meeting in wich Divine Goodness
was Pleased in mercy to own us with his
Living Power and Presence to the
comforting & refreshing of menny Present sevral friends
appear'd in Testimonie & some in Solem
Prayer, friends ware advised to be pure in
their love to the Lord & not to have their minds
to much set on the Things of this world the Low
& feeble ones, ware Incouraged to press forward
and trust in the Power of the Lord who will be
unto such strength in weakness Riches in Poverty
& a present help in the needfull time

verso

1814

1mo[January]=9th was at our first day [Sunday] meeting it felt
a little refreshing, it was held in Silence
in the A,[fter]Noon my Wife walk'd with Bro:
& Sistor &et to C[hipping]Norton, intending to be at
the monthly Meeting there to morrow
=10 I walk'd with some more friends
to C,[hipping]Norton to our monthly meet'g –
it was not very large yet felt pretty com=
=fortable some strangers ware there who
are on a religious visit to friends families
viz Jos Lamb Thos Harris & Ann Ashby
they all appeard in the way of Testimonie which
felt to be attended with the Living Power
one friend appear'd in Solemn Prayer
in the A,[fter]noon walk home with my Wife
& some more friends
14, this A,[fter]noon the friends who are on a Religious
visit to friends families arived at Charlbury
15, this morning the friends above mentioned
Paid I & my Wife a visit it felt to be a refresh=
=ing season they ware concerned to Incourage us
to persevear with simplicity & godly sincerity in the
way of welldoing signifying it was not only

Page 107

necessary to feel a state of Resignation & willing
to do the will of the Lord but that we should
be concern'd to feel his Instructions and Guidance
in our undertakings & Labours – that we
might do the Lords work in his own way
and time
=16, the visiting friends set out this morning
for southnewington intending to be at a
Funeral there, I was at our first
day meeting, altho I feel feeble and
weak as to a spiritual state yet I feel
it to be my duty to Indeavour to press for=
=ward in the little pointins of duty useing
diligence to Labour after that food which

I so much stands in need of, and nourishes
up the soul unto Eternal Life, the
meeting felt a little refreshing
=17, this morning Joseph lamb &et left us
and we ware visited by another friend viz:
Elizth Caggeshall from America & by her
desire a Public meeting was held in the
Evening it began at 6 oclock

verso

1814

---

it was pretty large and I trust a satisfac=
tory meeting Eliz: appear'd a pretty wile in
Testimonie indeavouring to turn the mindes of
the People Inward to the living Power, the Word
nigh in
the heart & in the mouth which if they would
believe in it and obey it, it would cleanse and
purify their Hearts and make them wise unto
salvation she also signified the ministers
of Christ ware not Hirelings, but as
they freely received so they freely adminis=
=tered to the People
18, a Deepish snow I went with E. Caggshall
to C,[hipping]Norton had a trying Journey it
snowing & the winde blowing pretty
much ware favour'd to get there safe
I return'd in the A,[fter]noon –
-20, was at our fifth day [Thursday] meeting
-23, was at our first day [Sunday] meeting it felt a
little refreshing
of late it has been cold Weather and much
snow lying on the ground so that People
and Coachs have been hindred from Travel=
=ing at times, & some People have lost their
lives by the severity of the weather, and it
being such that some Poor People have
been hindred from their Labour fireing
also being scarse a Colection has been made

Page 108

1mo[January] 1814

---

for the Poor I have been Imploy'd at times
with others in attending to giving away wood &
Coal &et
to the Poor
=30 was at our first day [Sunday] meeting, it was
held in Silence yet I trust it was a profitable
meeting to the travilers Zion ward
2[February]=3 our week day meet'g was held in
Silence
=6 was at our first day [Sunday] meet'g, I was
Desireous to draw near to the Lord
in solem Silence, that I might be
favour'd to feel my strength renewed
as I finde it necessary to Labour out=
=wardly got outward food to support the
outward Body so daily I feel it Necessary
to Labour Spiritualy to Obtain Spiritual
food to keep my Soul alive to refresh &
Nourish it and to Inable me to perform
that Labour and Duty unto the Lord,
which is necessary for the Salvation of
my Soul
=13 was at our first day [Sunday] meeting ware
fav'd
with the Company of the friends who have
been on a visit to friends Families viz:

verso

1814

T. Harris J Lamb & Ann Ashby the meeting
felt comfortable, and I trust friends ware
drawn into a patient waiting upon the Lord
to feel after an acquaintance with Him in
spirit, and to feel their strength renewed
one friend appear'd in Solem Suplication
2mo[February] 14 was at our Monthly meeting,
held at
this Place (Charlbury) the visiting friends who
ware at our monthly meeting yesterday ware at
our monthly meeting to day, it was rather

small, -altho little was said by way of Tes=
=timonie yet Divine Goodness was pleas'd
to own us with his Lifegiving Power to
the renewal of our strength & to the Incourag=
=ing us to persevear in the way of Truth
& Righteousness – the buisness was gone through
pretty comfortabley, a friend expressed friends
should Indeavour to expearince our meetings
to be governed by the Athority & Power of God,
and not in mans Wisdom that we might be
Inabled
to support the Law & the Testimonie,
=20 was at our first day [Sunday] meeting, it felt
comforting
in which Divine Goodness was pleased to re=
=fresh & strengthen such as ware concern'd to
draw near unto him in spirit and seek an In=
=ward acquaintance with him,

Page 109

I was concern'd to speak theirin, to set
forth the benifit of Solem silence, signifying
tis in Stillness god is known & to such
as Patiently wait upon him he is pleas'd
to appear by his Power manifesting to
them their states & Conditions showing
them what is evil & what is good and
as they are concerned to live in Obidience
to his Divine Power strengthening and
Inabling them to refuse the evil & do
that which Good,
=27 was at our first day [Sunday] meeting, I trust
it was a profitable meeting altho held
in Silence,
3[March]=6 was at our first day [Sunday]
meeting it was
held in Silence, it was my fervent desire
we might be concern'd spiritualy to Labour
to feel the Springings up of the living
power & word of Life to Inable us to
Worship the Lord in Spirit & in Truth
=13 was at our first day [Sunday] meeting such
as ware concerned to wait patiently
upon the Lord, I trust ware favour'd to feel

verso

1814

their Spiritual strength renewed,
3mo[March]=14th walk'd to our monthly
meeting held at Witney
smallish meeting it felt to be a low time amoungst
us, yet I trust we ware favoured with the over=
=shadowings of Divine Goodness which united
us
in a Spiritual Labour for the Prosperity of
the Truth, after meeting call'd to se some
of the friends, sat a little with Thos Smiths
Daughter
& Jno Hankins Daughter who ware both very
poorly I was concern'd to Incourage them
to love the Lord & seek unto him for
Comfort & refreshment, return'd Home in the
Even'g
=20 took a walk to Burford found sistor
poorly was at the first day [Sunday] meet'g their,
I was concern'd to Incourage friends to be
diligent in the attendance of their religious
meetings to wait upon the Lord & Worship
him, after Dining at sistors & sitting a little
with she & her Children, walked Home with
her Daughter Ann
=27 was at our first day [Sunday] meeting it was
held
in silence, & I trust profitable to such
as ware concern'd to exercise Patience & Labour'd
to know the Lord who hath begun a good work
in them, by his Power to carry it on to his own
Glory & their Peace and Joy in the Holy Gost,

Page 110

1814

4mo[April] 3rd yesterday Bro'r Gibbs came and
fetch'd
my Wife to sibford to pay her Relations
a visit their, this day was at our first
days meeting, I trust we ware favoured to
feel the goodness of the Lord to refresh & Com=

=fort us, I was concerned to Incourage
friends to Faithfullness & to Indeavour to
live up to the Principal which we Profess,
it was our Preparative meeting in which the
Queries ware answer'd I express'd to the
youth that I believed they had felt the visitation
of Divine Love to the tendering & contriteing
their Spirits and bowing them in Humility
before the Lord, & I wish'd them to live in
Obidience to the instructions of his Spirit
& then I believed he would cause his bles=
=sings to rest upon them - - -
=4 took a walk to our monthly meeting
held at Burford it felt comforting
& I trust friends ware refreshed being
sensible Divine Mercy was extended to
them some advice was given in Testimonie
Dind at Thos Huntleys, towards Evening
took leave of Relations and return'd Home

verso

1814

4mo[April] 10th was at our first day [Sunday] meeting, we
ware I trust favoured to feel Divine Love
to be present amoungst us, to the tender=
=ing our hearts & Contriteing our Spirits
before the Lord, blessed be his Name
=12 took a walk with my Wife & some more friends
to Witney, to our Quarterly meeting, it felt
comforting Divine Goodness continuing to be
gracious & to own us with his living power,
sevral friends appear'd in Testimonie, to
turn the mindes of the People inward toward
Christ the true Light that enlighteneth every man
that cometh into the world Incouraging them
to live in Obidience theirunto Praying that they might
be Inabled to Worship the Lord in the
Beauty of Holiness & newness of Life
after meeting spent a little time with friend
in the Evening I and my Wife walk'd Home
with menny friends, -
=17, was at our first day [Sunday] meeting it felt com=
=forting Indeed it is very precious to feel Divine
Love to flow amoungst us I was concern'd to
speak a little theirin to Incourage the youth
in Perticular to love the Inward and Spiritual

Page 111

---

appearance of the Dear Redeemer –
=24th walked to Witney to the funeral of Thos
Skinners Eldest Daughter Ann she was a young
woman about 18 years old Just in the blume
of life, who a few weeks back appear'd
Healthy & Blooming is now numberd with
the silent Dead, which is as a warning
to youth to prise their time, & Indeavour
always to live in a state of preparation
for Death as not knowing but that they
may be call'd away as at the third Hour
of the Day, before the Judge of all the
Earth, to give an account how they have
spent the precious time which hath
been afforded to them, and to receive a
reward according to their Works, O! how
solemn, May every one duly consider
of those things in time, lest the pale face
messenger should be sent to them in an
unlooked for & an Unprepared state –
it was a pretty large meeting on the
occation a pretty menny Neighbours being present
who behaved solid & Commendable, Joseph
Lamb & Ann Ashby ware their

verso

1814

---

sevral friends appeard in Testimonie
and one in Prayer after meeting spent a
little time with some friends, in the Evening
walk'd Home,
5[May]=1, was at our first day [Sunday] meeting, silent meet'g
=5, this morning alittle before friends went
to meeting R Spendlove was taken with
a kind of fainty fitt, which is very alarm=
=ing for one of his age, he being at times
taken suddainly poorly before, and altho

he has been favoured as yet to recover
it appears to be a warning from the Almighty
to him and others, through Divine assistance
to Labour to be ready to bid adieu to this
World and all the things thereof when=
=ever the Lord shall se meet to remove
from works to Rewards –
=8, was at our first day [Sunday] meeting it felt re=
=freshing in which the Lord was pleased
to own us with his Lifegiving Power &
presence, I was concern'd to speak theirin
to set fourth the Preciousness of the Truth
signifying it was more to be desired than
any thing thing this world affords because
it inables through faith in Christ to Obtain
an Inheritance in his Everlasting Kingdom

Page 112

5[May]=9 walk'd to Monthly Meet'g held at C[hipping]Norton
my Wife going yesterday with some friends
one friend appear'd in Solem Prayer,
the buisness was gone through pretty agreeabley
Din'd at Sam'l Atkins's they are very kinde
friends, return'd Home pretty soon after Din'r
=15 was at our first day [Sunday] meeting I was
concern'd to wait in Patience upon the
Lord to feel a renewal of strength being
greatly sensible of the necessiety their
is for so doing, the meeting was held in silence
=22 was at our first day [Sunday] meeting it was
held in Silence, the desire of my minde
is that I may attend to the teachings of
the Truth within my own breast, & live
in Obidience thereunto, so as to feel sweet
Peace to flow in my minde, as the Prophet
signified, the Lord will keep that man in
Perfect Peace whose minde is stayed on
him because he trusteth in Him, -
=29 was at our first day [Sunday] meeting I trust
friends ware favour'd to pertake of
Divine Refreshment, I spake a little
theirin to Incourage friends to trust in the
Lord with all their Hearts & to Love & fear Him

verso

1814

6mo[June] 5th was at our first day [Sunday] meeting it
was held in silence I was desirous to
feel the Lords Power to Inable me a poor
weak Creature, to walk before Him in
truth with a clean & upright heart doing
that which is pleasing in his sight –
=7 this day the Husbands of two of Steph'n
Mathew's Daughters Drank tea with us
they having come from London for a
few days to se the contry ware their
Wives Mother formerly liv'd –
=9 at our weekday meeting was favour'd a little
to se the nature of true Silence, it felt to
me very precious, and good for the Children
of men to be acquainted with, Especialy in
their approaches & Worship to Almighty God,
to feel their own Wills runnings & Desires to be
silenced & to know a being brought of from the
lo, here is Christ and lo there is Christ unto Christ
the Power of God within the hope of Glory –
=12, was at our first day [Sunday] meeting I trust the
Heavenly Fathers love was felt to flow
amoungst us I trust to the bowing our Spirits
in Humility & Contritedness before the Lord
I was concern'd to speak a little therein as

Page 113

Truth appear'd to open the way & give ability
6mo[June]=13th was at our Monthly meet'g held here (Charlbury)
Pretty large & it felt pretty comfortable
spake a little therein, H Smith also appear'd
which felt to be in the Life, to friends Eddi=
=fication & comfort, the buisness was gone
through comfortabley, after meet'g a pretty menny
friends call'd to se us,
=19 was at our first day [Sunday] meeting, it was
held in silence, in which I trust friends
ware favour'd to feel a renewal of

strength, my secret Cries ware that
I might be preserved in a state of Innosciency
=25, took a walk to milton by Adderbury
Lodgd at Thos Malls who is an honest agreeable friend
call'd to se the other friends who live their
=26, was at the morning & Evening meetings
at adderbury I was concern'd to speak
theirin to Incourage friends to be faithfull
in answering the Lords requireing –
in the evening after meeting walk to Ayn[h]o,
to Cousin Whichleys Lodg'd their
=27, spent the morning with Cousin at Ayn[h]o
agreeabley, Afternoon took leave of them and return'd
to Adderbury Drank tea at Thos Plesters, in the Even'g

verso

1814

---

walk'd to Banbury to Cousin Jno Heads ware
I met with Bro'r & sistor Sess's Lodgd at J,H
6[June]=28, before the quarterly meeting began call'd
to see the friends, the meeting felt pretty comfortable
sevral friends appeard in Testimonie which felt
to be attended with living Power one or two friends
appeard in prayer, the buisness was gone through
agreeabley, - Din'd at Henry Stones, - after tea at
Cousin Heads, took my farewell of Relations &
friends, and walk'd to Sibford in Company with
Jeremiah Lamb & some young friends Lodgd at Bro:
Jno Gibbs, ware an Aged friend lay Dead 90
years old or more, her Name was sarah Smith
=29 took leave of my Relations & walk to Brails
with some young friends ware we refresh'd our=
=selves then walk'd to Shipstone was at the Quar=
=terly meeting their which was pretty large
sevral friends appear'd in Testimonie –
the buisness was gone through in a solid weighty
manner, which was to the Honnour of the Lord
and Reputation of its members, after meet'g
spent a little time with friends at Thos Wells's
ware I Din'd afterwards call'd to se some
friends Drank Tea at Saml Gillets who has lately
lost his Wife she having been removed by Death
which I believe is a great loss to him he having
sevral Children & She being a religious Industrous
carefull Wife I was concern'd to Incourage him
to labour after resignation to the Lords pure will

Page 114

1814

In the Evening walk'd with Bro'r & sistor
Cork & Cous'n M Bissell to Campden, Lodgd at C Corks
6mo[June] 30 spent the day with my Relations
& friends in a Religious agreeable manner
7[July]=1, was at friends meeting at Campden which
felt refreshing I was concerned to speak
theirin and also to appear in Prayer –
returned from meeting to Bro: WC to Din'r
afterward took leave of my Relations & walk'd
to stow spent a little time at Neighbour
Colletts they are Religious people & behaved
friendly & kinde, call'd also to se some Re=
=lations, walk'd down to Jno Peglers to Lodg.
they behav'd kinde tho J.P. had so much of
the concerns of this life to attend to I could
have but little of his Company
=2 after Breakfast took leave of J Pegler & his
Family & walk Home, found my Wife tolerable
well, O! may I ever Remr to be gratefull
unto the Lord for his mercies unto me a verry
poor Creature
=3 was at our first day [Sunday] meeting it felt refreshing
I trust the Lord is mercifull & gracious menny
times owning us with his Life giving power
to the renewal of our strength & to the Incourageing
us to Labour after Purity & holiness of Life

verso

1814

7mo[July] 10th was at our first day [Sunday] meeting it
felt to be a good meeting friends being
favoured to pertake of Divine Love to
their Joy and Incouragment to persevear in
the way of truth & Righteousness
in the A[fter] Noon set out towards Faringdon
walk with James Sessions to Witney Drank
Tea at the Widow Rutters, she is poorly
had a Comfortable sitting with she & some
friends, I was led to speak Incourageinly
to her to trust in the Lord be of good comfort
and He would strengthen her Heart and be
her support & Comfort –
afterwards call'd to se some more friends Lodgd at J.H.
11, walk'd to our monthly meeting held at
Faringdon it was small & nearly held in silence
except the Yearly meeting Epistle being read
after meeting Din'd at dehorn's I was concern'd
to advise them to love the truth and keep to
the plainness & purity which it leads them
that obey it into, and also to labour after the
Injoyment of Divine Love which Inables
us to unite in an Harmonious Labour for one=
anothers good Spiritual and temporal, afterwards
call'd to see the other friends, Drank tea at Robt
Renolds's Widow he having Died about three quarters of

Page 115

1814

a year ago, the Loss of her Husband & that
of their Eldest son a little before her Husbands
Death he Proving very Dishonest and undutifull
to them I believe, Proved a great Affliction
to her, O! how Ungratefull and sinfull it is
in Children when their Parent have used them
tenderly & Labour'd for their Spiritual and tem=
=poral good, the Lord I believe will not let
such go unpunished even in this Life but
cause them to feel sorrows Griefs troubles
Afflictions and anguish of minde, altho upon
sincear Repentance and amendment of Life
I hope they may be favour'd to feel
forgiveness, O may they that have Parents take
warning & Love the Lord and walk agreeable
to the pure truth which in mercy he hath
Placed in their Inward Parts, and then I trust
they will be preserved in their Duty to their
Parents, & be concern'd to love & Comfort them,
I was Concern'd to advise she & her Children
to Labour after Resignation of minde to the
will of the Lord to love fear sarve & honnour
Him, & then I believed he would be their support,
and comfort them with the Injoyment of
His Love, in the Evening bid them farewell
and walk'd to Witney ware I was kindly Entertaind
12, after breackfasting at Jno Hankings took leave
of friends and walk'd Home, with my Nephew,

verso

1814

7mo[July]=14th at our fifth day [Thursday] meeting to day I
trust friends ware favour'd to feel a
renewal of Strength in their patient
waiting upon the Lord in Silence –
=17 was at our first day [Sunday] meeting I trust
it was a time of Rejoiceing under a sence
that our Heavenly Fathers Love was
felt to flow amoungst us, I was concern'd
to Incourage friends to Labour to know
a sitting as under the Government of
Christ to be taught by his Spirit, in which
there is a breathing fourth Glory to God
in the highest, Peace on earth and good=
=will towards men towards the close
the Yearly meeting Epistle was read
=21 at our weekday meeting to day I trust
friends ware favour'd to feel a renewal of strength
in silent waiting upon the Lord –
24 was at our first day [Sunday] meeting, under a

sence of my own Weakness & unworthiness
I feel a necessiety to watch unto Prayer
28, a refreshing meeting in Silence, in which we ware
Inabled to unite in a Spiritual Labour for
Divine food to comfort & refresh our Souls
yesterday Cousin Jno Kewell came to se us from Londn
31 was at our first day [Sunday] meeting in our silent

Page 116

sitting, it appear'd to me as with out the Power
of the Dear Redeemer we can do no good
thing, therefore tis onely as we have our
Dependance upon him and are living in Obidience
to the guideance & Instructions of his Power that we can
do the will of our Heavenly Father
and I was concerned to speak a little on
that subject in meeting –
8[August]=2 Early this morning I was taken very Ill
with a sickness which continued great
Part of the day O how good it is to exercise
Patience in affliction and to dwell near to him
whome the winds and boistrous weaves of
the Sea obey, such as do, tho the billows
of afflictions and adversity, are suffer'd to
go over their Heads, I trust I will be favour'd
to feel a degree of Peace, & the Lords Power
will be an anchor to their souls preserve
them in safety and in the Lords time Inable
them to praise Him on the banks of Deliverance
=4, a little recover'd, at our fifth day [Thursday] meeting I
trust friends ware favour'd to feel refreshment
in Silence
7[July]= was at our first day [Sunday] meet'g, I trust we
ware favour'd to feel the Love of God to
the tendering our Hearts & Contriteing our spirits
before the Lord

verso

1814

In the A[fter] Noon walk'd over to Burford with
sistor and Relations spent the Evening
agreeabley at sistors
8mo[August]=10nthly meeting smalish, it felt to be a
low season "it is better to go to the House of
mourning than to the house of mirth"
after meeting spent a little time with Relati=
=ons Comfortable, in the evening I & my Wife
with some friends Return'd Home –
11, felt a little refreshed at our fifth day [Thursday] meet'g
14, was at our first day [Sunday] meeting it was held in
silence yet felt refreshing, having a sence of my
own Inability to do good and the Necessiety
their is to Labour for Divine Power &
refreshment to Inable one to Persevear in
the way of Truth & Righteousness, it ap=
=pears Necessary to watch unto Prayer,
18, at meeting was favour'd to feel a Degree
of Calmness to attend my minde, & it
appeared good to wait patiently upon the
Lord that I might be sensible when good
came from his Presence, but this Patient
waiting & retirdness of minde should be
expearenc'd not only when met together at a
place of Worship, but at other times & seasons,

Page 117

8mo[August] 21st was at our first day [Sunday] meeting, it felt
a little refreshing, I was concerned to
advise friends to watch unto Prayer
as believeing it good for us, that through
Divine Assistance we might be inabled
to offer up pure offerings, from sincear
clean Hearts, acceptable to the Lord, -
=28 at meeting altho sensible of weakness it felt
refreshing, I was led to consider of the nevver failing
love of God towards his poor contrited Children,

& I was concernd to speak theirof as an Incourage=
=ment for friends to trust in the Lord, to Love & fear Him,
9[September]=1, came home from Reap'g & attended our
week day meet'g, it felt refreshing, held in Silence
=4 was at our first day [Sunday] meeting, my minde much
Exercised on acct of my Religious dutys breathing
to the Lord that I might be directed aright, and
Inabled to perform them to the Lords Honnour and
my own Peace
lately heard that Michael Petiphor of Sibford Died
after a sevear Illness of about three days
he had been Poorly a little before, his Wife Died
about three days before him, he was buried
last sixday [Friday] & his Wife the day before

verso

---

a friend who came in by Convincement
he was a open Hearted Genorous Loving
friend Labouring to do good to friends, and
others very kinde to poor Widows & Fatherless
helping them to settle their affairs
altho His loss will be felt by menny I trust it is
his Everlasting Gain –
on 9mo[September] 3rd a Neighbour of ours Died very suddain=
=ly came home from Field Eate his Din'r
had his Horse brough out Intending to go
into the field (he being a Farmer) to se about
his Corn but finding himself Poorly his Wife
desired he would go lie down on the Bed a
little, she went up stairs with him he lay
down, she went down stairs & stop'd about
ten minutes went up again and found him Dead
a strikeing instance of the uncertainty of time
and a warning to others to live in the fear of the
Lord and Indeavour to be prepared for such an
awefull time, lest the Palefaced Messenger should
be sent to them in an Unprepared state
=11, was at our first day [Sunday] meeting, it felt refreshing
in the A.[fter]Noon my Wife went with on foot with
six friends to C[hipping]Norton, in order to be at the monthly meeting

Page 118

1814

-12th I took a walk to our Monthly meeting held at
C[hipping] Norton it felt pretty comfortable sevral friends
appear'd in testimonie I was concern'd to speak
theirin, the buisness was gone through pretty com=
=fortabley – after Dining at j. Kings call'd to se
a few friends and return'd Home to Tea
=14 took a walk to Witney to the Burial of Widow Rutter
who died about a week ago who Indured pretty
much affliction I believe she was a Woman
who lov'd the Lord in Sincerity and Incouraged her
Children to walk in the Truth and walk agreeable
to its pure leadings, and now I trust her Immortal
soul is safely landed in the Glorious Kingdom
of Everlasting Joy & Peace, at the meeting sevral
Testimonies ware born to Incourage the People to
live in the fear of the Lord & Not trust in Shadows
and forms of Religion, but Labour to Injoy the
substance of Religion even the Power of Christ
within the Hope of Glory, who leadeth his People in
the way of Truth & Righteousness, after meeting Din'd
with the children of the Deceas'd & other friends
afterward ware favour'd with a comfortable
sitting together and to feel Divine Love to flow
amoungst us, and some words ware spoken signify=
=ing there was no cause to Mourn But rather to be

verso

1814

thankfull to the Lord that He had been Pleased
to remove the Deceas'd out of a state of Affliction
into a state of Everlasting Joy & Peace –
= return'd Home with Bro: in the evening
9[September]=17 set out pretty early towards our Quarterly
meeting to be held at reading walk to shillingford
to Robt Greens ware I was kindly Entertain'd Lodgd their
=18 being first day [Sunday] stop't their Meeting, it felt
Comforting I trust friends ware favourd to feel
a renewal of Divine Love, I was led to speak
amoungst them, to Incourage them to wait upon
the Lord that they might feel their strength re=
=newed and be Inabled to persevear in the way
of Truth & Righteousness, & afterwards I appear'd
in Solemn Prayer, Din'd at Jno Sargoods who,
was very kinde, I have had sevral agreeable walks
with him but now the Infirmities of Old age comes
on so that he cannot take such long walks as he
used to so, in the afternoon call'd to se some other
friends I was concern'd to advise them to love the truth
and walk agreeable to its pure leadings & also to In=
=courage their Children to do the same, they ware
loving and appear'd tender, Lodgd at R Greens –
=19 after Breackfast walk'd to Reading reach'd there
about two A[fter]Noon – Din'd at Cousin Jno Tutteys
spent the A.[fter]N.[oon] in calling upon some of the friends
they ware Loving and appear'd glad to se me Lodgd at J, Tutteys

Page 119

9mo[September] 20th before meeting call'd to se some more of the
friends the meeting was not very large yet I trust
we ware favour'd to feel a little refresh'd &
believe Divine Mercy was a fresh extended to the
Disobidient Backsliding children, sevral friends
appear'd in Testimonie the youth ware advised to be Obidient
to the Lord, and live agreeable to our holy Pro=
=fession, be concern'd to learn of Christ who was
meek & lowly in Hear and to take his yoke upon
them which is easy and his Burden light that they
might be Inabled to supply the Places of the
Elders whome the Lord has seen meet to remove,
the buisness was gone through pretty comfortably
after meeting took leave of friends Dind at Cousin
Jnan Fardons & walk'd Homewards as far as
shillingford Lodgd at Robt Greens and on the
=21st after breackfasting with them, bid them
farewell and walk'd Home ware I found
my Wife tolerable well having had a pretty
comfortable Journey, May Gratitude flow in
mine Heart to the Lord for his mercies –
23 yesterday afternoon was concernd to go to some
of the People who kept Public House not to

verso

Incourage Revelling vain sports &et nor to
suffer Plays to be carried on at their Houses
but to fear the Lord & sarve Him, that they
might be favour'd to obtain mercy and be
prepared to meet Death, which hath been
sent to some suddain of late –
9[September]=25 was at our first day [Sunday] meeting my minde
was Exercised, I was concern'd to appear
in solemn Prayer Praying the Lord
to be mercifull to the Afflicted Exercised
mindes, who ware looking unto him for
help & support, and that he would be pleasd
to draw the youth as with the cords of His
Love, that they might be Inabled to run the
way of his Commandments with delight
and be concern'd to give Him the Praise –

in the A[fter]Noon took a walk to Burford found sistor
& rest tolerable well - -
10[October]=2 was at our first day [Sunday] meeting, it felt refresh=
=ing, altho a time of mourning to some, I was
concern'd to mention Blessed are they that mourn for
the shall be comforted,
=6 was at our fifth day [Thursday] meeting, I trust friends
mindes ware bow'd in Humility before the Lord
& he was pleased to administer Divine Refresh=
=ment to his humble dependant Children, I
was concern'd to speak a little theirin to set fourth

Page 120

the benifit of Solem awefull Silence &
prosteration of Soul before the Lord
10[October]=9 was at our first day [Sunday] meeting a pretty
menny young friends present it felt comforting &
I trust Divine Providence was pleased to feed
his dependant Children with Heavenly food,
I was concernd to speak a little theirin to In=
=courage the youth to be faithfull in sarving the Lord,
=10 was at our Monthly meeting held at Charlbury
it felt pretty comfortable sevral mouths
ware opened to Incourage friends to Love the
Lord & his precious Truth and be found walk=
=ing agreeable theirunto that Christ Jesus who
had been the Auther of their Faith might also be the finisher
theirof
=15, this morning Rachel Albt sein'r Departed
this Life it appear'd the Illness of which she
died was something of a Canser or nature under
her left arm which broke & run very much,
a few weeks before her Death she nor her Relations
did not I believe apprehend her end to be so near (but that it
might have been a lingering Illness) still a day or
two before she Died when she alter'd very much and
appear'd sensible to the last, going of very quietly,

verso

1814

she was a Woman I believe who Indeavourd
to live an Innofensive Religious life
and to act consistan with the Principal of
Truth being an Example to her Children &
others to live agreeable to the principal of
Truth and sometimes was concern'd to give
a word of Caution & advice to such as dis=
=obey'd the Principal of truth & did not keep to
the plainness & simplicity which it leads its
followers into
10mo[October] 16th took a walk to witney to the Burial
of Mary Barritt grand Daughter of Old Wm Barritt
a pretty menny Neighbours attended the funeral
and I think it was a renew'd visitation to menny
there was a pretty deal spoken by way of advise
to mind the teachings of Divine Grace which
hath appear'd unto all men - -
I was concern'd to appear in Prayer at the Grave
as was also Hanh Smith – I Din'd at my kinde
friends Jno Hankins's after Din'r went up to
Thos Skinners to see Cousins the Relations of the
Deceas'd and to attend the Funeral the Burial
being at the afternoon meeting, in the Eveneing
return'd Home
=20 attended the Funeral of rachel Albt it being
our weekday meeting a pretty menny friends

Page 121

Present at the meeting, which felt to be a
comforting refreshing season, in the fore=
=part of the meeting one friend appear'd in
solem Prayer after which sevral friends
appear'd in Testimonie, and T.H. appear'd
at the Grave in an awakening awefull
manner, in the A[fter] Noon bear'd the friends
Company at W. Albrights it felt to be
a solemn affecting season

=23 was at our first day [Sunday] meet'g, it felt refreshing
30 was at our first day [Sunday] meet'g, it felt refreshing
11[November],5, having felt drawings in my minde to attend
friends monthly meeting at Sibford walk'd
to sibford in the afternoon found Relations
and friends mostly pretty well Lodgd at Bro'rs
12, before meet'g call'd to see ann Petiphor
who had lately lost by Death her father
& Mother, She appear'd to be in an humble
tender frame of minde, I was concern'd to
Incourage her to bear Afflictions Patiently
Labour after Resignations to the will of the
Lord & to live in his fear also do her best to serve
& Honnour him & then I believed his Power
would be her support & Comfort,
it being first day [Sunday] was at the Preparative
meeting which felt refreshing, I was concern'd

verso

---

to appear in Solemn Prayer one friends appeard in
Testimonie, Din'd at Bro: Gibbs's in the afternoon I Bro:
& Sistor went to Cousin Wm Gibbs to drink Tea, I
went to supper I was concern'd to advise them to Love
the Lord & sarve him in the way of his pure requireings
& perticularly the Children to give up all and sarve the
Lord faithfully in the way of his leadings & then I believed
the blessings of the Lord would attend them they appear'd
tender and affectionate
11[November]=7, was at the monthly meeting, Truth felt to be low amoungst
us, yet I hope their are some sincear Honest hearted friends
who are concern'd to wrestle as for the Blessings and Labour
through Divine Assistance that Truth may be Exalted over
all, Din'd at J Lambs afterwards spent a little
time at Bro: Johns Comfortabley Lodgd their
=8, Breackfasted early took leave of Relations &
walk'd Home
=13, was at our first day [Sunday] meeting I was con=
=cern'd to speak a little theirin
=14, walk'd to Witney to our Monthly Meeting
it felt pretty comfortable some friends ap=
=peared in Testimonie and solemn Prayer
after meeting call'd to se some of the friends
return'd Home to Tea –
-20 was at our first day [Sunday] meeting I trust friends
ware favour'd to feel the flowings of Divine
Love I was concernd to advise friends faith=
=fully to follow their Heavenly Sheppard, that

Page 122

---

they might be favour'd to feel true
Peace to flow in their mindes, a state
in which their is no condemnation
11mo [November] 27 was at our first day [Sunday] meeting, I was con=
=cerned to have my minde centerd in a
patient waiting upon the Lord, that I
might be favour'd to feel his Power to
arise to refresh comfort & strengthen me
that I might be Inabled to do his Will feeling
myself to be a poor weak creature,
but there appears to be in a state of weakness
a Necessiety to keep striving on & Persevearing
in the way of duty, least greater weakness
should ensue
12[December]=4 was at our first day [Sunday] meeting it felt
refreshing – held in silence
=7 took a walk to the Funeral of Cousin
Jno Midwinters Wife of Blox[h]am she
was afflicted pretty much some years be=
=fore she Died with a paraletic Disorder,
& a Husband given to Drincking to Excess,
she was buried at Friends Graveyard at ad=
derbury, the weather being bad it was not a
very large meeting, yet felt pretty comfortable

verso

1814

Ann Ashby was their from Banbury, she
was concern'd to speak theirin the call was
extended to sinners to repent & turn to the Lord
that they might finde mercy, after the
funeral went to Blox[h]am & Din'd with my
Relations took leave of them and walk to Sib=
=ford Drank Tea at Jos: Lambs who ware
very kinde went to Bro: Gibbs's to Lodge,
-8, after breakfasting at Bro: bid them farewell
& return'd Home to Meeting it being fifth day
[Thursday]
=11 was at our first day [Sunday] meeting – in
the
afternoon walk'd with Bro: Robt to Burford
spent the evening comfortabley at Sistors with
she her family & Hanh Smith and her Daughter
=12 was at our monthly meeting held at Burford
it was not very large yet felt pretty com=
=fortable I was concern'd to speak theirin
H Smith also appear'd theirin the buisness
was gone through pretty agreeabley, after
meet'g Din'd at Sisters – tooke leave of them &
return'd Home
=18 was at our first day [Sunday] meeting, I was
concern'd
to Labour that I might feel the Lords Power, that
I might be
be taught by his unering Spirit & I was con=
=cern'd to mention what a priviledge it is for
us to sit as under our own vine and under

Page 123

our own fig Tree ware none can make afraid,
such witness the Lords power to sanctify &
cleanse them from Sin –
12mo [December]=19th about Noon set of for
our Quarterly
meeting to be held at Oxford rode their
with my Nephew in his Cart Lodgd at Oxford
-20 Quarterly meeting began at 10 oclock
it was not very large yet felt pretty
comfortable I was concerned to appear
in Prayer it was an exercise to my
minde to give up to such a weighty
concern, but being afraid if I did not
I should not Injoy sweet peace therefore
gave up and felt comfort, H Smith ap=
=peard in Testimonie to the eddification
and comfort of Friends
the buisness was gone through pretty
comfortabley, it has been under the con=
=sideration of Friends of the Q.M. to chainge
the places of
holding some of our Quarterly meetings
but the Conclusion of this meeting was
to hold them at the usual Places without
any alteration, after meet'g Dind with
some friends at Horse & Jockey, afterwards
return'd Home

verso

1814

12mo [December] 25th was at our first day
[Sunday] meeting
it felt refreshing I was concern'd to speak
a little theirin

1815

1mo[January] 1st was at our first day [Sunday]
meeting it
felt refreshing I was concern'd to speak
a little theirin concerning the uncertainty
of Life & the Necessiety of being prepared
for Death, -
=8, was at our first day [Sunday] meeting, I trust
the honest upright in heart ware
favoured in their silent & Patient
waiting upon God, to feel a renewal
of Strength also these maybe sensible
of great Poverty and weakness at times and may
have tryals and Exercises to go through yet may
these be Incouraged to persevear in the way of
their duty trusting
in the Lord and having their dependance on him
then I
trust he will strengthen and Inable them to do
what=

=soever he is pleased to require at their hands"In the Lord Jehovah is Everlasting Strength"
-15, was at our first day [Sunday] meeting, it felt re=
freshing ware favour'd with the Company
to Thos Harris Long compton, who came to se

Page 124

---

his Grandaughter, he appear'd in meeting,
signifying it is a mercy for us to be favour's
to sit together quietly to Worship the
Lord, but wishes none might be contented
with the form only but be concern'd to draw
near to the Lord in Spirit and then he would
be pleased to feed them with the Bread and Water of Life
=19 at our fifth day [Thursday] meeting to day I trust we
ware favour'd to feel a little of that
Heavenly Power which unites us and
causeth is to sympathise for oneanother
in Affliction & Exercises, & Inables
us to Labour to the Lords honnour &
our Peace & Comfort
=22 was at our first day [Sunday] meet'g it was
held in Silence,
=29 was at our first day [Sunday] meeting it felt
refreshing, I was concern'd to speak a
little theirin
4[th day, Wednesday]=2nd[February] yesterday heard of the Death of Cousin
Crosley Wife of [blank] Crosley and an Invitation
to me and my Wife to attend the Funeral
she being to be Buried at Longcompton, &
I and my Wife this morning went to the

verso

Funeral it was the weekday meeting at
Longcompton but they did not bring the
Corps till about 12 oclock, a pretty menny
relations & Neighbours attended & it appear'd
to be a satisfactory meeting, T. harris appear'd
a considerable wile in Testimonie in the meeting
House and at the Grave, I also was concern'd
to direct the mindes of the people to their true
Teacher the Comforter the spirit of Truth within
which reproves for that which is Evel and
as it is loved and obey'd leadeth into all Truth
after meeting Din'd at t. Harris's ware we
ware kindly entertaind bid them farewell &
return'd Home having had a pretty comfortable Journey
2mo[February] 5th was at our first day [Sunday] meeting, I trust we
ware favoured with a renewal of Divine Goodness
I was concern'd to speak a little theirin to In=
=courage friends to Faithfullness in answering
the Lords requirings
=8 walk'd to Witney was at the fourth day [Wednesday]
meeting, I trust kinde Providence was
pleased to favour us a little with his
Lifegiving Power, I was concern'd to speak
a little theirin, call'd to se some of the friends after
meeting, return'd Home to Tea –

Page 125

1815

2mo[February] 12th was at our first day [Sunday] meeting it felt a little
refreshing, the desire and breathing of my
spirit was to the Lord that he would be pleas'd
to Inable me to come up in the Discharge
of my duty unto him in the A,[fter]noon call'd
to se friend M Bowley, who has been very
Poorly for a long time, having a bad Coughf
& appears dropsycal so that she appears
not likely to live long - -
=13, was at our Monthly meeting held at this
place (Charlbury) it was small some
friends being poorly and bad travelling,
according to my feeling we are in a rather
Cloudy mournfull state may we be enoughf
sensible theirof and be concern'd to apply in
good earnest for Divine help & refreshment
to comfort us & cause the Cloudes to Disperse
I was concern'd to speak a little theirin, but
could not feel that relief I long to Expiearence
nevertheless it appears to be my duty to strive
to get forward in the Path that leads to blessed=
=ness in which true Peace is Injoyed and not
look back at the discouragements I have met

with & may be likely to meet with but with

verso

---

an Eye of Faith look to that Almighty Power which
hitherto hath been my support, & in the
greatest Tryals & Exercises when humane
help has failed, (as I have been concern'd to
trust theirin in), hath been as an anchor
to my soul which has preserved amidst
the Storms & Tempest in Safety, forever
blessed be the Lord Almighty
=19 was at our first day [Sunday] meeting I trust
friends ware favour'd to pertake of Divine
nourishment, I was concern'd to Incourage
friends to Labour after the Injoyment of
that Peace which this world cannot give,
neither can it take away, which can
only be Obtained through living in Obidience
to the Power & Spirit of the Dear Redeemer,
=26 was at the first day [Sunday] meeting it felt a
little refreshing, I was concern'd to appear
in Prayer, beseching the Lord for mercy and
that he would be pleased to be near unto those
try'd afflicted Exercised ones wether in minde or
body as there was a looking unto him for help
that he in mercy would be pleased to be the help
and support of these and such as had Backslided
from his Law and transgress'd his Commandments

Page 126

and ware concern'd to ask forgiveness &
Witness sincear Repentance & amendment
of Life Desireing the Lord would be pleas'd
to forgive them, and feed us with the Bread
& water of Life that we might be strengthened
and Inabled to sarve him in newness of
Life unto his Honour & Praise who is
worthy thereof for Ever - -
3[March]=2 at our fifth day [Thursday] meeting to day I trust
we ware favour'd with the Instructions
of the Lords Spirit, I was concern'd to
speak a little theirin
=5 was at our first day [Sunday] meeting I trust them
that ware concern'd Patiently to wait for
the arising of the Lords Power ware
favour'd to feel its Heavenly Influence
=12 was at our first day [Sunday] meeting it was
held in Silence yet I trust profitable
to those whose mindes ware turned to=
=wards the Lord and ware concern'd to
Posess their souls in Patience
=13 was at our own monthly meeting held at
Witney it was small yet felt pretty comfortable

verso

1815

sevral friends appear'd in testimonie the
buisness was gone through pretty comfortabley
Din'd at Thos Skinners in the evening return'd Home
3mo[March]=14th was at a meeting of friends and Neighbours
who met together to Establish a School after
the Lancaster Plain Rules ware produced
read & agreed to, a Commity was appointed
to se that a School is Established for
Boys to ented at 6 years old and Girls
at 5 years old also to se that the School
be conducted orderly according to the Rules
=19 was at our first day [Sunday] meeting, it was
held in Silence
=22 went to Witney to the Burial of Thos
Smiths Daughter sarah, she was about
13 years old, was taken Ill at Islington
school ware she had been about [blank]
years she Died in her way Home which
added to the Affliction of her Parents
& Relations, the meeting felt pretty com=
=fortable & I trust her Parents & relations
ware favour'd to feel Divine Goodness
to be their support, & to Inable them to
feel Resignation to the Devine Will, sevral
friends appeard in Testimonie

Page 127

3mo[March]=26th was at our first day [Sunday] meeting
4[April]=2 was at our first day [Sunday] meeting was favour'd

to get into a Patient waiting upon the
Lord for a renewal of strength of which I
felt the want of, more that ability to administer
any thing to others my Wife in the afternoon
Intended to go to Burford in order to be at the monthly
meeting on the morrow but being poorly was prevented
=3, I walked to Burford was at the monthly meeting
their it felt a little refreshing I was concern'd
to speak a little theirin – after Drincking Tea
at sistors bid Relations & friends farewell
and return'd Home,
=8, this morning Mary Bowly departed this
Life after a long and tedious Illness it being Inward
weakness & very bad Coughf at times for sevral years
wareby she was much reduced & Brought very thin
she was favour'd to go of quietly and tho it is
cause of mourning to her Relations & friends yet
I trust tis her great gain –
=9 was at our first day [Sunday] meeting it felt to be a
Comfortable meeting, I was concern'd to speak
theirin, to Incourage friends to learn of him
who was meek and Lowly of Heart, -

verso

1815

4mo[April]=12th I and my Wife went in Company with
other friends to Witney, to our Quarterly meeting
a pretty large meeting & felt comfortable
sevral friends appear'd in Testimonie I was
concerned to appear in Prayer, which is a
weighty Exercise to my minde but as my Peace
is concern'd theirin I give to what I believe is
my duty believing that whatsoever the Lord
requires He will give strength to perform
the Buisness was gone through pretty
agreeabley – return'd Home pretty soon
after Dinner with some friends –
=16, it being first day [Sunday] Mary Bowly was
Inter'd, we ware favour'd with a large and
solid Meeting on the occasion menny friends
and Neighbours being present & I trust it
was a renew'd visitation unto menny, sevral
friends appear'd in Testimonie by which
the People ware put in minde of the Lords
mercy in visiting them wile in their sins
and calling on them by his good spirit as in
the cool of the day, to for sake sin and Inicquity
and turn unto the Lord in the day of mercy
love and sarve him in the way of his requiring
that they might be favourd with an Inheritance
in his Glorious Kingdom when time to them
here should be no more

Page 128

1815

4mo[April]18th I called at R Spendloves to se the re=
=lations (before the parted) of the late M,
Bowly, I was favour'd to spake a little
matter unto them that appeard to be
my duty, to Incourage them to be diligent
in the attendance of meetings to wait
upon the Lord that they might be
favour'd to know the will of God concerning
them and also be favour'd with strength
to do it & more to that effect
=23 was at our first day [Sunday] meeting it felt
a little refreshing, sevral strangers
present, my minde pretty much exercised,
great watchfullness and attention to the Heavenly
Guide (the Light of Christ within) and
obedience thereunto, appears necessary in
Order to be found in the discharge of
Duty
=21, took a walk to Norton call to se some
of the friends, some of whome ware poorly
as Richd Fowler Saml Atkins and sarah
Paul I was led to simpathise with them
and to Incourage them to trust in the Lord &
seek unto him for help and support –

verso

1815

4mo[April]30th was at our first day [Sunday] meeting I trust
friends ware favour'd with the Incomes
of Divine Love & mercy to the comforting
& refreshing their spirits, I was concern'd to
speak theirin to Incourage friends to give
up all and sarve the Lord in the way of his
requirings
5mo[May]=1st this morning a piece of ground was mark'd
out up in the Plainclose in order to build
theiron a Charlbury Brittish School,
=7 was at our first day [Sunday] meeting it was held
in Silence in which true Spiritual Worship
is sometimes perform'd, as truly as when menny
Words are spoken, for in Silent humble wait=
=ing upon the Lord he is graciously pleased
to favour such with his pure Power
which makes them sensible of their own
weakness and Inability to do good without
Divine assistance and they are concern'd
to draw near in Spirit unto the Lord and Breathe
unto him for Instruction with respect of their
duty and a renewal of their strength that they
may be Inabled to persevear theirin, and the
Lord is pleased to arise by his Pure spirit unto
his humble dependant Child to the scattering
of their Enemies to the making hard

Page 129

things easy and bitter things sweet, to the
causing the mountains to skip like Rams
and the little hills like Lambs, to the re=
=moving those things out of the way or Inabling
them to overcome them, that have appeard
obstructions in the way of their duty
and also to the feeding them with Divine Re=
=freshment to the strengthening and Inable=
=ing them to persevear in the way of their
Duty with Joy & Delight O! Blessed for
ever be the Name of the Lord,
=14, was at our first day [Sunday] meeting I was
concerned to Wait Patiently upon the
Lord that I might be favour'd to feel
a renewal of strength, being sensible
of great weakness, knowing that the
Lord is the Physician of soul and Body
and that he is pleased to refresh & Comfort
the souls and Bodies of his Dependant
Children, glory Honnour and Renown
be given unto the Lord for Evermore
=18, this morning my Wife set out with
Bro'r Sistor & their son Jesse Sessions
and frd Gurney intending for the Yearly meet'g

verso

1815

held at London Jesse Sessions to be left
at Islington school my Wife & M Gurney
went on the out side, a pretty fine morning,
5[May]=21, was at our first day [Sunday] meeting it felt re=
=freshing I was concern'd to speak theirin
to set fourth the shortness of Life & the uncertain=
ty of it and the awefullness of Eternity –
=25 under a sence of weakness, it appear'd
good for me in Patientce to wait and
watch unto Prayer,
-28 was at our first day [Sunday] meeting it was
held in silence yet I trust it was a good
Profitable meeting, to those whose mindes
ware dependant on the Lord and ware turn'd
unto his Divine teaching in the secreet of
their souls
6[June]=4 was at our first day [Sunday] meeting I trust
the Lord is yet Mercifull & that we ware
favour'd to pertake of his goodness I was
concern'd to speak a little theirin –
=8, my Wife return'd with Bror & sistor Sess's
from the Yearly meeting
=11 was at our first day [Sunday] meeting I was concern'd
to advise friends to Labour after the Injoyment
of true Peace which is obtained by fearing the

Page 130

Lord and sarving him in the way of his
requirings
6mo[June]=12th, our Monthly meet'g held here
(Charlbury) not
very large, it felt to be a low & mournfull time
yet in the midst of Judgement the Lord was
pleas'd
to remember Mercy, I was concern'd to appear
in Prayer beseetching the Lord to be mircifull
and forgive such who through unwatchfullness
had
transgressed against him, as they ware concern'd
to seek for forgivness through sincear repentance
and Amendment of Life, and that he would
in mercy be pleased to strengthen the weak hands
and say unto the weak be strong and to such
as have no might of their own increase your
strength, and also that he would be pleased
to strengthen the youth & Inable them to live
to his praise and Honnour who is worthy to be
Praised & Honnoured for Ever, some friends
appeard
in testimonie, I trust it was a humbling
season, in which the mindes of some ware bowed
in humility and reverence before the Lord
the buisness was gone through pretty
comfortabley
=18, was at our first day [Sunday] meeting, it felt
a little re=
freshing, I was concerned to mention how the
Lord is
Pleased to visit the youth with his Power to the
tendering
and Contriting their spirits before him, and to
make them

verso

sensible of his Holiness & Greatness, which hath
Preserved them from giving way to rong words &
actions, and I desired they would keep near to
this
pure anointing Power of the Lord, and live in
Obidi=
=ence thereunto that they might know a growing
in Grace & Truth, -
6mo[June]=24th set out for our Quarterly
meeting to be held
at Banb'[ur]y, walk'd in the afternoon to Ded=
=ington call'd to se the friends their &
drank Tea at the Widow Farthings, after
ward walk to Thos Fardons adderbury mill
ware I was kindly entertaind Lodgd their
=25, after breackfast walk'd to adderbury
call to se some of the friends before meet'g
the meeting felt pretty comfortable Thos
Speakman from Reading their he appeard
in Testimonie I also was concern'd to speak
theirin, Din'd at Thos Lambs, drank tea
at Thos Plesters was at the evening meet'g
which began at 5 oclock – it felt pretty
comfortable
went to Cousin Witchleys Ayn[h]o to supper
they ware very kinde Lodg'd their
=26 after breackfasting with Cousins had a
comfortable sitting together and I was Inabled

Page 131

to give them good advise, - after Dining
with them, bid them farewell, & walk'd to ad=
=derbury & from thence to Milton found Thos
Mall Poorly seems like a person in a Decline,
He and his Wife are loving agreeable friends
Lodg'd their
6[June]=27 walk'd to Cousin J Heads to Banbury
breackfasted their, - it is a time of sorrow
and Mourning with sincear honest hearted
friends
on acct of the misconduct and backsliding
of some in Our Society, of the foremost rank,
the Quarterly meeting began at 10 oclock
not very large, but felt pretty comfortable
considering the low state of thinks , sevral
friends appear'd in Testimonie which sound=
ed an Allarm to the lukewarm & careless
ones, & friends ware Incouraged to give up
all and sarve the Lord faithfully, two
friends appear'd in Prayer, -
Din'd at Edward Atkins's, afterward calld to se
the friends at Banbury, found John Rutter
very poorly, as I sat with him & friends I
felt a little hope he might be favour'd to get
better – tooke leave of Relations & friends & in
the Evening walk'd to Sibford Lodg'd at Bro: J
Gibbs's

verso

1815

6mo[June] 28th after Breackfasting with my Relations
bid them farewell, & walk'd to c[hipping] Norton
call'd to se sevral of the families of the
Atkins who are in great distress, they being
in the Banking buisness, young Wm Atkins
was returning from the Bankers at London
in the Coach with a great number of
Bank Notes and Guineas to the amount
of menny thousand Pounds Value, He leaving
them in the Coach wile He supped ware the
Coach stopped, they ware all stolen out of
the Coach, it was thought a very careless
thing of W Atkins & People blame him very
much, Indeed I think some People having so much Paper
as Passeth for Money, it leadeth to high
mindedness & Pride, and to be off their gard,
so as not to act Prudently with respect to
the things of this Life, little thinking of
the dangerous state they are in, and how soon
they may fall into Ruins Confusion sorrow
and Distress and cause others to be so in a
great measure, as appears to be the Case with
them; People hearing of their Loss caused a great
run upon the Bank on which acct and in
order to prevent the lost Notes from passing,

Page 132

the Bank was shut, they having menny
Notes out, it causeth great uneasiness amoungst
People Complaints murmerings &et Reproaching
them and Friends also, as prettending to
be very good religious on which acct
they put Great confidence in them, but
now they prove as bad as others as are not
making such high prettentions as to re=
=ligion, Indeed I think it is Inconsistent
with the principels of friends to make
promisery Notes and Pass them for money
because of the dangers it exposes them
to and others, friends know in trading in goods
it is dificult to prevent Trust & how
hurtfull trusting to much is and that it has
been the ruin of menny a one, but this Bank=
=ing brings People in general to become
Creditors to Bankers when they have no
dealings at all with them, therefore Increaseth
an Unnecessary trust which proveth to the
anxiety disturbance sorrow trouble & ruin
of menny, I think it is a thing that ought
to be shunned by all Wise & good men –
I return'd Home at Night, -

verso

1815

7mo[July] 2nd was at our first day [Sunday] meeting
=9 was at our first day [Sunday] meeting it felt refreshing
my Wife set out in the A[fter] Noon towards
faringdon in order to be at the monthly meeting
=10 I rose early & walk'd to witney to breakfast
and from thence to Faringdon to our monthly
meeting it was not very large yet felt a
little refreshing I was concern'd to speak
a little theirin the yearly meeting Epistle
was read, Din'd at Robt Huntleys – towards
evening John Shepley who is on a Religious
visit, (Thos Heath accompanying him) came
to Faringdon, to attend a meeting which
was appointed to begin at 6 oclock – I stop'd
meeting sevral Neighbours came in, it
felt to be a good refreshing meeting J.
Shepley was pretty much drawn fourth in
Testimonie wareby I believe the pure witness
was reachd in menny & they ware convinsed
of the error of their ways, & Incouraged to live
in the fear of the Lord and be Obidient to his
Heavenly Power, then they would expierence
a pure chainge wrought in them even a Death
unto sin & a new birth unto Righteousness

Page 133

the meeting was concluded in Prayer, I sup'd
at the Widow Reynolds's with the friends,
most of the friends of Faringdon being there

after Supper we ware favour'd with a
refreshing season together J Shepley was
Inabled to speak to the states of some present
with Comforting and Incouraging language,
=11, after Breakfast bid friends Farewell
and walk'd to Witney J. Shepley and T.H. going
for Abingdon, I stop'd at Witney till
after Tea, in the Evening walk'd Home –
-13, in the Evening Martha Routh and
Ann Grace who are on a religious visit
came to Charlbury
-13, the above mentioned friends had a
meeting with friends it began at 10 oclock
in the morning it felt refreshing both
the friends Appear'd in Testimonie, in the Evening
a Public meeting was held by M. Rouths
desire, it was not so large as we have had
them sometimes but it felt satisfactory M
Routh appeard in Testimonie a pretty will it
felt to be hard Labour but I truth arose into

verso

1815

Dominion she treated on the necessiety
of waiting upon the Lord in Silence, in
order to aproach him & be acquainted
with true spiritual Worship, mention'd
the Discourse of the Dear Redeemer with
the Woman at Jacobs well, treated on
the qualification of true Gospel Ministers
she signified the Lord was pleased to call to
Preach the Gospel Femeales as well as
males & none could be true Gospel Minis=
=ters but such whome the Lord Jesus was
pleased to fit & qualify and send fourth
she also signified that grace & truth which
came by Jesus Christ was able & would if
People attended to its Devine Teaching & they
Indeavour'd always to live in Obidience
thereunto preserve them from sinning against
the Almighty & Inable them to work the
works of Righteousness, the Effects thereof
would be Peace altho People fell into
error & menny times transgressed against
the Lord it was for want of Watchfullness and
attention to the Gift of God in their own
Hearts, not through any Insuficiency thereof
the meeting was concluded in Prayer
7mo[July] 15th I went in the Evening as Guide
with the

Page 134

---

friends to C[hipping] Norton found friends there
in a Poor mournfull state –
7mo[July] 16 walk'd to Witney with some friends
to
to the funeral of a Child of Eliz: Longs
she was about eight years old had been af=
=flicted with a Disorder that for sometime
nearly took away the use of her limbs so
that her removal may be look'd upon a
mercy, as she appeard to be before she Died
in a sweet Innoscient state of minde,
signified the Almighty loved her and she
was desirous his Will might be done –
apretty menny Neighbours attended the
Funeral & I trust it was a satisfactory
meeting, some friends appeard in Testimonie
I Din'd with the Widow Long & her Child=
=ren with whome I had a Comfortable
Oppertunity, to incourage them to live
in the fear of the Lord and keep his
Commandments, - was at the afternoon
meeting, it began at three A.[fter]N.[oon] I think
it was a heavy trying meeting, as menny
appear'd to have enoughf to do to overcome
heaviness, on which acct in Summertime
I think it would be more profitable and

verso

1815

Comfortable to friends if it began at
five in the Evening, I drank tea at T.
Smiths afterwards I and my Company re=
turn'd Home –
7mo[July] 20th at our fifth day [Thursday]
meeting I trust in
our Patient waiting upon the Lord, we
ware favour'd to feel a renewal of strength
=23 was at our first day [Sunday] meeting I trust
friends ware favour'd to pertake of

Divine refreshment I was concern'd to
speak a little theirin signifying
the Lord is & has been gracious unto
us in extending his mercifull visitations
time after time and it would be well
for us to be found profiting thereby & Labour=
=ing to bring forth good Fruites answerable to
the
good things we have received of the Lord,
otherwise his mercies would turn to our
Condemnation, -
=27th was at our fifth day [Thursday] meeting,
in taking a
view of the things of this Life they appear in
a very unsettel'd Chaingable state menny ap=
=pear to have been lifted up by gain in Trade

Page 135

& having their views outward through a
covetious disposition have launched fourth
into am extensive way of trade beyond
what they had a Capital or Capacity to mannage,
which hath Prov'd their Downfall,
I feel it is a very good thing to retire in=
=ward often, and wait upon the Lord to feel
his pure Power to Direct & guide us in
all our undertakings, Temporals as well
as Spirituals and act agreeable theirunto
in all things, then I trust we shall witness
Preservation from the menny troubles and
Distressing Situations, that menny fall into,
and shall be favour'd with Food & Raiment
altho, it may be in a plain homely way
yet if we are Content and thankfull for it
a blessing will attend it, & it will be enoughf
to Comfort and satisfy Nature, -
30 was at our first day [Sunday] meeting, I trust
friends ware favoured to know the Com=
=fort their is in trusting in the Lord
& being favour'd to Injoy his Living
Power, which quickeneth & maketh a live

verso

1815

unto God, O that friends might not
rest contented without feeling a renewal
thereof day by day –
8mo[August] 3rd at our fifth day [Thursday]
meeting was very desirous
to draw near in Spirit unto the Lord that
I might feel my streength renewed,
and O the Breathing of my Spirit is unto
the Lord that he would be pleased to look down
and shew mercy also be the support &
comfort of the poor in Spirit Try'd Exersised
afflicted ones, who are breathing & seeking
unto him day by day for help & support well
knowing unless the Lord is Pleased to hear and
help & afford his good Power to support in vain
is the help of Man
=5 set out twds Armscutt [Armscote] meeting
walk'd to Thos
Harris's call'd to se some of the friends the
Widow Hodgkins
was poorly, was kindly Entertain'd at Thos Wells
&
Bro'rs – Lodgd their
=6, walk'd with some friends to Armscutt
[Armscote] meeting, it
felt comforting & I trust the Lord was pleased
to visit
us with his good Power to the tendering our
hearts
sevral Mouths ware opened to Instruct the People
in the
way of Life & Salvation & I believe the pure
witness

Page 136

was reach'd in People to the makeing them
sensible
of the error of their ways, they ware desired to
for=
sake wathsoever they knew to be wrong turn to
the
Lord and sarve him in purity and uprightness of
Heart that they migh finde acceptance of the
Lord, the meeting concluded in Prayer, went to
Cousin
Thos Fardons Tredington to Dinr, menny
friends Din'd there & they appear'd to Entertain
them very kindly walk from thence with
Bro J Gibbs to Sibford call'd to se Cousin
Gilletts Brails,

=7 rose pretty early, took leave of my Relations
and walk to Banb[ur]y to the monthly Meeting
held there, it was not very large and tho things
are low amoungst us yet I trust we ware favourd
to feel Divine Goodness to refresh &
Comfort us, I was concern'd to speak theirin
as was also another friend, signifying its is
faithfullness that causeth the spring of Life
and love to flow sweetly – Din'd at Cousin
Jno Heads, the meeting holding pretty long I did
not return till morning, but call'd to se some
of the friends had a little oppertunity with
one of the Widow Beesleys sons who to her
great grief has kept Company with a young
woman not of our Society & sometime attended

verso

1815

Public worship I spoke to him what rested
upon my minde, wishing he would live in
the fear of God and not sin against him
which he appear'd to take well, - Lodgd at J
Heads
8mo[August] 8th after breackfasting with
Cousins bid
them Farewell and walk Home call'd
to se Aunt Jones in my way, altho she is about
82 years old appeard pretty hearty and
chearfull, was glad to se me –
=13 was at our first day [Sunday] meeting, I trust
friends ware favourd to feel Divine
Goodness to be near to their comfort and to the
re=
=newing of their Strength, in the after=
=noon walk'd to Burford, was at the evening
meeting it felt a little Comforting spent the
evening agreeabley at sistors
=14 was at the monthly meeting which was not
very large I trust friends ware favourd
to feel Divine Goodness to be near to comfort
and Incourage them to press forward in the
Path of Duty. Din'd at Sistors in the Evening
return'd Home
20 was at our first day [Sunday] meeting a pretty
menny
young friends their, O! that they may rem'r
their Creator in the Days of their youth and

Page 137

Devote their strength & faculties to sarve
& Honnour the Lord, wile the Evel days
come not nor the years draw nigh when
thou shalt say I have no pleasure in them
then I believe altho the Days of Tribulation
and affliction may come and the things
of this world may cease to give Joy & Comfort
the Lord will be the support of these
and He will be their their Everlasting
Joy and exceeding great reward,
8mo[August] 23rd my Wife set out for Sibford
Campden &et
in order to pay a visit to her Relations
their, and left Mary Gilks, a Convinced
woman friend who hath been at our House about
two weeks to keep house
-25 yesterday M. Gilks being taken very
Poorly & this morning she being very desirous
to return to her Parents, I got a person to
go Home with her to Bladon near Woodstock
=27 was at our first day [Sunday] meeting it felt
refreshing
and I trust we ware favour'd to feel the lifting up
of the Light of the Lords Countenance upon us,
=30 this Evening my Wife return'd from her
Journey
to Sibford Campden &et

verso

1815

8mo[August] 31st at our weekday felt poverty &
lowness
in a Spiritual sence and that nothing will
support amidst all self abasement & Exer=
=cises but the Almighty Arm of Power,
O may I ever be favour'd to labour for its as=
=sistance and have Faith theirin and then
I trust I shall witness preservation in
the most trying seasons,
9[September]=3 was at our first day [Sunday]
meeting it felt to
be a refreshing season I was led to mention

that times & Seasons ware not at our command
but at the Lords, therefore it was out Duty
to labour to do good wile we ware favour'd with
time & Oppertunity, lest the time should
come that we might have a desire to do
good and should not be favour'd with strength
nor op=
=pertunity & more to that purpose,
this day Thos Jarvis's wife of Burton came to se
us
and be at our Meeting she appears to be a
well inclind woman & to have a love for
Truth & good friends, but not being rec'd into
membership, living ware no other family of
friends live and being much exposed to other
Company, it appears that she and such people
do require the sympathy and tenderness of
friends,

Page 138

and Friends should watch over them for good,
and Incourage them to persevear in faithfullness
in following the Lord, and answering his
requirings
9mo[September] 10 was at our first day [Sunday]
meeting it felt re=
=freshing, & I believe the Lord is near and
willing to do us good if we will but accept
of his mercy and assistance in his own way
and time, I was concern'd to advise such
as ware sensible of their backslideings
and transgressing the Divine Law,
to seek for forgivness & altho in order to feel
if they might have to bear that Chastising
hand of the Lord I believed it was to
cleanse them and to purge away their
sins & I believed if they bear'd it patiently
the would be restored into favour & know
their Peace to flow as a river,
11th walk'd to our Monthly Meeting held at
C[hipping] Norton
I was concern'd to speak a little theirin – the
buisness
held pretty long after meeting call'd to se most
of the friends after Tea I my Wife and friends
return'd Home
=14, I walk'd over to C[hipping] Norton to the
Burial of Rich'd Fowler who Died after a pretty
long Illness it being thought to be a wite swelling

verso

1815

I having visited him sevral times in his Illness
he appear'd to bear his Affliction with Patience
& to be resigned to the will of Divine Providence
I understood he went of so quietly that it was
hardly perceived whe he breathed his last
I believe he was a Sincear honest Hearted friend
whose chief delight was to sarve the Lord and
se truth Prosper, the meeting was pretty large
and satisfactory sevral friends appeard in
Testimonie I was Concern'd to speak theirin
also to appear in Solem Prayer at the Grave
it is trying to the Natural Part thus to be
Exercised
and nothing but an apprension of Duty can
Induce
me to appear in this manner, In the afternoon I
sat with friends at the House of the Deceas'd
& I trust we ware favour'd to feel a Degree of
solemnity
to cover us
afterwards call'd to se Samuel Atkins who is in a
a very feeble state not hardly able to get about
with two People to help him, in the Evening
return'd Home
9[September]=16 set out for our Quarterly
meeting to be
held at Reading, walk'd to Shillingford
was kindly entertaind at Robt Greens Lodgd
their
=17 was at the first day [Sunday] meetg at
Warborough
I trust friends ware favour'd to pertake of
Divine Refreshment I was Concern'd to speak =

Page 139

theirin, after meeting Din'd at Jno Sargoods
& drank Tea at the widow sargoods with
sevral friends whose Company felt comforting
and edifying, in the even'g sistor with her son
James & daughter Hanh came up to Shillingford
=18, walk'd with some friends to Stephen Greens
Wallingford to Breackfast & from thence
to Reading to Dinner, spent the afternoon in

visiting Relations & friends our meeting together I hope
was matter of Incouragment to us to persevear
in the way of Duty, sup'd at Cousin Jnan
Fardons who have sevral Children, the
appear Industrous agreeable friends Lodgd at the Widow Tutteys
=18 quarterly meeting began at 10
oclock, I trust Divine Providence was again
pleas'd to favour us with his lifegiving power
& presence altho menny have backslided from
his Righteous Law through unwatchfullness
& unfaithfullness to their Heavenly Guide
the Pure witness within them & the Lord was pleas'd
to Invite them by his servants to turn again for=
sake sin & Inquity sincearly repent theirof amend
their ways & Live and Incouragment was given

verso

to the sincear Honest friends to persevear
in the way of Duty two friends appeard in
solem Prayer, after meeting Din'd at Henry
Smiths, bid Relations & friends farewell and
return'd to Walingford Lodg'd at Stephen
Greens as did sevral more friends
=19 rose pretty early & walk'd Home was
favour'd with a pretty comfortable Journey
O! that I may nevver forget to be grate=
=full to the Lord for his mercies who I have
faith to believe, will nevver leave not
forsake them that trust in Him
but he will be with them in the way
they go and give them Plenty of Bread to
Eate and Raiment to put on
21, was at our fifth day [Thursday] meet'g I trust
friends ware refreshed in their silent
waiting upon the Lord, -
24 was at our first day [Sunday] meeting I was
very desireous to wait patiently upon
the Lord that I might be favour'd to feel
my strength renewed under a sence of
weakness in the A[fter] Noon walk'd to Burford

Page 140

was at their evening meeting it felt a little
refreshing spent the remainder of the evening
at Sistors Lodg'd their on the morrow return'd Home
9mo[September] 28, was at our fifth day [Thursday] meeting my chief
buisness appears to be to retire inward and
wait for the ariseing of the pure heavenly
Power & to be very attentive to its leadings
that I may feel preservation from the menny
snares & besetments of the Enemy of my Soul
well might the Dear Redeemer say, Watch
and Pray that ye enter not into Temptation
10[October]=1 was at our first day [Sunday] meeting I trust
it was a refreshing meeting in which
the Lords power was felt amoungst us,
=5 was at our fifth day [Thursday] meeting was oppress'd
in minde under a sence of menny people in the
town giving way to sin and Inicquiety & some
who are making a high profession Incouraging
vanity & Revelling
=8, was at our first day [Sunday] meeting I trust it
was a good meeting I was concerned to Prayer
that if it pleased Him the Lord he would arise in the

verso

Brightness of his Majesty to the bringing
down sin & Inicquiety in the Earth &
that he would make the wicked sensible
of their transgressions and favour them
with a day of Repentance, also that the
Lord in mercy would be with his Children
such as ware concern'd to sarve him with
Purity and uprightness of Heart that he would
be with them and be their support in
their tryals and Exercises & make them
sensible that he would Deliver out of
them all,
10[October]=9 was at our monthly meeting held
here (Charlbury) altho things are low
amoungst us I trust the Almightys
mercy is still extended towards us sevral
friends appear'd in Testimonie wareby
friends ware Cautioned not to be to much
entangled with the things of this Life but
in their commings to meetings to Indeavour
to have their Hearts prepar'd to Worship the

Lord in the Beauty of Holiness O How would
our Lights shine amoungst the People ware this

Page 141

our Chief concern and Delight –
10[October]=12 was at our fifth day [Thursday] meeting
it felt a little refreshing
=15 was at our first day [Sunday] meeting, it felt
refreshing in my silent waiting my
concern is to draw near in Spirit unto God
that I may be Inabled to put up my
Cries and Supplications unto him in
secreet for Preservation from the enemy,
and for help & Instruction to Inable me
to persevear in the way that leads to that
rest which is prepared for the Righteous
=19 was at our fifth day [Thursday] meeting, one
strainger was their viz Stephen Mathews
of London, his Father used to live at Milton
22 was at our first day [Sunday] meeting,
I trust friends ware favour'd with the lifting
up of the Lord Countenance amoungst them,
I was concern'd to speak theirin, the new
Governess was at meeting who came down from
London a few days ago to Instruct the Chil=
=dren at our British Scool
=25 took a walk to Witney was at friends fourth day [Wednesday] meeting

verso

1815

10mo[October] 29th was at our first day [Sunday] meet'g
11[November]=1, last night we ware allarm'd hearing
a Noise & very soon after our Chamber
window was broke by some mischeveous
Person, which is much the case when People
give way to Drinking late to excess, when
they Part they are Noisy and disturb & Injure
their peaceable Neighbours what a sorrow=
=full thing that it should be sufferd amoungst
People professing Christianity
=5 was at our first day [Sunday] meeting it fell
a good refreshing meeting, I was concern'd
to speak theirin Signifying we Injoyed
menny Priviledges as that of reading the
Scriptures friends books attending our Re=
=ligious meetings peaceabley in Order to turn
our mindes towards the Power of him who is
the fountain of all good from whence every
good & Perfect Blessing comes and it was
our Duty to Improve these oppertunities and
be concern'd to meditate in the Devine Law and be
obidient theirunto, and it would lead us to purity
and holiness of Life for I did believe such a
state attainable as being made Perfect & free

Page 142

from Sin or it would not have been com=
=manded by the Dear Redeemer, and it would
be happy for us to Expiearence such a state
and then I believe we should be sensible
that in our Heavenly Fathers House is Bread
enoughf and to spare wile some are
in poverty & hungry & our Heavenly Father
would be pleased to break bread & bless it, hand
it to his Desciples and his Desciples to the
Multitude
=12 was at our first day [Sunday] meet'g it felt a
little refreshing, - my minde much exercis'd
on account of being abused by some young
fellows, but as our Trust is in Divine
Providence and we are concern'd to look
unto him for help & Preservation I trust
as he hath hitherto being our Protector &
support so he will continue to be, for
Ever blessed be his Name –
=13 walk'd to Witney (my Wife went thither
with some Relations in a Cart,) to our
monthly meeting it felt pretty comfortable I was
concern'd to speak theirin to Incourage

verso

1815

friends to be quite given up to sarve
the Lord in the way of his requirings
it being the only way to Injoy Divine Love and

true Peace of minde, in the Evening return'd
Home
11[November]=19 was at our first day [Sunday]
meeting I was
led to speak a little theirin, to Incourage
friends to draw near in Spirit unto
the Lord desireing they might Indeavour
to remove every thing that hinders them
from drawing near in Spirit unto the
Lord and from seeking unto him for help and
healing virtue and thence I believed they
would be favoured to receive Divine
help & Comfort
=26 was at our first day [Sunday] meeting, it
was held in Silence, yet I trust it
was a profitable refreshing season,
to them whose mindes ware rightly
Exercised, altho my Heart of late hath
been much engaged in Prayer in my own
account & others for Divine Help & Refreshment
both spiritualy and Temporaly and also for Pre=
servation and Power that we might be Inabled

Page 143

to Labour to the Lords honnour and
the exaltation of the Everlasting Truth
a midst Discouragments Tryals &
Exercises which attend those who are
concerned for the Prosperity of Zion
yet now my minde is drawn into
awefull Silence
11[November]=29 went to Witney to the Burial
of Elijah Wearing an Old man
of about 84 years of age a pretty
large meeting of friends & Neighbours
tho not menny friends their strangers
a degree of Solemnity appear'd to cover
the meeting I was concerned to Incourage
the people to labour after silence &
stillness in which they might be favour'd
to feel the Power of God to shew them
their own states and Conditions and
to Inable them to refuse that which is
evel, and to do that which is good –
Hannah Smith also appear'd in Testimonie

verso

1815

12mo [December] 3rd was at our Preparative
meeting
the meeting for Worship was held in
silence yet I trust profitable, and I
believe Divine Teaching (to the truly
exercised mindes) may be as fully known
and felt in Silence as when menny
words are Spoken, however the Lords
Power must not be limited but he is
to be waited upon in Solem awefull
Silence and then wether He is pleased
to appear to teach the People by his pure
Spirit in the secreet of their Hearts or
to make use of poor Man or Woman to
convey his Power & Instruct them in
their duty I trust it will be received
and will prove to their Eddifacion
and Comfort,
=10 was at our first day [Sunday] meeting
which was I trust Profitable (altho
held in Silence,) to such whose mindes
ware concern'd to receive Instruction
by the unering Teacher in their own
Hearts, in the afternoon walked to

Page 144

1815

Burford with Bro'r & some friends
found Sistor Mander very poorly Lodgd their
12[December]=11 was at the monthly meeting
their
it felt pretty comfortable considering
the low state we are in, some friends
appear'd in Testimonie, I also was con=
=cearn'd to speak theirin, the buisness
was gone through pretty comfortabley one
friend Disown'd for Marrying out, I
have had to mourn that friends should give
way to Marry those of a Difrent Perswasion
as to Religion, If friends are concern'd to

Love the Lord above all & keep to near to
the Guideance of his pure truth they will
be preserv'd from so doing, If they are
Inclind to have an helpmeet, their Chief
concern will be to attend to the leadings
of Truth in this very weighty affair and
to chuse one who loves the Truth and are
concern'd to act consistend to it in all
things, then I trust they will be united theirby,

verso

& their Labours will tend to the Honnour
of the Almighty also to the Eddification
and Comfort of each other,
=17 was at our first day [Sunday] meeting held in silence
=21 was at our fifth day [Thursday] meeting
under a sence of exercise & weak=
=ness I was concerned to wait and
seek unto the Lord for help &
strength and it is much the ex=
=ercise and breathing of my Spirit
unto the Lord that he will be
pleased to hear the Cries of the
poor & Sighing of the needy who
under whatever tryals & Exercises
they may be and are Concern'd to
trust in Him seek unto Him for help,
comfort & support that He will
be pleased to arise for the help of them
and be their support and present help
in every needfull time,
=24 was at our first day [Sunday] meeting it felt a

Page 145

1815

little refreshing, held in Silence –
12[December]=26th took a walk to C[hipping] Norton, call'd
to se a friend who appears to be in a
Decline, after sitting a little with
her, I was favoured to give her a
little Instruction, she appeard ten=
=der & desireous to be resigned to the
will of Divine Providence –
call'd to se some other friends in
affliction, walk from thence to
sibford it was very wett & windy
so that I had a trying Journey, Lodg
at Bro'rs, they ware very kind to Dry
my Cloths administer to my Necessieties
=27 attended the burial of the Widow
of the late Joseph Harris a Minister,
the Meeting was not very large but
felt Satisfactory the People ware ad=
=vised to attend to the Inward teaching of
the Spirit of the Lord and live in Obi=
dience thereunto that they might be favour'd

verso

to be prepared for Death, after
meeting took leave of some friends
and return'd Home time not admiting
for me to go down to the House
ware the friend Died to dine with
the friends –
12mo [December] 30th was at our first day [Sunday] meet=
=ing it felt a little refreshing

1816

1mo[January] 7th was at our first day [Sunday] meeting
my minde much exercised I was
concern'd to appear in prayer,
desireing of the Lord that he would
be pleased to hear the Cries of the
poor and Sighing of the needy, and
that he would be pleased to be with
the tryed Exercised ones who ware
concernd to look unto him and seek
to him for help & Preservation that
he would be pleased to be the Help and
preserver of these

Page 146

1816

1mo[January] 8th set out for our Quarterly meeting
to be held at Oxford rode with Bror
& his Son in his Cart to Oxford
met with a pretty menny friends
at the Inn this side Oxford Drank
tea with them – we Lodgd their
=9 before the Quarterly meeting
began went into Oxford to se some
friends, - a strainger in the minis=
=try at the quarterly meeting viz
Richard Weston,
I trust it was a good refreshing meet'g
friends being favour'd to feel a degree
of solemnity to cover them, sevral
friends appear'd in Testimonie –
the buisness was gone through pretty com=
fortabley, after meeting Din'd with menny
friends at the Horse & Jockey, took leave
of them and return'd with my Relations Home –

verso

1816

1mo[January] 13th having heard of the Death of Aunt Grace
Hemmings of Epwell, in the afternoon walk'd to
Sibford call'd to se some of the friends their Lodg'd at Bro: J. Gibbs
=14 walked with Bro: J Gibbs to Epwell and
Breackfasted with Cousin Wm Hemmings son of the
Deceased he appear'd sorrowfull for the loss of his
Dear Mother being now left in a lonely situation
without a Housekeeper, yet I trust if he is concern'd
to fear the Lord and sarve him in the way of his
requireings and to seek unto him for support & preservation
He will be his support through all tryals & Probations
and will be a Father unto him will be with him
in the way he should go, give him Bread to eat &
Raiment to put on – menny friends & Neighbours
attended the Funeral, it was a pretty large meeting
Divine Goodness being pleas'd to own us with his Life=
=giving Power I trust to the tendering and contriteing
of the Peoples hearts before the Lord J. Lamb appeard
in Testimonie I was concern'd to appear in prayer
at the grave, after the Burial return'd with Cousin
to Epwell, and Din'd at his House with sevral Relations
and friends, spent the afternoon with them in a solid
weighty manner, after Tea return'd to sibford Lodg'd at Bro'rs
=15, set out pretty early and walk'd to C.[hipping]Norton
to our Monthly meeting it appear'd to be a mournfull
time with us, yet I trust the Lord has not forsaken us
but that he is still near to his poor Contrited Children

Page 147

who are concern'd to wait Patiently upon him, and seek
unto him for Counsel and support & He will be
near to these and be their support, and preserver through
every tryal and Exercise, blessed be his Name for
Evermore, after meeting before I return'd Home call'd
to se some of the friends - -
1mo[January] 21st was at our first day [Sunday] meeting I trust we ware Com=
forted and refreshed together in our Silent waiting
upon the Lord,
=25 was at our fifth day [Thursday] meeting, pretty
much exercised in minde, feeling a

great necessiety to be on my watch
Tower, that I may be sensible what
the Lord shall require of me by his
Pure Power, also may be favoured
to receive strength to do it,
=28, was at our first day [Sunday] meeting it
was held in Silence O that friends
in their silent sitting together might
have their mindes center'd towards that pure
Power which is profitable to Direct
then they would be directed and Inabled
to walk in the way of Truth & Righteousness

verso

1816

2mo[February] 4th was at our first day [Sunday] meeting,
I trust we ware favoured to feel
a little of the flowing of Divine
Love amoungst us, to the tendering
and contriteing our Spirits before
the Lord, - yesterday Thos Harris of
Longcompton call'd here in his way Home who had
been t his Brors funeral, (Saml Harris's)
-11 was at our first day [Sunday] meeting
it was held in Silence
=12 was at our Monthly meeting here
viz Charlbury I was concern'd to ap=
=pear theirin & another friend also –
=15 was at our fifth day [Thursday] meet'g
in the Afternoon as I was pulling
some faggots out of the pile it
fell upon me, I was in danger of
being much hurt but through Divine
Mercie was but little hurt to what
it might be expected O may I rem'r
to be truly Gratefull to the Almighty

Page 148

---

for all his Mercies and presarvations
unto me a poor Creature
2mo[February]=18th was at our first day [Sunday] meeting it
was held in Silence, I was desireous
to expearence "They that wait upon the
Lord shall renew their Strength,"
=22 was at our fifth day [Thursday] meeting my Wife gone
to Sibford with Cousin Jos: Harris & his
Daughter Jane
=23 Bro: Jno Gibbs Brot my Wife Home
on Horseback
24, was at our first day [Sunday] meeting it
felt to be a time of Poverty I had
nothing to communicate, O that these
seasons may wean us from a Dependance
on visibles things and Instrumental help
& Instructions, and cause us to feel after &
labour for the Injoyment of the Power
of God, that we may know the feet of our
mindes established upon the sure Rock

verso

1816

Christ Jesus, against which Satan
with all his snares besetments alurements & Tem=
=tation can never Prevail nor draw us
out of the oath of uprightness & Purity,
2mo[February]=28 took a walk to Witney was at
friends fourth day [Wednesday] meeting altho
small it felt a little comforting
=29 at our fifth day [Thursday] meeting felt a
little refresh'd
3[March]=3 was at our first day [Sunday] meeting it
was held in Silence
=5, sent a letter & a present to Cousin
Kewells, also sent a Letter to my
Nephew & Niece at Islington school
=7 our fifth day [Thursday] meeting was held in
Silence yet I trust the spiritual minded
ware favourd to feel their strength renewd
=10, was at our first day [Sunday] meeting it felt
refreshing I was concern'd to speak theirin
altho my faith in the Lords Power and leadings
appeared but as a grain of mustard seed

Page 149

---

for smallness yet as I gave up and was

obidient theirunto, I was favour'd to
feel Peace to flow in my minde
=11, took a walk to our monthly meeting held
at Witney, altho things are low amoungst
us yet the Lord is still gracious in
favouring us with his Power, I trust to
the tendering our hearts and contriteing
our Spirits I was concern'd to appear
in solem prayer, after meeting call'd
to se some of the friends return'd Home in the
A[fter] Noon
=12 took a walk to C[hipping] Norton to the
funeral
of Wm Coales's wife who died of a Decline
a meeting was held in the occasion it began
about Eleven, and felt to be a good eddifying
meeting, sevral friends appear'd in Testimonie
which through the Divine blessing ap=
=peared to have a good effect upon the
People their being a pretty menny Neigh=
=bours present, after meeting Din'd at Wm
Coles with a pretty menny friends, after

verso

1816

Dinner friends had a solid sitting together
and ware dipped into a sympathy and
concern for oneanothers good, some ware
led to exhort friends to fear the Lord
and be verry attentive unto his Power
also live in Obidience thereunto then
they would witness preservation from
the Power of the Devil, who is as a
Roaring Lion that goeth about seek=
=ing whome he may Devour
3mo[March]=17 was at our first days [Sunday]
meeting it
was held in Silence
=24, was at our first day [Sunday] meeting
it was held in silence, I was concern'd
to wait patiently upon the Lord that
I might be favoured to feel my strength
renewed,
=31 was at our first day [Sunday] meeting it was
held in Silence, feeling no opening in my
minde to speak any thing, our Preparative
meeting queries ware answered, -
My Wife gone with Bro: Sesss on foot to
Burford to be at our Monthly meeting to be

Page 150

1816

held there to morrow,
4mo[April] 1st walked to Burford was at our
monthly
meeting, it felt comforting Divine Goodness
being pleased to favour is with his lifegiving
Power Hanh Huntly was there who has been
from us a pretty wile, she appeared in
Testimonie & another woman friend,
the buisness was gone pretty agreeabley
after meeting Din'd at sistors, in the
evening I & my Wife walked Home with our
Relations
=7 was at our first day [Sunday] meeting it feels
to be a low time amoungst us in which
something like Poverty is felt, may we be
content to bear the trying proveing dis=
=pensations of the Lord without murmering
or repineing, then I trust they will work
together for our good,
=9 I & my Wife attended our Quarterly meeting
held at Witney it was pretty large & comfortable

verso

1816

sevral friends appear'd in Testimonie I
also was concern'd to advise friends to exercise
Patience in waiting upon the Lord & be
diligent in the attendance of their religious
meetings & then I believed they would be
favour'd to receive Divine refreshment
to their spiritual comfort and to the In=
ableing of them to do the will of the Lord
one friend appeard in solem Prayer,
the buisness was gone through pretty
agreeabley after meet'g din'd at T. Skinners
calld to se some of the friends in the

evening I and my Wife return'd Home
4[April]=11 was favoured to pertake of Divine
love and under the Influence thereof I
was constrained to advise friends to keep
the Commandments of the Lord mention=
ing that Scripture"if ye love me keep
my commandments ye are my friends
if ye do whatsoever I command you,
=14 was at our first day [Sunday] meeting I was

Page 151

concerned to draw near in Spirit unto
the Lord that I might be Instructed of
him and that I might be Inabled to
act consistant with his pure Power,
4mo[April]=21st was at our first day [Sunday] meeting
it was held in Silence,
=23, took a walk to Burford was at friends
third day [Tuesday] meeting it was held in Silence
=25, after being at our fifth day [Thursday] meeting
my Heart was tendered under a sence of
the Love of God to my soul in the days
of my youth when he show'd me how
dangerous it was to give way to my own
Inclinations & would not suffer me to be
easy or Enjoy Peace of minde in such a state
but made me sensible of I would pertake
of his love & mercy and Enjoy true Peace I must
Deny self take up my daily Cross & sarve Him
faithfully in the way of his requireings
O! may I nevver forget to be Gratefull unto the
Lord for his long sufferings and tender Compassion

verso

to me a poor unworthy Creature
4[April]=28 was at our first day [Sunday] meeting I trust
we ware favour'd to pertake of Divine
Goodness to our Spiritual refreshment
5[May]=5 was at our first day [Sunday] meeting it was
held in Silence, yet I trust it was a
good profitable meeting to such as ware
concerned to worship the Almighty in
spirit and in Truth,
=7 walk'd to our monthly meeting held at C[hipping]Norton
silent except one friend appear'd in solem
Prayer, after meeting Din'd at Saml Atkins's
saml still continues in a very helpless state
appears to bear his Affliction Patiently call'd
to se most of the friends before I return'd Home
-9 was at our fifth day [Thursday] meeting H. Huntley
appear'd theirin friends ware advised to be
diligent to labour after the Bread of Life
which nourisheth up the soul unto Eternal Life
=11 was at our first day [Sunday] meeting largish meet=
=ing sevral strangers ware present,

Page 152

I was concern'd to mention what a great
favour it is for us to be acquainted with
and Injoy the Divine teacher within
our selves, may the youth be Incouraged
to give up all and sarve the Lord in the
way of his requirings and then I believed
he would be with them in the way the
should go, and give them Bread to eate and
raiment to put on,
5mo[May] 16 of late I have been pretty much ex=
=ercised and burthened with observing the
youth spending their precious time in
vanity & vain amusements gaming Drink=
=ing to excess and such like evil practises
and some of them in perticular on the
first day [Sunday] of the week – I could not feel
quite easy & discharge my duty unto the
Lord without getting some papers Printed
as a warning to such as are giving way to
sinfull Practises and Advise to them to sincearly

verso

1816

repent thereof amend their ways and turn
to the Lord that they might be favour'd
to finde Mercy – therefore got some
Papers printed, and this morning was Im=
=ployd in distributing them,

5[May]=16 was at our fifth day [Thursday]
meet'g it felt refreshing
=18, rose early & set out on foot for our yearly
meet'g to
be held in London, reach'd Shillingford
about 3 oclock Din'd at Robt Greens who
ware very kind Call'd to se the friends
drank tea at my old friends Jno Sargoods
with him I have had menny comfortable
walks, but now he's advanced in years so
as not to be capable of taking long walks
=19 was at the first day [Sunday] meet'g at
Warbo=
=rough it felt refreshing I was concern'd
to speak theirin, as also to appear in Prayer
Din'd at Robt Greens, walked from thence
in the A,[fter]noon, to Henly Drank Tea at
Theobalds call'd to se Edwd Swain & his Family
and some other friends, lodg'd at young Jos:
Mays who was very kinde, his wife being from
Home

Page 153

5mo[May]=20th after Breackfast walked to
Maidenhead
call'd to se some of the friends their
Din'd & drank Tea at Nicholas Albrights
in the evening Nicholas went a little
way with me to put me in the road
through Winsor for stains, reach'd stains
about nine was kindly entertaind at
Robt Ashbys Lodgd their,
=21, in the morning call'd to se the Widow Ashby
who is about 82 years old looks pretty well,
appears to Injoy Divine Love & mercy
which preserves her in a Chearfull Patient
Resinged frame of minde –
call'd to se some other friends Thos Ashby was
poorly – had a early Din'r, set of for London
about noon, walk'd to the widow Harris's
Brendford
to Tea, afterward walk'd to London reach'd
Cous'n
T Kewells about 8 oclock at Night they appeard
glad to se me, Lodgd there
22 Yearly Meeting began at 11rn'g it felt to be a
good
refreshing Meeting sevral friends ware favour'd
to give good Advise & Counsell, the first that
appear'd mentioned that scripture wether we Eate
or Drink or whatever we do we should do it

verso

1816

all to the Glory of God – two appeals ware
Deliverd
in, the Representives call'd over & began reading
over the Answers to the Queries
A,[fter]noon met of 4 oclock five Testimonies or
accts
Brought in Concerning Deceased friends
ministers
5[May]=10, met at 11rn'g sevral more
Testimonies of
Deaces'd Ministering friends
A[fter] noon met at 4 oclock sevral Epistles from
America read which was Edifying and com=
=forting
=24, wrote a Letter to my Wife attended
Borrough
meeting it was large and Comfortable, sevral
friends appeard in Testimonie I was concernd
to speak theirin, I my Nephew & Cousin Thos
Whicheley Din'd with sevral more friends
at Thos Nortons ware we spent a little time
comfortabley, met at five A,[fter]noon the meet'g
for Buisness, a large Commity was appointed
to draw up answers to the Epistles also to
consider respecting rules for settlements some
alteration being proposed
=25 met at 11 oclock some alteration agreed to
respecting rule for Disownments meet'g
adjourn'd
to second day [Monday] morn 11 oclock I Din'd
at Jos Rutters

Page 154

1816

Drank Tea a Wm Dartons, their met with a
Convinced friend who came from Ohio in
America, had some agreeable conversation with

him he walk'd with me to Cousin Kewells and
there sup'd with us –
5[May]=26 first day [Sunday] morn'g went to the
Peel meeting which
was a favour'd meeting sevral friends appeard
in Testimonie & one in Solemn Prayer
se my Nephew & Niece Jesse & Rebecca Sess's
who ware glad to se me, Din'd at George
stringers, spent a little time there Comfortabley
A,[fter]noon attended Gracechurch=street
meeting,
it felt comforting, sup'd at Alexanders
=27, meet'g of Buisness began at 12rn'g
an amendment agreed to respecting a minute
Concerning Ministering friends laying a con=
=cern before a monthly meet'g to travel in
the work of the ministery, Din'd at Jno Pims
A,[fter]noon mett at 4 oclock the reports from or
Concerning Ackworth Islington schools &et read
and remarks made thereon, one of the ap=
=peals brought to a Conclusion,

verso

1816

---

we ware favour'd with a visit from the
women friends [blank] one of them
appear'd in Prayer the other in Testimonie
Din'd at A, astons – A[fter] noon met at 4
at the conclusion sevral Commities met
on various accounts
5[May]=29 took a walk with my Nephew and
Cousin to Radcliff meeting it felt a
satisfactory meeting sevral Living Tes=
=timonies born theirin, I was concerned to
advise friends to be diligent in the
attendance of their religious meetings
Din'd at frd Harris's Drank Tea at frd
Nights, met for buisness at 5 A,[fter]noon
=30 met at 10 oclock and again at 5 A[fter] noon
Epistles read over being answers to Epistles
from various parts agreed to – sup'd at J. Albts
31, met at 11rn'g ware favour'd with a visit from
the womens
meeting of five women friends, they ware
favour'd to give us good advise Din'd at J Elliotts
A,[fter]noon met at 5 I was concern'd to give
friends
advice, to keep under the coverings of the Lords

Page 155

Spirit and to take Counsel of Him,
the yearly meeting Epistle to friends in
great Britain & Elseware read over unani=
miously agreed to, order'd to be Printed,
the meeting of buisness concluded I trust
with gratitude and Thankfullness to the
Lord for his mercies and favours extended
to us – sup'd at Cousins –
6mo[June]=1st, went by Water & Land to strood
to se
Cousin Jno Kewell I believe we went about 28
miles by Water
which was new to me, it was a fine calm
morning had a fine view of the towns as
we went along landed at gravesend
we got to strood to Dinner I and my Relations
ware kindly entertaind at the friends ware
cousin Jno lives whose Names are Horsenail,
spent the A[fter] noon Comfortabley Lodgd at
friend Horsenails
2 was at friends fore and afternoon meetings
in the morning meeting I was concern'd to
Incourage
friends to be Diligent in the attendance of their
Religious meetings that they might be favour'd

verso

---

to know the Lords Power to bring forth the new
birth in them which being Expearenc'd it
would be their Delight to do the will of God
Dind at friend Horsenails drank tea at Robt
stiles's who keeps a Boarding school for boys
had a view of an old ruinous castle and other
high walling which appears to have been built
menny years ago, in the evening took a
walk along Rochester, I went upon a
high hill ware was a fortifacion
large Connons being Planted on top
how Horrible the appearance amongst
the Professors of Christianity being to
do good to Comfort to heal & preserve
Life, sup'd with my Relations at Saml
Wheelers

6[June]=3 after breackfast took my Farewell
of friends and walk'd to graves=end about
one oclock A,[fter]noon took Passage in a vessel
and set sail for London, the Wind was
high & boistrous, I became verry sick

Page 156

---

but was favour'd to get better before we
landed which we did and reach'd London about
6 in
the Evening, we saw a great menny
vessels in our Journey Cousin Kewells
ware pleas'd to us safe return, sup'd
with Cousins
6mo[June]=4th was at the Burrow meeting it felt
comfortable menny friends appeard
theirin, Din'd at Cousins, A[fter] noon took
a walk to se Cousin Wm Barrit & Wife
Cousin Wm continues to be afflicted with
the Palsy we also call'd to se Wm Barritt
Junr & his Wife he being lately married
drank tea with them, went from
thence to Islington school to se they
children, had Rebecca & Jesse Sessions
along with us to Cousin Kewell they ware
Pleased with their Visit, after Supper I
was led to Incourage my Relations to Love
and Sarve the Lord that it might be
well with them, took my Farewell of
them, and next morning being 5th rose early
and set out for Home

Page 157

1816

---

call'd at the Widow Harris's Brendford
she was very kinde, desired I would go
with them to a friends House to Dine
which I did, Kidds they ware very kinde
and friendly after Din'r the friend
brought me about five miles on the
way in his Carriage reach Robt Ashbys
stains to Tea, call'd to se thos Ashby who
had been very poorly found him a little
better Lodgd at R. Ashbys –
6[June]=6 after Breackfasting at R. Ashbys took
my farewell of him and his Family &
rose with his son Samuel in their Car=
=riage to Maiden Head was at friends
meeting their it felt a little refreshing
I was Concern'd to speak theirin Dind at
Nicholas Albrights, after Din'r walk to
Henly, Tea'd at young Jos: mays, walk in
the evening to Shillingford, Lodgd at R greens
=7 after breackfast bid them farewell and walkd
Home was favour'd to se my own weakness and

Page 157

---

the Necessiety to keep upon my watch
Tower that I might be favour'd to se my
Divine Leader and receive strength to do
my Heavenly Fathers will, -
was favour'd with a pretty comfortable
Journey and to return Home with a degree
of Peace, for which my minde is bow'd in
Humble thankfullness before the Lord
6[June]=9 was at our first day [Sunday] meeting
which felt comforting
-10 was at our monthly meeting
which felt pretty comfortable Hanh Huntly
appear'd theirin and another friend
16 was at our first day [Sunday] meet'g
=23 at our first day [Sunday] meeting ware
favour'd
with the Company of Wm Forster who
is on a religious visit, the meeting was silent
except I believed it right for me to advise
friends to turn their mindes Inward towards
the Divine Teacher in themselves
=24 my Wife set of for the Quarterly meeting
to be held at Banbury I was Prevented from
going on some perticular acct she return'd
on the morrow I understood Wm Forster &

verso

1816

Jno Kirkham ware at the Qr meeting
6[June]=28 Wm Foster attended a meeting at the
Malborough Arms in Woodstock appointed
by his desire to begin at six in the Evening
I and sevral friends attended the meeting

a pretty menny Neighbours came, I thought
they behaved well considering the place W=
Forster appear'd a pretty wile in Testimonie
I trust to the reaching of the pure witness in
menny and to the pointing out to them the
way of Life and salvation menny appear'd
to be affected and ware sensible of the Love
of God being extended towards them
after meeting Wm Forster return'd to Charlbury
29 W. Forster visited friends families, he
Drank Tea with us, he was Concern'd to
Incourage
us to faithfullness, he appear'd sensible of my
tryals and exercises altho known to few,
30, was at our first day [Sunday] meeting Wm
Forster
attended, appear'd in Testimonie, and at the
Conclusion of the meeting signified he should
like to have a public meeting appointed
accordingly a Evening meeting was appointed to

Page 158

begin at six, it was very full and appeard
satisfactory W.F. appeard a pretty wile in
Testimonie & Concluded the meeting in solem
Prayer
7[July]=7 was at our first day [Sunday] meeting,
in the after=
=noon I set out for our monthly meet'g to be
held at Faringdon walk'd to Witney drank
Tea at Daniel Rutters with him and his
relations and sevral young friends who
came from London afterward call'd to
se some of the friends, Lodg'd at Jno Hankins
=8, walk'd to Faringdon part of the way DR
was kinde as to let me ride in his Cart
the other part, the monthly meet'g felt pretty
comfortable one friend appear'd in Solemn
Prayer and sevral in Testimonie, the buisness
was gone through agreeabley, I Din'd at James
Renolds, James was gone to a funeral but his
Wife was at Home after calling to se some
of the friends walk'd to Witney Lodgd at J Hanks
-9 rose early and walk'd Home

verso

1816

7mo[July]=14th was at our first day [Sunday]
meeting it felt refreshing
=21, was at our first day [Sunday] meeting it felt
refreshing
I meet with tryals and Exercises and I believe
menny do as they pass through this vale of
Tears that are pretty much unknown to any
but the Lord alone and themselves yet I believe
if there is but a loving the Lord above all,
and a seeking to him for Help preservation
and support he will be the help and support
of these and he will nevver leave nor forsake
them altho he may se good to try their Patience
and Faith in his Almighty Power yet in
his own good time he will arise to the scattering
their Enemies and Inableing them to praise
him the God of their Salvation
=25 at our fifth day [Thursday] meeting I was led
to consider the weakness of humane
nature and the necessiety there is for us
to be constantly upon our watch even
unto Prayer, watch and Pray that he
enter not into Temptation, -
=28 at our first day [Sunday] meeting was
favoured to feel
Divine Love extended & I was concerned to men=

Page 159

=tion to feel Divine Love to flow in our hearts
it is a very great favour & I desired we
might indeavour to remove throug Divine
Assistance every thing that might hinder
the pure flowings theirof,
8[August]=1 was at our fifth day [Thursday]
meetings – felt very
desirous that our dear youth might love
the Lord in sincerity and be concerned to
sarve him in the way of his requirings
according to the mainfestations & Instructions
of his Divine Power within them, that the
Intent of their going to meeting and waiting
upon the Lord in Silence to feel the arisings
of his Power might Produce the desired Effect,

=3 set out for Armscutt [Armscote] meeting, call'd at Thos
Harris's Longcompton Drank tea their, in the
Evening Walk'd to shipstone was kindly enter=
tain'd at Thos Wells's Lodgd their
=4 call'd to se some of the friends, walk'd with
some friends to Armscutt [Armscote] meeting, it was
large of friends and Neighbours and felt comfortable
I believ'd it to be my duty to signify that without

verso

---

without the Power of the Dear Redeemer we could
do nothing, and it was good for us to be sensible
thereof, then there would not be so much trust
=ing in forms and ceremonies, but a waiting
to receive this Divine Power to strengthen &
Inable us to refuse that which is Evel and
do that which is good which was the reason
why we waited in Silence upon the Almighty
sarah Lambley was favour'd with a fine
oppertunity in testimonie, wareby she Indeavour'd
to turn the Peoples mindes Inward desiring they
might become acquainted with the Divine Teacher
in themselves, and yield Obidience to its Instruct=
=tions that they might know a being redeemed from
all Inicquity & be Inabled to sarve the Lord in
newness of Life, - concluded in Solemn Prayer
din'd at Sarah Lambleys ware friends had a com=
=fortable sitting together, drank Tea at Cousin
Thos Fardons ware I had the agreeable Company
of menny Relations and friends, in the Evening
walk'd to shipstone, went to Cousin Gilletts Brails to Lod'g
8mo[August]=5th walk'd to Bro'rs Sibford to Breackfast
Cousin Susanna very Ill with a fever,
it appear'd to be a time of mourning –

Page 160

---

after breackfast walk'd to the monthly meet'g
held at banbury a pretty comfortable meet'g
some friends appear'd in Testimonie
din'd at Cousin Jno Heads call'd to se some
of the friends with whome I had a little
friendly conversation, after tea return'd Home
8[August]=8, at our fifth day [Thursday] meeting I was so sensible
of my own weakness that it appear'd
necessary for me to walk humbley watch=
=fully & reverently as before the Lord
-11, was at our first day [Sunday] meeting no safety nor
Preservation with being constantly upon
the watch and attentive to the Divine Instructer
in the afternoon my Wife went with our Relations to Burford
=12 I walk'd to Burford to se our Relations and be
at the monthly meeting, the meeting felt pretty
comfortable H. Smith appear'd in solem Prayer
Dind at Sistors call'd to se some of the friends
in the Evening walk Home with Bro: & sevral friends

verso

1816

8mo[August] 15th was at our weekday meet'g it was held
in Silence as I was concern'd to wait Patiently
upon the Lord was favour'd to feel a re=
=newal of Strength,
=18 was at our first day [Sunday] meeting, it was pretty
full menny strangers ware present, yet it
did not feel very lively I was pretty much ex=
=ercised and very desirous to keep near to Divine
Goodness that I might feel preservation and
be Inabled to discharge my duty unto the Lord
whome I Love and desire to sarve above all things
=25 was at our first day [Sunday] meeting, it felt re=
=freshing, my mouth was opened to men=
=tion a little of the sufferings which friends
formerly underwent in bearing a testimonie
for the Truth and being faithfull in sarving
the Lord and be that means opened the way

for our ease & Liberty, therefore it behoves us to
be very thankfull & gratefull to the Almighty
for the mercies and favours we Injoy, and we
should

Page 161

show it by keeping to the Divine Law written
in our Hearts and bearing our Testimonie for
the Lord
8mo[August] 29th I have been pretty much
exercised of
late on acct of the wicked behaviour of some
yound People
who are often working wickedness, lately
they came the town with the Engin and
brought it before our door and because
I would not give them beer (I being afraid
so to do lest I should incourage druckeness
so displease the Almighty) they spouted
the water upon me and into the entry
against three of my windows broke one
of them pretty much caused the water to come
in at the windows to the dammage of my goods
I went to the man who had the management
of the pipe told him if he would get the
window mended I would look over the other
abuse he had sevral days to consider of it
but would not therefore 8mo[August] 30th I
went to the

verso

Justice accompanied by Bro: R Sessions &
a Neigh'r who se him play up against the
window and made my Complaint the Justice
granted a warrant to apprehend the man
who plaid against the house – to appear
before him on next third day [Tuesday] being
9mo: 3rd
9mo[September]=1st, was at our first day
[Sunday] meeting it felt
refreshing to my poor Exercised minde,
well may it be said, "The Heart knows its
own bitterness and a stranger does not
Intermeddle with its Joys" – at our Pre=
=parative meeting it was uniamously concluded
by the Men and women friends, to have a
afternoon
meeting, in the summer to begin at 5 in the
Evening, and
three oclock in the winter A.[fter]Noon, if the
monthly meeting
ware agreeable to it
=3 ware favour'd with a visit of Mary Dudly
& her Daughter, Maria Lamb of Reading bear'd
them Company also Jos: May, a meeting was ap=
=pointed on their acct to begin at 10 oclock in
the morning it felt to be a good satisfactory

Page 162

meeting in which the renewed visitation of
Divine
mercy was extended much Instruction was
given by way of Testimonie & in a Perticular
manner to the youth the meeting was
Concluded in Solemn Prayer
9mo[September]=5th attended our fifth day
[Thursday] meeting, silent
=7 this day the friends came back to
Charlbury who paid us a visit last third
day stop'd a little wile, and then went
on for witney, in the evening
=8, attended our first day [Sunday] meeting it
felt
refreshing it was held in Silence
=9 I & my Wife attended our monthly meet'g
held at C,[hipping] Norton, Joseph Allen & his
Wife ware their, they being on a Religious
visit Joseph was drawn fourth in Tes=
timonie in a Powerfull manner, another
stranger also appear'd in the ministery,
after meeting din'd at Wm Atkins Jun'r, call'd to
se a few friends before I return'd Home

verso

1816

9mo[September] 10th Mary Dudly her Daughter
and the other
friends that accompanied them here to day, and
by their Desire a Public meeting was held it
began at six oclock in the Evening it was pretty
large and I believe a good eddifying meeting
sevral young men there who have given way to a

reprobate life they appeard solid and the pure
witness was I believe reachd in them by the
Testimonie of Mary Dudly to the convincing them
of the evel of their ways, the meeting concluded
in Solem Prayer, I believe menny went away
refreshed & Comforted
=11 Mary Dudly and other friends took their affectionate
farewell of us and went to Oxford Intending
to hold a Public meeting their –
=15 was at our first day [Sunday] meeting it felt refreshing
the monthly meeting having signified their
consent for us to hold a afternoon meeting
on first day [Sunday], accordingly we began and this
day held an Evening meeting, it felt comforting
21 I set out for our Quarterly meeting to
be held at Reading call'd at Jno Jacksons's
& drank tea, reach'd Shillingford about eight

Page 163

was kinde entertaind at Robt Greens lodgd their
9mo[September] 22nd befor meeting at Warborough call'd
to se some of the friends, the meeting
felt pretty comfortable altho it is small
yet I think there is some sincear friends
attend it, I was concerned to appear in
Testimonie and in Prayer, - din'd at
Ann Sargoods, after dinner took my
farewell and walked to reading, supped at
Cousin Tutteys ware widow Tuttey lives,
sevral straingers ware their Ann Ashby
Richd Burlingham Hanh Huntley &et
we had a comfortable sitting together, some
friends spake by way of Incouragment for
us to love and sarve the Lord Lodgd at Cousin Tutteys
=23 call'd to se my Relations & friends, they
ware very kind and I hope our meeting to=
=gether through mercy was comforting and
Edifying to each other call'd to se a friend
who went from Charlbury he appear'd to be in

verso

a thoughtfull state, having lately been
bitten in the ear by his own dog which
they soposed was mad as it bit his man
and sevral dogs, he had the part that was
bitten took out of his Ear and he with
his man had been to the salt water, I Incourag'd
him to seek to the Lord for mercy and for
his Power to be his support and comfort
I think People should be carefull not
to fondle or Play with dogs but keep them
in their places, supped with sevral friends
at Cousin Jnan Farthings
=23 the Quarterly meeting began at 10 oclock
it felt to be a good refreshing meeting, it
being a renewed visitation of Divine Love
and mercy, sevral strangers ware present
as Mary Dudly & her Daughter Richard
Birlingham &et sevral friends appeard
in testimonie wareby friends ware ad=
vised to be diligent in the Lords work and
build up the Breaches that ware in the

Page 164

Walls of Zion, and wile they ware
thus doing to be carefull to maintain
their watch and keep near to the
Divine Power that they Enemy might
not anoy them or hinder them from
going on in the work of the Lord
in the meeting for Buisness sevral women
friends visited the men, and it was sig=
=nified the fields truly appeard wite
unto Harvest and there was a necessiety
of Faithfull Labourers in the Lords
Harvest, and friends ware Incouraged
to persevear in the Discharge of their
duty also to beware of the Goliahs who
bid defience to the Living God and Indeavour
through the mighty Power of the Lord to over=
=come them, like as little David did in an
outward sence on what was visible to out=
=ward observation, so might they trust in

verso

in the Lord having the shield of Faith
& putting on the breastplate of Rigteous=
=ness or being clothen therewith & the Helmet of
salvation on their Heads having the sword of the

spirit which is the word of God so might be
favoured to over come sin & Satan –
the Women taking up a pretty deal of time the
meeting was adjourn'd, friends met again about
four, A[fter] Noon, then went through the
remainder of
the buisness pretty comfortabley, - -
10mo[October] 24th set out pretty early for
Home call'd
at Robt Greens with other friends and had
some refreshment – reach'd Home about Eight –
=29 was at our meeting on first day [Sunday] –
10mo[October] 4th our weekday meeting was
held on this day
being sixday [Friday] onacct of Richd
Burlingham &
Ann Ashby who are on a religious visit &
visited our meeting it felt to be a comfortable
meeting, - they also visited friends Families
they had a sitting with me and my Wife
which was edifying and comforting one of
them appear'd to be dipped into a feeling sence
of my Exercises's,

Page 165

1816

10mo[October]=6 I went to C[hipping] Norton
with Rich'd Burlingham and Ann
Ashby as Guide Wm Albt Junr also went,
we ware at friends morning and afternoon
meetings which felt refreshing Rich'd Birlingham
and Ann Ashby I believe ware favour'd to
speak to the states of menny present,
=13, was at our first day [Sunday] meeting it felt
comforting
=14, was at our monthly meeting held at
Charlbury, I was concerned to appear
theirin, the Buisness held long, we are in
a low situation their is cause of Morning
the seed I think is oppressed & Truth hardly
ariseth into Dominion, -
=20 was at our first day [Sunday] meetings we
had the Company of Thos Harris of Long=
=compton they felt refreshing & I trust
Divine Goodness was pleased to favour us
with his living Power to the causing us to
rejoice under a sence of his Love, -
=24 was at our fifth day [Thursday] meeting, I
and my Wife
are in a mournfull state having lately heard
that sistor M. Gibbs is very Ill with a Fever,

verso

1816

10mo[October] 27 was at our first day [Sunday]
meeting
it felt refreshing I was concerned to
speak theirin signifying how acceptable
it is with the Lord to wait Patiently
upon the Lord to feel the arisings
of his pure power and to seek an
Inward acquaintance with him
I was also at the afternoon meet'g
my Wife being poorly was not at
meeting she being poorly on account a messenger
being come to Inform us of the
Death of her Sistor Mary Gibbs,
who liv'd at Sibford she died of a
Fever, it affected my Wife very
much she not going over to se her
in her Illness their appearing some
danger of taking the disorder – it is
a strifeing time with Brother J Gibbs his
only Daughter dying a little before of
the same Disorder and now his Wife, but
she being a Honest upright Hearted woman

Page 166

and one that loved to have friends keep to
the plainness & Simplicity of the Truth, altho it
is cause
of mourning to some who ware acquainted
with her Religious conduct & Conversation
yet I trust it is her gain & she is removed
out of a world of tryals and Exercises in to
that Glorious Kingdom ware all tears & sighing
are at an end and sorrows are known no
more, =31st I was at our fifth day [Thursday]
meeting,
11mo[November] 3rd was at our first day
[Sunday] meeting, it was

held in silence, in the afternoon was
again at meeting it felt refreshing silent
=7 was at our fifth day [Thursday] meeting my minde was
humble & I was concerned to sit as at the
footstool of Jesus to be sensible of the gracious
Instructions of his Spirit, also to receive
strength to do my Lords will
10 was at our first day [Sunday] meeting it felt refreshing
11, took a walk to our monthly meeting held at Witney
small meeting it being a winterly day yet it felt
pretty comfortable Hanh Smith appear'd in Prayer
I was concerned to speak a little theirin, in the Even'g return'd Home

verso

1816

11mo [November] 10 took a walk to C,[hipping] Norton with an
intent to meet Bro: Jno Gibbs but I
understood he was so poorly (thought it
was something of the Fever complaint)
could not come, met his Bro: Wm their
I was at the first day [Sunday] meeting at C[hipping] Norton
it felt refreshing I was concern'd to speak
theirin – Din'd at Wm Coles's, call'd to se
Saml Atkins, who appear'd a little better
return'd Home to Tea, -
=17 was at our first day [Sunday] meetings
=24 was at our first day [Sunday] meeting they felt
refreshing, wrote a letter to Bro: J Gibbs,
12[December]=1 was at our first day [Sunday] meeting –
Drank tea at Wm Albrights, spent a little
time with them Comfortabley
=8, was at our first day [Sunday] meeting I trust Divine
goodness was felt to be amoungst us, and
under the influence thereof I was constrain'd
to speak theirin in the afternoon walk'd
with Bro: Robt & my Niece A.M. to Burford
reach'd their about six in the evening –

Page 167

---

spent the evening comfortabley at sistors, Lodgd their
12[December]=9 was at our monthly meeting held at
Burford it was small yet felt refreshing
I was concern'd to speak a little theirin
din'd at sistors, pretty soon after dinner bid
them Farewell and walk'd Home –
=15 was at our first day [Sunday] meeting, at which was
a Funeral of Mary Veal who died last second day [Monday]
morning, a pretty menny Neighbours attended, (she
marring out was not a member) it felt to be a satis=
=factory meeting the People behaved in a still becoming
manner, my minde was pretty much exercised their
being no friend in the ministery there besides myself
I Indeavoured to keep near to the Divine Power, after
a time of Silence I felt a Concern to stand up which
I did and advised the People to prepare for their
latter end signifying the gracious visitation of the Lord was extended
towards them, & his pure Power showed them their states
and Conditions and made known unto them what they
had done amiss, as they ware concerned to minde this pure
Power and live in Obidience to it, it would Inable them
to forsake sin and do that which is good and pleasing unto

verso

1816

the Lord and by so doing they would finde mercy and
witness a being prepared for death, or words to that purpose,
12[December] 15th in the afternoon attended our meeting which was held in silence
=22 was at our first day [Sunday] meeting it was
held in Silence,
was also at our afternoon meeting
it felt refreshing I was led to speak
a little concerning Divine Love & the
comfort their is in dwelling together
in Unity & Love
=29 was at our first day [Sunday] meeting I was con=
=cearned to wait in Solem silence that
I might be favoured to receive Divine
Instruction, & I believe a degree of solem=
=nity was over the meeting & Silence prevailed
in which Divine Instruction may be received
as well as when words are spoken
was at our afternoon meet'g it felt re=
=freshing, it was held in Silence
there hath been so much wet of Late for several
months that we have had the longest Harvest
I ever remember some of the Corn was not
got in till the latter end of the 12:[November] or the be=
gining of the 13:[December] some of it much Damaged

Page 168

1817

1mo[January]=5th was at our morning and afternoon meetings
which felt refreshing
=12 attended our morning meeting
it felt comfortable –
=13 walk'd to our monthly meeting held at C[hipping] Norton
I was concern'd to speak theirin, it is a
low mournfull season or a time to mourn amoungst
us, O that we may dwell near to the Lord
and Indeavour to be guided by his pure
spirit in all our Labours & undertakings
then in the day of tryal & Probation we
shall have a strong tower and Rock of
Defence to flee unto and be safe –
= was at our first meeting on first day [Sunday], it
felt a little refreshing
the breathing and travail of my spirit is
unto the Lord that He will be pleased
to preserve my minde near unto himself
and also the mindes of those in Profession
with me, that in al things the may have
a single Eye to the Glory of God, then I

verso

1817

I believe in the greatest trials and
exercises he will not leave nor for=
sake them but will be their comfort
& support through all
was at the afternoon meeting, it was
held in Silence,
1mo[January] 22 was at the fourth day [Wednesday] meeting at
Witney at which was a Funeral,
=23, Poorly with a Coughf & Cold, my
Wife also Poorly, was at our fifth
day [Thursday] meeting, it felt a little refreshing
=26 was at our first day [Sunday] meeting, my minde
was comforted being sensible that Divine
Goodness was felt amoungst us, under
a sence theirof I was constrained to
speak theirin to Incourage friends to
press after Purity & Holiness of Life as
blessed are the pure in heart for they
shall se God, - was also at our after=

Page 169

=noon meeting in which Divine Love

was felt amoungst us, and I was
concerned to set fourth the preciousness
theirof, signifying we should be willing
to part with any thing this world affords
to Injoy Divine Love, it being an
Inestimable Blessing
1[January]=29 took a walk to C,[hipping] Norton old Wm Atkins
Wife was very Ill and not likely to
live long, Edwd Hopkins Wives mother
was in the same afflicted state, I went
to se her, she appear'd sensible her time
would not be long, and to be willing to
be removed
2mo[February]=2nd was at our first day [Sunday] meeting, I feel a
a great desire raised in my minde that
I may live near to the Lord and be found
daily in the Discharge of my duty unto
Him – was also at our afternoon meeting it
felt a little refreshing

verso

1817

2mo[February] 6th my minde much exercised on acct
of the Tryals that attend poor mortals
in this Life, I firmly believe that
they that Trust in the Lord & do sarve
him in the way of his requiring shall
be as Mount Zion that cannot be re=
=moved for the Lord will be with them
in all their Tryals and afflictions
to support preserve and Comfort them
=9 being first day [Sunday] took a walk to the first
day meeting at C[hipping] Norton it felt a little re=
=freshing speake theirin setting fourth the
blessed state of the Righteous and the great
Peace they Injoy who sarve the Lord in
the way of his requirings, in the A[fter] noon walk'd Home
-10 attended our monthly meeting held at
Charlbury my minde pretty much Exercised
being desirous my Will should be given up
or so brought into subjection to the Divine
Will as that I might do the will of the Lord
I was concern'd to appear theirin

Page 170

2mo[February]=11th took a walk to C.[hipping] Norton to the
Burial of the Widow Beavington (E, Hop=
kins motherinlaw) Sarah Lambley & Thos
Harris their, ministering friends, a pretty
menny friends and Neighbours attended the
funeral, S. lambley was favour'd to appear
in Testimonie a pretty wile, signifying there
was not cause to weep for the Dead but for
the living who ware gone into Captivity through
giving way to their own hearts lust & vain In=
=clinations, Inviting them to turn inward
to the manifestations of the Spirit of
the Lord and live in Obidience thereunto
in the day of his mercy, that they might
be favour'd to know a returning out of
the broad way which leadeth to Destruction
in to the straight & narrow way which
leadeth unto Life everlasting,
after meeting I dind with the friends at
Edwd Hopkins, after Dinner friends had
a Comfortable sitting together and under

verso

1817

---

the Influence of Divine Love of them ware
constrained to minister to others –
after calling to se some friend I return'd Home
2[February]=13, was at our fifth day [Thursday] meeting,
this day the new Coin of sixpence's shilling
& half Crowns began to be chaing'd for the
old which gives satisfaction to menny
there having been great uneasiness in
the Nation on acct of plain shillings &c
being refused to be taken by menny
but they have chaing'd most or nearly all of them Except
the french Coin –

=16 was at our first day [Sunday] meeting it felt refreshing
=20, I felt a little refreshed at
our weekday meeting – altho there
was a deal of rain the last half year,
yet now and of late we are favour'd with
fine open weather and but little frost,
the wheat looks very fine and the Gosbery &
some other Bushes, are comming out in
green leaf

Page 171

2[February]=23 was at our first day [Sunday] meeting,
it was held in silence yet I trust
friends ware favoured to feel a
renewal of strength
was also at our afternoon meeting
which was held in Silence, -
=27 was at our fifth day [Thursday] meeting
my minde of late hath been pretty
much exercised, the breathings of my
Spirit is unto the Lord that it may
work together for my good, and that
this may be the day of the Lords merci=
full visitation unto my soul –
3[March]=1, took a walk to Sibford found Bro: Jno
Gibbs finely recover'd he having been Ill
of a Fever, he appeard much tried his only
Daughter & Wife being lately removed by Death
& he left in straitened sircumstances hardly knowing
what to do for the best, I advised him to exercise
Patience trust in the Lord love and fear him
and I hoped the Lord would be his support and Comforter,

verso

1817

Lodg'd at Jno Enocks
3mo[February]=2nd was at the first day [Sunday] meeting at Sibford
it was not very large yet it felt refreshing
I was concern'd to speak theirin signifying
the fear of the Lord is a fountain of Life
which preserves from the snares of Death
desireing they might live in his fear love and
sarve him in the way of his requirings that
they might feel Preservation
Dind at the Widow Frenchs afterward went
to Epwell with Bror drank Tea at Cousin W.H,
=3, walk'd with my relations to Adderbury,
call'd to se some of the friends before
the Monthly meeting began – was at the
monthly meeting it felt to be a low time
for want of friends, keeping near and living
in Obidience to that Power which preserves
in purity and holiness of Life –
I din'd at Cousin Fardons who live at the
mill, Drank tea at Thos Plesters
went to the widow Malls to Lodge he Hus=

Page 172

=band Thos Mall being removed by Death
about a half a year ago he was a friend
whome I much loved I believe he was
a honest sincear friend and loved such
as kept to the plainness and simplicity
which Truth leades into, the Widow
entertained me very kindly was glad to se
me = 4th after breakfasting with her I
took my farewell of her and return'd Home
3mo[April]=6th attended our fifth day [Thursday] meeting which I am
in the Practice of, and altho often
in a low Exercised state yet I am
concerned in Patience to Labour for Divine held
and Spiritual refreshment through
mercy am favoured to receive it, -
=9 was at our first day [Sunday] meeting was refresh'd
and comforted under a sence Devine Goodness
was felt to be present & I was concernd to
speak theirin signifying it was a great
Priviledge to sit under the Lords teaching
desiring they might all be concern'd to meet in

verso

his Name, and then I believed He would ful=
=fill his gracious promise that ware but
two or three ware met together in his name
there He would be in the midst of them

this being taught of the Lord would be as
sitting under their own vine and under their
own figtree ware none can make afraid
3[March]=10 walk'd to witney to our monthly
meeting
held their H Smith appear'd theirin,
I also was concern'd to appear theirin
Dind at Daniel Rutters, call'd to se some
of the friends before I return'd Home
=16, was at our first day [Sunday] morning &
afternoon meetings
which ware held in Silence, yet I trust
profitable & refreshing, to such as whare
concern'd to Labour for that meat which
Perisheth not, but nourisheth up the
souls of those that receive it, unto Eternal life
=23 attended our first day [Sunday] meeting
also attended our afternoon meeting both
held in Silence I may we in our meeting

Page 173

together to worship the Lord not have our
dependance on man but on the Lord
and may it be our chief concern to
be Instructed and governed by his spirit
then I trust our meetings will tend
to the Lords honnour & our Eddification
& Comfort
3[March]=30 was at our first day [Sunday]
meeting which
felt comforting, I was concerned to
advise friends to attend to the Divine
monitor in their own Hearts, which bears
a Testimonie against that which is
evil & is displeasing unto the Lord,
and as it is obey'd we living under its
heavenly Influence are Inabled to
do the will of God
4[April]=6 was at our first day [Sunday] meet'g
it felt
a little refreshing it was held in Silence
in the afternoon walk'd with my Re=
=lations to Burford spent the Evening
comfortabley at sistor Manders lodg'd their
=7, was at our monthly meet'g held at Burford

verso

not very large it felt a little refreshing
I was concern'd to advise friends to make
good use of the time they ware favour'd with
and so to number their days as to apply
their Hearts unto Wisdom which is profitable
to direct & doth guide in the way of true
Peace, - Din'd at sistors, call'd to se
some of the friends, after tea walk'd Home
4mo[April] 13 was at our first day [Sunday]
meeting ware
favour'd with the Company of Jos: Lamb
my minde was exercised being very de=
=sirous to be found in the discharge of my
duty, I was concerned to appear in solemn
Prayer, afterward Jos: Lamb appear'd
in Testimonie he signified in comming to
sit with us his minde was comforted & he
rejoiced under a sence that Divine Good=
=ness was near, he believed it good for us
often to put the question to ourselves
"am I in the way to the Kingdom",
was also at our evening meeting it felt com=
forting, I was Inabled to Incourage friends to

Page 174

1817

Faithfullness as the only way to Expearence
Preservation and the blessings of the Lord,
4[April]=15 I and my Wife attended our
Quarterly
meeting held at Witney, a pretty large &
Comfortable meeting – sevral friends ap=
peared in Testimonie I also was concern'd
to speak theirin concerning the greatness
and purity of the Almighty therefore we ought to
be very carefull not to do any thing dishonest
or Impure to offend him, who hath power
to kill and to cast both soul & body into
hell, - the buisness was gone through
pretty agreeabley, Din'd at Thos Skinners
drank tea at T. Smiths, in the evening walk'd
Home
=20 was at our first day [Sunday] meeting it felt
refreshing I was concern'd to advise
the youth to refrain from Earthly
Pleasures as "they that live in Pleasures
are dead wile they live", and Indeavour

to turn their mindes Inward to the
teaching of the Divine Spirit and be
obidient theirunto that they might Expear=
=ence a Groth in the Truth

verso

1817

4mo[April] 27th was at our first day [Sunday] meeting, as my Spirit is drawn near
to the Lord I feel fervent Desires
that our youth may Love the Lord
fear to offend him be Zealous for
his Glorious cause of Truth and
Righteousness in the earth, if this
be their happy expearence I trust the
Lord will delight to be with them
and he will be their Shield & Exceeding
great Reward – attended our evening
meeting it felt comforting, I was con=
=cern'd to speak theirin setting forth
the Preciousness of the Living word &
Light of Christ, which to them that
love and Obey it, shines Brighter and
brighter, unto the Perfect day
5[May]=4 was at our first day [Sunday] meeting, my minde
was exercised on the youths account, and
I was concern'd to mention it was a happy
state to be quite given up to sarve the Lord in the
way of his requirings, altho this cannot be

Page 175

obtain'd in our own wills and in our
own time yet it may through Divine
assistance, by being watchfull and attentive
unto the Divine Teacher in our own Hearts
and through living in Obidience thereunto,
5[May]=11 was at our first day [Sunday] morning meeting
held in Silence, yet I trust Profitable
to such as ware concerned to wait upon
the Lord in the Silence of all flesh –
was also at our evening meeting it felt
refreshing and comforting
I was concerned to speak concerning
the Power of the dear Redeemer and
of the necessiety there is to press through
the crowd of difficulties and touch
him, having faith in his living Power
then I believed we should be favour'd
to receive comforting healing power from Him,
=18 was at our first day [Sunday] meeting, held in Silence
was at our Evening meeting it was held in silence
yet I trust Profitable to the mindes of them

verso

1817

who ware concerned to Profit thereby
5mo[May]=22nd I attended our fifth day [Thursday] meeting
my Wife set out last sixth day [Friday] morn'g
with Bro'r & Sistor sessions for London
to attend the yearly meeting –
=25 attended our first day [Sunday] morning meet'g
am poorly with a Cold a Coughf at=
=tending it, & through tryals and Ex=
=ercises am in a low Humble situation
of minde, in which state I feel desirous
that the Lord in mercy may strengthen
and Inable me to do his Will,
was also at our evening meeting it
felt refreshing, I believed it right
to Incourage friends to love the Lord
above all and Sarve him in the way
of his leadings, as that Passage of
Scripture which signifieth, all things
work together for good to them that
love God is matter of Incouragment
to the truly religious mindes

Page 176

5mo[May] 29th was at fifth day [Thursday] meeting –
this morning heard of the Death of
Wm Barritt Adderbury,
6[June]=1 was at our first day [Sunday] meeting –
as this day is set appart for Religious

Duties, I was concern'd to advise friends
and the youth in Perticular to spend
it in a retired weighty manner not
giving way to Indulge themselves in law=
=full things, but be concerned to read
the Scriptures and friends books and
also to Profit thereby, then I believed
the Lord would be pleased to tender their
hearts and Contrite their Spirits before
Him, was also at our first day [Sunday] evening
meeting it felt comforting, Robt
spendlove was at meeting twice to
day who is above ninety years old
it sets fourth his love to attend meetings
to be retired in Spirit & wait upon
the Lord & I believe he is favour'd to feel
a renewal of Spiritual strength altho

verso

1817

as to the outward man he gets weaker
6[June]=8 was at our first day [Sunday] morn'g meeting
it was held in Silence – was also
at our evening meeting which felt re=
=freshing, as we ware concern'd to wait
upon the Lord I trust we ware favourd
to feel the Springings up of the water
of Life to the watering the young &
tender Plants, and to the re=
=freshment of such as love the Lord
=10, this evening My Wife (Bro'r & Sistor)
returned Home from London, she was
favour'd to be at menny comfortable
meetings, I understood it was a comfortable
and satisfactory yearly meeting –
=15 was at our first day [Sunday] meeting it was
held in Silence was also at our evening
meeting I was concern'd to speak theirin
signifying they that loved God would
be concerned to keep his Commandments
and in all their ways Acknowledge
Him
=22 was at our first day [Sunday] meeting it felt re=

Page 177

freshing I was concern'd to advise friends
to Indeavour through Divine assistance
to have their Hearts & wills at the Lords
disposial, even to have their own will
brought into Subjection to the Divine Will
a state in which the new birth is ex=
=piearanced that of being born again, and
becoming as little children fitted & prepared
to Injoy the Kingdom of Heaven –
6[June]=26 attended our fifth day [Thursday] meeting which
I am constantly in the Practise of
Except any thing very perticular prevent me
=27 attended our monthly meeting held
at Charlbury this day to accomodate
a Commity of friends who attended
it, it felt comfortable, sevral living
Testimonies ware born wareby friends
ware advised to keep low and humble in
the fear of the Lord, to have their depen=
=dance upon him and be concerned to wait
for the arising of his Light & Grace in
their hearts, that they might be favoured

verso

to have a sence of their duty and
be strengthened to do it, and such as
whare in a low mournfull exercised state
whare Incouraged to bear their tryals
with Patience and not let go of their con=
=fidence in the Lord but be concern'd to
trust in him, and when the Lord had
tried them he would bring them fourth
as Gold, - -
6mo[June] 29th set out for our Quarterly meeting to be
held at Banbury reach'd south newington
to meeting it was small only three besides
myself, yet I trust we ware favoured to
Pertake a little of Divine refreshment
Din'd at Wm Harris's, spent about one
Hour with them agreeabley then walk'd
to milton drank tea at sarah Malls
walk'd with she to adderbury evening meetg
it felt refreshing I was concern'd to speak
therein, and also to pray, after meetg call'd
at A Barritts & the Widow Barritts stop'd a

little, went from thence with Cousin Wycheleys
to Ayn[h]o, Lodg there they ware very kinde

Page 178

6[June]=30 spent the morning comfortabley with Cousins
after Dining with them was favoured to
give them some advice to Incourage them
to love the Lord and sarve him faithfully,
return'd from thence to adderbury call'd
to se some the friends, understood
Joseph Lamb (who was settel'd at Reading
and came their chainge of air) was very
Ill being in a decline and not likely to
live long drank tea with Cousin Fardons at
the mill – in the evening walk'd to Banb'[ur]y
Lodg'd with Cousin Jno Heads –
7mo[July]=1st attended our Quarterly Meet'g strangers
present Richard Gilks & Thos Brown
who are on a religious visit in these
parts, we ware favoured with a com+
=fortable meeting sevral friends appear'd
in Testimonie, they whose faces ware turn'd
Zionward ware Incouraged to press forward
such as had gone astray ware advised sincearly
to repent of their rong doings & return to the
flock of Christ wile mercy was extended
the mourners in zion ware comforted, blessed
be the Lord he Inabled me to Incourage the

verso

youth and others to love the Lord above
all and be strip'd of their own Righteous=
ness that they might be clothed with the
righteousness of God by living in Obidience
to his Spirit, at the close of the meetg
the yearly meet'g Epistle was read,
which manifest that meetings fervent desire & concern
for the good & establishment in the Truth
of their Brethren & Sistors & their Ofspring
in what situation soever they may be and ware
ever their lot may be cast sevral minutes
of much weight and concern came from the
yearly meet'g which are left for further
consideration, after meet'g Din'd at H
Stones, drank tea a Jno Heads in the Even'g
return'd Home,
7mo[July] 3rd at our fifth day [Thursday] meeting I felt as a
very poor Creature, & a great Necessiety
to look unto the Lord and seek [illegible] to him for
a renewal of strength and ability to do
his will
=6 was at our first day [Sunday] meeting it
felt refreshing held in Silence, it is a

Page 179

happy thing for friends to Expearence a being
brought into such a solemn awefull silence
as to have their mindes bowed in Reverence
before the Lord & to be taught by his pure
spirit was also at our Evening meet'g
which was a refreshing meet'g
sistor Mander this afternoon and two
of her Children came to se us &
ware at meet'g - -
7[July]=13 was at our first day [Sunday] meeting, was a
little refreshed, I was concern'd to
mention that the injoyment of the
love & favour of God is more to be des=
=ired than all other things, & I wishes
we might be sensible theirof –
in the afternoon set of for our Monthly Meet'g to
be held at Faringdon, walk to Witney spent
the evening their with friends Comfortabley
found Hanh Smith in a very weak state Lodgd at Jno Hankins
=14, walked alone to Faringdon, the monthly
meetg was small, and felt but little of the arise=
=ings of Divine Power & its Injoyment, after
a time of Silence the yearly meeting Epistle was
read which contain'd much Good Instruction

verso

1817

after meeting Din'd at the Widow Reynolds's
with she & her family and sevral friends,
the Widow appear'd in a loving humble

frame of minde, afterward call'd to se
some of the friends, in the evening returnd Home
7mo[July] 16th walk'd with my Wife to Burford
she being set out on a visit to her
Relatives at Campden &c
spent the A,noon comfortabley at sistors
& in calling to se some of the friends
in the evening I return'd Home
=20 attended our first day [Sunday] meeting it
was held in silence, at the conclusion
the yearly meeting Epistle was read
which contain'd a deal of good Instruction
O! that is was more minded and received
in that Love from which it springs,
especialy by our young friends, then
would it tend to their good and advance=
=ment in the Path of purity, the alone
way which leads unto the Glorious Kingdom
also attended our afternoon meet'g

Page 180

7mo[July]=24th attended our weekday meet'g –
sensible of great weakness therefore
am concerned to breathe and seek unto
the Lord for strength and ability to
do his will,
=25 being appointed visitor this week to
the Brittish school, have attended
constantly twice a day as it appear'd
necessary to keep the Children in an
orderly becoming manner, -
=27, was at our first day [Sunday] morn'g
meeting, I was
concern'd to mention the happiness such
enjoy that know the Lord for themselves
& are concern'd to sit under his Divine
Teaching the Teaching of the holy spirit
and as there is a constant watchfullness and
a keeping close be obidient to the Heavenly
Teacher, altho the Enemy may beset those
and lay his temptations and baits yet cannot
he prevail against them nor draw them
in to any Evel for the Light of Christ in
them makes manifest all his besetments and

verso

1817

Temptations and preserves out of
them – was at our Evening meeting
it felt to be a good refreshing meeting
and I felt an evidence that the Lord
owned us theirin, Praises be unto Him
for his mercies and the enjoyment
of his Living power,
7mo[July] 31st was at our fifth day [Thursday]
meetg we
ware favour'd with the company of
Richd Gilkes & Thos Brown who are on
a religious visit, ware favour'd with
a good refreshing meeting R Gilks ap=
=pear'd in testimonie, he signified it was
a favour in our meeting together to be
sensible of Divine goodness & he believed
there ware Present who ware Established
upon the sure foundation and altho they
might have tryals and exercises to meet with
yet he was led to speak encouraging to them
signifying they would be favour'd to drink of the
living
water to there refreshment that springs
up unto Eternal Life –

Page 181

this evening my Wife return'd with her
niece who has been out about two
weeks a paying a visit to our Relations
at Campden, Brails Sibford &c
8[August]=3 was at our first day [Sunday]
meeting
I was concern'd to set forth the Purity of
the Dear Redeemer and how he was
Pleased in the day of his visitation to cause
his heavenly light to shine into our mindes
thereby showing us our states & conditions
& manifesting unto us that which is of
an evil tendancy & hinders our growth
in the truth, desiring that friends
might endeavour to put away every hurt
full thing – was also at our afternoon
meeting it felt refreshing, I was pretty

much exercised concerning Prayer believing
true pure spiritual Prayer would
be acceptable unto the Almighty but
alas how menny their are at this day
that use formal Prayers day by day
& yet are much straingers to this Spiritual

verso

Prayer which findes acceptance with
the Lord and obtains what the sould
stands in need of, -
8mo[August] 10 in our first day [Sunday] meeting as I
sat in Silence, strong desires was
raised in my minde that I might be
strengthened & enabled to persevear in the
way of my duty – in the A,noon walk'd
to Burford found Sistor & Cousins tolerable
well spent the evening with them Comfortabley lodgd their
=11, was at our monthly meeting
held at Burford, it felt pretty comfortable
I was concerned to appear theirin & E Atkins
also appear'd in Testimonie – Din'd at
sistors, call'd to se some of the friends in the
eveing return'd Home with Bro: Robt & some of his Children
=14 was at our fifth day [Thursday] meeting, I feel
it necessary to labour after a Humble
watchfull & Circumspect state of minde depending
on the Lord daily for Instruction and
ability to do his Will
-17 was at our first day [Sunday] meeting in our silent
sitting before the Lord, it appeard good

Page 182

to watch unto Prayer, - was also at
our evening meeting it felt refreshing
held in Silence –
8[August]=21 at our weekday meeting, my chief
Buisness appeared to be, to Labour after
a retired inward & Spiritual acquaintance
with the Lord that I might feel my
spiritual strength renewed and bodily
also, for I do believe the Lords truly
dependant Children who are afflicted & tryd
in minde & Body and are concern'd to seek unto him for
refreshment & strength, He is pleased to
administer it to both soul & body,
=24 was at our first day [Sunday] meeting, sat
in a low exercised state of minde,
I think it is good in a Spiritual state
to know how to suffer want and to
know how to abound, was also at our
evening meeting, continues in a low ex=
=ercised state, yet the meeting felt re=
=freshing
=28 was at our fifth day [Thursday] meeting, was re=

verso

1817

=freshed and comforted being sensible
of the flowings of Divine Love amoungst us
8mo[August]=31 at our first day [Sunday] meeting we ware
favoured with the company of Thos
Clarke who is on a religious visit in
these parts, we had the company also of
a few friends who ware appointed to visit
the preparative meetings, it was a satisfac=
=tory meeting – in the evening we had another
Public meeting by the desire of Thos Clark, it was
very full menny Neighbours attended who
behaved orderly and attentive to what was
deliver'd, T, Clark was favoured
with a good oppertunity to Preach the
Gospel to the People he Laboured
to turn their mindes from relying on
outward observations & forms, to an
acquaintance with the Truth within them=
=selves signifying it was a Pearl of great
Price, mentioning the words of Christ
for this end was I born and for this

Page 183

cause came I into the world that
I should bear witness unto the Truth,

9mo[September]=1st, I went as Guide with T,C,
to sibford R, Ashby
and his Wife accompanying us, reach'd their
just in time to attend their monthly Meeting
T,C, appear'd in Testimonie and some other
friends which through mercy was to the ed=
-dification of friends, I dind at Jno Enocks
after spending a little time with friends I re+
turn'd Home, 4th attended our weekday meeting
=7 attended our first day [Sunday] meetings, a
pretty
menny straingers ware their, & I trust Divine
Goodness was please to appear amoungst us
to our comfort & spiritual refreshment
=8, walked to our monthly meeting held
at C,[hipping] Norton was at the select meet'g
which felt comfortable, such as are
in the station of Ministers & Elders
ought to be Perticular carefull to walk
orderly and to set good Examples in their
Conduct & Conversation unto others –

verso

---

our monthly meeting was pretty large &
comfortable
after meeting call'd to se some of the friends
Saml Atkins who has been in a very
feeble state a long time not able to get
about, - is now much better & gets about
a little, in the evening I return'd Home
8[August]=13 set out for our Quarterly Meet'g
to
be held at Reading, reach'd Shillingford
about 5 oclock in the evening was
kindly entertaind at Robert Greens Lodgd there
=14, stop'd their first day [Sunday] meeting,
it is a smallish meeting yet I believe
their are a few sincear Honest friends
belonging to it, was favoured with a
comfortable meeting – after meeting call'd
to se some of the friends whose company was
agreeable and comforting, Sistor Sess's and
her son & Daughter came at Night, we Lodgd
their
15, I rode with my Relations to Reading, reach'd
their about middle of the day Din'd at the
widow Tutteys, or at her sons with whome
she lives they entertain friends kindly
afterward call'd to se some of my Relations

Page 184

in the Evening was at the select meeting
it felt to be a refreshing time, I was
concern'd to speak theirin signifying it
is good for friends to walk lowly & humbley
before the Lord & to learn of him who was
meek and lowly in Heart that they might
finde rest unto their souls, -
sup'd at Cousin Jnan fardons whose Company
was comforting, Lodgd at Tutteys
=16, was at the Quarterly Meeting
sevral straingers present as John
shepley Ann Crawly &c sevral
Testimonies ware born, such as had
been slothfull with respect to their
labouring to do their days work in the
day time ware warned to be more dili=
=gent lest the Palefaced Messenger should
be sent to them at unawares,
two friends appear'd in solem Prayer
the Buisness was gone through pretty
agreeabley. Dind at Henry Smiths,
Pretty soon after Dinner bid relations

verso

1817

and friends farewell, and return'd
back to shillingford as did a number
more of friends, some of whome lodgd at
R, Greens, I lodgd with Jos: Lamb of Sibford
who was very poorly with a soar Leg,
9mo[September]=17 after Breackfasting with
friends we
all set our for Home, I call'd at Jno
Jacksons's, they ware tolerable well I call'd
at the Horse=&=Jockey to se the Landlady
who is now a Widow, she appeard sorrow=
full, I signified it is good to bear Tryals
and afflictions Patiently and Indeavour to
be resigned unto the will of the Lord –
reach'd Home about eight at Night
=18 was at our weekday meeting –
=21 was at our first day [Sunday] meeting, M,
Ashby
appear'd theirin, to the eddification of friends

A,[fter]N,[oon] was at our evening meeting
=29 was at our first day [Sunday] meeting, it felt re=
=freshing I was concern'd to appear in solem
Prayer, desiring that the Lord in mercy would
be pleased to be with his servants & Children

Page 185

who ware Afflicted, try'd and exercised and
help with a little help, strengthen and
Enable them to sarve him faithfully, that
he might be praised who is worthy of all
Praise Honnour & Obidience for Evermore
= was also at our evening meeting was
comforted feeling Divine Love to be
Present,
10mo[October] 2nd at our fifth day [Thursday] meeting to day we
ware favour'd with the Company of Jno
sheply from [blank] saml Hanham accompany'd
him, it was a good refreshing meeting, he
was led to speak comfortabley to the mourners
in Zion and to Incourage to faithfullness
setting forth the mercies and blessings the
righteous pertake of and altho they may have
in the discharge of their duty to go through
menny tryals and exercises, yet he had to
declare Fear not, for the Lord would be their
shield & exceeding great reward,
=5 took a walk to Witney to se Hanh
Smith who has been very Ill had a
little sitting with she and her Daughter who

verso

is often poorly I felt Divine Goodness
to be near to the tendering our Hearts and
bowing our Spirits in humility before
the Lord & I was concern'd to Pray unto
the Lord for mercy, - was at the morning
and afternoon meetings which felt a little
refreshing, I was concern'd to speak theirin
return'd Home in the evening, -
10mo[October]=9th was at our fifth day [Thursday] meeting, held in Silence,
I was concerned to wait patiently upon the Lord
that I might feel my strength renewed,
feeling a great necessiety to depend on the Lord
for strength and ability to do his pure will
=12 was at our first day [Sunday] meeting, it was held
in silence, yet I trust profitable to those
whose dependance was on the Lord
13 was at our Monthly meeting held at
Charlbury it felt satisfactory, I was
concern'd to advise friends to have their
dependance on the Lord, it being their
way to be Instructed by Him and also to
receive ability to do his pure will, -
=16 was at our fifth day [Thursday] meeting, one friend
appeard theirin, it felt a little refreshing

Page 186

1817

10mo[October] 19th was at our first day [Sunday] meeting
it was held in silence, saml Atkins
at our meeting, he has been at Charlbury
a few days, he is so feeble it is hard
work for him to get to meeting and back
again with a stick & Crutch, altho
throug mercy he is much better than
he was, as sometime back he could
not go at all,
I was also at our afternoon meeting
it felt refreshing I was concerned
to advise friends to Labour daily
after the bread & water of Life that
they might feel their spiritual
strength renewed
=23 was at our fifth day [Thursday] meeting, it felt
a little refreshing
26 was at our first day [Sunday] meeting I
was concerned to seek the Lord and wait
Patiently upon him that I might
feel my strength renewed & might
be favour'd to know when to keep silence

verso

1817

and when to speak, that I might
minister of the ability that God giveth
that God in all things might be Glorified
was at our afternoon meeting, silent
10mo[October] 29 took a walk to witney was at
the fourth day [Wednesday] meeting, it was small
yet felt a little refreshing, call'd to se
Hanh Smith who still continues in a
very weak state, & I believe resigned
unto the will of Divine Providence
=30, was at our fifth day [Thursday] meeting,
11[November]=1, took a walk to Sibford
Intending
to be at the monthly meeting to be held
their, spent the evening at Jos: Harris'
he and his family ware very kinde to
me, Lodgd their three nights
=2, before meet'g went to se Bro: J, Gibbs
was at the first day [Sunday] meeting at Sibford
was favour'd to feel a renewal of strength
Din'd at Brothers, drank tea at Cousin Wm
Gibbs who lives at a lone house about a
mile of, spent the afternoon in a religious
and I hope in an Eddifying manner,

Page 187

11mo [November] 3rd after Breackfasting at Jos:
Lambs
call to se some of the friends before meet'g
the monthly meeting felt pretty comfortable
I was concerned to appear theirin, as was
also Ann Ashby, Din'd at Jos: Lambs
Drank tea at Bro: J, Gibbs
=4 after brackfasting at Jos: Harris's
with his family & some more friends
we had a comfortable sitting together
before we parted, I returned Home
call'd at C,[hipping]Norton to se some friends
their saml Atkins continues better
=9, was at our first day [Sunday] meeting
my minde was exercised in Silence
yet I believe it was a refreshing meet'g
=10 took a walk to our monthly meeting held
at witney it felt pretty comfortable
I was concerned to appear in solem prayer
fervently desiring that the Lord would be
pleased in mercy to strengthen the weak
Hands and confirm the feeble nees , and
as he had seen meet to remove some,

verso

of the Elders from works to rewards He
would be pleased to raise up their
offspring as they ware concerned to
Love & fear Him, fit & qualify them
to Labour for the Honnour of His great
Name, who is worthy of honnour Praise
and Obedience for Evermore
11mo [November] 16 at our first day [Sunday]
meeting I was
concerned to wait Patiently upon the
Lord that I might be favoured to
receive Instruction from Him
=23 was at our first day [Sunday] meeting it
felt refreshing, my minde was
a little exercised concerning the living
Faith, which is the Gift of God,
and it is as we are found in the exer=
=cise theirof that we are enabled to
offer up such offerings as are accept=
=able unto God
27 attended our weekday meeting,
-30 was at our first day [Sunday] meeting I was
concerned to sit in a lowly humble state
before the Lord being led to meditate on

Page 188

the uncertainty of Life, and to mention
we have no continued sitting here
but should seek a City to come, whose
builder and maker God the Lord is, -
12[December]=7 was at our first day [Sunday]
meeting it
felt a little refreshing, I was Concernd
to mention that the Life of a Christian
is a continual Warfare, desireing we
might seek unto the Lord for help that
we might be Enabled to make War
in Righteousness so be Enabled to over=
=come the man of sin and the things
of the World that hindereth our

Progress Zion=ward –
in the A,[fter]noon my Wife went to Burford
with some of our Relations to be at M. meet'g
=8,I rose early and walk to Burford in time
to be at the select meeting which felt
satisfactory, the monthly meeting was not
large but felt a little refreshing, I & my
Relations Dind at Sistors, the funeral of

verso

---

of Hannah Smith being to be on the morrow
I stop'd at Sistor Manders all Night
spent the evening with sistor & Cousins
in a Comfortable eddifying manner,
12mo [December]=9, after breackfasting at
sistors took leave
of my Relations and walk'd to Witney to
the Funeral of Hanh Smith, meeting
began about 11 oclock attended by menny
friends, as well as menny Neighbours
sevral Friends in the ministery their
the Corps according to her desire was put
into the Grave before they went into the
meeting House, there was a solemn pause
at the grave, Thos Harris signified that
it was happy for those who Died thee Death
of the Righteous & if we would Die such
a Death we must Indeavour through
Divine assistance to live the life of the Righteous
after which friends went into the meeting
House and ware favour'd with a Solemn
refreshing meeting, sevral friends appeard
in Testimonie, I was concern'd to mention
that the mercifull visitation of the Lord
was renewed and to call the People to
repentance and amendment of Life

Page 189

---

also to Pray for forgiveness, that they
might be favour'd to finde mercy, -
a pretty menny friends din'd at Thos
Smiths, and afterwards they ware
favoured with a Comfortable sitting
with the Family, & sevral friends
had something to say by way of advise
& Caution to the family & friends also advised
the family to be resigned unto the
Divine Will Trust in the Lord love
& fear Him then He would be their
Preserver & Comforter –
she was a Woman of a meek & quiet
spirit one that Loved the Lord in sin=
=cerity & in Truth was glad & rejoiced
to Incourage the work of Religion in her
Neighbours as well as friends & to turn
their mindes inward to the Power & spirit
of the Redeemer which as it is loved and
obeyed cleanseth & Purifieth the Heart also
brings

verso

---

into a State of acceptance and fel=
=lowship with the Lord, she went through
much affliction of Body and her family
also for a pretty menny years which was
cause of bowing her minde in Humility
before the Lord who was pleased to be
her support & to Enable her to bear afflic=
with Patience & Resignation to the Divine Will,
12[December]=14 was at our first day [Sunday]
meeting
I felt such a poor Creature that
I thought sometimes I was favoured
to make some advancement in a re=
ligious Life but at other times I
could hardly make any progress
theirin, I finde nothing better than to have
my dependance on the Lord and to be
daily seeking unto Him for Counsel Instruction
and ability to do his pure Will then as
I am concerned to do it, I trust I shall
be favoured to grow in the rate of Pure
undefiled Religion altho their may be

Page 190

---

but little appearence as to the outward,
was also at our afternoon meeting
it felt refreshing, speak a little
theirin
12[December]=15 about middle of the day set
out
for Oxford Quarterly meeting reached
Oxford about 4 oclock in the afternoon
Rode in a Cart with my Relations
was at the select meeting it felt
refreshing & some friends appear'd

in Testimonie, quarter'd at the Horse
& Jockey with a pretty menny friends,
after supper a friend or two ware
led to give good advise unto others
=16 quarterly meeting began at 1o
which felt comfortable and was
owned by our great Lord & marster
sevral friends appeared in Testimonie
to the comfort and Eddification of
friends the buisness was gone through in
a weighty manner, - after Dinner return'd
Home with my Relations

verso

12mo[December]=21st was at our first day
[Sunday] meeting
morning & afternoon which felt re=
=freshing, in the evening Cousin Jno
Head call'd to se us
=28 was at our first day [Sunday] morning
meeting, it felt to be a refreshing
meeting it was held in Silence – was
also at our afternoon meeting it
was held in Silence
=31, was at our weekday meeting held to day
on account of it being a fair to morrow

1818

1mo[January]: 3rd wrote a few lines to the
Duchess of Beaufort, I having had some
acquaintance with her & believing her
to be desirous of living a religious good
life and also concerned to Instruct her
Children and servants to do the like
by example & Precept, I wrote unto
her Encouraging her thus to do Daily
signifying then the blessing of the Lord
would rest upon them, - - -

Index of Persons

Index of Places

Index of Subjects